A Companion to
T. S. Eliot

D0796729

Blackwell Companions to Literature and Culture

This series offers comprehensive, newly written surveys of key periods and movements and certain major authors, in English literary culture and history. Extensive volumes provide new perspectives and positions on contexts and on canonical and post-canonical texts, orientating the beginning student in new fields of study and providing the experienced undergraduate and new graduate with current and new directions, as pioneered and developed by leading scholars in the field.

Published Recently

A COMPANION TO
T. S. ELIOT

EDITED BY
DAVID E. CHINITZ

WILEY Blackwell

Library of Congress Cataloging-in-Publication Data

A companion to TS Eliot / edited by David E. Chinitz.
        p. cm. – (Blackwell companions to literature and culture)
     Includes bibliographical references and index.
   ISBN 978-1-4051-6237-1 (cloth) – ISBN 978-1-118-64709-7 (pbk.)
   1. Eliot, T. S. (Thomas Stearns), 1888–1965–Criticism and interpretation–Handbooks, manuals,
etc.   I. Chinitz, David.   II. Title: Companion to T.S. Eliot.
   PS3509.L43Z64945 2009
   821′.912–dc22
                                        2008047763

A catalogue record for this book is available from the British Library.

Cover image: T. S. Eliot at his desk at Faber & Faber, c.1926. Photo © National Portrait Gallery,
London
Cover design by Richard Boxall Design Associates

Set in 11 on 13 pt Garamond 3 by Toppan Best-set Premedia Limited
Printed in Malaysia by Ho Printing (M) Sdn Bhd

1   2014

Contents

Notes on Contributors

Ann Ardis is the author of *New Women, New Novels: Feminism and Early Modernism* (1990) and *Modernism and Cultural Conflict, 1880–1922* (2002) as well as coeditor of *Virginia Woolf Turning the Centuries* (2000), *Women's Experience of Modernity, 1875–1945* (2002), and *Transatlantic Print Culture, 1880–1940: Emerging Media, Emerging Modernisms* (2008). She is currently working on a book-length study of periodicals on both sides of the Atlantic at the turn of the twentieth century that sought to engage an increasingly diverse public in discussions of "modern" literature, art, and politics.

Richard Badenhausen is Professor and Kim T. Adamson Chair at Westminster College, Salt Lake City, where he teaches classes in literature, trauma studies, and theories of place. He has published many articles on Eliot and is the author of *T. S. Eliot and the Art of Collaboration* (2005). He is currently completing a book entitled *T. S. Eliot's Traumatic Texts*.

Sarah Bay-Cheng is Associate Professor of theater at the University at Buffalo–SUNY, where she teaches avant-garde drama, modernist film and theater, and contemporary intermedia and virtual reality performance. She is author of *Mama Dada: Gertrude Stein's Avant-Garde Theater* (2004) and editor of *Poets at Play: An Anthology of Modernist Drama* (forthcoming). Her essays have appeared in journals such as *Theatre Journal* and *Theatre Topics*, and in anthologies such as *A Companion to Twentieth-Century American Drama* (Blackwell, 2005) and *Theatre and Film* (2005).

Jewel Spears Brooker, Professor at Eckerd College, Florida, has written scores of essays and has written or edited eight books, including *Reading "The Waste Land": Modernism and the Limits of Interpretation* (1990) (with Joseph Bentley), *Mastery and Escape: T. S. Eliot and the Dialectic of Modernism* (1994), and *T. S. Eliot: The Contemporary Reviews* (2004). She is coeditor of two forthcoming volumes of Eliot's *Complete Prose*. Dr. Brooker has served as a member of the National Humanities Council and as president of the T. S. Eliot Society and the South Atlantic Modern Language Association.

Edward Brunner teaches American literature at Southern Illinois University, Carbondale. He has published books on Hart Crane, W. S. Merwin, and the Cold War poetry of the years just after World War II.

Christine Buttram, Associate Professor of English at Winona State University in Minnesota, has published articles in the *Journal of Modern Literature, English Language Notes, Essays in Criticism*, and the *Yeats Eliot Review*. Her book on Eliot and the human body is nearing completion. For several years, she has served on the Board of the T. S. Eliot Society.

Bryan Cheyette is Chair in Modern Literature at the University of Reading, UK. He is the editor of seven books and author of *Constructions of "the Jew" in English Literature and Society* (1996) and *Muriel Spark* (2001), and he is now completing *Diasporas of the Mind: Literature and "Race" after the Holocaust*. He has recently guest edited the journal *Wasifiri* and is coeditor of volume VII of the *Oxford History of the Novel in English*, on the British and Irish novel, 1940–2000 (forthcoming).

David E. Chinitz is serving as Vice President of the T. S. Eliot Society and as Inter-disciplinary Chair of the Modernist Studies Association while completing a book on Langston Hughes. His publications include *T. S. Eliot and the Cultural Divide* (2003) and articles in such journals as *Callaloo, Modernism/Modernity, American Literary History*, and *PMLA*. He is a Professor of English at Loyola University Chicago.

John Xiros Cooper is a Professor of English at the University of British Columbia. He has written three books on T. S. Eliot and edited a collection of essays on Eliot and music. He is the author of *Modernism and the Culture of Market Society* (2004) and is currently writing a book on Eliot's British publisher, called *Modernism in the Mainstream: The Case of Faber and Faber*.

Michael Coyle, Professor of English at Colgate University in Hamilton, NY, is founding president of the Modernist Studies Association. Since *Ezra Pound, Popular Genres, and the Discourse of Culture* (1995), he has edited *Ezra Pound and African American Modernism* (2001), *Raymond Williams and Modernism* (2003), *Broadcasting Modernism* (with Debra Rae Cohen and Jane Lewty, forthcoming), and *Ezra Pound and Education* (with Steven Yao, forthcoming). He is currently finishing *Professional Attention: Ezra Pound and the Career of Modernist Criticism*.

Anthony Cuda is an Assistant Professor of English at the University of North Carolina–Greensboro, where he teaches American literature and twentieth-century poetry. He has published essays in *Twentieth Century Literature, Modern Language Quarterly*, the *Journal of Modern Literature*, and elsewhere; is finishing a book called "The Passions of Modernism: Eliot, Yeats, Woolf, Mann"; and is coeditor with Ronald Schuchard of the forthcoming *Complete Prose of T. S. Eliot*, volume 2.

Elisabeth Däumer is Professor of English and American literature at Eastern Michigan University, with specialties in literary theory and twentieth-century poetry. She has published essays on T. S. Eliot, Muriel Rukeyser, and feminist theory. She is also coeditor (with Shyamal Bagchee) of *The International Reception of T. S. Eliot* (2007).

Kevin J. H. Dettmar is W. M. Keck Distinguished Service Professor and Chair of the Department of English at Pomona College in Claremont, California. He has published books and articles in both modernist studies and popular music studies, and is the general editor of the *Longman Anthology of British Literature*.

Frances Dickey is an Assistant Professor at the University of Missouri. She has published on Whitman, Frost, Eliot, and Bishop; her essay "Parrot's Eye: A Portrait by Manet and Two by T. S. Eliot" received the Kappell Prize from *Twentieth Century Literature* in 2006. She is writing a book on portraiture in modern American poetry.

Leonard Diepeveen is Professor of English at Dalhousie University. He is the author of *The Difficulties of Modernism* (2003) and *Changing Voices: The Modern Quoting Poem* (1993). As well, he is coauthor, with Timothy van Laar, of *Art with a Difference: Looking at Difficult and Unfamiliar Art* (2001) and *Active Sights: Art as Social Action* (1998).

Barry J. Faulk is an Associate Professor at Florida State University, where he teaches Victorian literature and cultural studies. He is the author of *Music Hall and Modernity* (2004) and has published articles in *Modernism/Modernity, Cultural Critique*, and *Victorian Literature and Culture*.

Nancy K. Gish is Professor of English and women's studies at the University of Southern Maine. She is the author of *Time in the Poetry of T. S. Eliot* (1981) and *"The Waste Land": A Poem of Memory and Desire* (1988). She has also published books on Hugh MacDiarmid and articles on contemporary Scottish poets. Her most recent book, coedited with Cassandra Laity, is *Gender, Desire, and Sexuality in T. S. Eliot* (2007).

Jason Harding is a Lecturer in English at the University of Durham, UK. He is the author of *The Criterion: Cultural Politics and Periodical Networks in Inter-War Britain* (2002) and coeditor (with Giovanni Cianci) of *T. S. Eliot and the Concept of Tradition* (2007). He is currently editing a volume in the *Complete Prose of T. S. Eliot* under the general editorship of Ronald Schuchard.

Christina Hauck is an Associate Professor of modern British literature at Kansas State University. She has published articles on Virginia Woolf, T. S. Eliot, Marie Stopes, Lord Alfred Douglas, and others, and she is currently writing a book on sexual reproduction and modernist identity. She is also a Dharma Teacher in the Kwan Um School of Zen and a co-founder, with Margaret Wheeler, of the Tall Grass Zen Center in Manhattan, Kansas.

Aaron Jaffe is an Associate Professor of English at the University of Louisville, Kentucky. He is the author of *Modernism and the Culture of Celebrity* and the coeditor of two forthcoming essay collections: *Modernist Star Maps* (2009) and *The Year's Work in Lebowski Studies* (2009).

Michael Levenson, William B. Christian Professor of English at the University of Virginia, is the author of *A Genealogy of Modernism* (1986), *The Spectacle of Intimacy* (with Karen Chase, 2000), *Modernism and the Fate of Individuality* (2005), and the forthcoming *Modernism*. He is also the editor of the *Cambridge Companion to Modernism* (1999).

James Longenbach is the Joseph H. Gilmore Professor of English at the University of Rochester, NY. He is the author of six books of literary criticism, most recently *The Art of the Poetic Line* (2008), and three books of poems, most recently *Draft of a Letter* (2007).

Randy Malamud is Professor of English at Georgia State University in Atlanta. He is the author of five books, including *T. S. Eliot's Drama: A Research and Production Sourcebook* (1992) and *Where the Words are Valid: T. S. Eliot's Communities of Drama* (1994), and the editor of *"The Waste Land" and Other Poems* (2005) and, most recently, *A Cultural History of Animals in the Modern Age* (2007). He is a regular contributor to the *Chronicle of Higher Education* and a frequent collaborator with the photographer Britta Jaschinski.

Marc Manganaro's scholarly interests have centered on the relation of modernist literature and anthropology. He has authored *Myth, Rhetoric, and the Voice of Authority: A Critique of Frazer, Eliot, Frye, and Campbell* (1992) and *Culture, 1922: the Emergence of a Concept* (2002), and he edited and introduced *Modernist Anthropology: From Fieldwork to Text* (1990). Formerly Professor of English and a Dean at Rutgers University, he is presently Dean of the College of Arts and Sciences at Gonzaga University in Spokane, Washington.

Gail McDonald is Senior Lecturer in English at the University of Southampton, UK. Her work on Eliot includes *Learning to be Modern: Pound, Eliot, and the American University*. Her most recent book is *American Literature and Culture, 1900–1960* (Blackwell, 2007). She is a founder of the Modernist Studies Association.

John Timberman Newcomb is Associate Professor of English at the University of Illinois. He has published two books – *Wallace Stevens and Literary Canons* (1992) and *Would Poetry Disappear: American Verse and the Crisis of Modernity* (2004) – and numerous articles and reviews on American poetry. His current book project is "The Poetry of Modern Life: American Verse on the Urban Boulevard, 1910–1925."

Lee Oser's books include *The Return of Christian Humanism: Chesterton, Eliot, Tolkien, and the Romance of History; T. S. Eliot and American Poetry*; and *Out of What Chaos: A Novel* (all 2007). He is currently working on full-length studies of Shakespeare and Newman.

Jeffrey M. Perl is the author of *The Tradition of Return: The Implicit History of Modern Literature* (1984) and *Skepticism and Modern Enmity: Before and After Eliot* (1989). He is founder of the journal *Common Knowledge*, which he has edited since 1992. Currently Professor of English literature at Bar-Ilan University in Israel, he taught for many years at Columbia University and the University of Texas.

Cyrena N. Pondrom is Professor of English and women's studies at the University of Wisconsin–Madison, and a recipient of NEH, ACLS, and Fulbright Fellowships. Her publications include *The Road from Paris: French Influence on English Poetry, 1900–1920* (1974), *The Contemporary Writer: Interviews with Sixteen Novelists and Poets* (with L. S. Dembo, 1972), and numerous essays on Gertrude Stein, Hilda Doolittle (H.D.), Marianne Moore, Edith Sitwell, T. S. Eliot, and other modern figures. She is at work on a book-length study titled *T. S. Eliot and the Performativity of Gender*.

Patrick Query has published articles and chapters on Eliot, W. B. Yeats, Evelyn Waugh, Graham Greene, and W. H. Auden, as well as numerous reviews. His recently completed book manuscript, entitled *The Idea of Europe in Ritual and Writing, 1919–1939*, deals with the ways in which British and Irish writers of the interwar years used verse drama, bullfighting, and Catholic ritual to explore ideas of European identity. He is currently Assistant Professor of English at the United States Military Academy at West Point, New York.

Lawrence Rainey is founding editor of the scholarly journal *Modernism/Modernity*. He has authored *Revisiting "The Waste Land"* (2005) and edited *The Annotated "Waste Land" with Eliot's Contemporary Prose* (2005). In 2006 these books were jointly awarded the Robert Motherwell Prize for an outstanding contribution to the study of modernism. He has also written *Institutions of Modernism* (2000), edited *Modernism: An Anthology* (2005), and edited and translated *Futurism: An Anthology* (2009). He has received research fellowships from the Guggenheim and Leverhulme Foundations, and numerous other scholarly awards.

Gareth Reeves is Reader in English at Durham University, UK. He is the author of two books on Eliot – *T. S. Eliot: A Virgilian Poet* (1989) and *T. S. Eliot's "The Waste Land"* (1994), for Harvester's Critical Studies of Key Texts series – and of *The Thirties Poetry: Auden, MacNeice, Spender*, with Michael O'Neill (1992). He is the author of two volumes of poetry, *Real Stories* (1984) and *Listening In* (1993), and of many essays on twentieth-century English, American and Irish poetry.

Sanford Schwartz teaches literature at Penn State University. The author of *The Matrix of Modernism: Pound, Eliot, and Early Twentieth-Century Thought* (1988) and various essays on modern literary, cultural, and intellectual history, he recently completed a study of C. S. Lewis's Space Trilogy in its twentieth-century context (2009).

Tony Sharpe was for several years Head of the Department of English and Creative Writing at Lancaster University, UK, where he teaches modern and American literature. He is the author of *Vladimir Nabokov* (1991), *T. S. Eliot: A Literary Life* (1991), *Wallace Stevens: A Literary Life* (2000) and, most recently, *W. H. Auden* (2007), as well as of various articles and chapters reflecting his interest in modern and contemporary poetry. He is currently working on a study of Auden's use of North Pennine places.

Vincent Sherry is Professor of English at Washington University in St. Louis. He is currently writing the Blackwell biography of Ezra Pound and a book-length study of European Decadence and modernist literature in English. His publications include *The Great War and the Language of Modernism* (2003); *James Joyce: Ulysses* (1995; 2nd ed. 2004); *Ezra Pound, Wyndham Lewis, and Radical Modernism* (1993); and *The Uncommon Tongue: The Poetry and Criticism of Geoffrey Hill* (1987). He also edited the *Cambridge Companion to the Literature of the First World War* (2005).

Carol H. Smith is Professor Emerita of English at Rutgers University. She is the author of *T. S. Eliot's Dramatic Theory and Practice: From "Sweeney Agonistes" to "The Elder Statesman"* (1963) and of articles on modernism and twentieth-century writers. She is currently working on a study of H.D. (Hilda Doolittle) and her circle.

Jayme Stayer has taught at the University of Toledo, the University of Texas A&M–Commerce, Universidad Centroamericana in San Salvador, and John Carroll University, Ohio. His scholarly publications include work on Beethoven, Bakhtin, Stravinsky, and Eliot, and on rhetoric. He is currently working on a book on the rhetoric of voice and audience in Eliot's early poetry. A Jesuit, he joined the Society of Jesus in 2003. And, no, he is not particularly fond of Eliot's post-conversion poetry.

Preface

Critical work on T. S. Eliot has undergone a renaissance since the early 1990s, bringing new ideas and methods to bear on a much-studied writer whose depths, by then, were long supposed to have been plumbed. Key developments have included innovative work in the areas of sexuality and gender; new insight on Eliot's relations with popular culture and mass media; more closely historicized readings of his political, social, religious, and philosophical views; a more sophisticated understanding of his role in the definition and dissemination of modernism; and rekindled debate over his prejudices. Meanwhile, *The Varieties of Metaphysical Poetry*, a major addition to the canon of Eliot's prose, appeared in 1993, providing important new material for literary scholars; and *Inventions of the March Hare*, a fascinating collection of early poems and drafts that had been lost in manuscript for decades, was finally published in 1996, further altering critical assessments of Eliot's development, influences, and social views. Between then and now, *Cats* (for which Eliot had been posthumously awarded a Tony) ended its marathon run on Broadway; Eliot was named "Poet of the Century" in *Time* magazine; and journalism on some of the scholarly controversies kept Eliot in the public eye to an unusual degree.

A *Companion to T. S. Eliot* presents the "new" T. S. Eliot in a series of chapters covering, from a contemporary perspective, the full range of Eliot's output and career. Part I of the *Companion* comprises eight chapters elucidating the forces that shaped Eliot as writer and thinker, with attention given to influences high and low; Eastern and Western; aesthetic, biographical, historical, philosophical, and scientific. Part II guides the reader through Eliot's entire oeuvre, analyzing richly every phase of his poetry, drama, and critical prose.

Part III contextualizes Eliot in a variety of ways. By examining his work through the lenses of race, gender, sexuality, religion, and politics, several chapters shed light on the new developments in Eliot studies and the controversies surrounding Eliot in our own time. Two chapters consider facets of Eliot's career – his work as a publisher and his founding and editing of the *Criterion* – that were adjunct to his writing, yet crucial to the immense authority he wielded as a cultural figure. Others give informative glimpses into his reception and reputation among several readerships, or highlight aspects of his poetics that help to account for his literary eminence and continuing influence.

A Companion to T. S. Eliot is not merely the most comprehensive book of its kind, but also the first to synthesize broadly the resurgence of Eliot studies under a new, post-postmodernist critical regime, and with the inspiration of fresh primary material. A number of projects underway at this writing, including the compilation at long last of Eliot's *Complete Prose*, the resumption of his *Letters* (hitherto suspended since the publication of volume 1 in 1988), and authoritative new editions of his poems and plays, promise to keep the momentum of today's scholarship on Eliot going, and quite likely to accelerate it further, for some time to come.

Until those new editions of Eliot's work appear, readers confront a haphazard assortment of texts. Several collections of Eliot's poems and prose are available, with those published in the United States differing from those published in Britain, each with its own unique content, pagination, and typographical errors. While any selection among these editions is inevitably arbitrary, it seemed better, for the purposes of this *Companion*, to make some selection than to make none, so that references could be standardized around a consistent and accessible set of texts. The editions in use here are listed in the *Companion*'s "Bibliography of Works by T. S. Eliot." Creative works appearing in the *Complete Poems and Plays 1909–1950* (Harcourt) have been referenced to that text in preference to any others where they may also appear; similarly, essays are referenced primarily to *Selected Essays* (new ed., Harcourt). Prose pieces not included there are cited, if possible, in the listed editions of Eliot's other collections (*The Sacred Wood, On Poetry and Poets*, etc.); uncollected pieces – which still constitute the majority of Eliot's prose – are referenced, perforce, to their original sources. Writers and editors, as well as students and other readers, can look forward to a future in which such limitations, frustrations, and inconveniences are no longer a part of their experience of Eliot.

I would like to thank Julia Daniel for her assiduous and capable assistance with the editing of this *Companion*, and Loyola University Chicago for the research-support grant that sponsored Julia's work. For their advice, my thanks go to Debra Rae Cohen, Michael Coyle, Kevin J. H. Dettmar, Lawrence Rainey, and Jayme Stayer. Emma Bennett and the editorial staff at Blackwell have been most helpful, and I am grateful to Al Bertrand for engaging me in this project. I would also like to acknowledge the contributors to this volume for their generous cooperation with my editorial activism. And to Lisa, Michael, and Raina: thank you, as always, for being with and bearing with me.

D. E. C.

Acknowledgments to Sources

The editor and publisher gratefully acknowledge the permission granted to reproduce the copyright material in this book. Excerpts from the following works by T. S. Eliot are reprinted by permission of Faber & Faber Ltd.: *The Complete Poems and Plays: 1909–1950, Inventions of the March Hare: Poems 1909–1917, The Letters of T. S. Eliot, 1898–1922, Poems Written in Early Youth*, and *The Waste Land: A Facsimile and Transcript of the Original Drafts*. In addition, the following works are reprinted by permission of Houghton Mifflin Harcourt Publishing Co.: excerpts from "Five-Finger Exercises" and "Landscapes" in *Collected Poems 1909–1962* by T. S. Eliot, copyright ©1936 by Houghton Mifflin Harcourt Publishing Company and renewed 1964 by T. S. Eliot; excerpts from *The Letters of T. S. Eliot, 1898–1922*, copyright ©1988 by SET Copyrights Limited; and excerpts from *Inventions of the March Hare: Poems 1909–1917* by T. S. Eliot, copyright ©1996 by Valerie Eliot.

Every effort has been made to trace copyright holders and to obtain their permission for the use of copyright material. The publisher apologizes for any errors or omissions in the above list and would be grateful if notified of any corrections that should be incorporated in future reprints or editions of this book.

Abbreviations Used for Works by
T. S. Eliot

ASG	*After Strange Gods*
"C"	*Criterion* Commentaries
CC	*Christianity and Culture*
CP	*Collected Poems 1909–1962*
CPP	*The Complete Poems and Plays 1909–1950*
EAM	*Essays Ancient and Modern*
EED	*Essays on Elizabethan Drama*
FLA	*For Lancelot Andrewes*
IMH	*Inventions of the March Hare*
KE	*Knowledge and Experience in the Philosophy of F. H. Bradley*
OPP	*On Poetry and Poets*
SE	*Selected Essays*
SP	*Selected Prose of T. S. Eliot*
SW	*The Sacred Wood*
UPUC	*The Use of Poetry and the Use of Criticism*
VMP	*The Varieties of Metaphysical Poetry*
WLF	*The Waste Land: A Facsimile and Transcript of the Original Drafts*
TCC	*To Criticize the Critic*

For the particular editions of Eliot's works referred to in this book, see the "Bibliography of Works by T. S. Eliot," p. 460.

Note: Endnote references in SMALL CAPITALS refer to chapters in this volume.

Part I
Influences

1

The Poet and the Pressure Chamber: Eliot's Life

Anthony Cuda

Over the course of his long career, T. S. Eliot preferred to think about poetry not as the communication of ideas but as a means of emotional relief for the artist, a momentary release of psychological pressure, a balm for the agitated imagination. In 1919, he called poetic composition an "escape from emotion"; in 1953, a "relief from acute discomfort" (*SE* 10; *OPP* 98). At first, poetry alleviated for him the mundane pressures of a bank clerk who lived hand-to-mouth, caring for his sick wife during the day and writing for the *Times Literary Supplement* at night; later, it lightened the spiritual pressures of a holy man in a desert of solitude with the devils conniving at his back. Most frequently, though, it eased the pressure of an artist doubting his talent, an acclaimed poet who wrote more criticism than poetry, ever fearful that the fickle Muse had permanently left him. The most intensely creative stages of Eliot's life often coincided with the periods in which he faced the most intense personal disturbances and upheavals.

But where do we, as students of Eliot, begin to account for that pressure? "The pressure," as he himself called it, "under which the fusion takes place" and from which the work of art emerges (*SE* 8)? We could begin with the bare facts. Eliot was the youngest of seven children, born on September 26, 1888 in St. Louis, Missouri. His family traced its roots to the early colonies in New England, and his grandfather, a Unitarian minister, moved the family from Boston to St. Louis in 1834 and founded the Church of the Messiah, the first Unitarian church west of the Mississippi. Eliot's father, Henry Ware Eliot, chose to diverge from his own father's footsteps in the ministry and pursued a career as president of the Hydraulic-Press Brick Company, while his mother, Charlotte Champe Eliot (a teacher, social worker, and writer) introduced the children to art and culture. But where among these facts, which are barely even "memories draped by the beneficent spider," does the author of *The Waste Land* begin to emerge (*CPP* 49)?

Maybe it's better to begin in two places at once. For 14 years while Eliot was young, his family divided its time between St. Louis and coastal New England,

A Companion to T. S. Eliot, First Edition. Edited by David E. Chinitz.
© 2014 John Wiley & Sons, Ltd. Published 2014 by John Wiley & Sons, Ltd.

spending summers near Gloucester, a deep-sea fishing port in Massachusetts where his father eventually built a summer cottage. The yellow fog that winds through "Prufrock" and the brown river-god of "The Dry Salvages" both reflect the time he spent as a boy in the industrialized city of St. Louis. The urban imagery of his early poems, he admitted much later, "was that of St. Louis, upon which that of Paris and London have been superimposed" ("Influence" 422). The peaceful sailing scenes and serene coastal imagery of poems like "Marina" and *Ash-Wednesday*, on the other hand, arise from his summers in Gloucester, where he learned to sail with his brother. This is where the pressures of Eliot's creative life seem to begin: somewhere between the hard, claustrophobic inwardness of the city and the open, romantic expanses of the New England shores.

Boston and the Mind of Europe, 1906–1915

Eliot attended private academies as a young man – Smith Academy in St. Louis and then Milton, just south of Boston – before entering Harvard in 1906. Though a lackluster student at first, he joined the editorial board of the Harvard literary magazine, the *Advocate*, and became increasingly fascinated with literature and philosophy. After three years he went on to pursue graduate work in philosophy, apprenticing himself to influential American intellectuals at Harvard. Josiah Royce, Irving Babbitt, and George Santayana were all among the renowned professors who offered the young student not only footholds in the Western intellectual tradition but also invaluable models of the kind of public intellectual he would eventually strive to become.

Every writer feels the need to tell a conversion narrative, a story that distinguishes "the bundle of accident and incoherence that sits down to breakfast" (in W. B. Yeats's words) from the artist he or she has become. Eliot was fortunate enough to have two: one literary, the other, religious. The first revolves around a fortuitous discovery at Harvard in December 1908, when he apparently stumbled upon a copy of Arthur Symons's slim introduction to the nineteenth-century French literary tradition, *The Symbolist Movement in Literature* (1899), a book that profoundly changed the direction of Eliot's creative energies. Before then he had read the odes of Keats and Shelley and the dramatic monologues of Browning and Tennyson, and he had imitated the amalgam of violent spiritual energy and demotic speech that he found in late Victorian English poets like John Davidson and Lionel Johnson. He showed a growing interest in Elizabethan drama and a love for Dante's *Commedia*, which he learned to read in the original Italian and which remained an imaginative touchstone throughout his career. Under Symons's influence, however, Eliot's attention veered toward more recent French poets like Jules Laforgue and Charles Baudelaire, whose laconic wit, ironic pose, and fascination with urban landscapes helped him develop a wry, detached idiom to match his growing interest in philosophical skepticism.

Second in importance only to Symons's book in Eliot's early education were his courses with Irving Babbitt, the Harvard professor with whom he was to share a lifelong intellectual kinship. Babbitt's mistrust of emotional excess and individualism turned Eliot against the romantic literary tradition and toward classicism, which espoused the need for limitations and discipline to curb the natural human appetites and inclinations. The opposition between romanticism and classicism that Eliot encountered in Babbitt's class deeply influenced his early criticism, especially once he found support for it a few years later in the forceful and uncompromising rhetoric of modernist poet and essayist T. E. Hulme, whose theories he likely first encountered in 1916. Hulme proposed a classicism based on original sin, the Christian doctrine that proposes human nature to be essentially flawed. This was a radically "new attitude of mind," Eliot wrote when he reviewed Hulme's *Speculations* in 1924, and it "should be the twentieth-century mind, if the twentieth century is to have a mind of its own" ("C [Apr. 1924]" 231).

From 1910 to 1911 Eliot spent a crucial year in Paris, studying at the Sorbonne and attending lectures by the well-known, provocative French philosopher Henri Bergson at the Collège de France. In the world of contemporary art and philosophy, he later reflected, "the predominance of Paris was incontestable" ("C [Apr. 1934]" 451). He studied French with novelist Alain-Fournier, plunged into the chilling fiction of Dostoevsky in translation, and wrote poetry that drew from his reading in the social realism of Charles-Louis Philippe (especially *Bubu de Montparnasse*) and the psychological realism of Henry James (as in *Portrait of a Lady*). He also met and nurtured a close friendship with a fellow lodger in his Paris pension, Jean Jules Verdenal, whose death in World War I Eliot later memorialized in the dedication to his first book.

Eliot returned to Harvard in 1911 to begin a PhD in philosophy. He undertook an intense study of Eastern literary and philosophical traditions, studied primitive myth and ritual with Josiah Royce, and took a class with Bertrand Russell, a prominent British philosopher visiting at Harvard, whose skepticism and intellectual precision he admired. He began his dissertation and, in the following year, accepted a fellowship to study abroad, first at Marburg University in Germany, then at Merton College, Oxford, where he was to work one-on-one with a prominent expert on the philosophy of F. H. Bradley. Soon after he arrived in Europe, however, Germany declared war, compelling the young American to interrupt his studies and head for England early. The change of plans proved immensely fortunate.

A far more important galvanizing agent than any of the professors he encountered at Oxford was the gregarious American expatriate and avant-garde poet Ezra Pound, whom he met just before classes began in September 1914. Pound had been energetically making his presence known in London's literary circles for six years by the time the two met, and he immediately brought Eliot under his wing. His judicious eye for the most experimental, provocative literary talent soon fell upon Eliot's early poem, "The Love Song of J. Alfred Prufrock," which he promptly sent to the prominent Chicago literary magazine, *Poetry*. "This is as good as anything I've ever seen," Pound told his new protégé (Hall 263). To Eliot, he offered the guidance and unflagging encouragement that the young poet sorely needed; to others, he sang Eliot's praises tirelessly.

Friends from this period describe Eliot as grave, bookish, and reticent – one unforgivingly labeled him "the Undertaker" – and this side of his personality does resemble the brooding, cynical personae of his early poems (Gordon 139). But we now know that Eliot was also a great lover of popular culture, and his imagination drew as much from forms of "low" culture like contemporary slang and popular music as from conventionally "high" forms like classical poetry, philosophy, and opera. In London he frequented popular locales like the Old Oxford Music Hall, where he admired the outlandish comedians' "savage humor" and the self-assured bravado of their performances. In Eliot's eyes, "lowbrow" entertainment was an art with explosive potential for institutional change.

Eliot's temporary academic sojourn in Europe soon began to assume the look of permanence. The atmosphere at Oxford was stifling, he told his long-time friend Conrad Aiken, and in the midst of seeking release elsewhere he met Vivien Haigh-Wood, a spirited, adventurous, and artistic young woman six months older than he. They were married in June 1915, only a few months after their first meeting, and within the same few months, his early poems – including "Prufrock," "Rhapsody on a Windy Night," and "Portrait of a Lady" – began to emerge in print. Eliot returned to America in 1915 to tell his family the unexpected news – not only of his marriage but also of his decision to abandon a promising academic career for the capricious whims of the literary life.

Toward *The Waste Land*, 1916–1921

Eliot's return from America marked the beginning of a low, dark period of his life. He soon learned of Vivien's lifelong battles with chronic physical and mental illness. His new wife could be vibrant and wildly creative, but she was also prey to nervous collapses, bouts of migraine and exhaustion, prescription-drug addictions, even suicide attempts, all of which grew increasingly severe. Exhausted physically and intellectually from caring for her and teaching a number of ill-paid, evening extension classes (for "continuing education" students, as we would call them), Eliot himself began to sink into depression and physical enervation. His mentor Bertrand Russell, the philosopher whom he met at Harvard and caricatured in "Mr. Apollinax," had returned to Cambridge and befriended the struggling couple soon after their marriage. When he learned of their financial worries, he offered them a room in his London flat, where in the coming months the notorious womanizer began a sexual affair with Vivien that would continue for four years. Eliot's discovery of it, likely sometime in 1917, was crushing. It was a double betrayal – by his new wife and his trusted teacher, who treated Eliot "as if he were my son" (Bell 313) – and it exacerbated the disgust and revulsion toward sex and the spirit of savage, biting satire that together pervade the poems composed during this period.

Eliot took a position in the Colonial and Foreign Department at Lloyds Bank, then the second largest bank in England, in March 1917 in the hopes of gaining a degree of economic stability. In addition to continuing his evening lectures, he oversaw the publication of his first book, *Prufrock and Other Observations* (1917), and assumed an assistant editorship at *The Egoist*, an avant-garde literary magazine. He worked late into the evenings composing dozens of iconoclastic reviews and essays that aimed at revolutionizing the Victorian and Georgian ideals of artistic decorum and propriety that still dominated the literary establishment. The contentious and authoritative tone of these essays reflects the young American's desire to break into the "safe" (as he put it) of the insular London literary world (*Letters* 392). Through his connections with Pound and others in London, Eliot met Leonard and Virginia Woolf, W. B. Yeats, Wyndham Lewis, Aldous Huxley, James Joyce, and other literary giants of early modernism. In 1920, the appearance of his second volume of poetry (published as *Ara Vos Prec* in England; as *Poems* in America) and a collection of critical essays, *The Sacred Wood*, had firmly secured him a reputation as both a radical innovator in poetry and a voice of piercing critical acumen.

As his creative life was coming together, however, his personal life was rapidly falling apart. With their cycles of debilitating illness, Eliot and his wife struggled as if they were locked in a cage together, each feeding off of the other's physical and nervous ailments in an alarming downward spiral. The roles were often reversed: Vivien cared for Eliot when he was ill and wrote letters on his behalf. "We feel sometimes," he wrote to his mother in 1918, "as if we were going to pieces and just being patched up from time to time" (*Letters* 235). The makeshift patchwork came apart in 1921 after a strenuous visit from his family, when Eliot suffered something like a nervous breakdown and was forced to take three months' sick leave from the bank for psychiatric treatment. He went first to rest at Margate, a tranquil seaside town in southern England, and then to a clinic in Lausanne, Switzerland, where he sought the help of renowned psychologist Roger Vittoz.

It was during this period of collapse and convalescence that he began to assemble fragments of old poems and to compose new segments that would eventually coalesce to become *The Waste Land.* Despite its elliptical allusions and apparent detachment, *The Waste Land* is a profoundly personal poem. One of his close friends who read the manuscript soon after its completion called it "Tom's autobiography" (Gordon 147). This is surely an overstatement, but the poem's tapestry of classical allusions does align startlingly well with the intricate, tangled patterns of Eliot's personal distress. From the lascivious "cauldron of unholy loves" implied in the quotation from St. Augustine ("To Carthage then I came" [*CPP* 53]), to the wind-tossed lovers Paolo and Francesca trapped in Dante's inferno for eternity ("What is the wind doing? / Carrying / Away the little light dead people" [*WLF* 13]), many of the poem's spiritually vacuous personae are chilling echoes of Eliot's personal nightmare.

On his way home from Switzerland, Eliot stopped in Paris and met up with Pound, who undertook a massive revision of the unwieldy manuscript. He cut long sections, questioned the unity of others, and (along with Vivien, who also read the drafts) recommended additions and revisions. There followed months of anticipation, during which time publishers offered enormous payments for rights to a manuscript they hadn't yet seen. When *The Waste Land* was published in its final form in 1922 (first in the *Dial* and the newly launched *Criterion*, then in book form by Boni and Liveright), it was half its original length and twice as fragmented, condensed, and lyrically daring.

After *The Waste Land*, 1922–1930

In 1922, with the help of a wealthy patron of the arts, Lady Lillian Rothermere, Eliot founded the *Criterion*, an international periodical of literature, culture, and politics that became the staging ground for modernism's most heated debates in the coming years. He was already at work on a new creative project in 1923, an experimental verse drama called *Sweeney Agonistes*, when he sent a personally inscribed copy of his most recent volume of poems to a woman with whom he had not spoken for years. While he was still a graduate student in Boston, Eliot had met and fallen in love with Emily Hale, now a teacher of drama and literature. That she shared his feelings was uncertain to him in 1912, however, and when next he saw her, he was a married man who had settled in England. As the coming years proved, however, his early love for her held an undiminished place in his memory. By the time he reached out to reestablish contact with Hale, he had recognized that the only way out of the "chaos and torment" that he and Vivien inflicted upon one another was separation, though years passed before he acted upon this knowledge (Seymour-Jones 414). The copy of *Ara Vos Prec* that Eliot sent to Hale bore a telling inscription from Dante's *Inferno*: "keep my Treasure," the quotation reads in Italian, "where I yet live on, and I ask no more" (XV.119–20). It seemed a rich if typically cautious promise that he had not forgotten her.

The newly launched general publishing house of Faber & Gwyer (later Faber & Faber) asked Eliot to join the firm as literary editor in 1925. The position offered him a highly influential position in the London literary community and a ready forum for publishing the authors he most admired, including Joyce, Pound, and Marianne Moore. In testament to his growing prominence in literary and academic circles, Eliot was invited to give the prestigious Clark Lectures at Cambridge during the following year. Published only recently as *The Varieties of Metaphysical Poetry* (1993), the 1926 lectures expand his preoccupations with the seventeenth-century metaphysical poetry of John Donne, George Herbert, and Richard Crashaw, tracing their imaginative lineage back to Dante and the Italian poets of the *dolce stil novo*. He discusses a "tendency toward dissolution" that first began to divide thought from feeling in the English poetry of the seventeenth century (*VMP* 76), and he applauds the intellectual and emotional superiority of medieval religious thinkers like Richard of St. Victor, Thomas Aquinas, and John of the Cross. In the latter half of the decade, Eliot's imagination gravitated strongly toward the intellectual structure and emotional self-scrutiny of religious thinkers like these. He held fast to the conviction that art could not be a substitute for religion, but he also came to believe that religious sentiment could be a potent catalyst for artistic and emotional forces.

Eliot's creative energies were moving steadily toward the unity of thought and feeling he found in religious writers, and his personal energies were not far behind. During a visit to Rome later in 1926, he shocked his companions by descending to his knees in front of Michelangelo's *Pietà* at St. Peter's. From a philosophical skeptic and poetic ironist, this seemed an unprecedented gesture of devotion and surrender. Perhaps, however, his companions would have been less surprised had they realized that Eliot had been on this path for some time. How could they have known that during a walking tour almost a decade before, he had startled Pound in the same way by confessing unexpectedly: "I am afraid of the life after death" (Schuchard 119)?

Eliot began to meet regularly with William Force Stead, an American chaplain at Worcester College, Oxford. In May 1927 he confided to Stead the exciting news that he had received an unexpected letter from Emily Hale, and that it had "brought back something" to him, as he put it, that he "had not known for a long time" (Gordon 234). He had also turned to Stead in November 1926, when he decided to be confirmed into the Church of England. The baptism and confirmation were both performed with great secrecy at Eliot's request. He knew that his conversion would likely be greeted with dismay by the literary public, for whom he was still the seemingly nihilistic, iconoclastic author of "Gerontion," *The Waste Land*, and "The Hollow Men."

When he publicly declared his conversion – writing in the 1928 volume of essays, *For Lancelot Andrewes*, that he was "classicist in literature, royalist in politics, and anglo-catholic in religion" (vii) – it was as he suspected. To many, it seemed an effortless escape from the spiritual devastation and ruins of modernity that he had once so fiercely recaptured; to him, it was the most demanding path possible, a way to face not only the ruins but the vast abyss that lies beneath them. In effect, Eliot chose to follow his beloved Arnaut Daniel, the soul in Dante's *Purgatorio* who voluntarily plunges into "the fire that refines" (XXVI.148). In his eyes, this demanded a life of sacrifice, devotion, and celibacy.

Eliot almost immediately turned his attention back to Dante. The medieval poet who had once provided *The Waste Land* with models for its haunting scenes of infernal torture now offered him a different set of images, one to which he had been drawn years before but had not yet fully grasped: that of spiritual purgation and self-sacrifice. In the essay "Dante" (1929), his imagination moves from the torments of *Inferno* to the strivings of *Purgatorio*, as well as to his master's earliest visionary work, sensing in the *Vita Nuova* ("New Life") the very paradigm of discipline, imaginative sublimation, and renewal that he had long sought in his own life. His immersion in Dante also helped him to map the emotional terrain for his own purgatorial poem, *Ash-Wednesday* (1930), in which he attempted to reconfigure the *Vita Nuova* for himself. Written between 1927 and 1930, *Ash-Wednesday* came together just as *The Waste Land* had, in pieces and segments that gesture separately toward the emotional consequences of surrender, sacrifice, and self-denial. If, as Lyndall Gordon suggests, "Eliot's poems of 1927–1935 move toward a pulsating moment or a vision of radiant light" (241), they do so slowly, arduously, and with the same fear and hesitation that characterized his earliest poems of circuitous disbelief and self-torment in *Inventions of the March Hare.*

"Into the Rose-Garden," 1932–1939

Eliot returned to the United States in 1932, for the first time since the fraught visit in 1915 on the heels of his unexpected marriage, to give the prestigious Charles Eliot Norton lectures at Harvard. He arranged to meet Emily Hale while he was there and found tremendous relief in their long-awaited reunion. In a letter to Pound, he admitted that he now felt torn between his thriving career in England and the peaceful domestic pleasures he had rediscovered across the Atlantic.

Before Eliot came back from America, he sent Vivien a request for a formal separation, which she received with shock, desperation, and outright refusal. Friends said that he looked "10 years younger" ("hard, spry, a glorified boy scout," Virginia Woolf observed) upon his return to England in June 1933, but in private Eliot was committing himself to an ascetic, prolonged solitude (Woolf: 178). For six months he lived in a cramped cabin outside the ramshackle farmhouse at Pike's Farm, owned by his friend and colleague at Faber, Frank Morley. His demeanor, Morley recalled, was that of "a man who is climbing his private mountain of Purgatory" (Tate 106). Once back in London he effectively went into hiding from his wife, whose frantic pleas for his return grew steadily more public and intrusive. At St. Stephen's Church, where he attended daily prayer services, he met and befriended Eric Cheetham, an Anglican priest who offered him a place to stay in his presbytery. The austere living conditions at 9 Grenville Place conformed to Eliot's increasingly ascetic tastes and his desire for a chastened daily routine of reflection, prayer, and atonement. There were few visitors to entertain, the pipes froze frequently, and the walls shook when the train passed by below. He soon took up the position of Vicar's Warden at St. Stephen's, a post which obliged him to look after the business affairs of the parish. Emily Hale's visit to England around this time and the pair's walking tour of the magnificent grounds at the English manor house Burnt Norton – during which he apparently experienced a visionary sense of release and rejuvenation – only intensified the conflict and self-division that he suffered. He found himself torn between the simple, shared happiness he desired and the chastened, rarefied ideals he associated with the spiritual life.

Once again, however, Eliot released and transfigured the mounting pressures of this internal conflict by transmuting them into the desperate spiritual struggles that confront his protagonist, the medieval English Archbishop Thomas Becket, in *Murder in the Cathedral* (1935). Boldly experimental and steeped in the vocabulary of self-doubt and temptation, Eliot's first complete play opened to unexpected and widespread acclaim. He had long been interested in Greek and Roman tragedy, in the haunting, incisive wit of the Elizabethan dramatists, and in the practical intricacies of poetic drama in general. Verse drama now offered him a new and challenging forum for the dramatic impulse that was so clearly present in such early monologues as "Prufrock" and "Portrait of a Lady," and in turn, it cleared a space in his poetry for a new, more meditative and discursive style. The variegated styles of *The Waste Land* were splitting apart: the tumultuous voices of dramatic personae that echo through the poem now found a more traditional medium in actual stage characters, while the solemn voice of the thunder at its conclusion soon found its own place in the *Quartets*.

The year 1936 saw the publication of two significant collections of Eliot's mature work. *Essays Ancient and Modern* reasserted his position not only as an influential and authoritative literary critic but as a steadfast public intellectual, one whose sweeping range of interests encompassed social policy, political institutions, national education, and the uses of culture. His new collection of verse, *Collected Poems 1909–1935*, represented the concentrated poetic achievement of almost two decades and concluded with his new long poem, "Burnt Norton," in which philosophical meditations on temporality and irrevocable loss coalesced with memories of his serene visit to the manor house with Hale several years before. Eliot addresses her implicitly in the poem, questioning himself about "the passage which we did not take" and "the door we never opened," but in the end, turning away from comfort and nostalgia to plunge toward a "darkness to purify the soul" (*CPP* 117, 120).

By the summer of 1938, Vivien had grown desperate and inconsolable over Eliot's abandonment and refusal to return to her. She began to wander the streets nightly in distress, and according to her brother, was picked up by the police and committed to a sanatorium called Northumberland House soon thereafter. It seems likely that Eliot did not have a hand in her committal, but he neither prevented it nor attempted to contact her before she died there in 1947. Again Eliot felt the pressures of his personal life escalating, and again he found a release valve in the composition of his second play, *The Family Reunion* (1939). There the protagonist, Harry Lord Monchensey, returns to his ancestral home to confront his guilt over the mysterious death of his wife, for which he fears he may have been responsible. In the play's conclusion, he must decide between the comfort and reassurance offered by his newfound lover and the uncertain, lonely path of solitude and purgation offered by the ghostly Eumenides. Harry chooses the latter, claiming "I would not have chosen this way, had there been any other": "it is at once the hardest thing and the only thing possible" (*CPP* 280). Though it was not, in truth, the only one possible, Eliot made this choice as well. Over the coming years Emily Hale realized that he did not intend to marry her, and the two drifted apart.

War and the *Quartets*, 1939–1947

With his editorial energy flagging, his disappointment over *The Family Reunion*'s lackluster reception, and his growing despondency over the certainty of a second world war, Eliot brought the 17-year run of the *Criterion* to an end in 1939. Despite the incipient political chaos, he capitalized on his increasingly broad appeal as public intellectual and offered a timely series of lectures, published as *The Idea of a Christian Society* (1939), in which he emphasized the crucial need for religion, community, and culture in refashioning a society that might withstand the despotic aggressions of a tyrant like Hitler. It is telling that, although many of the poems in the book had already circulated privately among his friends at Faber, *Old Possum's Book of Practical Cats* also appeared at this time. With their jovial lightness and lilting rhythms, perhaps these delightful poems (which eventually gave rise to the blockbuster musical *Cats*) were meant to signal his farewell to an era of civilization that he sensed radically threatened by the oncoming war. In Eliot's eyes, the historical and cultural richness that he had so avidly sought when he left Harvard over twenty years before – what he called then the "mind of Europe" (*SE* 6) – was coming undone.

He had yet to compose a magnum opus, a long work that would be representative of his mature creative abilities. In the strife-filled years between 1939 and 1942, when many theaters closed and public arts organizations folded, Eliot returned to poetry and to the composition of what he now envisioned would extend and complete the creative project he had undertaken four years before with "Burnt Norton." As he now foresaw it, each new sequence would follow an identical structure, revolve around a particular, familiar locale, and expand outward from "an acute personal reminiscence" (as he put it) toward more universal meditations on time and redemption (Gardner 67). Eliot was hopeful that the poem would bring him the kind of "reconciliation and relief" that he sensed stirring in Beethoven's late Quartets: "I should like to get something like that into verse before I die," he admitted (Spender 132–33). But he often doubted the value of his work amid such violence and chaos. "Morning after morning spent fiddling with words and rhythms," he wrote searchingly, "often seems so pointless" (Browne 158).

During World War II Eliot enlisted as an air-raid warden in Kensington, where he would spend two sleepless nights each week watching for fires caused by German attacks. As the strain wore on him, he took to living outside of London for part of the week, commuting into the city to attend to his publishing responsibilities and assume his fire-watching duties from the roof of the Faber office building. In the midst of it all, the second volume of his long "war" poem, "East Coker," appeared in 1940; "The Dry Salvages" in 1941; "Little Gidding" in 1942; and the *Four Quartets* as a whole, "[t]he complete consort dancing together," later in the same year (*CPP* 144).

The Smiling Public Man, 1943–1965

After the war ended Eliot returned to live full-time in London and shared a flat at 19 Carlyle Mansions with John Hayward, an avid bibliophile and exacting literary editor whose opinions he deeply valued. In the eleven years they shared the flat, Eliot appreciated both the solitude and the social life that Hayward's friendship permitted. Other friends from this period recall him living between the usual extremes. At times, the 55-year-old poet was intensely solitary and reclusive, keeping to his part of the shared flat, a sparse bedroom with a large crucifix and writing desk. At others, he was surprisingly jovial and social, giving private readings of his poetry or reciting from memory long passages from Sherlock Holmes, one of his long-time favorites.

After 1948, Eliot lived the life of a "sixty-year-old smiling public man" (as W. B. Yeats memorably referred to himself) (Yeats 216). He enjoyed a private audience with the Pope during a visit to Rome in 1947, gave national broadcasts for BBC public radio, and spent a year at the prestigious Institute for Advanced Study at Princeton University. The man who had once taught evening courses for a meager living was now invited around the world to give literary lectures. In 1948 alone he lectured in Brussels, Germany, and South Africa. In the same year he was awarded both the prestigious Order of Merit in England and the Nobel Prize for Literature in recognition of "his outstanding, pioneer contribution to present-day poetry" (*Le Prix* 56). When he visited the United States he was welcomed as a celebrity and immediately greeted by the press and groups of fans. One lecture that he gave in Minneapolis, "The Frontiers of Criticism," famously drew an audience of 14,000 listeners. Despite such impressive accolades, however, he maintained regular hours at the publishing house. An interviewer in 1960 recorded his daily schedule, which seemed the routine of an anonymous office clerk: "He left his flat . . . wearing an impeccable dark blue suit and carrying a tightly rolled umbrella, walked one block to the No, 49 bus stop. When the bus came, he mounted to the upper deck, unfolded his *London Times* to the crossword puzzle, and fell to" ("Reflections" 22). From his office at Faber, Eliot the publisher turned his attention to promoting and nurturing the literary talent of young writers like W. H. Auden, Djuna Barnes, and later Ted Hughes.

Though he continued to add to his prolific critical writings, Eliot wrote little poetry after the *Quartets*. The popular stage now consumed his creative energies, even if he claimed to possess no natural talent for dramatic composition. In his later plays, he worked tirelessly to balance the formal elements of dramaturgy with the release of personal pressures that poetry had once provided. In *The Cocktail Party*, for instance, a semi-comedy which opened to great acclaim in New York in 1949, Eliot examined the kind of suffering he knew from his years of severe and self-imposed solitude: "What is hell? Hell is oneself, / Hell is alone" (*CPP* 342). The popular success of *The Cocktail Party* landed him on the cover of *Time* magazine, but he remained dissatisfied with its imperfections and soon set about trying to remedy them in *The Confidential Clerk*. In his fourth major play, he strove to achieve an even more colloquial, less "poetic" style. "Cut out the poetry," Eliot once surprisingly remarked, "That's what I've been trying to do all my life" (Matthews 159).

When his sister Margaret died suddenly in 1956, the 68-year-old poet somberly asked his friend E. F. Tomlin, "How does one set about dying?" (Gordon 500). Yet in the nine years remaining to him, he finally discovered the domestic happiness that had eluded him for so long. A few months later he proposed to Valerie Fletcher, his 30-year-old secretary at Faber, and the two were married early in the morning on January 10, 1957 in a private ceremony at St. Barnabas Church, where (as Eliot learned) Jules Laforgue had been married almost a century before. After a honeymoon in the south of France, Eliot returned to his play-in-progress, *The Elder Statesman*, now lightening the play's darker undertones and integrating a kind of tender love poetry unknown in his work until then. He was uncharacteristically affectionate with his new wife in public: the man who had seemed to be preparing for death now told reporters that he was considering taking dancing lessons with her. Despite his continuous and increasingly severe health problems, it was a period of profound and liberating peace for Eliot.

After a series of debilitating illnesses, Eliot died of heart failure at his home in London on January 4, 1965. He entertained some remarkable visitors and correspondents during his final months – renowned composer Igor Stravinsky and nuclear physicist J. Robert Oppenheimer among them – but perhaps none so singularly entertaining as the comedian and film star Groucho Marx, with whom he drank whiskey, traded photographs, and smoked cigars. News that the famous comedian was coming to London to visit him, he later told Marx, had inestimably improved the poet's own reputation around town. "Obviously," Eliot mischievously wrote, "I am now someone of importance" (Marx 162).

References and Further Reading

Ackroyd, Peter. *T. S. Eliot: A Life*. New York: Simon, 1984.

Bell, Robert H. "Bertrand Russell and the Eliots." *American Scholar* 52 (1983): 309–25.

Browne, Martin E. *The Making of T. S. Eliot's Plays*. London: Cambridge UP, 1969.

Dante Alighieri. *The Divine Comedy*. Trans. Allen Mandelbaum. New York: Knopf, 1995.

Gardner, Helen. *The Composition of Four Quartets*. New York: Oxford UP, 1978.

Gordon, Lyndall. *T. S. Eliot: An Imperfect Life*. New York: Norton, 2000.

Hall, Donald. *Their Ancient Glittering Eyes: Remembering Poets and More Poets*. New York: Ticknor, 1992.

Le Prix Nobel En 1948. Stockholm: Imprimerie Royale, 1949.

Levy, William Turner, and Victor Scherle. *Affectionately, T. S. Eliot: The Story of a Friendship, 1947–1965*. Philadelphia: Lippincott, 1968.

March, Richard, and Tambimuttu, eds. *T. S. Eliot: A Symposium*. Chicago: Henry Regnery, 1949.

Marx, Groucho. *The Groucho Letters*. New York: Simon, 1967.

Matthews, T. S. *Great Tom: Notes towards the Definition of T. S. Eliot*. New York: Harper, 1973.

"Reflections: Mr. Eliot." *Time* 6 Mar. 1950: 22–26.

Schuchard, Ronald. *Eliot's Dark Angel: Intersections of Life and Art*. New York: Oxford UP, 1999.

Sencourt, Robert. *T. S. Eliot, A Memoir*. New York: Dell, 1971.

Seymour-Jones, Carol. *Painted Shadow: The Life of Vivienne Eliot*. New York: Random, 2001.

Spender, Stephen. *T. S. Eliot*. New York: Viking, 1998.

Tate, Allen, ed. *T. S. Eliot: The Man and His Work*. New York: Dell, 1966.

Woolf, Virginia. *The Diary of Virginia Woolf: Volume 4, 1931–1935*. New York: Harvest, 1983.

Yeats, W. B. *The Collected Poems of W. B. Yeats*. 2nd rev. ed. Ed. Richard Finneran. New York: Scribner, 1996.

2
Eliot's Ghosts: Tradition and its Transformations

Sanford Schwartz

"You told me your thesis was about the influence of Shakespeare on T. S. Eliot," she said.
"So it is," he replied. "I turned it round on the spur of the moment, just to take that Dempsey down a peg or two."
"Well, it's a more interesting idea, actually."

— David Lodge, *Small World* (1984)

The small world of Persse McGarrigle, ingénue hero of David Lodge's globe-trotting academic satire, has just become substantially larger and immeasurably more complex. In an effort to outshine Robin Dempsey, his apparent rival for the beautiful and brainy Angelica (the "she" of the epigraph above), Persse has tripped upon the reversal of cause and effect that might have turned his humdrum thesis into "the influence of T. S. Eliot on Shakespeare," the paradoxical but more provocative study of a later poet's influence upon his predecessor. But unlike the antediluvian Dempsey, few of Lodge's own readers would be startled by Persse's spur-of-the-moment inspiration: "'Who can hear the speeches of Ferdinand in *The Tempest* without being reminded of 'The Fire Sermon' section of *The Waste Land?*'" (52). After all, the idea that literary tradition is a two-way street had been around for most of the century, and Persse's rather tame formulation misses its more radical implication – that the present shapes our comprehension of the past as much as the past influences the present. Ironically, the most influential articulation of this view harks back to Eliot's own essay "Tradition and the Individual Talent" (1919), and to the subsequent stream of lectures, articles, and full-length volumes that consolidated the poet's position as the arbiter of literary taste in the middle third of the century. By the time of Lodge's novel, Eliot had acquired a posthumous reputation as the epitome of a stifling traditionalism, and in this respect Persse McGarrigle's actual study of Shakespeare's influence on Eliot is behind the times not only in its old-fashioned approach to literary tradition but also in its focus on a poet whose once unassailable canonical status had been rapidly disintegrating. The fact that Eliot himself was

A Companion to T. S. Eliot, First Edition. Edited by David E. Chinitz.
© 2014 John Wiley & Sons, Ltd. Published 2014 by John Wiley & Sons, Ltd.

responsible for the more dynamic concept of tradition to which Persse owes his sudden upsurge of individual talent is the unspoken joke that the writer shares with his reader. But it is uncertain whether Lodge's more militantly "postmodern" readers, eager to represent "modernism" as a spent cultural force, were prepared to accept the joke. Now that we have come to recognize the "postmodern" dimension of "modernism" itself, we seem better poised to enjoy Lodge's ironies. More importantly, we may also be in a position to appreciate anew the poet who once astonished the world with the ingenuity of his verse, challenging the authority of his nineteenth-century forebears even more successfully than his late twentieth-century critics contested his own.

"Tradition and the Individual Talent"

"Tradition and the Individual Talent" is the locus classicus of Eliot's concept of tradition. The essay first appeared in two installments (September and December 1919) in the avant-garde journal the *Egoist*. It achieved broader circulation in Eliot's first prose collection, *The Sacred Wood* (1920), and later served as the lead article of his most influential volume, *Selected Essays* (1932). Eliot cited the essay repeatedly in subsequent works, such as *After Strange Gods* (1934), *Notes towards the Definition of Culture* (1948), and, as late as 1964, his Preface to a reissue of *The Use of Poetry and the Use of Criticism* (1933). Nearly a century after its initial appearance, scholars continue to debate a multitude of issues raised by this pivotal essay: its sources in Eliot's literary and philosophical background; its place in the artistic and intellectual ferment of the early modernist movement; its affiliations with contemporaries as different as Ezra Pound and Walter Benjamin; its internal divisions and discrepancies, such as the discontinuity between its two major sections – the first focusing on "tradition," the second on "the individual talent" – and its fluctuation between descriptive and prescriptive stances; its subsequent development in Eliot's own critical and cultural writings and its relations to more recent work on tradition and cultural memory; and perhaps above all, its relationship to Eliot's own poetic output both before and after it appeared. Does the essay serve as a reliable gloss on the use of tradition in Eliot's verse, as many of his early admirers seemed to assume? Or does the essay provide a justification for a poetic practice that may be more complex than the essay itself indicates, a practice that may in turn expose the rifts and ruses within Eliot's literary program, as some of his later critics came to believe? Should we approach Eliot's allusive habits as a nostalgic longing for a lost tradition or as a detached and distinctively modern (if not postmodern) orientation to a heritage that has become an "imaginary museum" (Malraux 13),[1] operative only in the ironic mode of "citability" (Benjamin 38), pastiche, and parody? However we address these concerns, Eliot's seminal essay remains a flash point for modern reflection not only on the problem of literary tradition and its attendant concerns with canonicity, influence, and authority, but also on the increasingly urgent issue of cultural transmission in a world that seems caught between irreversible rupture from the past and uncompromising reversion to it.

"Tradition and the Individual Talent" is often read through the lens of Eliot's later and more ideologically freighted criticism, particularly the oft-quoted remark that his leanings were "classicist in literature, royalist in politics, and anglo-catholic in religion" (*FLA* vii). Indeed, there is much in Eliot's early essay that seems to anticipate this elevation of traditional authority over the individual autonomy implicit in romantic literature, egalitarian politics, and Protestant religion: the paradoxical assertion that the most "individual" aspects of a poet's work are those in which "the dead poets, his ancestors, assert their immortality most vigorously" (*SE* 4); the claim that any poet worth his salt must write "with a feeling that the whole of the literature from Homer and within it the whole of the literature of his own country has a simultaneous existence and composes a simultaneous order" (4); and the focus on the poet's "continual surrender of himself as he is at the moment to something which is more valuable," his "continual extinction of personality" (6–7). Under the weight of the venerable "mind of Europe," there seems to be limited room for the development of an individual voice or new forms of expression that are adequate to the changing conditions of the world we inhabit (6). Seen from this perspective, Eliot retains the acute historical sensibility of nineteenth-century intellectuals, but in the process of rejecting the evolutionary or developmental paradigm that characterized their thought, he transforms "the historical sense" into a seemingly ahistorical awareness of a permanent and authoritative tradition (4). Even as he shifts from "tradition" to the creative "individual talent" in the second half of the essay, Eliot couches the act of poetic invention in a markedly anti-romantic "Impersonal theory of poetry" that transmutes personal emotion into the "*significant* emotion, emotion which has its life in the poem and not in the history of the poet" (7, 11). This account of poetic "depersonalization" seems to confirm the prevailing image of the reactionary Eliot and offers us little reason to see the young poet-critic as significantly different from the one who became the sitting target of wave after wave of cultural antagonism in the decades after his death.

However satisfying this reading may be to a later generation, it presents only half of Eliot's equation in "Tradition and the Individual Talent":

> The necessity that [the artist] shall conform, that he shall cohere, is not one-sided; what happens when a new work of art is created is something that happens simultaneously to all the works of art which preceded it. The existing monuments form an ideal order among themselves, which is modified by the introduction of the new (the really new) work of art among them. The existing order is complete before the new work arrives; for order to persist after the supervention of novelty, the *whole* existing order must be, if ever so slightly, altered; and so the relations, proportions, values of each work of art toward the whole are readjusted; and this is conformity between the old and the new. Whoever has approved this idea of order, of the form of European, of English literature, will not find it preposterous that the past should be altered by the present as much as

the present is directed by the past. And the poet who is aware of this will be aware of great difficulties and responsibilities. (*SE* 5)

A critical eye will find it easy to fault this formulation. If nothing else, the focus on "existing monuments" implies an elitist aesthetic, says little about the social framework of artistic production, and begs a variety of questions concerning canon formation and the complex interaction among various literary voices, styles, and forms that coexist and often compete for cultural dominance. Nevertheless, in its own time Eliot's emphasis upon the "simultaneous" and "ideal" order was a means of extricating voices from the past from an increasingly pedantic historical method that tethered them to their own bygone age. Eliot may well have been echoing his friend and editor Ezra Pound, who expressed the same shift from historical to aesthetic criteria a few years earlier: "All ages are contemporaneous. . . . What we need is a literary scholarship, which will weigh Theocritus and Yeats with one balance, and which will judge dull dead men as inexorably as dull writers of today, and will, with equity, give praise to beauty before referring to an almanack [*sic*]" (6). Pound was engaged in raising ghosts from the past to "make it new" in the present, and his hostility to the forms of modern life, like Nietzsche's, led increasingly to the search for lost traditions – and the values implicit in them – that the modern world had abandoned, suppressed, or distorted beyond recognition. Eliot for his part hews closer to the "main current" of tradition, while reminding us that the vital center "does not at all flow invariably through the most distinguished reputations" (*SE* 5–6).

Also evident in Eliot's reference to an "ideal order" is the patently modern recognition, articulated with precision in his 1916 doctoral dissertation on the philosopher F. H. Bradley, of "the relativity and the instrumentality of knowledge" (*KE* 169), including our knowledge of the past. As he states in his thesis, the development of any science is "rather organic than mechanical"; it provides a provisional if efficacious "point of view" that establishes a framework for new inquiry and is in turn modified by its own discoveries "into something new and unforeseen" (61). In a similar way, the elements of tradition constitute an "ideal order" that sets the stage for the "supervention of novelty" that alters "the *whole* existing order." Of course, the organic notion of tradition as "a living whole" has been a cornerstone of modern conservative thought ever since Edmund Burke issued his famous *Reflections on the Revolution in France* (*SE* 7). But in light of his more radical Bradleyan perspective, Eliot comes close to turning the tables on Burke. If as a result of "the really new" work of art, the past is "altered by the present as much as the present is directed by past," then the tail of innovation begins to wag the dog of tradition. The same is true of the "Impersonal theory of poetry" that dominates the second half of the essay. If the upshot of the poet's "self-sacrifice" is a "medium . . . in which impressions and experiences combine in peculiar and unexpected ways," Eliot's dissociation between "the man who suffers and the mind which creates" is far less a program for self-suppression in favor of an authoritative tradition than a call to the "transmutation" of passions and feelings into something "new and unforeseen" (8–9).

The countervailing tendencies in Eliot's essay allow us to seize it by either end of the stick, or to play one tendency against the other. As the mid-century hegemony of the New Criticism began to decline, critics found it tempting to set the second half of the essay in opposition to the first, teasing out the discrepancies between the self-declared "classicist" and the closet "romantic" whose works attest to the very aesthetic he sought to supersede. In the process of unseating Eliot's own authority, this revisionist tendency brought to the fore the more personal poetic voice and the more self-divided critical stance that was there all along. At the same time, with the release of Eliot's doctoral dissertation (first published in 1964), it became increasingly apparent that the mind of the young philosopher was more dialectical than dogmatic, more inclined to Bradley's emphasis upon the limitations of conceptual knowledge than to his notion of the Absolute. In his early literary essays, which began to appear soon after the completion of the thesis, Eliot employs the same strategy through which he exposes the one-sidedness of "idealism," which privileges mind over its objects, and "realism," which starts with objects and then tries to account for their representation in the mind. Most of Eliot's readers are well acquainted with his attempt to offset an excessive subjectivism in late romantic poetry – the literary equivalent of philosophical idealism – by emphasizing dispassionate receptivity to the objects of experience (which include the poet's own emotions and feelings). Less well known is his criticism of excess in the opposite direction – the objective extremes of fictional and dramatic realism – by insisting that the artist should not seek to represent the existing world (which is only a product of social convention) but should constitute a new world, or as he puts it in "Hamlet and His Problems" (1919), "intensify the world to his emotions" (*SE* 126). The same double movement may be at work in the conflicting currents of "Tradition and the Individual Talent," which appeared at the same time as the essay on *Hamlet*. In other words, it is unnecessary to set the "classical" Eliot against the crypto-"romantic," the poet who conforms to "tradition" against the "individual talent" who produces "new and sudden combinations" (185). Admittedly, the rhetorical force of the essay lies more on one side than the other, and it would be a mistake to ignore this telling asymmetry or its effects upon Eliot's readers, both advocates and adversaries alike. Nevertheless, the concept of tradition developed in the first half of the essay is not only open to innovation but actually depends upon the individual creativity explored in the second half. And as we shall see, the specific type of novelty explored in the latter portion of the essay does not arise *ex nihilo* from the uncreated depths of individual genius but from the selective retrieval and reworking of the tradition itself.

Talent and the Individual Tradition

Taken together, the two halves of "Tradition and the Individual Talent" speak to the pervasive counterpointing of past and present in Eliot's early verse, which seems to hold out the same set of interpretive options prompted by the opposing tendencies of his essay. If the section on "tradition" directs us to the swarm of allusions that establish parallels and contrasts with the state of modern life, the ensuing section on "individual" creation calls attention to the "new combinations" that these allusions produce. On the one hand, the various modern personae who populate the early poetry, whether or not they are aware of it, are situated in a field of textual references that awaken the sense of something other and elsewhere – a tradition that elicits the remembrance of a spiritual legacy that still reverberates in the "deeper, unnamed feelings which form the substratum of our being, to which we rarely penetrate" (*UPUC* 149). Prufrock, "Apeneck" Sweeney, Gerontion, Madame Sosostris, as well as the anonymous "Hollow Men," are animated largely by their ruptured relationship to this heritage or to the even more distant primitive and immemorial rites that position us as creatures "[b]etween two worlds" (*CPP* 141). On the other hand, past and present are fused together "in peculiar and unexpected ways" that compel our attention through the surprising and often complex relations they establish (*SE* 9). Hence the tradition is at once the site of a lost order as well as the repository of images, voices, and literary techniques that generate new forms of expression commensurate with the belated and ironically self-aware situation of the modern artist.

The remarkable staying power of Prufrock's "Love Song," Eliot's first major poem (1910–11), is attributable at least in part to this double-pronged appropriation of the past:

> But though I have wept and fasted, wept and prayed,
> Though I have seen my head [grown slightly bald] brought in upon a platter,
> I am no prophet – and here's no great matter;
> I have seen the moment of my greatness flicker,
> And I have seen the eternal Footman hold my coat, and snicker,
> And in short, I was afraid. (*CPP* 6)

Much is made of the obscurity and obliqueness of Eliot's allusions, but even if the full appreciation of these lines depends upon our biblical literacy (Mark 6.14–29; Matthew 14.1–12), we have little difficulty comprehending the transposition of prophetic lament – "wept and fasted, wept and prayed" (echoes of 2 Samuel 1.12, 12.21) – to the spiritually impoverished but psychologically exacting rituals of exchange in the modern drawing room. Such trademark allusions call up a tradition that hovers between presence and absence, haunting us with the remembrance of that which we can no longer embrace but cannot rid ourselves. At the same time, this union of spiritual anguish and social decorum, the resolutely self-sacrificial and the fastidiously trivial, also exhibits those "new and sudden combinations" that Eliot associates with poetic creativity – the "gift for combining, for fusing into a single phrase, two or more diverse impressions" that he found in Shakespeare, Donne, and their contemporaries, as well as in Laforgue and the French symbolists, and cultivated throughout the first half of his career (*SE* 185). Of course, not all of Eliot's poetic allusions display this talent for "amalgamating disparate experience" (247), and many of his "new compound[s]" arise from sources other than the intersection of past and present (8). But in the union of these two processes – recollection of the past and formation of new combinations in the present – we find the voice that is at once steeped in tradition and thoroughly modern; and, in their uncanny blending of pathos and humor, such compounds express both the crisis of modernity and the quickening power of the resources, compensations, and perhaps even recuperative possibilities still available to it.

Many of the allusions in Eliot's early poetry operate in this double fashion, simultaneously eliciting an estranged tradition and transforming it into a distinctively modern idiom. At the same time, Eliot's readers continue to struggle with, and often object to, the elusive references, the scraps of verbal citation that require both immense learning and considerable patience to wrest whatever significance they may have. These difficulties may be most evident in the epigraphs that appear in many of the poems prior to *The Waste Land,* a significant portion of which are unidentified or in a foreign tongue. At the gateway of "Prufrock," for instance, stands the block of italicized words that some might recognize as Dante's Italian, but most will stare at bemusedly. The conventions of the epigraph allow us to jump, however hesitantly, from the title to the first line of the poem, but if nothing else, this enigmatic mass seems to indicate that we are entering a dense terrain that may demand as much erudition as the poet himself possesses. Part of the message appears to be, as the poet puts it in his famous essay, that tradition "cannot be inherited, and if you want it you must obtain it by great labor" (*SE* 4). But for those undaunted readers who are prepared to expend that labor (or take the shortcut of a reader's guide), the fragment offers a beguiling perspective on the voice of the lines to follow:

> If I but thought that my response were made
> to one perhaps returning to the world,
> this tongue of flame would cease to flicker.
> But since, up from these depths, no one has yet
> returned alive, if what I hear is true,
> I answer without fear of being shamed. (*Inf.* XXVII, 61–66)

The speaker of these lines, Guido da Montefeltro, has been consigned to the niche reserved for false counselors in the densely populated eighth circle of Hell. In this instance the deceiver becomes the victim of his own self-deception, revealing his identity to Dante in the mistaken belief that his auditor must be a permanent resident of the underworld. What appears to be a private confession to one of the dead turns out to be a public disclosure to the world of the living. In this respect the epigraph not only sets the stage for the subsequent portrait of the modern inferno, dramatizing the all-consuming rift between self and world entailed in the struggle "[t]o prepare a face to meet the faces that you meet" (*CPP* 4). By simultaneously accentuating and blurring the boundary between private and public utterance, the epigraph also points to the peculiar suspension between lyric and dramatic voices, between internal musing and conversational speech, that underscores the central conflict between the effort to sustain an autonomous identity and the disorientation that ensues from immersion in the sea of "human voices" (7). Seen from this perspective, Guido's speech displays a double movement akin to Eliot's more transparent allusions. The shades of the dead establish similarities-in-difference to the situation of the present, while the modern journey to the past brings forth a poetic speech that is neither interior monologue nor an address to an auditor (the province of Victorian dramatic monologue), but something "rich and strange" that inhabits the uncertain space between them.[2] Already in this early poem (1910–11), the individual talent had constructed "a new compound," a fusion of poetic forms that cannot be identified with any voice in our actual experience, but that, like the work that combines disparate or contrasting emotions into "a new art emotion," intrigues and haunts us through the dissonant union of its constituent voices (*SE* 8, 10).

In *The Waste Land,* these complex relations between tradition and the individual talent expand into a structural principle, which (according to his appended Notes) Eliot derived from James Frazer's anthropological classic, *The Golden Bough* (1890–1915), and Jessie Weston's related study, *From Ritual to Romance* (1921), and developed into something akin to the "continuous parallel between contemporaneity and antiquity" that Eliot found in the "mythical method" of Joyce's *Ulysses* (*SP* 178). The allusions to a lost cultural tradition continue to operate as they did in "Prufrock," "Gerontion," and other early poems, but instead of an individual persona we now have a panorama of different figures, primarily though not exclusively modern, situated within an enduring archetypal framework that highlights the failure and futility of their condition. As in previous poems, the allusions in *The Waste Land* still provide the compensatory satisfaction of forming new composites: "But at my back from time to time I hear / The sound of horns and motors, which shall bring / Sweeney to Mrs. Porter in the spring" (*CPP* 43) – where Marvell's memorable carpe diem, chiming with the more obscure echo of Actaeon and Diana in John Day's *Parliament of Bees* (mentioned in Eliot's Notes [52]), modulates into the frenetic cacophony and routine sexuality of the modern waste land, at once continuous with and cut off from the past. But in addition to these "words perpetually juxtaposed in new and sudden combinations" (*SE* 185), *The Waste Land* is assembled through the juxtaposition of larger blocks of disparate material – vignettes, pastiches, apostrophes, songs, etc. – interspersed with a variety of passing references, brief tags, or mere noise, and woven together through a network of motifs and recurrent symbols. These juxtapositions reflect primarily a change in scale, and therefore Eliot's attempt at a modern long poem may be regarded as the further development of the principles and practices of his earlier verse. But to the extent that we take our interpretive cues from the references to Frazer and Weston in Eliot's Notes, there is something unsettling about a framework that grounds the spiritual legacy of Western culture – and more specifically the foundational event of the life, death, and resurrection of the Son of God – in a more comprehensive pattern of vegetation ceremonies based on the naturalistic cycle of the seasons. Does our tradition bear within it the voice of transcendent authority and the power of spiritual redemption, or does the anthropological grounding of religious tradition establish a new and seemingly universal vision only at the cost of taking us one step further in the modern "disenchantment of the world"?[3]

For similar reasons there is also something disturbing in the ostensibly curative sequence formed by Eliot's ingenious juxtapositions, which seem to move, however tentatively, from death (winter) to renewal (spring) in the last two sections of the poem. Once we have passed through the remedial calm of the moral injunction – Datta (give), Dayadhvam (sympathize), and Damyata (control) – what are we are to make of the final cascade of "fragments" that reprise the discontinuous character of the poem itself (*CPP* 50)? Does the dazzling collage of disparate voices throughout the poem culminate in a movement toward possible regeneration, or are we left with a "heap of broken images" that signify the terminal state of a tradition in ruins? Most would agree that the pieces coalesce poetically into something "rich and strange," but in the end the poem seems to hover between unity and fragmentation, the unity at once tentatively affirmative and ironically qualified by the very principle that informs it, the fragmentation perhaps dispiriting but also indicative of the enormous "variety and complexity" that must be assimilated in any adequate reconstruction of our cultural heritage (*SE* 248). Even for those who dismiss such reconstruction as mere nostalgia for a world well lost, the poem stands as a monument to the drastically altered circumstances in which we live, while its "variety and complexity" bears witness to a future dependent upon acceptance if not joyous celebration of life among the fragments.

Orthodoxy and the Individual Heresy

In the wake of his religious conversion, Eliot modified his concept of tradition as well as his allegiance to the kind of allusions that inspired his early poetic creation. In the infamous and never reprinted *After Strange Gods: A Primer of Modern Heresy* (1934), tradition is no longer an organic system composed of individual aesthetic monuments but a more inclusive notion, virtually synonymous with "culture" in the broadest sense of the term, which "involves all those habitual actions, habits and customs, from the most significant religious rite to our conventional way of greeting a stranger, which represent the blood kinship of 'the same people living in the same place'" (18). This reformulation clears the way for the introduction of "orthodoxy," which is the enduring standard of authority by which we examine, correct, and renew the tradition as it actually exists (22). If tradition is a largely unconscious process embedded in feeling and action, the maintenance of orthodoxy "calls for the exercise of all our conscious intelligence" (31). As a criterion for right living and thinking, orthodoxy can deliver some harsh strictures, and as its self-appointed guardian Eliot is no more tolerant of the "heretical" secular tendencies of major modern poets than he is of the culturally disruptive presence, as he puts it, of "any large number of free-thinking Jews" (20).

Eliot would come to regret such scandalous remarks, but before we dismiss his later work on the basis of such missteps (as telling as they may be), we should consider some of the more successful essays of his immediate post-conversion years.

If orthodoxy can trigger inquisition, it can also lead to insight, as it does in Eliot's little-known 1927 piece on Machiavelli's *The Prince* (*FLA* 47–65), which detaches this seemingly "modern" work from the new secular spirit with which it is usually associated and shrewdly resituates it within the tradition of late medieval Christian thought. The same is true of his more familiar 1930 essay on Baudelaire (*SE* 371–81), which rescues the poet from his association with late nineteenth-century aestheticism and recovers the traditional religious sensibility that informs (and dramatically enriches) his groundbreaking lyrical portraits of the modern city. We should also consider the judicious discussions of tradition in such essays of the 1940s–50s as "Yeats" (*OPP* 295–308), "What is a Classic?" (53–71), "The Social Function of Poetry" (15–21), and "American Literature and the American Language" (*TCTC* 43–60), his long deferred acknowledgment of a considerable literary debt (Oser 20–21). These later writings sometimes suffer from excessive qualification and from the conscious effort to achieve the equipoise of the seasoned sage. But they take us well beyond the scope of "Tradition and the Individual Talent" in their sensitivity to the varieties of literary expression; to the various time frames – one's own generation, the immediate past, the preceding era, the longer arc of the epoch, the enduring tradition – that inform any significant creative achievement in the present; and to the interactions between literary creativity and the evolution of the language, the social fabric, the national character, and the balance between stability and change that no civilization can afford to take for granted.

Significant changes also appear in the lyric poetry composed after the mid-twenties. Gone is the gallery of modern personae who are unaware of or unable to affirm the larger pattern embedded in the poetry itself. Gone as well is the allusive practice that perpetually fuses past and present into "new and sudden combinations." Donne gives way to Dante, and instead of the succession of metaphysical ironies we have the more measured, often meditative voice of the pilgrim whose journey forward is also an effort to recover what has been lost or forgotten, a return to what we are always in danger of allowing to slip away. The poet still draws his inspiration from the voices of the dead, but they are more companionable shades that bear witness to the same authority, and like the "familiar compound ghost" who appears in his last major poem, "Little Gidding," they share the recognition that "last year's words belong to last year's language," and answer to the common call, which never changes but is never the same, "[t]o purify the dialect of the tribe" (*CPP* 140–41). Similarly, as he shifted his creative energies increasingly toward the theater, Eliot continued to employ the scaffolding of ancient myth and ritual that he adopted in *The Waste Land,* but instead of the juxtaposition of radically disparate materials he comes closer to Joyce's own "mythical method" by staging a single sustained plot that establishes "a continuous parallel between contemporaneity and antiquity." We still find characters who are oblivious to the pattern in which they participate, but the center of attention now shifts to figures who traverse the gap between past and present and project the sense "that they are living at once on the plane that we know and on some other plane of reality from which we are shut out" (*EED* 173).

It is difficult to overestimate the significance of the struggle between tradition and innovation, the heritage of the past and the unique conditions of the present, in the political, social, and artistic debates of the last two centuries. Indeed, the modern concern with tradition is inseparable from the pervasive sense of the increasing distance between past and present that arose in the eighteenth century and accelerated dramatically in the wake of the French Revolution and the massive upheavals of industrial transformation in the nineteenth century. In this respect, Eliot is a relatively late arrival in a longstanding dispute, and he arrived upon the scene at a moment in which the evolutionary model – and its attendant notion of "progress" – through which many nineteenth-century intellectuals negotiated the rival claims of stability and change, was cracking under the ever-intensifying pressure from the very forces that produced it. Whether or not he rebounds from the current slump of his literary fortunes, Eliot remains a compelling if controversial case of early twentieth-century efforts to balance these opposing allegiances. In the years since his death, it has become more and more common to subsume Eliot within his own dogmatic creed – classicist, royalist, Anglo-Catholic – or to divorce his poetry (or at least his early poetry) from his prose and treat him as an exemplary instance of the peculiar association between avant-garde aesthetics and reactionary politics that we find in Pound, Yeats, Wyndham Lewis, and other luminaries of the modernist movement. The very persistence of the first view suggests that it is not entirely without foundation, and the second has much to recommend it even as it calls for further explanation. As a literary and cultural critic, Eliot leans decisively in one direction, but as we have seen in his seminal program piece, his concept of tradition contains an irreducibly radical element, and his notion of individual "surrender" and "self-sacrifice" is associated not with the commitment to shopworn literary forms but to the creation of new and surprising "combinations." We find the same doubleness in the perpetual juxtaposition of past and present in the early poetry, which may be read either as an elegiac lament for a lost tradition or as an ingenious staking of new poetic ground, but ultimately turns on the tension between them. This tension reaches its maximum in the discord between unity and fragmentation in *The Waste Land*. We may focus, as did Eliot's New Critical followers, on the vegetation ceremonies, at once sexual, social, and spiritual, that underlie its network of recurrent symbols and weave together its many divergent voices. Or we may direct our attention to the assemblage of stylistic pastiche and to the radical fragmentation that anticipates the irreducible multiplicity of the postmodern condition. The poem lends itself to either view, but the enduring fascination of Eliot's masterpiece lies in its power to pull us simultaneously in opposite directions, toward a tradition that may or not offer the prospect of redemption, and to a historically unprecedented situation that shuffles between the pride of its coming of age and the uncanny persistence of ghosts that refuse to stay away.

NOTES

1 Malraux's phrase, "le musée imaginaire," appears as "museum without walls" in the English translation.

2 "[R]ich and strange" comes from Ariel's song in *The Tempest* (I.ii.397–403), Eliot's favorite means of alluding to the process of metamorphosis or magical transformation.

3 "Disenchantment of the world" is Weber's famous phrase, "Entzauberung der Welt" (221). For more on Eliot's use of Frazer and Weston, see "FISHING, WITH THE ARID PLAIN BEHIND ME": DIFFICULTY, DEFERRAL, AND FORM IN *THE WASTE LAND*.

REFERENCES AND FURTHER READING

Benjamin, Walter. *Illuminations*. Ed. Hannah Arendt. Trans. Harry Zohn. New York: Schocken, 1969.

Bloom, Harold. *The Anxiety of Influence: A Theory of Poetry*. New York: Oxford UP, 1973.

Burke, Edmund. *Reflections on the Revolution in France*. 1790. Ed. J. C. D. Clark. Stanford: Stanford UP, 2001.

Cianci, Giovanni, and Jason Harding, eds. *T. S. Eliot and the Concept of Tradition*. Cambridge: Cambridge UP, 2007.

Dante Alighieri. *Inferno*. Trans. Robert Hollander and Jean Hollander. New York: Random, 2000.

Flinn, Anthony. *Approaching Authority: Transpersonal Gestures in the Poetry of Yeats, Eliot, and Williams*. Lewisburg: Bucknell UP, 1997.

Gadamer, Hans-Georg. *Truth and Method*. 1960. 2nd ed. New York: Seabury, 1975.

Jay, Gregory S. *T. S. Eliot and the Poetics of Literary History*. Baton Rouge: Louisiana State UP, 1983.

Levenson, Michael H. *A Genealogy of Modernism: A Study of English Literary Doctrine 1908–1922*. Cambridge: Cambridge UP, 1984.

Litz, A. Walton. "The Allusive Poet: Eliot and His Sources." *T. S. Eliot: The Modernist in History*. Ed. Ronald Bush. Cambridge: Cambridge UP, 1991. 137–51.

Lodge, David. *Small World*. London: Secker, 1984.

Longenbach, James. "'Mature poets steal': Eliot's Allusive Practice." *The Cambridge Companion to T. S. Eliot*. Ed. A. David Moody. Cambridge: Cambridge UP, 1994. 176–88.

——. *Modernist Poetics of History: Pound, Eliot, and the Sense of the Past*. Princeton: Princeton UP, 1987.

Lucy, Seán. *T. S. Eliot and the Idea of Tradition*. New York: Barnes & Noble, 1960.

Malraux, André. *The Voices of Silence*. 1947–49. Trans. Stuart Gilbert. Princeton: Princeton UP, 1978.

Oser, Lee. *T. S. Eliot and American Poetry*. Columbia: U of Missouri P, 1998.

Pearson, Gabriel. "Eliot: An American Use of Symbolism." *Eliot in Perspective: A Symposium*, ed. Graham Martin. New York: Humanities, 1970. 83–101.

Pound, Ezra. *The Spirit of Romance*. 1910. New York: New Directions, 1968.

Rabaté, Jean-Michel. *The Ghosts of Modernity*. Gainesville: UP of Florida, 1996.

——. "Tradition and T. S. Eliot." *The Cambridge Companion to T. S. Eliot*. Ed. A. David Moody. Cambridge: Cambridge UP, 1994. 210–22.

Reeves, Gareth. "T. S. Eliot and the Idea of Tradition." *Literary Theory and Criticism: An Oxford Guide*, ed. Patricia A. Waugh. Oxford: Oxford UP, 2006. 107–18.

Riquelme, John Paul. *Harmony of Dissonances: T. S. Eliot, Romanticism, and Imagination*. Baltimore: Johns Hopkins UP, 1991.

Sauerberg, Lars Ole. *Versions of the Past – Visions of the Future: The Canonical in the Criticism of T. S. Eliot, F. R. Leavis, Northrop Frye and Harold Bloom*. New York: St. Martin's, 1997.

Shils, Edward. *Tradition*. Chicago: U of Chicago P, 1981.

Shusterman, Richard. *T. S. Eliot and the Philosophy of Criticism*. New York: Columbia UP, 1988.

Svarny, Erik. *"The Men of 1914": T. S. Eliot and Early Modernism*. Philadelphia: Open UP, 1988.

Weber, Max. *The Protestant Ethic and the Spirit of Capitalism*. 1905. Trans. Talcott Parsons. New York: Scribner, 1958.

3

T. S. Eliot and the Symbolist City

Barry J. Faulk

Symbolism and the City

T. S. Eliot's *The Waste Land*, modernism's most celebrated global text, presumes that the history of the planet can be situated within the world city of London. As Joseph McLaughlin observes, the poem depicts the metropolis as Eliot experienced it: as "a linguistic and cultural Babel, an urban jungle, and both the heart and frontier of Empire" (25). The increasing globalization of culture, enabled by the rise of European imperialism, is the social foundation of this epic vision. As the first generation of poets who developed a poetic practice and a notion of culture adequate to the modern experience of the global metropolis, the French Symbolists enabled Eliot to conceive his wildly ambitious poem. It was the Symbolist Poets who provided Eliot with a means of conceptualizing London in its new immensity as both world city and center of world decay. Indeed, a philosophy of culture derived from the Symbolists underlies both the poetry and the criticism that Eliot wrote in the most productive years of his career, between 1917 and 1925.

It may seem counterintuitive to assert that the supposedly otherworldly Symbolists were capable of mentoring anyone in worldly matters. The movement that began in Paris during the last decades of the nineteenth century, with Stéphane Mallarmé at its center, rejected conventional expectations that poetry should strive for clarity and express common sentiments. The Symbolists sought to create poetry that evoked mysterious forces outside of everyday life, or expressed vague, abstract moods or mental states. They greatly admired Arthur Rimbaud and Charles Baudelaire from the previous generation of French poets. They sought to extend Baudelaire's claims (in *The Flowers of Evil*) to have discovered poetic symbols that served as "correspondences" between the visible world and a spiritual realm. And they esteemed poet-prodigy Rimbaud for writing visionary prose poems that proclaimed the need to transform modern life into an adventure. The Symbolists believed that poems should be as ambiguous and open to interpretation as a dream; indeed, they were interested

A Companion to T. S. Eliot, First Edition. Edited by David E. Chinitz.
© 2014 John Wiley & Sons, Ltd. Published 2014 by John Wiley & Sons, Ltd.

in dreams and the irrational as a source of poetry well before the Surrealists. Exalted visions, private reveries, and seedy locales were the frequent subject matter of their poems. Above all, the Symbolists were obsessed with words: their tones; their shapes; and their power, when properly arranged, to exceed literal statement, and, like music itself, to become infinitely expressive.

Like Rimbaud, Symbolist poets like Mallarmé and Jules Laforgue broke with conventional verse forms and developed highly idiosyncratic styles of writing – Mallarmé paradoxically seeking to describe the ineffable with precise diction, and Laforgue incorporating conversational idioms and slang in a unique poetry of ideas. Eliot's debt to these poets is profound, but modernism as a movement is equally obliged to the Symbolists for its image of the authentically modern artist. The notion of the "poète maudit" – the poet as antihero striving to achieve vision through, in Rimbaud's words, a "long, involved, and logical *derangement of all the senses*" by cultivating intoxication, blasphemy, and obscenity (*I Promise* 33) – became crucial to the popular image of the poet, and to a large degree, to the modernist artist's self-conception.

It is well known that the Symbolists prized their remove from mundane life. Mallarmé held that poetry was sacred, and that the poet was a sort of secular priest. In "The Book as Spiritual Instrument," he articulates a complex argument about the unique capacity of the book to combine matter with ideal forms, which nonetheless draws sharp lines between mere prose and the purified speech of poetry. Mallarmé famously advised poets to retreat from the world and remove themselves to their "ivory tower," a space above the fray.

Yet the closer we examine the major ideas of Symbolism, the propositions that helped unite the movement, the more we find a bewildering range of practice that belies the movement's collective identity. Take for instance the scholarly commonplace that the Symbolists wrote poems that drew on the model of music. Baudelaire inaugurated the music/poetry analogy in a commentary on Wagner's *Tannhäuser*, which Baudelaire believed constituted a new, uniquely expressive sort of poetry, linking sounds with mood, atmosphere, emotion, colors, even concepts. Baudelaire advised poets to organize words in a manner that was analogous to the way composers arranged tones, with the aim of evoking moods that exceeded mere emotion and blended thought with feeling. In contrast, Paul Verlaine took a more basic approach to the music-as-poetry analogy, relying on assonance and alliteration to make his verse more sonorous. But the argument that the Symbolists wrote musical verse runs aground in the cases of Rimbaud and Laforgue, the two Symbolist poets who most influenced Eliot. Laforgue incorporated colloquial speech in free verse and abandoned musical forms in poetry, except when he used verse structures from popular songs of the day to substitute for the stanza. Rimbaud's poetry is remarkable for its ability to combine concrete detail with abstractions, but not for any sonorous tonal quality. Mallarmé's highly sophisticated efforts to conflate writing poems with musical composition resulted in such supremely unmusical poems as "Un Coup de Des" ("A Roll of the Dice"), where the arrangement of words as print matter on the page becomes part of the meaning of the poem, with no notable regard for sound, not to mention verse form, grammar, or syntax. Such contradictory practice suggests that we cannot grasp the significance of Symbolism solely by acquainting ourselves with the explicit aims of the movement, or by relying on critical formulae. To comprehend the essence of the movement, we must look outside the Symbolists, to the context in which they lived and worked.

Clearly this is a job for Raymond Williams. In "Metropolitan Perceptions and the Emergence of Modernism," Williams situates the rise of avant-garde practice in the context of the new phenomenon of the imperial city. For Williams, migration is the enabling condition of avant-garde activity, specifically the movement of provincial intellectuals to the global metropolis. Laforgue and Rimbaud provide specific instances of this trajectory from the provincial city to the metropolis, as does Eliot himself. The cosmopolitan character of Symbolism has long been recognized. "Symbolism was not French; it happened in Paris," Anna Balakian reminds us, and as a cosmopolitan movement it anticipated the international character of subsequent avant-gardes (9–10). The Symbolists were centered in the metropole, and the alienating experience of urban density and cultural diversity was decisive in their development; it underlies the Symbolist mistrust of language in its ordinary usage, and explains their efforts to compensate for the increasingly marginal role of the extraordinary language of poetry in their society.

Cities like Paris and London were, as Williams writes, "the place where new social and economic and cultural relations beyond both city and nation . . . were beginning to be formed" (44); they were nodes in an emerging world system, and metropolitan artists were aware both of the rapid transformation in their midst and their uneasy situation in the new world order. The metropolis offered new, unprecedented possibilities for free, untrammeled expression, while at the same time, traditional social and cultural forms, developed under conditions of aristocratic hegemony, persisted. The metropolis was no mere melting pot, but a crucible where new forms of expression were born. Amid the linguistic diversity of the city, the rules of language seemed increasingly arbitrary to the discerning mind, a product of mere conventions genuine artists might defy with impunity. The situation was conducive to artistic experiment, but it also created a prejudice that the best poems somehow dramatize or acknowledge their status as artifacts, and confirm the poet as supreme technician of language.

The Symbolists were acutely conscious of the newly beleaguered status of poetry among the other discourses that proliferated in the city; this perception encouraged a greater awareness of their chosen medium, language itself. As Mallarmé emphatically claimed, poems were made of words, not ideas. Poems such as "Un Coup de Des" go one step further, exploiting the matter of the book, turning the spatial arrangement of black ink on white spaces into the poem's masterful orchestration of language. The Symbolists imagined their poems as constituting an alternative practice to middle-class communication: poets make language do more than the bourgeois – more than signify things, commemorate history, call for action, or evoke simple emotions. They arranged words for their own sake, in a supremely disinterested activity that set the poet above the journalist. As with any practice that exalts form or technique over content or shared experience, Symbolism could tend toward a cult of expertise.

This is to say that Symbolism was an avant-garde practice, and, as Williams argues, such practice was as much an effect of urban experience as an autonomous activity. Understanding Symbolism as a byproduct of metropolitan experience explains the universal agreement of the Symbolists that the movement's master was a poet from an earlier generation, the premier poet of urban street life, Charles Baudelaire. It was Baudelaire who forced lyric poetry to deal with seedy Parisian realism. In "The Painter of Modern Life" (1863), Baudelaire praises the flâneur, the detached observer of Paris crowds, as a philosopher of street life. Moreover, he conflates the flâneur with the modern artist, suggesting that the latter is distinguished by his way of life as much as by the kinds of art he produces (Gendron 35). Whatever their emotional genesis, Baudelaire's own poems returned obsessively to the social reality of Paris, with vivid, timely detail; his poetry is peopled by the city's demimonde, as well as the dispossessed poor made homeless by Baron Haussmann's mid-century grand plan to gentrify Paris. Baudelaire expanded the notion of modern poetry to include contemporary circumstance such as the changing spaces or demography of the modern city.

Eliot's Decadent Initiation

Taking this larger view of the place of the Symbolists in the world city into account, it would seem a mistake to insist on too rigid a separation of the Symbolists – those poets like Mallarmé committed to avant-garde discipline and an exalted notion of poetry – from the less ascetic Decadents. The Decadents, represented in England by Walter Pater, Oscar Wilde, Arthur Symons, and Aubrey Beardsley, were devoted to the cult of art for art's sake. While it would be erroneous simply to conflate the Decadents with the Symbolist artists they revered, it is also true that if you subtract from Symbolism such elements of Decadent ideology as occultism, drug use, and the vehement rejection of traditional religious morality, you take away most of Symbolism's distinctive content (Balakian 115). The art produced by both Symbolists and Decadents is fundamentally shaped by the circumstances of life in the secular, global city.

Eliot was introduced to the French Symbolist writers by the English Decadent poet Arthur Symons, whose *The Symbolist Movement in Literature* (1899), Eliot later stated, "was of more importance for my development than any other book" (*IMH* 395–96). His initial encounter with the Symbolist poets was transformative, and Symons and the Decadent poets of the 1890s framed his understanding of the movement.

Symons introduced Eliot to poets like Laforgue and Mallarmé, who had broken with conventions of French poetry and established *vers libre* as the most appropriate form for modern poetry. Laforgue's poetry in particular had a powerful effect on Eliot. "Portrait of a Lady," "The Love Song of J. Alfred Prufrock," and "La Figlia che Piange" are all written in a free verse adapted from Laforgue's *Derniers Vers*, an extremely loose form with "rhyming lines of irregular length" that substitute for stanzaic structure a conversational expression of an emotive idea – Baudelaire's precise definition of music (Ramsey 202). Soon after reading Laforgue, Eliot adopted the poet's unique version of dramatic monologue, which gave voice to a specific social type: a highly educated man, both philosophically inclined and somehow streetwise, perpetually uncomfortable in social situations, and a perennial failure in romance. This character is emotionally blocked and sexually repressed, coping with life by recourse to a cultivated insouciance and a highly developed sense of irony, directed at others but also at himself. Such is the central protagonist of the Laforgue monologue; we also recognize him as the chief persona in Eliot's first book, *Prufrock and Other Observations*. No wonder Frank Lentricchia describes Eliot's discovery of Laforgue as the poet's "Laforguian conversion": it is impossible to imagine Eliot writing his early, breakthrough poems without the enabling example of Laforgue's repertoire of voices, idioms, and poses (242).

Symons's book brought a generation of experimental poets to Eliot's attention and revolutionized his technique. The Symbolists also represented an expanded notion of what counted as the life of the mind. Their poems were ambiguous and often obscure, designed to convey the complex sorts of experience possible for sophisticated urbanites. They endeavored to engage their limited audience deeply, and with unprecedented intimacy. Poems such as Rimbaud's "Cities [II]" – "Some of the upper parts of town are inexplicable: a boatless arm of the sea unrolls its blue sleeve of delicate hail between piers loaded with giant candelabras" – were full of unearthly yet somehow precise juxtapositions (*Season* 53). In the process, the Symbolists moved verse away from the notion of a naturalistic poetic voice toward the construction of highly wrought poetic text.

Besides introducing Eliot to contemporary experiments in verse, Symons's book presented Eliot with a new mode of poetic self-presentation. The Symbolists that Symons surveys are all poet-intellectuals, often poet-critics or poet-philosophers. Again, the crucial figure here is Baudelaire; as Balakian writes, "Baudelaire makes poetry an intellectual rather than an emotional activity, and in this light the poet assumes the character of the sage or seer, rather than that of the bard" (47). More than anyone else in French letters, Baudelaire transformed the notion of the poet from someone who feels deeply and is at his or her most compelling when chronicling personal history or a national conquest, into a superior thinker, bent on deciphering the universal condition of being human. Accordingly, Baudelaire is the nineteenth century's great cosmopolitan, to whom no culture or experience is exotic or alien. Balakian argues that Baudelaire's cosmopolitanism is precisely the reason for the poet's appeal to the younger generation of Symbolist poets, "who will become in the years of 'the end of the century' the most denationalized group of writers that ever worked together," since the Paris in which they convened was now a world city (47).

Eliot knew well that Arthur Symons self-consciously affiliated his work with the movement in France. Eliot praised Symons's poetry – "Mr. Symons is himself, we must remember, no mean poet" (*IMH* 395) – while slighting Symons's capacity to assimilate Symbolism fully, at least compared with Eliot: "I must be grateful to him for putting me in touch with the work of the French poets, and for not having got out of them, for his own poetry, what I was to find there myself" (396). This remark should not cause us to underestimate Symons's influence on Eliot as a cosmopolitan poet-intellectual in his own right. Eliot's assertion that the "influence of Baudelaire upon Mr. Symons was manifestly genuine and profound" pays the elder poet a significant compliment (395). Like Baudelaire, Symons was a practicing poet who treated writing criticism, studying history, and writing poems as complementary occupations.

If anything, Symons's stature as interpreter of the Symbolists was underscored for Eliot by Symons's existential authority. Symons's career taught Eliot the important lesson that a modern poet and poetry could thrive not only in Paris, but in London as well. Symons made it a point of pride to acquaint himself with all aspects of urban modernity, including London nightlife (van den Beukel 136). He traveled to Paris to meet Verlaine and Mallarmé, introducing Mallarmé to W. B. Yeats and J. M. Synge. Symons adopted Baudelaire's interest as a poet in the universal human; he wrote prolifically on painting, music, and ballet as well as on Europe's major cities.

The city is the constant mise-en-scène of Symons's poetry and criticism. He treated dance as a mode of symbol production in the essay "The World as Ballet," a notion that Mallarmé expounded in "Ballets." While Symons, like Baudelaire, wrote verse on the image of the female dancer, this abstract discourse "required" Symons's nightly visits to music-halls in Leicester Square in the 1890s, which Karlien van den Beukel describes as a "a gaudy entertainment center where youths watched shows and became drunk" (136). Symons wrote essays on both Wagner and music-hall dance, unafraid of the music hall's associations with low culture.

Eliot didn't follow Symons's example to the point of making nightly raids on London's subcultures, but Symons reinforced the notion of the Symbolist poet as a cultural connoisseur. The extensive range of Symons's interests and obsessions seems to have had a major impact on Eliot's early poetry, which alludes to diverse cultural practices from Henry James to jazz, and on his early criticism, which pivots from the Jacobeans to Marie Lloyd, the music-hall singer. Symons balanced his intellectual seriousness with a bohemian lifestyle, with lasting consequences for Eliot's own notions of the breadth and scope of culture. Eliot's debt to Symons's book on Symbolism goes far beyond the introduction it gave him to Laforgue and Mallarmé. The book and its author left Eliot with an ideal that he upheld throughout his life: that the genuine modern poet was an urban, cosmopolitan intellectual.

Cultural Spaces

Major cities have always been centers of commerce and cultural production, but late nineteenth-century London and Paris, especially, were more than densely populated areas with various commercial interests or cultural cliques. With the rise of mass entertainment in the new metropolis, there was for the first time a concerted effort by capitalist entrepreneurs to rezone the city according to cultural differences. As lines blurred between culture and commerce, entrepreneurs provided myriad opportunities for city dwellers to take sides, and to patronize entertainments that accorded with their class status. The respectable middle class might distinguish themselves from the poor, or even from the merely bourgeois, by exclusively patronizing the upscale while avoiding common amusements. Yet cities like London and Paris offered both popular and elite entertainment to citizens who saw fit to patronize both. One could find opera *and* music hall in Leicester Square; and even the culinary landscape of central London was increasingly marked by an international diversity.

The global metropolis seemed to be a place without clear boundaries, but the citizens who sought distinction could redefine themselves as consumers, and thus reinstate the class hierarchies that seemed to collapse in the urban maelstrom. In contrast, fin-de-siècle poets responded to the rezoning of the city by refusing to be identified with a single stratum of taste; instead, they reveled in the opportunities the city allowed for losing identity. Rather than affiliate with a single class, they sought to survey the whole of culture, and to achieve a universal vantage point, the prerogative of the cultural exile that consciously remains without a spiritual home in the city. It goes without saying that this sort of mobility is available only to those who can afford it.

Eliot's early poems presume the kind of social mobility and knowledge of the streets embodied by the Symbolist flâneur. Memories of night walks through dimly lit streets among a demimonde haunt the monologist in poems as various as "Preludes," "Rhapsody on a Windy Night," "Portrait of a Lady," and, of course, "The Love Song of J. Alfred Prufrock." These memories of urban sites usually serve a dramatic function, highlighting the contrast between an emotionally impoverished high culture, characterized by propriety and self-restraint, and a vernacular life that the male protagonist of these poems finds both seductive and threatening. Prufrock wonders whether he should interrupt afternoon tea to state aloud what he has witnessed in his street rambles: "Shall I say, I have gone at dusk though narrow streets / And watched the smoke that rises from pipes / Of lonely men in shirt-sleeves, leaning out of windows?" (*CPP* 5). In "Prufrock's Pervigilium," an omitted episode from "The Love Song of J. Alfred Prufrock," the recollection of sights glimpsed on dark, narrow streets includes prostitutes soliciting men under gas lamps, dangerous-looking boys who smoke cigarettes and hold themselves aloof from Prufrock's gaze, and dilapidated homes (*IMH* 43–44). The memory of "a street piano, mechanical and tired," playing "some worn-out common song" has the capacity to unnerve the "self-possessed" narrator in "Portrait of a Lady" (*CPP* 10). "Rhapsody On A Windy Night" compiles realistic street images while giving voice to a street lamp; in true Symbolist fashion, the poem alternates between matter-of-fact description and a vague diction that sacrifices sense for sound:

> Along the reaches of the street
> Held in a lunar synthesis,
> Whispering lunar incantations
> Dissolve the floors of memory
> And all its clear relations (14)

The "crowd of twisted things" thrown up by the narrator's memory appear to be the residue of years of chronic flânerie.

Symbolists and Decadents alike resisted the bourgeois formula that equated patronizing a place with assuming a specific identity, in an effort to embody a universal human perspective. Arthur Symons's response to the city's cultural diversity was not different in practice from that of a supposed elitist like Mallarmé. The topics of Mallarmé's essays — Parisian fairgrounds, pantomime, ballet, melodrama, women's fashions — mirror those of many Symons essays.[1] The sheer variety of Mallarmé's interests, indicating his core urban cosmopolitanism, are enough to suggest to recent scholars the extent of Mallarmé's empathy with aspects of human experience that lie outside the traditional concerns of poetry (Catani 5).

Symbolism provided Eliot with a coherent philosophy of culture, a notion of the poetic vocation that fit the part of a serious intellectual. Eliot also learned from the practical example of Decadent poets like Symons, and their limitless (admittedly, in Symons's case, often prurient or voyeuristic) curiosity about the breadth of urban culture, in a city that encompassed both the sophisticated arts and popular entertainment. The Symbolist flâneur is the likely source of Eliot's lifelong — and essentially solitary — interest in reviving poetic drama in the modern age. Edmund Wilson explains Eliot's seemingly quixotic obsession with reviving verse drama as an unconscious recognition of his undoubted gift for writing poems with strong personae — the repressed J. Alfred Prufrock, the savage Sweeney — who attain the status of real-life characters (95–96). But more than self-promotion is at stake in essays such as "The Possibility of a Poetic Drama" (1920): a complex theory of culture underlies Eliot's interest in the form.

In *T. S. Eliot and the Cultural Divide*, David Chinitz claims that Eliot had a formula for understanding culture that still has relevance for postmoderns: that the Eliot who liked "a good show, a good thriller, a good tune, as well as a 'great' poem" provides an "early model . . . for our own engagement with culture of all kinds" (18). If this is the case, we should recognize the roots of Eliot's largesse in Symbolist practice, in the attempts of its partisans to achieve a disinterested survey of the entire range of culture, high and low, at hand in the global city.

As an American immigrant in London, Eliot discovered in the London music hall an entertainment where song lyrics were given dramatic presentation by highly stylized performers, resulting in an experience that appeared to Eliot to combine poetic skill with the capacity of entertaining mass audiences. As Chinitz writes, "The music hall, for Eliot, represents a vanishing possibility of reconciliation between diverging levels of culture"; its practice suggested a strategy that Eliot argued strenuously that modernist poets should adopt (103). In several essays — "A Dialogue on Dramatic Poetry," "The Need for Poetic Drama," "Poetry and Drama," and "The Future of Poetic Drama" — Eliot offers precise instructions on how poets could resuscitate a genre that had functioned in the past as a crossover art. The return to poetic drama should not take the form of a self-conscious "revival," spearheaded by reform-minded intellectuals; it can succeed only after poets undertake a careful study of current practice in the popular arts. Modern poets must build on the techniques of practitioners of contemporary arts like music hall, emulating the unique ability of music-hall singers such as Marie Lloyd for creating a strong, sympathetic bond with audiences, especially her urban, working-class public. Above all, Eliot wants modern poets to resist the temptation to write plays merely for the coterie audience that already exists for modern verse.

As we have seen, the gulf between art and entertainment was exacerbated in the space of the world city itself. Eliot's lifelong interest in the fate of poetic drama reveals itself as an attempt to overcome the modern cultural divide and resist poetry's increasingly marginal status (Chinitz 68–72). By adapting and appropriating the techniques of popular music-hall singers, Eliot argues, poets might reclaim a mass audience for modern poetry.

What concerns us here are the assumptions about cultural diversity that underlie Eliot's arguments about the relations between high and low art. Eliot's championing of music hall might seem to set him apart from the Symbolists, who often insisted on the gulf separating poetry from everyday language, and the poet from the journeyman. But just as clearly, Eliot's concern with popular art, and his envy of popular singers like Marie Lloyd, has a precedent in fin-de-siècle poets like Arthur Symons and even Mallarmé, who balanced a high esteem for poetry with a voracious interest in a range of modern urban entertainment. Eliot's fantasy of becoming a modern poet who can replace the music-hall singer in the hearts and minds of mass audiences has its roots in the Decadent dream of losing your identity, including your class status, by merging with the denizens of night life, and vanishing, flâneur-like, into the city crowd. The fact of social privilege needn't hinder such a fantasy; in fact, privilege enables it.

We should not confuse the fin-de-siècle dream of a disembodied, universal view of the city with either a postmodern cultural eclecticism or cultural relativism. As it turns out, Eliot's interest in the popular arts is not incompatible with cultural hierarchy. Throughout "The Possibility of a Poetic Drama," Eliot emphasizes that, in the process of learning from music hall how to reach a mass audience, the modern poet will also refine this popular form in some obscure way. Eliot defines fine art as "the refinement, not the antithesis of popular art" ("Marianne Moore" 595). And again: poets should "take a form of entertainment, and subject it to the process which would leave it a form of art." There is no reason to doubt his claim to appreciate popular art, but here at least, he implies that a clear hierarchy exists between poetry and vernacular forms.

Like the Symbolists, Eliot both feared and reveled in what the imperial city represents – the disintegration of national boundaries, of cultural hierarchy, and even of personal identity. His various comments on the relation between popular entertainment and poetry suggest that, like the previous generation of poets, he was capable of imagining a new order of things, growing out of the end of the old world, while savoring to some degree the sight of cultural boundaries collapsing.

Urban Anthropology

Whether or not *The Waste Land* is a narrative or a discontinuous series of London vignettes, the poem is organized by a series of narrators who, much like the fin-de-siècle poet, wander the city and survey its diversity while recording their responses. The poem's unfixed perspective recalls the flâneur's impressionistic, disinterested view of the city. *The Waste Land* alternates between a passionless, alienated view of cultural breakdown and seemingly desperate efforts to reestablish cultural hierarchy out of anarchy by means of a perspective achieved through a poetic arrangement of disparate "fragments." One could argue, perhaps, that the broken pieces of culture cohere, at least in the performance of the text itself.

Eliot had a lifelong interest in primitive culture. Like many intellectuals of his generation, he read deeply in anthropology, ethnography, and Freudian psychology during the same years he discovered the Symbolists.[2] The major insight gained from this course of reading, a notion that underlies Eliot's *Poems* (1920), *The Waste Land* (1922), and *Sweeney Agonistes* (written 1924–25), is that of a fundamental continuity between primitive modes of experience and modern culture (Chinitz 77–78). Neither the emergence of secular reason and scientific method, nor the forms of social propriety that accompany bourgeois hegemony mean that primitive consciousness and emotion have disappeared from modern civilized society. Anthropologists like Lucien Lévy-Bruhl, Sir James G. Frazer, and Francis M. Cornford taught Eliot that civilized life, especially the civilized arts, had a lineage in primitive custom and ancient ritual; primitive emotion and exalted states of consciousness persist just under the surface of modern life. Eliot insisted that a proper grasp of modern art required comprehending the survival of pre-logical mentalities in contemporary practice, claiming in a review of Wyndham Lewis's novel *Tarr* that the artist "is more primitive, as well as more civilized, than his contemporaries, his experience is deeper than civilization" ("Tarr" 106).

However, Eliot's concern with "savagery" is highly selective and has little in common with, say, the barely concealed anti-immigrant chauvinism evident in Arthur Conan Doyle's stories of Sherlock Holmes, which Eliot revered. Eliot was interested most of all in the claim of anthropology that a more vital and complex primitive experience persisted into modern times. He was especially taken with, in Robert Crawford's words, "the idea that such intense experience [as the primitive's] might even now be available to modern man" (80; cf. Chinitz 76–80). Eliot would have found these insights confirmed in the Symbolist poets he admired. The Symbolists often incorporated elements of the primitive in their work, invariably situating the theme in relation to the city. The Symbolists famously responded to the shock of city life by affecting the aloof, above-it-all stance of the dandy; but their poetry frequently expressed a contrary desire to lose one's composure and experience extraordinary passions and heightened states of consciousness. Crawford's claim that "Baudelaire and the Symbolists were at once poets of the urban world and of the savage" captures the dual notion of the poet implied in Symbolist practice: the poet-as-sorcerer, wishing to change the structure of reality through words, and the poet-as-technician, who manipulates language for its own sake (82). At times, the Symbolist interest in the primitive seems limited to nostalgia or exoticism, as with Baudelaire's celebrations of the sexuality of his mulatto mistress, Jeanne Duval, or Rimbaud's passionate denial of his European ancestors in order to assert his "savage" heritage, in "A Season in Hell." But such Rimbaud poems as "Cities" [1 and 2] juxtapose images of primitive life with scenes of modern Paris in a manner that clearly had considerable impact on Eliot, who wrote an enthusiastic appreciation of *Illuminations*, the book that includes these poems, in 1917 (Crawford 83). A poem like Baudelaire's "To a Madonna," which presumes the essential continuity between extreme religious emotion and sexuality, no doubt also had a lasting effect on Eliot, who would have recognized the similar genealogy of religion in anthropology and Freudian psychology, and who yearned, like the Symbolists, to experience in everyday life the heightened emotional states that enlightened reason had relegated to the margins of modern life (Crawford 81).

Urban detective fiction, such as the Sherlock Holmes stories, equated the primitive with the foreign and sought to find ways to contain the threat, at least in the realm of imagination. For the Symbolists, the primitive was not the other, but a capacity within modern consciousness. Moreover, the residue of the savage mind in modern society was, for the Symbolists and Eliot alike, a hopeful sign, a portent that modernity might take a utopian turn and reconstitute itself as a complex hybrid of intellectual accomplishment and passionate feeling, thus healing the "dissociation of sensibility" that Eliot lamented (*SE* 247). Unlike detective stories, or most cultural anthropology, both of which presented the persistence of primitive behavior as anachronistic at best and perilous to civilization at worst, the Symbolists depicted primitive mentality as metaphor as much as historical fact, an existential truth about the universal human. Reading Durkheim, Frazer, and Lévy-Bruhl convinced Eliot that moderns had access to the kinds of heightened emotion and experience that bourgeois secularism associated with remote primitives; reading the Symbolists confirmed in Eliot both the possibility and desirability of reconnecting with this powerful world outside the modern everyday, without adopting a primitive "chic" or rejecting modernity. In fact, the double vision that can encompass the composite of primitive and sophisticate characteristic of the modern mind requires more intellect, not less. The notion of the Symbolist mélange of the modern and the primitive requires an ideal reader, capable of acknowledging the deep interpenetration of primitivism with modernity.

The new anthropology of Symbolist poetry requires a new notion of culture as well, one that is broader and more inclusive. It is clear that this enhanced concept of culture serves as the foundation on which Eliot builds the major poem of his career, *The Waste Land*. Eliot learned to associate city life with a complex overlay of cultures; the Symbolists equipped the poet with a concept of culture wide enough to include such diversity. *The Waste Land* submits the Symbolist understanding of culture to a trial by fire; it is a poem of unique density, crowded with different class dialects, literary references high and low, mythology, ritual, and ragtime. The poem is at its most

Symbolist in assuming that the proper arrangement of language can transform our perception of reality, and perhaps the nature of reality itself. The "collocation" of fragments that serves as the poem's mode of meaning production presumes the Symbolist demand that poetry encompass the widest possible range of cultural data. As Michael Levenson writes, the poem "collocates in order to culminate. . . . The poem is not, as it is common to say, built upon the juxtaposition of fragments; it is built out of their interpenetration. Fragments of the Buddha and Augustine combine to make a new literary reality which is neither the Buddha nor Augustine *but which includes them both*" (190; emphasis added). *The Waste Land* provides readers with a novel, complex arrangement of cultural traditions intended to supplant the previous order and to produce, like the Symbolist poem, a new system of knowledge.

As the first poets who embodied the new, co-dependent relation between modern cities and modern art, the Symbolists remained Eliot's guide to understanding the modernist sensibility. Faced with the paralyzing experience of what Raymond Williams calls "visual and linguistic strangeness" in the cosmopolitan metropolis, the Symbolists staked out claims for a new community based on a shared faith in the power of the poet's principal medium, language (46). They pitted their skill at word organization against what they perceived as a general coarsening of discourse by commerce and politics. In this way, they provided Eliot with the means to write poems that made unique cognitive and emotional demands on readers, and that decisively linked modernity with the kind of experience and perceptions unique to life in the city. Further economic and geopolitical changes produced a wider readership for Eliot's poetry than the Symbolists themselves achieved. By the time he wrote *The Waste Land*, readers around the globe were prepared to accept that modern Englishness, manifest in the world city of London, was no longer merely English (cf. Marx 199).

NOTES

1   The titles of some of Symons's essays published between the years 1896 and 1898 suggest the extreme variety of his subject matter: "The Gingerbread Fair at Vincennes: A Colour-Study," "In Carnival," "The Lesson of Millais," "The Isles of Aran," "An Apology for Puppets," "Moscow," "Naples," and "Ballet, Pantomime, and Poetic Drama."

2   See MIND, MYTH, AND CULTURE: ELIOT AND ANTHROPOLOGY.

REFERENCES AND FURTHER READING

Balakian, Anna. *The Symbolist Movement: A Critical Appraisal*. New York: New York UP, 1977.

Catani, Dominic. *The Poet in Society: Art, Consumerism, and Politics in Mallarmé*. New York: Lang, 2003.

Chinitz, David E. *T. S. Eliot and the Cultural Divide*. Chicago: U of Chicago P, 2003.

Crawford, Robert. *The Savage and the City in the Work of T. S. Eliot*. Oxford: Clarendon, 1987.

Gendron, Bernard. *Between Montmartre and the Mudd Club: Popular Music and the Avant-Garde*. Chicago: U of Chicago P, 2002.

Lentricchia, Frank. *Modernist Quartet*. Cambridge: Harvard UP, 1994.

Levenson, Michael. *A Genealogy of Modernism: A Study of Literary Doctrine 1908–1922*. New York: Cambridge UP, 1984.

Marx, John. *The Modernist Novel and the Decline of Empire*. Cambridge: Cambridge UP, 2005.

McLaughlin, Joseph. *Writing the Urban Jungle*. Charlottesville: U of Virginia P, 2000.

Ramsey, Warren. *Jules Laforgue and the Ironic Inheritance*. New York: Oxford UP, 1953.

Rimbaud, Arthur. *A Season in Hell and Illuminations*. Trans. Wyatt Mason. New York: Modern Library, 2005.

——. *I Promise to Be Good: The Letters of Arthur Rimbaud, Volume II*. Trans. Wyatt Mason. New York: Modern Library, 2003.

van den Beukel, Karlien. "Arthur Symons' Night Life." *Babylon or New Jerusalem? Perceptions of the City in Literature*. Ed. Valeria Tinkler-Villani. Amsterdam: Rodopi, 2005. 135–53.

Williams, Raymond. "Metropolitan Perceptions and the Emergence of Modernism." *The Politics of Modernism*. Ed. Tony Pickney. New York: Verso, 1989. 37–49.

Wilson, Edmund. *Axel's Castle*. 1931. Glasgow: Collins, 1984.

4
Not One, Not Two:
Eliot and Buddhism

Christina Hauck

The ten thousand things return to the one.
Where does the one return?

— Zen Koan, Forty-fifth Case of the *Blue Cliff Record*

The Ten Thousand Things Return to the One

T. S. Eliot invites us at crucial junctures to read his poetry and plays in relationship to two great Indic religions, Hinduism and Buddhism. It seems that Hinduism was the more obvious influence; at any rate, references to various Hindu texts, especially the *Bhagavad-Gita*, abound and have received considerable scholarly attention. But Buddhism seems to have held a deeper attraction: according to Stephen Spender, Eliot, at the time he was writing *The Waste Land*, considered becoming a Buddhist (qtd. in Kearns 67). What drew Eliot to Buddhism was perhaps what averted his conversion: Buddhism's radical difference from both Hinduism and Christianity. Unlike those religions, which rely on concepts of an eternal self (*atman* and soul, respectively) whose purpose is to be reconciled with an all-powerful, all-knowing deity, Buddhism propounds *anatman* or non-self, which is neither separate from nor identical with *shunyata* (generally if problematically translated as *emptiness*). In Buddhist teaching, there is no self and there is no God – at any rate, no God not subject to the law of impermanence – propositions Eliot could not ultimately accept.

This is not to say that Hinduism and Christianity are more alike than different. Indeed, the differences are profound. Two in particular mattered to Eliot. First, Hinduism presupposes reincarnation. The self or *atman* gradually attains liberation from the cycle of birth and death through the course of innumerable lifetimes. Second, Hinduism presupposes the ultimate co-identity of *atman* with *Atman* (Brahman or god). Liberation *entails* the discovery that *atman* was always already *Atman*. In contrast, Christianity supposes that the soul is granted only one lifetime to achieve

A Companion to T. S. Eliot, First Edition. Edited by David E. Chinitz.
© 2014 John Wiley & Sons, Ltd. Published 2014 by John Wiley & Sons, Ltd.

salvation, and, crucially, that the soul may, indeed must, approach God but is never co-identical with Him.

It would be equally untrue to say that Buddhism and Hinduism differ completely. They share common features, notably a belief in reincarnation and an insight that ultimately the individual is not an ontologically distinct entity. However, in the Buddhist tradition, what is reincarnated is not the self but the "mind stream" generated by the "self"; the self is only a "heap" of phenomena (*skandhas*) in a continual state of dissolution and formation. Buddhism, moreover, affirms that all compounded things are subject to decay; nothing that exists is eternal or unchanging, including God or Brahma. There is a Buddhist pantheon, but from a Buddhist perspective, even the gods are compounded. From his first discourse at the age of 35 to his last utterance at the age of 80, the Buddha taught the law of impermanence and the necessity of determined effort in achieving nirvana: *vayadhammaa sankhaaraa appamaadena sampaadethaa*: "all things are perishable, through vigilance Awaken!" (Jayarava).

It is well established that Eliot had a far from casual interest in all three religious traditions. Raised in the Unitarian Church (nominally Christian), he spent a good part of his adolescence and early adulthood in search of religious faith. While a graduate student in the philosophy department at Harvard, he studied both Sanskrit and Pali, reading a variety of Hindu and Buddhist texts, the "subtleties [of which] make most of the great European philosophers look like schoolboys." These studies "left [Eliot] in a state of enlightened mystification," as he struggled to "erase from [his] mind all the categories and kinds of distinction common to European philosophy from the time of the Greeks" (*ASG* 43–44). Jeffrey M. Perl argues that what Eliot discovered in the Buddhist texts was a philosophical approach that permitted him to cut through the central dilemmas of the Western philosophic tradition, exemplified by the subject–object dichotomy and the ceaseless effort to transcend it. As propounded by the second-century CE Indian philosopher Nagarjuna, neither subject nor object exists except as points of view. Subject and object are convenient fictions used to navigate the field of phenomena we call "reality," but they do not exist apart from that field. Using an incisive, rigorous method of argument, Nagarjuna concludes that there is no self. Thus, there is no one and no thing to transcend: "Samsara [the world as we know it] is nothing essentially different from nirvana [the world as it is] / Nirvana is nothing essentially different from samsara" (qtd. in Perl 53).

According to Cleo MacNelly Kearns, it is not clear that Eliot read Nagarjuna or even needed to in order to have discovered this set of ideas, which were common to the early (Hinayana) Buddhists and which deeply influenced later (Mahayana) Buddhists (80), both of whom Eliot did study. Eliot was also deeply familiar with the idealist philosopher, F. H. Bradley, and Bradley's system of analysis closely resembles Nagarjuna's, as numerous scholars have noted (Kearns 103). Like Nagarjuna, and like Buddha before him, Bradley rigorously denied the existence of the self. But whereas Nagarjuna's simultaneous commitment both to philosophical rigor and Buddhist faith leads him to reject the very concept of transcendence, Bradley's commitment to thinking keeps him enmeshed in the quest for transcendence. His dialectic begins with "immediate experience," which is "not simply a primitive state but a continuing dimension of life" (Kearns 122). In opposition to this arises a sense of subject and object, a state whose transcendence lies in the perception of the Absolute. But the Absolute turns out to be nothing more than the "finite center" of "immediate experience," and hence the subject is trapped in a never-ending solipsistic circle (Kearns 122–23). In brief, Bradley does not so much deny the self as invest the self with the power to transcend the self, a hopeless task.

Eliot focused his dissertation, *Knowledge and Experience*, on Bradley. "A great deal of the argument in *Knowledge and Experience* is determined by a clearly perturbed sense of the problem of solipsism and an attempt to solve it without recourse to a semi-mystical hypothesis," such as Bradley's Absolute (Kearns 123). This Eliot does by creating two new terms, "point of view" and "half-object." What enables escape from solipsism is the ability to switch "point of view," to see things from a different per-spective. This switching entails "half-objects," anything seen from two perspectives simultaneously. These related terms let Eliot view Bradley's "finite center" not as a fundamental condition of subjectivity, but rather as a problem created by the effort to establish a point of view outside of reality (Kearns 123–6). These terms also move Eliot closer to a Buddhist point of view, without actually forcing him to relinquish belief in the self (who switches or creates).

It is not clear how well Eliot understood *shunyata*, but it seems that most of his critics have not grasped it. One mistake some critics make is to divide *shunyata* into positive and negative aspects. But strictly speaking, *shunyata* is not pleasant or unpleasant or even neutral; those distinctions arise from and perpetuate a belief in the self. A more common mistake has arisen because of the common translation of *shunyata* as "emptiness," which has led some critics to understand it as nothing, a blank, a void, a state of non-being. Such critics read Eliot's many references in *The Waste Land*, for example, to "nothing" as allusions to *shunyata*. But *shunyata* might be better translated as "no self-nature" or "no metaphysical essence." There is no thing and no place that can be said to exist except in relation to other things and places. (Buddha calls this "co-dependent origination.") Everything everywhere is *shunyata*, which might be envisioned as a matter–energy–mind flow with no beginning and no end. Practically speaking, a human being is very different from a rock or waterfall or bird-song. But ultimately all are *shunyata*, empty of metaphysical essence. The attainment of this point does not require or lead to passivity or inertia. Meditation alerts the meditator to *shunyata*. Meditation is balanced, aware and relaxed: the very mirror of *shunyata*. The life of the Buddha guarantees that the realization of *shunyata* invigorates: after attaining enlightenment, he began to teach, crisscrossing India and Nepal for 45 years.

Finally, it needs to be said, the attainment of *shunyata* does not entail a loss of the self or a destruction of the ego or any such thing, as apparently Eliot (or his critics) feared, for one cannot lose or destroy what does not exist except as a set of temporary conglomerations (*skandhas*) interacting in a field which cannot be exited. Suffering arises because of the ceaseless activity of identifying with those conglomerations. The alleviation of suffering is not predicated on detachment from either the "subject" or the "objects" of the "self." Attachment and detachment are both deluded actions; both give rise to suffering. Rather, Buddha advocated the middle way of non-attachment, which permits the experience of *shunyata*, not as a destination or a state of mind or an object to be obtained or interacted with, but as the complete set of temporary conglomerations emerging from and dissolving into itself: the ten thousand things return to the one.

Where Does the One Return? Narrative Structure(s) in *The Waste Land*

It would seem that Eliot's most profound expression of the core insights of Buddhism appears in *Four Quartets*. This sequence reveals not only Eliot's deep experience of the Four Seals of Existence (suffering, impermanence, *anatman*, and *shunyata*), but also what critics have noted as his remarkable method, which in the words of Kearns has the "mind-bending effect" of the Zen Buddhist koan, "a question apparently unanswerable, from which we get relief only by a sharper insight than any provided by its initial terms of reference" (134). Kearns finds these effects to be the most pronounced when Eliot does not refer directly to Buddhism, and I tend to agree. Nonetheless, there is value in examining Eliot's Buddhist allusions. In this chapter, I will bracket *Four Quartets*, for the most part, focusing instead on an early poem, *The Waste Land*, and a late play, *The Cocktail Party*. My purpose will be first to tease out some of the difficulties attendant on Eliot's use of Buddhism and second to draw attention to the various ways that Eliot shuttles back and forth between a Christian and a Buddhist sense of self.

In "Individuation and Awakening: Romantic Narrative and the Psychological Interpretation of Buddhism," Richard K. Payne abstracts the narratives structuring Christian and Buddhist views of the self in order to show how profoundly different they are. According to Payne, the Christian view of the self derives from the Genesis account of creation. It is a story of three successive states: innocence, sin, redemption. From the eighteenth century onward, this emphatically religious perspective has been secularized. Not only does it underwrite the familiar dialect of Western philosophy, it is foundational, Payne argues, to modern analytical psychology, which views the self as beginning first in a idealized state of "unconscious unity," followed by "a period of disruptive interaction with the actualities of the world," and culminating in "a final reintegration [of the self] at a higher state" (42–43).

Drawing on an influential Buddhist text, Sántideva's *Bodhicaryavatara*, Payne abstracts a Buddhist narrative of the self that also moves through three successive states: ignorance, desiring to awaken, awakening. Although Payne does not acknowledge it, the story of the Buddha's life probably serves as the ultimate model for this narrative. Raised in extremely privileged surroundings, kept ignorant of the ordinary course of existence, he did not become aware of suffering until he was 28 years old, when he belatedly learned about sickness, old age, and death. These facts troubled him so deeply that he felt he could not rest without discovering their cause. He left home and became a mendicant monk or *bhikku*. After many years of severe asceticism, finding himself near death and yet no closer to his goal, he recalled a moment in his childhood when he had spontaneously entered into a state of *samadhi*, or serene concentration and awareness. So, he sat down under a tree, vowing to remain there until he attained enlightenment or died. Here he awakened. What he attained was not the individuation so prized in the European tradition, but rather liberation from the processes that give rise to the self: " 'My heart's deliverance is unassailable. This is the last birth. Now there is no renewal of being' " (qtd. in Ñanamoli Thera).

Apart from the convenient tripartite structures, there are very few points of equivalence between these two narratives. Innocence is not ignorance. In the Christian worldview (and its secularized versions in philosophy and psychology), innocence precedes suffering (cast as sin or alienation), but does not cause it. However, in the Buddhist worldview, ignorance, along with greed and hatred, causes suffering. Moreover, the state of sinfulness (alienation) is not cognate with the state of desiring to be awake, although it may give rise to a desire to atone or be forgiven or achieve union with that from which one is alienated – but that is only to say that both religions require some kind of effort. Above all, the state of redemption is not the state of being awakened. Redemption is a state of transcending sin (or alienation), whereas awakening is a state of recognizing *anatman* and its cognate, *shunyata*.

Eliot makes extensive use of the tripartite structures underlying Western religious and secular understandings of the self in *The Waste Land*, which can be read as a quest narrative driven by a guilt-ridden protagonist, whose sin remains unnamed. Although quest narratives are Christian in orientation, usually entailing a search for the Holy Grail, Eliot famously draws on Jessie Weston's *Ritual and Romance*, which locates their origins in European prehistory. According to Weston, the "Fisher King," a character common to all quest narratives, is a refashioning of the pagan scapegoat whose annual sacrifice was required to release the rain and restore the land to fertility. These earlier vegetation myths assimilated easily to Christian myth in that a single scapegoat bears the guilt for the entire community. His or her (ritual) murder appeased the gods and secured the life of the tribe.

Eliot extends the geographical and cultural scope of *The Waste Land* via James G. Frazer's *The Golden Bough*, an anthropological compilation that records worldwide variations of this story (and numerous others, as well). But Eliot does not foreground African or Polynesian accounts of drought caused by sin and relieved by sacrifice. Rather, he alludes extensively to the analogous Vedic myths of a land suffering from "drought or sterility caused by some evil force or blockage" (Kearns 32). This becomes most apparent in the poem's final section, "What the Thunder Said." The location is "Ganga" (the Ganges River), ancient India. The situation is one of extreme drought. Indra, the god of the thunderbolt and the breaker of drought, speaks, DA DA DA, releasing the rain (*CPP* 49). In contrast to European versions of this narrative, the

Vedic version has no scapegoat. Rather, a priest mediates between the offended god and the suffering people, interpreting his ambiguous utterance. As Kearns eloquently argues, Eliot uses this myth to align his role as modern poet with that of ancient priest.

Eliot less successfully yokes Buddhism to Christianity in *The Waste Land*. The title of the poem's third section, "The Fire Sermon," draws directly from Henry Clarke Warren's translation of the "Addita-Pariyaya Sutta," the third of the Buddha's recorded discourses, which recapitulates the lessons of the first discourse (on the Four Noble Truths) and the second (on non-self). In the "Addita-Pariyaya Sutta" the Buddha addresses his first mass audience, a group of 1,000 fire-worshiping ascetics. In his typically thorough way, he argues that the entire universe is on fire. The metaphor is an apt one, for he aims to persuade his audience that they are enthralled by the very source of their suffering.

He begins with the eyes, the first of the "six internal bases" or roots, and asserts that the entire threefold field of the visual is on fire: eyes are burning, any form that yields visual impressions is burning, and the consciousness of the contact between the sense organ and the form perceived is burning. He then asserts that whatever arises from the experience of seeing is also burning; it does not matter if what arises is experienced as pleasant or unpleasant or neither. The entire field of the visual is burning: with lust (or greed or craving), hatred (or anger or aversion), and ignorance (or delusion).

Having established that the first of the six internal bases is aflame, he makes nearly word-for-word identical points about each of the others: ear/hearing, nose/smelling, tongue/tasting, body/feeling, and mind/thinking. He concludes that any part of the mind–body that human beings are accustomed to identifying with the self is suffering. This recapitulates the First Noble Truth, the fact of suffering, and the Second, the causes of suffering: lust, hatred, ignorance. Recognition of these truths, continues the Buddha, leads to *nibbida* of the sense organ/perception processes. Warren translates *nibbida* as "aversion," but more recent scholars have translated it as "disenchantment" (Thanissaro Bhikku) or "estrangement" (Ñanamoli Thera). The difference is crucial. The words "disenchantment" and "estrangement" point toward the cultivation of non-attachment to those elements of our experience we commonly identify as "self." Non-attachment leads to *nibbana* (nirvana). But "aversion" is a form of hatred, and hatred is one of the three causes of suffering. Rather than promote the cessation of suffering, Warren's translation tends to suggest a way to prolong it.

Eliot's "Fire Sermon" compounds Warren's error by construing "lust" as sexual desire: this part of *The Waste Land* depicts one despicable sexual act after another. But in the context of the "Addita-Pariyaya Sutta," "lust" is better understood as "greed" or "insatiable craving," not only for sexual pleasure, but also for all forms of self-gratification, including sensual pleasure, wealth, power, fame, etc. The Buddha does not here counsel the cultivation of aversion, nor does he caution exclusively against sexual expression; rather, he encourages his audience to deliver themselves from the spell of whatever appears before their senses and whatever arises in their mind as a result of sense perception.

Eliot claims in a footnote that "the Buddha's Fire Sermon . . . corresponds in importance to the Sermon on the Mount," thereby creating a parallel between Jesus and Buddha (*CPP* 53). Attractive as it may be, the comparison overwrites major differences: whereas Jesus offered himself as the way, promising salvation to his followers (John 14:6), Buddha persistently told his followers that he could not liberate them – they would have to liberate themselves: "Self is savior of self; / what other savior could there be?" (qtd. in Ñanamoli Thera). Moreover, Jesus promised his followers eternal life. But according to the Buddha nothing is permanent. Liberation as a Buddha (salvation, if you will) requires nothing more than a profound experience of the Four Seals of Existence. In Christianity, what Christ saves is the soul; what he saves it from is eternal burning in Hell. In Buddhism, what is liberated is the self; what it is liberated from is its belief in itself.

Another difficulty emerges in Eliot's introduction of St. Augustine (354–430 CE) in the line "To Carthage then I came" (*CPP* 46). As he records in his *Confessions*, Augustine was sent to Carthage to study rhetoric. During the months he waited for his father to raise the money for his tuition, he began, in Christian parlance, to sin, and his licentiousness continued for years afterward: "Burning burning burning burning" (46). But sex was not Augustine's only sin, or even his most dangerous. During his years in Carthage, he embraced Manichaeism, a syncretic, extremely dualistic religion developed in the third century CE. From a Roman Catholic (early Christian) viewpoint, Augustine burned for many years in intellectual as well as sensual error. The introduction of Augustine thus relaxes Eliot's obsessive focus on sex, opening the poem up to a more Buddhistic understanding of "lust" as insatiable physical and mental craving. Moreover, from a Roman Catholic perspective, the central error of Manichaeism is its dualism, the division of the universe into Good and Evil. Here would seem to be a point at which Eliot successfully draws Christian and Buddhist doctrine into productive collaboration, for the Buddha regarded dualism as a fundamental error as well.

The "collocation of" Augustine and the Buddha may not have been an "accident," as Eliot's footnote tells us (*CPP* 53), but it certainly implies a view of the self that from a Buddhist perspective is mistaken. Both Buddha and Augustine renounced their pursuit of sensual pleasure, but whereas the Buddha discovered he had no self, Augustine reified his self and in so doing, paved the path for generations to follow: what he produces in the *Confessions* is nothing less than "the unified, transcendent 'I' of [the] autobiographical tradition" (Anderson 207). It may be that Eliot evokes the Vedic myth in "What the Thunder Said" as a way to mediate between the extremely coherent self presented in the *Confessions* and the *anatman* presented in the "Addita-Pariyaya Sutta." If so, we have to say his effort failed, for despite the resolution intimated by the mantra-like repetitions of DA DA DA and "shantih shantih shantih," much of the end of *The Waste Land* comprises a painful disintegration, a fragmented series of voices speaking from archaic European poems and plays, all divorced from their original narrative context, all performing some kind of suffering, even insanity (*CPP* 50).

"Several Kinds of Sanatoria": Buddhism in the Plays

{M}y only hope of really penetrating to the heart of {the} mystery would lie in forgetting how to think and feel as an American or a European: which, for practical as well as sentimental reasons, I did not wish to do.

(*ASG* 44)

As Kearns and other critics have argued, Eliot's conversion to the Anglican Church in 1927 did not abate his interest in Hinduism and Buddhism. Indeed, approaching them from the security of his Christian faith, Eliot seemed less threatened by elements in them that had previously unsettled him. *Four Quartets* (1935–42) goes even further than *The Waste Land* in its use of Hindi thought and narrative, most pertinently in the near-paraphrase of the *Bhagavad-Gita* in "The Dry Salvages" (*CPP* 133–34). Certain lines from *Ash-Wednesday* (1930) and *Four Quartets*, moreover, suggest the Middle Way of the Buddha.[1] Indeed, *Four Quartets* seems permeated from beginning to end with Eliot's awareness of the Four Seals of Existence, expressing impermanence ("In my beginning is my end"), extreme suffering ("Where is there an end of it, the soundless wailing"), assertions of non-self ("You are not the same people who left that station / Or who will arrive at any terminus") and (possibly) *shunyata* ("the still point of the turning world") (123, 131, 134, 119).

What remains perplexing is the question of the purpose served by continued evocations of Buddhist insight in Eliot's post-conversion poetry and plays. To approach that question (or is it a koan?), I will turn to *The Cocktail Party*. Not only is it (arguably) Eliot's best play, it suggests the futility, even folly, of trying to affix Eliot. Of him we may say indeed, "the play" – of words and ideas – "is the thing."

The Cocktail Party (1949) begins with a gathering, a cocktail party, whose hostess, Lavinia, is absent. It ends with another cocktail party – or rather, takes place as Lavinia and her husband, Edward, await the arrival of their guests. The play builds on a motif of departure and return (or return and departure) that is of undisputed importance to Eliot's mature work. This motif suggests cycles of experience and understanding that can be read as simultaneously philosophical, literary, and psychological. It evokes the familiar movements of dialectic from thesis to antithesis to synthesis, as well as paradigmatic narrative structures, whether those be "Western" (the path from innocence to sin to redemption) or "Vedic" (turning on the wheel of birth, death, and rebirth) or Buddhist (the path from suffering to enlightenment). Above all, this motif evokes a sense of self that balances between the extreme coherence, even rigidity, of the Augustinian view and the extreme fluidity of the Buddha's view. Or, as Reilly tells Edward in *The Cocktail Party*, "one is an object / As well as a person" (*CPP* 307).

In *The Cocktail Party*, as throughout his dramatic oeuvre, Eliot uses three main character types: those such as Lavinia and Edward, who secure their identities through their sense of physical or social place; those such as Celia Coplestone and Peter Quilp, who secure their identities through their vocation; and those whose point of view encompasses and mediates between the others, such as Reilly (and possibly Julia Shuttlethwaite and Alexander MacColgie Gibbs). Much of the play centers on Reilly's efforts to help first Edward and Lavinia, then Celia. Eliot makes the dilemmas of the first two character types explicitly cognate with those of *The Waste Land*. The connection seems especially clear in the case of Celia: both of her possible paths "avoid the final desolation / Of solitude in the phantasmal world / Of imagination, shuffling memories and desires" (*CPP* 365), an unequivocal allusion to the opening lines of *The Waste Land*: "April is the cruellest month, breeding / Lilacs out of the dead land, mixing / Memory and desire" (37). Prophetic and nearly omniscient, the "one-eyed" Reilly is something of a Tiresian figure, though significantly less passive than his *Waste Land* counterpart; and as a psychiatrist, he may be the modern equivalent of the ancient Vedic priest whose incantations ease the drought, and thus an avatar of the poet. Like the protagonist(s) of *The Waste Land*, the characters of *The Cocktail Party* struggle to break the seal on their excruciating isolation and enter into community (or communion) with one another.

In his first conversation with Edward, Reilly expounds a view of the self that reflects Eliot's rethinking of Bradley's solipsism. Reilly appears as "an uninvited guest," a stranger. Mysteriously, he seems to know better than Edward himself what Edward is experiencing following his wife's abrupt departure a day earlier:

> There's a loss of personality;
> Or rather, you've lost touch with the person
> You thought you were. You no longer feel quite human.
> You're suddenly reduced to the status of an object –
> A living object, but no longer a person.
> It's always happening, because one is an object
> As well as a person. But we forget about it
> As quickly as we can. (*CPP* 307)

This expresses well Eliot's idea of the "half-object." Reilly goes on to identify moments of extreme stress as those in which we are likeliest to be shaken out of our solipsistic subjectivity, to see ourselves as others might. He gives the example of surgery. Before the operation, one is "still the subject / The centre of reality," but "stretched on the table / You are a piece of furniture in a repair shop / For those who surround you, the masked actors" (307). Lack of space keeps me from explicating the tantalizing allusion to "Prufrock" or the metaphor of performance; let me simply say that the phrase "centre of reality" surely echoes Bradley's "finite center."

Reilly represents such moments of crisis as opportunities for "finding out / What you really are" (307). He offers a view of the self that comes extremely close to that

of the Buddha – "You are nothing but a set / Of obsolete responses" (309) – if one
were to substitute *skandhas* for *responses*. But why obsolete? Because

> we die to each other daily.
> What we know of other people
> Is only our memory of the moments
> During which we knew them. And they have changed since then.
> To pretend that they and we are the same
> Is a useful and convenient social convention
> Which must sometimes be broken. We must also remember
> That at every meeting we are meeting a stranger. (*CPP* 329)

This sense of daily death (and the unspoken concomitant of daily rebirth) comes even
closer to a Buddhist conception of the self. Not only is the self comprised of *skandhas*,
those "heaps" are in a state of continual flux, ceaselessly dissolving and re-forming.
Their seeming solidity arises because we mistakenly believe in their permanence. The
metaphor of death (and of birth) usefully introduces the concept of reincarnation,
which occurs not only over countless lifetimes, but countlessly within each lifetime.
Loosening our attachment to every manifestation of self, "ceas[ing] to believe in [our]
own personality," is the Buddhist way to liberation (348).

Edward construes this sign of health as a symptom of mental illness. When he
consults Reilly several weeks later, he demands to be placed in a sanitarium because
he has "ceased to believe in [his] own personality." But Edward is lying – to himself
and to Reilly. He believes all too strongly in his personality, and even in the moment
of crisis remains "absorbed in the endless struggle / To think well of [himself]" (*CPP*
348). Reilly wisely refuses to help Edward reify himself in this way. Perceiving that
Edward's suffering is separate from neither his habits of deceitful self-representation
nor his unhappy marriage, he brings Edward's wife, Lavinia, whom he has also been
treating, into the session. This breach of several protocols of psychotherapy is remarkably effective at getting these characters to recognize the causes of, and take responsibility for alleviating, their suffering. Indeed, from this point forward Reilly treats
them more like a Zen Master might treat a pair of particularly obstinate students.
His prescription has the flavor of a Zen koan: Edward is a man incapable of loving,
Lavinia is a woman incapable of being loved. What can they do? This presentation of
their dilemma has the effect koans can have on students: they feel completely stuck.
"[W]hat can we do," Lavinia exclaims, "when we can go neither back nor forward?
Edward! / What can we do?" (356). Some measure of the efficacy of Reilly's treatment
can be discovered in their newfound (if belated) concern for their cast-off lovers,
Celia and Peter, whom they suddenly recognize as being "people" as well as "objects."
Eliot confirms Reilly as an avatar of the Buddha with Reilly's parting benediction:
"work out your salvation with diligence" (368) directly cites Warren's translation of
the Buddha's last words as recorded in the "Mahaparinibbana Sutra": *appamadena
sampadetha* (109).

It may seem at this point in the play that Eliot is tipping the scales in favor of a Buddhist sense of the self and the world. But intentionally or unintentionally this phrase reveals a considerably more ambivalent attitude. It seems literally to mean something like, "with nonheedlessness, exert yourself," or, less awkwardly, "with mindfulness, exert yourself" (Sangharakshita 24). Warren's translation of *appamadena* as "diligence" is not misleading, although it seems to flatten out the meaning of a word that denotes "the cornerstone of all skillful mental states" (Thanissaro Bhikku, "Practice"). However, his translation of *sampadetha* as "work out your salvation" is extremely problematic, not least because the syntax of his translation implies a self. It is not clear how *sampadetha*, which seems to be a reflexive verb ("exert yourself"), became translated into the familiar subject–verb–object formation of "work out your salvation," though it seems to be a common mistake. Perhaps to translate it differently requires a degree of "forgetting how to think and feel as an American or a European" (*ASG* 44) – because thought itself is so dependent on grammatical formations. Equally vexing is Warren's use of the word "salvation," which has such powerful connotations in Christian doctrine. As we have seen, from a Buddhist perspective, there is no one to save. I am tempted to say that the entire phrase, "work out your salvation with diligence," makes nonsense of both Buddhist and Christian points of view: the Buddha seems to suggest that right effort and "salvation" (liberation, enlightenment) are always already the same, and Christ alone can offer the gift of salvation.

On the other hand (and with Eliot, there is always another hand), it may be that Eliot intends to collocate Buddha and Christ. Christ's dying words, "Father, forgive them; for they know not what they do," suggest that a degree of mindfulness – *appamadena* – deeply connects Buddhist and Christian teaching. Reilly's treatment of Celia bears this out, to a degree. Unlike Edward and Lavinia, Celia possesses "an honest mind" which is "one of the causes of her suffering" (*CPP* 352). She presents two chief symptoms. First, in the wake of the end of her affair with Edward, she has discovered that "one is always alone" (360). Second, she finds herself suffering from "a sense of sin," not because of the adulterous affair, but because she has become aware of a feeling "of emptiness, of failure / Towards someone, or something, outside of myself; / And I feel I must . . . *atone*" (360, 362). Reilly offers two options for treatment. He can "reconcile [her] to the human condition," which would permit her to enter a life much like that Edward and Lavinia achieve, a life of tolerance and contentment (363), or he can send her on a journey that "is unknown" and "requires faith – the kind of faith that issues from despair" (364). Celia unhesitatingly chooses this path. If the language she and Reilly use to describe her ailment and treatment – sin, atonement, faith – were not enough to convince us that Eliot is casting her dilemma and its solution in explicitly Christian terms, her ultimate fate should. In the third act we learn that she "join[s] an order" and works at a mission on the island of Kinkanja (in "the East"), nursing the sick (380). Caught in the crossfire of a conflict between indigenous groups, she refuses to leave her dying patients and is "crucified / Very near an ant-hill" (381).

Insofar as the news of Celia's death is probably the most moving and climactic of all scenes, it might seem at the end of the play that Eliot gravitates toward a Christian view of the self. There are good reasons to avoid this conclusion, however, including the distinctly satiric circumstances of her death. Indeed, Eliot's depiction of Christians is unflattering. In Kinkanja the "natives" who convert prosper because they eat the monkeys they formerly worshiped. But when the monkey-worshipers begin cannibalizing the Christians, they hastily reconvert. This little parable undoubtedly conveys something of Eliot's own xenophobia, but it is equally likely he is holding a mirror up to European and American Christians who mistake prosperity for grace. If Eliot is affirming Christianity over Buddhism, it is surely not Christianity as the majority practice it.

In the end, it is futile to try to pin Eliot down to any one point of view, religious or otherwise. Rather, what seems useful is to consider his work in relation to one or more aims that might help explain the recurring return to religion as both theme and motif. Chief among these aims, I would like to suggest, from the beginning to the end of his career, is that of achieving respite from psychological isolation. This is simultaneously Eliot's deeply felt personal need and his perception – even diagnosis – of a wider cultural malaise. Religion offers one solution, or set of solutions, because it brings people into a larger community and offers possibilities for communion with something even larger. In *The Cocktail Party*, Eliot secularizes the quest for community and communion. Ultimately, there is no solitary isolated self in this play, but rather a series of compounded impermanent selves all interacting. This view of self is not *anatman*, but rather a carefully considered compromise between *anatman* and the unified transcendent Augustinian self so implicated in the secularized Euro-American view. *The Cocktail Party* doesn't merely dramatize this compromise. The very work of bringing it to the stage creates a community – a writer, producer, director, actors, technicians, stagehands – all working in concert. And the staging of the play draws the audience into this community as well, if only for the duration of its performance.

NOTES

1   See, for example, "Teach us to care and not to care" (*CPP* 61), "torment / Of love unsatisfied // The greater torment / Of love satisfied" (62) or "the devil of the stairs who wears / The deceitful face of hope and of despair" (63). And see especially "There are three conditions which often look alike / . . . / Attachment to self and to things and to persons, detachment / From self and from things and from persons; and, growing between them indifference" (142).

REFERENCES AND FURTHER READING

Anderson, Linda. *Autobiography*. London: Routledge, 2001.

"Forty-fifth Case." Trans. Seung Sahn Sunim. *The Blue Cliff Record*. Cumberland, RI: Kwan Um School of Zen, 1994.

Jayarava. "The Last Words of the Buddha." *The Jayarava Rave*. Blogspot, 25 Feb. 2006. Web. 23 June 2008.

Kearns, Cleo McNelly. *T. S. Eliot and Indic Traditions: A Study in Poetry and Belief*. Cambridge: Cambridge UP, 1989.

——. "T. S. Eliot, Buddhism, and the Point of No Return." *The Placing of T. S. Eliot*, ed. Jewel Spears Brooker. Columbia: U of Missouri P, 1991. 128–35.

Ñanamoli Thera. "Three Cardinal Discourses of the Buddha." *Wheel* 17 (1981). *Accesstoinsight. org*, 1995. Web. 23 June 2008.

Payne, Richard K. "Individuation and Awakening: Romantic Narrative and the Psychological Interpretation of Buddhism." *Buddhism and Psychotherapy across Cultures: Essays on Theories and Practices*. Ed. Mark Unno. Somerville, MA: Wisdom, 2006. 31–51.

Perl, Jeffrey, M. *Skepticism and Modern Enmity: Before and After Eliot*. Baltimore, MA: Johns Hopkins UP, 1989.

Sangharakshita. "Conze's Introduction to Buddhism: Its Essence and Development." *Dharmachakra*. Western Buddhist Order, n.d. Web. 23 June 2008.

Thanissaro Bhikku, trans. "Addita-Pariyaya Sutta: The Fire Sermon." *BuddhaSasana*. Binh Anson, 22 May 1998. Web. 23 June 2008.

——. "The Practice in a Word." *Accesstoinsight.org*, 1999. Web. 23 June 2008.

Warren, Henry Clarke. *Buddhism in Translations*. 1896. New York: Atheneum, 1976.

Weston, Jessie. *From Ritual to Romance*. Cambridge: Cambridge UP, 1920.

5
Yes and No: Eliot and Western Philosophy

Jewel Spears Brooker

Early in 1922, T. S. Eliot invited Ezra Pound to comment on a draft of his "long poem," *The Waste Land*. In the scene describing the tryst between the typist and the clerk, Eliot included the following quatrain:

> She turns and looks a moment in the glass,
> Hardly aware of her departed lover;
> Across her brain one half-formed thought may pass:
> "Well now that's done, and I am glad it's over." (*WLF* 46)

Pound circled the contingent "may" in the third line and scrawled in the margin: "make up yr. mind / you Tiresias / if you know / know damn well / or / else you don't." Please sir, yes or no, black or white. Pound's impatience points to a distinguishing characteristic of Eliot's mind. Beginning with his undergraduate writings, Eliot shied away from straightforward statements. In poems such as "The Love Song of J. Alfred Prufrock," this hesitancy appears as fear of language, fear that leads to social paralysis. In essays such as "Tradition and the Individual Talent," it surfaces as a resistance to binary thinking resulting in a simultaneous embrace of such opposites as tradition and originality. In his philosophical writings, Eliot's reluctance to affirm appears as principled ambivalence leading first to relativism, then to skepticism, and finally, to humility. In *The Waste Land*, his refusal of omniscience admits multiple voices and incorporates jarring angles, each present and each transcended in the poem as a whole. By the time *Four Quartets*, his last and greatest poem, appeared, the early ambivalence had modulated into a dance of opposites supporting a Christian epistemology of paradox. From first to last, the underlying impulse seems to have been an awareness of finitude, especially in regard to epistemology (what and how it is possible to know). Eliot was not Tiresias, nor did he aspire to be. He has been caricatured as dogmatic, in part because of his strong and authoritative prose style, but in the context of his overall achievement, this portrayal is unmasked as a distortion.

A Companion to T. S. Eliot, First Edition. Edited by David E. Chinitz.
© 2014 John Wiley & Sons, Ltd. Published 2014 by John Wiley & Sons, Ltd.

Eliot's signature ambivalence did not suddenly appear in the midst of his philosophical studies. As readers of such early poems as "The Love Song of J. Alfred Prufrock" know, he was divided within and against himself by the time he finished his undergraduate studies. His public proclivity to "measure out [his] life with coffee spoons" (*CPP* 5) and his private longing "to dance, dance faster . . . in the circle of desire" (*IMH* 62) can be explained in part by family, class, and religion. His family, one of America's most distinguished, was self-consciously dynastic, enlightened, public-spirited, and respectable, all characteristics that facilitated a gap between public and private, outer and inner. In regard to religion, his forebears were Unitarians, high-minded rationalists who had made their peace with the Enlightenment by exorcizing enthusiasm and demythologizing Protestantism. By the time Eliot finished his undergraduate studies, he had come to believe that this religious rationalism had shortchanged him. In a 1936 letter to his brother, he explained that his attraction to Bergson, his Indic studies, and his "abortive attempt to make [him]self into a professor of philosophy" had been motivated by a "religious preoccupation" that eventually led to his baptism at Finstock Church. Such a preoccupation, as Lyndall Gordon suggests, can be seen in Eliot's discarded poems on saints and martyrs (57–64). In 1912–13, it was entangled with awareness of a troubling gap between intellect and feeling, an awareness that attracted him to philosophical idealism and enabled him to philosophically ground the ambivalence that appears in much of his writing.[1]

The larger intellectual context that informs Eliot's philosophical studies includes two clusters, both strong in the late nineteenth and early twentieth centuries, and both relevant to his consciousness of the gap between the subjective and objective in his own life. The first is the strenuous critique of dualism occurring in philosophy and science, and the second is the tenuous promise of overcoming dualism contained in the emerging social sciences. The assault on dualism was described in September 1926 in a leading article in the *Times Literary Supplement* as "The Dethronement of Descartes." The writer claims that Descartes and the great physicist-philosophers of the seventeenth century had been unseated by the physicists and philosophers of the early twentieth, ushering in a new dispensation in intellectual history. A few years earlier, in an essay on the metaphysical poets, Eliot had made a parallel point about literary history. He argued that the triumph of dualism in the wake of seventeenth-century thinkers had led to "a dissociation of sensibility" in which thought and feeling, subject and object, fell apart. Consequently, poets thought and felt by starts and fits (*SE* 241–50). Eliot repeated and extended this argument a few years later (1926) in his Clark Lectures at Cambridge University (published in *VMP*).

In 1929, in his landmark study, *The Revolt Against Dualism*, A. O. Lovejoy explored this turn in intellectual history in some depth. Descartes, Locke, and Newton, he argued, had dominated Western thought for three centuries, their bedrock assumption being that the precondition for understanding the world was the strict separation of subject and object. Early twentieth-century philosophers and scientists attempted to escape from the epistemological dualism of subject and object as well as from the parallel psychophysical dualism of mind and matter (1–4). The realization that subject and object are connected in a systematic way and that mind and body are aspects of a single world turns Descartes on his head. Lovejoy's argument was resumed by such intellectual historians as Thomas Kuhn and Gerald Holton. His thesis, like theirs, is helpful in approaching modern thinkers in many fields. Many of the figures who shaped the twentieth-century mind, figures as diverse as Bradley, Freud, Heisenberg, Picasso, Royce, and Eliot, have in common an about-face on the subject–object question and the mind–matter question; they all try to discredit the dualism that arbitrarily divides the world into this and that.

The second aspect of intellectual history that is important for understanding Eliot's work in philosophy is the rise of the social sciences in the second half of the nineteenth century. In 1859, Darwin published *The Origin of Species,* and in 1871, *The Descent of Man.* His thesis that life evolved from primitive forms through natural selection anticipated and facilitated the turn against dualism; by positing underlying unity, both in time and among forms of life, it laid the foundation for the assault to come. By century's end, Darwin's theory had been extended to the human sciences, resulting in an explosion of activity in theology, anthropology, sociology, and psychology. The Darwinian principles from which the social sciences emerged include (1) continuous evolution over time, with "missing links" hypothesized to fill in the record; (2) descent with modification from a common ancestor; (3) survival and improvement through natural selection; and (4) possible recovery of primal unity through the comparative study of surviving fragments. These principles undergird the work of pioneers across the social sciences, including Sigmund Freud in psychology, Émile Durkheim in sociology, Lucien Lévy-Bruhl in anthropology, and William Robertson and J. G. Frazer in comparative religion. In *The Golden Bough*, for example, Frazer tried to demonstrate a single evolutionary sequence in the development of religion from primitive to modern, and as Darwin had postulated a common ancestor for humankind, he postulated a common ancestor for all religious narratives. He believed in the original unity of human consciousness and in its continuous evolution from prehistory to the present. He assumed, moreover, that although the Ur-narrative (parent myth) had broken up in prehistoric times, it could be reconstructed through a comparative examination of its evolved fragments, a theory Eliot used structurally in writing *The Waste Land*.

Eliot's university education, spanning the decade between 1906 and 1916, was influenced by his awareness of his own doubleness. Consciously or not, he chose to study figures who in combination reflected the objective and subjective division in his own makeup. He was attracted to the realism of Aristotle and the idealism of Plato; to the subjectivity of the East and the objectivity of the West; to the vitalism of Henri Bergson, whose work he was to encounter in Paris, and the objectivism of Bertrand Russell; to the empirical idealism of F. H. Bradley and the pragmatism of William James.[2] In all of these studies, he was indebted to the Darwinian method of the social sciences. While he rejected both Darwin's materialism and the social scientists' progressive liberalism, he found much of use in their methodology.

Further, he appreciated their hypothesis regarding primitive social and religious unity and the historicist implications of their emphasis on change over time.

Eliot's chosen field of study was strongly shaped by both the philosophical debate about dualism and the contemporaneous debate about the importation of Darwinian methodology to the human sciences. As an undergraduate at Harvard, he focused on comparative literature, studying German, French, Greek, and Latin language and literature, as well as ancient and modern philosophy. This work reinforced his skepticism and deepened his tendency to hold contrasting (even contradictory) perspectives simultaneously. After graduating in 1910, Eliot left America to spend a year at the Sorbonne in Paris, where the new ideas in philosophy and the social sciences were all the rage. This year was pivotal in Eliot's intellectual odyssey, turning him toward a career in philosophy. Years later, he looked back: "At the Sorbonne, . . . the sociologists, Durkheim, Lévy-Bruhl, held new doctrines; Janet was the great psychologist; . . . and over all swung the spider-like figure of Bergson" ("C [Apr. 1934]" 452). Eliot attended Bergson's lectures and was fascinated by the Frenchman's vitalism, a post-Darwinian attempt to overcome dualism by dissolving the barriers between mind and world. He was intrigued by Bergson's valorization of subjectivity and by his account of the relation of consciousness to time and memory, an interest evident in poems he wrote that year, notably "Rhapsody on a Windy Night." In the reflections quoted above, Eliot admitted that he himself had been momentarily caught in the spider's web.

By the end of his year in Paris, Eliot had decided to pursue a career in philosophy, and in 1911, he returned to Harvard University to work on a PhD. His areas of advanced study included Indic literature, the social sciences, and Western philosophy. The first two areas are covered elsewhere in this volume.[3] In regard to the third: Eliot took three courses in successive years that can be seen as especially formative in his intellectual development. In 1911–12, he took "Descartes, Spinoza, and Leibniz," a course that highlighted the Enlightenment commitment to Cartesian dualism. In 1912–13, he took a seminar on the philosophy of Immanuel Kant, the monumental figure whose work is the first real critique of dualism. In 1913–14, he took a seminar on logic with Josiah Royce, a neo-idealist who struggled to substantiate underlying unity through the application of post-Darwinian scientific methodologies to philosophical problems. Upon completion of his coursework at Harvard, Eliot in 1914–15 studied Aristotle and Bradley at Merton College, Oxford, a capstone experience that included writing his doctoral thesis on Bradley.

The course in "Descartes, Spinoza, and Leibniz" dealt with three iconic figures of the European Enlightenment and their role in the triumph of rationalism in Western thought. A decade after taking this course, Eliot, in his Clark Lectures at Cambridge University, described their revolution in philosophy as a disaster initiated by Descartes

> when he compared the impression of "ideas" on the mind to the impression of the seal
> on the wax; and when he clearly stated that what we know is not the world of objects,

but our own ideas of these objects. The revolution was immense. Instead of ideas . . .
as references to an outside world, you have suddenly a new world coming into existence,
inside your own mind and therefore . . . inside your own head. (*VMP* 80)

Continental rationalism was answered in succeeding generations by British empiricism. Empiricists such as John Locke and David Hume refuted the rationalists'
concept of two separate worlds, one consisting of mind and the other of independent
and largely unknowable bits of matter. They claimed, rather, that the world of objects
was to some extent dependent on human experience of it, that it was furnished and
shaped by its encounter with the human mind. Despite obvious differences, both
rationalists and empiricists were essentially dualistic, with rationalists focusing on the
subject/object binary and empiricists on the experience/experienced binary. Both took
Newton's *Principia* as scripture and Newtonian mathematics as their central doctrine.
In the late eighteenth century, rationalism and empiricism were answered by Kant,
whose work was a bold attempt to synthesize Descartes and Hume and thus to mend
the split in the European mind.

Kantian critical idealism, foundational in all post-Enlightenment philosophy, was
central in Eliot's own understanding of modern thought. In the 1912–13 seminar,
Eliot wrote three essays, the first of which deals with Kant's epistemology, and more
specifically, with his attempt to reconnect the subject with the object of thought.
Kant's ambition was to transcend dualism by establishing a subjective basis for objective knowledge. He maintained that instead of the mind corresponding to objects,
objects must correspond to the mind. At the same time, he distinguished between
phenomena, that is, what is knowable through experience; and *noumena*, that is, what
is not knowable because it is the thing-in-itself, existing apart from any knowing of
it. As Eliot suggested in his seminar papers, Kant solves some problems but creates
others. He counters Cartesian dualism (mind/world; subject/object), but in the process,
he introduces Kantian dualism (*phenomena/noumena*). As expressed in a passage Eliot
underlined in the introduction to his edition of Kant, "however far we may carry our
investigations into the world of sense, we never can come into contact with aught but
appearances" (37). For Descartes, then, the object does not exist; for Kant, it exists
but is unknowable. Descartes dissolves the outside world; Kant puts it beyond reach.[4]

The third course from the Harvard years is the capstone seminar in logic Eliot took
with Josiah Royce in 1913–14. Royce's seminar, offered regularly over many years,
had by 1913 achieved legendary status at Harvard. Royce, who was to become Eliot's
mentor and direct his dissertation, based the course on his belief in an underlying
unity connecting the arts and sciences, and in collaboration with students, he explored,
comparatively, different methodologies from the new science that would enable a
transcendence of various dualisms in philosophy. The seminar, the notes of which
have been published, consisted of a spirited discussion of papers read by visiting
scholars and seminar participants (see Smith). Royce was a soldier in the revolt against
dualism described by Lovejoy. His metaphysics was a synthesis of European idealism
and American pragmatism as outlined by his senior colleague, William James. His

major contribution to the effort to overcome dualism, pursued in the seminar and in his books, was an insistence on the connection between hermeneutics and reality – that is, between the work of communities of interpreters and the progressive realization of the world in which we live (Hocking xvii).

Eliot had been intensely interested in problems of language and interpretation for years. As J. Alfred Prufrock laments, "It is impossible to say just what I mean!" (*CPP* 6). This is a point where Eliot's interests and those of Royce intersected. On December 9, 1913, Eliot read a paper, "The Interpretation of Primitive Ritual," to the group. His stated purpose was to evaluate the extent to which the methods of sociology could be considered scientific, and if scientific, the extent to which such methods could be applied to religion. His argument, which drew on his reading from Bradley, had several main points: (1) science consists of generalizations from facts; (2) all facts are functions of preexisting definitions and categories; without the definitions, facts are not facts; and (3) definitions cannot exist apart from interpretation. His conclusion is that a science of religion is impossible due to confusion between definition and interpretation.[5]

By the time Eliot finished his coursework at Harvard, he had decided to do his doctoral thesis on the philosophy of F. H. Bradley. In June 1913, he bought his own copy of *Appearance and Reality*, and in March 1914, he received a fellowship to spend a year at Bradley's Oxford college, Merton, where he was to study Aristotle and Bradley with Harold Joachim, Bradley's friend and disciple. The year at Oxford represents a turning point in Eliot's intellectual and professional life. He began the year with the idea of becoming a professor of philosophy; he ended it committed to a life in literature. The moment between his work at Harvard and his work at Oxford is crucial in understanding his mind and art. This is the moment in which he crossed the Atlantic, both literally and metaphorically, and thanks to his letters, it is possible to get a snapshot of his mind at this pivotal moment, July 1914. After a brief visit with his family, Eliot left for Europe, first to attend summer school at Marburg University in Germany, and then to spend the academic year at Oxford. He arrived in Marburg in mid-July, but within weeks was forced to leave by the outbreak of the Great War. On August 1, Germany declared war on Russia, and on August 2, the university cancelled summer school and asked foreign students to leave. Eliot made his way to London, arriving on August 21.

The letters most revealing of Eliot's state of mind as he goes from America to Europe are to his Harvard friend Conrad Aiken. These letters from July 1914 vividly demonstrate that the struggle with dualism was not purely an academic issue. It was part of a personal spiritual and psychological quest for wholeness. The letters display his divided self, and also, his consciousness of dualism on several levels. First, Eliot was aware of a gap between his own mind and body; second, he was sensitive to the corresponding epistemological split between how intellectuals know the world and how non-intellectuals know it; and third, he was thinking about the philosophical distinction between appearance and reality. In late July, settled in Marburg with a Lutheran family, he writes that he spends his mornings studying Greek and his evenings reading Hüsserl, but also that he continues with poetry, in evidence of which he encloses drafts of "Oh little voices of the throats of men" and "The Love Song of St. Sebastian."

Eliot's dualism is evident not only in his letter to Aiken (abstruse texts in German and Greek / dirty jokes, bawdy verses), but also in the poems he enclosed. "Oh little voices of the throats of men" is written from the point of view of a slightly mad, highly self-conscious intellectual who is dozing in an armchair just before dawn. The shadows in the room are leaping and dancing, and the wind is rattling the windows. In the opening stanza, he hears in the wind in the chimney "little voices" that "come between the singer and the song," and he imagines "twisted little hands of men held up" rending "the beautiful." The stanza concludes:

> Yet you do well to run the ways you run
> Yes you do well to keep the ways you keep
> And we who seek to measure joy and pain
> We blow against the wind and spit against the rain
> For what could be more real than sweat and dust and sun
> And what more sure than night and death and sleep? (*Letters* 45)[6]

The contrast is between a poet and ordinary working men, between the fruitless life of searching "dialectic ways" and the "real" life of physical labor. (A similar contrast can be seen in other early poems, including "Preludes," where an ironic but sensitive narrator broods on images of "muddy feet" pressing "to early coffee stands" and "hands / ... raising dingy shades / In a thousand furnished rooms" [*CPP* 12]). This conflict between an effete intellectual and the hardier members of the working poor stimulates the cerebral narrator to ponder a key distinction, both in his own life and in the history of philosophy, i.e., the distinction between appearance and reality:

> Appearances appearances he said
> I have searched the world through dialectic ways
> I have questioned restless nights and torpid days . . .
> And always find the same unvaried
> Interminable intolerable maze . . .
> Appearance appearances he said
> And nowise real; unreal, and yet true;
> Untrue, but real (*Letters* 45)

The echo of Eliot's early poems is a reminder that his awareness of the great Cartesian divide reached back to his own situation as a self-conscious urban intellectual. The narrator's twofold approach to the situation – searching dialectic ways (philosophy) and questioning restless nights (existence) – was to continue in Eliot's work at Oxford.

Eliot kept in touch with the Harvard Philosophy Department primarily through Professor James H. Woods, to whom he sent periodic updates on his work. On

October 5, the day before he went up to Oxford, he reported: "I have been plugging away at Hüsserl [in German], and find it terribly hard . . . I have also broken ground by going through most of the *Metaphysics* [Aristotle] for the first time in Greek" (*Letters* 60). On October 6, he arrived at Merton College, and a few weeks later, he checked in again with Professor Woods, this time listing his courses, three of which consisted of close readings of Aristotle: (1) *Metaphysics* [with Joachim]; (2) *Posterior Analytics* [Joachim]; and (3) *de Anima* [R. G. Collingwood]. But the work on Aristotle, intensive by any measure, was only one of two tracks he was following. The other was his work on Bradley.

Eliot's thesis deals with Bradley's metaphysics (what reality is or isn't) and his epistemology (how one can know). In regard to metaphysics, Bradley is part of the long conversation on mind/matter dualism initiated by Descartes. The French rationalists, as noted, had been answered by the British empiricists, who had been answered in turn by the German idealists. But Kant's synthesis, again as noted, ended by replacing one form of dualism with another. Kant's successor, Hegel, responded by arguing that the real and the rational were one and the same. Bradley demurred, pointing out, quite rightly, that Hegel's solution overcomes dualism by tossing out the material world. He tried to reintegrate the world of human experience into his own version of the Absolute, thus creating a model that includes both the world of nature and the world of ideas. In a 1927 essay, Eliot warns against overestimating Bradley's debt to Hegel, maintaining that, unlike Hegel, "Bradley is thoroughly empirical" (*SE* 403). Clearly attracted to Bradley's simultaneous commitment to wholeness and human experience, Eliot quotes a brilliant passage from *Principles of Logic*:

> It may come from a failure in my metaphysics, or from a weakness of the flesh which continues to blind me, but the notion that existence could be the same as understanding strikes as cold and ghost-like as the dreariest materialism. . . . Our principles may be true, but they are not reality. They no more *make* that Whole which commands our devotion than some shredded dissection of human tatters *is* that warm and breathing beauty of flesh which our hearts found delightful. (qtd. in *SE* 397)

"There is but one Reality," Bradley argues, "and its being consists in Experience. In this one whole all appearances come together" (*Appearance* 405, 403). He does not collapse the distinction between appearance and reality, but he does reconnect them by defining "appearance" as reality in any less than complete aspect; appearances are all that anyone can know of reality. "The Absolute *is* its appearances, it really is all and every one of them" (431).

Bradley's epistemology, a major topic in Eliot's thesis, descends from his metaphysics. If reality is an all-inclusive "experience," then subjects and objects in themselves are not ultimates but rather parts of something larger than either one. One can never discover truth through analyzing subjects and objects, because analysis by its very nature divides reality into this and that, temporal and spatial, mind and matter. How, then, can one ever know anything? Knowledge, Bradley claims, does not begin with thought but with feeling. He posits an epistemological triad: "immediate experi-ence," "intellectual experience," and "transcendent experience," with the first and third phases made up of feeling, and the intermediate term made up of thought. This is how he describes the feeling that comes *before* thinking:

> We in short have experience in which there is no distinction between my awareness and that of which it is aware. There is an immediate feeling, a knowing and being in one, with which knowledge begins; and, though this . . . is transcended, it nevertheless remains throughout as the present foundation of my known world. (*Essays* 159–60)

It is the nature of immediate experience to fall apart, to make way for perception in terms of self and not-self. This is the level of analytical (intellectual) experience, the dualistic level of knower and known, subject and object. Although most people never get beyond this level, a few transcend it, achieving a sort of non-analytical compre-hensive wisdom. This wisdom, in Bradley's view, involves a return to the wholeness and unity of immediate experience. Whereas immediate experience is characterized by a *knowing and feeling* that comes before thinking, transcendent experience is char-acterized by a *thinking and feeling* that comes after and is achieved through thought. This is the level that Eliot refers to as "a direct sensuous apprehension of thought, or a recreation of thought into feeling" (*SE* 246). One of Bradley's terms for transcendent experience is "felt thought," a term Eliot appropriated in contrasting seventeenth- and nineteenth-century poets: "Tennyson and Browning are poets, and they think; but they do not feel their thought as immediately as the odor of a rose" (247). In his thesis, Eliot accepts the idea that intellectual experience is enclosed in an envelope of pure feeling: "We are led to the conception of an all-inclusive experience outside of which nothing shall fall." He admits that the first and last terms in this triad can only be known hypothetically, but maintains that they are necessary postulates because thinking occurs only in time (*KE* 31).

The experience of simultaneously devoting oneself to an intensive study of Aristotle and Bradley would have been provocative, to say the least. Aristotle, after all, is the father of realism, and Bradley is an idealist. Aristotle associated reality with particular things, but Bradley associated it with an all-encompassing whole. Aristotle was devoted to scientific analysis, but Bradley believed that analysis was a stage in a process, a stage that had to be transcended on the journey towards wisdom.

By the end of his fall term at Oxford, Eliot was exhausted. He spent part of the Christmas break at the seashore with friends and the remainder in London. On New Year's Eve 1914, alone in London, he wrote to Aiken. "In Oxford, I have the feeling that I am not quite alive – that my body is walking about with a bit of my brain inside it, and nothing else" (*Letters* 74). The Oxford term had only intensified his feeling of self-division. Less than a week later, he confessed in a letter to fellow student Norbert Weiner that, on both a personal and a professional level, his "search through dialectic ways" had brought him to a dead end. "[A]ll philosophizing is a perversion of reality: for . . . no philosophic theory makes any difference to practice. . . . It invariably involves cramming both feet into one shoe" (80). Although Eliot admired both Aristotle and Bradley, he could accept neither realism nor idealism at face value. Neither could claim to be true without willfully ignoring the arguments that undercut its position. Having decided that the only truth is the whole truth (*KE* 163), he now identified himself as a relativist. "[O]ne has got to neglect some aspects of the situation, and what relativism does . . . is to neglect *consciously* where realism protests that there is nothing to neglect, and idealism that it has neglected nothing." The "lesson of relativism," he claimed, is "not to pursue any theory to a conclusion, and to avoid complete consistency" (*Letters* 80–81). In regard to his thesis, Eliot added: "my relativism made me see so many sides to questions that I became hopelessly involved, and wrote a thesis perfectly unintelligible to anyone but myself" (81).

Back in Oxford on January 28, Eliot checked in with Professor Woods, reporting that he was continuing with Professor Joachim on Aristotle and taking a class with Professor Stewart on Plotinus. In regard to the thesis:

> I had great difficulty, even agony, with the first draft, owing to my attempt to reach a positive conclusion; and so I should like to turn it into a criticism . . . of the Bradleian metaphysic, for it seems to me that those best qualified for such tasks are those who have held a doctrine and no longer hold it. (*Letters* 84)

He adds that he now agrees with Professor Santayana that philosophy is a species of literary criticism, words about words, not words about reality. Bradley described the intellectual prison, but did not give him a working key; Bradley led him to believe in an envelope of pure feeling, but on one end, it was irrecoverably lost; on the other, it was unreachable.

Several questions suggest themselves. The first is: given Eliot's state of mind at the end of the fall term, why did he not abandon philosophy? Why finish the year at Oxford? Why revise the thesis? The answer, contained in letters to his mother, is that he did it out of a sense of gratitude and duty, primarily to his parents, but also to his professors at Harvard. The second question is: why did Eliot then turn to poetry? In his 1926 lectures at Cambridge, the overall subject of which is the relationship between philosophy and poetry, he indicates that he had come to believe that poetry could deliver what philosophy could not. The best poetry unifies intellect and feeling, fuses thought into a complex that is experienced as feeling. "It is a function of poetry . . . to draw within the orbit of feeling and sense what had existed only in thought" (*VMP* 50–51). The best philosophical poetry is that in which "an idea, or what is ordinarily apprehensible as an intellectual statement, is translated in sensible form; so that the world of sense is actually enlarged" (53–54). Good poetry, in other words, takes abstractions, thoughts, and ideas and transforms them so that they are experienced, at least momentarily, as feelings rather than thoughts, in the body instead of the brain. Genuine poetry "elevates sense for a moment to regions ordinarily attainable only by abstract thought, or . . . clothes the abstract, for a moment, with all the painful delight of flesh" (55).

A final question: was anything that is relevant to Eliot's creative work retained from those patient hours, weeks, years of surrender to Kant, Aristotle, and Bradley? The answer is a resounding yes. Although it is not possible in this chapter to provide an illustrated catalog of the philosophical elements in Eliot's art and criticism, it is possible to mention three general qualities of mind that can be associated with his studies. The first, an emphasis on individual "facts" and analysis, can be associated with Aristotle (buttressed, as Richard Shusterman suggests, by Bertrand Russell); the second, an emphasis on "experience" and on systematic wholes, can be associated with Bradley; and third, a relativism that modulates into principled ambivalence and into Christian humility, can be associated with the essential limitations of both realism and idealism.

The indebtedness to Aristotle is most evident in Eliot's early criticism, but interestingly, the indebtedness to Bradley is evident in the very same essays. In "The Function of Criticism," for example, Eliot says that "[c]omparison and analysis . . . are the chief tools of the critic" and that "putting the reader in possession of facts" is the critic's raison d'être. Further, he argues that philosophical speculation is not fruitful in literary criticism (*SE* 21–22). But in the very same essay, he makes the case for a concept of art that could have been written by Bradley himself:

> I think of . . . the literature of the world, of the literature of Europe . . . not as a collection of the writings of individuals, but as "organic wholes," as systems in relation to which, and only in relation to which, individual works . . . have their significance. (*SE* 12–13)

"Tradition and the Individual Talent," similarly, focuses simultaneously on scientific analysis and organic wholes. This double allegiance had been outlined in one of the more poignant passages in his thesis:

> [T]he life of a soul does not consist in the contemplation of one consistent world but in the painful task of unifying . . . jarring and incompatible ones, and passing, when possible, from two or more discordant viewpoints to a higher which shall somehow include and transmute them. (*KE* 147–48)

A parallel commitment is evident in his poetry. In *The Waste Land*, for example, the "facts" consist not just of "empty bottles, sandwich papers, / Silk handkerchiefs, cardboard boxes, cigarette ends," but of those "facts" as *experienced* in autumn memories by one who recognizes them as the residue of "summer nights" and as *experienced* by a reader who recognizes them as part of the cultural and literary detritus of civilization over many centuries (*CPP* 42). These "facts" are not, as Aristotle would suggest, ultimate, but rather, as Bradley would insist, connected to larger contexts in human experience. The simultaneous commitment to separate things (including multiple voices) and to larger wholes is perfectly realized in the form of *The Waste Land*, a poem made up of facts on one level, and on another, of an abstraction that goes back to the beginning of human consciousness – that is, to the Frazerian monomyth.[7]

By the time Eliot finished his formal study of philosophy in 1916, he was in the midst of a personal crisis, and Europe was mired down in what seemed a never-ending war. For various reasons, some indicated in this chapter, he had come to the conclusion that "no knowledge will survive analysis" (KE 157). But as Shusterman indicates, Eliot's philosophical position was not static, and his skepticism was itself in time and changing. As it evolved into a more complex ambivalence, it merged in the late 1920s with Christian humility, the artistic fruit of which can be seen in his crowning achievement, *Four Quartets*.

NOTES

1 Astute critics agree that Eliot's ambivalence is philosophically grounded and fruitful. Habib, for example, helpfully associates the ambivalence with Eliot's use of irony. And Shusterman takes a long view of Eliot's philosophical thinking, seeing him as moving through several stages, including objectivism, hermeneutical historicism, and *phronesis*, or practical wisdom. Perl, who has contributed much to our understanding of Eliot and Western philosophy, has a chapter in this volume that discusses ambivalence in Eliot's poetry; see DISAMBIVALENT QUATRAINS.

2 What these philosophical antitheses share is a contrast between the personal/inner world (in idealism, the idea; in subjectivism, the ego; in vitalism, the organism; in rationalism, the mind or reason) and the impersonal/outer world (in realism, the world apart from any perception of it; in empiricism, the common world of experience; in objectivism, objects). Bradley's synthesis is an attempt to bridge the polarity between mind and world by putting both under the umbrella of Experience. James's pragmatism, insofar as it is mechanistic, tends toward the objective side, but also shifts the argument by emphasizing process instead of being, what works instead of what is. The point in regard to Eliot is that his studies gave roughly equal time to both sides and that his personal quest involves not only acknowledging both, but also transcending them.

3 See NOT ONE, NOT TWO: ELIOT AND BUDDHISM and MIND, MYTH, AND CULTURE: ELIOT AND ANTHROPOLOGY.

4 For summaries of the three Kant papers, see Habib 97–125.

5 This extraordinarily interesting paper on the hermeneutical implications of attempts to understand the primitive mind is quoted and discussed at length in Gray 108–42.

6 The poem also appears in *IMH* 75–76.

7 For a fuller discussion, see Brooker 110–22.

REFERENCES AND FURTHER READING

Bradley, F. H. *Appearance and Reality: A Metaphysical Essay*. 2nd ed. Oxford: Clarendon, 1897.

——. *Essays on Truth and Reality*. 1914. Oxford: Clarendon, 1950.

Brooker, Jewel Spears. *Mastery and Escape: T. S. Eliot and the Dialectic of Modernism*. Amherst: U of Massachusetts P, 1994.

"The Dethronement of Descartes." *Times Literary Supplement* 9 Sept. 1926: 1.

Gordon, Lyndall. *Eliot's Early Years*. Oxford: Oxford UP, 1977.

Gray, Piers. *T. S. Eliot's Intellectual and Poetic Development*. Atlantic Highlands, NJ: Humanities, 1982.

Habib, M. A. R. *The Early T. S. Eliot and Western Philosophy*. Cambridge: Cambridge UP, 1999.

Hocking, Richard. "The Philosophy of Royce." Smith xi–xxiii.

Holton, Gerald. *Thematic Origins of Scientific Thought*. Cambridge: Harvard UP, 1973.

Jain, Manju. *T. S. Eliot and American Philosophy*. Cambridge: Cambridge UP, 1992.

Kant, Immanuel. *The Philosophy of Kant as Contained in Extracts from his Own Writings*. Trans. John Watson. New ed. Glasgow: MacLehose, 1908.

Kuhn, Thomas S. *The Structure of Scientific Revolutions*. 2nd ed. Chicago: U of Chicago P, 1970.

Lovejoy, Arthur O. *The Revolt Against Dualism: An Inquiry Concerning the Existence of Ideas*. 1929. La-Salle, IL: Open Court, 1955.

Perl, Jeffrey. *Skepticism and Modern Enmity: Before and After Eliot*. Baltimore: Johns Hopkins UP, 1989.

Shusterman, Richard. "Eliot as Philosopher." *The Cambridge Companion to T. S. Eliot*. Ed. A. David Moody. Cambridge: Cambridge UP, 1994. 31–47.

Smith, Grover, ed. *Josiah Royce's Seminar: 1913–1924*. New Brunswick, NJ: Rutgers UP, 1963.

6

A Vast Wasteland? Eliot and Popular Culture

David E. Chinitz

"An artificial and unimportant distinction"

In May 1961, Newton Minow, the newly appointed chair of the Federal Communications Commission, lectured the National Association of Broadcasters on the quality of television broadcasting in the United States. At the crux of his oration, which urged the broadcasters forcefully to raise the cultural bar, Minow deployed one of the twentieth century's most influential metaphors:

> I invite you to sit down in front of your television set when your station goes on the air and stay there without a book, magazine, newspaper, profit-and-loss sheet or rating book to distract you – and keep your eyes glued to that set until the station signs off. I can assure you that you will observe a vast wasteland. (24)

Minow's address, officially titled "Television and the Public Interest" but known ever after as the "vast wasteland speech," struck a chord that reverberated for years in American discourse on the media. Its climactic if unacknowledged invocation of T. S. Eliot was no accident.

Few intellectuals of stature would have disputed the proposition that Western culture was in decline in 1961. Americans and Europeans, by common consensus, were addicted to the lowest forms of amusement, from romance novels and hard-boiled detective fiction to the movies, and, by now, to television. The purveyors of these and other forms of commercial culture were "leveling down" their standards in order to appeal to the widest possible audience, which further eroded the already-low taste of the misguided majority. Meanwhile, and as a direct consequence, the fine arts were losing their prestige and patronage. It was given to a small and beleaguered minority to defend and preserve the best of traditional high culture and to put popular culture back in its place. This critique of contemporary culture, influentially articulated by F. R. Leavis in the 1930s and developed with varying emphases by other important

A Companion to T. S. Eliot, First Edition. Edited by David E. Chinitz.
© 2014 John Wiley & Sons, Ltd. Published 2014 by John Wiley & Sons, Ltd.

critics over the next two decades, was so well established by the Cold War years – and so strongly associated with Eliot – that by uttering the single keyword *wasteland*, Newton Minow could bring down its entire weight on the television industry.

Indeed, Eliot has long been an iconic figure for a militant advocacy of high culture against low. Whereas Minow and his contemporaries were eager to cite Eliot as an ally, later critics have more often treated Eliot as a figurehead for a snobbish and ill-informed critical posture. (One typical remark applauds the discipline of cultural studies for rejecting "the blanket dismissal of popular culture by elitists in the Eliot tradition, a dismissal which effectively stigmatized all current forms of popular art" [Fowler 166].) Both sides rely on the same oversimplified and finally inaccurate representation of Eliot as a (or *the*) leading stalwart in high culture's last stand. In fact, Eliot's relations with popular culture were far more involved, more ambivalent, and in short, more interesting than either his past enthusiasts or detractors cared to admit.

What did Eliot himself have to say about works of popular culture, or about the relations between high and low culture? In his later criticism, he sometimes sounds like the Eliot we have learned to expect, inveighing against the mechanization and globalization of culture. Elsewhere, though, and, especially, early in his career, Eliot's thinking about popular culture was richer and more bracing. "[F]ine art," he wrote in 1923, "is the *refinement*, not the antithesis, of popular art" ("Marianne Moore" 595), suggesting a continuum of cultural expression that is not reducible to aesthetic worthiness. ("Tradition and the Individual Talent" explicitly rejects any equation of "refinement" with superiority: art may become more sophisticated, but such a development "is not, from the point of view of the artist, any improvement" [*SE* 6].) "Popular art," for Eliot, is neither a degradation of high art nor the enemy of high art, as most of his contemporaries believed. He warns that the accepted high–low dichotomy is an "artificial and unimportant distinction" that has "dangerous consequences" for culture ("Marianne Moore" 594).

Was this purely a matter of theory, or did Eliot actually find something of value in, say, the best-selling novels of his day? Did he himself not dwell in the "refined" world of high art, immersing himself in only the "best" literature and sneering at the melodrama of popular fiction? In the 1927 essay "Wilkie Collins and Dickens," Eliot argues that readers should not have to choose between these things. Far from being inimical to great art, melodrama is a vital constituent of it, and for the "serious" novelists of his time to dismiss this element of the aesthetic is a grave mistake (*SE* 409, 417–18). Eliot perceived, too, that the opposition between high and low culture was not a permanent condition, but an historical development of modern origin: even as recently as the mid-nineteenth century, "such terms as 'high-brow fiction,' 'thrillers' and 'detective fiction'" had yet to be "invented." Without the interference of these categories,

> there was no such distinction. The best novels *were* thrilling; the distinction of genre between such-and-such a profound "psychological" novel of today and such-and-such a masterly "detective" novel of today is greater than the distinction of genre between

Wuthering Heights, or even *The Mill on the Floss*, and [Ellen Wood's bestselling melodramatic novel] *East Lynne*. (409–10)

The literary fiction of his own time becomes "dull," Eliot charges, as it abandons melodrama to the commercial novel (416). And he predicts: "If we cannot get this satisfaction out of what the publishers present as 'literature,' then we will read – with less and less pretense of concealment – what we call 'thrillers'" (409).

As if to underscore this point, Eliot personally reviewed twenty-four works of crime fiction and two nonfiction works on the subject of murder in the 1927 *Criterion*. Thirty-five years later he confessed, or perhaps boasted, that he had read no "'serious' prose fiction" since that time (Stravinsky 92). The fiction he admitted to reading was of another sort: the comic stories of P. G. Wodehouse, and the detective novels of Raymond Chandler, Agatha Christie, and others. Eliot was in reality no friend of the sacralization of high culture that readers came to associate with him.

Though often ambivalent, Eliot was productively engaged with popular culture in some form at every stage of his working life. His attraction to such cultural forms as American vaudeville, English music-hall comedy, comic strips, mystery novels, and popular song had an essential influence on his art and his career. Only with this recognition can we account for the fact that he devoted the entire creative effort of his last 30 years – bracketing only the last three *Quartets* and a handful of negligible "occasional" verses – to an effort to develop a popular verse drama. The attempt was an embarrassment to his many supporters, who were never more discomfited than when Eliot appeared to be succeeding, and particularly in 1950, when *The Cocktail Party*, starring Alec Guinness on Broadway and Rex Harrison in London, became one of the year's hit plays. It was as a critic and as a poet, in the traditional sense, that Eliot had made his considerable reputation; why did he not remain, in that same sense, a poet? Just as the "serious novel" appeared moribund to Eliot if it could not close the gap with popular fiction, he thought that poetry, too, needed to take on a new shape – one that would reembody in a popular form the poet's skills with language and rhythm. The theater, he speculated, might be "the best place in which to do this" (*UPUC* 147). By working in a popular genre, Eliot noted, the poet also wins the opportunity to engage with a substantial public, to address as well as entertain a relatively "large and miscellaneous" (i.e., diverse) audience (146). In this way the poet could claim, or reclaim, "some direct social utility" (147). Eliot would later dub such uses of the poetic craft "applied poetry" (qtd. in Lehmann 5).

Culture Contact

It is not only in his late work as a playwright that we find the evidence of Eliot's engagement with popular culture, but from the very beginning of his career. In Part III of "Suite Clownesque" (1910), for example, J. Alfred Prufrock's urban wanderings are restaged as a kind of vaudeville comedy:

If you're walking down the avenue,
Five o'clock in the afternoon,
I may meet you
Very likely greet you
Show you that I know you (*IMH* 35)

The poem's snappy rhyming style is modeled on the Tin Pan Alley lyrics of the day, and the persona, sure enough, soon alludes to the contemporary hit song "By the Light of the Silvery Moon" and expresses his excitement at finding himself on "Broadway after dark!" A stage direction calling for music from "the sandboard and bones" mixes a minstrel element into the poem's cultural mélange, and current slang phrases – "I guess," "up to date," "all right" – add further local color. With the stride and in the rhythms of modern popular culture, the speaker celebrates his young, American self as "First born child of the absolute / Neat, complete, / In the quintessential flannel suit." Yet an underlying anxiety surfaces from beneath his apparent confidence: "I guess there's nothing the matter with us! / – But say, just be serious, / Do you think that I'm all right?" (35). The speaker's monologue ends with this uncomfortable plea, an expression of the ambivalence Eliot felt, or felt he should feel, toward the popular elements that suffuse his poem. "A man," as he would write later, "will often love what he spurns" (*CPP* 184).

Although Eliot's use of song rhythms owes much to Jules Laforgue, the French symbolist whom the young Eliot adopted as his master in 1909, apprentice poems like "Suite Clownesque" reveal a further influence: American jazz – or, more accurately, given the early date, ragtime. It was "the *convergence* of these elements," as I have argued elsewhere, "that produced the masterpieces of the *Prufrock* period": "Laforgue showed Eliot how to adapt his voice to the popular material around him, and jazz gave Eliot a way to bring Laforgue into contemporary English – that is, a way to incorporate the inflections of his own language in a form of verse derived from another" (*T. S. Eliot* 36). An untitled poem written during Eliot's 1910–11 stay in Paris makes this confluence the more obvious. Here the heavy blue smoke and the "torpid" ambiance of a cabaret create a decadent atmosphere in which Eliot's speaker languishes. The poem's first verse paragraph establishes this lethargic, almost hypnotized mood; the second shatters it as a live musical performance suddenly catches the speaker's wandering attention. At this moment, the poem's verse – to this point repetitive, abstract, and long-lined – changes direction sharply:

What, you want action?
Some attraction?
Now begins
The piano and the flute and two violins
Someone sings
A lady of almost any age
But chiefly breast and rings
"Throw your arms around me—Aint you glad you found me"

> Still that's hardly strong enough—
> Here's a negro (teeth and smile)
> Has a dance that's quite worth while
> That's the stuff!
> (Here's your gin
> Now begin!) (*IMH* 70)

The closing lines are not without irony, yet the poetic energy generated by Eliot's innovative use of popular-song rhythms is undeniable. Besides quoting an actual lyric of the day, Eliot again assimilates the popular idiom ("That's the stuff," "What, you want action?") while sketching a scene from the incipient Jazz Age. The poem all but advertises the source of its volatile rhythms and erratic rhymes in the ragtime lyrics of the period. The italicized popular-song excerpt stands out in no way, apart from its length, from Eliot's original lines, precisely because Eliot's lines have taken the ragtime lyric as their model. As Philip Furia explains, ragtime "licensed the vernacular as a lyrical idiom and forced the lyricist to construct a lyric out of short, juxtaposed phrases marked by internal rhymes and jagged syntactical breaks" (49). Eliot went to school to this music in becoming Eliot.

For Eliot did not merely experiment with this verse form: in the space of a few months, he learned how to make great poetry of it. The cadences of "The smoke that gathers blue and sinks" and of "Suite Clownesque" are also the cadences of "Preludes":

> And now a gusty shower wraps
> The grimy scraps
> Of withered leaves about your feet
> And newspapers from vacant lots;
> The showers beat
> On broken blinds and chimney-pots. (*CPP* 12)

They are refined in "Prufrock":

> And indeed there will be time
> To wonder, "Do I dare," and, "Do I dare?"
> Time to turn back and descend the stair,
> With a bald spot in the middle of my hair (4)

And they remain perceptible in *The Waste Land*, in, for instance, "The pleasant whining of a mandoline / And a clatter and a chatter from within / Where fishmen lounge at noon" (45), not to mention "O O O O that Shakespeherian Rag— / It's so elegant / So intelligent" (41). The sounds of popular music inspired Eliot's rhythms, his treatment of rhyme, the shaping of his lines – inspired, in short, the distinctive traits that make Eliot sound like Eliot.

Other pioneering aspects of Eliot's work are likewise rooted in demotic influences. Before Eliot whittled *The Waste Land* down to half its original length with the editorial assistance of Ezra Pound, the poem was to have opened not with "April is the cruellest month," but with a rowdy scene of popular entertainments, and was to have included, on its first page, quotations from such songs as George M. Cohan's "Harrigan," the sentimental "Maid of the Mill," and the "coon songs" "By the Watermelon Vine" and "My Evaline" (*WLF* 5; Chinitz, "Shadows" 451–54; 459–60). This opening scene, too obviously influenced by the Circe episode from *Ulysses*, was deleted in its entirety, leaving the ballad of Mrs. Porter (ll. 199–201) and the "Shakespeherian Rag" (ll. 127–30) the sole popular song quotations to survive in *The Waste Land*.

Michael North has argued that the modernist form of *The Waste Land* can be traced to the minstrel show, another "art of mélange" (*Dialect* 85–86). Minstrel shows, which burlesqued other cultural forms at will, were in fact filled with allusions and gave the materials they referenced new meaning through jarring juxtapositions – as one finds in Eliot:

> But at my back in a cold blast I hear
> The rattle of the bones, and chuckle spread from ear to ear.
> A rat crept softly through the vegetation
> Dragging its slimy belly on the bank
> While I was fishing in the dull canal
> On a winter evening round behind the gashouse
> Musing upon the king my brother's wreck
> And on the king my father's death before him.
> White bodies naked on the low damp ground
> And bones cast in a little low dry garret,
> Rattled by the rat's foot only, year to year.
> But at my back from time to time I hear
> The sound of horns and motors, which shall bring
> Sweeney to Mrs. Porter in the spring.
> O the moon shone bright on Mrs. Porter
> And on her daughter
> They wash their feet in soda water
> *Et O ces voix d'enfants, chantant dans la coupole!* (*CPP* 42–43)

In the second line of this passage, the phrase "rattle of the bones" weirdly conjoins two divergent scenes: the phantasmagoric cityscape of the succeeding lines, and the minstrel stage, where the ear-to-ear grin and the bones – played as a percussion instrument – were standard features. This reference is sandwiched between an echo of Andrew Marvell's "To His Coy Mistress" and a Gothic transposition of Shakespeare's *The Tempest*. The closing lines fly, in the same way, from seventeenth-century lyric (Marvell and John Day) to a bawdy popular parody of the sentimental song "Red Wing" (into which Eliot inserts his own character, Sweeney), and then, thanks to the common element of the footbath, to the resolution of the Grail quest as recounted in

Paul Verlaine's sonnet on Wagner's opera *Parsifal*. These 18 lines illustrate in concentrated form the "famous techniques of quotation and juxtaposition" that made *The Waste Land* the technical breakthrough that it was (North 85). That a reference to the minstrel show leads off the passage seems telling, especially since, as North points out, the allusions to "My Evaline" and "By the Watermelon Vine," which Eliot had spliced together on his deleted opening page, would have provided the first examples of Eliot's jarring new poetics. It does not matter that these songs were ultimately cut from the poem: the popular form leaves its trace in Eliot's profoundest modernist innovations. Nor is minstrelsy the only popular genre behind Eliot's practices: vaudeville and its English music-hall cousin were similarly miscellaneous, and jazz was notorious for its omnivorous assimilation, juxtaposition, and parody of any and all musical sources.

The underlying variety-show character of *The Waste Land* is on full display in Eliot's next project: the unfinished verse-drama *Sweeney Agonistes*. It was here that Eliot made his first attempt at "applied poetry" – again, the deployment of poetic craft in a hybrid medium that would entertain a large audience and give the poet "some direct social utility" (*UPUC* 147). An astonishing variety of popular genres are audible in the words and visible in the design of *Sweeney Agonistes*. Among the constituents of Eliot's pastiche, Rachel Blau DuPlessis lists "melodrama, tabloid shock, working-class sentimental poetry, true-crime confession, bartender's parable, Gilbert and Sullivan operetta, as well as minstrel and vaudeville" (99); to these one might add musical comedy, burlesque, Tin Pan Alley song, and music hall. The first scene of the uncompleted play, which Eliot called "Fragment of a Prologue," comprises a syncopated, deliberately jazzy dialogue; the second scene, the "Fragment of an Agon," is punctuated by parodic songs.[1] The play harnesses popular cultural forms as a vehicle for Eliot's rather nihilistic vision of life. His strategy is closely related to his musings on the origin of drama in ritual – the *ur*-form of culture, "popular" in the most literal sense of the term ("Beating" 12; "Marianne Moore" 597; "Dramatis" 305–06). But Eliot's attempt to make a ritual drama of *Sweeney Agonistes* undoes any popularizing effect that his use of vaudeville, crime stories, or jazz might have had. The imposition of ancient ceremonial structures and symbols on the play makes it esoteric – rich fare for an avant-garde readership, yet unlikely to speak to the "large and miscellaneous audience" Eliot coveted. He would have to bear the yoke of existing dramatic conventions and audience expectations if he was to achieve a genuine popularity.

Perhaps the conflicting impulses behind *Sweeney Agonistes* had something to do with Eliot's failure to complete the play. His next project, "The Hollow Men," picks up some of the frayed threads of *Sweeney Agonistes*, but it does so in the familiar medium of "pure" (as opposed to "applied") poetry, returning Eliot to his comfort zone. The poem's epigraph recalls a popular ritual familiar, at any rate, to all its English readers: the annual burning of Guy Fawkes in effigy to celebrate the defeat of the 1605 Gunpowder Plot, and the depiction of the hollow men as effigies themselves ("Leaning together / Headpiece filled with straw" [*CPP* 56]) permeates the poem. Its last movement uses nursery rhyme to distill Eliot's bleak portrait of the modern world in the well-known closing lines:

> *This is the way the world ends*
> *This is the way the world ends*
> *This is the way the world ends*
> *Not with a bang but a whimper.* (59)

This eschatological chant is juxtaposed with fragmented stammerings of the Lord's Prayer ("For Thine is / Life is / For Thine is the"), recalling the earlier moment when, venerating their shattered idols, the hollow men mutter "prayers to broken stone" (59, 58). As a whole, "The Hollow Men" reinforces the idea that popular culture is grounded in ritual, adding the further suggestion that culture degenerates as the faith behind the ritual disintegrates.

Artists and Audiences

One of the crucial documents in Eliot's relations with popular culture is his elegiac 1923 essay on the music-hall comedian Marie Lloyd. Here Eliot accounts Lloyd's recent death an "important event" in the development of English culture. Lloyd, he argues, was not only an "artist" of "genius," but a significant and emblematic cultural figure. She was the greatest and most popular music-hall performer of her time, the most beloved of her largely working-class audience, because she, better than anyone else,

> succeeded . . . in giving expression to the life of that audience, in raising it to a kind of art. It was, I think, this capacity for expressing the soul of the people that made Marie Lloyd unique, and that made her audiences, even when they joined in the chorus, not so much hilarious as happy. (*SE* 406)

Lloyd's "superiority," for Eliot, was a product of "her understanding of the people and sympathy with them, and the people's recognition of the fact that she embodied the virtues which they genuinely most respected in private life" (406–07). Her performances distilled and expressed "that part of the English nation which has perhaps the greatest vitality and interest" (405).

Most critics have treated "Marie Lloyd" as an anomaly in Eliot's oeuvre. Those who have not ignored it have often expressed an admiration coupled with puzzlement at its existence (Chinitz, *T. S. Eliot* 14–15). Taken seriously, the essay prescribes a philosophy of art, an attitude toward popular culture, and a gauge of artistic excellence that seem hard to reconcile with either the austere complexities of Eliot's poetry or the mandarin erudition of his criticism – a criticism that had famously argued, only two years earlier, that "poets in our civilization, as it exists at present, must be *difficult"* (*SE* 248). The framing of that imperative is revealing, however: Eliot is not advocating difficulty as an artistic ideal but asserting that poetry must respond even to such unfavorable conditions as the chaos and incoherence of modernity. Difficulty under the circumstances is a regrettable necessity. The *ideal* may be judged from one of the few passages in *The Waste Land* that portrays an enclave of cultural vitality:

> "This music crept by me upon the waters"
> And along the Strand, up Queen Victoria Street.
> O City city, I can sometimes hear
> Beside a public bar in Lower Thames Street,
> The pleasant whining of a mandoline
> And a clatter and a chatter from within
> Where fishmen lounge at noon. . . . (*CPP* 45)

Somehow, amid the "arid plain" of the City (50), London's commercial district and the center of its malaise, endures the oasis of the fishmen's pub, where a working-class clientele mingles to music, and where even the ragtime rhythms of Eliot's early poems return to breathe fresh air into the urban wasteland. Here, as in "Marie Lloyd," an organic culture is still accessible among "the people" – but in both cases Eliot represents that culture as endangered by a besieging modernity.

In "Marie Lloyd," the threat comes, specifically, from mass culture:

> The lower class still exists; but perhaps it will not exist for long. In the music-hall comedians they find the expression and dignity of their own lives. . . . With the decay of the music-hall, with the encroachment of the cheap and rapid-breeding cinema, the lower classes will tend to drop into the same state of protoplasm as the bourgeoisie. (*SE* 407)

The difference between music hall and film, for Eliot, has much to do with the audience's engagement, or lack thereof, with the medium: "The working man who went to the music-hall and saw Marie Lloyd and joined in the chorus was himself performing part of the act; he was engaged in that collaboration of the audience with the artist which is necessary in all art and most obviously in dramatic art" (407). A good modernist, Eliot is convinced that the bourgeois relation with the arts ranges from ersatz reverence to uncomprehending boredom. Art is received, if at all, in a state of "listless apathy" (407). The techniques of mechanical reproduction only intensify this alienation, Eliot believes, because the element of participation, of active involvement, is missing; one cannot interact with a projection on a screen or with a disembodied voice on a recording. (In *The Waste Land*, the impassive conduct of the typist – she remains uninvolved even during sexual intercourse – finds its objective correlative in her playing of "a record on the gramophone" [*CPP* 44].) The decline of the music hall, epitomized in the death of Marie Lloyd, therefore represents not merely the disappearance of a treasured form of entertainment, but a mounting social disaster.

To conclude, however, that Eliot's position can be summarized neatly as an advocacy of "popular art" against "mass art" – that is, of art issuing from the people vs. art foisted on the people by the "culture industry" – would be an oversimplification. James Naremore generalizes about modernism that what it abominated was not popular culture per se, but "a commodified, mass-produced . . . culture that took the form of slick-paper magazines, Books-of-the-Month, and big-budget productions from Broadway and Hollywood" (44). Though useful as a summary of modernism as a whole, this formulation may not accurately represent the views of any given modernist. Marianne Moore, a fan of professional baseball and boxing, considered vaudeville shows to be "insulting wigwaggery" (107), while E. E. Cummings, who loved vaudeville and Charlie Chaplin films, thoroughly detested radio (174–75, 194–96). Eliot, by contrast, considered Chaplin a pernicious genius because his success abetted the proliferation of the movies ("Dramatis" 306), yet he saw merit in radio and supported that medium from early on, making over eighty broadcasts of his own between 1929 and 1963 (Coyle 32–33).[2] As we have seen, he was also (ambivalently) attracted to and influenced by genres, such as jazz and Tin Pan Alley song, that are not easily classified by any neat distinction between "popular" and "mass" culture. Each modernist, one might conclude, was groping toward a critical evaluation of modern expressive forms and media, no two to precisely the same conclusion. Few, though, even among those most receptive to popular culture, went as far as the patrician Eliot when he spent the second half of his career retraining himself as a playwright whose works would become "big-budget productions" in the theaters of London and New York.

Broadway and Beyond

Eliot's career as a dramatist takes him, slowly and not steadily, but inexorably, away from the experimentalism and high-modernist "difficulty" of *Sweeney Agonistes* and toward a compromise with the middle-class, theater-going audience. *The Rock*, a 1934 "pageant play," is hard to place along this arc; but that is in part because Eliot only wrote the words to fit a scenario created by others, and in part because the play was commissioned for a specific purpose.[3] A work of frank propaganda intended to generate funds for the construction of new church buildings in the diocese of London, *The Rock* had to appeal to a general audience, and, through the use of a music-hall "variety" format that embraced song, comedy, folk legend, dance, pantomime, and other entertainments, it largely succeeded. Yet, as Eliot understood, the audience that came to see *The Rock* did so in part out of a sense of religious obligation, and not because he had realized his ambition of inventing a new form of verse drama that brought poetry into the popular theater. (Much of the play, actually, was in prose.) That quest would continue in Eliot's next theatrical efforts.

Murder in the Cathedral (1935), a historical drama about the assassination of St. Thomas Becket of Canterbury, has been the one securely canonical play in Eliot's oeuvre. Critics have found here the magnificence of language and the intellectual "seriousness" that they value in Eliot's poetry. Like *The Rock*, though to a lesser degree, *Murder in the Cathedral* incorporates popular genres: there is a whiff of contemporary detective fiction, a quotation from a well-known Sherlock Holmes story, and a central place for Christian liturgy (though religious ritual, despite Eliot's eager construal, is not a popular genre in quite the same sense). The play also features a chorus of ordinary women intended to speak for and to a popular audience. Yet its elevated diction, richly "poetic" imagery, and deliberately conspicuous versification do not point the way toward a verse drama that could, as Eliot hoped, compete for audiences with prose drama. Convinced that a poetic dramatist should "not let the audience forget that what they are hearing is verse" ("Need" 995), Eliot produced a powerful poetry that offers much to the relative few who appreciate his "pure" poetic masterpieces:

> Now I fear disturbance of the quiet seasons:
> Winter shall come bringing death from the sea,
> Ruinous spring shall beat at our doors,
> Root and shoot shall eat our eyes and our ears,
> Disastrous summer burn up the beds of our streams
> And the poor shall wait for another decaying October. (*CPP* 176)

Whether a play written in this mode is likely to appeal to a "large and miscellaneous audience" is another question.

Though it is a profound and aesthetically rich work, *Murder in the Cathedral* did not satisfy Eliot's stage ambitions. Both the far-off historical setting and the stylized versification, he came to feel, had "transport[ed] the audience into [an] imaginary world totally unlike its own, an unreal world in which poetry is tolerated." Eliot did not want poetry to be "tolerated": he wanted to create a verse drama that was genuinely popular; and to do this, he saw, he would need "to bring poetry into the world in which the audience lives and to which it returns when it leaves the theater" (*OPP* 82). All of Eliot's plays after *Murder in the Cathedral* are set in the present, and his verse, put in the mouths of contemporary characters, came to sound less and less obviously "poetic," and more like modern spoken English.

With its present-day drawing-room setting and attenuated poetic lines, Eliot's next play, *The Family Reunion* (1939), takes him part way to his goals. His retention of the "mythical method" – the play is loosely based on Aeschylus's *Oresteia* and requires the Eumenides or "Furies" of the myth to appear on stage – and his continuing use of a chorus, however, indicate that Eliot was not ready to submit wholeheartedly to the generic conventions of modern popular drama. Unsurprisingly, the theater-going public responded by not attending, and the play closed after only five weeks (Bush 209). Eight years, four *Quartets*, one world war and a Nobel Prize later, Eliot would try again, this time conscientiously suppressing any avant-garde impulses and dispensing with any obvious high-literary devices. He was determined, as he told one skeptical interlocutor, to keep on "[u]ntil I can convince people that I know how to write a popular play" (qtd. in Smidt 61). In *The Cocktail Party* (1949) Eliot wove his ideas about redemption, community, and human relations into an appealingly "theatrical" comedy, and he was rewarded with a popular hit. The play ran for over 400 performances on Broadway and over 300 in London. That *The Cocktail Party* was written in verse did not keep audiences away.

Chastened, perhaps, by the failure of *The Family Reunion*, Eliot had reversed his position on the perceptibility of the verse in poetic drama. While remaining convinced that the application of poetic craft could add a great deal to the emotional effectiveness of a play, he believed now that such results had to be achieved "unconsciously" – that the audience must *not* be "aware" that it is listening to verse ("Aims" 13). *The Cocktail Party* is written in an irregular, scarcely detectable four-stress meter. "Poetry" here comprises a light-handed manipulation of tone and cadence, well-chosen words, and the occasional elevation of language, at emotional moments, just beyond the confines of everyday speech:

> Henry, you simply do not understand innocence.
> She will be afraid of nothing; she will not even know
> That there is anything there to be afraid of.
> She is too humble. She will pass between the scolding hills,
> Through the valley of derision, like a child sent on an errand
> In eagerness and patience. Yet she must suffer. (*CPP* 368)

This is about as "poetic" as *The Cocktail Party* gets, and Eliot reported himself "pleased . . . that several critics left the theater without having decided whether the play was meant to be in verse or in prose" ("Aims" 13). His last two plays, *The Confidential Clerk* (1954) and *The Elder Statesman* (1959), are in more or less the same vein, though neither matched the success of *The Cocktail Party*.

Later critical assessments of Eliot's plays (apart from *Murder in the Cathedral*) have been generally unenthusiastic, and his long pursuit of a popular verse drama has raised a number of significant questions. Is Eliot to be commended for seeking a rapprochement with the bourgeoisie, or did the attempt "sabotage" his art, as Frank Kermode has argued? In subduing his earlier modernist antagonism to the middle class and its conception of art, did he lower his standards? Should he have put his effort, instead, into developing the kind of expressionist drama suggested by the uncompleted *Sweeney Agonistes*? Did he give up too easily on the "social utility" of "pure" poetry? Following the trajectory of these questions beyond their intersection with Eliot, one might ask whether any boundary-crossing artist – a "classical" composer who attempts to write a musical, say, or a "literary" novelist who assays journalism or screenplay writing – is misdirecting his or her talent, or putting that talent to a different but not inappropriate use. And what of the rock musician with symphonic ambitions or the cartoonist who collaborates with a poet? What *is* the relation, or what should it be, between popular culture and the fine arts, between culture and class, and – if the distinction is not too problematic to be meaningful – between popular arts and mass culture?[4] Is television, is the Internet, are the movies a "vast wasteland," and, if so, what, can or ought to be done? Such issues are not only for aestheticians but for societies collectively to resolve. Through both his writing on these subjects and his artistic practice, Eliot has put the questions before us. The task of evaluating and answering them is ours.

NOTES

1 For more on this play and its influences, see *SWEENEY AGONISTES*: A SENSATIONAL SNARL.

2 David Trotter, it should be added, has argued that despite the notoriety of his most purely negative remarks on the subject, Eliot actually bore "an enduring preoccupation" with cinema, "one with definite consequences for his development as a writer" (237).

3 For more detailed accounts of *The Rock* and the other plays discussed here, see ELIOT'S 1930S PLAYS: *THE ROCK, MURDER IN THE CATHE-DRAL*, AND *THE FAMILY REUNION* and ELIOT'S "DIVINE" COMEDIES: *THE COCKTAIL PARTY, THE CONFIDENTIAL CLERK*, AND *THE ELDER STATESMAN*.

4 The relation between class and the production of culture, in particular, is a topic that Eliot treats at length in *Notes towards the Definition of Culture* (see especially the first two chapters, CC 93–122). See also IN TIMES OF EMERGENCY: ELIOT'S SOCIAL CRITICISM.

REFERENCES AND FURTHER READING

Bush, Ronald. *T. S. Eliot: A Study in Character and Style*. New York: Oxford UP, 1983.

Chinitz, David E. "In the Shadows: Popular Song and Eliot's Construction of Emotion." *Modernism/Modernity* 11 (2004): 449–67.

———. *T. S. Eliot and the Cultural Divide*. Chicago: U of Chicago P, 1993.

Coyle, Michael. "'This rather elusory broadcast technique': T. S. Eliot and the Genre of the Radio Talk." *ANQ* 11 (1998): 32–42.

Cummings, E. E. *Selected Letters of E. E. Cummings*. Ed. F. W. Dupee and George Stade. New York: Harcourt, 1969.

DuPlessis, Rachel Blau. *Genders, Races, and Religious Cultures in Modern American Poetry, 1908–1934*. Cambridge: Cambridge UP, 2001.

Fowler, Bridget. "The 'Canon' and Marxist Theories of Literature." *Cultural Studies* 1 (1987): 162–78.

Furia, Philip. *The Poets of Tin Pan Alley: A History of America's Great Lyricists*. New York: Oxford UP, 1990.

Kermode, Frank. "What Became of Sweeney?" Rev. of *The Elder Statesman*, by T. S. Eliot. *Spectator* 10 Apr. 1959: 513.

Leavis, F. R. *For Continuity*. Freeport, NY: Books for Libraries, 1933.

Leavis, F. R., and Denys Thompson. *Culture and Environment: The Training of Critical Awareness*. London: Chatto, 1937.

Lehmann, John. "T. S. Eliot Talks about Himself and the Drive to Create." *New York Times Book Review* 29 Nov. 1953: 5+.

Minow, Newton N. ["Television and the Public Interest."] *How Vast the Wasteland Now?* New York: Gannett Foundation Media Center, 1991.

Moore, Marianne. Rev. of *Sweeney Agonistes,* by T. S. Eliot. *Poetry* 42 (1933): 106–09.

Naremore, James. *More Than Night: Film Noir in Its Contexts*. Berkeley: U of California P, 1998.

North, Michael. *The Dialect of Modernism: Race, Language, and Twentieth-Century Literature*. New York: Oxford UP, 1994.

———. *Reading 1922: A Return to the Scene of the Modern*. New York: Oxford UP, 1999.

Smidt, Kristian. *The Importance of Recognition: Six Chapters on T. S. Eliot*. Tromsø: n.p., 1973.

Stravinsky, Igor. "Memories of T. S. Eliot." *Esquire* Aug. 1965: 92–93.

Trotter, David. "T. S. Eliot and Cinema." *Modernism/Modernity* 13 (2006): 237–65.

7

Mind, Myth, and Culture: Eliot and Anthropology

Marc Manganaro

The Anthropological Method

By far the most famous use of anthropology in modernist literature occurs in Eliot's 1922 masterwork, *The Waste Land*. Eliot's borrowing from anthropology in the poem is made obvious in his famous Notes, which were appended to the poem proper when it was first printed as a book. In the preface to the Notes, Eliot states that "[n]ot only the title, but the plan and a good deal of the incidental symbolism of the poem were suggested by Miss Jessie L. Weston's book on the Grail legend: *From Ritual to Romance*" (*CPP* 50). Eliot then goes on to comment, "To another work of anthropology I am indebted in general, one which has influenced our generation profoundly; I mean *The Golden Bough*; I have used especially the two volumes *Adonis, Attis, Osiris*. Anyone who is acquainted with these two works will immediately recognize in the poem certain references to vegetation ceremonies" (50).

Eliot's invitation to readers to consult the Weston and Frazer books as guides to his poem — and indeed, he noted that "Miss Weston's book will elucidate the difficulties of the poem much better than my notes can do" (*CPP* 50) — proved irresistible to generations of critics trying to "crack" *The Waste Land*. From the year of the poem's publication, 1922, critics rightly pointed to the parallel between Eliot's invocation of a dead land (37–38), waiting through winter to be born again in the spring, and the imagery of decaying and sterile lands in ancient and tribal cultures that are symbolically revived through rituals — "vegetation ceremonies," Eliot calls them — in which a god or king is revived or reborn. Weston's book puts forward a thesis that such rituals are not limited to the ancient or modern "primitive," notes the parallels between the Arthurian legend of the Fisher King and ancient Egyptian ceremonies having to do with the rise and fall of the Nile, and identifies the Tarot pack as a survival of those ancient imageries.

Iconoclastic, ritual characters are presented in the first section of the poem by "Madame Sosostris, famous clairvoyante," who "had a bad cold," but "nevertheless /

A Companion to T. S. Eliot, First Edition. Edited by David E. Chinitz.
© 2014 John Wiley & Sons, Ltd. Published 2014 by John Wiley & Sons, Ltd.

Is known to be the wisest woman in Europe, / With a wicked pack of cards" (*CPP* 38). Sosostris as impaired contemporary seer places cards of the Tarot deck one by one in front of the unnamed narrator – "the drowned Phoenician sailor," "Belladonna, the Lady of the Rocks, / The Lady of situations," "the man with three staves," the "Wheel," "the one-eyed merchant," and "this card, / Which is blank, is something he carries on his back, / Which I am forbidden to see." She notes finally that "I do not find/ The Hanged Man" (*CPP* 38–39). These characters recur significantly throughout *The Waste Land,* and it is the absence (or possible presence) of the Hanged Man as sacrificed king or god, with allusions to Christ, that stands as an indicator of whether the land and culture of the poem is indeed renewed. In his note to this passage of the poem, Eliot makes quite clear the importance of the fate of the "Hanged Man" and the link of this character to the ancient sacrificed gods – including Christ – as chronicled in Frazer's *The Golden Bough*:

> I am not familiar with the exact constitution of the Tarot pack of cards, from which I have obviously departed to suit my own convenience. The Hanged Man, a member of the traditional pack, fits my purpose in two ways: because he is associated in my mind with the Hanged God of Frazer, and because I associate him with the hooded figure in the passage of the disciples to Emmaus in Part V. (*CPP* 51)

As critics have observed since the poem's appearance, Eliot's purposeful paralleling of contemporary and ancient characters (e.g., Madame Sosostris to the Greek seer Sibyl) and events (e.g., World War I to the First Punic War) was influenced by the rather freewheeling comparisons of evolutionary anthropologists, primarily Frazer, between ancient cultural rituals and contemporary "primitive" tribal practices. Indeed, one of the great modernist innovations of Eliot's poem, and something most readers have found puzzling, is the use of sudden, abrupt juxtapositions between ancient and modern settings and characters. While the influence of collage as practiced in then-contemporary painting and cinema is sometimes cited, the comparative organization of anthropological texts of the period, and again of Frazer's especially, is a source that Eliot acknowledges and even advertises.

Perhaps nowhere does Eliot so famously acknowledge the anthropological basis for this practice of juxtaposition as in his 1923 review of James Joyce's *Ulysses.* There Eliot defends Joyce's novel against charges that it is formless, and that Joyce is a "prophet of chaos" (critic Richard Aldington's claim) by arguing that the novel is indeed structured, organized, but not by the conventional "narrative method" of storytelling. Rather, Eliot explains, Joyce is using the "mythical method," by employing the Ulysses myth, as rendered in Homer's *The Odyssey*, as a contrastive framework for modern-day Dublin and Dubliners. Eliot proclaims that

> [i]n using the myth, in manipulating a continuous parallel between contemporaneity and antiquity, Mr. Joyce is pursuing a method which others must pursue after him. . . . It is simply a way of controlling, of ordering, of giving a shape and a significance to the immense panorama of futility and anarchy which is contemporary history. (*SP* 177)

At the conclusion of his review, Eliot identifies the works that have paved the way for Joyce's use of the "mythical method": "Psychology . . . ethnology, and *The Golden Bough* have concurred to make possible what was impossible a few years ago. Instead of narrative method, we may now use the mythical method. It is, I seriously believe, a step toward making the modern world possible for art" (178).

Eliot's argument here is historically important, not only as a way to approach Joyce's controversial novel, but also as a clarion call for how to compose future, modernist, literature. It is, moreover, a way of reading his own work of 1922, *The Waste Land*. In effect, the new social sciences – psychology, ethnology (a term for pre-modern, pre-twentieth-century anthropology) and Frazer's work (which is given its own category) – activate mythology as a non-narrative device for capturing modern history and experience in art. However, it is not really *myth* as such that comprises or illustrates that method, for myth itself is by definition narrative, a form of traditional storytelling; rather, it is the way that then-modern social scientists, and primarily anthropologists, *organize* myth in their texts – and that is, by juxtaposing the myths, stories, and rituals of ancient and modern peoples. What Eliot is pointing to here is the anthropological method that held sway from the mid-nineteenth to the early twentieth century, and is most famously exemplified in Frazer's *The Golden Bough*, in which the myths and rituals of diverse peoples, ranging from "primitive" to "civilized," and from ancient to modern, are dramatically juxtaposed for the purposes of illustrating cultural similarities (and sometimes, cultural differences).

Ironically, at the time that Eliot was so openly advertising the usefulness of Frazer's brand of comparative anthropology, anthropologists, especially Franz Boas and his disciples, were challenging the comparative method and the evolutionary assumptions of Frazer and his colleagues. As early as the 1880s, Boas had called for an anthropology, and museum display, that organized cultural materials (e.g., eating utensils, bows and arrows) according to the tribes that used them, rather than according to their "level of civilization," their place on a hypothesized evolutionary ladder. Also noteworthy is that 1922, the year of the publication of *The Waste Land* and *Ulysses*, was also the year in which Bronislaw Malinowski's paradigm-shifting ethnography *Argonauts of the Western Pacific* was published. *Argonauts* importantly called for a "functionalist" approach to understanding a particular culture, in which tribal practices and attitudes are to be understood with regard to how they relate functionally to one another. In other words, the kind of comparative evolutionary anthropology that Eliot was proclaiming a profound influence on the new literature was at that moment rapidly becoming outmoded within the field of anthropology itself.

Mystical Mentality

Eliot's advertisement of Frazer, however, should not suggest that he was ignorant of the anthropological currents of his day, nor that he was simply a believer in Frazer's brand of anthropology. In fact, Eliot was an extremely well-read and discerning student of anthropology. As a graduate student at Harvard he composed, for a seminar taught by the eminent philosopher Josiah Royce, an essay, "The Interpretation of Primitive Ritual," which investigated the interpretive capabilities and weaknesses of a range of evolutionary anthropologists, including Frazer, Edward Tylor, and the Cambridge Hellenists (mainly Jane Harrison). Later he wrote a number of reviews of current anthropological publications by authors such as the Frenchmen Émile Durkheim and Lucien Lévy-Bruhl.

Eliot's literary and social criticism also contained numerous references to anthropological works beyond Frazer, including texts of the missionary anthropologist R. H. Codrington, the eminent British anthropologist W. H. R. Rivers, and Malinowski's contemporary E. E. Evans-Pritchard. And as editor of the influential multidisciplinary journal the *Criterion* in the 1920s and 1930s, he published work by anthropologists (such as an essay on gambling and primitive mentality by Lévy-Bruhl) and commissioned reviews of just-published works of anthropology (such as a review by Robert Graves of a recent Malinowski book).

The range of anthropology Eliot read is evidenced in the uses to which he put this material in the early literary criticism and poetry. For one, clearly Eliot was extremely interested in then-current anthropological theories on the nature of so-called "primitive mentality." The anthropologist whom Eliot most often cites on the issue is Lévy-Bruhl, whose first book on "primitive mentality," *Les Fonctions mentales dans les sociétés inférieures*, translated in English as *How Natives Think* and published in 1910, Eliot had read in the original French no later than 1913. In this volume Lévy-Bruhl asserts that the mentality of the "primitive," which he calls "pre-logical" and "mystical," differs essentially from that of modern man in that it does not operate according to rules of Aristotelian logic. Rather, the natives' perception has a mystical and emotional base that produces a completely different kind of thinking. According to Lévy-Bruhl, what some anthropologists (e.g., Frazer) see as faulty perception on the part of the "savage" is just another way of apprehending reality.[1]

Eliot himself was fascinated by the theory of the "mystical" basis of "primitive" mentality, and by Lévy-Bruhl's assertion that the "savage" operates according to the "law of participation," wherein "objects, beings, phenomena, can be, though in a way incomprehensible to us, both themselves and other than themselves" (61). Eliot writes of Lévy-Bruhl in a 1916 review of a book by Clement C. J. Webb – a volume that criticized Lévy-Bruhl's theories. Here Eliot defends Lévy-Bruhl effectively by using one of the anthropologist's own examples, that of the Bororo tribe of Brazil, who held a parrot for a totem:

> Now, according to M. Lévy-Bruhl, this is not merely the *adoption* of parrot as an heraldic emblem, nor a merely mythological kinship or participation in qualities; nor is the savage *deluded* into thinking that he is a parrot. In practical life, the Bororo never confuses himself with a parrot, nor is he so sophisticated as to think that black is white. But he is capable of a state of mind into which we cannot put ourselves, in which he *is* a parrot, while being at the same time a man. In other words, the mystical mentality,

though at a low level, plays a much greater part in the daily life of the savage than in that of the civilized man. (116)

In spite of this final assertion, one idea emerging in Eliot's early criticism that owes much to Lévy-Bruhl is that in modern societies, the "mystical" power of the "primitive" actually does exhibit itself in the poet. In a September 1918 review in *The Egoist*, Eliot concludes a review of Wyndham Lewis's novel *Tarr* by asserting that "The artist, I believe, is more *primitive*, as well as more civilized, than his contemporaries, his experience is deeper than civilization, and he only uses the phenomena of civilization in expressing it. Primitive instincts . . . are confounded in the ordinary man" (106).

Now while Lévy-Bruhl himself does not suggest that the contemporary artist is able to bridge the gap between "primitive" and civilized mentalities, clearly Eliot has Lévy-Bruhl in mind when he presses that point. In *The Use of Poetry and the Use of Criticism*, published fifteen years after his review of *Tarr*, Eliot refers to an essay by E. Cailliet and J. Bede, offering the following summary: "The authors, who have done field work in Madagascar, apply the theories of Lévy-Bruhl: the prelogical mentality persists in civilized man, but becomes available only to or through the poet" (141). Eliot then goes so far as to say that "poetry begins, I dare say, with a savage beating a drum in a jungle, and it retains that essential of percussion and rhythm; hyperbolically one might say that the poet is *older* than other human beings" (148).

It might seem ironic that Eliot, often viewed in his time and ours as the most "civilized" and intellectual of modern writers, also asserts that the modern poet has a "primitive" aspect, taps into the primal, and operates according to "prelogical" principles. However, Eliot is not alone among modernist artists and thinkers in suggesting "primitive" filiations to modern art, and indeed the beginning of the twentieth century saw an upwelling of interest in the "primitive" among literary as well as visual artists – Picasso comes most readily to mind, and among modern writers, D. H. Lawrence. Significantly, modern artists both borrowed from the formal or organizational aspects of "primitive" art, and incorporated thematic concerns or beliefs about the "primitive" – for example, Lévy-Bruhl's assertions about "pre-logical mentality," and Lawrence's idea of "blood consciousness."

It would be a mistake, however, to claim that Eliot was simply a primitivist – that he believed that so-called "primitive" or primal ways of living and making art were superior to the "civilized." And indeed, Eliot's anti-romantic tendencies include resistance to the general notion that man in his natural state is admirable. He does assert, though, that the "civilized" poet brings the primal "essential of rhythm and percussion" (*UPUC* 148) into modern poetry. Eliot refers to this quality as "the auditory imagination," which he describes as "the feeling for syllable and rhythm, penetrating far below the conscious levels of thought and feeling, invigorating every word; sinking to the most primitive and forgotten, returning to the origin and bringing something back" (*UPUC* 111). This sense of "syllable and rhythm," this bridge between "primitive" and "civilized," Eliot notes in other essays, is that which ties poetry essentially to drama – and is a primary reason why Eliot, as late as the 1950s, composed his own plays in verse. It is also what bonds audience to poet as performer. In 1923 Eliot published an essay entitled, indicatively, "The Beating of a Drum." Here he seeks to show that the prototype of the Fool in Elizabethan drama can be found in the "primitive" shaman or medicine man, who is, after all, the wielder of sacred words, but more generally Eliot maintains, along the lines of Cambridge Hellenist F. M. Cornford, that drama as a genre has "primitive" ritual origins. The essence of drama, Eliot tells his readers, is rhythm, and when that is lost, the magical relationship between performer and audience disappears. He then goes on to illustrate his point with contrastive examples from modern art and popular media:

> It is the rhythm, so utterly absent from modern drama, either verse or prose, and which interpreters of Shakespeare do their best to suppress, which makes Massine and Charlie Chaplin the great actors that they are, and which makes the juggling of Rastelli more cathartic than a performance of [Ibsen's] "A Doll's House." (12)

Dissociation

Common to many of Eliot's invocations of the "primitive" in art is the premise that art has a primal, original purpose or function that is integrally, centrally, tied to the welfare of the culture or tribe. In his late-career essay "The Social Function of Poetry" (1945), for example, he discusses the "deliberate, conscious social purpose" of poetry in "its more primitive forms . . . some of which had very practical magical purposes – to avert the evil eye, to cure some disease, or to propitiate some demon" (*OPP* 15–16). While Eliot is not saying that art must return to those purposes solely and wholly, throughout his career he is very concerned with what is lost of that integral social function as art becomes more "civilized" and removed from the "practical" and "magical." This concern is replayed in both of his major works of social criticism, *The Idea of a Christian Society* and *Notes towards the Definition of Culture*. And as early as 1923, in a review of a work by anthropologist W. J. Perry, Eliot acknowledges but queries the distinctions between "primitive" and modern artistic functions:

> The arts developed incidentally to the search for objects of talismanic properties. The Egyptians who first fashioned gold into a likeness of a cowrie-shell, the Cretan who designed an octopus on his pottery, the Indian who hung a necklace of bear's-teeth about his neck, were not aiming primarily at decoration, but invoking the assistance of life-giving amulets. At what point, we may ask, does the attempt to design and create an object for the sake of beauty become conscious? At what point in civilization does any conscious distinction between practical or magical and aesthetic beauty arise? (490–91)

Central to Eliot's literary and social criticism is the tenet that modern man – that is, since the seventeenth century – has seen a division between the practical and mundane on the one hand and the artistic on the other, as well as between the spiritual and material aspects of social structure. This idea is perhaps most famously encapsulated in his essay "The Metaphysical Poets" (1921), where he notes a division between two types of poetic thinking and practice: that of Donne and poets previous to him, in which all the varieties of human experience are part of a whole and are expressed as such in the poetry; and the poetry after Donne, in which the disparate experiences of the poet have no seeming relation to each other, in which "dissociation of sensibility" has "set in." The latter Eliot typifies in the poetry of Victorians Browning and Tennyson, who, Eliot asserts, "do not feel their thought as immediately as the odor of a rose" (*SE* 247). This dissociative state he contrasts to the mentality of the Metaphysical poet:

> A thought to Donne was an experience; it modified his sensibility. When a poet's mind is perfectly equipped for its work, it is constantly amalgamating disparate experience; the ordinary man's experience is chaotic, irregular, fragmentary. The latter falls in love, or reads Spinoza, and these two experiences have nothing to do with each other, or with the noise of the typewriter or the smell of cooking; in the mind of the poet these experiences are always forming new wholes. (*SE* 247)

This argument clearly owes much to Lévy-Bruhl's notion of "primitive mentality." Lévy-Bruhl, discussing the "law of participation" that governs the thinking of "primitive man," notes how every object for the "primitive" contains mystic properties that tie that object to other objects, to the individual, and to the communal tribe. The result is a complex network of spiritual links and the belief that, in Lévy-Bruhl's words, "there is no phenomenon which is, strictly speaking, a physical one" (30). This is a version of reality wholly accepted by the "savage," but modern man cannot grasp this concept of unitary thinking because he has made divisions between the physical and the spiritual, and in the process has excluded the possibility of perceiving the spiritual in the material. It is this process of division that Lévy-Bruhl terms, in the original French, "dissociation," and asserts that, as long as it does not occur, "perception remains an undifferentiated whole" (31). This concept played a major role in Eliot's own reformulation of the literary canon, in which the Metaphysical poets were in the ascendancy and post-seventeenth-century poetry, especially that of the nineteenth century, tended to be disparaged.

Lévy-Bruhl's notion of "primitive" mentality, as well as those of other anthropologists of the period, played a role in Eliot's own poetry as well. In general terms, the poetry Eliot wrote before his conversion to Anglo-Catholicism portrays a society of dissociation, a civilization that separates the physical from the spiritual to the extent that the non-physical is no longer considered "real." This poetry of dissociation, which culminates, one might say, in *The Waste Land* and "The Hollow Men" (1925), often presents personae who realize the spiritual impotence of their environments but are powerless to act upon their longings to unite the physical and spiritual realms. Prufrock is just such a character, one who knowingly lives in a world divested of mystical connections between the seen and unseen. Prufrock *does* have intimations of the mystical, but these links are private rather than collective, and are expressed in terms of lack, absence, and alienation. When the spiritual can be entered into, entry is only temporary, and threatens dire consequences: "Till human voices wake us, and we drown" (7). This disparity between ideal private vision and the reality of a fragmented culture is virtually nonexistent in Lévy-Bruhl's version of "primitive" society, as it is in Eliot's version of pre-dissociation poets – but in Prufrock's world it acts as a profoundly destructive force.

Eliot's Prufrock is typical of pre-conversion personae who inhabit contemporary urban settings that are at odds with anthropological versions of "primitive" tribal life, which is said to be at one, both practically and spiritually, with the natural environment. At the same time, "Prufrock" and other early poems suggest a mentality that in some ways approximates a breakdown of the logical, the rational, and the civilized. Several of Eliot's personae display "primitive" or specifically "pre-logical" ways of thinking and behaving. Sweeney, a character featured in two early poems, "Sweeney Erect" and "Sweeney Among the Nightingales," is a prototype, even a stereotype, of the mind-numbing, instinctual, brutish modern savage. Somewhat akin to Eugene O'Neill's character Yank in the 1922 play *The Hairy Ape*, "Apeneck Sweeney" is a semi-comical throwback to an earlier evolutionary stage in human history (*CPP* 35). In other poems a less negative version of the "primitive" emerges, one more aligned to Lévy-Bruhl's pre-logical "primitive." In "Rhapsody on a Windy Night" Eliot portrays a protagonist who wanders the city streets one night recollecting the various images from his past in a pattern that has no apparent logical connections. The world presented to the reader is typically "modern" – lonely, desolate, sterile – yet the mode of recollection, as described by Eliot in the first stanza, represents memory in anything but rational or civilized terms, and indeed, suggests that the process of recollection is "pre-logical":

> Twelve o'clock.
> Along the reaches of the street
> Held in a lunar synthesis,
> Whispering lunar incantations
> Dissolve the floors of memory
> And all its clear relations,
> Its divisions and precisions (*CPP* 14)

In "Gerontion" (1920), often seen as a prelude to *The Waste Land*, the absence of any sense of mystical "participation" as described by Lévy-Bruhl, and the reduction of all phenomena to the merely physical, are clearly indicated in Gerontion's own account of his condition:

> Vacant shuttles
> Weave the wind. I have no ghosts,
> An old man in a draughty house
> Under a windy knob. (*CPP* 22)

Yet Gerontion, like Prufrock, at least attempts to make the connection between the seen and the unseen, even though he is powerless to alter his own condition. He recognizes the link between his own physical decline and his spiritual destitution, and, much like the narrator (or narrators) of *The Waste Land*, in describing his infirmity he affirms the "primitive" belief (à la Lévy-Bruhl and others) that no bodily condition or illness is merely physical. As Lévy-Bruhl says of the "primitive," Gerontion as well regards illness or disease "as the product of an invisible, intangible agent" (233).

In "The Hollow Men," the persona, who speaks in the first person plural for all of the hollow men, bemoans their dissociative state in a vague waste land, "the dead land," a "cactus land," a "valley of dying stars" (*CPP* 57–58), in which all impulse is checked by the "Shadow" that falls "Between the idea / And the reality / Between the motion / And the act" (58). Like Gerontion, the speaker of "The Hollow Men" expresses frustration at his inability to forge connections among fragmented pieces of his existence in this landscape of modernity, a desolate setting wherein, one might say, Lévy-Bruhl's "law of participation" uniting the physical and spiritual is forgotten. The hollow man's lament registers as more specifically anthropological, however, when we realize that Eliot's "dead land" strongly suggests Lévy-Bruhl's account of a West African belief in "Dead-land" ("pays des morts" in the original French). Lévy-Bruhl takes his description of "Dead-land" from the anthropologist A. B. Ellis's account of twin spirits, the *kra* and the *srahman*. The former is a spirit that exists in the world and, upon the death of the body it inhabits, roams the earth until it is reincarnated into another being. The *srahman*, on the other hand, is a ghost that commences its career only when the body dies, and carries its life out in "dead-land," a lifeless duplicate of the real, living world, whose "mountains, forest and rivers are . . . the ghosts of similar natural features which formerly existed in the world" (67).

The parallels between Eliot's "dead land" and that of the West Africans, as chronicled by the anthropologists, are striking. The hollow men's abode, like the West African "Dead-land," is a shell of a world – as Eliot calls it, a place of "Shape without form, shade without colour" (*CPP* 56) – and the beings who inhabit it, like the *srahman*, are simulacra of living beings, resembling scarecrows: "stuffed men / Leaning together / Headpiece filled with straw" (56). Just as the *srahman* ghost is cut off from its *kra* after the death of the body, so are the hollow men separated from others of their kind, from "Those who have crossed / With direct eyes, to death's other Kingdom" (56). To the West African this "other kingdom" is the *kra*'s new life in another body in the living world, a reincarnation which the *srahman* is not permitted to join, for, as in the hollow man's case, the "eyes" (symbolizing "[t]hose who have crossed") are "not here . . . / In this valley of dying stars" (58). For the hollow men, as for the *srahman*, such a reunion is "The hope only / Of empty men," since the dead land for both is, as Eliot expresses it, "this last of meeting places" (58).

With his conversion to Anglo-Catholicism in 1927, the poet looks primarily to Christianity as a redeeming force, as a way out of the darkness, the "shadow," that falls upon Prufrock, the characters of *The Waste Land*, and the hollow men. Still, "primitive" or animistic figures or forces, as influenced by anthropology, do emerge in the post-conversion poetry, most notably in *Ash-Wednesday* and *Four Quartets*. In the latter work, recalling Lévy-Bruhl, spiritual forces are articulated, at times, as mystical apprehensions of reality previously shared by ancestors in a collective fashion (for example, the rustic dance in "East Coker," and the invocation of "the dead" in Part I of "Little Gidding"). In Eliot's post-conversion drama as well, we see the enactment of primal ritual that sometimes seems more shamanistic than Christian (in *The Cocktail Party*, for example, and even in the overtly Christian drama *Murder in the Cathedral*).

The Definition of Culture

The most far-reaching anthropological dimension of Eliot's later career, however, is doubtless found in his major works of social criticism of the 1930s and 1940s, *After Strange Gods* (1934), *The Idea of a Christian Society* (1940), and *Notes towards the Definition of Culture* (1948). While these works have been decried by many critics as elitist, conservative, reactionary, and, in the case of *After Strange Gods*, anti-Semitic, the later social criticism, especially *Notes towards the Definition of Culture* (hereafter referred to as *Notes*), proposes complex theories of culture and social formation that engage in anthropological theorizing on culture and put forward models for culture that would greatly influence later cultural theorists.

Perhaps ironically, given that Eliot's professed purpose in *Notes* was to "limit" the use of the word *culture*, in order to "rescue this word" from abuse (*CC* 89), Eliot's effort to delimit *culture* produced a complicated, highly variable, and elastic formulation of the term that encouraged further debate. Even the brilliant Marxist critic Raymond Williams conceded that Eliot, "in his discussion on culture . . . has carried the argument to an important new stage." Williams asserted that if one does not, for example, take on Eliot's formidable insistence that *culture* be regarded in several complex, interpenetrating levels – at the level of "the individual," of "the group or class," and of "the whole society" – a critic might as well "retire from the field" (227).

Despite the reputation of Eliot's definition of culture as elitist, central to his "definition" is the broad anthropological concept of culture. In his first chapter, in fact, he cites the Victorian evolutionary anthropologist Edward Tylor's seminal definition of culture as a "complex whole" (Tylor 1; *CC* 94). Eliot also discriminates "the necessity that a culture should be analyzable, geographically, into local cultures" (87), a statement that owes less to evolutionary anthropology than to the more "modern" anthropological understanding of a culture as defined according to the territory it inhabits, developed especially in the work of Franz Boas and his disciples Margaret Mead and Ruth Benedict.[2]

So we see in *Notes* an attempt to integrate an evolutionary and a more modern, Boasian version of culture. Eliot also incorporates Victorian critic Matthew Arnold's humanist notion of culture as "the best that has been thought and said in the world." Complicating his use of Arnold's definition, however, is his critique of what Eliot terms the "thinness" of Arnold's conception of culture: Arnold conceives of culture as being possessed by the individual, which, according to Eliot, erroneously assumes that culture is only consciously possessed or aimed at. Arnold ignores, Eliot claims, the relation of the individual human's possession of culture to that of the larger social organism. In that sense, Eliot asserts, Arnold's argument lacks a certain "social background" (*CC* 94).[3]

Essentially Eliot maintains that understanding "culture" means keeping conscious of its numerous possible definitions – anthropological, humanist, individual-based, group-based, and even internationally based – all at the same time. For this reason it is not even possible in complex modern societies, Eliot argues, for one individual to "contain" or incorporate all conceptions of culture – only society as a whole can do that. However, in simpler social organizations, Eliot argues in an anthropological vein, cultural intent and meaning are unified:

> It is obvious that among the more primitive communities the several activities of culture are inextricably woven. The Dyak who spends the better part of a season in shaping, carving and painting his barque of the peculiar design required for the annual ritual of head-hunting, is exercising several cultural activities at once – of art and religion, as well as of amphibious warfare. As civilization becomes more complex, greater occupational specialization evinces itself. (*CC* 94)

While Eliot is, again, no primitivist pure and simple, no believer that we can actually return to a simpler way of life, the above passage does show a certain admiration for a so-called "primitive" society that fuses, in "inextricably woven" fashion, its cultural activities, both religious and secular-occupational, into a whole. It does in a sense represent that society before the "dissociation of sensibility" set in. Indeed, a prime criticism of Arnold's definition of culture in Eliot's volume is that Arnold attempted to separate culture from religion; and in fact, Eliot in *Notes* professes his own intent "to expose the essential relation of culture to religion" (*CC* 87), even in such a complex, highly differentiated society as that of mid-twentieth-century Great Britain. One might say that this fusion of religion and culture that has as its basis an anthropological conception of tribal culture can be found in Eliot's work of 25 years before *Notes*, *The Waste Land*. Indeed, the material of Eliot's poem of 1922 – the "fragments I have shored against my ruins" (*CPP* 50) – are fragments of cultures both ancient and modern, pieces of culture, if you will, that collectively represent a lack of such fusion.

At the same time, some of those cultural "fragments" are from historical cultures of religious-social union and hence represent cultural richness, at least in comparison to the present-day of the poem. See, for example, the quotations from Dante and St. Augustine, and the invocations from cultural-religious sacred books of both West (the Bible) and East (the Upanishads), the latter of which are invoked, one could argue, as our only hope for revival, for putting ourselves, our fragments, back together again. In that regard, *The Waste Land* and *Notes towards the Definition of Culture*, separated from each other by a quarter-century, each written in the wake of a world war, both may be said to suggest ways in which a unified culture might be reestablished.[4]

The motives and methods of Eliot's two works on "culture," *The Waste Land* and *Notes*, underscore that the relation of anthropology to Eliot's works is not one simply of influence, though deep influence can be found. Indeed, Eliot was engaged in an effort in the early twentieth century to compose modern literature out of anthropological materials and in anthropological contexts, and he worked as well with (or, one might say, against) anthropology to produce new conceptions of "culture." The range of Eliot's work attempts both to create a new art for a new age and to answer questions about how to define, describe, and interpret culture, questions at the heart of the modern anthropological enterprise.

NOTES

1   The relation between Lévy-Bruhl's conception of "primitive mentality" and Eliot's work is developed further in Manganaro, "Dissociation" 98–109.
2   For a detailed historical account of this work, see Stocking.
3   *See also* IN TIMES OF EMERGENCY: ELIOT'S SOCIAL CRITICISM.
4   For an extended argument on the continuities between the two works, see Manganaro, *Culture* 16–55.

REFERENCES AND FURTHER READING

Crawford, Robert. *The Savage and the City in the Work of T. S. Eliot.* Oxford: Clarendon, 1987.

Gray, Piers. *T. S. Eliot's Poetic and Intellectual Development.* Sussex: Harvester, 1982.

Harmon, William. "T. S. Eliot, Anthropologist and Primitive." *American Anthropologist* 78 (1976): 797–811.

Hegeman, Susan. *Patterns for America: Modernism and the Concept of Culture.* Princeton: Princeton UP, 1999.

Lévy-Bruhl, Lucien. *How Natives Think.* 1910. Trans. Lilian A. Clare. New York: Knopf, 1925.

Longenbach, James. *Modernist Poetics of History: Pound, Eliot, and the Sense of the Past.* Princeton: Princeton UP, 1987.

Manganaro, Marc. " 'Beating a Drum in a Jungle': T. S. Eliot on the Artist as 'Primitive.' " *Modern Language Quarterly* 47 (1986): 393–421.

——. *Culture, 1922: The Emergence of a Concept.* Princeton: Princeton UP, 2002.

——. "Dissociation in 'Dead Land': The Primitive Mind in the Early Poetry of T. S. Eliot." *Journal of Modern Literature* 13 (1986): 97–110.

——. *Myth, Rhetoric, and the Voice of Authority: A Critique of Frazer, Eliot, Frye, and Campbell.* New Haven: Yale UP, 1992.

Stocking, George W. "The Ethnographic Sensibility of the 1920s and the Dualism of the Anthropological Tradition." *The Ethnographer's Magic and Other Essays in the History of Anthropology.* Madison: U of Wisconsin P, 1992.

Tylor, Edward Burnett. *Primitive Culture: Researches into the Development of Mythology, Philosophy, Religion, Language, Art, and Custom.* 1871. Vol. 1. London: Murray, 1920.

Vickery, John. *The Literary Impact of The Golden Bough.* Princeton: Princeton UP, 1973.

Williams, Raymond. *Culture and Society: 1780–1950.* 1958. New York: Columbia UP, 1983.

8

"Where are the eagles and the trumpets?": Imperial Decline and Eliot's Development

Vincent Sherry

When T. S. Eliot sailed to Europe in July 1914, he was resuming a journey he had begun in October 1910 – on several levels. As a student, he had spent that earlier academic year in Paris, where he attended lectures at the Sorbonne and officially, if somewhat diffidently, furthered his work toward a doctorate in philosophy at Harvard. As a poet, however, he drew deeply from the Parisian scene. One of the primary sites in the poetics of urban modernity, the city offered him the spirits of Charles Baudelaire and Jules Laforgue and the legacy of a potent French Decadence. The atmosphere went straight to his head and crested in the major work of 1910–11. Now, in 1914, the doctoral student was pursuing a fellowship to bring his dissertation to completion, beginning with summer study at the University of Marburg in Germany and continuing at Merton College, Oxford. The mood was professional, dutiful, resigned. And the maturing poet . . . well, this poet was not, in his own view, maturing at all: the correspondence from that summer shows him already thinking of himself, in the conceit of one of his favored later witticisms, as a young poet with a great future behind him.

Outgrowing the suit of poetic clothes that Parisian Decadence has tailored for him? Yes, in one sense, but the power of that style's initial appeal to him is no simple whim of fashion. It bespeaks an intensity of connection which, if lost at the moment, will be regained and strengthened in these next years. In this period, which includes his taking up residence in London, an evidently reckless marriage, his shifting between jobs, and his rather swift affiliation with English life, he is also – and most notably – experiencing the national struggle of the Great War. This is a richly difficult history. It affords the young American a new understanding of a sensibility peculiar to Europe and specific to Decadence: an imaginative apprehension of living in a late historical age, of time winding down, all in all, of Decay as a condition of general existence. Not that some presentiment of this kind was unavailable to Americans, especially to Americans of Eliot's cultural class. Many of them felt or fancied the authority of their privileged condition as a connection to an earlier and purer modus of American life,

A Companion to T. S. Eliot, First Edition. Edited by David E. Chinitz.
© 2014 John Wiley & Sons, Ltd. Published 2014 by John Wiley & Sons, Ltd.

and they reacted to its vulgarization, as they perceived it, by the immigrant waves of the nineteenth century. But this experience of lost dominance is qualitatively different from the one recorded in the older European states of France, Spain, and Great Britain. Here, longer histories locate the present as a perceptibly later, older moment. World War I will make this feeling intensely real as one of exhausted vitality, weighing out proof for it in dead bodies by the millions. This experience of immense and unprecedented levels of death is also recalibrated, in the imaginative language of national ambition, as the climacteric in the gradual, or not so gradual, collapse of empires. Imperial decline provides an expressive topos in the historical vocabulary of literary Decadence and, as we shall see, in the affective rhetoric of Eliot's own poetic lexicon.

In these next years, then, it is the difficult privilege of Eliot's experience to find in the shaking earth of the Great War a ground and warrant of the Decadence he had taken on in easier days. His earlier attraction to that sensibility may have drawn on his membership in that imperiled American gentry, but a new historical content and depth, a fresh intellectual volume and resonance, will be afforded him by the broadly European, specifically British circumstance of his writing life in the later teens and twenties. Beginning our consideration in the work he did between 1910 and midsummer 1914, we may establish a basis of comparison for the subsequent poetry, and then proceed to read the verse of *Poems* (1920) as the record of a Decadence that has been seasoned by the material experience of an authenticating history. A concluding consideration of *The Waste Land* (1922) will demonstrate the lengthened life cycle of the poetics of Decadence.[1] Its developmental curve describes the main lines of Eliot's growth as a poet.

The Singing Schools of Decadence

Probably the first poem Eliot wrote after arriving in Paris in November 1910, "Fourth Caprice in Montparnasse" offers a primer in the poetics of Decadence. It also witnesses the ambitions and limitations of Eliot's engagement with that sensibility:

> Here is a landscape grey with rain
> On black umbrellas, waterproofs,
> And dashing from the slated roofs
> Into a mass of mud and sand.
> Behind a row of blackened trees
> The dripping plastered houses stand
> Like mendicants without regrets
> For unpaid debts
> Hand in pocket, undecided,
> Indifferent if derided. (*IMH* 14)

The tradition of painterly poetry had been revived in mid-nineteenth-century France, and, in his opening representation, Eliot's Parisian scene certainly recalls the canvases of an urban impressionist like Whistler. If the combination of pictorial and literary genres was taken by traditionalists as a fall from generic purity in the arts, and so as one more entry in the swelling census of artistic Decadence, it is, in Eliot's poetic painting, a very soft fall indeed. His evocative lines share their drab cityscape with the 1890s verse of, for example, Arthur Symons, but Eliot draws the line here at the feverish perception, the fascination with the artificial, and the "perverse" that Symons and his cohort professed. This is an atmospheric Decadence, a climatic condition, a sort of emotional twilight, and, in the first six lines especially, it sounds the tonic chord into which Eliot will resolve many of the poetic prospects in *Prufrock and Other Observations*. The turn the verses take in the seventh line moves on the trope of "mendicants" toward that underside of urban modernity, the beggars and misfits who are the habitués of Baudelaire's poetry. As soon as Eliot strikes this note, however, the rhythm shifts markedly, unpredictably, turning the measured cadence into the hurdy-gurdy rigmarole of a Gilbert and Sullivan multiple-syllable rhyme. He forces those profounder chords of Decadence into musical burlesque, a rhythm that trivializes the disturbance he was just on the verge of stirring up.

A second poem of 1910, "Convictions (Curtain Raiser)," offers another primer on Decadence, appearing as it does as the second piece in *Inventions of the March Hare*, Eliot's notebook collection of early poems. It raises the curtain on that collection with a recitation of the convictions of the Decadent, who speaks through the personages introduced in these opening lines. "Among my marionettes I find / The enthusiasm is intense":

> And even in this later age [my marionettes]
> Await an audience open-mouthed . . .
>
> And over there my Paladins
> Are talking of effect and cause,
> With "learn to live by nature's laws!"
> And "strive for social happiness
> And contact with your fellow-men
> In Reason: nothing to excess!"
> As one leaves off the next begins. (11)

The speaking marionette, the human puppet-doll: this conceit is familiar, indeed central to cultural Decadence. The artifact-man configures the supremacy of the new aesthetic values, which were developed discursively by Pater and asserted variously, most infamously perhaps by a dandy like Wilde's Lord Henry Wotton, who would subdue human nature to the forms and standards of artifice. This convention-flaunting sensibility speaks its unbeliefs, in Eliot's poem, as the mainstream values of nineteenth-century Progress, of Reason in all things, which, accordingly, are placed within these inverted commas as heckling echoes. Eliot also historicizes this condition accurately, assigning it to "this later age" of history and dating its slogans as a dying fall in the language of the master culture.

Here, then, are the presumptive understandings of the Decadent sensibility in a primer, a textbook-perfect demonstration, or, one might say, just a paint-by-numbers depiction. Other scenes in the poem are keyed equally closely to the Decadent's script, featuring the "tissue paper roses" of nature as artifice and a more extensive, but not more incisive, representation of these humanized marionettes. And where is the poetic diction itself keyed to the dying fall of the master language? Eliot includes the establishing attitudes of this sensibility, but he does not convert these (un)convictions into an art that is their necessary outcome. While the verse he publishes from this period in *Prufrock* will certainly succeed as tone-poems in the key of Decadence, it may be fairly said that the more daunting aspects of this sensibility remain an undertone at the edge of consciousness, a musical theme that vanishes when listened for directly.

These more challenging aspects are forced to a revealing focus in "The Love Song of St. Sebastian." Eliot first mentions the poem in a letter of July 19, 1914 to Conrad Aiken, which combines a description of his new German locale with an allusion to A. C. Swinburne: "Marburg is . . . a wonderfully civilized little place. . . . The houses have beautiful unkempt gardens, with great waves 'where tides of grass break into foam of flowers'!" (*Letters* 40–41). The quotation is from Swinburne's "Laus Veneris," or "Praise of Venus," which, as the proximate muse for Eliot's "*Love Song* of St. Sebastian," invokes for this poem one of the most potent spirits in the legacy of literary Decadence. Probably the most important advocate for Baudelaire in mid-late nineteenth-century England, Swinburne had aggressively defended the French poet's representation of the diseased condition of humanity (*Les Fleurs du Mal* may be translated *Flowers of Evil* or *Flowers of Illness*) and offered his own probing explorations of the agon and pathos of human sexuality. Eliot takes this wheel a turn further in his representation of erotic psychopathology in his "St. Sebastian." In this tortured song of thwarted eros, the speaker ranges across a spectrum of sadomasochistic fantasies: a self-loathing wish to be annihilated in the sexual act dovetails into a compulsion to murder the beloved, a vision that Eliot spells out thus in manuscript: "You would love me because I should have strangled you / And because of my infammy [*sic*]. / And I should love you the more because I had mangled you" (*Letters* 47). In the margins of this transcription Eliot alters "infammy" to "infamy" and overwrites "<u>Not</u> to rhyme with 'mammy.'" He can joke about a slip which, if it can not be rid of psychological content for the Freudian reader, does at least in this correction avoid the sort of involuntary comedy he falls into in that pratfall triple-syllable rhyme of "strangled you" and "mangled you." Entering the Decadent's labyrinth of sexual malady, then, Eliot reaches a moment of poetic extremity where, once again, the rhythms of musical farce cadence a swerve, or lurch, from a confrontation with the more difficult aspects of this sensibility.

In a second letter to Aiken of July 25, which includes the manuscript copy of the poem, Eliot presents an interestingly contradictory record of his attitude to the *materia poetica* of the Decadent. On one hand he suggests that he has come to a poetic impasse: "I enclose some *stuff* . . . [I] wonder whether I had better knock it off for a while – you will tell me what you think. Do you think that the "Love Song of St. Sebastian" part is morbid, or forced?" (*Letters* 44). *Morbidity*, as an attribute of the art of Decay, was most often assigned to Decadence by mainstream critics, and Eliot is using the word to reject the poetics he has been unsuccessful in implementing in the St. Sebastian poem. On the other hand he is unable to jettison the poetics of Decadence as his primary template of literary ambition. The rest of this letter projects a sequence that will use the "Love Song" as the load-bearing element – weakened beam or not – for a poetic structure which arises, in this prospectus, as a virtual Temple of literary Decadence. There will be a "recurring piece quite in the French style," which is the national language of Decadence, where a young woman who "[w]raps her soul in orange-coloured robes of Chopinese" will lead the reader to a masked ball, the state occasion for a celebration of life as artifice. And St. Sebastian, otherwise known as the martyr and victim of the homosexual subculture? "[T]here's nothing homosexual about this," Eliot protests (too much) to Aiken (44). In that contested trait he is identifying the point of sexual transgression for which he is unwilling to accept authorship – not necessarily for a homosexual tendency of his own but as a most indicative instance of the fall from the norm, the establishing condition for an art of Decadence.

Given these exceptionally high levels of tension, it is not hard to understand why Eliot feels he might need to "knock it off for a while." In his developing relation to the poetics of Decadence he has reached a kind of choking point, where the literary conventions of this sensibility are overfeeding a mind that has been undersupplied by the actual, establishing circumstances of the sensibility. In retrospect, we can say that he needs to experience the unreason of history, to realize the impossibility of progress, to understand the lie that human nature gives to the idealizing constructions of nineteenth-century humanism. In prospect, however, he hardly knew that this was coming. "We rejoice that the war danger is over," he remarks at the end of this second letter to Aiken. The forward irony of his comment would be realized in less than a week, when, with the fated innocence of other young men in the summer of 1914, he would be carried toward the conflagration of his generation.

War, Empire, and the Lexicons of Decadence

"[I]f I could only get back to Paris," Eliot writes to Aiken on September 30, 1914 from London; "But I know I never will, for long. I must learn to talk English" (*Letters* 58). In his five-finger exercises in Decadence, Eliot *has* been writing a kind of French poetry in English, and this letter, which expresses dissatisfaction with almost everything he has composed since "Prufrock," declares an awareness that a change needs to be made. In the next few years he will find the location of this change, where the attitudes and practices of French Decadence will undergo not so much a breach as an expansion – in the awareness history visits on him.

The record the war leaves in Eliot's poetry of the late teens is not nearly so explicit a history as may be found in other civilian poets. What is visible and consistent in this verse is an end-of-empire feeling, which finds an intense literary witness in Eliot's own lengthened end-of-the-war moment. With a complexity, with a density that registers the historical thickness of his work of this period, he marks his sense of late imperial time. The feeling of loss that is centered and enlarged in this framework of imaginative reference is the primary matter in Eliot's recovery of an historically enriched poetics of literary Decadence. Thus, we may first follow his representation of the failing state of Empire in the verse of the late teens, so to establish the historical basis for a literary language of Decadence.

Eliot's references to the decline of Empire emerge through the poetic form that dominates his prosody at this moment: the rhymed quatrain. In this stanza an extreme regularity of cadence, formalized by often strong rhymes, effects an energy of palpably mechanical character. Eliot probably needed to ramp himself up thus in order to break the nearly three-year-long writing block that followed upon his arrival in Britain. But the cadence also reverberates suggestively with the headlong mobilization of these modern days, this modern war. Its costs are recorded as the fall of an ideal of empire that he represents initially, most recognizably, in the elegiac mode. The elegiac measure emerges *within and in dissonance to* the dominant prosody, the mechanical-piano gambol that may represent Eliot's poetic apprehension of the machine-made farce of modern history. Sidelong moments of exalted feeling, of loss as exalted as the fall of imperial order in the current day: this is the conceit of Eliot's modern imperial elegy, and two poems show it in an exemplary way.

"Sweeney Among the Nightingales" opens in caricature, rhythmical as well as imagistic:

> Apeneck Sweeney spreads his knees
> Letting his arms hang down to laugh,
> The zebra stripes along his jaw
> Swelling to maculate giraffe. (*CPP* 35)

The bestiary trope extends through the poem into a virtual zoology of human types, including a "silent vertebrate in brown," and "Rachel *née* Rabinovitch," who "[t]ears at the grapes with murderous paws." The animal-mechanical feeling is prosodic, too, featuring an octosyllabic that gallops – the eight syllables shorten occasionally for variety and change of pace, but Eliot does not use this variation as an expressive inflection. The rhythm and feeling shift perceptibly, however, into the majestic cadenza of this finale:

> The host with someone indistinct
> Converses at the door apart,
> The nightingales are singing near
> The Convent of the Sacred Heart,
>
> And sang within the bloody wood
> When Agamemnon cried aloud

> And let their liquid siftings fall
> To stain the stiff dishonoured shroud. (36)

These perfectly iambic tetrameter lines create and maintain a sense of processional solemnity. The cadence goes strong but is also strange and fateful as the first word of the final stanza marks a formal turn with its coordinate conjunction, and the rhythm builds into the sublimity of the final prospect. Here the beauty of the wood, lit up with the incandescence of the nightingales' song, mingles with the terrible memory of Agamemnon's violent demise. The hero returning from the Trojan War to the murderous plot of his wife Clytemnestra is doubled by Sweeney, surrounded in the seedy bistro of contemporary London by a mélange of women as menacing as that "Rachel *née* Rabinovich." In view of this modern counterpart's simian character, however, the likeness should hardly entail the exhilaration of sublimity. So, where does the majestic sentiment of this finale come from?

I suggest that it comes from a poet's *pre*sentiment about the events that background the Sweeney character and that deepen his identity with the mythic double. For Sweeney is a returning soldier, too. Those "zebra stripes along his jaw" depict the creases of fat cut into the neck by the tight, stiff collar of the military dress uniforms that were worn at this time.[2] When he later reappears in *The Waste Land*, it is to visit Mrs. Porter, the madam of a Cairo brothel known for infecting British soldiers with venereal diseases. The song of "Mrs. Porter and her daughter" was sung by troops in the Dardanelles campaign (Southam 168). This contemporary context is of primary importance; indeed, until the Agamemnon epigraph was added to "Sweeney Among the Nightingales" in the last moment of the poem's composition, the final classical allusion had lacked a structural resonance (*IMH* 381). In the finished poem, the classical hero functions in a rhetoric of ironic imaginative comparison, recalling a standard which Sweeney fails but which also makes available a range of exalted feeling in the poem, here of exalted loss. And no small sense of loss attends the perception that Britain's "Great War for Civilization" is being fought – and lost – by this "Apeneck" Irishman, the simian representative of that unevolved province and now insurgent colony.

This sense of downturn in the current war also locates a moment of powerful feeling in "A Cooking Egg." Initially, this poem might be dismissed as the brittle and trivial wit of Eliot's quatrain art, his music-box prosody. The dominant voice is the know-nothing know-it-all, a sort of rhetorical zero:

> I shall not want Honour in Heaven
>   For I shall meet Sir Philip Sidney
> And have talk with Coriolanus
>   And other heroes of that kidney.
>
> I shall not want Capital in Heaven
>   For I shall meet Sir Alfred Mond.
> We two shall lie together, lapt
>   In a five per cent. Exchequer Bond. (*CPP* 27)

This caricature-in-voice is interrupted and significantly altered, however, as the poem turns toward conclusion:

> But where is the penny world I bought
> To eat with Pipit behind the screen?
> The red-eyed scavengers are creeping
> From Kentish Town and Golder's Green;
>
> Where are the eagles and the trumpets?
>
> Buried beneath some snow-deep Alps.
> Over buttered scones and crumpets
> Weeping, weeping multitudes
> Droop in a hundred A. B. C.'s. (27)

Syntactically, "The red-eyed scavengers are creeping / From Kentish Town to Golder's Green" recalls "The nightingales are singing near / The Convent of the Sacred Heart." And where those two lines in "Sweeney" lead to the "turn" of the final stanza, which pivots on the initial coordinate conjunction, a similar modulation occurs in "A Cooking Egg." For the cadence changes in the next verse, the quatrain stanza-pattern breaks in the single free-standing line, and the variation marks a difference in aesthetic emotion that matches the shift in the finish to "Sweeney." The intensification in "A Cooking Egg" includes, too, an allusion to present conditions in the Great War. The human cost of this first mass war is scaled to the proportion of "[w]eeping, weeping multitudes" and imaged in the pathos of its conscripted masses' typical lives, in the figures of the "buttered scones and crumpets" that are served in a hundred public canteens, the Allied Baking Companies. Eliot is sustaining a frame of war reference from the earlier mention of "Sir Alfred Mond" and the "five per cent. Exchequer Bond," where the minister in the war cabinet is linked, from his former career as prominent financier, with the instruments used to fund the war.

As in "Sweeney Among the Nightingales," Eliot is taking the war as a source of poetic feeling that is amplified through a framework of imperial reference. The softly sardonic comedy in the rhyming of "crumpets" and "trumpets" includes a muted, ironically protected perception of the relation between the common food of the cannon fodder and the insignia of Empire's pageant, "the eagles and the trumpets" of a Roman *triumphus*. A gloss on the imperial content of these images comes in Eliot's later (1932) poem "Triumphal March," from *Coriolan*, where that rite of the Roman Empire, a procession of treasure and captives through the capital city, is featured in these images for the regalia of a modern military parade: "You can see some eagles. And hear the trumpets" (*CPP* 85). Fancied in 1932, already foregone in 1917: that rhetorical question asks, *ubi sunt*, where are these numinous things of yesteryear? It is as a lost source of order and authority that this memory of the Roman triumphal march exerts its particular poetic power, which is measured, indeed, in its distance, its *ir*relevance – in the poor, bare, *un*accommodated lives of these somber conscripts in the mass army of the failing empire. If Eliot can experience the imperial episteme really only as a fallen or compromised ideal, he comes back again (and again) to the war as the event that establishes his relation to empire as *materia poetica* – as a subject for memory and desire, for nostalgia, for elegy.

This historical circumstance generates the idiolect of a specifically British Decadence, and the key to this literary language lies in the Latin meaning at the root of the English word – de*cad*ere, "to *fall* away." It preserves a memory that bridges some of the differences between its iterations in literary history, most notably, in the late phases of Roman and British *imperia*. If the long fall of British imperial fortunes begins in the previous century, it afforded the circumstance of a Decadence that was specifically English and at the same time highly conscious of its historical precedents. As Linda Dowling has demonstrated in *Language and Decadence in the Victorian Fin de Siècle*, the literary sensibilities of Pater and Swinburne reached back to comparable circumstances in late antiquity, and a prescient memory of imminent ends entered their activity as writers. In Pater's *Marius the Epicurean*, for instance, the historical fiction of the title character's late imperial life comes through a literary language that is mired in a heavily Latinate vocabulary and syntax, an English "buried" as it were in the crypt of its classical roots and word-systems. In the elaboration of this "dead language" factor in their imaginative vocabularies, the English Decadents are inscribing a *memento mori* to their own national language and its supporting historical institutions, which included a British Empire now in its own incipient decline.

As again now, in 1917, in the verbal liturgy of "Mr. Eliot's Sunday Morning Service":

> Polyphiloprogenitive
> The sapient sutlers of the Lord
> Drift across the window-panes.
> In the beginning was the Word.
>
> In the beginning was the Word.
> Superfetation of τὸ ἕν
> And at the mensual turn of time
> Produced enervate Origen. (*CPP* 33–34)

"In the beginning was the Word" invokes a pristine original moment of language, some Adamic unity of sound and meaning, of transparency between word and referent. This quality has obviously fallen into the polyglot composite of words that are otherwise not in referential life and use, of words learned or obsolete or rare or unusually formed, of words that all look back to ancient roots that do not stir with current life. If there is a piece of Eden in each root, the root is dead, and the composite language of the passage, preposterous or indeed *post*posterous as it is, is just this dead matter of fossilized radicals. This is the linguistic condition of a decadent script, of the Scripture of Decadence.

Evidence of the historical provocation for this usage is not hard to find in the poem, though it appears in the last stanza with a suddenness that registers, arguably, the

inexorable force of current political circumstance. Here comes Sweeney again, unlikely
hierophant in the Sunday Service of Mr. Eliot: "Sweeney shifts from ham to ham /
Stirring the water in his bath" (*CPP* 34). The Irish caricature is broad and blunt –
Paddy's pig provides the basis for the word-play in representing the character's
"hams," the parts to which he is reduced, whose "stirring" invokes by a subtler syn-
ecdoche the motions of other Paddies, the Easter Rising of Sweeney's countrymen in
1916. (Similar images and verbal figures in the poem's companion piece, "Sweeney
Erect," help to translate the bawdy pun of its title almost irresistibly into "The
Irish[man] Rising.") Most important, this powerful presentiment of a waning imperial
age underwrites the language of a New Decadence, Eliot's dead language lexicon, in
the poem's overture.

The Irish Question emerges in another unlikely site, Venice, which provides the
location for "Burbank with a Baedeker: Bleistein with a Cigar." The connection surfaces through Eliot's correspondence around the time of the poem's composition. In
a letter to the British novelist and travel-writer Douglas Goldring, he refers to the
controversy Goldring had touched off with his 1917 critique of the Irish literary
revival, *Dublin: Explorations and Reflections of an Englishman*. This book singled out for
criticism one of the more conspicuous spokespersons of the Celtic movement, Ernest
Boyd, who retaliated with "Broadbent's Baedeker" – a review of Goldring's volume
in the Dublin weekly, *New Ireland*, which accused Goldring of cultural imperialism.
Goldring's ironically patronizing riposte, "The Importance of Being Ernest," stirred
a further rejoinder from Boyd, "A Boy of the Bulldog Breed."[3] Writing to Goldring
on November 10, 1918, Eliot refers to "the cuttings from *New Ireland*" and claims:
"my opinions nearly coincide with yours." Whatever difference "nearly" intimates,
the "Baedeker" reference and the conspicuous alliteration of "b"s in Eliot's title obviously recall the headlines in the *New Ireland* controversy. Not that this reference is
necessary to establish a theme of imperial decline in the Venetian scene: the city situated on its coastal plain is perceived to be ever surrendering its cultural treasure,
which is the booty of marine empire, into the sea. But those reminders in Eliot's title
of the decline of empire in Ireland establish the theme at a closer focus, which may
account for the particular imaginative intensities and linguistic interests of this poem.

Eliot's closing quatrain does justice to the potential for themes of imperial fall in
Venice, citing St. Mark's lion as the image of temporal devastation, of a glory already
fallen, always foregone. Into this topos, however, he strikes a particularly English
allusion as his final note:

> Who clipped the lion's wings
> And flea'd his rump and pared his claws?
> Thought Burbank, meditating on
> Time's ruins, and the seven laws. (*CPP* 24)

The "seven laws" make reference to *The Seven Lamps of Architecture*, where
Ruskin enumerates the "laws" of moral order in public construction, in general,

and in Venice, in particular. Here, as in *The Stones of Venice*, the image of "ruins," "Time's" and tides' but also of "laws," that is, of ethical as well as material degeneration, holds the controlling focus. Ruskin's motives in *The Stones of Venice* included a wish to turn the story of its fall into a cautionary tale for England as a maritime imperial power (1: 15), and Eliot's last stanza answers that warning with his representation of imperial power in diminuendo. It is the assimilated point of the history he has experienced in the preceding years, most closely in the Irish trouble that underlies his title.

This reference draws its chief significance and implication as an attitude toward the material of cultural history. For Eliot, this is primarily an attitude toward the stuff of poetic language, which, in the waning days of Empire, in the late historical age of Decadence, appears as the prime site of decay. Language is a material always already lapsing into the unliving condition, which is the unvoiced condition of a printed existence only; it is the material of words going . . . going . . . gone from vital exchange, of an increasingly paleographic craft. And so we read of one of those high-end denizens of Venice extending a "meagre, blue-nailed, phthisic hand" (*CPP* 24). The outlandishly rare and recherché (and unpronounceable) adjective – *phthisic* means *decaying* – provides the last Word in the poetics of English Decadence, a word sent like a message in a bottle from that floating island of perennial Decadence. Outwardly Venetian, inwardly English, this location shows its emotional proximity and poetic productivity for Eliot as he deploys the diction and tropes of literary Decadence in this one summary instance.

The Waste Land: Dracula's Shadow

Eliot's development of an historically enriched poetics of Decadence is a process that is recapitulated in the manuscript history of a single passage in *The Waste Land*. This first draft is dated by Valerie Eliot to 1914:

> A woman drew her long black hair out tight
> And fiddled whisper-music on those strings
> The Shrill bats quivered through the violet air
> ~~Sobbing~~ Whining, and beating wings.
>   distorted
> A man, ~~one withered~~ by some mental blight
>   contorted
> Yet of abnormal powers
> { Such a one crept
> I saw him creep head downward down a wall
> And upside down in air were towers
> Tolling reminiscent bells –
> And ~~there were~~ chanting voices out of cisterns and of wells. (*WLF* 113)

The figure of the man crawling "head downward down a wall" suggests very forcibly a memory of the vampire Dracula in the first sighting by Bram Stoker's narrator Jonathan Harker: "But my very feelings changed to repulsion and terror when I saw the whole man slowly emerge from the window and begin to crawl down the castle wall over that dreadful abyss, *face down*, with his cloak spreading out around him like great wings" (39). In the double "down" of "head downward down," Eliot replicates the force of the shock that Harker's emphases strike into the *"face down"* of his representation. And the likeness that Harker draws between the cloak and "great wings" may account for the presence here of the figure of the bats, from which the human figure in this scene emerges and into which he disappears in the published, 1922 version. The penultimate version of late 1921 records this stage of development:

> A woman drew her long black hair out tight
> And fiddled whisper music on those strings
> And bats with baby faces in the violet ~~air~~ light,
> Whistled, and beat their wings
> A ~~man~~/form crawled downward down a blackened wall
> And upside down in air were towers
> Tolling reminiscent bells, that kept the hours.
> And voices singing out of empty cisterns and exhausted wells. (*WLF* 75)

Though deleted, the "man" preserves the human figure into this last draft and so locates the Dracula character as the main point of continuity and development over these years.

Dracula is a major figure in the hermeneutics of cultural Decadence. The vampire represents a reversion from the Progress mythology of Western European civilization, an atavism that stands as a reminder of the very fragile character of human improvability. More particularly, Dracula emerges from an Eastern European locale that serves diversely in the literary constructions of this time as a recurring topos of such backward-sliding attitudes.

In the first casting of this passage in 1914, the Dracula figure prompts a rhetoric of censure that emerges from a vantage shared with the standards of meliorist civilization, the values which this figure so explicitly contests. This rhetoric is weirdly overheated but revealing nonetheless as a measure of the strongly conditioned quality of Eliot's earlier sensibility. He is holding onto the values that Decadence defies but that history has not yet given the lie to, at least on the grand scale of the Great War. The exercises in literary Decadence that he has inscribed heretofore have been woven largely out of his head; they represent an appropriation, often a masterful appropriation, of the postures and gestures that are available to him from a strictly literary tradition.

The recasting of this passage in 1921–22 demonstrates Eliot's assimilation of the history that has intervened. He relocates the scene from the never-never land of the "evening" and "violet air" of 1914 and inserts it into a geographical and historical prospect that he labels quite specifically, in his note to this section of the published poem, as the "present decay of Eastern Europe" (*CPP* 53). This eastern European location takes the atavistic challenge that the Dracula figure represents into the instigating site of the Great War. And this challenge is writ large in the epic perspective of those "hooded hordes swarming / Over endless plains" (48) – the vision of a European continent overrun by barbarian hordes recalls the end of the Roman Empire and, just so, invokes the present day as a moment in a history whose chaos is also framed as imperial decline.

Unsurprisingly, then, Eliot provides an epigraph to the 1921 manuscript of the poem that reads as the last words of the imperial dream – "The horror! The horror!" from Conrad's *Heart of Darkness*. Kurtz's final words are uttered at the outer verge of commercial empire; they locate the *terminus ad quem* of the imperial project, the limit where Western meliorism and rationalism fail. Suppressing this epigraph at Pound's direction, Eliot nonetheless leaves this evidence of an end-of-empire feeling as a creative, instigating presentiment for the poem. *The Waste Land* includes a number of other references that together inscribe a *memento mori* to imperial ambition. The marine empire of Phoenicia is seen in the body of the drowned Phoenician sailor, which circulates through the text; a major moment of reversal in imperial fortunes is recalled in the naval battle at Mylae (l. 70); the early and late days in Britain's maritime empire are bracketed by the Thames, which "sweats / Oil and tar" (ll. 266–67) nowadays, but runs back through the allusions to Spenser (ll. 176, 183) and Elizabeth (ll. 279ff.) to the sap years of marine imperial reign. References to the life-cycle of empire dominate the opening scene of "A Game of Chess" (ll. 77–96), where allusions to Cleopatra and Dido recall the figures linked to Antony and Aeneas in the history and mythology of the Roman Empire. The "falling towers" of major imperial capitals – "Athens Alexandria Vienna London" (ll. 374–75) – restate the same feeling of inevitable historical loss. The Conrad epigraph puts these other references in perspective and frames the ruined monument of the imperial project as the poem's major imaginative space. It is here that the Decadent sensibility Eliot has been developing for nearly fifteen years finds its local habitation and name, its signature vision.

NOTES

1 For more on the Decadent movement in English poetry, see T. S. ELIOT AND THE SYMBOLIST CITY.

2 In 1974, Marshall McLuhan told me that Eliot had said to him that the model for Sweeney was an Irish-Canadian airman, billeted in London during the war.

3 Ernest A. Boyd, "Broadbent's Baedeker," *New Ireland* 19 May 1917: 24–25; Douglas Goldring [signed "Broadbent"], "On the Importance of Being Ernest," 26 May 1917: 49–50; Boyd, "A Boy of the Bulldog Breed," 2 June 1917: 62–63.

REFERENCES AND FURTHER READING

Dowling, Linda. *Language and Decadence in the Victorian Fin de Siècle*. Princeton: Princeton UP, 1989.

Hobsbawm, Eric. *The Age of Empire: 1875–1914*. New York: Vintage, 1989.

Ruskin, John. *The Seven Lamps of Architecture*. 1849. Boston: Estes, 1900.

——. *The Stones of Venice*. 1851. 3 vols. Boston: Estes, 1899.

Sherry, Vincent. *The Great War and the Language of Modernism*. New York: Oxford UP, 2003.

Southam, B. C. *A Guide to The Selected Poems of T. S. Eliot*. 6th ed. San Diego: Harcourt, 1994.

Stoker, Bram. *Dracula*. 1897. Ed. Nina Auerbach and David Skal. New York: Norton, 1997.

Part II
Works

9

Searching for the Early Eliot:
Inventions of the March Hare

Jayme Stayer

It is a common story. An adolescent – an incoherent clump of nerves, hormones, idealism, and contrarianism – picks up a notebook to record thoughts and impressions. In the notebook will be found attempts at role-playing, the trying on of masks to stretch the limits of identity. Also making an appearance will be questions of ultimate meaning: God, the universe, and metaphysics contrasted with the idiotic, quotidian scenery that is a torment to the author. The confusion of sexuality and the anguish of love will prompt some dark broodings – and perhaps a bawdy limerick or two. In the usual turn of events, such notebooks are mercifully lost or destroyed, and all are spared the embarrassment of the wretched scribblings therein. What is uncommon in the story of T. S. Eliot's early poetry is that his notebook was saved, and that many of the verses turned out to be not wretched at all.

The whereabouts of the notebook were unknown for many years, after John Quinn, the patron to whom Eliot sold the notebook, died in 1924. At the time of the transaction, Eliot had implored Quinn to keep the poems to himself "and see that they are never printed" (*IMH* xii). In his later years, Eliot was glad to think the notebook had been lost, but it came to public attention after Eliot's death when the New York Public Library announced that it had acquired the leather-bound notebook. Finally published in 1996, the notebook has been ably edited and richly annotated by Christopher Ricks under the title *Inventions of the March Hare* – Eliot's whimsical inscription written, then deleted on a flyleaf at the front of the notebook. As the title intimates, the contents of the notebook do not reveal a sure, linear progress from apprenticeship to mastery, but an ad hoc experimentation that results in awkward poems alternating with masterpieces, a record of the ebb and flow of Eliot's mind and technique as he absorbed new influences, set himself new tasks, and, in effect, invented himself as a serious poet.

A Companion to T. S. Eliot, First Edition. Edited by David E. Chinitz.
© 2014 John Wiley & Sons, Ltd. Published 2014 by John Wiley & Sons, Ltd.

Searching for Precedents: The Juvenilia

The notebook poems are all the more interesting when contrasted with what Eliot had been writing before. In the years prior to starting the notebook, Eliot had composed stories and verses – mainly schoolboy exercises – the worst of them dull, the best of them competently formulaic.[1] A. David Moody has identified the authors whose effects Eliot was copying as Wordsworth, Tennyson, Thomas Gray, and Edward Fitzgerald, among others. But though the language is drawn from these poets, Moody argues, it is "undisturbed by the young author's own direct sensations," the result of which is that the adolescent's poetry is "not impersonal but remote and artificial, its images not originals but reproductions" (17).

The tone, manner, and content of these poems reflect the constricted upbringing of one born into the Boston Brahmin class. Women appear as either blandly virginal or vaguely dangerous; exhortations of *carpe diem* are rendered in Jonsonian meter; flowers alternately bloom and decay. Other constraints that muffle the verse include the impossible generic expectations of the graduation ode, of which Eliot wrote two. His 1905 address given at the commencement exercises of Smith Academy (apostrophized as "O queen of schools") includes such ghastly bombast as: "Great duties call – the twentieth century / More grandly dowered than those which came before, / Summons" (*Poems Written* 13). The 16-year-old Eliot does manage to strike the appropriately elegiac note, but mainly he flounders inside the sage-voice he has puffed up for the occasion.

Even the juvenilia whose occasions are less grand fail to find a signature style. Eliot's 1907 poem – "Song" ("When we came home across the hill") – attempts a description of loss, but both image and emotion are stock and insipid. Beginning in the idyllic setting of spring, the poem ends with the contrast: "But the wild roses in your wreath / Were faded, and the leaves were brown" (*Poems Written* 18). Another "Song" published two years later also observes the failure of the ideal in an affectless monotone. Surrounded by white flowers, the passive speaker queries an inadequate beloved: "Have you no brighter tropic flowers / With scarlet life, for me?" (22). To search for precedents of Eliot's style and manner in these poems is to be baffled by their desultory flatness, the lack of a distinctive voice. The poems do not sound like Eliot.

Searching for a Voice

In December of 1908 – around the same time that he published the wooden poem complaining of emotional poverty – Eliot picked up a copy of Arthur Symons's *The Symbolist Movement in Literature* in the library of *Advocate* (*Letters* xx).[2] Symons's brief description of Jules Laforgue inspired Eliot to order the complete works of the French poet, which set arrived some time in 1909. After a period of quiet gestation, the longed-for passion burst forth in a flurry of poems. Imitating the voice of a French

poet, Eliot created a voice that was recognizably his own, and the results would moti-
vate him to buy a notebook in order to collect the experiments and continue exploring.
Unlike the imaginative space in which the young Eliot composed scripted assign-
ments, set-pieces for school periodicals, or farewells for graduation – the audiences
for which were oppressively authoritative – the notebook was a private workshop
where novel creations could be tried and failures could be hidden.

"Nocturne," one of Eliot's first poems to register Laforgue's influence, brims
with sardonic energy.[3] Gone are the wispy longings, conventional flowers, and
orotund rhetoric. In their place is a riveting, blisteringly ironic poem with a polemical
viewpoint:

> Romeo, *grand sérieux,* to importune
> Guitar and hat in hand, beside the gate
> With Juliet, in the usual debate
> Of love, beneath a bored but courteous moon (*Poems Written* 23)

In sonnet form, Eliot reworks the innocent, tragic love of Romeo and Juliet as a tale
of urbanity and satire. In the young poet's vision, the love scene is so clichéd that
even the moon – who is supposed to be sanctioning the courtship – is only "bored
but courteous," grudgingly fulfilling her duties as scene-setter. Regretting the trite-
ness of the episode, the poet interjects some drama by having Juliet stabbed. The
speaker is fascinated by the theatricality that results: "Blood looks effective on the
moonlit ground." The poet's delight in the macabre turns to contempt when he considers the inability of "female readers" to interpret his gruesome intervention properly.
Misreading the death scene, such women project their own fantasies of a *Liebestod*
ending: " 'The perfect climax all true lovers seek!' "

For this poem, Eliot has found an edgy voice as well as a theme: the artificiality of
romantic expectations and the suffocating inconsequence of class rituals such as courtship. In imagining an audience for such satire, Eliot has also targeted an anti-audience:
those "female readers" whose sentimentality has been shaped by nineteenth-century
gender roles and culture. The influence of Jules Laforgue, with his masks and irony,
his scorn for sentimentality, and his breezy, colloquial style, made possible this transformation in Eliot. Laforgue's sensibility as a whole spoke powerfully to the impres-
sionable Eliot, but it was a terrific piece of luck that Symons chose "Autre Complainte
de Lord Pierrot" as the only poem of Laforgue's to be quoted in full. Voiced through
the persona of a stock *commedia dell'arte* character – the naïve and ridiculous Pierrot
– Laforgue's poem records the increasingly absurd exchanges between a woman's gasps
of love and a man's mocking non sequiturs. Beginning in the unlikely banality of
geometry and ending in death, the mask of the poem manages both to disguise and
to reveal, in Symons's analysis, "suffering and despair, and resignation to what is, after
all, the inevitable" (61). With such a poem as a provocative model, Eliot's first
attempts – especially "Nocturne" and "Conversation Galante" – seem less like studious imitations of Laforgue and more like discharges of pent-up pressure.

In the November 1909 burst of writing that produced these poems, an expansion of technique and theme is evident. The influence of Laforgue and other French symbolists enables a broader intellectual scope and encourages a close inspection of the ugly, the boring, and the conventional. One result of this attention to the sordid is an honest appraisal of the ambivalence of the modern condition. Eliot has also achieved a richer tonal palette, with a continuum of nuance as well as sudden shifts. Note, for example, the opening of "Nocturne," where Eliot swoops into an arch timbre with the terse *Frenchisme:* "Romeo, *grand sérieux.*"

In her own analysis of the notebook poems, Helen Vendler has identified various competing discourses with which Eliot had to grapple in order to achieve a lyrically authentic voice and to move beyond the influence of Laforgue. Enumerating the available discourses of class, culture, and generation which Eliot adapted and resisted, Vendler writes:

> [Eliot] has mimicked, satirically, the inherited repressive discourses of his class, but has been unable to dismiss them utterly – admitting, by his recurrent recourse to such straightened exchanges, their importance in his aesthetic and ethical formation. He has fled gratefully at first to the foreign example of Laforgue, finding in irony a refuge from the inanities of both social and sexual upper-class conversation; he has nonetheless realized that ironic alienation cannot be a permanent discursive solution for a poet who also wants a lyric voice with which to speak directly and honestly on matters of the soul. He has judged the jazzy but semiotically empty discourse of the smart set as a language suitable only for "shaking cocktails on a hearse," usable as a decorative accent but not as a substantial matrix. (100)

While Vendler's compelling analysis explains how Eliot mobilized competing discourses, a problem with her thesis is that it valorizes the lyric voice as the authentic, "pure" voice for which Eliot was reaching, and appraises all the adopted or oblique voices as merely preparatory.

David Chinitz has offered a quite different view of how Eliot used the available discourse of the emerging Jazz Age. Far from seeing it as a "decorative accent," Chinitz argues that popular culture sank its roots deeply into Eliot's consciousness. He complicates the standard account of how Laforgue's poetry gave breath to Eliot's voice by revealing how the metrical rhythms of American popular music undergird Eliot's first efforts:

> What the apprentice poems of *Inventions of the March Hare* now enable us to see is that the acknowledged influence of Laforgue was complemented by the nearly suppressed yet indispensable influence of American jazz. It was the *convergence* of these elements . . . that produced the masterpieces of the *Prufrock* period. Laforgue showed Eliot how to adapt his voice to the popular material around him, and jazz gave Eliot a way to bring Laforgue into contemporary English. (36)

Discussing in detail the popular music of the 1910s, Chinitz shows how its movement, rhymes, and tonalities become transformed into "Eliot's patented cadences" (38).

Whatever discourses, adoptions, or resistances go into the shaping of a voice, one needs a voice not for its own sake, but as a means to an end. The specific contours of Eliot's voice – its scope and technical makeup, its various registers of irony, obliquity, and directness – were a function of the ideas and emotions with which the poet was grappling.

Searching for Meaning

In his attempts to make sense of his experience and the world, the young Eliot frequently revisits certain difficulties in his notebook: (1) the problem of the self's relationship to the Absolute, which in Eliot's case includes a nascent spiritual awareness; (2) the problem of solipsism, or how the internal self relates to external realities, especially realities that are sordid or at odds with conventional feelings; and (3) the problem of the sexual impulse and how to negotiate between its insistent claims and socially proper modes of expression and behavior. Eliot's mature poetry would find compelling solutions to these problems, but it is in the notebook that the poet first maps out their terrain.

The Absolute and its enemies – time, women, sexual desire, social customs – are ubiquitous in the notebook. As Absolute, as God, as silence, or as shadow, some presence appears to interrupt, disturb, or render implicit judgment by its contrast with a world that is more meaningless than fallen. In its philosophical guise, this presence emerges in the poem "Spleen," where the object of the poet's animosity is the "dull conspiracy" of social ritual.[4] In the final stanza, the meticulously dressed figure of Life – a precursor of the balding Prufrock – waits "(Somewhat impatient of delay) / On the doorstep of the Absolute" (*Poems Written* 26). Casting about for some larger meaning against which to oppose his ennui, the poet remains stuck on the doorstep, neither inside nor outside, unable to make a decisive commitment. Even more ominously, the presence appears in the final poem of "Suite Clownesque," in which a vaudeville show reaches its high-spirited conclusion. In the midst of a denouement of dancing milkmaids, revealed identities, and narrative resolutions, a comedian reappears with a sinister dismissal, his unexpected entrance falling across the stage "like a shadow dense, immense" (*IMH* 38).

In its numinous guise, the presence materializes in "Silence." The silences in Eliot's early poetry are often uncomfortable ones: awkward gaps in conversational banter that reveal social clumsiness and the risks of intimacy. But in "Silence," Eliot was coming to terms with a different understanding, one that Ronald Schuchard has described as "an ecstatic visionary experience" (121). In the poem, the outward forms of busy life are described as "garrulous waves" of passersby who chat and quarrel about a "thousand incidents." The speaker imagines it all falling away to disclose some inner stillness. The portent of this silence paralyzes him, its undeniable reality leading him to the conclusion: "There is nothing else beside" (*IMH* 18).

"Silence" is not a conversion poem, but the terrifying peace is a felt experience rather than an abstract value or rational truth. In her biography of Eliot, Lyndall Gordon gives the poem particular weight in the development of Eliot's spiritual life. She argues that Eliot was at first not conscious of the religious implications of the silence, only that it was opposed to the world of ordinary sense experience: "The revelation in the spring of 1910, at the age of twenty-one, had no immediate repercussions but remained the defining experience of his life" (49). The beginnings of the spiritual search evident in "Silence" in 1910 and extending to the saint poems of 1914 were cut short, Gordon argues, by the more immediate concerns of 1914–1915: Eliot's rejection of family expectations, his hasty marriage to the unstable Vivien Haigh-Wood, and his precipitous transformation from philosophy professor-apparent at Harvard to unknown artist in an adopted country.

While the visionary experience could be rendered lyrically in "Silence," Eliot was more often unsure of the epistemological ground on which he stood. As a result, his access to experience, whether physical or metaphysical, foundered on the shoals of solipsism. The intellectual lineaments of this problem can be traced in his student philosophy papers and dissertation, but its emotional force pressed through in the notebook poems.[5] A poignant expression appears in "Introspection," which might more properly be entitled "Solipsism," for it describes not the serene analysis of one's mind, but a desperate agon from which the mind cannot escape. The poem presents a series of interlinked images describing the tautology of the mind's self-exploration. The first image – "The mind was six feet deep in a / cistern" (*IMH* 60) – has the mind buried as if in its grave, blocked from the world. The poem continues with the image of a snake's head eating its tail "like two fists / interlocked." The struggle of the mind is triply depicted in an image (cistern/grave) interlocked with a metaphor (snake) interlocked with a simile (fists). Starting from such a brute premise, the poem can only end, swiftly, at its logical conclusion: the snake's head futilely banging against the cistern wall. As the starkest statement of the philosophical problem, it is a failed poem and an aesthetic cul-de-sac. The more successful poems of the notebook will hazard tentative forays and risk tenuous connections between the self and the world, implicitly rejecting the radical incommunicability of this self-made prison.

Eliot's search for meaning included not only metaphysical questions of the Absolute, and philosophical questions about the nature and reliability of experience, but physical questions of sexuality. While many early poems ridicule the meaninglessness of courtship rituals, the poet – ever the product of his class and upbringing – still paradoxically seeks intimacy within those structures. "Entretien dans un parc," for example, describes the charged atmosphere between a man and a woman walking in a park. Only after tense moments of irresolution does the speaker momentarily abandon his reserve, provoked by "a sudden vision of incompetence" to catch hold of her hand. His advance accepted, the speaker nonetheless feels exasperated, responding with a typically Laforguian dismissal: "All the scene's absurd!" (*IMH* 48). The final stanza fantasizes a way out of these romantic difficulties: "if we could have given ourselves the slip / What explanations might have been escaped." In this hypothetical world, in which their awkward selves have been evaded, no explanations would be required, no confusion over "ends unshaped" (49). Even though this fantasy is deflated by reality – "We are helpless" is his conclusion – the poet is nonetheless intrigued by the vague promise of her acceptance, however ambiguously interpreted and however threatening to his own composure.

Women are largely rendered as unsympathetic in the notebook, and the women of Eliot's class are never seen as sexually refulgent beings: they remain objects, sexless if still desired. Such an untenable psychological formulation has its warped underside in Eliot's violent, scatological, and sadistic verses, including the mock epic of "King Bolo and his Big Black Kween" (*Letters* 86). These poems raise a number of problems for critics, not least of which is what to call them (see Poirier, Johnson). There is no agreement as to whether "bawdy," "ribald," or "blue verse" cast a sufficiently wide net to capture these dark inventions.

Another problem of these verses is their relationship to the rest of the notebook, a problem first caused by Eliot himself, who cut out the offending pages before selling the notebook to John Quinn. Christopher Ricks's editorial decision to include the poems – found in the Ezra Pound papers at Yale University – in the published edition has resulted in a separate appendix. Thus, their excision and not-quite-reinsertion into the published notebook reflect Eliot's own and critics' subsequent ambivalence about them. A further problem is one of attribution: such "scabrous exuberances," as Ricks calls them (*IMH* xvi), exist in a lively oral tradition of repetition and variation. Some of the poems seem clearly inventions of Eliot's, while others are either transcriptions of variations Eliot has heard or improvisations he has attempted (Chinitz, "Blue"; Ricks "To Keep," "Crabby").

There is a fierce comic energy about these verses, but of the kind that produces more heat than light. Of all of Eliot's early verses, the meter here is the most clunky, a rhythmic unease that mirrors the hammering, hectoring quality of the content: "Take up my good intentions with the rest / And then for Christ's sake stick them up your ass" (*IMH* 307). Perhaps the most noteworthy element of these verses is not their misogyny, racism, adolescent fixations, or depraved sexuality, but the sobering fact that they are mostly not very funny. Missing is that ineffable mixture of frolicking rhythms, comedic wordplay, and crude observation that raise blue verse to a high art form. Instead, there is a litany of raping and fucking and shitting and whoring. But these verses are not an anomaly in Eliot's work. As elsewhere in the notebook, Eliot is testing the limits of what can be said and how to say it. If we are looking to disapprove of the poet, then we should recall that the erotic thrives on the crossing of boundaries, including the taboo.

Between the sexless depictions of aristocratic women and the pornographic invective of the blue verse, Eliot managed to find an oblique manner for addressing the problem of sex. Prostitution and the homoerotic were the themes he addressed in this indirect manner, and such themes were likewise elliptically related to the sexual mores of his class. Depictions of prostitutes and working-class women in the notebook carry about them the air of non-moralizing nostalgia, as if such squalid lives at least did not suffer from the artificialities and trivialities of the poet's own social milieu. These women have real bodies: "Women, spilling out of corsets, stood in entries" (*IMH* 43); and they have real desires: "behind her sharpened eyes take flight / The summer evenings in the park / And heated nights in second story dance halls" (56). But such women remain outside the poet's ambit. Similarly, some of the poems explore the sadomasochistic and the homoerotic. "The Love Song of St. Sebastian," for one, transforms the homoerotic connotations of St. Sebastian and blends them with religious delirium (see Kaye). But as with his depiction of lower-class women and prostitutes, such an attenuated eroticism is detached from the poet's everyday experience and is forced into service for a spirituality of suffering that is attitudinizing and pointless.

This problem of sex and class achieves equilibrium in the masterpiece of the notebook, "The Love Song of J. Alfred Prufrock." There, Prufrock imagines the women who will observe and judge him at tea, with their "Arms that are braceleted, and white, and bare / (But, in the lamplight, downed with light brown hair)" (*IMH* 41). The crucial "But" conjoins by contrast the civilized bracelet of class charms with the animality of body hair, its frisson whispered through those very Eliotic parentheses.

Searching for an Audience

The problem of audience is one which Prufrock dramatizes – to whom does the lonely prophet speak, and to what effect? For an author to address an audience involves both the imaginative creation of a discourse community to whom one wants to speak, as well as the discovery or invention of its attitudes and expectations vis-à-vis the author's message. In "Humouresque," the vituperative marionette is described as having a "Half-bullying, half-imploring air" (*IMH* 325) – a good description of the ethos of the speakers of these early poems, who alternately beg or browbeat their audiences.

We have seen how a numinous presence intrudes in "Silence," but an auditing presence, almost as threatening, makes itself felt in the poem: a skeptical "You" who appears in the antepenultimate line: "You may say what you will, / At such peace I am terrified. / There is nothing else beside" (*IMH* 18). This "you" – a skeptic who would say something otherwise about such an experience – is for Eliot some projection of the restrictions of class and culture that hamper any straightforward description of the numinous. In placing such an anti-audience inside the poem, Eliot is asserting more imaginative control over his audience and has moved some way toward exorcising such ghosts by insisting on the primacy of his own experience over social expectations. But not all "yous" of the early poems are skeptics who must be defensively preempted. Whoever else that "you" is in the opening line of "Prufrock" – "Let us go then, you and I" – whether reader, or beloved, or mirror of the "I," it is a you who is in league with the speaker (*CPP* 3).

In addition to the imaginative creation of an audience, a related though distinct task is finding an actual public venue and publishing for a real audience. For a young man of Eliot's refinement and family connections to describe the exploration of poor districts and the meeting of prostitutes required some mental border-crossing on his part, some coded obliquity in his expression, as well as some overt self-censorship when it came to choosing which poems to publish and which to leave in the privacy of the notebook.

The obliquity of Eliot's method can be seen in the third of his "Preludes," whose origins derive from Charles-Louis Philippe's novel *Bubu de Montparnasse*. But while Philippe's sordid atmosphere is retained, the explicit description of the streetwalker's profession is absent in Eliot. This obliquity is even more apparent in the trail of the original epigraph. Written in the notebook as "Son âme de petite putain" ("her little whore's soul"), it is expunged before the poem is published (*IMH* 335).

This self-censorship sometimes creates a pregnant evasiveness, but it can also lead Eliot to leave some of his aesthetic successes unpublished. Two poems written around the same time illustrate how Eliot handles the theme of female sexuality for two different audiences. The first poem, "Morning at the Window," which Eliot published, is the more reserved. Attending in detail to the dreary routines of the working poor, the speaker notes a woman with an "aimless smile" that lingers briefly, then evaporates (*IMH* 343). Grover Smith is critical of "the imprecision of the verbal conceits" of the poem, complaining that "the damp souls of housemaids" is not a cogent image (30–31). In its attempt to be reserved, the poem ends up becoming unintentionally baffling.

Contrast this poem with "Paysage Triste," whose emotional and sexual content is more explicit than "Morning at the Window." As in "Morning," the speaker passes an anonymous female with whom he makes a momentary connection. In "Paysage Triste," the speaker sees a beautiful "girl" on a bus. Used to getting attention for her looks, she responds casually to his hungry gaze by ignoring him without embarrassment. She is possibly a prostitute, but perhaps only because the speaker wishes it so: it is he who labels her an "almost denizen of Leicester Square" – an upscale entertainment spot where prostitutes found lucrative trade (*IMH* 52).

The rest of the poem contrasts the poet's imaginative tryst with this woman to the impossibility of their union ever being respectable. As a woman from the lower classes, she would be unfamiliar with the conventions of upper-class courtship and would be ignorant of the subtle conventions of reserve and intimacy that govern it. The lower-class woman, who might easily give her body to the speaker in another situation, would therefore be afraid to violate the boundaries of intimacy at the opera in the way his upper-class companion can do: she leans across him, her elbow on his lap, to claim her opera-glasses from a child. But this evocative contrast of erotic intimacies remains in the notebook, unpublished.

Eliot's imagining of an audience and his search for publication venues went beyond merely developing an oblique style behind which he could hide. Rather, once established in literary London, his horizons widened considerably, and he even published "Preludes" and "Rhapsody on a Windy Night" in Wyndham Lewis's audacious *Blast* – a magazine that outraged Eliot's conservative parents when they were sent a copy

(*Letters* 131). That Eliot would align himself with the avant-garde so soon after leaving decorous Boston is a measure of how far his sense of audience had developed.

Voice, Theme, and Audience: Two Poems

So far in this chapter, the rhetorical elements of Eliot's early poetry have been separately explored: a voice is constructed, a theme is struck, and an audience is addressed. But such processes do not occur separately. As a summation, let us look at two poems from that first outpouring of poems in 1909 to observe the missteps Eliot made, the risks he took, and the aesthetic lessons he learned. Though written in the same month as Eliot's first Laforguian creations, the companion poems "First Caprice in North Cambridge" and "Second Caprice in North Cambridge" both strain against the limits of their French models, attempting to redirect the Laforguian voice, broaden the theme, and grope toward a more nuanced sense of audience.

Laforgue's irony turns out to be a double-edged sword for the young poet: it gives him a voice for his disgust and irritation, but it also undermines any attempts at emotional sincerity. "First Caprice in North Cambridge" records Eliot's discovery of the aesthetic problem that corrosive irony presents. Set in the slum district just north of the Harvard campus, the poem begins with a direct treatment of the sordid. Images such as "dirty windows" and "Trampled mud and grass" seem to be building to something momentous, but that movement is broken off with a dismissive conclusion: "Oh, these minor considerations! . . . ." (*IMH* 13; ellipses in the original). The poet, fearing he has drifted into the sentimental, reaches too quickly for its ironic antidote. After such a crippling turn, the poem can only be abandoned.

The companion poem "Second Caprice in North Cambridge" continues the exploration of the sordid while attempting to fix the aesthetic problem of abrasive irony. Though physically close to Harvard, the poor section of North Cambridge exists "Far from our definitions" studied in philosophy courses, and far from the "aesthetic laws" that govern high art. Its seedy images nonetheless stimulate "pity" in the reader (*IMH* 15). The "charm" and "repose" evoked by fields and vacant lots are presumably aesthetic in nature, because the poet betrays irritation at his own repetition of the cliché "rack the brain." He testily objects to his own breaking of the aesthetic law: "(What: again?)" As with the final line of "First Caprice," this sneer is Laforguian in origin, though here its brittle irony is cordoned off from the rest of the poem: it is both parenthetically enclosed and buried in the middle of a stanza, whose sonorous tone continues uninterrupted, as if the contemptuous aside had never intruded (15). The consequences of the dismissive gesture – which in "First Caprice" dooms the poem to failure – are contained here rather than carried through. More adroitly managed than in "First Caprice," Eliot's solution for defusing irony in "Second Caprice" is still a cheap one, but it shows that he is working to solve the aesthetic problem raised by the first poem.

In "First Caprice," detritus stands metonymically for human misery. But because such sentiments have been dismissed by his own pen as "minor considerations," the poet must shore up in the second poem the rhetorical transaction he has destabilized in the first. So in "Second Caprice," Eliot directs the mechanics of pity by insisting didactically on its effects. The poem begins:

> This charm of vacant lots!
> The helpless fields that lie
> Sinister, sterile and blind –
> Entreat the eye and rack the mind,
> Demand your pity. (*IMH* 15)

This didacticism is not an aesthetic advance over the first poem; rather, it is a sign of insecurity on the poet's part as to whether or not his new-found tools are working. The rhetorical sleight-of-hand specifies the work of pity and includes an unconvincing shift to the second person. The "you" whose pity is "demand[ed]" is not a hostile audience, but neither is it to be trusted to reach its own conclusions. The speaker attempts to soften its unintentionally coercive force by assuming the second person plural in the second stanza: "Let us pause."

In attempting to solve the aesthetic problem of "First Caprice," Eliot instead stumbles onto another. Human misery is the ostensible subject of the first poem, but its nearness to sentimentality alarms the ironically defensive poet and destroys the planned movement of the poem. Thus, the problem which the now-wiser poet takes up in the second poem is not the problem of human misery, but how that problem might be handled rhetorically. That the speaker is concerned with this problem is evident in the first noun of the poem: "charm." Its descriptive qualifier – "This charm" – points to a specific ideology that is shared (or so the poem presumes) with the reader. *This* charm is nervously asserted even before the first, un-charming image is allowed to enter the scene: "vacant lots!" The strained exclamation point – a punctuation that Eliot would later deploy to more subtle effect – likewise attempts to compel the reader. Unlike the neutral descriptors that begin "First Caprice" ("dirty," "broken," "frail," "Trampled"), with their negative, if morally neutral connotations, the adjectives of "Second Caprice" are explicitly moralizing: "helpless," "Sinister," "sterile." The switch from neutrality in the first poem to moralizing in the second is a function of the speaker's uncertainty: the images of sordidness cannot be trusted to do the work he intends. His rhetorical solution is forced, but at least in this second poem the tension is productive and not merely contradictory.

With "Nocturne," one of Eliot's first Laforguian poems, in its confident and unified voice, in its sureness of tone, its urbanity and anti-romanticism, we can detect the beginnings of an Eliotic manner. But the poem is wholly derivative, never moving beyond its Laforguian borders. Its audience holds assumptions that turn out to be just as constricted as those of the "female readers" it deplores: the expectation that the earnest and the sentimental will be hooted off the stage. It is this narrow audience that is feared in "First Caprice," and that provokes the speaker to dismiss preemptively his own imagined ridiculousness.

With "First Caprice" and "Second Caprice," however, Eliot struggles to move beyond the mimicked voice of "Nocturne" in order to integrate the larger concern of human suffering into his poetic range. It is not surprising that such first experiments fail, nor that their attempted solutions only raise more intractable difficulties. What is remarkable is that a 21-year-old, in the same productive month in which he has written three successful Laforguian poems, has already reached the limits of what his short but fruitful apprenticeship with Laforgue has taught him. In "Nocturne," Eliot finds a Laforguian springboard for a confident, sardonic voice and a narrow audience to applaud his hostile irony. In "First Caprice" and "Second Caprice," he leaps from that springboard in a more hesitant voice, to a theme that is more generous, albeit vexed, imagining imperfectly an audience whose adventurous expectations are coextensive with his own quickly broadening purview. Within three months of this experimenting, Eliot will have penned part of "Portrait of a Lady"; within a year, two "Preludes"; and within two years, "The Love Song of J. Alfred Prufrock," "La Figlia che Piange," and the remaining portions of "Preludes" and "Portrait" – all major poems and aesthetic triumphs that are drafted and perfected in the notebook.

The story of the notebook is how it prepared Eliot for the public stage of poetry: how a shy, reserved boy with strong internal and external restrictions on his manner of expression came to imagine a self that exceeded the boundaries delimited for him by his family, class, culture, and education. The chaff of the notebook – its rhetorical uncertainties, self-defeating gestures, and pornographic excrescences – Eliot will sweep away, and to the public he will present the wheat that is left over: the telling allusions, hallucinatory squalor, transcendent intimations, muted suffering, electric fear, and bilious ennui, all of it spoken, sung, or growled in virtuosic registers of irony, obliquity, deadpan, and directness. This accomplishment, achieved in the notebook, would make the honeyed tones and staid pieties of Edwardian verse seem hopelessly dull and antiquated, and would come to define not only Eliot's poetry but the modern moment. It is an uncommon story.

Notes

1 The extant juvenilia were originally published in school periodicals, *Smith Academy Record* and *Harvard Advocate*. They were later collected as *Poems Written in Early Youth*, privately printed in 1950 and made widely available in a corrected trade edition in 1967. These verses can also be found in British editions (1969 and later) of *The Complete Poems and Plays of T. S. Eliot* (Faber & Faber).

2 See T. S. Eliot and the Symbolist City.

3 The exact chronology of these early experiments is uncertain, but Ricks identifies six of them as having been written or published in November 1909 (*IMH* xxxix). Only five poems are actually listed under Ricks's November dating, "Conversation Galante" having been inadvertently left out.

4 Neither "Nocturne" nor "Spleen" appears in the notebook. Originally published in the *Harvard Advocate* (Nov. 1909 and Jan. 1910,

respectively), they were collected with the other juvenilia in *Poems Written in Early Youth*. But their publication dates, along with their style and content, place them with the Laforguian inventions of the notebook.

5 On Eliot's epistemology, see YES AND NO: ELIOT AND WESTERN PHILOSOPHY and DISAMBIVALENT QUATRAINS.

REFERENCES AND FURTHER READING

Chinitz, David. *T. S. Eliot and the Cultural Divide*. Chicago: U of Chicago P, 2003.

——. "T. S. Eliot's Blue Verses and Their Sources in the Folk Tradition." *Journal of Modern Literature* 23 (1999): 329–33.

Gish, Nancy K. "Disincarnate Desire: T. S. Eliot and the Poetics of Dissociation." *Gender, Desire, Sexuality in T. S. Eliot*. Ed. Cassandra Laity and Nancy K. Gish. Cambridge: Cambridge UP, 2004. 107–29.

Gordon, Lyndall. *T. S. Eliot: An Imperfect Life*. New York: Norton, 1999.

Johnson, Loretta. "T. S. Eliot's Bawdy Verse: Lulu, Bolo and More Ties." *Journal of Modern Literature* 27 (2003): 14–25.

Kaye, Richard A. "'A Splendid Readiness for Death': T. S. Eliot, the Homosexual Cult of St. Sebastian, and World War I." *Modernism/Modernity* 6 (1999): 107–34.

McIntire, Gabrielle. "An Unexpected Beginning: Sex, Race, and History in T. S. Eliot's Columbo and Bolo Poems." *Modernism/Modernity* 9 (2002): 283–301.

Moody, A. D. *Thomas Stearns Eliot: Poet*. 2nd ed. Cambridge: Cambridge UP, 1994.

Poirier, Richard. "The Waste Sad Time." *New Republic* 28 Apr. 1997: 36–45.

Ricks, Christopher. "Crabby." *New Republic* 9 June 1997: 48.

——. "To Keep the Ball Rolling." *Times Literary Supplement* 6 June 1997: 17–18.

Schuchard, Ronald. *Eliot's Dark Angel: Intersections of Life and Art*. New York: Oxford UP, 1999.

Smith, Grover. *T. S. Eliot's Poetry and Plays: A Study in Sources and Meaning*. Chicago: U of Chicago P, 1960.

Symons, Arthur. *The Symbolist Movement in Literature*. 1919. New York: Dutton, 1958.

Vendler, Helen. "T. S. Eliot: Inventing Prufrock." *Coming of Age as a Poet*. Cambridge: Harvard UP, 2003. 81–113.

10
Prufrock and Other Observations: A Walking Tour

Frances Dickey

Publication and Reception

The 1917 publication of *Prufrock and Other Observations* marked the beginning of an era in modern poetry. Surprisingly, however, most of the poems collected in this volume had been written at least six years before. Eliot began "Portrait of a Lady" and "Preludes" in 1910, completing them the following year along with "The Love Song of J. Alfred Prufrock" and "Rhapsody on a Windy Night" during his study abroad in Paris and Munich. "La Figlia che Piange" followed shortly afterward. Not until 1915 did Eliot venture to publish these poems separately in periodicals; two years later the Egoist Press brought out his first book. The core poems of the *Prufrock* volume thus predate Eliot's graduate training in philosophy, the tragic wartime death of his Paris friend Jean Verdenal (to whom he later dedicated the book), and his unhappy marriage to Vivien Haigh-Wood; they are the work of a 23-year-old. More importantly, these poems also belong to a very different world than the one that received them. They were written before or at the same time as many of the defining moments of Anglo-American modernism, such as the first Post-Impressionist Exhibition in London (1910), visits to London by Futurist F. T. Marinetti (1910 and 1912), the launching of Imagism (1912), the publication of Freud in English (1913), and, most importantly, the outbreak of World War I (1914). *Prufrock and Other Observations* appears now so quintessentially modern not because it bears the stamp of these upheavals but because it profoundly shaped literary modernism. Many aspects of the book actually reflect a nineteenth-century context, including its literary frame of reference, its anxiety about urbanization and prostitution, and its philosophical rather than Freudian approach to psychology.

The poems of *Prufrock* had to await the founding of literary journals prepared to publish avant-garde work in English: "The Love Song of J. Alfred Prufrock" appeared in 1915 in *Poetry* magazine (in existence since 1912), quickly followed by "Preludes" and "Rhapsody" in *Blast* (established 1914), and "Portrait of a Lady" in Alfred

A Companion to T. S. Eliot, First Edition. Edited by David E. Chinitz.
© 2014 John Wiley & Sons, Ltd. Published 2014 by John Wiley & Sons, Ltd.

Kreymborg's *Others* (established 1913). The publication of the collected volume was modest, consisting of 500 copies, secretly subsidized by Ezra Pound. Pound conducted a blistering defense of the work in response to an unfavorable review comparing Eliot's poems to the behavior of a drunken slave (Brooker 4–6). Most reviewers, however, including Marianne Moore, Conrad Aiken, May Sinclair, and Babette Deutsch, called attention to the quality and importance of the poems, even while recoiling from Eliot's depiction of human nature (1–17). The title poem established Eliot's reputation as a poet and is now among the most familiar works of modernism and perhaps of American poetry altogether.

Background and Major Sources

The background to *Prufrock and Other Observations* consists of everything that the precocious Tom Eliot read before and during his creative burst of 1910–11.[1] Jules Laforgue's influence is paramount as the source from which Eliot received Symbolism and introduced it into American poetry. Eliot had read Arthur Symons's *The Symbolist Movement in Literature* in the winter of 1908–09, and many of Symons's quotations from Laforgue appear in barely disguised form in the early *Prufrock* poems, such as "Enfin, si, par un soir, elle meurt dans mes livres" ("At last, if one evening she dies among my books" [Symons 110]), transposed to "and what if she should die some afternoon" in "Portrait" (*CPP* 11). Even passages from Symons's prose echo in the poems, as when "In Laforgue, sentiment is squeezed out of the world before one begins to play at ball with it" (109) becomes "to have squeezed the universe into a ball" in "Prufrock" (*CPP* 6). Prufrock traces his lineage to Laforgue's debonair and flippant "Pierrot" (a version of the stock character of the foolish romantic found in pantomime and *commedia dell'arte*). From Laforgue Eliot learned an attitude of ironic detachment, the technique of free verse, and a method of endowing apparently unpoetic modern objects with significance. Eliot's "objective correlative" (proposed in "Hamlet and His Problems," 1919 [*SE* 124–25]) essentially theorizes the symbolist technique that he first encountered in Laforgue and tried out in "Prufrock."

Eliot had already read widely before he came to Laforgue. In later years he tended to downplay his debts to Victorian poetry, making this frame of reference more difficult for us to see. His most important poetic inheritance, however, may have been the Victorian dramatic monologue (see Langbaum; Christ). Symbolist poetry tends to minimize characterization to achieve a universal or generalized speaker. By contrast, Victorian poets drew on contemporary advances in the novel to transform the romantic lyric "I" into a vehicle for exploring the individual and his or her relation to society and convention. "Prufrock" and "Portrait" inherit this project, particularly from Robert Browning's *Men and Women* (1855). Like Prufrock, the Browning speaker distinguishes himself as belonging to a particular time and place, and this historical specificity is often combined with personal peculiarity or social isolation.

Eliot's poetic speakers differ from Browning's and Laforgue's, however, in the greater intensity of their introspection. Three figures in particular contributed to Eliot's knowledge of and interest in the new field of psychology: Harvard philosophy professor William James, who had published the first American textbook on psychology in 1890; his novelist brother Henry James; and the French philosopher Henri Bergson. Debts to Henry James's fiction can be found throughout the *Prufrock* poems, from the title of "Portrait of a Lady" to the narrative device of indecision and missed opportunities. Eliot's use of interior monologue in "Prufrock" and "Portrait" reflects James's narrative technique and his attention to consciousness as the site of meaningful action. The Jameses shared their interest in consciousness, and particularly the idea of "flow" (i.e., "stream of consciousness," a term coined by William) with Bergson, whose lectures and books deeply, if temporarily, influenced Eliot in 1911. William James and Bergson had mutually influenced each other for 20 years, and in 1909 James had hailed the younger philosopher for helping him to see that "reality, life, experience, concreteness, immediacy, use what word you will, exceeds our logic, overflows, and surrounds it" (725). Bergson's distinction between pure experience – as flow or duration – and measured or "extended" experience underlies much of the *Prufrock* volume.

Another important aspect of Eliot's background was city life, experienced both in person and in his reading. Raised in downtown St. Louis and educated in Cambridge, Eliot was an inveterate urbanite, drawn to wandering the streets of working-class districts in Boston and Paris. While in Paris, Eliot read three novels of Fyodor Dostoevsky, including *Crime and Punishment*, in which the narrative orientation around the protagonist's fevered consciousness dovetails with description of the modern city. Dostoevsky represents urban life as having an unhealthy effect on the mind, whose aimless thoughts and attraction to dark passages resemble the protagonist's nighttime wandering through poor neighborhoods (he sets off on such a walk at the opening of the novel, just as Prufrock does). The novels of Charles Dickens, and more directly James Thomson's poem "The City of Dreadful Night" and John Davidson's "Thirty Bob a Week" also contributed to Eliot's vision of the city (Crawford 35–60). Their London is the literary substratum for "Prufrock," "Preludes," "Rhapsody," and "Morning at the Window," over which is laid the Paris of Baudelaire, Laforgue, and Charles-Louis Philippe (author of *Bubu de Montparnasse* [1901], which opens with an evening stroll in a red-light district of Paris, and of *Marie Donadieu* [1904]). The nineteenth-century city that Eliot encountered in life and in his reading was at once a center of fashion and culture – represented by the leisured, strolling dandy – and a cesspool of poverty and exploitation resting, at the bottom of the social hierarchy, on the sale of sex by destitute girls. Eliot's concern with the city reflects a squalid social reality that seemed at the time to expose an awful crime at the heart of human nature.

Finally, Eliot drew on the standard texts of a nineteenth-century education, including the Homeric epics, Virgil's *Aeneid*, Dante's *Divine Comedy*, the plays of Shakespeare and other Renaissance works, and the Bible. Eliot's epigraphs, which were mostly added later, perhaps overstate the importance of these monumental sources. Allusions can often be traced through a more contemporary work; for example, the line "to have squeezed the universe into a ball" may echo Andrew Marvell's "Let us roll all our strength, and all / Our sweetness, up into one ball" (in "To His Coy Mistress" [51]), but it also has a closer source in Symons. Even Hamlet was mediated for Eliot by Laforgue's humorous fictional depiction of the character. The exception to this mediation is Dante, whom Eliot read early and often.

"The Love Song of J. Alfred Prufrock"

> Let us go then, you and I,
> When the evening is spread out against the sky
> Like a patient etherized upon a table (*CPP* 3)

These opening lines are at once famously memorable and utterly enigmatic. To whom does Prufrock speak? Himself or someone else? He sets out on a journey, but the destination remains vague, as does the "overwhelming question" that he never asks (3). Most enigmatic of all, the image of the etherized patient hovers over the entire poem as an emblem of Prufrock's numbness and his inability to take action. It exemplifies his profound confusion between tenors and vehicles in his metaphors; his vehicles (the "patient") point inexorably back to his emotions rather than outward to describe the world (the "sky"). This confusion is a linguistic symptom of Prufrock's indecisive negotiation between, on the one hand, the outdoor urban space of male companionship and anonymity, and, on the other, the feminine indoor space of social convention (at the "table" where tea is served, and where he feels he is being cut open). This spatial division also corresponds to the problematic boundaries of Prufrock's selfhood, between the interior of his thoughts and emotions and the exterior world of things and other people.

Eliot situates Prufrock's utterance at the crepuscular or twilight hour, a favorite time of day for French Symbolists and British fin-de-siècle poets, signifying the transition to nighttime and the demi-monde, and suggesting personal or historical decline. The month of October is an analogous time on the calendar. Prufrock's departure for the city streets as the sun is setting indicates the meeting of realms that are ordinarily kept apart: bourgeois and underworld, work and private life, waking and dreaming. His entrance into the "underworld" opens a journey indicated by the progression of verb tenses. Beginning with a future orientation ("Let us go" and "there will be time" [*CPP* 3–4]), Prufrock shifts into the present tense ("the afternoon, the evening, sleeps so peacefully" [5]), and then shows hesitation in the conditional "should I" that tests out the possibility of an action (6). A moment of crisis comes and goes, indicated by Prufrock's transition to the past conditional ("would it have been worth while?" [6]). This progression tells the story of a missed opportunity that is nowhere explicitly narrated but constitutes the action of the poem.

As he progresses in time, Prufrock also moves through space, conducting his journey or quest through city streets and a series of "rooms." As his mind looks forward anxiously to an indoor destination presided over by women – "In the room the women come and go / Talking of Michelangelo" – his feet take him by urban venues that these women would have been sure to avoid fastidiously (*CPP* 4). The strict nineteenth-century distinction between marriageable girls and sexually available ones is mapped out in the poem between genteel reception rooms and "one-night cheap hotels," and accounts for some of the poem's barely controlled panic (3). After outdoor mortifications ("pools that stand in drains" [4]) and indoor ones, Prufrock's final crisis takes place in the inner sanctum of feminine domesticity and convention: "After the cups, the marmalade, the tea, / Among the porcelain, among some talk of you and me" (6). Yet, the poem ends in a space outside the parameters set by the opening lines, on the beach and "in the chambers of the sea" (7).

Prufrock's journey, with its succession of challenges culminating in a test of courage that becomes a crisis of identity, traces the outline of the quest narrative that Eliot later mined explicitly for *The Waste Land*. As indicated by the epigraph from the *Inferno* (which replaced an earlier quotation from the *Purgatorio*), Eliot has a Dantean model in mind, with echoes of Homer in the singing mermaids (Manganiello 18–25). Paralleling this narrative is the looser romantic frame of an encounter with nature, which reconnects the isolated speaker with other people and the divine in a moment of epiphany. Prufrock's experience, however, subverts or disappoints the expectations built into both of these patterns: at the moment of the crisis, rather than taking heroic action, he backs down, says nothing; nor does his walk produce any transcendental insight or knowledge except that he is merely a "Fool" (*CPP* 7). Eliot deploys the Laforguian technique of deflated expectations, but not for humorous ends: Prufrock has nothing to fall back on to reassure him of his own and the world's solidity, which may explain why we find him drowning at the end of the poem.

Prufrock's quest to establish his identity and make contact with his beloved has a philosophical underpinning, explained by Eliot's "temporary conversion to Bergsonism" in 1910–11 (*IMH* 411). "When the evening is spread out against the sky" corresponds quite exactly to Bergson's 1889 account of "spreading time out in space" in *Time and Free Will* (133). Bergson distinguished between pure time, or duration, experienced as continuous and in flux, versus clock time, which imposes a quantitative framework on something essentially unquantifiable (Childs 68–73). Selfhood, too, may be either "pure" and undifferentiated, or "spread out" and subdivided according to the demands of social convention. Bergson argued that language itself accomplishes this division: "Little by little . . . [our conscious] states are made into objects or things; they break off not only from one another, but from ourselves" (*Time* 138). His objections to the spatialization of time and selfhood account for Eliot's negative images of clock time – "I have measured out my life with coffee spoons" (5) – and sociality: "there will be time / To prepare a face to meet the faces that you meet" (4); "When I am pinned and wriggling on the wall" (5); "as if a magic lantern threw the nerves in patterns on a screen" (6). In each of these images, the spatial "spreading out" of experience seems unnatural and even violent. Prufrock's discomfort with the passage of time (it seems to move both too quickly and too slowly for him) and with social situations thus reflects what Bergson viewed as a fundamental human predicament: the dissonance between the flow of experience and the fixed conventions of language, measurement, and social roles.

One of the most striking stylistic and perceptual characteristics of the poem is fragmentation, a phenomenon predicted by Bergson as a consequence of extension in space. Time, self, other people, and visual scenes are broken up into "a hundred visions and revisions": "I have known the eyes already, known them all . . . / I have known the arms already . . . / Arms that lie along a table, or wrap about a shawl" (*CPP* 5). Prufrock is incapable of seeing a whole person. Even his beloved is seen only as disconnected body parts. The fragmentation of his vision is reflected in the incompleteness of his speech; his thoughts begin with "and" and end with ellipses.

Prufrock's difficulty seeing other people and his tendency to make the external world into a symbol of his own state of mind suggest solipsism or, less radically, self-absorption. He, not the evening, is "like a patient etherized upon a table"; his own thinking, not the streets, is "a tedious argument / Of insidious intent" (*CPP* 3; Childs 68). Prufrock internalizes everything as a metaphor, again in a way that Bergson explains: "Consciousness . . . substitutes the symbol for the reality, or perceives the reality only through the symbol" (*Time* 128). The case of Prufrock's pin shows how this process works: "My morning coat, my collar mounting firmly to the chin, / My necktie rich and modest, but asserted by a simple pin" (*CPP* 4). Prufrock adorns himself with a little ornament intended to mark him as a dandy, at home in the sophisticated world of the drawing room. Yet soon the pin pierces him: "when I am formulated, sprawling on a pin" (5). This line transforms the pin from an object in the external world to a metaphor for his (interior) feelings. The pin, of course, is a particularly apt symbol for internalization, because it is a material object that enters the body with violence.

To call Prufrock a solipsist, however, would be too simple, for the example of the pin demonstrates his extreme sensitivity to the pressure of other people, even if he can't perceive them fully. As he puts on the pin, signifying his submission to the social codes that govern his appearance in the drawing room, he sees himself alternately as he would like to be seen and as he fears he will be judged: "[They will say: 'How his hair is growing thin!']" (4). This nervous alternation of points of view dramatizes Prufrock's fundamental bifurcation into at least two selves, as hinted by his opening address to "you and I." Whereas Bergson diagnoses a "true" self that persists in dreams and memory, overlaid by a second "social" self, both of Prufrock's selves here seem social. Soon these multiply into a series of possible roles: a crab ("I should have been a pair of ragged claws"), John the Baptist ("I have seen my head [grown slightly bald] brought in upon a platter"), Lazarus ("'I am Lazarus, come from the dead'"), and finally Polonius ("an attendant lord . . . / Almost, at times, the Fool") (5–7). Although his consideration of these roles is primarily negative ("I should have been," "I am no prophet," "No! I am not Prince Hamlet" [7]), their proliferation suggests a model of identity based on role-playing, rather than on a core self that precedes and underlies social convention.

The "Hamlet" passage (*CPP* 7) was one of the earliest portions that Eliot wrote, and he insisted on retaining it against Pound's advice, which suggests that the link between Hamlet and Prufrock was central to his conception of the poem. Hamlet is like Prufrock in experiencing "a hundred indecisions" (4), but unlike him in finally taking violent and decisive action. The primary similarity between them is that each plays multiple roles within a single drama, and keenly perceives the performative aspect of life. Prufrock's "performativity" – to use a term Eliot would not have recognized – raises questions about free will as an aspect of subjectivity: do we choose our actions or does convention choose them for us? Perhaps by not acting at all Prufrock is attempting to exert negative agency, refusing to enter into the prescribed role of "lover."

The performative aspect of "Prufrock" also raises the issue of genre: is the poem dramatic or lyric? Eliot's title indicates it is a "love song," placing it in the category of lyric, the predominant form of English romantic poetry. The romantic lyric aspires to a universal voice, avoiding historical and geographic identifiers that would mark the speaker as a specific individual in time, and preferring metaphor over narrative as a method of development. The rest of the title, however, denotes a particular person with the unique name of "J. Alfred Prufrock" (the last name has been traced to a St. Louis tailor; it also reflects the poet's undergraduate signature, T. Stearns Eliot). Prufrock may call his utterance a song, but he speaks in dramatic monologue, and his alienation is a feature of this genre. His isolated condition persists up to the last 12 lines of the poem, where rhyme and alliteration push his speech towards lyric as he listens to the mermaids singing. The final six lines squarely enter the realm of song, adopting the inclusive pronoun "we" for the first time. This "we" offers a brief transcendence from personal isolation to social communion, though "human voices" then immediately cause the speaker to "drown" (7). Eliot's closing gesture toward lyric partly explains the mysterious satisfaction that readers of "Prufrock" experience, despite the speaker's manifest failure to achieve any of his own goals.

"Portrait of a Lady," "Conversation Galante," and "La Figlia che Piange"

Along with "The Love Song of J. Alfred Prufrock," these poems were written, as Eliot affirmed, "under the sign of Laforgue" ("sous le signe de Laforgue" [*IMH* 407]). The four Laforguian poems particularly make use of dramatic speech and take a man's encounter with a woman as their core subject matter. Two painting genres also shape "Portrait," "Conversation," and "La Figlia": the portrait, and the eighteenth-century "conversation galante" scene depicting a man and woman in amorous dialogue (Roper; *IMH* 191). The shared basis of painting and drama, as foregrounded in these poems, is the act of *posing*. Like "Prufrock," these poems raise questions about our relation to convention: are our interactions, and even our feelings, scripted by social forms?

Eliot draws our attention to the dramatic element of "Portrait" at once: "Among the smoke and fog of a December afternoon / You have the scene arrange itself – as it will seem to do – / With 'I have saved this afternoon for you'" (*CPP* 8). These lines introduce a complex speaking situation and power dynamic. Though the poem has the appearance of a dialogue between a man and a woman, in fact it is the interior monologue of a man, in which he repeats or hears the woman's half of their conversation; although he addresses her as "you," we hear only what he thinks and not what he says to her. Thus he is in some sense her "stage manager," casting the woman in a particular role for his own or our benefit. He begins, however, by accusing her of trying to arrange *him* in the role of Romeo to her Juliet. As he silently resists her efforts, the speaker portrays her as an ageing socialite and patroness whose desires have been shaped by Victorian sentimentality, particularly Matthew Arnold's poem "The Buried Life" (1852). Most of her utterances can be traced back to this work, which articulates the idea of a "buried" interiority only accessible through intimate or romantic friendship. For his part, he makes her belief in intimacy look ridiculous: he reaches for his hat as she claims that "I am always sure that you understand . . . / Sure that across the gulf you reach your hand" (*CPP* 9). He, too, has an idea of interiority, but it's quite different from hers: "Inside my brain a dull tom-tom begins / Absurdly hammering a prelude of its own . . ." (9).[2] Their struggle takes place along at least three different axes: along gender lines (as in "Conversation Galante"); between generations, with modernity defining itself by mocking the Victorian; and geographically, between the center of culture and its periphery. Though Eliot became associated with the "establishment," he began his career as a provincial outsider, a disadvantage he struggled self-consciously to overcome. "Portrait," begun in January 1910, dates from that early period.

Like "Prufrock," "Portrait" moves between contrasting outdoor and indoor locations, beginning in the Lady's "darkened room" (*CPP* 8), then passing outside briefly for a masculine interlude: "Let us take the air, in a tobacco trance . . . / Then sit for half an hour and drink our bocks" (9). This is in December (section I); the speaker sees her next in the spring (section II), when again he escapes her company for a more masculine outdoor activity: "You will see me any morning in the park / Reading the comics and the sporting page" (10). At this point he hears "a street piano, mechanical and tired . . . / Recalling things that other people have desired. / Are these ideas right or wrong?" (10). This is the "overwhelming question" of "Portrait," to which the speaker returns at the end: "Not knowing what to feel or if I understand / Or whether wise or foolish, tardy or too soon . . ." (11). While the Lady has Arnold's "The Buried Life" to tell her what to feel, the speaker has no such guide, and he wonders whether feelings themselves might be a matter of acting or "arranging." His crisis occurs in section III, in October (almost a year after their first meeting) when she finally realizes that his feelings *do not* "relate" to hers. The confrontation reduces him to "a dancing bear." Ultimately, the question of what to feel becomes one of performance: "Would she not have the advantage, after all? /. . . . And should I have the right to smile?" (11). Their relationship resolves into a struggle between poses competing to be the more "successful."

"Conversation Galante," based on Laforgue's "Autre complainte de Lord Pierrot," takes a lighter approach to the conflict of wits between a man and a woman. Eliot has borrowed Laforgue's dialogue form (with the last line of each stanza devoted to a response), but reversed the genders of the speakers, so that the male "I" is the more voluble and romantic, while the woman delivers deflating one-line replies. This poem, written in 1909, shows Laforgue's raw influence in the flippant tone of the interlocutors, their tongue-in-cheek discussion of the moon ("It may be Prester John's balloon"), reference to the "absolute," and humorously unpoetic polysyllabic rhymes, such as "vacuity" and "refer to me" (*CPP* 19).

"La Figlia che Piange," Italian for "the girl who weeps," departs from the ironic tone of the other poems of the volume, suggesting an autobiographical incident to some readers, although the presumed date of composition, late in 1911, would rule out any reference to Eliot's graduate-school flame Emily Hale. The speaker is not dramatized as a character (as in the other Laforgue poems), but rather as a director of a scene. Derek Roper associates the poem with the late Victorian portrait genre depicting a woman in a garden, and identifies the speaker as an interpreter of such a painting, who feels sympathy for her and constructs a simple narrative of betrayal to explain her expression (227). Placed at the end of the *Prufrock* volume, "La Figlia" parallels "Prufrock" by coming to rest in the past conditional: "And I wonder how they should have been together! / I should have lost a gesture and a pose" (*CPP* 20). Thus the volume's loose narrative of romantic disengagement, as well as its thematic question of whether feelings are spontaneous or staged, are brought to a close in a fittingly inconclusive way.

"Preludes," "Rhapsody on a Windy Night," and "Morning at the Window"

These city poems form a group with similar works found in *Inventions of the March Hare*, such as the "First Caprice in North Cambridge," "Fourth Caprice in Montparnasse," and "Interlude in London," titles that reveal the varied origins of Eliot's urban landscape. The prelude and rhapsody, along with the caprice and interlude, refer to musical forms: single-movement works that each explore a mood or musical problem, played either in a series or singly. Frédéric Chopin's piano compositions in these forms were widely performed in the nineteenth century, as suggested by the Lady in "Portrait." Eliot's musical allusion indicates that the focus of each poem is a state of mind, atmosphere, or impression rather than a determinate event or character.

The title of "Preludes" additionally points to a thematic concern with waiting and expectation: the "you" of section III waits, the cab horse "steams and stamps" (I), the "conscience of the blackened street" is "impatient" (IV), and even the times of day are described as if preparing themselves for something ("the winter evening settles down," "the morning comes to consciousness") (*CPP* 12–13). But waiting for what? Laforgue's pessimistic "Préludes Autobiographiques," which undoubtedly provided another model for Eliot's poem, describes the future as an "éternullité" (Laforgue 20). The four preludes cycle through transitional times of day: evening and morning rush hours (sections I and II), nighttime before dawn (III), and back to evening rush hour. The passage of time appears futile and without goal, an idea that the closing lines also imply: "The worlds revolve like ancient women / Gathering fuel in vacant lots" (*CPP* 13). Bergson's influence clearly underlies this negative representation of time, measured out and reduced to a meaningless, mechanical repetition. Similarly, "His soul stretched tight across the skies" (13) literalizes the Bergsonian idea of extension, and echoes the opening of "Prufrock" (completed three months before Prelude IV). As in "Prufrock," fragmentation is pervasive: the day is divided into hours, persons into hands, feet, eyes, and "short square fingers stuffing pipes" (13); the city into "a thousand furnished rooms" (12); and the point of view disorientingly shifts from "you" (section I), to "one" (II), to another "you" in III, and then in IV quickly moves from "His soul," to "I," and back to "you." "Preludes" achieves one of the most condensed and sensuously apprehended representations of fragmentation in modern literature, without clearly attributing a cause.

Coinciding in the same poem with Eliot's abstract critique of Western metaphysics is his densely detailed, morbidly sensitive recording of urban life, presumably based on experience as well as his reading of Philippe's *Bubu of Montparnasse*, the unvarnished narrative of a prostitute who contracts syphilis. The only character who emerges clearly from the fragmented impressions of "Preludes" is the "you" of section III, her gender indicated by the curling papers in her hair and by her passive, sexualized pose ("You lay on your back, and waited" [*CPP* 12]). Her patient, but by no means heroic suffering, as well as her location in a "furnished room," are reminiscent of many passages in *Bubu* ("there was the unmade bed where the two bodies had left their impress of brownish sweat upon the worn sheets – this bed of hotel rooms, where the bodies are dirty and the souls as well" [49]). Like Philippe, Eliot treats the exploitation of women as a gritty reality, and simultaneously as a moral problem for the "conscience." (The speaker may be implicating himself in the situation by describing her in this intimate way.) "Preludes" does not distinguish between the metaphysical and the social causes of alienation; both contribute to the same "vision of the street" (*CPP* 13). "Morning at the Window" (1914) conveys a similar vision, though perhaps with less sympathy for the "damp souls of housemaids," who are seen from above rather than at eye level (16).

"Rhapsody on a Windy Night" may represent the culmination of Eliot's Bergsonism, or else his repudiation of it, but either way is considered his most explicit engagement with the French philosopher (Childs 50–51). Bergson's distinction between pure and practical memory informs the opening action, in which

> lunar incantations
> Dissolve the floors of memory
> And all its clear relations
> Its divisions and precisions (*CPP* 14)

The street lamp operates as the selective, practical process of recollection, while the moon sheds light on all the heterogeneous contents of unconscious memory ("a crowd of twisted things" [14]). Though the moon prevails temporarily, the lamplight of selective memory reasserts itself at the end when the speaker catches sight of his house number, which draws him back into practical life. "The last twist of the knife" (16) likely refers to Bergson's account of how the practical memory "presents nothing thicker than the edge of a blade to actual experience, into which it . . . penetrate[s]" (*Matter* 130). The negative tone of the poem, however, is difficult to interpret, whether as frustration with Bergson or with the difficulty of accessing pure memory. Like "Preludes," "Rhapsody" revolves around the ambiguous figure of the prostitute, treated with a mix of revulsion and sympathy: she is an image picked out by the lamp on the city street, then she becomes the moon ("A washed-out smallpox cracks her face / Her hand twists a paper rose, / That smells of dust and eau de Cologne"), and she leaves behind "female smells in shuttered rooms" that are part of the speaker's pure "reminiscence" (*CPP* 15).

In terms of the structure of *Prufrock and Other Observations*, "Rhapsody" reaches farthest into the surreal "spaces of the dark," into memory and irrationality (*CPP* 14). Picking up Prufrock's foray through "muttering retreats," "Rhapsody" brings the protagonist (or antihero) of the volume to an empty street at midnight, lit by lamps that actually "sputter" and "mutter" (15). This is the journey into consciousness. In the other narrative of the volume, concluded with "La Figlia che Piange," the protagonist anxiously negotiates interpersonal relationships and social codes of behavior.

"The *Boston Evening Transcript*," "Aunt Helen," "Cousin Nancy," "Mr. Apollinax," and "Hysteria"

The short poems that fill out the rest of the *Prufrock* volume were written in England in 1915, after Eliot's departure from graduate school, and they reflect his reaction to polite Cambridge (Massachusetts) society. They correspond in style to the satirical portraits that Ezra Pound – now Eliot's close collaborator – was writing for *Lustra* (1916). The object of their critique is social, rather than metaphysical or personal, but they share with the other poems of *Prufrock* a resentment or resistance to convention.[3] In each satire, the disorderly, subterranean energies of modernity and sexuality rise up against genteel New England culture: "evening" and "appetites" in "The *Boston Evening Transcript*" (*CPP* 16), the dalliance of the housemaid and footman in "Aunt Helen," smoking and "modern dances" in "Cousin Nancy" (17), and the Dionysian, priapic Mr. Apollinax, who forever unseats the hegemony of teacups in the house of Harvard "Professor Channing-Cheetah" (18). Mr. Apollinax is based on the British analytic philosopher Bertrand Russell, who visited Harvard in 1914 and may have been instrumental in dispelling Eliot's Bergsonism.

Apollinax's laughing "like an irresponsible foetus" (*CPP* 18) connects him with the laughter in "Hysteria," but while Apollinax's vitality merely threatens propriety, this prose poem represents sexuality as consuming and terrifying. Hysteria was a common diagnosis of women in the late nineteenth century for nervous anxiety thought to be brought on by sexual dissatisfaction. (Since there was no corresponding diagnosis for men experiencing emotional distress, the term "shell shock" was coined in World War I to describe symptoms of trauma, a condition explored in *The Waste Land*.) Here, the male speaker becomes "involved" in the woman's literally hysterical laughter – her mouth looks to him like a devouring womb or vagina – until it seems that he himself is suffering from hysteria (19). This work offers a medical or psycho-analytic, rather than philosophical, explanation of the perceptual fragmentation that is everywhere in the poems of *Prufrock*. "Hysteria" also identifies sexuality, rather than social convention, as the primary challenge to the integrity of the self. Between "Conversation Galante" of 1909 and "Hysteria" of 1915, each representing a conversation between a man and a woman, Eliot's first book "observes" the changing meaning of "love" from the end of the Victorian era to the beginning of the modern, Freudian, postwar world.

NOTES

1   See T. S. ELIOT AND THE SYMBOLIST CITY and YES AND NO: ELIOT AND WESTERN PHILOSOPHY.

2   The reference to the tom-tom has particularly interested critics for the way it seems to align the speaker's mentality with "primitive" cultures, a subject of artistic and anthropological interest at the turn of the century. See MIND, MYTH, AND CULTURE: ELIOT AND ANTHROPOLOGY.

3   On this resentment, see also DISAMBIVALENT QUATRAINS.

REFERENCES AND FURTHER READING

Bergson, Henri. *Matter and Memory*. Trans. Nancy Margaret Paul and W. Scott Palmer. New York: Macmillan, 1911.

——. *Time and Free Will: An Essay on the Immediate Data of Consciousness*. Trans. F. L. Pogson. London: Allen, 1913.

Brooker, Jewel Spears. *T. S. Eliot: The Contemporary Reviews*. New York: Cambridge UP, 2004.

Childs, Donald. *From Philosophy to Poetry: T. S. Eliot's Study of Knowledge and Experience*. New York: Palgrave, 2001.

Christ, Carol. *Victorian and Modern Poetics*. Chicago: U of Chicago P, 1984.

Crawford, Robert. *The Savage and the City in the Work of T. S. Eliot*. New York: Oxford UP, 1987.

Gray, Piers. *T. S. Eliot's Intellectual and Poetic Development, 1909–1922*. Atlantic Highlands, NJ: Humanities, 1982.

James, William. *A Pluralistic Universe. Writings 1902–1910*. New York: Library of America, 1987.

Laforgue, Jules. *Selected Poems*. Trans. Graham Martin. New York: Penguin, 1998.

Langbaum, Robert. *The Poetry of Experience*. New York: Random, 1957.

Lowe, Peter. "Prufrock in St. Petersburg: The Presence of Dostoyevsky's *Crime and Punishment* in T. S. Eliot's 'The Love Song of J. Alfred Prufrock.'" *Journal of Modern Literature* 28 (2005): 1–24.

Manganiello, Dominic. *T. S. Eliot and Dante*. New York: St. Martin's, 1989.

Marvell, Andrew. "To His Coy Mistress." *The Complete Poems*. Ed. Elizabeth Story Donno. Harmondsworth: Penguin, 1972. 50–51.

Mayer, John T. *T. S. Eliot's Silent Voices*. New York: Oxford UP, 1989.

Moody, A. D. *Thomas Stearns Eliot, Poet*. New York: Cambridge UP, 1994.

Philippe, Charles-Louis. *Bubu of Montparnasse*. Intro. T. S. Eliot. New York: Shakespeare, 1951.

Roper, Derek. "T. S. Eliot's 'La Figlia che Piange': A Picture without a Frame." *Essays in Criticism* 52 (2002): 222–34.

Sigg, Eric. *The American T. S. Eliot: A Study of the Early Writings*. New York: Cambridge UP, 1989.

Symons, Arthur. *The Symbolist Movement in Literature*. London: Constable, 1908.

11

Disambivalent Quatrains

Jeffrey M. Perl

Eliot's career is often assumed to fall into two phases. The break between these is said, for convenience, to occur with Eliot's announcement that he was "classicist in literature, royalist in politics, and anglo-catholic in religion" (*FLA* vii), though it is understood that the transition – his conversion from one sort of Eliot to another – could not have been so abrupt. While sensitive to the dissonance in Eliot's writing, we tend to assume that his discordant tones are sounded not simultaneously but in succession. His career, however, does not divide comfortably into phases – and certainly, an agnostic, materialist, avant-garde phase was not followed by its inverse. His conversion was an expression, one among many, of unresolved ambivalence. At different times he responded in different ways, but his ambivalence was constant and consistent. He appears to have wanted, sometimes desperately, to feel "concentrated in purpose" (*CPP* 62). Occasionally, temporarily, he would succeed. But he was liable, even after 1927, to turn and turn again. "Because I do not hope to turn again" is the first line of his post-conversion poem *Ash-Wednesday* (60).

A better way of understanding Eliot's ambivalence is to read his prose in the context of his poetry, and his poetry in the context of his prose. It is a teacherly commonplace that when, for example, Eliot was most insistent in his critical essays on maintaining classical standards in verse, his own verse was at its most romantic. This syndrome of Eliot's is regarded by many as a ploy. He was not called Old Possum for nothing: Ezra Pound, who gave him the name, meant that his staid demeanor was an act. But the contradictions between Eliot's poetry and prose are less a question of camouflage (or protective coloring) than they are of his enduring need to have things both ways. Of this need Eliot was not unaware. Wavering line by line, *Ash-Wednesday* solicits grace for ambivalent converts – those "who chose thee and oppose thee, / Those who are torn on the horn between season and season, time and time" (*CPP* 65). Eliot learned to live with his ambivalence, and eventually, in the interplay of voices of *Four Quartets*, its poles or terms appear untraumatically together on the page.

A Companion to T. S. Eliot, First Edition. Edited by David E. Chinitz.
© 2014 John Wiley & Sons, Ltd. Published 2014 by John Wiley & Sons, Ltd.

These terms or poles are not easily formulated – or rather, the formulations that proliferate are misleading. One pole is best defined in connection with Eliot's Harvard papers. These philosophical texts have been characterized in diverse ways, but anyone who has had access to them (most are unpublished) needs to account for both their skeptical rhetoric and the conventionalist upshot of their arguments.[1] Eliot calmly presupposes that a superfluity of facts exists to support almost any understanding of any object or state of affairs. The outcome of this alarming premise might be that "anything goes," but Eliot concludes, instead, that we must accept what "goes" now. The so-called real world is constructed, rather than found or discovered or revealed; and it is constructed over time, which means that wholesale alterations of it may endanger reality per se. Eliot takes for granted that all constructs are unsatisfactory; they are vague, approximate, merely practical, and self-contradictory. He would not retain any construct out of affection for it (as a conservative might) or out of belief in it (as a positivist would). Eliot would retain and develop constructs already in use, rather than introduce any "noticeable change," because "reality," as his dissertation insists, "is a convention" (*KE* 98). If we want to have reality, a real world, at all, we must accept (which is to say, suffer) the unsatisfactory conventions already in place.

However radical his premises, then, Eliot's conclusions are a bowler hat and umbrella. Since every explanation is correct from some viewpoint and incorrect from another, a philosophy has value to the extent that it returns us to the understanding of reality with which we began. To be true a proposition must be nearly tautological: it must cohere with truths already accredited. Hence, all knowledge depends on a prior "*faith*." These claims were made many years before Eliot's conversion – faith did not yet mean for him adherence to religious doctrines. Faith meant "intending" the same objects as are conventionally intended by others.[2]

Subjectivity and objectivity – self and world – have reality only in relation to each other: "The self, we find, seems to depend upon a world which in turn depends upon it; and nowhere, I repeat, can we find anything original or ultimate. And the self depends as well upon other selves; it is not given as a direct experience, but is an interpretation of experience by interaction with other selves" (*KE* 146). Everything must depend concurrently upon everything else (nothing is "original or ultimate," irrelative or irrelevant) for there to *be* anything at all. The only reality is "continuous reality" – a web reinforced by its infinite complexity and yet, for all that, "fragile and insecure" (156, 162). Why insecure? Because no real world per se exists. The self-denying ordinance of conventionalism, its denial of unshared truths and private languages, is itself denied in the closing chapters of Eliot's dissertation: the real world that we intend together, he adds there, is fragile because the "things of which we are collectively certain, we may say our common formulae, are certainly not true. What makes a real world is difference of opinion. . . . All significant truths are private truths. As they become public they cease to become truths; they become facts" (165). In the rift between truths and mere facts was lush soil for Eliot's ambivalence. If a soul maintains its private truths against established facts, then shared realities will be to that extent weakened. But if a soul disowns its truths in favor of established facts, shared realities will be no less destabilized. It is the investment of private significance in public realities that gives them what power they have. Therefore, each soul intends realities that (compared with its own) are trivial and defective. Otherwise there would be no common reality – no *world* – at all.

Small wonder, then, that Prufrock fears to eat a peach. "Do I dare to eat a peach?" intensifies, rather than undercuts, his prior question: "Do I dare / Disturb the universe?" (*CPP* 7, 4–5). *Prufrock and Other Observations* is not a book of philosophical poetry, but its avenues "follow," Prufrock says, "like a tedious argument / Of insidious intent" (3). The poems that Eliot wrote in his twenties recoil from philosophical arguments he found compelling around the same time. The upshot of philosophical conventionalism – the upholding of rules (against exceptions) and of common attitudes (against private conviction) – is hell on earth for souls as cut off and peculiar as the central intelligences of these poems. Forces of hearty objectivity, meanwhile, are on the move across the page:

> Miss Nancy Ellicott
> Strode across the hills and broke them
> . . . .
> Miss Nancy Ellicott smoked
> And danced all the modern dances (17)

Cousin Nancy, Cousin Harriet, the female interlocutors of "Prufrock," "Hysteria," "Portrait of a Lady," and "Conversation Galante," the consumers of steak in "Preludes," the talking street lamps of "Rhapsody on a Windy Night" – these all fit comfortably in their time and place because the "common formulae" satisfy their personal, or personified, requirements. Prufrock and other speakers in these poems are uncomfortable because they must satisfy, not their own needs, but the common need for norms. Their own needs are too unusual for any common formula to accommodate.

In *Prufrock and other Observations*, consensual reality is overbearing, brisk, complacent, superficial, dense, bland, "indifferent and imperious"; or rather, its representatives in the poems are (*CPP* 20). Their advantage over more diffident personae is power – the power that their rapport with consensual reality confers. A Prufrock may condescend to them privately ("The readers of the *Boston Evening Transcript* / Sway in the wind like a field of ripe corn" [16]) but in any encounter is left "wriggling on the wall" (5) by those holding "sway" – the personae with social skills, steaks at six, and unambivalently conventional beliefs. Eliot was an ambivalent conventionalist: while persuaded that the maintenance of convention is imperative, the conventions of his own era and society were for him unbearable. As a consequence, he neither had his cake nor ate it. Without such reward as either conventionality or unconventionality can bring, he paid the price of both; and his first book shows the strain. Only one poem in it intimates a kind of resolution:

> I mount the steps and ring the bell, turning
> Wearily, as one would turn to nod good-bye to La Rochefoucauld,
> If the street were time and he at the end of the street,
> And I say, "Cousin Harriet, here is the *Boston Evening Transcript*." (16–17)

The speaker affiliates with the august dead to separate himself – urbanely, wearily – from relationships of mere blood and place, class and time. He nods conspiratorially, almost romantically, at an associate too continental or irregular for the company of honest provincials like his cousin. The reader may understand the gesture as nostalgic, but the nostalgia is of a special type. Glancing warmly over one shoulder, the speaker shows a cold shoulder momentarily to Cousin Harriet at the door. His nostalgia is passively aggressive, an evasion of obvious (in favor of elective) affinities, a momentary escape from unwanted fellowship in a community whose appetite is for skimming transcripts of the lives of others.

The speaker in this poem is poised between two communities, or communities of two kinds. He terms them, generically, "others" and "some." "Some" have "appetites of life" that quicken in the evening; "others" have the local news, sport, and weather reports as substitutes. This "some" includes La Rochefoucauld (1613–80), maker of maxims still fresh in 1915, plus the speaker, who compares the poem's "others" with "ripe corn." The "others," to whom the speaker has blood ties, are *cornlike* in that they "sway," but only with the wind; and *corny* in that their language, thought, and way of life are moving on from ripe to rancid. These two generic categories embrace characters residing outside the poem as well. Pound, Wyndham Lewis, Ford Madox Ford, members of the *Egoist* circle, and advanced practitioners of the arts (James Joyce, for example) known to Eliot as Pound mentors or Pound protégés, were among, or would soon be among, Eliot's exclusive group of "some." Included also was a large but by no means comprehensive contingent of the august dead, and in their writings – as in the company of breathing modernists – Eliot took refuge from his "others."

Fellowship with backward-looking innovators – membership in a league of *cognoscenti* whose doings, Pound said, comprised the "real history" of their time – afforded Eliot a social remedy for his metaphysical dilemma. In a sense, the problem had always been sociological: Eliot defined reality as a convention, and conventions are social constructions. Philosophical conventionalism tends to produce a laissez-faire attitude toward conventions. Any set may underwrite an effective "real world," so long as it is widely and deeply enough accepted. But the modernists with whom Eliot was affiliated regarded their culture in anything but laissez-faire terms: in its modern form, the West was for them decadent – untrue to itself, fraudulent, and (as evidenced by the Great War) suicidally deranged. Eliot, on the evidence of his poetry from these years, was relieved to conclude (though temporarily) that conventionalism was not, did not have to be, yoked to majoritarianism and "the error of pure contemporaneity" (*TCC* 119). This relief he expressed, in his *Poems* (1920) quatrains, as indignation. His poems of 1917–19 are resentful of the social order that, in the love songs of *Prufrock*, he had tried grimly to embrace.[3] In order to appreciate the tone of these quatrains, it must be heard as an aftertone. A man who had felt "pinned and wriggling on the wall" (*CPP* 5), freed now, as if by Cavaliers, to join them, confronts the Giants (mostly female, some of them cousins) who had bullied him, then taunts them in daring strophes and rhyme.

The quatrain poems exhibit, they make an exhibition of, a sudden want of Eliot's characteristic ambivalence. Not that these poems are unambiguous; after nearly a century's effort, criticism has yet to disambiguate them. What they are, for lack of a proper word, is "disambivalent." Uptightly suave, brusquely proficient, satirically dismissive of other perspectives and human beings, these exercises in unfree, epigrammatic verse are the counterparts to essays – later disparaged by Eliot as arrogant, vehement, cocksure, and rude – about the "dissociation of sensibility" and related kinds of decadence (*SE* 247). One of these essays, written the same year as his earliest quatrain poem, gives assurance that "the coming of a Satirist" ("no man of genius is rarer") would prove the vitality of "formal rhymed verse" (*TCC* 189). Then the genius himself adds: "there is no freedom in art" (184). This manifesto, "Reflections on *vers libre*," heralded a group program – the program of a group of two. Years later, Pound explained, in Eliot's journal the *Criterion*, that "at a particular date in a particular room, two authors . . . decided that . . . floppiness had gone too far and that some counter-current must be set going. . . . Remedy prescribed 'Emaux et Camées' (or the Bay State Hymn Book)" ("Harold Monro" 590). The sloppiness of free verse was to be swept aside in favor of Théophile Gautier's intimidatingly accomplished quatrains as a standard for American avant-garde verse. The reference to New England hymnals was an elbow in Eliot's Puritan side, and Pound had a point. With the exception of "The Hippopotamus," titled as an homage to Gautier's "L'Hippopotame," Eliot's quatrains are more Bay State than French, omitting rhyme in the first and third lines of each stanza, as American hymns, with relative insouciance of style, were free to do.

Apart from their resistance to formal "floppiness," the *Poems* (1920) quatrains devolve from patterns set in "The *Boston Evening Transcript*." The personae, who are again no more than names, divide once more into "some" and "others." The speaker in "Whispers of Immortality," for example, postulates an "our lot" (meaning "us guys," laddishly; or "our team") consisting of himself, John Webster, and John Donne. These Jacobeans, however, differ functionally from La Rochefoucauld in the earlier collection. Though he died as they did in the seventeenth century, he survives in a tenseless conditional – "If the street were time and he at the end of the street" (*CPP* 17) – while they subsist only in perfect-tense verbs. Not simply dead, Donne and Webster are *thematically* dead and were "much possessed by death" even when alive. Unduped by skin (l. 2) or breasts (l. 3) or lips (l. 4), in life they saw through face to skull, and flesh to bones. Still, Donne and Webster found bones arousing, and bones appear to have a sex life of their own. Marrow suffers anguish; skeletons, ague; and bones, fever – a fevered longing to be seized and penetrated by "tightening . . . lusts" of "thought" (*CPP* 32–33). Reason too thus has its eros and "clings" to *corpora* of the bookish dead – but also to a body among the living. The "Abstract Entities" of idealism are described as

satellites of Grishkin's "charm," a "bust" so formidable that the verb used for this rotation is "circumambulate" (a term reminiscent of Magellan). Unrelenting double meanings leave the reader guessing what is and is not metaphorical.

"Expert beyond experience" (l. 12) is reassurance that Donne was not a practicing
necrophiliac, but there is no guarantee that the speaker may not be so. Its title situates the poem generically as rumor (and "Immortality" minus one letter would make
it an allegation). The speaker acknowledges that "Grishkin is nice" – a disingenuous
expression of ambivalence (as the exclamation point in line 6 disingenuously expresses
surprise). But loath himself to circumambulate, the speaker is drawn to "breastless
creatures" (of no specified sex or even species). Invitingly, they lean "backward,"
though not on loveseats, in their graves: "our lot crawls between dry ribs / To keep
our metaphysics warm" (*CPP* 33). Books have spines, not ribs. "Ribs" may thus evoke
shelves, as in a library; if so, "metaphysics" should bring to mind what dictionaries
say it means. But the rule throughout this poem has been double-entendre – body
words suggesting bookish words, and vice versa – or in one case, triple-entendre,
where "balls" means the "eyes" of the cultural past (l. 5). We may wonder, then, what
bits of a warm body we are invited to imagine as "metaphysics" (l. 32). In any case,
we are asked to read love for the past as lust for the dead. Sublimation is not what
this poem enacts.

From a guarded nod in "The *Boston Evening Transcript*" at a ghost from the *ancien
régime* we come, in this later poem, to a disclosure of nostalgia so erotically charged
as to be virtually necrophilia. So much for "our lot," the personae that "Whispers of
Immortality" esteems. The personae disesteemed are one louche cosmopolitan – her
name Grishkin (*griskin* with a Russian accent) means "the lean part of the loin of a
bacon pig" – and her avatar, a fast and savage Amazon cat. These two differ from
Cousin Harriet, another disesteemed persona, in that she lacks, while they embody,
"appetites of life" (*CPP* 16). Between Grishkin's skeleton and skin is the "promise"
of "bliss" – for those for whom mascara, "effluence of cat," and rendezvous in pieds-
à-terre are compelling. (Speakers in the *Prufrock* volume are uncompelled by "female
smells" and "shaking . . . breasts" [15, 19].) Thus the opposition between "them" and
"us" in *Poems* (1920) is not one between intellect and flesh, or culture and nature, or
past and present, or religious and secular; otherwise the valences assigned to contrasting personae and pursuits could not, as they so remarkably do, reverse while remaining
vehement. The terms of reference for "us" and "them" appear versatile and slippery,
even ambivalent – but what they are, most accurately, is unfamiliar: unfamiliar, that
is, in the reader's context.

These poems construct a context of their own by which ours is to be exposed, then
judged; and they do so by disrupting expectation. In "Mr. Eliot's Sunday Morning
Service," "The Hippopotamus," and "A Cooking Egg," the speaker condescends to
those (Origen the heresiarch, the Church, and Pipit, respectively) deficient in "appetites of life," just as the speaker does to Cousin Harriet in *Prufrock and Other Observations*. In "Whispers of Immortality," however, the speaker aligns himself with those
whose appetite is for the dead. What are appetites of life if necrophilia (metaphorical

or otherwise) is among them? And what manner of vice – these questions are related – lends itself this earnestly to priggishness?

> The ladies of the corridor
>   Find themselves involved, disgraced,
> Call witness to their principles
>   And deprecate the lack of taste (*CPP* 26)

– as if sex workers "sate upright" like a Pipit or a Boston Eliot (26). But the occasion of disgrace in "Sweeney Erect" is the "hysteria" of an epileptic (after sex with a rough client), and the "principles" to which the "ladies . . . / Call witness" are those of a prostitutes' moral code. The decadent and prim, the appetitive and theological, are not counterposed; they are conflated in these poems. Not only do "Abstract Entities" orbit Grishkin's "charm," her "bust / Gives promise of pneumatic bliss" (33) – an exact rendering of the Christian promise of salvation (*pneuma* meaning "spirit" in Greek). Moreover, where one might expect an overlap of figuration between Grishkin and the hippopotamus (since "mating time" is key to both, and both are "merely flesh and blood" [30]), the overlap in their two poems is between Grishkin and the Church. Grishkin is compared, for a quarter of her poem's length, with a jaguar that can hunt while "couched," and in "The Hippopotamus" the Church is said to "sleep and feed at once" (33, 31). In contrast to both, the hippo's "day / Is passed in sleep; at night he hunts" (30) – a bohemian's schedule, apparently; but at least someone in these poems is not poised to hunt, kill, and consume prey around the clock.

"Burbank with a Baedeker: Bleistein with a Cigar" makes this point clearer, though in Latin: *"Tra-la-la-la-la-la-laire – nil nisi divinum stabile est; caetera fumus"* (*CPP* 23). "Only the divine endures; the rest is smoke," this epigraph begins, but what can "divine" mean in the context of "tra-la"? "Divine," as in the *Divine Comedy*? The divine Sarah Bernhardt? In 1919 the tango was divine, sublime. The long epigraph to "Burbank," in burlesquing superscriptions to Psalms (*xxxiv* in particular), intimates it is a psalm itself. "The Hippopotamus," whose second epigraph situates it, comically, as an epistle of St. Paul's, rhymes Peter's "rock" with "nervous shock" (and "odd" with "God") (30). The incarnation of divinity as frivolity in these poems – "Mr. Eliot's Sunday Morning Service" rhymes "Paraclete" and "feet" (34) – suggests a line of argument. To say, as Eliot's dissertation does, that "reality is a convention" is not to say that talk about reality is not grave. "Whispers of Immortality" offers terms useful for this discussion: convention as bones, and fashion as flesh. Flesh is "nice" but transient, superficial, cruel; bones are (like quatrains) dry but solid, always there, dependable. Fashion, whose charms are novelty, evanescence, and distraction, can be mistaken for reality – which is to say, convention – once reality is understood as conventional. But (borrowing terms, now, from "Sweeney Erect") fashion is convention "of the corridor." Fashions move on in haste, as prostitutes and their clientele do, yet can appear sublime by recalling conventions of sublimity (in lieu of sublime passion, erotic commerce; in lieu of sublime justice, peer pressure). The crisis of the present is that leading institutions follow fashion, not convention. The City of God apes the City of Man. The "True Church" (in "The Hippopotamus"), romantic transcendentalism ("Sweeney Erect"), Enlightenment idealism ("Whispers of Immortality"), *Golden Bough* ritual and myth ("Sweeney Among the Nightingales") – all are examples of failed religion or of failures to substitute for failed religions. In "Burbank," the dilettante's church of the holy Baedeker is despised, and in the same breath Jews like Bleistein are disdained for not practicing (let alone teaching) "the seven laws" (24) – rules of basic decency – set down for gentiles by the Talmud.

On grounds surprisingly comparable, Eliot's family religion – scholastic Protestantism – is rejected with contempt in "Mr. Eliot's Sunday Morning Service." The Mr. Eliot of this poem is less likely Thomas Stearns than his grandfather William Greenleaf, founder of the "Eliot Seminary." In either case, the poem frowns equally on Sweeney and on the "sapient sutlers of the Lord," religious intellectuals who preach far over Sweeney's head (*CPP* 33). Eliot's "Service" opens with an erudite sermon ("Polyphiloprogenitive / . . . Superfetation of τὸ ἕν") and ends by juxtaposing an ignoramus with scholastics who neglect (but should edify) him:

> Sweeney shifts from ham to ham
> Stirring the water in his bath.
> The masters of the subtle schools
> Are controversial, polymath. (34)

But who is Sweeney to shame this intelligentsia, and why does he figure so prominently (three titles, five pieces) in the Eliot corpus? Based on the "demon barber" of horror fiction, a Boston Irishman who gave Eliot boxing lessons, and a murderer who drowned his victim in her bath (near the Eliots' London flat), Sweeney finds himself naked in the "Service" of "Mr. Eliot," and erect in the company of Ralph Waldo Emerson. (Emerson knew William Greenleaf Eliot – both were Unitarian ministers – and dubbed him "Saint of the West.") "Sweeney Erect" figures its hero as subhuman or mechanical – jackknife, sickle, cyclops, ape – but equally disdains Emerson for his naive anthropology. Interrupting (even the syntax of) the narrative, the quatrain in parentheses is anything but parenthetical:

> (The lengthened shadow of a man
> Is history, said Emerson
> Who had not seen the silhouette
> Of Sweeney straddled in the sun.) (26)

Emerson's innocence was culpable. Understanding little of *Homo erectus*, Emerson and his successors – the "enervate" clerisy of Mr. Eliot's "Service" (34) – are offered pulpits from which to preach inspirationally about the higher primates. Eliot said of Wordsworth that he was innocent of feelings apart from those in which he specialized ("Reflections I" 119); and of Matthew Arnold that, while "the horror and the glory" of life were "denied" him, "he knew something of the boredom" (*UPUC* 98–99). Horror and glory are paired on one side of this divide; boredom stands apart on the other. Eliot connected boredom with the "nearly soulless," the "never born and never dead," drifting in the foyer of Dante's hell. Compared with their liminal condition, even horror is a blessing: "damnation itself is an immediate form of salvation – of salvation from the ennui of modern life" (*SE* 379). The *Poems* (1920) quatrains are more concerned to distinguish tedium and frivolity from horror and glory ("Grishkin is nice," but skeletons are nicer) than to distinguish glory from horror, because boredom (defined as "cheery automatism") is worse than evil. "[I]t is better, in a paradoxical way" – so Eliot judged Baudelaire's Satanism – "to do evil than to do nothing" (380). Good and evil are paired against the decadent norm; still, these poems by no means idealize innocence. Decadence couples readily with sophistication, but here just as easily with naiveté. Princess Volupine (consumptive disingénue) and Burbank (Jamesian naif) "were together" (in her "shuttered barge"), "and he fell" (*CPP* 23–24). Meanwhile, Princess Volupine couples too with Sir Ferdinand Klein, whose surname rhymes with an identically placed word – "Declines" – eight lines earlier (a record for rhyming distance, but unmistakably intended). Thus the princess hooks up, in the course of eight quatrains, with a stock decadent and a stock naif. Burbank is paired as well with Bleistein, of course, the colon in the poem's title implying a parallel or even equation (contrast would require a semicolon or comma). The Baedeker of the title couples with a cigar, the iconographical attribute of a Jewish cynic, watchful and worldly, like Bleistein from Vienna – and given this association with Freud, Burbank's guidebook may suggest voyeurism more than sightseeing.

Whatever it may be, then, the opposite of decadence must be the opposite of innocence as well. The presence of this uncorrupted norm is attested by a short list of personae: Doris, the prostitute with "broad feet," who brings spirits to a colleague spurned for tasteless epilepsy (*CPP* 26); "the Baptized God" with "unoffending feet" and the Umbrian painter who "designed" him; a swarm of "bees / With hairy bellies" that performs (unlike the clergy) their "office of the epicene" enthusiastically (34); three from the literary past (Sidney, Webster, Donne) who kept "Honour" and "metaphysics" warm (27, 33); and palpably, one hippopotamus. To this list should be added the occasional reader (Pound, Lewis, Joyce, the Woolfs) who has understood the epigraphs without help. What does this varied cohort share? *The Waste Land* offers Eliot's best response: "the hand expert with sail and oar" – a hand masterly with culture's most elegant devices, trustworthy with the reader's "heart" ("your heart would have responded / Gaily, when invited" is in the second person), and calm but candidly erotic (*CPP* 49–50).

In comparison with this image, the like of which is barely prefigured in *Poems* (1920), other images of human conduct suggest incompetence, boredom, chaos, exhaustion. The conspirators of "Sweeney Among the Nightingales" are less murderous than they are clueless. The "person in the Spanish cape" conceals a dagger, perhaps, but "Slips and pulls the table cloth / Overturns a coffee-cup," then "yawns and draws a stocking up." Another slapstick bungler, "the man with heavy eyes," declines participation, "shows fatigue" – and the conspiracy (or is it a ceremony?) ends scatologi-cally (*CPP* 35–36).

If it is a ceremony that these nightingales perform, it is a failed ritual – and the poem too may fail since, unlike other Eliot quatrains, it lacks the bull's-eye that satire requires. Its zoo words are read as degrading to Sweeney; but, while he may be the target of personae in the poem, he does not seem to be Eliot's target. The poem's first word, succeeding a Greek epigraph from *Agamemnon*, may suggest more – or perhaps less – than that Sweeney should have shaved. "Apeneck" has the look of transliterated Greek (and the first word of the previous poem in this collection is "Polyphiloprogeni-tive"). The association of Sweeney with animals – all favorites at the London Zoo – may indicate costuming: J. G. Frazer mentions animal-skin vestments in *The Golden Bough*. And if the nightingales of the title are (as slang would have it) prostitutes, may not ape and zebra, "silent vertebrate" and giraffe, connote erotically as well (*CPP* 35)? Sweeney "spreads his knees"; his ape neck swells "to maculate giraffe" – maculate as opposed to immaculate (the conception here being dirty). By indirection we learn that Sweeney is erect again, his neck swelling to the scope of a giraffe's. Shrinkage follows ("the shrunken seas"), and then a "person" of covert gender tries "to sit on Sweeney's knees." The "silent vertebrate" (presumably Sweeney) "Contracts and con-centrates, withdraws," and a rabbi's daughter ("*née* Rabinovitch") tears at some "grapes with murderous paws" (35). The poem's images of fruit – "Bananas figs and hothouse grapes" – are iconographically male, and its epigraph is the wail of a man's man as his wife butchers and castrates him in his bath. (How, then, should we hear the verb "Circumscribe" in line 32?)

At this point it is worth clarifying that the "hornèd gate" that "Sweeney guards" (*CPP* 35) cannot be the *Aeneid*'s "gate of horn," as critics who regard Eliot as a fancy poet have long maintained. For while "hornèd" may indicate cuckoldry or sexual urgency, and perhaps imply a sacred place (the altar of Exodus features horns), *hornèd* cannot mean *made of* horn. Yet critics are not accountable for such mistakes. While images in the poem may suggest rental costumes, its words really are off-the-rack. Their job is to tart-up some things as other things, then cloak the rest. The poem is stocked with terms of evil augur, drawn almost randomly from *The Golden Bough* and representing more contexts, temporal and cultural, than a contextualist like Eliot should deploy in good faith. The result: Christianity appears, in this poem, as hea-thenism in disguise. Anthropologists at the time wrote triumphally, for example, of the "Sacred Heart of Dionysus" (so who knows what goes on in that "Convent" in stanza nine?). Pound, in the genre of his conspiracy with Eliot, drew a logical infer-ence: "Christ follows Dionysus, / Phallic and ambrosial" (*Mauberley* 62). One begins, in this supercontext, to suspect even denotative words – especially "host" in line 33 – of double agency (36). Eucharist itself is a cover (or *involucrum*: those wafers are not really bread). Still, is Christianity the privileged butt of a poem whose title mocks Elizabeth Browning and ends with guano showering the conqueror of Troy? The question remains of whether a satire so lacking an object should be judged entirely competent.

It was in part his omnicompetence and purposefulness that made Odysseus the hero of modernism, and he is just enough evoked in *Poems* (1920) for us to notice his absence there. "Nausicaa and Polypheme," the sweetest and the sourest of Odysseus's interlocutors, are bracketed in "Sweeney Erect" (*CPP* 25), and another Greek sailor, Theseus, is likewise recalled and not named. The epigraph and opening stanzas invite comparison of these two: as Nausicaa is to Odysseus, so Ariadne is to Theseus. Daughters of island kings, they rescue visitors they fancy, then are abandoned. But where Odysseus leaves his princess charmed (and everyone he meets – the cyclops "Polypheme" included – eager for another chance at him), Theseus, in this variant of the myth, leaves Ariadne suicidal. The "perjured sails" of stanza 2 invoke another suicide, Theseus' father's, provoked by the son's fecklessness (25). This focus may respond to metaphorical uses that, at this time, Joyce and Pound were making of Odysseus's voyage home to Ithaca. The suicides relating to Theseus in "Sweeney Erect," like the murder of Agamemnon in "Sweeney Among the Nightingales," stand as reminders that, in antiquity as at present, returning home means catastrophe more often than it does renewal. "The nightingales are singing" as conspirators encircle Sweeney, and the same birds "sang . . . When Agamemnon cried aloud" – the progression of tenses effects a parallel, not contrast, between modern prole and classic king (36). The reader is expected to picture Agamemnon, not as described in mythographies or student cribs, but as the preening, macho brute presented in the *Oresteia*. "All societies," Eliot came to summarize his view, are "corrupt" (*TCC* 74), but that "all" equalizes nothing except eras and social orders. His disambivalent hierarchy – the distinction in these poems between "us" and "them" – is stark and self-defeating. Untranslated and unattributed, the epigraph to "Sweeney Among the Nightingales" pre-selects for the reader's contempt almost any reader the poem might ever come to have.

The appeal of, and to, a standard both normative and normal in the past is disambivalent (rather than confident) and, thus, insecure. Eliot conflates Agamemnon with Sweeney because one is "stiff," the other "erect," with dire consequences for the vulnerable (*CPP* 36, 25). When Eliot parallels Sweeney with Christ (both naked in their baths), his contempt falls on flaccid men whose knowledge of Greek metaphysics redeems no one. Lines Eliot cancelled from the text of "A Cooking Egg" have the speaker recalling his arousal, in the past, at glimpsing Pipit's tongue and stockings (*IMH* 358). "Where are the eagles and the trumpets?" is laughably posed, but when put honestly – "where is the penny world I bought / To eat with Pipit behind the screen?" – the question hurts (*CPP* 27). He has turned from disappointment to a fantasy of life with the historic dead, but his choice of "Bride" (Lucretia Borgia) is evidence that he is suicidal. Care for the "weeping multitudes" who "Droop" restored to Eliot's verse the "mess of imprecision of feeling," which bore him from *The Waste Land* to *Four Quartets* (128). It was *caritas*, in other words, that released Eliot from unsound certainties, which, for a time, he was desperate to have shared. Christianity became, ironically – though the Christian God *is* of three minds – the guarantor of Eliot's ambivalence.

NOTES

1 Eliot's philosophical position was a variety of skeptical doubt so radical that it leaves the skeptic no reason (as Eliot put it) "for believing anything else" than what is conventionally believed in the context of his or her time and culture ("Christianity and Communism" 383). Eliot's main sources for this "conventionalism" are to be found, he said, in Montaigne's essays and in texts of the Buddhist philosophical tradition (predominantly of the Ma¯dhyamika school); see also NOT ONE, NOT TWO: ELIOT AND BUDDHISM. For present-day conventionalist philosophy, see Rorty.

2 Eliot developed the argument outlined here in a series of papers he wrote as a Harvard graduate student. See Perl, ch. 4, esp. 66–71, which includes direct quotations from several of those papers.

3 The poems in quatrains and their original places of publication are: "The Hippopotamus," *Little Review*, July 1917; "Mr. Eliot's Sunday Morning Service," "Sweeney Among the Nightingales," "Whispers of Immortality," *Little Review*, Sept. 1918; "A Cooking Egg," *Coterie*, May 1919; "Burbank with a Baedeker: Bleistein with a Cigar," "Sweeney Erect," *Arts and Letters*, Summer 1919. For Donald Gallup's inventory of the TSS and MSS in the Berg Collection of the New York Public Library, see *Times Literary Supplement*, 7 Nov. 1968: 1238–40.

REFERENCES AND FURTHER READING

Cameron, Sharon. *Impersonality: Seven Essays.* Chicago: U of Chicago P, 2007.

Ellmann, Maud. *The Politics of Impersonality: T. S. Eliot and Ezra Pound.* Cambridge: Harvard UP, 1987.

Gautier, Théophile. *Poésies complètes de Théophile Gautier.* Paris: Nizet, 1970.

Kenner, Hugh. *The Pound Era.* Berkeley: U of California P, 1971.

Laity, Cassandra, and Nancy K. Gish, eds. *Gender, Desire, and Sexuality in T. S. Eliot.* Cambridge: Cambridge UP, 2004.

Lewis, Wyndham. "Early London Environment." *T. S. Eliot: A Symposium.* Ed. Richard March and M. J. Tambimuttu. London: Editions Poetry, 1948.

Perl, Jeffrey M. *Skepticism and Modern Enmity: Before and After Eliot.* Baltimore: Johns Hopkins UP, 1989.

Pound, Ezra. "Harold Monro." *Criterion* 11 (1932): 581–92.

——. *Hugh Selwyn Mauberley.* 1920. *Selected Poems of Ezra Pound.* New York: New Directions, 1957. 61–77.

Ricks, Christopher. *T. S. Eliot and Prejudice.* London: Faber, 1988.

Rorty, Richard. "Quietism and Naturalism." *Philosophy as Cultural Politics: Philosophical Papers.* Vol. 4. Cambridge: Cambridge UP, 2007.

12

"Gerontion": The Mind of Postwar Europe and the Mind(s) of Eliot

Edward Brunner

If T. S. Eliot's poetic output seems small by comparison with other poets, it is not just because he was also essayist, book reviewer, cultural critic, editor, and dramatist (and for a time, bank employee): it is because he reserved his poetry for the serious disruptions in his life as it was lived intellectually and emotionally. All his major poems are, in the strongest possible sense, transitional works. They emerge from a crisis that is often personal, sometimes public, frequently both. "Gerontion" can surely be counted among the most important of these writings. The product of what one Eliot scholar has called quite simply "the worst year of [Eliot's] life" (Schuchard 6), it also sets in motion the possibilities that will lead to the writing of *The Waste Land*.

A number of firsts distinguish "Gerontion." It is the poem in which Eliot solidly commits to an allusive style that is a pastiche of phrases, lines, and passages from predecessors whose presence will deepen readers' appreciation. It confirms a trend new to Eliot, a tendency to take public issues and reshape them as a cultural crisis experienced in personal terms. It promotes a role for the poet as a self-aware figure, not only standing in his own historical moment but surveying a horizon that extends to the history of Europe. It openly asserts what "Sweeney Among the Nightingales" had foreshadowed: Eliot's abiding interest in sacred rituals and religious feelings, here used as a foil to the limits of a rational "scientific" skepticism. And finally, it offers itself as a counterpart – perhaps as an equal – to the rigorous conceptualizing expected in a philosophical argument, even as it conveys its meanings not logically or discursively but in constellations of imagery and in syntax where gaps operate like pauses in music. As darkly ambivalent as the situation in "Gerontion" is, Eliot's text is nothing if not ambitious – a remarkable expansion of his prowess as a poet.

A Companion to T. S. Eliot, First Edition. Edited by David E. Chinitz.
© 2014 John Wiley & Sons, Ltd. Published 2014 by John Wiley & Sons, Ltd.

A Postwar Vacuum

"Gerontion" steps directly into the postwar moment, as a product of the months during which, as Eliot wrote to his mother on October 2, 1919, the Peace Conference had resulted in "obviously a bad peace, in which the major European powers tried to get as much as they could, and appease and intimidate as far as possible the various puppet nationalities which they have constituted and will try to dominate" (*Letters* 337). The defective peace treaty indicated the war had produced no winners and losers. It had left behind, in Eric Sigg's words, "[b]attlefield casualties, unscrupulous war profiteers, political collapse": "Fought to uphold idealism and preserve a status quo, the war demolished both," a paradox, Sigg suggests, that "generates the emotional and intellectual issues 'Gerontion' addresses" (174).

"Gerontion" serves as the introductory poem in Eliot's second commercially published volume, *Poems* (1920). While degradation is present throughout this work, traces of the recent war are never obvious in the so-called "quatrain" poems that comprise the majority of the book.[1] At least twice, in important letters to confidantes, Eliot defended the quatrain poems in the weeks before the book's publication, calling them *"very serious"* (*Letters* 311, original emphasis) and "intensely serious" (363). Their cutting tone clearly invites the charge that Eliot is operating satirically. Updated versions of an international England previously limned by Henry James but now deposed by a sensibility cognizant of Baudelaire, these verses enter settings that are emotionally impoverished, overtly sexual, and brutally manipulated. Packaged in tetrameter units with knife-sharp rhymes, the poems are dominated by stereotypes and caricatures. By contrast, "Gerontion" establishes a tone unequivocally "serious." Presented in a free verse that falls in and out of traditional meters, its events unfold in an emotional range that exceeds the stark light of the quatrain poems. The "dry thoughts" of its recollecting protagonist are anything but. They are all too familiar, disturbing, even ominous, and their allusions, once perceived, only further their complications.

The poem's ambiguity begins with Gerontion's blurred identity. Just who he is, where he stands, what he represents, and why he is known only generically (the title translates from ancient Greek as "little old man") are ongoing problems. This is not a text like "Prufrock" with roots in the dramatic monologue tradition, with a speaker in a recognizable setting and who has understandable anxieties. "Prufrock lives as a personality," Grover Smith has asserted; "Gerontion, as a recording memory" (63). Caught up in remembrances that jump from one topic to another, that lead to a string of indirectly connected observations, all considered with tormenting regret, Gerontion's motives for speaking so intensely, and even his expectations in doing so, resist easy explanation. "None of the co-ordinates of 'Gerontion' – the speaker, his world, the poet, the present his voice inhabits – has any referential substance," writes Eric Svarny. "The deictics of the poem do not locate us in a knowable environment" (176).

Since Eliot withholds an explanatory context for Gerontion, our stipulations about who or what he could be largely determine what stance we take toward the work. Writing in 1935 with an eye on political events in Germany and Italy, Stephen Spender was ready to grant Eliot's protagonist allegoric status. "Gerontion is an objective poem," he asserted, noting that the speaker's extreme age was easy to explain: the poem was "written in the belief that the decline of civilization is real, that history is, as it were, now senile" (Spender, *Destructive* 142). Spender's observation inaugurated a line of thinking best summarized in David Perkins's remark that Gerontion is "less a character than a historical phase of the European mind" (498). That a poet should aspire to speak for an entire culture had been set forward by Eliot in "Tradition and the Individual Talent," whose first half appeared in the September 1919 issue of the *Egoist*. "The historical sense" that Eliot asserted to be "nearly indispensable to anyone who would continue to be a poet beyond his twenty-fifth year" would compel one to write "not merely with his own generation in his bones, but with a feeling that the whole of the literature of Europe from Homer and within it the whole of the literature of his own country has a simultaneous existence and composes a simultaneous order" (*SE* 4). The poet "must be aware that the mind of Europe – the mind of his own country – a mind which he learns in time to be much more important than his own private mind – is a mind which changes" (*SE* 6). Eliot allows, in his extended series of appositions, for a poet who brings "the mind of his own country" to bear on a Europe that is not his native land.

Certainly "Gerontion" conveys a broad sense of Europe in postwar crisis. If the poem naturally falls, as John Crowe Ransom observed, into five movements as "a sort of symphony . . . or at least the perfect miniature of one" (94), then each segment is more or less 13 to 16 lines, and each is punctuated by a brief, self-deprecating afterthought. The poem's first movement introduces a figure that speaks for a Europe now in ruins, while the remaining movements sketch aspects of a concept Eliot was in the process of developing in his essays: the "dissociation of sensibility" (*SE* 247). Eliot would not hit upon this descriptive phrase until his 1921 essay "The Metaphysical Poets," where it describes a turn that Eliot thought symptomatic of early modernity. Around 1600, self-conscious thinking arises, at odds with spontaneous emotion; thought and feeling, that is, are no longer supportive of each other but take on oppositional roles. The poem's second movement, then, describes this condition and recalls what has been lost: a common culture held together by religious ritual. The third movement explains the inadequacy of that which has replaced faith-based ritual – an understanding of history as secular, rational, and skeptical – while the fourth incriminates that replacement as amplifying a general disorientation, until a concluding section expresses sorrow for the possibilities that have been extinguished.

Considering the poem as an analytic response to a present-day crisis that is also intent on conveying the disorder and anxiety of that crisis, a detailed summary would show that the opening section (ll. 1–16) is intent on presenting the dilemma in its starkest terms. All that is youthful, all that promises a future, seems remote; the young prop up the old, who regret lost opportunities. The metaphor of a "house" occupied by temporary inhabitants, overseen by a figure of stereotypical malfeasance (the antipathetic figure of the Jew associated with the immigrant, the cosmopolitan), evokes not only architecture but genealogy, suggesting that the intellectual lineage of Europe is being undone. If the authority and power of ritualized religion had, in the past, actively guarded European civilization, then today's secular society, as the next segment implies (ll. 17–33), views religion from within a secular framework, like Pharisees who once demanded proof (Matt. 12:38): "'We would see a sign!'" (l. 17). Such a demand anticipates modern skepticism, and becomes a step toward undermining the wisdom of a religious tradition that refused the bluntness of the evidentiary sign, preferring the "darkness" of a "word within a word" that required the faith upon which a community might be built. (Eliot's phrasing draws from a 1618 Christmas sermon by Lancelot Andrewes.) Yet the outcome of this new secularism is atomization. Ritual is no longer binding and instead is replaced by diverse and individualized activities, embraced as if they offered salvation to one at a time, "divided" and performed by an international cast that obsessively collects delicate place settings (Mr. Silvero), slavishly honors the masterpieces of another culture (Hakagawa), presides over ghostly séances (Madame de Tornquist), or poses provocatively at thresholds (Fraulein von Kulp). Indeed, the old man of this debased culture has "no ghosts": he sees in a clear light that exposes these modern substitutes for ritual. The secular frame flattens such pursuits into strategies for coping. At the same time, the existence of such compulsive activity reveals a longing for a commonality that no longer exists: there are ghosts everywhere, though they go unacknowledged.

"After such knowledge, what forgiveness?" In the next segment (ll. 34–48), Gerontion insists that modern knowledge brings not clarity but an excess of information. As we "Think now" (for thinking is that which, in our current circumstances, only occurs willfully), we can rely on no comfortable, familiar, and apparently true-by-intuition framework of inherited understanding, and so we are easily overwhelmed. "History" is figured in this passage as sometimes a *femme fatale*, sometimes a dark woman, sometimes a lost girl – an identity that shape-shifts with a feverish allure. The gifts we receive from her as we exercise our thought – in five lines, variants of "gift" appear six times – are paradoxical, effusive, baffling, and likely to turn into their opposites. History's maze-like corridors lead toward distractions that beguile but cannot satisfy, ending obscurely in strange alliances, tangled relationships. Eliot uses Gerontion's musings to examine what is lacking in a fourth segment (ll. 49–61), drawing upon imagery recalling the tiger in *Songs of Experience* that William Blake paired with the lamb in *Songs of Innocence*. When skeptical knowledge now envisions religious feeling as no more than a primitive reaction to the seasonal turnings of the new year, then spring turns barbaric, no longer a stage in a cycle of larger revitalization. Debunked rituals that only mark seasonal regularity can never serve as a basis for anything, much less restore hope. Such routine only further ages us, never freeing us from the burden of accumulated knowledge. To "[s]tiffen in a rented house" (l. 51) is only to descend into age, though the phrase might, in another poem, suggest a new resolve or even a physical arousal. And what one longs for, the kind of deep and intimate encounter with another (the "you" in this segment is unidentified because it is whoever is most desired) now seemingly recedes into a distance. Without passion, there are no senses that can be trusted. And if the only words left are purposive words that ache for a meeting "honestly," there cannot be that "closer contact," only questions that register confusion and longing.

Gerontion's vision of the world has shifted away from the stony emptiness of the opening segment where all fires gutter and a cold wind persists, but it has developed into a place of divided emotions, of minute adjustments that offer titillation (in references to "delirium," "the membrane," and "pungent sauces" that evoke contemporary pleasures and pains), even as massive cycles of birth and death only become more evident. The spider and the weevil, agents of change and decay, are inevitable. Realizing that, the speaker's final impressions are surprisingly moving, and when a list of names now appears, those who are identified are no longer accompanied by dismissive traits but are curiously honored. Though they will fracture into atoms, their proximity to death gives them a grandeur that opens onto final lines that, we know from manuscript revisions (*IMH* 352), Eliot added at a late stage in the poem's composition: "Gull against the wind, in the windy straits / Of Belle Isle, or running on the Horn, / White feathers in the snow, the Gulf claims. . . ." Gerontion in a sense tempers his dismay at not having "fought in the warm rain" (l. 4) by intuiting a fate associated with the wind, whose presence in the poem now becomes retrospectively paramount, in "windy spaces" (l. 16), in "vacant shuttles" that "Weave the wind" (ll. 30–31), in "a draughty house / Under a windy knob" (ll. 32–33), as if he had been buffeted by winds of change and winds of chance. These are "the Trades" (that may also stand for trade wars) that lead not to a climax but to exhaustion, to a "sleepy corner," with only traces left like "white feathers in the snow" dissolving into their background. Thus the last sentences, fragments all, with no directing syntax, retain the absence of order as well as the pain and confusion of the present.

Versions of Exile

Yet to depict "Gerontion" as if it were a stage upon which Eliot was channeling "the mind of Europe" has never sufficed to explain all the poem's aspects. Why is this, rather than a straightforward essay, successful as a format for serious thinking? More pointedly, how is the poem an example of elements larger than just Eliot's idea of "the mind of Europe"?

Since the 1990s, scholars interested in examples of the cultural work accomplished by modernist poetry have explored "Gerontion" and other writings for evidence not only of the attitudes that Eliot was aware of but of attitudes whose implications escaped him. Among the evidence unearthed, one passage in "Gerontion" has generated considerable controversy:

> My house is a decayed house,
> And the jew squats on the window sill, the owner,

> Spawned in some estaminet of Antwerp,
> Blistered in Brussels, patched and peeled in London (ll. 7–9)

For several critics, the poem's general tendency to offer provocative juxtapositions that have no basis in recognizable settings turns disturbing here. Why would the owner of a house squat "on the window sill"? Why is his birth described as if he were a creature? Why is his outward appearance registered as deteriorated architecture? The passage appears to nominate a scapegoat that exposes how European civilization was *really* "invaded." The loss of a common culture results from an infestation of alien (Jewish, not Anglo-Saxon) races whose progeny, as it swarmed from Antwerp to Brussels to London, left behind a wake of destruction. Relevant in this regard is a passage in Eliot's 1933 University of Virginia lectures, collected as *After Strange Gods*. In setting out to describe "the very best living tradition" (19), Eliot notoriously remarks that "reasons of race and religion combine to make any large number of free-thinking Jews undesirable" (20).

Historically, anti-Semitism is expressed as innuendo, through coded phrases embedded in a legitimizing discourse. Prejudice survives by refusing to proceed in an open, clear, linear fashion where it might be challenged by counterexamples, exposed to requirements for logical thinking, and confronted with rigorous questioning. At the same time, as it works through intimation, allusion, and suggestion, it also inhabits a linguistic environment similar to the Symbolist poetics that Eliot derived from modern French poets.[2] Symbolist poetry, in Donald Davie's words, moves with "deliberate vagueness" by asserting "a relationship between items which is impossible or highly unlikely in the world we observe" (202, 204). For Rachel Blau DuPlessis, intent upon disclosing the subterranean meanings that lurk in modern poems, it is no coincidence that Eliot was drawn toward the hazy edges of the Symbolist aesthetic: "Eliot's cultural work involved the sub rosa threading of ideologically charged materials and chronic socio-cultural stereotypes into the poetic texture (by allusion, metonymy, prosodic displacement, deep denotation, transegmental aural drift and other tactics)" (154). Eliot's usage of the Jewish landlord becomes, in DuPlessis's reading, deeply constitutive – "part of a heteroglossic marginal scene" that allows Eliot to maintain "an interior debate . . . on possible cultural gains and losses from the vibrant, if suspect, power of this figure" (143). Even more pressing is Anthony Julius's 1995 contention: he maintains that Eliot's artistry lay in his ability to transform racist clichés and exhausted stereotypes into powerful, haunting figures: "anti-Semitism did not disfigure Eliot's work, it animated it" (173).

In seeking to counter such claims, Jewel Spears Brooker differentiates Eliot from the characters he invents: "Gerontion's mind is a metaphor for the mind of Europe, a collapsing mind with which Eliot had little sympathy" (111). All events in the poem, Brooker maintains, "exist in Gerontion's demented mind," and all figures, including Gerontion, are "represented as withered and repulsive remnants" (112). For Brooker, the poem's gaps and omissions signal Gerontion's distorted consciousness. Yet her distinction between Symbolist poetics and mental breakdown, or poet and persona, while generally legitimate, may also be too sharp. The distance Eliot displays toward the feckless Prufrock or the cartoonish Sweeney is less evident in Gerontion's agonizing struggles. Speaking before the T. S. Eliot Society in 2002, Marjorie Perloff, proposing that the "argument for Gerontion as a fictional persona is never quite convincing" (29), pondered Eliot's remarks in a July 1919 letter to his brother that "[o]ne remains always a foreigner" (*Letters* 310) and suggested that Eliot may have been invoking a despised stereotype in this controversial passage as an opportunity to reflect on his own alienation, as an American out of place in England.

Yet the inclination to contextualize this controversial passage by recovering the circumstances at the time the poem was written might also include a return to a text widely read in intellectual circles in 1919. First readers of "Gerontion" would have been ready to compare the voice of its "little old man" with that of another out-of-place American: Henry Adams, whose autobiography, privately printed in 1907, was published to much acclaim in 1918 as *The Education of Henry Adams*.

Writing in the persona of an aged man on the verge of a new century, Adams used the occasion to meditate on the loss of stable values that had once concentrated responsibility in the hands of the elite, educated class of which he was a charter member. As if personally offended by history's unexpected surprises, he complained bitterly that his scholarly investigations had failed to disclose any meaningful pattern to historical events despite his search for underlying "laws." From the medieval past, he did recover evidence of the religious awe that had once unified Europe. But as the editor of Adams's letters noted, in "the masculine world of power, the Virgin enters as a symbol recovered from the past and as a still effective historical force" (Levenson 594). And just as the modern-era electric dynamo replaced the medieval icon of the Virgin, so a shallow new breed of diverse citizenry replaced the patrician families raised on Anglo-Saxon customs. Anti-Semitic remarks do not prevail in Adams's autobiography, but when they do appear, they are striking. The Jew either appears as a disturbing, invasive figure, "a furtive Yacoob or Ysaac still reeking of the Ghetto, snarling a weird Yiddish to the officers of the customs" (238), or as a lurking, guileful presence, "the complex Jew" (272) or "the Jew banker" (285) who had changed his name from Cohen "in order to please his wife" but whose mind remained "Cohen" (214). To Adams, as a young Harvard graduate, his education on the continent exposed him to the "derisive Jew laughter of [Heinrich] Heine [that] ran through the university and everything else in Berlin" (79).

Eliot might well have felt affinity with Adams: in a letter home, dated May 4, 1919, he mentioned that he would be reviewing the *Education*, and he noted that Adams was "a cousin of ours" (*Letters* 290). To John Quinn, in a letter of July 9, he wondered what "American opinion" would think of his "article on Adams," adding: "but it is a type that I *ought* to know better than any other" (*Letters* 313). No less important, however, would have been Eliot's equally strong recoil from Adams as "a type." This attraction and repulsion, Ronald Bush speculates, was already evident in the figure of Burbank in "Burbank with a Baedeker: Bleistein with a Cigar." Written a year before Eliot's review but at a time when the *Education* was in print, the poem was a "serious exercise" in sketching an "Adams-like compatriot" who displays the New Englander's "inability either to understand the beauty or the evil of the Old World. . . . Burbank is immature, all intellect and no sensation" (25). If Burbank is the cartoon sketch that can be used to illustrate the fatal modern divorce between thought and emotion, then Gerontion may be the detailed portrait or the life-size depiction.

Moreover, as an American in Europe just becoming sensitized to the remarkable loss of American political prestige in 1919, Eliot may have been struck as well by Adams's readiness to portray himself as an American unable to fathom European conventions, often confessing puzzlement over diplomatic maneuvering. Writing to his mother at war's end on December 29, 1918, he described the arrival of President Woodrow Wilson at Buckingham Palace as "an extraordinary and inspiring occasion": "I do not believe that people in America realize how much Wilson's policy has done to inspire respect for Americans abroad. . . . Politics here are in a complete chaos at present" (*Letters* 264). But his workplace duties that year involved settling the bank's prewar accounts with Germans, bringing him in direct contact with what he called "that appalling document, the Treaty of Versailles" (qtd. in Matthews 63). Not ten months later, Eliot is writing home that "at the Peace Conference, the one strong figure was Clemenceau, who knew just what he wanted. . . . Wilson went down utterly before European diplomacy" (*Letters* 337).

Adams's autobiography, in short, gave Eliot much to think about, and when he came to the *Education* in a review entitled "A Skeptical Patrician" in the May 23, 1919 *Athenaeum*, just weeks before the July draft of "Gerontion" began circulating among friends, he used the occasion effectively. Glimpses of the origins of Eliot's poetry are always breaking the surface of his essays and reviews, and this period was no exception, especially since his reviews for the *Athenaeum* were numerous and various. Twenty were produced in 1919 alone, though Eliot's stint as a reviewer did not begin until April, and they encompassed topics as diverse as translations of North American Indian poetry, *Cyrano de Bergerac*, and a French history of sixteenth-century Italian philosophy. Laboring under increased responsibilities at Lloyds Bank in the position to which he had been newly promoted in March, continuing to teach his extension course, and nursing Vivien through illnesses, he had to use his time more shrewdly than ever. An unsigned review of a book memorializing young poets killed during the war ("The New Elizabethans and the Old") in the April 4, 1919 *Athenaeum* cites a Lancelot Andrewes sermon: "*Christ is no wild-cat*, said Bishop Andrewes" (135) – a quote that confirms the error in Gerontion's readiness to address Christ as "the tiger." And a review of Rudyard Kipling in the May 9, 1919 issue ("Kipling Redivivus") drew Eliot's attention to oratory and its limits: Kipling's work is "music just as the words of the orator or preacher are music; they persuade, not by reason, but by emphatic sound" (297) – an observation that aligns with the insistent and repeated verbs "Think now" and "Gives" and "Think at last" in the third and fourth segments of "Gerontion."

As probative as notions in these reviews might be, neither was as seminal to "Gerontion" as reviewing the *Education*. Eliot's review is remarkable not only for

identifying flaws in Adams's character but for offering corrections. In Eliot's estimation, Adams thought too abstractly, never realizing that "education – the education
of an individual – is a by-product of being interested, passionately absorbed. . . .
[M]en ripen best through experiences which are at once sensuous and intellectual
. . . . [M]any men will admit that . . . their keenest sensuous experience has been as
if the body thought" ("Sceptical" 362). In conclusion, he compares quotes by Adams
and Henry James, each recording his first impression (albeit two decades apart) of
Liverpool. Adams is all conceptualization, offering one predigested observation only
to surround it with another, as he describes "a coffee-room in November-murk" and
cumbersomely asserts "the romance of red sandstone architecture." James, by contrast,
is all concrete detail and amazed perception as he seeks out the dynamic of the
moment, and ends with an unlikely, modest, yet vivid example of "the plate of buttered muffin and its cover" (qtd. in "Skeptical" 362).

F. O. Matthiessen, who recognized that Eliot was alluding to Adams's description
of spring in Washington when Gerontion described a "depraved May," stressed the
importance of the conflict between Adams and James: "Deeply impressed by the
acuteness of Adams's intelligence, Eliot yet felt a lack of full ripeness in his writing
when compared with that of James's" (12). But Matthiessen held back from the next
step: that Eliot might have been inclined to represent the sensibility of an Adams by
using the strategies of a James, to convey the thin and dry intellect of Adams through
Jamesian sensory reporting. To replicate the voice of Adams alone might have been
all too easy – indeed, it could have produced work uncomfortably close to the brittle
harshness of the recent quatrain poems. But to give a tactile dimension to an abstract
intellect, to convey the feel of disorientation, old age, and desiccation, might have
attractions for Eliot. From such an angle, the poem's various stylistic subtleties
become evident and intriguing. The work establishes a stony sullenness at its opening
in which most detail is banished – generalizations dominate and stereotypes rule,
whether it is "the jew" who is a patchwork of survivalist tactics that leave disarray in
their wake or "the woman" who fails to ignite a fire. Its analysis of religious intensity
is fragmentary, and it minimizes the passion and mystery at the heart of belief or
dismisses them fearfully. Although the cosmopolites who pursue their separate rituals
resemble the caricatures in the quatrain poems that Eliot sketched with dismissive
contempt, they are not simply derided here; and by hesitating to judge them severely,
Eliot prepares us for the affecting, even generous identification of similar figures – de
Bailhache, Fresca, Mrs. Cammel – as those whose loss actually matters in the final
lines of the poem. If the segment that mulls over the "contrived corridors" of history
is among the longest of all the passages, it may reveal the speaker's attraction to the
tangled secrets that he ostensibly condemns, as he is drawn back compulsively to
revisit them. And the climax that resounds so compellingly just before the speaker's
voice dies down – "Gull against the wind, in the windy straits" – may disclose an
element of self-pity, as the speaker battles alone, tragically unrecognized.

When James is invoked as an interactive presence to attend to the voice of the
Adams-like speaker, the complications of the poem become focused. "Gerontion" is

a sympathetic but distanced reconceptualizing of a type Eliot would disavow. (And the anti-Semitic gesture toward the landlord Jew becomes one of many moments in which Eliot inhabits a point of view that he may want to reject – though some critics would be quick to point out the limitations of using James as a lens to correct anti-Semitic distortions [Posnock; Freedman]). Since Gerontion is the one whom he would *not* be and whom he fears he may be or may become, it is less surprising that the poem unfolds in a space free of referents. This poem may work, for Eliot at least, as a charm – or perhaps better, a purgative spell, as if poetry that dons a persona only to empty it could be *the* modern variation on a religious rite.

Since a degree of uncertainty remains throughout the poem, casting Eliot into a state that is both punitive and restorative, it is not surprising to learn that "Gerontion" once included a second epigraph, a passage from Dante's *Inferno*: "*Come 'l mio corpo stea / nel mondo su, nulla scienza porto*" ("how my body stands / in the world above, no knowledge have I") (*IMH* 351). Fra Alberigo is explaining, from his perspective at nearly the deepest point in Hell, that under certain conditions, the damned who are guilty of betraying those who had entrusted themselves to them have their souls taken even as they still live. Eliot may have discarded the epigraph because the gulf between Gerontion and Alberigo is too great. But his interest in the *Inferno* still pervades this poem. In an essay on Dante written in March 1920 (*Letters* 374), Eliot sharply disagreed with Walter Savage Landor's depiction of the damned as allegorical types designed to carry a didactic message. For Eliot, Dante's figures in Hell reached an apotheosis of sorts: "it is a part of damnation to experience desires that we can no longer gratify. For in Dante's Hell souls are not deadened, as they mostly are in life; they are actually in the greatest torment of which each is capable" (*SW* 166). They have become larger than they were in life, so it is possible to say, as Eliot says of Brunetto Latini (Canto XV): "so admirable a soul, and so perverse" (166).

Gerontion in all his torment – intensely reliving past moments whose loss he is constitutionally unable to appreciate – may be Eliot's first serious effort to imitate the voice of a Dantean subject. Responding to the opening lines, Spender once exclaimed: "One can almost see Gerontion seated in Hades" (*T. S. Eliot* 60), and Bush's 1983 study attends to Gerontion as a scandalous figure, with "no desire to think" except to find "a substitute for thought" (36), and his poem a "dazzling exposition of rhetorical insincerity" (40). Gerontion's monologue, then, may be doubly virtuosic: it is not only Eliot's evocation of the type of the New England intellectual like Henry Adams, with Adams channeled through the counterforce of a James who hears Adams's thin words by surrounding them with thick experience; it is also Eliot's strongest attempt so far to emulate the indelibly complex voice of the Dantean subject, suffering intensely because experiencing its weaknesses so fully. So seen, "Gerontion" foreshadows Eliot's great imitation in "Little Gidding" of a Dantean encounter, though the "familiar compound ghost" in that 1944 poem speaks within a *terza rima* frame that Eliot does not attempt in 1919 (*CPP* 140).

Eliot's modern Hell, of course, is internal and psychological, not a spiritual and archetypal construct like Dante's. Eliot criticized Pound's "Hell Cantos" (XIV, XV,

XVI in the *Cantos*) because its inhabitants were so unquestionably bad. Eliot's wry list of Pound's damned begins with "politicians, profiteers, financiers, newspaper proprietors" and continues with "liars, the stupid, pedants, preachers" (*ASG* 46). "Mr. Pound's Hell, for all its horrors," Eliot concludes, "is a perfectly comfortable one for the modern mind to contemplate," because "it is a Hell for the *other people*" (47, original emphasis). Dante's Hell, however, is populated by those like us or those we could be like. Experiencing how close the damned are to us grips our attention as nothing else could. And while Gerontion's trains of thought may be not our own, and his reveries from the past may differ from ours, he cannot be dismissed as if he were wholly evil. The errors he makes, as well as his frustrated longings, unfounded assaults, and self-pitying postures, are all too familiar to Eliot's readers.

Even as Eliot gives voice to a character immersed in desperation and diminished to the point of ruin, he also presents him as still longing for a transformative change. Out of the testing that produced this complex figure, a mix of himself as he might be yet would not be, Eliot found himself occupying a new, terribly honest position. Pound rejected Eliot's suggestion, at a late point in their reshaping "He Do the Police in Different Voices" into *The Waste Land*, that "Gerontion" might stand as the long poem's prologue. Whatever the wisdom in Pound's advice, Eliot's proposal was a sure acknowledgement of the earlier poem's importance. It would be impossible for Eliot, after completing this multiply voiced, deeply divided, allusion-drenched text, so haunted by a lost world of religious ritual, to avoid the enormous issues he would spend the rest of his career confronting.

NOTES

1 On the quatrain poems and the war, see also "WHERE ARE THE EAGLES AND THE TRUMPETS?": IMPERIAL DECLINE AND ELIOT'S DEVELOPMENT.

2 See T. S. ELIOT AND THE SYMBOLIST CITY on the influence of French symbolism, and ELIOT AND "RACE": JEWS, IRISH AND BLACKS on Eliot's relation to what Bryan Cheyette terms "Semitic discourse."

REFERENCES AND FURTHER READING

Adams, Henry. *The Education of Henry Adams*. Cambridge, MA: Riverside, 1918.

Brooker, Jewel Spears. "Eliot in the Dock." *South Atlantic Review* 61 (1996): 107–14.

Bush, Ronald. *T. S. Eliot: A Study in Character and Style*. New York: Oxford UP, 1983.

Davie, Donald. "Pound and Eliot: A Distinction." *The Poet in the Imaginary Museum*. Ed. Barry Alpert. Manchester: Carcanet, 1977. 191–207.

DuPlessis, Rachel Blau. *Genders, Races and Religious Cultures in Modern American Poetry, 1908–1934*. Cambridge: Cambridge UP, 2001.

Freedman, Jonathan. "Henry James and the Discourses of Antisemitism." *Between "Race" and Culture: Representations of "the Jew" in English and American Literature*. Ed. Bryan Cheyette. Cambridge: Cambridge UP, 1996. 62–83.

Gordon, Lyndall. *Eliot's Early Years*. New York: Oxford UP, 1977.

Julius, Anthony. *T. S. Eliot, Anti-Semitism and Literary Form*. Cambridge: Cambridge UP, 1995.

Levenson, J. C. "The Etiology of Israel Adams: The Onset, Waning, and Relevance of Henry Adams's Anti-Semitism." *New Literary History* 25 (1994): 569–600.

Matthews, T. S. *Great Tom: Notes towards the Definition of T. S. Eliot*. New York: Harper, 1974.

Matthiessen, F. O. *The Achievement of T. S. Eliot: An Essay on the Nature of Poetry*. Oxford: Oxford UP, 1935.

Perkins, David. *A History of Modern Poetry: From the 1890s to the High Modernist Mode*. Cambridge: Harvard UP, 1976.

Perloff, Marjorie. *Differentials: Poetry, Poetics, Pedagogy*. Tuscaloosa.: U of Alabama P, 2004.

Posnock, Ross. *The Trial of Curiosity: Henry James, William James, and the Challenge of Modernity*. New York: Oxford UP, 1991.

Ransom, John Crowe. "Gerontion." *T. S. Eliot: The Man and His Work*. Ed. Allen Tate. New York: Delta, 1966. 133–58.

Schuchard, Ronald. "Burbank with a Baedeker, Eliot with a Cigar: American Intellectuals, Anti-Semitism, and the Idea of Culture." *Modernism/Modernity* 10 (2003): 1–26.

Sigg, Eric. *The American T. S. Eliot: A Study of the Early Writings*. Cambridge: Cambridge UP, 1989.

Smith, Grover. *T. S. Eliot's Poetry and Plays*. Chicago: U of Chicago P, 1956.

Spender, Stephen. *The Destructive Element*. London: Cape, 1935.

——. *T. S. Eliot*. Harmondsworth: Penguin, 1975.

Svarny, Eric. *"The Men of 1914": T. S. Eliot and Early Modernism*. Philadelphia: Open UP, 1988.

13

"Fishing, with the arid plain behind me": Difficulty, Deferral, and Form in *The Waste Land*

Michael Coyle

In July of 1922, some three months before its appearance in the *Criterion*, American poet Ezra Pound affirmed that "Eliot's *Waste Land* is I think the justification of the 'movement,' of our modern experiment" (Pound, *Letters* 180). In 1922 such justification seemed necessary enough. Indeed, few writers of the time and even fewer readers would even have known that there was "a movement" afoot. Less than a century later, however, we run the opposite risk of taking for granted the astonishing strangeness of the poem, and of thinking that Eliot's radical poetics were somehow either inevitable or unproblematic. *The Waste Land* is a disturbing poem that is designed to disturb; it is a difficult poem whose design discourages simplification; it is a deeply conservative poem that nonetheless presents as radical a challenge to what remain our customary ways of assessing value as any text has ever mounted. There is, in other words, a real danger in simply nodding our heads dutifully at casually somber mentions of its "greatness."

At the same time, having troubled the attention and even the sleep of generations of readers and students, *The Waste Land* has become a synonym for what is too often perceived as a peculiarly academic kind of difficulty. Ever more burdened library shelves might even seem (falsely) to suggest that Eliot shared James Joyce's conviction that the way to guarantee his immortality was to fill his work with "so many enigmas and puzzles that it will keep the professors busy for centuries arguing over what I meant" (qtd. in Ellmann 521). From the beginning, from Pound's initial heralding to John Crowe Ransom's 1923 affirmation that *The Waste Land* "is the apotheosis of modernity" (Brooker 106), to James Longenbach's contention in the present volume that *The Waste Land* is "the most radically innovative and pervasively influential poem written in the twentieth century,"[1] most everyone has sensed that this is a poem that *stands* for big things. But although there is today general agreement on what those things might be, there remains considerable debate over how they cohere – and to what ends.

To be sure, *The Waste Land* is difficult. But rather than quote Joyce we would do better to paraphrase Vladimir Nabokov: modernist literature cannot be read, it can

A Companion to T. S. Eliot, First Edition. Edited by David E. Chinitz.

only be reread. This chapter emphasizes not *what* the poem means but rather *how* it means, how design and form press readers and shape their experience of the poem. It explores how *The Waste Land* can at once be tightly structured and yet still feel "open" in form. Most importantly, this chapter works to save *The Waste Land* from its reputation, and, rather than explain away its very real difficulty, it suggests how the experience of difficulty and unease is integral to the poem.

The very structure of the poem, which at first seems simply to unfold in five parts, poses difficult questions. The poem more properly can be said to include six parts, since when Eliot first published it in book form he appended notes to the end of the poem. In 1956, nearly a quarter-century after he published the poem, Eliot dismissed these notes as something he added only because his poem "was inconveniently short" for publication in book form (*OPP* 109); as several scholars have established, however, Eliot had been thinking about notes well beforehand. In effect, the notes function as a kind of a posteriori epigraph, working to reshape how readers experience the poem. In Jo Ellen Green Kaiser's words,

> Eliot's notes . . . [shift] the central issues of the poem from questions of modernity to questions of interpretation. For although the poem radically questions the possibility of order, and thus the foundations of modernity, the notes assume that order not only can be achieved but already exists. While at least one speaker of the poem knows only "a heap of broken images," the author of the notes knows that the poem has a "purpose" and a "plan." (87)

Read in this way, Eliot's prose notes comprise an integral part of the poem. But the question of *The Waste Land*'s structure proves still more complex. In 1972 Valerie Eliot published a facsimile edition of Eliot's original manuscripts and typescripts, including his own and Ezra Pound's editorial comments and reproducing the considerable material that they decided to cut. This material adds no further sections to the poem, but, particularly in Parts I, III, and IV, includes long narratives whose preservation, while not changing the thematics of the poem, would have changed its texture a great deal. However inadvertently, the later publication of Eliot's manuscripts and typescripts complicates further our sense of what comprises the wholeness of this poem.

As published, *The Waste Land* presents no unnecessary word. Despite the numerous and lengthy cuts that Eliot made at Pound's suggestion prior to publication, it is missing nothing important to the design of the poem. For this reason, readers might take as emblem the figure in Eliot's epigraph – the Cumaean Sibyl, who wished for the wrong things and got them. In other words, those readers who seek the comfort and unity of narrative will likely look for one in *The Waste Land*, and at least initially, or partially, find one. A richer experience of the poem awaits those who resist chasing shadows. The poem is not narrative, although it contains fragments of narrative. There is no "story" to this poem; it sustains no one locational or temporal logic; there is no consistent speaker for this poem. Where narratives appear, we tend to get only parts of them, or to part from them unsatisfied. The single longest story in the poem occupies the heart of "The Fire Sermon": the story of the young typist and her visitor, "the young man carbuncular," a "small house agent's clerk" (ll. 231–32). In this case we witness their emotionless assignation from beginning to end, but excepting the Clerk's perfunctory orgasm, the story has no climax and leads nowhere, not even to regrets on the part of the typist. It is a story that implicitly mocks the expectations of narrative.

For all of its use of myth and legend, *The Waste Land* militates against the narrative impulse to set things "once upon a time." In *The Waste Land*, time past is time present, and our modernity offers us no privileged vantage. In fact, the modern impulse to assume superiority over history appears to be a contributing factor to our spiritual malaise. This attitude is particularly noticeable in Part II: in the allusion to the old (even in 1922) popular song "That Shakespearian Rag"; or the apparent ignorance of the woman at her vanity regarding the significance of the "withered stumps of time" (l. 104) that adorn her boudoir; or the snidely arrogant way in which Lil's friend tells her that she "ought to be ashamed . . . to look so antique" (l. 156). The anti-narrative design of *The Waste Land* is of more than thematic importance, however. Principally, it functions to render more difficult readers' efforts to see stories as being "about" something other than their own lives. Anti-narrative design works to defer any closure that does not involve conscious awareness of one's own interpretive activity.

The pub scene that concludes "A Game of Chess" offers a characteristic example of how anti-narrative form functions in *The Waste Land*. In this case, we engage the story *in medias res*, where an excited storyteller is already well underway. We listen, as though overhearing from an adjacent seat in the pub, as she unsympathetically discusses "Lil" and her troubles and suggests her own designs on Lil's husband (ll. 139–67). Just as the story would seem to be approaching its point, the account breaks off as the unnamed speaker and her friend walk out of the pub, still in conversation. Until that moment, the poem has placed us, as in a dramatic monologue, in the position of that auditor, of the actual addressee; but the way it ends, with the barkeep saying goodnight to his regulars as they leave at closing time, returns us unceremoniously to the position of one who overhears and observes.

This particular handling of narratives or narrative fragments suggests another of the organizing techniques of *The Waste Land*: the poem positions us as that artist-as-spectator-of-modern-life whom Charles Baudelaire called the *flâneur*: a figure who observes (and overhears) the lives of ordinary people not from a sociological perspective but from an artistic one. Some of the most vibrant scenes in *The Waste Land* read as though snippets of conversation overheard by a strolling *flâneur*: lines 10–18 of "The Burial of the Dead," for instance, which are set in Munich's Hofgarten, or lines 60–76 of the same section, which describe a walk across London Bridge, surging with a crowd of office workers on their way into London's banking district ("the City"). Even, perhaps, the opening lines of "The Fire Sermon" (173–84), which according to Lawrence Rainey are the last lines that Eliot added to the poem. But there are other sections where it is either difficult to imagine a *flâneur*, or where the poem needs to make special allowance for such a figure – as Eliot does in his endnote for line 218, which informs us that "Tiresias, although a mere spectator and not indeed a 'character,' is yet the most important personage in the poem, uniting all the rest" (*CPP* 52). Scholars have debated the importance of this note, and indeed the importance of Tiresias, but the fact that he is not a "character" establishes his presence as an observer, and because he "perceived the scene, and foretold the rest" (l. 229), he enables Eliot to be in the bedrooms of both the wealthy couple of the first half of "A Game of Chess" and also the typist in "The Fire Sermon." That Eliot takes care to identify Tiresias as something other than a character indicates that the poem is not about him; if we understand that "personage" as a *flâneur* we can see that the poem is about the transformation of these often sordid scenes into something that is neither sordid nor even necessarily depressing. *The Waste Land* is about a world gone wrong, but the very existence of so energetic a poem suggests that the lifelessness and soullessness of the world depicted is not inevitable. To put it another way, the form of the poem gives the lie to its content.

The figure of Tiresias does something else for us besides. Much has been written about what Eliot was after in adapting this figure from Homer and other ancient writers, but fundamentally he represents a confusion of binary oppositions. Ancient accounts about him differ in detail, but he is always a complexly liminal figure, confounding the boundaries between important oppositions: he has lived as both man and woman, as both sighted and blind, in both this world and the next – where he continues to function as a seer, with command of time past, present, and future. Furthermore, in Sophocles's Theban trilogy, it is he who sees the cause of the city's suffering. In other words, like virtually all the motifs in *The Waste Land*, the presence of Tiresias in the poem is overdetermined.

As developed by Sigmund Freud in *The Interpretation of Dreams* (1899), overdetermination allows that a feature of a dream may have both multiple causes and multiple interpretations.[2] This is not so much to say that any interpretation could be equally valid as to suggest that unrelated, even apparently contradictory, interpretations are not only possible but even necessary. In the context of a non-narrative, even anti-narrative poem like *The Waste Land*, overdetermination functions as an informing principle. Consider, for instance, the opening of "The Fire Sermon," mentioned above. Describing an autumnal riverscape, the speaker observes "no empty bottles, sandwich papers, / Silk handerkerchiefs, cardboard boxes, cigarette ends / Or other testimony of summer nights" (ll. 177–79). Given that the speaker identifies the young women who might ordinarily have been partying along the banks with "their friends, the loitering heirs of city directors" (l. 180), as "nymphs" (l. 179), we might want to read this scene as one of restored purity. After all, this part of the poem is called "The Fire Sermon," after Buddha's famous sermon about freeing oneself from desire. But at the same time, this imagery of "the brown land" unmistakably connects with the waste-land of the previous two sections. Is this emptiness a sign, then, of spiritual cleansing, or of sterility? For the poem to do its work both interpretations need to be there, each destabilizing even as it implies the other. "Overdetermination" is not a word Eliot himself ever used, and the poet himself had no interest in psychoanalysis; but I invoke the term here to characterize one of the salient features of this poem – its ability not only to sustain but actually to invite contradictory interpretations.

This doubleness is another aspect of the "liminality" mentioned above: that quality where the poem apparently inhabits both sides of an opposition. Other examples are to be found in every part of the poem, but none is more illuminating than one that emerges in Eliot's endnotes to the poem, which open by pointing readers to two purportedly inspirational sources: Jessie L. Weston's *From Ritual to Romance* and Sir James Frazer's *The Golden Bough*. Eliot describes both works as anthropological, and expresses indebtedness to both. In fact, no two books could differ more in either character or purpose. Frazer was a loyal son of the Enlightenment, a rationalist who regretted the enduring power of religion (which he was inclined to lump together with superstition) over the modern world. Weston, by contrast, was a spiritualist and mystic who affirmed that "the Otherworld is not a myth, but a reality" and believed that the half-forgotten folklore of the pre-Christian World enshrined enduring truth (186). In other words, Frazer was a champion of the modern (which is not the same thing as identifying him as a "modernist"). Weston, by contrast, was a primitivist. Frazer urged that what troubles us moderns is our continuing adherence to myth and superstition. Weston believed that what troubles us is that we have lost touch with myth, treating it as nothing more than so many silly stories. The argument between these two writers was hugely important in Eliot's day and persists into our own; consider, for instance, Madison Avenue's enduring fondness for images of the primitive as signs of vitality, or the recent use of "cave-girl" images by dance divas aiming to project "raw" sexuality, or even the primitivist trappings of hugely popular TV shows like "Survivor." A number of scholars, following the lead of Leon Surette, have taken to equating modernism with primitivism. The textuality of *The Waste Land* suggests, instead, that what defines modernism is the tension between Frazer's and Weston's positions, and invites readers to see the poem as informed by it. One of *The Waste Land*'s least acknowledged accomplishments is its evasion of fashionable primitivism while yet maintaining a fascination with antiquity.

Nevertheless, the effect of Eliot's note about Weston and Frazer has more often led to expectations of narrative structure than of informing tensions. In particular, early critics expected that Eliot structured *The Waste Land* so as to reflect the basic pattern of the Grail quest, as found in the many tellings from Thomas Malory's fifteenth-century *Le Morte D'Arthur* to *Monty Python and the Holy Grail*. In its simplest terms, this pattern takes something like the following form: there is a kingdom that, because of an impious act of the King (often a "fisher king"), falls under a curse; it is revealed that this curse cannot be lifted until a knight-questor, pure of heart, makes his way to the Chapel Perilous and, once there, asks the right questions. These questions, Weston explains, have to do with primeval fertility myths and are fundamentally simple: what are these objects and whom do they serve? In effect, this way of responding to Eliot's note would have the Grail legends function for *The Waste Land* in more or less the same way that Homeric legend functions for Joyce's *Ulysses*. From our perspective today, this older response to Eliot's note suggests the enduring temptation to look for narrative in this insistently anti-narrative poem.

Other changes in Eliot's reception history are equally important to the engagement of twenty-first-century readers with *The Waste Land*. A generation ago, Eliot's purported hostility to popular culture was a critical commonplace, but that commonplace has recently been challenged. Scholars like David Chinitz, chiefly, but among others, have demonstrated Eliot's lifelong attraction to popular culture, albeit noting that his attraction was by no means undiscriminating.[3] In other words, popular culture figures in *The Waste Land* in ambiguous and sometimes self-interfering ways (as in the reference to "nymphs" noted above). In the bleak scene between the man and the woman at the beginning of "A Game of Chess," a scene which describes the outlines of a shared life even as it shows that life has no substance, the woman struggles desperately to establish connection between herself and her silent partner: "Are you alive, or not? Is there nothing in your head?" Again, the man refuses or is unable to reply, but we see that in his head he carries the tune to a ditty from the 1912 Ziegfeld Follies, "That Shakespearian Rag" (ll. 128–30). This tune could be said to be the "nothing" in his head (l. 126), but, as Chinitz notes, it is also the only lively thing in this bleak setting. The song itself condescends to elite culture, suggesting that Shakespeare was so good that he might *even* have been able to make it on Broadway. We can imagine this attitude as symptomatic of a modern emptiness, and of a modern myopia that can only see things in presentist terms. But we could also see it as representing a more vital relation to the past than is evident in the looming presence of the unrecognized or misunderstood "withered stumps of time" with which the woman has filled her dressing room. Here again, this detail can be called overdetermined. The past does not always trump the present in this poem, any more than does the modern surpass the ancient. Neither modernist or primitivist, in this sense, *The Waste Land* effectually collapses time, suggesting that the struggles of humankind to find love and connection remain what they always have been. That, in itself, represents a critique of the modern world's superficial faith in progress, and while the poem finds the hectic mechanism of modern life wanting, it does not allow us to think ourselves somehow especially singled out by history. It does not allow us to conceive of ourselves as exceptional in any way.

Eliot's line, "O O O O that Shakespeherian Rag," is all the same unmistakably modern (l. 128). There is more syncopation in the extra syllable of Eliot's "Shakespeherian" (as opposed to "Shakespearian") than there is the whole of the original song, "ragtime" though it purports to be. But if Eliot here enjoys flirting here with an unmistakably modern rhythm, throughout much of the poem he plays with what he had called in 1917 "the ghost of [a] simple meter" (*TCC* 187). The opening lines of "A Game of Chess" offer a telling example: often described as being blank verse, they admit in fact of considerable irregularity. In truth there are just enough instances of unrhymed iambic pentameter to arouse the expectation of a pattern that never fully establishes itself. Something similar happens, repeatedly, with end-rhymes in "What the Thunder Said." The first and third lines of the opening stanza rhyme ("faces" and "places"), but thereafter only lines 4 and 8 ("crying" and "dying") follow in suit. Similar things happen further into the section. The first four lines of 378–85 set a rhyme pattern of ABAB, but the stanza ends CDDE. The poem plays with pattern without developing a sustained organizing rhyme scheme or meter. Rhyme is present here, but is – ghostlike – gone as soon as we apprehend it.

But while rhyme and meter are not repeated in regular ways, the poem does exhibit regular patterns – and these become most noticeable as the poem accumulates resonance. In "What the Thunder Said," individual words and images repeat both from earlier sections and also from previous stanzas in this section. For example, the "torchlight red on sweaty faces" (l. 322) and the dry rocks of lines 331–51 recall the "red rock" sequence of 19–29; the inclusive "Unreal" of 377 recalls the objective correlative of "the brown fog of a winter dawn" that produces the same Baudelairean descriptor (60); and "kept the hours" (383) connects with St. Mary Woolnoth church near the end of London Bridge (67). But within "What the Thunder Said" other words reappear in portentous ways: *hooded* (ll. 364 and 369); *cracked/crack* (370 and 373); *towers* (374 and 383); *violet* (373 and 380); *black/blackened* (378 and 382).[4] These echoes manage to make of repetition a surprise, appearing sometimes when or where expected, and sometimes not. *The Waste Land* exhibits a poetic texture that challenges readers to look for pattern, and sometimes to discern pattern where it is present in no obvious way. Which is to say that the texture of the poem is disruptive enough, defamiliarizing enough, to call attention to the very processes of interpretation. *The Waste Land* is not a puzzle waiting to be solved; it is a poem that challenges ideas about puzzles. Through it all, Eliot's prosody is inseparable from the many ways in which it foregrounds its own interpretation. This is a poem where the most important things happen on the level of form.

"I sat upon the shore / Fishing, with the arid plain behind me": so begins the final stanza of the poem (ll. 424–25). For Christian readers the idea of fishing is inevitably freighted with significance, but the poem does not necessarily invite us to go that way. In telling us that he sits on the shore, the speaker situates himself once again in a liminal space: a shore is at once neither land nor sea, and both at once. That the speaker sits "with the arid plain behind" him suggests that he has turned his back on the Waste Land and its empty promises ("the empty chapel, only the wind's home" [l. 389]). But that he is fishing does not necessarily suggest he is expecting deliverance. In this case, fishing is . . . waiting. And we can see that by relating this image to those that immediately follow. Setting one's "lands in order" is preparing a last will and testament, making ready for death – waiting (l. 426). In the same vein, the child's game alluded to in the next line is a waiting game: the players walk in circles under the raised arms of two others, who will bring the "Bridge" down around whomever happens to be at that point when the song ends (427). Subsequent lines further set this pattern of waiting. The quotation from Dante's *Purgatorio* is from a soul (the poet Arnaut Daniel) waiting to be purged of his sins (428); the Latin line from the *Pervigilium Veneris* returns to the story of Procne and Philomel, with Procne wondering, waiting "When will my Springtime come?" (429). In the next fragment, French poet Gérard de Nerval presents himself as "the man of gloom, – the widower, – the unconsoled, / The Prince of Aquitania, his tower in ruins": ruins too represent a liminal state, a place that is no longer present but not quite gone, either, and here the prince awaits the return of "the Italian Sea" (430). The next line, among the most famous in the poem, takes this suggestion of ruins and runs with it. Indeed, like most lines in Part V, and like all previous lines in this verse except 426, it has no terminal punctuation; it literally "runs into" the following line, from the Elizabethan play-wright Thomas Kyd, in whose *The Spanish Tragedy* the Hamlet-like protagonist, Hieronymo, resolves to feign madness until he sees how best to act (432) – another instance of waiting.

The portentous line "These fragments I have shored against my ruins" (431) figures in virtually all interpretations of the poem and has been understood in many ways. The "fragments" in question would seem to refer to the preceding poem. That the speaker has used them to "shore" his ruins connects, of course, with the shore upon which he is sitting, but more immediately suggests that he has deployed them in a way to hold himself together – to "shore" himself up. Here too we find the language of waiting, since something that has been shored up is in a temporary condition, awaiting the right moment or materials to be repaired permanently; the work of shoring may keep ruins from falling, but it can't restore their wholeness. Once more, in *The Waste Land*, binary oppositions like fragmentation/wholeness break down.

If the "fragments" line feels portentous, the penultimate line of the poem represents an actual portent. It repeats the three forms of the Sanskrit "Da," which Eliot's endnote to line 402 identifies as from the "fable of the meaning of the Thunder . . . found in the *Brihadaranyaka – Upanishad*, 5, 1" (*CPP* 54). However, Eliot's note for the concluding line, "Shantih shantih shantih" is often misunderstood: the point is not so much an invocation of a "Peace which passeth understanding" as it is "a formal ending to an Upanishad" (55). It represents a putting of oneself in the hands of God, and then waiting.

Waiting is as fundamental to the experience of reading the poem as it is to the experience of the figures in the poem. In this sense, readers do well to recognize Eliot's grasp of that modernist aesthetic principle so evident in other writers like Joyce, Woolf, or Pound. When Pound urged the "direct treatment of the 'thing' whether subjective or objective" (*Literary Essays* 3), he was insisting on the importance of poetic *presentation*: present, don't tell – the poet should never need to *tell* readers what to make of a scene; rather, that making should be shaped by the poet's making. When, for instance, the moment arrives for Gabriel Conroy's after-dinner speech in Joyce's "The Dead," no narrative voice tells readers that Gabriel delivers a boring speech; instead, Joyce presents the speech directly, clichés and all. And when Eliot, in his oft-cited essay "Hamlet and His Problems," charges that "*Hamlet* the play is the primary problem, and Hamlet the character only secondary" (*SE* 121), when he judges that "Shakespeare was unable to impose this motive successfully upon the 'intractable' material of the old play," his point is precisely that in *Hamlet* we are told that "something is rotten in the state of Denmark" without feeling it (123). *The Waste Land* accomplishes something very different. Only rarely, as in Tiresias's comments, are readers "told" anything. More often the poem engages readers in the kinds of experience being represented, and of these waiting is among the most important.

"What the Thunder Said" presents the most sustained working-out of this principle in the poem. It begins with a familiar grammatical construction: "*after* this, *then* that." But the opening takes us to an indeterminate rather than a structured space: the "then" clause never materializes. Here again Eliot has taken a familiar form, used it to raise certain expectations, but then, by not completing the form as expected, turns those expectations against themselves. In this way, the opening inaugurates what may be the most intense experience of waiting the poem has yet produced. Indeed, as the unidentified speaker plays with the combination of a small number of elements, contemporary readers might be reminded of the patter of the clown-protagonists of Samuel Beckett's *Waiting for Godot* (1956):

> If there were water
> And no rock
> If there were rock
> And also water
> And water
> A spring
> A pool among the rock (ll. 346–52)

These lines reproduce the broken form of the section's opening lines, beginning with a subjunctive, "if," that leaves us waiting for the "then" clause to complete the thought – the thought that is never fully told. The verse paragraph that follows opens similarly, with an unanswered question ("Who is the third who walks always beside you?" [l. 360]), while the next poses riddles – "What is that sound high in the air," "Who are those hooded hordes," and "What is the city over the mountains" – that point to an endless historical cycle and thus are incapable of resolution (367–77).

Waiting takes new, anaphoric form in lines 378–85. Six of the eight lines in this stanza begin with "And," but it is never clear to what these *and*s are leading. Instead, Eliot's description of bats crawling "head downward down a blackened [bell-tower] wall" suggests a world stood on its head. The "towers / Tolling reminiscent bells," too, are "upside down in air" – in air, which is to say apparently without foundation. The next stanza moves to the "Chapel Perilous," a scene that remains important even without the sustaining narrative structure of a Grail Quest. This "empty chapel, only the wind's home" (389), conceals no truths and reveals nothing. There is no one there to answer a Questor's (or a reader's) questions. But this passage ends with a series of promising events: the crowing of a cock in a flash of lightning, and the rising of "a damp gust / Bringing rain" – the rain for which the parched wasteland has been waiting (390–95). But, in the classic dynamic of waiting, these promises prove empty. The next stanza reports: "Ganga was sunken, and the limp leaves / Waited for rain, while the black clouds / Gathered far distant, over Himavant" (ll. 396–98). With the river sunken from drought, the leaves limp for lack of water, we are returned to the enactment of ongoing process, and so of waiting, that opens the poem. In this way the poem gathers force and moves toward conclusion.

Once again, a thought from "Hamlet and His Problems" might serve to set the point: "the work of art cannot be interpreted; there is nothing to interpret" (*SE* 122). Because *The Waste Land* has been the subject of interpretive debate for so long, and because in so many ways it seems to urge attention to its significance, the expectation of a unifying meaning seems almost inevitable. It is not. The anti-interpretive stance Eliot outlines in "Hamlet" represents a commitment to poetry as experience, a refusal of the common sense of a poem as a pretty package with a surprise meaning inside, like some kind of Cracker Jack box. It is a denial that meaning could ever be that simple, a rejection of the poet as dutiful public sage. The legendary difficulty of *The Waste Land* is an integral part of the poem. The sense of meaning escaping one on every side, the sense that at any given point there is more going on than the reader can take in, is integral to the experience of the poem, a crucial part of Eliot's design. This difficulty is not, in other words, to be explained away.

That difficulty is a feature of the poem and not an inadvertent consequence of other things relates immediately to the question of meaning in *The Waste Land*. Eliot's poem delivers an excoriating critique of modern life, particularly of the ways in which the false gods of convenience and freedom have transformed the dynamics of love and connection. But there is a crucial difference between saying that the poem "delivers" such a critique and saying that it "is" such a critique – especially in view of Eliot's anti-interpretive stance. That the poem delivers, suggests, offers, or frames such a critique allows that it does such a thing in the dynamic context of other processes – and precisely by means of these other processes. To insist that the poem *is* a critique, by contrast, denies *The Waste Land* its identity as a poem and limits its resonance to sociological or political discourse. In a perhaps inevitably paradoxical formulation, Archibald MacLeish, a younger poet much influenced by and friendly with Eliot, famously concluded that "A poem should not mean / But be" (141–42). The claim is paradoxical because MacLeish makes it in the conclusion to his 1926 poem "Ars Poetica": it is inevitable (the recent experiments of the "Language poets" notwithstanding) that a poem, being made out of words, must mean.

A poem can, therefore, generate meanings without losing its poetic status. An important element of what I've tried to demonstrate above is that *The Waste Land* repeatedly and deliberately generates contradictory interpretations, and that the experience of the poem requires this ambiguity. But any attempt to extract meaning from the experience of the poem through an immersion in its formal dynamics necessarily *trans*forms the poem, substituting paraphrase for Eliot's language. The influential New Critic Cleanth Brooks first made this argument in 1947 (*Well* 192–214); that he was still urging the point – and about *The Waste Land* in particular – in 1965 says much about the allure of the Siren call of meaning.[5] Nearly a century of criticism has amply demonstrated that no interpretation of the poem can ever account for all its complexity, let alone stand in for it.

And so we return at last to the radical (as in "of or relating to the root") nature of this poem: its ability to inspire expectations of meaning and coherence without ever finally satisfying them; its ability to resist attempts to separate its meaning from the experience of the poem. This is what a growing number of critics are after when, like Kaiser, recognizing the extent to which the poem's capacity to disturb comes from its refusal to *allow* the Cracker Jack reading, they conclude that *The Waste Land* is a poem *about* interpretation itself. In this way, *The Waste Land* might prove after all to be the apotheosis of the modern movement.

NOTES

1 See RADICAL INNOVATION AND PERVASIVE INFLUENCE: *THE WASTE LAND*.
2 Freud first introduces this concept in *Studies in Hysteria* (1895), co-written with Josef Breuer.
3 See Chinitz, *passim*, and Rainey, *Revisiting*, especially pp. 53–70, which discuss the motif of the typist in contemporaneous popular fiction. In particular, Rainey observes the final differ-

ence between Eliot's handling of the typist's post-coital reflections and what was more commonly found in period melodrama (66).
4 For further demonstration of how this dynamic plays out in the text of *The Waste Land*, see Levenson, particularly 170–71.
5 See the special chapter on *The Waste Land* in Brooks, *Modern* 136–72.

REFERENCES AND FURTHER READING

Brooker, Jewel Spears, ed. *T. S Eliot: The Contemporary Reviews*. Cambridge: Cambridge UP, 2004.

Brooker, Jewel Spears, and Joseph Bentley. *Reading The Waste Land: Modernism and the Limits of Interpretation*. Amherst: U of Massachusetts P, 1990.

Brooks, Cleanth. *Modern Poetry and the Tradition*. New York: Oxford UP, 1965.

——. *The Well Wrought Urn: Studies in the Structure of Poetry*. New York: Reynal, 1947.

Brooks, Cleanth, and Robert Penn Warren. *Understanding Poetry*. 1938. 4th ed. New York: Holt, 1976.

Chinitz, David. *T. S. Eliot and the Cultural Divide*. Chicago: U of Chicago P, 2003.

Diepeveen, Leonard. *The Difficulties of Modernism*. New York: Routledge, 2003.

Ellmann, Richard. *James Joyce*. New York: Oxford UP, 1982.

Feldman, Jessica R. *Gender on the Divide: The Dandy in Modernist Literature*. Ithaca, NY: Cornell UP, 1993.

Frazer, James. *The Golden Bough*. 1890. 3rd ed. 12 vols. London: Macmillan, 1915.

Freud, Sigmund. *The Interpretation of Dreams*. 1899. Trans. Joyce Crick. New York: Oxford UP, 1999.

Kaiser, Jo Ellen Green. "Disciplining *The Waste Land*, or How to Lead Critics into Temptation." *Twentieth Century Literature* 44 (1998): 82–99.

Levenson, Michael H. *A Genealogy of Modernism: A Study of English Literary Doctrine 1908–1922*. Cambridge: Cambridge UP, 1984.

MacLeish, Archibald, *The Human Season: Selected Poems 1926–1972*. Boston: Houghton, 1972.

Pound, Ezra. *The Letters of Ezra Pound 1907–1941*. Ed. D. D. Paige. New York: New Directions, 1950.

——. *Literary Essays of Ezra Pound*. Ed. T. S. Eliot. New York: New Directions, 1954.

Rainey, Lawrence, ed. *The Annotated Waste Land with Eliot's Contemporary Prose*. New Haven: Yale UP, 2005.

——. *Revisiting the Waste Land*. New Haven: Yale UP, 2005.

Surette, Leon. *The Birth of Modernism: T. S. Eliot, W. B. Yeats, and the Occult*. Montréal: McGill-Queen's UP, 1993.

Weston, Jessie. *From Ritual to Romance*. 1919. Gloucester, MA: Smith, 1983.

14
The Enigma of "The Hollow Men"

Elisabeth Däumer

An In-Between Poem

Despite Craig Raine's recent claim that "The Hollow Men," when "approached . . . directly, is a simple poem" (15), this five-section suite has proved a remarkably elusive and enigmatic work. As a transitional poem, looking backward to *The Waste Land* and forward to the explicitly spiritual, more musically than cinematically inspired poetry of Eliot's post-conversion period, it may not have been the entirely new beginning Eliot had in mind when he declared, in 1922, that *The Waste Land* was "a thing of the past" (*Letters* 596). Nevertheless, for novice readers of Eliot, especially those who have just traversed *The Waste Land*, developing, perhaps, a grudging admiration for its jazzy juxtapositions, complex allusiveness, and abrasive realism of voice and scene, "The Hollow Men" is bound to come as somewhat of a shock. Such readers frequently express dismay at the poem's "abstractness." What happened to the new poetic, as formulated by Pound? Where, in this poem, does Eliot "go in fear of abstractions" (Pound 85)? Where is the "direct treatment of the 'thing' whether subjective or objective" (84)? Where the realism of character, voice, and scene? Where the dialogue? The Eliot of *The Waste Land*, as one of my students has remonstrated, would never have written "Shape without form, shade without colour, / Paralyzed force, gesture without motion" (*CPP* 56). Instead he would have found an object or event to evoke that sensation of paralysis in and for the reader.

But how "abstract" is the poem? Its language and imagery are "disarmingly simple" (Southam 97), neither abstract in the way Pound taught his contemporaries to eschew, nor realistic in the manner Eliot's earlier poetry leads us to expect. Instead, we find a return to Symbolism and its approximation of the indefiniteness of music, which was meant to take poetry beyond the borders of language to a realm freed from the fetters of representational meaning. The poem's musical, rather than narrative, development of theme, its choral alternation between individual and collective voices, its rhythmic reiteration of sounds, words, and phrases cast a decisively musical spell,

A Companion to T. S. Eliot, First Edition. Edited by David E. Chinitz.
© 2014 John Wiley & Sons, Ltd. Published 2014 by John Wiley & Sons, Ltd.

eerily melodious and prayer-like in some places, manically cheerful in others, halting and apocalyptically threatening in the end. Both the topography of the poem – the tumid river, hollow valley, cactus land, twilight kingdom – and its imagery of eyes, stars, broken columns, and the Shadow arouse no "ordinary feelings" (Moody 121). The poem is not strictly symbolist, however; its images are neither idiosyncratic nor esoteric as those of symbolists like Valéry or Mallarmé, but conventional, we might even say "universal," and yet enveloped in the aura of an uncanny melodious mystery (130).

Even without knowing anything of Dante's symbology in the *Divine Comedy*, most readers bring to the poem's refrain of hollowness as well as to the images of eyes and stars enough cultural associations (including memories of Eliot's own poetry) to intuit the emotional drama of the poem. Since eyes and seeing are commonly associated with insight, intimacy, love, and judgment, the speakers' fear of eyes they "dare not meet in dreams" and their simultaneous longing for the presence of eyes serve as immediate clues to the emotional and spiritual state of the hollow men (*CPP* 57). Similarly, we need not be familiar with the relevant lines from Dante to be alive to the symbolic weight of stars in "The Hollow Men." The contrast of the fading stars of "death's dream kingdom" with the one "perpetual star / Multifoliate rose" suggests the hollow men's longing for a passion so transcendent that it will lift them from the broken valley of death's dream kingdom, "this valley of dying stars" (57–58).

Such intuitions may function as a guide into the poem, allowing readers to experience its symbolism as inviting, and indeed requiring, their participation. This is especially true with regard to the ominous Shadow, which enters in the final segment as an unfathomable presence, positioned in the in-between and endowed with an enduring symbolism, encompassing biblical associations with sin and death and the popular fascination with crimes and dreams, the unconscious, and the abject. The poem's confusingly similar yet emphatically distinguished kingdoms of death might prove its most formidably elusive element, requiring explication of the different realms of death in Dante's *Divine Comedy*; still, for novice readers of today, death's dream kingdom can resonate powerfully with the hollowness of a virtual realm, produced by the dream industry of modern media – one that offers little insight or intimacy, but only the spectral shapes of trend and fashion. By contrast, death's twilight kingdom and, even more so, death's other kingdom are suffused with ambivalent longing for connection and intimacy: there is talk of a "final meeting," if a feared one, in part II, and trembling "[l]ips that would kiss" in part III.

Orientation through Allusion

Although much can be gathered about this elusive poem, then, without any knowledge of its central allusions – certainly an indication of the unobtrusive way in which allusions function in this poem – the study of its sources, foremost among them Dante's *Divine Comedy* and Conrad's *Heart of Darkness*, proves infinitely rewarding. A first-hand encounter with Dante's trilogy enriches our experience of Eliot's hollow men, who belong to the damned in hell, and specifically to those consigned to its antechamber, where the tepid – the cowardly fence-sitters, those neither for nor against – suffer a double expulsion, despised by heaven and hell alike. Such an encounter will do more than introduce readers to Dante's allegory, with its different realms of death – the inferno, purgatory, and paradise, including their discrete circles and pouches; after all, any commentary can do that. More importantly, readers will gain a glimpse of Dante's visual language – of the richly detailed tapestry of settings, characters, stories, moods, and thoughts brought to the mind's eye with sudden vividness by the judiciously selected references in Eliot's spartan poem. The stars in "The Hollow Men" are more resonant if we are familiar with the marvelous lines describing Dante's joy in the first canto of *Purgatory*, when after his harrowing escape from hell he welcomes the "sweet azure of the sapphire . . . gathering on the serene horizon" (185) and is overcome by the beauty of the "four stars / unseen by mortals since the first mankind" (186). And the image of the hollow men "[g]athered on this beach of the tumid river" in section IV immediately recalls at least two graphically detailed scenes: first, the train of the "nearly soulless / whose lives concluded neither blame nor praise" (Dante 14); and, second, the damned souls gathered in the dim light of the sad river Acheron – the "lost / violent souls" (*CPP* 56) eager to find their way across the water, "for here / Divine Justice transforms and spurs them so / their dread turns wish: they yearn for what they fear" (Dante 16).

Readers also familiar with Conrad's *Heart of Darkness* are bound to have an even richer visual experience, as for them the "tumid river" will bring to mind both the Acheron and, as in a photographic superimposition, an image of a modern inferno, this one on the banks of the Congo, where Conrad's narrator Marlow steps into the "gloomy circle of some Inferno" and encounters "[b]lack shapes" that "crouched, lay, sat between the trees, leaning against the trunks, clinging to the earth, half coming out, half effaced within the dim light, in all the attitudes of pain, abandonment, and despair" (31). Marlow's nightmare vision of the colonialist enterprise in Africa, of its implacable grayness and moral ambiguity, which becomes for him the condition of life in general, serves as a crucial atmospheric counterpoint to Dante's vision of hell, which despite its despair and gloom is relieved by a sense of its divinely appointed order, justice, and love. In Conrad's modern inferno, created by the "imbecile rapacity" of European imperialism (38), it is the white intruders who are the hollow men – men like Kurtz and his cohorts who mask their brute acquisitiveness by the trappings of an allegedly superior civilization: clothes, poetry, and the eloquence of a language utterly divorced from truth. Idolized, envied, and feared by whites and natives alike, Kurtz is the archetypal hollow man (Marlow calls him a "hollow sham" [85]). What redeems him in Marlow's eyes, however, is his willingness, on the threshold of death, to face the truth about himself. Kurtz's dying words proved so resonant for Eliot that he had originally placed them as epigraph to *The Waste Land*:

Did he live his life again in every detail of desire, temptation, and surrender during that supreme moment of complete knowledge? He cried in a whisper at some image, at some vision, – he cried out twice, a cry that was no more than a breath –
   'The horror! The horror!' (*WLF* 3)

The theme of self-knowledge acquired through the unflinching confrontation with the shadow that falls between ideal and reality is central to "The Hollow Men," whose speakers evade what Kurtz had the courage to face with "direct eyes": the truth about themselves. The other two major allusions – to Guy Fawkes and Shakespeare's *Julius Caesar* – direct us to the tragic gap between political ideals and personal ambitions. Neither Brutus nor those collaborating in the Gunpowder Plot shrank from decisive action in pursuit of their political ideals; at the same time, neither came to realize the dubiousness of personal motive and self-delusion undergirding their apparently selfless, if violent, pursuits on behalf of their communities.[1]

Such closer familiarity with the contrasting, yet profoundly related, worlds of Dante and Conrad – with the assurance of Dante's ordered universe and the abysmal doubt of Conrad's – provides us with important guideposts for reading the landscape of "The Hollow Men." Section I plunges us into hell, death's dream kingdom, the world of the hollow men, whose eviscerated sense of self and community is conveyed by two paradoxes: the men are "hollow," yet "stuffed"; they speak as a group, but, with their "quiet and meaningless" voices reduced to the repulsive sound of "rats' feet over broken glass," they are deprived of any means of genuine communication (*CPP* 56). Their sense of insignificance and lack of motion, initiative, and volition ("Behaving as the wind behaves") is developed in subsequent parts of the poem, as is the symbolic terrain of death's dream kingdom, the "dead land" and "cactus land" of part III, in which "stone images / Are raised" (57) – an allusion to the worship of idols, or in contemporary terms that Eliot would surely not eschew, of material commodities like Kurtz's ivory. Most of all, this realm of death – really the death-in-life that Eliot explored in *The Waste Land* – is a world of utter solipsism: the speakers are "[s]ightless" (58) and, in their unwillingness or inability to cross "[w]ith direct eyes" (56), they take a sort of despairing, self-destructive comfort in the absence of the eyes of another, whose presence they long for, but only in the transfigured aspect of unconditional love – as the "[m]ultifoliate rose."

Death's dream kingdom, as the reference to "this beach of the tumid river" in part IV indicates, is located in hell's vestibule, a place and spiritual state that proved of consuming interest for Eliot, who had merged it in *The Waste Land* with limbo – the place for the virtuous but unbaptized – to epitomize in a most condensed manner the hell of contemporary civilization and its peculiarly modern spiritual disease: spleen, ennui, *acedia* (spiritual lethargy). In a significant departure from Dante's geography, the limbo of the hollow men is bounded by the River Acheron, and those who traverse it eventually find themselves not in hell, but in "death's other kingdom," a place of sunlight, trees, wind, and voices, whose imagery mirrors both that of Dante's paradise and, more ominously, that of Marlow's sojourn in the heart of darkness, with its trees "swayed by the wind" and its "jabber" of voices, "silly, atrocious, sordid, savage, or simply mean, without any kind of sense" (64–67). Death's twilight kingdom, invoked only twice in the poem (ll. 38, 65), is a transitional realm that loosely corresponds with Dante's arduous ascent of Mount Purgatory toward the Earthly Paradise: he passes through a wall of refining fire and submits to being humbled and shamed by a fearsome Beatrice, who reminds him of his sins and unfaithfulness. In Eliot's revised topography of hell, purgatory, and paradise, the twilight kingdom is the shadowy realm that needs to be crossed with "direct eyes" confronting the horror of self-knowledge.

Disorientation through Language

Taking as its blueprint Dante's progression down the narrowing circles of hell and up to the ever-more light-filled reaches of paradise, this confident mapping of the poem's emotional and spiritual terrain does not, of course, do justice to the experience of reading "The Hollow Men." The dreamlike fragmentation and strangely formless landscape of Eliot's poem are more akin to the impalpable fogginess of Conrad's world than to the ordered assurance and teleology of Dante's universe. Nor does the poem offer the luxury of a Virgil, guiding and teaching us about the distinct spheres, patiently responding to our perplexed questions or informing us about the ultimate goal of our journey. What we have for orientation are the words themselves, and these are frequently so ambiguous, even at their most emphatic, and mysterious even at their most transparent, as to leave us groping, from line to line, stanza to stanza, to find a foothold or a sense of direction. Indeed, the frequently repeated pronouns and adverbs "this," "these," and "those," "here" and "there," with their insistent promise of delineation, prove at best illusory guides, intercepting and frustrating the reader's desire for a clearly definable path or forward movement, and as often as not, looping us back to the pit of the hollow men's broken valley.

Part I sets up the central emotional binary of the poem, the contrast between the "here" of the speakers' damnation – their sterile, paralytic hollowness – and the "there" of death's other kingdom, a binary which corresponds to the poles of inferno and paradise, damnation and beatitude, in Dante. In part II, however, the strangely free-floating appearance of "These" and "There," in addition to the use of dislocating enjambments, destabilizes this binary:

> Eyes I dare not meet in dreams
> In death's dream kingdom
> These do not appear:
> There, the eyes are
> Sunlight on a broken column
> There . . . (*CPP* 57)

With their two enjambments, the first three lines immediately confront the reader with a series of choices. Though the open end of line 1 invites the expectation that the next line will continue the thought or statement, the plural pronoun "These" introducing the third line prompts us to rearrange the syntactic relation between the previous two lines. For now the meaning is no longer "Eyes I dare not meet in dreams in death's dream kingdom," but "Eyes I dare not meet in dreams. . . do not appear" "in death's dream kingdom." This seemingly haphazard slippage in meaning, as minute as it is profound, shifts the emphasis from the fear of eyes to their absence. Moreover, if we read the subsequent "There" as referring back to death's dream kingdom, our supposition of a wishful evasion of the eyes is confirmed. "There" the eyes have been transformed into symbolic substitutes (Smith 104) – "Sunlight on a broken column" – and the human body possessing the eyes has evaporated into disembodied "voices" in the "wind's singing," invoking a sense of comfort or, if the dissonant strain of Conrad's nightmare melody obtrudes, an eerie remoteness (*CPP* 57).

However, if we take it as pointing us away from "here," the word "There" leads us away from death's dream kingdom to a luminously invoked elsewhere, whose "romantic imagery" and mysterious melody, its recurrent sounds "permuted with Sestina-like virtuosity" (Kenner 185), are reminiscent of Dante's paradise. The second stanza of part II lends credence to this latter choice, since its comparative use of "no nearer" and "also" returns us back to the "here" of death's dream kingdom, its fear of confrontation, its retreat into unreality, which differs, if ever so slightly, from the absence-by-substitution of the eyes in the melodiously evoked elsewhere (*CPP* 57). The concluding plea, "Not that final meeting / In the twilight kingdom," does not resolve the ambiguity, but suggests instead a curious continuity between death's dream kingdom and death's other kingdom, as if the imagined luminescent remoteness of the latter were no more than a mirage of the former – the central dream, perhaps, of death's dream kingdom, which threatens to slip into a nightmare – and not the absolute state of blessedness procured by the disciplined education of desire and the rigorous acquisition of knowledge that Dante envisioned in *Paradiso*.

The fluidly obscure imprecision of the poem's emotional, moral, and spiritual terrain persists in subsequent sections of the poem, culminating in the anti-apocalyptic "whimper" of section V (*CPP* 59). Sections III and IV each begin with an emphatic return to the speakers' "here," their fundamentally vacuous existence (57, 58). Section III is the only one clearly divided into only two verse paragraphs (rather than three or six). Beginning "This is the dead land" and reiterating "this" and "here" (57), the first prepares us for the difference of death's *other* kingdom, taken up in the second. In a small but significant indication of difference, the opening of the second verse paragraph displaces "this" from the beginning to the end of the line. What appears to set death's other kingdom apart is not so much the terrain (desert and stones) as the speakers' emotion, shifting from numbness to palpitating tenderness. The raised stone images of death's dream kingdom, beseeched and worshiped by "a dead man's hand" (57) – an uncanny image of physical and spiritual mutilation – recur as the "broken stone" in death's *other* kingdom (58). And if the piercingly intimate vision of "Waking alone / At the hour when we are / Trembling with tenderness" appears to transport us worlds away from the stony death imagery of death's dream kingdom, the next lines, with their implication of impeded intimacy – "Lips that would kiss / Form prayers to broken stone" – blur any clear contrast between the present and the desired *other* realm of the hollow men (57–58). Similarly, the "broken stone" of death's dream kingdom, echoing the "broken column" of the luminous mirage in section II, suggests at first the destruction of idols, and with that the possibility of a concomitant spiritual transformation. Yet such hopeful reading falters under the weight of textual ambiguity, above all the hint of a painful emotional displacement, which may well be related to a noteworthy absence: there is not a single reference to "eyes" in this section of the poem.

Eyes do reappear in section IV, which some critics have regarded as the emotional and structural crux of the poem. For here the absence of eyes that, in section II, the speaker dared not "meet in dreams," is lamented – "The eyes are not here / There are no eyes here" (58) – and for the first time in the poem, there is a sense of what it might take to be delivered from this hell of sterile vacuity:

> Sightless, *unless*
> The eyes reappear
> As the perpetual star
> Multifoliate rose
> Of death's twilight kingdom
> The hope only
> Of empty men. (*CPP* 58, emphasis added)

The use of "empty" instead of "hollow," Friedrich W. Strothman and Lawrence V. Ryan have argued, signals an important spiritual change in the collective speaker of the poem, whose ability to envision salvation by the multifoliate rose – "the *corpus Christi mysticum*, a symbol of maximum fulfillment" – hinges on a "complete emptying of the human soul of everything that is not God" (426–27). In answer to such an optimistic gloss, musically reinforced by the slant-rhyme of "sightless" and "unless," we might point to the fundamental passivity with which the speakers imagine the reappearance of the eyes. What, we might ask, has happened to that fearsome crossing with *direct* eyes, to that "final meeting / In the twilight kingdom" (*CPP* 57)? And might not the resigned note of the speakers' lament testify to their deepened sense of spiritual impotence?

Section V certainly does not help us solve the enigma of "The Hollow Men." If anything, this section materializes the poem's pervasive ambiguity in the shape of the Shadow that falls, with fatal inevitability, between the poles of idea, conception, and intention on the one hand and their realization or fulfillment on the other. But is the Shadow purely a force of inhibition and impediment – hindering, as Grover Smith suggests, "even the attempt at prayer through which the speaker might come into the 'Kingdom' of pure actuality beyond" (107) – or an in-between space, a gap, temporal or spatial, that to those undaunted by it provides the grounds for unexpected, perhaps shattering, insight?

Reorientation through Criticism

When we turn to the poem's critical reception for clarification, especially with regard to the astonishingly ambiguous and typographically complex last section, we encounter an illuminating variety of responses, some of them describing the poem, with its "barely glimpsed possibility of Christian hope plung[ing] to crazy childishness," as Eliot's "most blasphemous" (Crawford 154), and others, by contrast, detecting in the children's prickly pear dance a "poetic expression of [Eliot's] groping first steps away from despair-inspiring relations toward religious faith and transcendence" (Freeman 42). According to an early consensus, cemented by the authoritative triumvirate of F. O. Matthiessen, Grover Smith, and Hugh Kenner, "The Hollow Men" was the last gasp of Eliot's *Waste Land* phase. As a poem focused on the state of "social, moral, historical, and poetic vacuity" (Kenner 194), devoid of plot or motivated actions, it was an extension of *The Waste Land*'s "design of quest and failure" (Smith 104). "In fewer words than *The Waste Land* has lines," Kenner concluded, the poem "articulates . . . everything remaining that *The Waste Land* for one reason or another omitted to say" (194). In the late 1950s, Strothman and Ryan challenged this by-then conventional interpretation and contended that "The Hollow Men" marked a decisive transitional stage between the despair of Eliot's *Waste Land* poetry and his later, spiritually affirmative poetry. Their argument rests, as implied above, on a special interpretation of "empty," which they approached in light of the writings of the Spanish mystic St. John of the Cross, who used the word "not in the sense of 'hollow' but of 'receptive, capable of being filled'" (426) to refer to a "state of grace," a sensual and intellectual deprivation that is "the absolutely necessary condition for eventual union with God" (427). Other critics also found evidence in the poem suggesting its distance from *The Waste Land*'s anguish and despair. Thus Eliot's biographer Lyndall Gordon viewed "The Hollow Men" as a record of the spiritual struggles of a "potential convert, still hollow of belief, [who] tries to make the Lord's Prayer . . . his own prayer": "On the right of the page are the eloquent responses of the given prayer; on the left, the potential convert struggles to utter the words, in vain" (211). A. D. Moody, tracing the poem's evolution from aborted drafts, discovered in "The Hollow Men" a distinct progression of feeling drawn from *La Vita Nuova*, Dante's record of his successful struggle to sublimate his love for Beatrice until carnal love was transmuted into a higher, ideal love, epitomized in the cult of the Virgin Mary (124–25).[2]

The elusive Shadow of section V has provoked the most searching interpretations. For many, it is the embodiment of some fatal obstruction, falling, as Kenner noted, "with a gesture of decisive inhibition" (192), a reminder of some inevitable "discrepancy between intention and achievement" (Crawford 157) or of the "hideous dream" opening between "the acting of a dreadful thing / And the first motion" described by Brutus in *Julius Caesar* (2.1.63–65). For Gordon, the Shadow is the struggling convert's lingering hesitation and doubt. More recently, Ronald Schuchard's psychologically inflected study proposed that the Shadow is a projection of Eliot's "Dark Angel" – the intense visitations of violent sexual feelings that tormented his spiritual life, proving "at once his fury and his muse" (3). The Shadow terrifies the hollow men as the knowledge of an irrevocable chasm between "potential passion and any actualization possible in life" (Eliot, "Beyle" 393). Nancy Gish, in turn, views the Shadow as a materialization of "unbearable desires that cannot be owned even if recognized in moments of horror" (119). In Strothman and Ryan's determinedly positive interpretation, the Shadow represents the benign presence of death, desired by the hollow men as the only way toward entrance into God's kingdom (428–29).

The observation that the italicized lines "*For Thine is the Kingdom*" and "*Life is very long*" (the latter from Conrad's *An Outcast of the Islands*) assume the visual force of a shadow falling between stanzas suggests yet another way to make sense of Eliot's nebulous figure (*CPP* 59). The Shadow, as discussions with my students have taught me, can then be seen as a space that challenges us to question what we think we know about God and life, including the religious, ethical, and epistemological certainties founded on the sort of dualistic thinking epitomized by the list of binary pairs – idea/reality, motion/act, conception/creation, etc. – at the center of part V.[3] Jewel Spears Brooker's study of the revolt against dualism advanced in Eliot's philosophical essays on Kant and in his dissertation on F. H. Bradley lends credence to such an interpretation. Brooker attributes Eliot's fascination with intermediate states to his adoption of Bradley's central insight "that the world is one, that reality is one, that dualism always leads to self-contradiction" (178). She explains that the frequent tropes of binary opposites, paradoxes, and contradictions in Eliot's poetry – from "Gerontion" to *Four Quartets* – "displace focus from term to relation," with the effect of directing "readers to an absence or a gap or a puzzle and then leav[ing] them there to reflect on what can only be guessed, glimpsed, imagined, half-heard" (159).[4] Brooker's semi-deconstructive perspective does not disambiguate "The Hollow Men" or transcend the oppositional interpretations that have polarized the poem's critical reception. Instead it foregrounds ambiguity as a central structural device that produces, or reveals, a twilight realm of uncertainty and undecidability, a gap or *aporia*, which can be at once impediment and "fertile impasse" (159), depending on the hollow men's, or our own, willingness to cross "with direct eyes." Of course, even this interpretation runs the risk of forcing too coherent a conclusion – of demanding the bang of a triumphal will-to-meaning rather than the infinitely less glorious "whimper" of continued uncertainty and doubt. Nevertheless, in view of the violent political upheavals that scarred the last century, as they continue to mark this one, the poem's anti-apocalyptic, anti-triumphalist admission of defeat and vulnerability bears the tentative hope for new or alternative meanings of the kind invariably eradicated in the "bang" of a final revelation.

NOTES

1 Of course, both of these sources function in more various and always evocative ways, inviting readers' interpretive ingenuity. The epigraph "A penny for the Old Guy" refers to Guy Fawkes Day (*CPP* 56), commemorating the failed attempt of Catholic extremists to seize power by killing King James and the ministers at the State opening of Parliament on November 5, 1605. Guy Fawkes was arrested in the cellars of the House of Lords, where he guarded nearly two tons of gunpowder. The circumstances of the Gunpowder Plot are referred to in line 10 ("dry cellar"), line 16 ("violent souls"), and in the final "whimper," an allusion to the failed explosion and, perhaps, the wail of pain with which the tortured Guy Fawkes gave away the names of his co-conspirators (Southam 97–98). With their ceremonial burning of stuffed effigies ("the old guy"), the annual celebration of Guy Fawkes Day also harks back to pagan rituals, as does the dance around the "prickly pear," suggesting the poem's concern with the "degradation of essential ritual" (Crawford 154). The multiple allusions to Shakespeare's play *Julius Caesar* reinforce the poem's theme of hollowness, juxtaposing the helpless paralysis of the hollow men with the envy of Cassius and self-deception of Brutus, which spurred their violent betrayal.

2 For the publication history of "The Hollow Men" from individual sections previously published in conjunction with poems excluded from the five-part sequence as it appeared in 1925, see Bush 81–101, Moody 118–27, and Southam 134–35.

3 This essay owes much to the enthusiasm and intrepid interpretative ventures of my students at Eastern Michigan University. I would like to thank all of them, and in particular Travis Schreer, Dana Blaisdell, Alyssa Brewer, Scott Caddy, Rachel Lebron, Brigette Lootens, Jantzen Norwood, Kristin Porchia, Laura Quashnie, Lindsay Sarin, Kathleen Whitman, and Nadine Yonka. My gratitude also goes to Leonore Gerstein for her perceptive comments on an earlier draft of the chapter.

4 On Eliot's "revolt against dualism," see YES AND NO: ELIOT AND WESTERN PHILOSOPHY.

REFERENCES AND FURTHER READING

Brooker, Jewel Spears. *Mastery and Escape: T. S. Eliot and the Dialectic of Modernism*. Amherst: U of Massachusetts P, 1994.

Bush, Ronald. *T. S. Eliot: A Study in Character and Style*. New York: Oxford UP, 1983.

Conrad, Joseph. *Heart of Darkness*. Ed. Ross Murfin. 2nd ed. Boston: St. Martin's, 1996.

Crawford, Robert. *The Savage and the City in the Work of T. S. Eliot*. Oxford: Clarendon, 1987.

Dante Alighieri. *The Divine Comedy*. Trans. John Ciardi. New York: Norton, 1970.

Freeman, Venus. "'The Hollow Men': Between the Idea and the Reality." *Yeats Eliot Review* 10.1 (1989): 41–43.

Gish, Nancy K. "Discarnate Desire: T. S. Eliot and the Poetics of Dissociation." *Gender, Desire, and Sexuality in T. S. Eliot*. Ed. Cassandra Laity and Nancy K. Gish. Cambridge: Cambridge UP, 2004. 107–29.

Gordon, Lyndall. *T. S. Eliot: An Imperfect Life*. New York: Norton, 1998.

Kenner, Hugh. *The Invisible Poet: T. S. Eliot*. New York: McDowell, 1959.

Matthiessen, F. O., and C. L. Barber. *The Achievement of T. S. Eliot: An Essay on the Nature of Poetry*. 1935. Enlarged ed. New York: Oxford UP, 1958.

Moody, A. D. *Thomas Stearns Eliot, Poet*. Cambridge: Cambridge UP, 1979.

Pound, Ezra. "A Retrospect." *Poetry in Theory: An Anthology 1900–2000*. Oxford: Blackwell, 2004. 83–90.

Raine, Craig. *T. S. Eliot*. Oxford: Oxford UP, 2006.

Schuchard, Ronald. *Eliot's Dark Angel: Intersections of Life and Art*. New York: Oxford UP, 1999.

Shakespeare, William. *The Oxford Shakespeare: The Complete Works*. Ed. Stanley Wells et al. 2nd ed. Oxford: Oxford UP, 2005.

Smith, Grover. *T. S. Eliot's Poetry and Plays: A Study in Sources and Meaning*. 1950. 2nd ed. Chicago: U of Chicago P, 1974.

Southam, B. C. *A Guide to the Selected Poems of T. S. Eliot*. New York: Harcourt, 1968.

Strothman, Friedrich W., and Lawrence V. Ryan. "Hope for T. S. Eliot's 'Empty Men.'" *PMLA* 73 (1958): 426–32.

15
Sweeney Agonistes:
A Sensational Snarl

Christine Buttram

"{T}he problem {of poetic drama} is much more of a tangle than it looks."
    – T. S. Eliot ("John Dryden II" 681)

Just after "The Hollow Men" and, again, just before *The Rock*, Eliot thought that his "poetry was over," that he had "written [himself] out" ("T. S. Eliot Talks" 5). Respectively, these periods correspond to the 1926–27 *Criterion* publication of his Sweeney play and its 1932 publication as *Sweeney Agonistes*, Eliot's most densely transitional work. The years from its conception to its final iteration, 1920–1936, saw changes in Eliot's marriage, profession, nationality, and religion. During this period, Eliot's aesthetics changed too, and he turned from dramatically inclined poetry to poetic drama.

To the end of his career, Eliot would emphasize how much the poet attempting drama had to learn and labor. So humbling was the creation of *Sweeney Agonistes* that Eliot would never refer to it as his first play and would rarely refer to it at all; in 1962, Eliot did not include it in *Collected Plays*. In 1936, he had collected it as an "Unfinished Poem" and said in a broadcast interview that he had written this piece over two nights, in the wee hours, with help from "a bottle of gin" (qtd. in Litz 10). Yet in the same year, Eliot described *Sweeney* as the "most *original* thing" he had written (qtd. in Schuchard 99–100).

Modern drama and contemporary theater were dead, Eliot thought from the outset. The reign of dramatic realism, the stagnancy of poetic drama, and the lack of dramaturgical convention had caused this dreary demise, as had actors' performing their personalities instead of roles. In 1924, Eliot stated that a "revolution in principles" must occur in the theater (*SE* 91), and in his prose of the late 1910s through the mid-1930s, he routinely examined the problems of the modern stage and explored solutions to them. This writing also reveals Eliot's active, wide-ranging involvement in the performance arts of his time. Attending plays and other staged productions regularly, keeping abreast of current writing in and on the theater, and sharpening his knowledge

A Companion to T. S. Eliot, First Edition. Edited by David E. Chinitz.
© 2014 John Wiley & Sons, Ltd. Published 2014 by John Wiley & Sons, Ltd.

of dramatic history, Eliot developed a multiform theory of poetic drama. Emerging quickly, these theories would stimulate but then stymie his first play.

"Toward a New Form"

Eliot was contemplating a Sweeney drama as early as 1920 (Woolf 68). In early 1922, he was "trying to read" Aristophanes (*Letters* 504); Ezra Pound advised that less "depressing" and more exciting would be the "native negro phoque melodies of Dixee" (505). Eliot would take this cue, yet not immediately. Later in 1922, he wrote that *The Waste Land* was "a thing of the past": "I am now feeling toward a new form and style" (596). Nevertheless, the Sweeney play lay unbegun for some time. In April 1924, he informed his patron John Quinn that he felt stimulated to start the work he had "in mind," a work "more ambitious than anything" he had theretofore written (*WLF* xxix).

Between *The Waste Land* and late 1924, Eliot forged a draft outline, a handwritten sketch based on an Aristophanic paradigm as filtered through F. M. Cornford's *The Origin of Attic Comedy*.[1] Dissecting Aristophanes's comedies to display their protodramatic antecedents in ancient fertility rites, Cornford furnished an appendix parsing Aristophanic plots in view of their vegetation-ceremony motifs. These analyses provided Eliot with a structure for his own outline, which delineated the Sweeney play as having a prologue, parados, agon, parabasis, scene, second parabasis, chorikan, second scene, and exodus (Stage Sixty). *Sweeney Agonistes* consists essentially of the first four units. Behind this scheme lurks Eliot's "mythical method" (*SP* 177–78). So emptily chaotic was modernity, he thought in the early 1920s, that its art could acquire meaning and order only through a sustained congruency between modern material and past patterns. This parallel seemed all the more necessary for drama, given its origins in religious ritual.

Eliot's prose of the early 1920s shows that avant-garde ballet and age-old Noh theater were also formative models for Eliot's new objectives. In its richly conventional depersonalization of actors, who wore iconic masks, the Japanese Noh relied on stylized gesture, not expressive diction. With no diction and all gesture, the ballet performers, particularly those of the Diaghilev *Ballets Russes* productions, inspired Eliot likewise. The ballet intrinsically carried ancient energies, Eliot believed, a wild and sacred power that Stravinsky musically underscored. (One draft of the Sweeney play includes an odd ballet interlude.) Both modern ballet and Noh drama tended toward percussiveness, and this raw rhythmical power was, to Eliot, more stirring than the drab realism that bred subjective acting. In 1933, he advised that actors in *Sweeney Agonistes* should wear masks (Flanagan 83).

Another inspiration for Eliot during these years was the best of the obsolescent music-hall stars, whose stage miens drew his utmost praise. For over a decade, Eliot perceived in music-hall performance an exquisite equilibrium between thespian detachment and audience engagement. In addition to generating comedy and songs that had popular appeal, music-hall artists, Eliot observed, performed a rooted ritual, a relevant mythos, on which a playwright could cultivate drama grounded in a tradition that he deemed distinctively English: a ferocious comedy, one that folded tragedy, horror, and vulgarity into brands of humor, farce, and satire.[2] These subjects are ubiquitous in Eliot's prose of the time. To his mind, music-hall artists brought into the present much of what was salvageable from England's dramatic inheritance, a native legacy from English plays *circa* 1600, plays interfusing comedy and tragedy – a binary of which Eliot was increasingly suspicious.[3]

Between late 1924 and late 1926, Eliot drafted parts of the Sweeney drama, wrote a draft scenario for its envisioned entirety, and entertained diverse titles and epigraphs. In the first of the two epigraphs on which he settled, Orestes's solitary perception of the Furies, ghastly specters of moral retribution, provides the single most important clue to Sweeney's role once his character reached final form. The words of Aeschylus's Orestes precede the epigraph from *The Ascent of Mount Carmel*, by the Spanish Carmelite St. John of the Cross (1542–1591), a writer of theology and poetry. Linked by "Hence," the epigraphs together seem to say that because morality is dreadfully real, one should seek a "divine union," and to do so, one should be "divested" of "the love of created beings" (*CPP* 74). In the *Ascent*, one must actively purge attachments to sensory phenomena and their mental counterparts because anything not God – including other people – is nothingness; this psychophysical askesis empties the self and opens it to passive purification enacted by God. It is spiritual progress, not crisis, which is the "dark night of the soul." Of all the play's personae, Sweeney is the only one to whom the epigraphs might even begin to apply unironically. While Sweeney is by no means devoted to contemplation of divine union, the first stages of moral terror have resulted in his dissociation from other humans. His recognition of pervasive nothingness is another promising sign. Inadvertently, he has entered a condition the spiritual ramifications of which exceed his own awareness.

The drafts demonstrate that Eliot had almost as much titular as epigraphical indecision. Of uncertain date, "The Superior Landlord" (an epithet Sweeney would give himself in triumph over Pereira) is one of the titles appearing in the drafts of the play. In the 1927 "Fragment of an Agon," a different title appears, framing both fragments since Eliot had ended the first with "[t]o be continued." Typographically diminished, *Wanna Go Home, Baby?* enters as an apparent afterthought, suggesting that the fragments have a home, that they have been excerpted from a complete work. American slang (Everett 246), this jazzy sexual proposition plays into Eliot's exposure of his characters' polyvalent homelessness and plays on his own artistic search for ritual origins – at best a dubious quest, he was realizing. By the mid-1920s, as his prose reveals, Eliot had become skeptical about his mythical method, about whether dead rituals could in fact be revived without a concurrent revival of the belief system that gave them cultural meaning. Between his two publications of the Sweeney fragments, perhaps earlier, Eliot tiptoed diagonally away from his Cornfordian-Aristophanic approach. The text had begun to work against itself: the fertility-ritual device had generated a drama of insterility; the death-rebirth cycle could spiral only to more of the same, and since the mythic paradigm could lead nowhere new, the modern play that led backward would lead nowhere too (Crawford 179–80; Kenner 216; Chinitz 120–22).

In 1932 Eliot published the fragmentary piece as *Sweeney Agonistes*, a title that cannot but echo Milton's *Samson Agonistes*, which only later in life did Eliot laud. As complex as Eliot's ambivalence toward Milton is just how Milton's play works, or does not, in thematic adjacency to *Sweeney*. Whereas Eliot's earlier incarnations of Sweeney align somewhat with the scriptural folk hero of Judges, Eliot's new Sweeney and Milton's Samson have little in common. All the same, in Samson's despairing realization of his own guiltiness, an insight auguring spiritual growth, and in his isolating recognition of an unredeemed life as death and a sacred death as life, Milton's Samson does abut Sweeney. Both characters are *agonists* – figures engaged in psychological struggle with classical and Christian resonance.

Perhaps Milton's Samson is not as allusively important to *Sweeney* as the generic orientations of *Samson Agonistes* were to Eliot. Milton took a Christian quasi-comedy (Samson is saved) and made it a classical tragedy, and Eliot took a quasi-Christian tragedy (the modern world is amoral) and made it a classical comedy. Within this syncretism, though, lies the fact that *Samson Agonistes* was – explicitly – never meant for the stage. In choosing his Miltonic title, Eliot may have been re-imagining his play as a non-theatrical dramatic poem. His attitude toward closet drama was chiefly negative, but introducing his mother's, *Savonarola*, in 1926, Eliot sanctions certain non-performative plays, and he drops Seneca's name suggestively (xii).

In 1927, after the Sweeney "FRAGMENTS" had seen print, Eliot turned his prose-writing to Seneca, a major presence behind the Sweeney play. In a "form which might be interesting to attempt in our own time," he asserted, Seneca's plays were "curious freak[s] of non-theatrical drama" meant for recitation (*SE* 55). His characters are "like members of a minstrel troupe sitting in a semicircle, rising in turn each to do his 'number,' or varying their recitations by a song or a little back-chat" (54). Significantly, this declamatory tenor could accommodate lines to make one's flesh creep; it was, in fact, the horrors of Senecan and kindred later plays that had pushed Eliot's dramatic theory and first play to a new level. A sensitivity to horror lurks within the tragicomedy of *Sweeney* and gives it a melodramatic "thriller" interest. With the corpse in the bathtub and Doris in the stewpot, the grisly details of the Sweeney play, along with its adaptations of popular music, were products of Eliot's progressive sense that dramatists of his time needed to draw a wider audience to the theater. Maybe, then, melodrama was needed to subtend or subvert the mythical method. But an *Aristophanic* melodrama?

Etymologically, *melodrama* denotes a drama with songs – which *Sweeney Agonistes* is indeed – and historically, the term acquired various meanings, with which Eliot was closely acquainted. In the late 1920s, he published a good bit of prose about detective fiction, blood-curdlers, mysteries, and crime stories. Recognizing the popularity and art of such stories, Eliot was prompted to assess them critically, and in doing so, he probed the aesthetics and longevity of melodrama. Its "golden age" having passed, melodrama survived in the cinema and "thriller" fiction, Eliot held in 1927. People would get their excitement somehow: "melodrama is perennial and . . . the craving for it is perennial" (*SE* 409). The best drama and the best melodrama, Eliot believed, partook of each other.

At least one conventionally melodramatic element does hover over *Sweeney Agonistes*. There is violent evil in the air. To be sure, the would-be villain has the only moral awareness on the stage, and the would-be victim is far from innocent, but Doris fears death, and Sweeney plays on these fears. For some, the title *Sweeney Agonistes* calls to mind *Sweeney Todd*, one of the most successful melodramas of the 1800s. Popular murder and popular music, it seems, together account most plausibly for Eliot's calling the play a melodrama. Eliot would lure through thrills and trills so that audiences, drawn in, might be permeable to less sensationalistic strata of the work. And strata there are in *Sweeney*. Good poetic drama occurs on "two planes at once," according to Eliot; it has a "double reality," an "under-pattern" (*EED* 173–74).

A further doubleness in *Sweeney* involves Eliot's attempt to meld poetic cadence with everyday modern speech. But which vernacular should be used: English? American? Canadian? Irish? Eliot chose not to choose, but instead creolized colloquiality for purposes of both aesthetic power and cultural commentary. In particular, differences between American and English speech rumble into Eliot's dialogue. The crossings of language and geography obliquely echo Eliot's portraying a psychological crossing into new, equally complex, territory (North 90) – a strangely bounded land where morality may claim its reality against the void of life and language. All the same, language must be used, and Eliot at this time saw the "people's speech" as the necessary benefactor and beneficiary of poetry (*UPUC* 5), and therefore of drama. Composing the diverse demotic idiom was, however, inseparable from composing the new metric to which Eliot aspired.

Blank verse was a dead end, he knew; its regularity did not fit modern entropy, and besides, he thought, no one could do it better than Shakespeare had. As Eliot wrote *Sweeney*, he felt Aristophanic rhythms approximated to modern dialogue, contemporary colloquial speech pounding some ancient beat and setting in motion the ritual-drama dance ("Beating" 12). Yet the modern world had become so mechanized that its rhythmical sensibility fused everyday language with the "internal combustion engine" or "street drill" ("Intro. to *Savonarola*" xi; Flanagan 82). Is the meter of *Sweeney* mechanistic? Is it barbaric? Many different drums lie behind its thumps and throbs. Among Eliot's relentlessly varied meters may also lurk medieval accentual patterns recalling the Old English line of four stresses (Gardner 24–29) and stichomythic Senecan rhythms similar to the accentual flow of early jazz.

From Eliot's time to our own, readers have commented upon what has typically been called the work's jazzy syncopation. Current interpretations of Eliot's jazzy meters in *Sweeney* tend to focus on the racial, cultural, and national dynamics that the piece enacts through its integration of this originally African-American music, a deeply traditional art that soared into multinational prominence among both the general public and artists who sought "primitive" sources. The "uncivilized" avant-garde folkishness of jazz and corollary musical genres inspired many a modernist seeking stylistic innovation. Eliot not only drew on such new techniques, but also recognized that within such songs and sounds dwelt complex sociohistorical issues with thematic possibilities. *Jazz* at this time was not just a type of music; it was, more broadly, a descriptor for much of modernity itself. Certainly, Eliot's spotlight on jazziness radiates in several vibrant directions at once.

A Mostly Flat Party

Similarly emissive are the textual energies of the play's protagonist. Readers who know Eliot's early embodiments of Sweeney may be, and have been, baffled by Eliot's staging *him* as the repository of intelligence, vision, and life itself (*UPUC* 146–47). Just who Eliot imagined his Sweeneys to be is not a matter of agreement. Different interpretations of the Sweeney pieces have brought to the fore different glosses of the Sweeney figure. Apparently, Eliot himself thought of Sweeney as "a man who in younger days was perhaps a professional pugilist . . . who then grew older and retired to keep a pub" (Coghill 86). Whatever his antecedents, Eliot's theatrical Sweeney "is so different a character from the 'apeneck Sweeney' . . . that Eliot might better have given him a different name" (Matthiessen 159).

To understand how Sweeney, of all figures, should be the one who contests that degeneration of which he was in the late 1910s an icon is to perceive how seriously Eliot took his 1927 belief that the "frightful discovery of morality" is an event of "permanent" dramatic potential, an "eternal tragedy . . . of the not naturally bad but irresponsible and undeveloped nature, caught in the consequences of its own action." In such cases, one "becomes moral only by becoming damned" (*SE* 142). For Eliot, it followed that moral excellence was less interesting than wrestling with right and wrong: "It is in fact in moments of moral and spiritual struggle . . . that men and women come nearest to being real" (*ASG* 46). These 1933 thoughts may shed light on just how shockingly Eliot's new Sweeneys depart from his prior Sweeneys, who do not even speak in the earlier poems.

In *Sweeney Agonistes*, Eliot gave Sweeney voice, a quite articulate voice at that, and invested him with metaphysical insight. At the crux of this work writhes Eliot's modulation of Sweeney into a modern Orestes with cuspy Christian potential. Sweeney is an ordinary man whom an extraordinary experience has altered utterly. Eliot does not tell us what it is. We may infer, with Hugh Kenner, that the effect of the experience "has rendered quotidian pleasures meaningless, and protracted life a preliminary death" (248). It is little wonder that "[n]o one on stage has the faintest idea what Sweeney is talking about" (222). Sweeney is impelled to verbalize his gnomic experience, but language cannot convey it; he is compelled to share it, but the experience is solipsistic. Yet if Sweeney might discover – or be discovered by – shadows of semi-morality, then any person might. And so Sweeney must try, as a comic agonist, to reanimate the living dead of the first "Fragment."

Qua prologue, though, Eliot's does not seem all that fragmentary, for it stages all the exposition one would want, and more, as Eliot extended it to include the choral entry, or parados. His 1933 opinion that the prologue-fragment was "not much good" is puzzling (Flanagan 83). Maybe in having presented characters who were meant to be uninteresting, Eliot thought that he had outdone himself. Nor is the dramatic action, such that it is, very interesting. The main events before the guests arrive are prevarication and prognostication, respectively putting off and peeping into the future. Doris and Dusty talk about men and think about who will gather at their flat that night. Like Madame Sosostris's tarot-reading in *The Waste Land*, their cartomancy is both a satirical object and a means for the poet to shuffle myth into method.

Dually meaningful as well is Pereira's telephoning and the women's response to his call. Turning the telephone into a speaker both places Eliot among avant-garde dramatists who were staging the autonomy of machines and demonstrates his mythical imagination: the telephone tingalings as a classical-drama Messenger, an ancient herald who brings troubling news (Grove 72). Doris and Dusty do not kill the messenger; they simply hang it up after lying through it. And who can blame Doris for dodging a visit from an untrustworthy man to whom she is sexually obligated? Then again, her lying dodge reveals her evasion of the reality that this sex pays her rent. Postponing Pereira's collection of his due is equivalent to denying the consequences of her casually deadening life. Dusty thinks she's lying when she says that Doris is sick, but Doris is sick, and Dusty is too. They do not see how they ail metaphorically.

Dusty, an ashen double of Doris, plays a remarkably unremarkable role after the prologue, but her name in both fragments recalls the stale decay of their mindless amusements. The women's having sex for fun or rent is only the most patent manifestation of their amorality; the inert triviality of their conversation and actions is as damning a post-mortem exposé. At issue is whether Doris might be revivified. When the Queen of Hearts is read as Mrs. Porter, Doris and Dusty speculate that the card might mean either of them. If Doris is a Porterian prototype, she might be resurrectable. While Sweeney's spring visit to Mrs. Porter in *The Waste Land* implies an annual fertility cycle that Eliot may be casting ironically, in the drafts of the Sweeney play, Mrs. Porter is slain by Sweeney in a second sort of agon, and then re-enlivened in a death–birth paradigm that both of them know will take its course. Eliot never published Mrs. Porter's murder–rebirth, so her thematic understudy, Doris, had to play some of this part.

Generally, though, Doris and Dusty are two of the same, and the male guests who arrive in the parados are more of the same – good-time guys calling on good-time gals. To use his 1934 words about Marston, all of Eliot's characters but Sweeney sound like a "tedious rattle of dried peas," funny but not funny; in their "empty and irrelevant gabble," they convey "significant lifelessness in this shadow-show" (*EED* 167). No more than Doris do the men know of an ancient comic pattern that would enact regeneration. No matter: Eliot's Greek model required a chorus, and his vision demanded that it be both mythic and modern. Satirized satyrs, the chorus comprises three pairings, and every character is largely interchangeable with his partner.

Regular visitors to the flat, Lieutenant Sam Wauchope and Captain Horsfall, both of the Canadian Expeditionary Force, have been living in London. Horsfall has no individual lines, yet Wauchope compensates for his counterpart's silence by being a choral leader of sorts. Moreover, he is a flimsy foil for Sweeney. Sam does not threaten the easy routine of fun. The women therefore see him as trustworthy and deem him a "gentleman" (*CPP* 75), a class distinction emptied of its status and defined instead by a pleasant participation in the *status quo*. Through Sam and Horsfall's geographical and social unrootedness runs a more profound nomadism, one that diffuses their and others' individuation. The same character split into two, Klipstein and Krumpacker mistakenly see Sam as culturally grounded. Their view that Sam is a "real live Britisher," "at *home* in London," says more about them than him (79). And Sam's calling them "gentlemen" obversely reflects his own careless attitude toward identity.

Americans in London for business, Klipstein and Krumpacker have only a choral function in the first fragment, but they dominate the second section of the second fragment. In Eliot's stunted parados, they exchange pleasantries, at some length, with Doris and Dusty. The two Americans repeat each other's words, finish each other's sentences, and talk as much to each other as with the women with whom they are supposedly chatting. Their clichés turn them into caricatures: their stale unreality and their sort-of-suave amorality classify them among the metaphorically moribund, as does the satire of martial heroism that Eliot has them perform. Klipstein and Krumpacker served in the Great War with the Canadians, who are giving them a "swell," "slick" introduction to London. In Klipstein's "did our bit" and "got the Hun on the run"; in Krumpacker's remembering the war as a poker game; and in the informality of "Loot" and "Cap," Eliot condemns them as men who speak breezily about the war (*CPP* 78–79).

Klipstein and Krumpacker's expressive range is that of colloquial American English, which Eliot reproduces with great skill. He saw – keenly ambivalently – that American popular language and culture were seeping into England's modes of speaking and thinking ("American Prose"). In Snow and Swarts, Eliot amplified the sounds of the American-English backtide, and he drew on the names of real musicians (Schuchard 114). Further diversifying the choral demographic, these two are Englishmen who, in the chorus, become blackface minstrels, Tambo and Bones, and thus perform not only an American art form, but also a popular aesthetic that entunes racial complexities and African-American dynamics into Eliot's unresolved chords of keyless identities. In the same chords, Klipstein and Krumpacker as Americans are postcolonial entities, and as Jews – the Jewish name of one suggests the Judaic ethnicity of both – they are diasporic figures. Wauchope and Horsfall are products of a less ancient diaspora, that of settler-colonies' dispersion away from, but still directed toward, the colonial center. Presumably of Irish stock, Sweeney seems to have been living in London, so he too enacts a postcolonial displacement. There is no sense of home in this play of "deterritorialization" (North 87–88). In 1928 Eliot wrote that in his "unsettled age," "everyone is conscious of nationality and race . . . but no one is sure of who or which or what is what or which race, . . . and we suspect that the more we know about race the more clearly we shall see that we are all merely mongrels" ("Idealism" 106). Through Swarts and Snow's blacked-up backup as end-men, Eliot accented the national and historical vertigo of the play, and he accelerated its racial–cultural syntheses (North 88–89) as he gradually shaped the play to question permutations of selfhood. Eliot in 1925 wrote that "the problem of race" is one constituent of "the universal problem of differences which create a mixture of admiration, love, and contempt, with the consequent tension" ("Rev. of *All God's Chillun*" 396).

Agon Without End

Tense differences multiply in the Sweeney–Doris dialogues of the agon fragment. Sweeney seduces Doris into listening to what he has come to realize: that at its most basic, physical life is nothing but "[b]irth, and copulation, and death" (*CPP* 80); that this stark triad has an epistemological abyss as its backdrop; and that, within and maybe despite this void, life and sex and death and their unknowable ontological context might hold moral realities investing life, terribly, with regenerative opportunities. Yet Sweeney himself is still resisting the new life. He may not want to be born anew, to undergo a metamorphic demise, but he senses that guilt exists and that it insists on itself. The phantasmal agents of moral reality have made eggs and isles, murder and milk, anything and everything, appear frighteningly symbolic and chillingly farcical to him. Had Sweeney begun the dialogue with Doris with a straight account of his situation, she would undoubtedly have been bored even more quickly by the conversation. So Eliot has Sweeney approach Doris on her level: naughty flirtation. She is immediately engaged.

It is Doris who casts Sweeney, right away, as the cannibal. In reverse-casting her as the missionary, Sweeney just develops the story along her lines. She is titillated by the scenario, which has no real meaning for her. Meanwhile, Sweeney is performatively self-conscious. It is he, not Doris, who ends the foreplay of failed rhetoric; she is flirty, not frightened, so Sweeney restrategizes. He uses a visual aid, an egg, a traditional emblem of (re)birth, and transfers its stark simplicity to an island-trope, using the trappings of Doris's good-time culture to make the island comprehensible to her. But he does so mainly negatively: none of the modern conveniences and amusements that she likes would be on this island. There would be nothing but basic natural existence, he prods her to picture. The word *nothing* dominates the section, and in the end, there is "[n]othing at all but three things," "[b]irth, and copulation, and death," a phrase leveled fivefold. Doris soon grows tired of the conversation. She would be bored on the isle.

The two semichoral songs are bisected by Doris's literal-minded responses to Sweeney. Just as Doris cannot grasp the symbolic meaning of the egg ("I don't like eggs"), she cannot grasp the abstract significance of the island (*CPP* 82). The songs that interrupt the Sweeney–Doris dialogue reveal what Doris is thinking. The choral rendition of the immensely popular American song "Under the Bamboo Tree" (1902) dissolves the lyrics about a Zulu courtship of sweet decorum and deflates, to some extent parodically, the complex cultural dynamics infusing the original, of which only the title and a couple of lines appear unaltered in Eliot's song (Chinitz 112–22). Instead, Eliot's characters sing an "Under the Bamboo Tree" of packaged and prurient tropical pastoralism, a send-up of cinematic stereotypes of golden-age South-Sea sites (Brooks 329), where "Gauguin maids" might be taken into, and taken in, the woods (*CPP* 81). Any fresh egg in any wood will do for them: all women and all trees become one and so none, just as all sounds on the island become one and none, and just as one, two, and three get screwed into numerical nonsense. The second half-choral song, an extension of the first, likewise projects Doris's misperception of Sweeney's meaning. For Sweeney, time has become a terrifying problem; for the chorus, time disappears in an idyllic, easy-sex fantasy with no problems and no worry. Their diminuendo, a diminished snatch of "Ain't We Got Fun," mixes times of day and night, and ends the song idealizing, hence counter-realizing, what Sweeney has said.

No character has been affected by Sweeney's agonistic parlay. Sweeney's abstruse verbal shell-game with life–death–life is so far beyond Doris's perception that she can respond only insipidly. "Why I'd just as soon be dead," she says in ignorance of the fact that she already is. "Life is death," Sweeney tersely states (*CPP* 82). Before he elaborates, Sweeney makes another rhetorical move that might draw Doris into his liminal domain. This time, the persuasive bait is a lurid murder story, a bait hooking all the better because of Doris's heebie-jeebies about "the COFFIN." While the cannibalistic play has not unsettled her, this apparently real-life story of "a man once did a girl in" is not fun at all (83). Such grisly murders did occur frequently, the newspapers catering to the public's – including Eliot's – desire to read about them. Yet Sweeney's tale of a woman's dead body preserved for months in a tub is so ghastly that it distracts from the ghastliness of the murderer's experience, which is his ultimate focus. Doris "dont [*sic*] care for such conversation," and she repeats the hackneyed "A woman runs a terrible risk" (83). She withdraws almost totally from the conversation.

Snow and Swarts take her place. They are "very interested" in the story, but even as they propel it – "Let Mr. Sweeney continue his story," Snow twice says – they dispel it into "another story" and into questions that "dont apply" (83). These characters hear the murder anecdote just as they would read a newspaper account of a gruesome slaying. They stop listening to Sweeney as they debate whether such murderers always get "pinched in the end." Sweeney resumes his story, but his listeners' what-happened-nextism shows that they are stuck in plot progression, not struck by figurative import. "What did he do?" is not the right question (83). "What did he become, and why?" would be a question in keeping with Sweeney's looming point. None of the characters think to ask whether Sweeney himself was the murderer, but others have dwelt on this issue. The text gives no definitive answer.

Another avidly interpreted angle of Sweeney's murder story turns on his statement "Any man has to, needs to, wants to / Once in a lifetime, do a girl in" (*CPP* 83). With this suggestion that depravity might erupt in anyone, the thematic interest shifts from the dead to the deadener, a clue to whose situation emerges in Eliot's 1917 story "Eeldrop and Appleplex, I": A "man murders his mistress. The important fact is that for the man the act is eternal, and that for the brief space he has to live, he is already dead. He is already in a different world from ours. He has crossed the frontier" (9). Sweeney's story, like that of Eliot's earlier character, is a gruesome exemplum.

Interrupting Sweeney irrelevantly, his flat-party audience induces frustration that impels him into monologue, but not before he declaims, in reaction to his listeners' inability to see beyond his story, that he "gotta use words" when he talks to them (*CPP* 83). Words are all that might exist between him and the others, so even though there is no "joint" linking him to them, or anyone to anyone else, linguistic significa-tion must suffice. Sweeney's monologue rattles into resignation – "We all gotta do what we gotta do" – yet the agonist musters a final rhetorical jab, hitting Doris with a reminder of how she pays for such amusement: "somebody's gotta pay the rent." She responds, "I know who" (84). Does Doris, vacantly, still view Pereira as the rent-payer? Or, has she recognized that she, as a kept woman, has a sexual sublease – that with her body, *she* pays the rent? For Sweeney to reanimate her in this agon, he must lead her to see rent-paying as a trope of moral consequentiality, and she must see the Furies that attend the rent-collector and the milkman and their linked figurative force in a death-to-life drama. Metaphysically, we are all merely tenants, Eliot hints; unhomed in so many ways, our lives are leases.

According to Cornford, the Aristophanic chorus ultimately endorses the agon-victor. Whether Sweeney has won, and whether the last chorus expresses his perspec-tive, are open questions. The answer depends on how one views their hangman. In this song, one's culpability disrupts routine structures of existence. The chorus is addressed to "you," to anyone. You may awaken from a nightmare, but this waking might be a dream, and in this sleeping wakefulness, you may sense the hangman's presence (behind which may dangle the Hanged Man's ritual presence), and you may be alive or dead. This state is, like Sweeney's new knowledge, beyond verbal articula-tion, so aptly the song ends only with hoo-ha's, which are themselves followed only by knocks. Both sounds vibrate with several waves of allusion.

To classify *Sweeney Agonistes* as an "Unfinished Poem," as Eliot ultimately did – though not before authorizing its performance – was not necessarily to belittle the piece, for Eliot greatly admired many unfinished poems. Eliot's abandoning this major work may be explained by his developing doubts about whether his dramatic theory and practice could in fact concur, whether his mythic methods would in fact interest modern audiences, whether the theatrical conventions of the past might in fact serve the needs of the present, and whether social usefulness and popular entertainment ought in fact be separated.[4] *Sweeney Agonistes* remained unfinished, but Eliot was not finished with it. In a late interview, he said that if there was "something good" in an unfinished composition, it would stay in the "back of [his] mind" and become "trans-formed into something else" ("Art of Poetry" 57). Thus was the Sweeney play trans-formed. In Eliot's later poems and plays, one finds many connections to his first entanglement with poetic drama.

NOTES

1 The drafts mentioned in this chapter are housed in the Hayward Bequest, King's College Library, Cambridge University.

2 For more on Eliot's attraction to ferocity, see ELIOT'S POETICS: CLASSICISM AND HISTRIONICS.

3 For the issues summarized here, see – in addition to works cited elsewhere in this chapter – Eliot's uncollected essays "Noh," "Poetic Drama," "Romantic," "Dramatis," "Ballet," the four "London Letters" listed in this volume's Eliot bibliography, "C [Apr. 1924]," "C [Oct. 1924]," "C [Jan. 1925]," "Intro. to *Wheel*," "John Dryden – II and III"; and, in *Selected Essays*, "'Rhetoric' and Poetic Drama," "Christopher Marlowe," "Ben Jonson," "Marie Lloyd," "Shakespeare and the Stoicism of Seneca," and "A Dialogue on Dramatic Poetry."

4 In 1958 Eliot unconvincingly explained that he did not finish *Sweeney Agonistes* because the rapid rhythms made the dialogue unperformable ("T. S. Eliot Talks" 14).

REFERENCES AND FURTHER READING

Brooks, Cleanth. "T. S. Eliot: Thinker and Artist." *T. S. Eliot: The Man and His Work*. Ed. Allen Tate. New York: Delta, 1966. 316–32.

Chinitz, David E. *T. S. Eliot and the Cultural Divide*. Chicago: U of Chicago P, 2003.

Coghill, Nevill. "*Sweeney Agonistes (An Anecdote or Two)*." Roby 115–19.

Cornford, Francis Macdonald. *The Origin of Attic Comedy*. [1914.] Ed. Theodor H. Gaster. Ann Arbor: U of Michigan P, 1993.

Crawford, Robert. *The Savage and the City in the Work of T. S. Eliot*. Oxford: Clarendon, 1987.

Everett, Barbara. "The New Style of *Sweeney Agonistes*." *English Satire and the Satiric Tradition*. Ed. Claude Rawson. Oxford: Blackwell, 1984. 243–63.

Flanagan, Hallie. *Dynamo*. New York: Duell, 1943.

Gardner, Helen. *The Art of T. S. Eliot*. New York: Dutton, 1959.

Grove, Robin. "Pereira and After: The Cures of Eliot's Theater." *The Cambridge Companion to T. S. Eliot*. Ed. A. David Moody. Cambridge: Cambridge UP, 1994. 158–75.

Kenner, Hugh. *The Invisible Poet: T. S. Eliot*. New York: Harbinger, 1959.

Litz, A. Walton. Introduction. "Tradition and the Practice of Poetry." By T. S. Eliot. *T. S. Eliot: Essays from the Southern Review*. Ed. James Olney. Oxford: Clarendon, 1988. 7–10.

Malamud, Randy. *T. S. Eliot's Drama: A Research and Production Sourcebook*. Westport, CT: Greenwood, 1992.

Matthiessen, F. O. *The Achievement of T. S. Eliot: An Essay on the Nature of Poetry*. 3rd ed. New York: Oxford UP, 1958.

McNeilly, Kevin. "Culture, Race, Rhythm: *Sweeney Agonistes* and the Live Jazz Break." *T. S. Eliot's Orchestra: Critical Essays on Poetry and Music*. Ed. John Xiros Cooper. New York: Garland, 2000. 25–47.

North, Michael. *The Dialect of Modernism: Race, Language and Twentieth-Century Literature*. New York: Oxford UP, 1994.

Roby, Kinley E., ed. *Critical Essays on T. S. Eliot: The Sweeney Motif*. Boston: Hall, 1985.

Schuchard, Ronald. *Eliot's Dark Angel: Intersections of Life and Art*. New York: Oxford UP, 1999.

Smith, Carol H. *T. S. Eliot's Dramatic Theory and Practice: From Sweeney Agonistes to The Elder Statesman*. Princeton: Princeton UP, 1963.

Stage Sixty Theatre Club. *Homage to T. S. Eliot: A Programme of Poetry Drama and Music*. Prod. Vera Lindsay. Globe Theatre, London. 13 June 1965.

Woolf, Virginia. *The Diary of Virginia Woolf*. Vol. 2, 1920–1924. Ed. Anne Olivier Bell. San Diego: Harcourt, 1980.

16
"Having to construct": Dissembly Lines in the "Ariel" Poems and *Ash-Wednesday*

Tony Sharpe

In his preface to *For Lancelot Andrewes* (1928), Eliot proclaimed himself "classicist in literature, royalist in politics, and anglo-catholic in religion" (vii); within, he identified with "[t]hose of us who lay no claim to being modern" (*SE* 425). Such declarations publicized his current commitment to views radically different from those imputed to him by some admirers of *The Waste Land* (1922). That poem's modernistic "different voices" had apparently been superseded by a more unitary utterance, such as was embodied in the poem with which – responding to Geoffrey Faber's suggestion that he contribute something to their firm's "Ariel" series of poetry pamphlets – he broke the silence afflicting him since "The Hollow Men" (1925). Eliot composed an Ariel poem every year from 1927 to 1931; this endeavor also led, indirectly, to the sequence *Ash-Wednesday*, published shortly after Easter in April 1930. "Journey of the Magi" (August 1927) opens quoting an Andrewes sermon, so Andrewes's voice literally inaugurates this period of poetic reinvigoration – "the voice," as Eliot described it, "of a man who has a formed visible Church behind him, who speaks with the old authority and the new culture" (*SE* 301–02).

1926, when he wrote those words, was the year in which, Eliot implied in his final *Criterion* editorial (January 1939), he first became aware of the exhaustion of modernism as a cultural force; yet the new order reflected in the poetry he wrote next projected neither the self-certainties suggested by his preface's formulations, nor the linguistic assurance of an Andrewes, who "takes a word and derives the world from it" (*SE* 305). A poetry evoking fragments and ruins was not, at a stroke, replaced by one extolling formed visible churches; but evidently the "ideal order" of literary "monuments" (*SE* 5) *had* been supplanted by a different authenticating framework. Also in 1926, visiting Rome, Eliot fell to his knees before Michelangelo's *Pietà*, and later that same year initiated procedures for joining the Church of England. Simultaneously, he applied for British citizenship, and he would soon signal his interest in "the relation of poetry to the spiritual and social life of its time and of other times" (*SW* viii).

A Companion to T. S. Eliot, First Edition. Edited by David E. Chinitz.
© 2014 John Wiley & Sons, Ltd. Published 2014 by John Wiley & Sons, Ltd.

This period, then, offers redefinitions of Eliot's self through gestures of assent and declarations of affiliation. But accompanying these constructions is, in the poetry, a deconstructive process, signifying his awareness that the self unmade precedes the self remade. "I who am here dissembled" (*CPP* 61) shows a more fractured and uncertain subjectivity than does the profession of classicism, royalism, and Anglo-Catholicism. The movement between world and word is more complicated than for Andrewes, the "ecstasy of assent" (*SE* 305) he compels modified by awareness that sincerity sometimes consists in confession of insincerity: "Consequently I rejoice, having to construct something / Upon which to rejoice" (*CPP* 61). These extraordinary, daringly clunky lines indicate a necessary dissembling, where willfulness substitutes for spontaneity, and the truest poetry is indeed the most feigning. The *Book of Common Prayer* defines baptism as "a sign of Regeneration or new Birth" (353); at his own (June 1927), for "such as are of riper years," Eliot would have heard the priest pray for his "triumph, against the devil, the world, and the flesh" (176, 178). His ensuing poems, however, were not triumphalist, but instead explored the inertia inhibiting spiritual regeneration, that "Shadow" impeding an attempt to pray encountered in the final part of "The Hollow Men" (*CPP* 58–59). For in professing Christianity, Eliot did not abandon a position of unillusioned skepticism: rather, as his 1926 essay on F. H. Bradley asserted, "skepticism and disillusion are a useful equipment for religious understanding" (*SE* 399).

This chapter will examine the poetry from "Journey of the Magi" to "Marina" (September 1930). "Triumphal March" (1931), initially an Ariel poem, was subsumed into the never-completed *Coriolan* sequence alongside the same year's "Difficulties of a Statesman"; "The Cultivation of Christmas Trees" (1954) comes from a different period. Given the overlapping composition of these Ariel poems and *Ash-Wednesday*, the question arises of what differentiates them. The answer may be that while the Ariel poems depict types and stages of spiritual progress, in none can the speaker simply be conflated with the poet himself, whereas in *Ash-Wednesday* the "I" seems personally implicated.

The Ariel Poems

"I *hate* spectacular conversions," wrote Eliot (qtd. in Seymour-Jones 447). The speaker of his first post-baptismal poem, "Journey of the Magi" (*CPP* 68–69), undergoes no spectacular conversion, but resembles those unwillingly awoken at the beginning of *The Waste Land* or discomfited by "Christ the tiger" in "Gerontion" (21). Mentioned only in Matthew 2, the Magi witness the Nativity and then are reconsigned "into their own country" (which Eliot's imagery implies to be exotically Oriental).[1] Despite borrowing Andrewes's language, this magus does not "speak with the old authority and the new culture" (*SE* 301–02), but draws strength from neither, in an era before Christianity has become established. He has been moved to do something, yet resents its consequences; he has heard no angels' voices, but accusations of "folly." He has seen a sign but is reluctant to interpret it, and does not unambiguously feel that impulsion which had led Eliot, in 1926, to venerate a statue of the Holy Mother: his is the situation of a man stranded between two worlds, who has lost old meanings without embracing new ones.

The poem's own meaning, however, seems accessible; it breaks with the disjunctive practices of much of Eliot's previous poetry, offering a decodable narrative sustained by that most reassuring of structural devices, the journey, here linked to the Christmas story (his final Ariel poem concerns Christmas trees). Yet the effect of rehearsing this familiar episode is to defamiliarize it, as its speaker finds that the end of all his exploring is to arrive where he started and not know the place. The poem's language enacts this process. Its parataxis adds one detail to another in mimesis of the spatio-temporal succession of his journey; but, simultaneously, its changing deployment of definite and indefinite articles subverts the sense of a mission completed. Apart from a few indefinite articles principally contained in Andrewes's quotation, the first part almost hypnotically utilizes "the" in its descriptive catalogue, producing an effect of semantic domestication: "the camels," "the silken girls," "the camel men," "the night-fires" are presented in a way that suggests they – like "the cities," "the towns," "the villages" – conform to type. In the second part, however, "a temperate valley," "a running stream," "a water-mill," and "an old white horse" all introduce a world uncharacterized by comforting behavioral predictability: this mill's "beating the darkness" and that horse's galloping away (contrasting with the camels' explicable lying down, earlier) denote unpurposive, unaccountable activity. The magus travels into a landscape whose significations he cannot unravel: the "three trees," dicing hands and "pieces of silver" are referable by us to the Crucifixion story, but remain incomprehensible to him. The last part shows how recurring memories of that distant journey define his present displacement: "no longer at ease," the magus is estranged equally from categorical efficiencies of language, as "birth" and "death" juggle meanings, and from "these Kingdoms," their previous exotic specificities now generalizable as "an alien people clutching their gods."

Eliot's magus knows neither what he found nor, rationally, why he looked for it – the incertitude of his perceptions perhaps suggested by predominantly feminine line-endings, which mimic the closure of rhyme without achieving it. His poem does not show revelation compelling ecstatic assent, but, rather, implies historical process. This can also be seen in 1928's Ariel poem, "A Song for Simeon" (*CPP* 69–70). Simeon is another marginal figure, appearing only in Luke 2, described as a devout man to whom it was revealed that he would not die before seeing Israel's savior. When Mary and Joseph present Jesus in the temple at Jerusalem, he takes the baby in his arms, uttering the metrical prayer liturgically incorporated as the "Nunc dimittis" – or, in the *Book of Common Prayer*, "the Song of Symeon [*sic*]" (43) – asking to be released from life. Eliot assumes that Simeon is old, and that (unlike the Cumaean Sybil in *The Waste Land*'s epigraph, who longs to die but cannot) his wish will be granted.[2] Eliot's "song" is not notably jaunty: "Dust in sunlight and memory in corners / Wait for the wind that chills towards the dead land" is reminiscent of earlier poetry. Both

Simeon and the magus are somewhat unwillingly awoken; but unlike its predecessor, "A Song for Simeon" sets up a pattern of irregular line-end rhymes, and its final word, "salvation" (the last two lines summarize the "Nunc dimittis"), offers a more apparently hopeful conclusion than the earlier poem's "death." Yet the future Simeon has foreseen is uncomfortable. Historically he is a Jew under Roman colonial authority, and, as a result of Christ's mission, ahead lie not only the consequences predicted for Jesus and Mary, but political suppression, persecution, martyrdoms. At Evensong, the "Nunc dimittis" invokes fulfillment and hope for the future; Eliot's poem based upon it fractures its sequence, instead emphasizing suffering and struggle. Although Simeon knows he will not be called upon to endure "the ultimate vision," the glimpse he has had of "thy salvation" makes him want to die; as with the Sibyl, the gift of prophecy can be a species of curse.

Eliot's Christianity could seem spiky. "Animula" (1929; *CPP* 70–71) is a case in point: A. D. Moody finds in it a "detachment, amounting to alienation, from the actual experience of growing up" (135). We move from old men contemplating death, to an infant setting forth in the context of a well-provided turn-of-the-century childhood, such as Eliot's had been. The title derives from a brief Latin poem – "*Animula vagula blandula*" ("Little soul, wandering, pleasant") – whose initial affectionate diminutives ironically recur, describing death: "*Pallidula, rigida, nudula*" ("Pale, stiff, naked"). Such austerity is tonal in Eliot's poem, which opens quoting from a passage in *Purgatorio* XVI (cited in the same year's "Dante" essay) where questions of free will and responsibility for sin are illustrated by an extended image of infancy. There is considerably less indulgent affection toward the "simple soul" in Eliot than in Dante: the line "Irresolute and selfish, misshapen, lame" is frigidly adjudicative, repudiating Wordsworthian notions of the soul's "fair seed-time," closer to Beddoes's "bodiless childful of life in the gloom" (qtd. in *OPP* 98).

"Animula" sets itself against cozy versions of childhood (the last of A. A. Milne's popular "Winnie the Pooh" books had been published the previous year): this little soul's dominant characteristic is quizzical dissociation, an essential loneliness of being. The first sentence's extended syntax – effectively the poem's first "part" – moves from pure immediacy of sensory perception, through awkward physicality and rudimentary awareness, to an incipiently constructed world: human entities are intuited beyond encountered "arm" and "knee" to emerge, with the acquisition of language – and in the language of acquisition – as "servants" who "say" things. The line lengths and rhyme scheme of this poem are more regular than in its predecessors, imparting a formality appropriate to the buttoned-up being of this isolated, studious child. In the second stage, constituted by the next two sentences, "The heavy burden of the growing soul" emerges in the form of increasingly vexatious philosophical ("'is and seems'") and ethical ("may and may not") disparities, whose resolution is defensively sought in the realm of codified knowledge – "the *Encylopaedia Britannica*," presumably read with back turned on the external world beyond the window. "The pain of living and the drug of dreams" underlines this small soul's damaged withdrawal. After so lonely and repressed a childhood, inevitably the adult who emerges – "from the hand of time," commencing the third stage – is self-distrustful, life-denying, and profoundly inauthentic. Describing this outcome, the poem clusters its rhymes ("gloom" negatively amalgamates "good" and blood"), mounting to a denunciatory crescendo:

> Fearing the warm reality, the offered good,
> Denying the importunity of the blood,
> Shadow of its own shadows, spectre in its own gloom.
> Leaving disordered papers in a dusty room;
> Living first in the silence after the viaticum. (*CPP* 71)

The "viaticum" denotes the last rites administered to the dying. The poem up to this moment has been making an increasing amount of noise, but then enacts the "silence" spoken of, in the stanza-break preceding the rhythmically distinct and unrhymed closing part; where prayers are solicited for identified and unidentified individuals, all presumably dead. "Boudin" (translatable as "blood-pudding") has suffered the same fate as T. E. Hulme in the Great War; "Floret," glimpsed in pseudo-medieval vignette, has been killed not by a wild boar but by the dog that hunts it. Each perplexingly suggestive name resonates as *European*, in this poem's Anglophone register, perhaps to imply a world elsewhere, beyond too "Britannic" a mindset. The last line adjusts the Roman Catholic "Hail Mary," asking intercession in the hour not of "our death" but of "our birth."

The previous poems anticipated death; here it is multiply encountered. "Animula" ends in a very different place from its beginning: the affectless vocabulary setting forth the "flat world" of the rudimentary soul (recognizably our own "reality") is at the close replaced by vocative injunctions exhorting emotional investment in orders of existence less easily categorizable, and certainly remoter from us. This presents acute problems of interpretation and evaluation: is Eliot's tale of the progress of the "simple soul" which starts poorly and ends worse a generalizable case, as in Dante? To assume so would lead to the position that we're bound to make a mess of life and are spiritually maladjusted to the world in which we "live," where accumulating experience merely deepens estrangement from our origins in "God." Therefore "Guiterriez" *et al.* exemplify different types of failure; for it is no less true of them than of the little soul, that they are effectively born when they die ("leaving" is "living"). Thus, the poem axiomatically installs reversed meanings of "life" and "death" implicit in its forerunners, to enunciate a doctrine which, if you are a devout believer, may make sense but which, if you are not, perplexes and offends.

Moody has objected to the poem's falsifying "take" on childhood. More recently, Craig Raine, while conceding that it "depicts a psychically damaged, confined soul corroded by its own caution," denies that the object is to universalize this as the human condition, suggesting, rather, that it implies the importance of other ways of being: *admitting* the blood's importunity and seizing "the opportunity to live fully" (Raine 2, 3). In Raine's reading, the poem's closing section offers, not additional illustrations of life's futility, but types who have embraced its possibilities, even to their own destruction; the "simple soul" described, by contrast, he aligns with the various examples in Eliot's poetry of those who have declined to inhabit their own lives fully. Such an interpretation rescues "Animula" from that automated disdain for the world, institutionalized by unsympathetic criticism as the poetic fruit of Eliot's religion; the poem, instead, endorses "the warm reality, the offered good" – in its surprising and habitually overlooked phrases.

"Marina" (*CPP* 72–73) reads very differently. It seems affirmative in ways the other Ariel poems aren't, admitting the feminine, the potential of shared human love and pleasures of the natural world. Whereas the dominant movement in its predecessors was away from familiar toward defamiliarized states, the sense here is rather of reunion and recovery, albeit fragmentarily apprehended. Its present tense is more permissive than the prescriptively sequential present continuous of "Animula," and the contrast is emphatic between that poem's extended, straitlaced opening syntax and the irregular, unpunctuated effusion, as of a mind reassembling itself, with which "Marina" begins:

> What seas what shores what grey rocks and what islands
> What water lapping the bow
> And scent of pine and the woodthrush singing through the fog
> What images return
> O my daughter. (*CPP* 72)

Where "Animula" had surveyed its growing child objectively, as from a somewhat lofty pulpit, "Marina" is intensely subjective, in its hesitant articulations: "unknowing, half-conscious, unknown." Although, as with the magus, a journey occurs, implying passage between different states of being, the element of narrative is less pronounced: the poem advances by means of dramatic juxtaposition rather than logical sequence. The "woodthrush," common to North America but not found in Britain, unobtrusively locates "Marina" – with the pines and the fog – on the eastern seaboard of Eliot's boyhood summers, as well as recalling *The Waste Land*'s hermit-thrush and pine-trees (another link is the "garboard strake," retrieved from a passage Pound excised [*WLF* 65]).

If this is a scenario of "return," what, then, caused separation? The implied answer is the ensuing comminatory list, which it is perhaps less important to *interpret* (as suggesting the deadly sins of anger, pride, sloth and lust), than to *hear* accumulating, through formulaically emphatic repetitions, a massively destructive potential which is miraculously dispelled by the rhythmic shift, subversively dismissing their clamor for attention: "Are become unsubstantial, reduced by a wind." "Marina" alludes to two intentionally opposed recognition scenes, each characterized by questions echoed in its own interrogatory mode. In Seneca's *Hercules Furens*, providing the epigraph, Hercules returns to lucidity from the frenzy during which, he will discover, he has slaughtered his children; in Shakespeare's *Pericles*, Marina (named for her birth at sea, when her mother apparently died and was cast overboard in a "caulk'd and bitumed" coffin [III.1]) at length is joyfully reunited with her father, Pericles. Although *Pericles* provides the dominant reconciliatory tone of the poem, the insensate rage of Hercules is represented in the hammer-blows of "Death" resounding in its list: one hero wakens to unimaginable horror, the other to ecstatic restoration. "Whispers and small laughter between leaves and hurrying feet" is imagery anticipating "New Hampshire" and *Four Quartets*; and the situation inferrable from "Marina" is encapsulated in a phrase from "Burnt Norton": "accepted and accepting" (*CPP* 118). This defines the poem's reciprocity, making possible provisional accommodation with a world whose evoked sensory details of sound, smell, and feeling are of a piece with, rather than antithetical to, the life of the spirit, in a balanced state of "grace dissolved in place." The reverse position – rejected and rejecting – might describe the "misshapen" soul of "Animula": we also have it in us to act more like Hercules than Pericles, for our destructive impulse, like a semi-submerged sea-rock, "in the sombre season / Or the sudden fury, is what it always was" (133).

Unlike its three predecessors, there is no overt doctrinal context for "Marina," whose sources are literary; while it may indicate the proximity of some transcendent threshold, what it overtly yearns for is recovery of a specifically human relationship. It is different, also, in its formal circularity, its ending almost exactly where it began; but in between it has rejected the meanings of death, affirmed the body (as the vessel whose dilapidations it exactly itemizes), and embraced possibilities of renewal: "The awakened, lips parted, the hope, the new ships." Such an account risks turning the suggestive hesitancies of its variable lines into thumpingly affirmative allegory; the poem needs to be *heard*, properly to conceive the relation between its "speech" and its "unspoken." I have implied that it is circular; but what may distinguish the opening from the closing scenes is that the first is remembered and the last anticipated: "Marina" ends with landfall yet to be made.

Ash-Wednesday

When Leonard Woolf (who had in 1928 heard Eliot read a shorter, earlier version) received a presentation copy of *Ash-Wednesday*, he replied: "It is amazingly beautiful. I dislike the doctrine, as you probably know, but the poetry remains and shows how unimportant belief or unbelief may be" (238). This early ambivalence has turned out to be characteristic: Ronald Schuchard observes that "after almost sixty years of reading and explication, critics still leave it in exasperation" (150). Moody finds it "life-denying" (154), and Denis Donoghue argues that "Its main impulse is to commit itself to the reality it contemplates, without disowning the sensuous memories and desires that officially count as obstacles" (149). Schuchard tries to reverse the trend of seeing this merely as Eliot's "conversion poem," protesting that it is "an extraordinary love poem of great personal intensity and spiritual discipline" (150) – relating these aspects to the reappearance in Eliot's life of his former love, Emily Hale: "*Ash-Wednesday*, though dedicated to his wife, was in fact a modern *Vita Nuova* for [Hale]"

(160). Ronald Bush quotes a letter in which Eliot tried to fend off the label of "devotional verse": "Between the usual subjects of poetry and 'devotional verse' there is a very important field still very unexplored by modern poets – the experience of a man in search of God, and trying to explain to himself his intenser human feelings in terms of the divine goal. I have tried to do something of that in 'Ash Wednesday'" (131). But later, publicly, in the first of his Norton Lectures (1932), Eliot disclaimed any serious intent:

> If a poem of mine entitled *Ash-Wednesday* ever goes into a second edition, I have
> thought of prefixing to it the lines of Byron from *Don Juan*:
> . . . .
>   I don't pretend that I quite understand
> My own meaning when I would be *very* fine;
>   But the fact is that I have nothing planned
> Unless it were to be a moment merry. (*UPUC* 21)

That rather obvious diversionary tactic probably derived from his impatience with the "devotional verse" tag, which simplified his poem's attitude and overlooked its evocation of "intenser human feelings." Byronic merriment, however, is not entirely absent from a sequence whose opening poem once took its title from a vaudeville comedy routine – although Schuchard makes the point that this ("All aboard for Natchez, Cairo and St. Louis"), terminating at Eliot's American birthplace, served to point up his state of exile. Other (abandoned) titles drew on Dante; and Dante and the liturgy are probably the two most notable influences on *Ash-Wednesday*. Soon afterwards Eliot wrote to Paul Elmer More that "my last short poem 'Ash Wednesday' is really a first attempt at a sketchy application of the Vita Nuova to modern life" (qtd. in Schuchard 150). His 1929 essay includes illuminating remarks about this work of Dante's, which, provoked by the death of Beatrice, consists of love poems and a linking prose commentary interpreting her as his means of salvation:

> [T]he *Vita Nuova*, besides being a sequence of beautiful poems connected by a curious
> vision-literature prose, is, I believe, a very sound psychological treatise on something
> related to what is now called "sublimation." There is also a practical sense of the realities
> behind it, which is antiromantic: not to expect more from *life* than it can give or more
> from *human* beings than they can give; to look to *death* for what life cannot give. The
> *Vita Nuova* belongs to "vision literature"; but its philosophy is the Catholic philosophy
> of disillusion. (*SE* 235)

This sounds tough but, notwithstanding, does not entail complete rejection of the physical world. In *Ash-Wednesday*, the feelings requiring sublimation were those toward his wife Vivien (who in 1928 told friends he couldn't stand the sight of her) and Emily Hale: despair (the Heraclitean "way down") and hope (the "way up") that might effectively be "the same," if diverting his passion from its truer object – to which, blood shaking his heart, the *Pietà* had compelled his ecstatic assent.

The poem's title (hyphenated as in the *Book of Common Prayer*) denotes the first day of Lent, 40 days' abstinence preceding Easter in the Christian calendar. As an Anglo-Catholic, Eliot would probably have taken Communion on that day, when the first Lesson, from Joel 2, included the phrases "Turn ye even to me, saith the Lord, with all your heart . . . and turn unto the Lord your God: . . . Who knoweth if he will return, and repent . . . ?" (78). Prayers attached to the service of Commination could also be used on Ash Wednesday: one of these begins, "Turn thou us, O good Lord, and so shall we be turned" (198). These liturgical resonances coinhabit the opening poem of the sequence (*CPP* 60–61), alongside the "turn" derived from translating Cavalcanti's poem of exile, saluting his lady in distant Tuscany. The diminished repetitions in Eliot's first three lines create an effect almost as of an engine that refuses to start; the opening section exhibits a pronounced loss of energy, both rhythmically and, in the enervated grandiloquence (lines 8 and 10), semantically. "I" occurs 19 times, setting up its own slightly irritating sonic insistence; potentially oxymoronic collocations suggest something obstinately not making sense: "agèd eagle," "vanished power," "infirm glory," and the dry bathos of "one veritable transitory power." Matins for Ash Wednesday specifies Isaiah 58:1–13, including "thou shalt be like a watered garden, and like a spring of water, whose waters fail not"; a longer line echoes these possibilities of renewal, only to deny them: "There, where trees flower, and springs flow, for there is nothing again." "Again" is used repeatedly, in constructions that precisely negate opportunities for alteration.

These lines seem to present not regenerative contrition, but a willfully anti-transcendental sluggishness: time is time, place place, in the poem's rigorous present tense. Perversely, what it renounces is "the blessèd face," rather than the devil and all his works. Its repetitiousness suggests the twistings of a caged animal, whose predicament is finally formulated: "And I pray that I may forget / These matters that with myself I too much discuss / Too much explain" – whose enjambment hints at yearning for enlargement, as elsewhere in the poem. The line "And pray to God to have mercy upon us" is notable perhaps as much for the introduction of "us" as of "God"; the earlier, ironic-sounding verb "rejoice" has semi-accidentally led to this impulse to "pray," reaching beyond self-enclosure: the poem's sequence of entrapping *because*s gives way to potentially progressive *and*s, as its "I" gives way to "we." The preponderantly negative mode – with "not" and "no" predominant – adjusts to include the positive as well: "Teach us to care and not to care." Included, at the end, in a community, albeit one of sin, the "I" is in a position to fare forward from a stillness that is preparatory, rather than inert.

The slowly gathering pulse and rhymes which *just* keep this poem going imply an instinct for renewal at odds with its apparent message. The next poem's vocative immediacy and liveliness of scene (*CPP* 61–63) offer a contrast, amplified by employment of the past tense. Many have commented on its debt, in particular, to cantos XXVIII and XXIX of *Purgatorio*, where in the Earthly Paradise Dante encounters a lady with whom he observes a "Divine Pageant." Eliot said of this: "It belongs to the world of what I call the *high dream*, and the modern world seems capable only of the *low dream*" (*SE* 223) – the sense of which is that we more readily interpret dreams as emanations from the subconscious than as a type of wisdom. The distinction is relevant to this poem, where all possible sources of subconscious motivation – "my legs my heart my liver and that which had been contained / In the hollow round of my skull" – have been expressly annihilated: the body, so often problematical in Eliot, is no more. Somehow an "I" survives this radical dismantling, associated with but not identical to the "bones," which speak as "we"; both address the "Lady" evidently not discomposed by the scattering to which her attention is drawn, and who functions, iconically, as the still center of the scene: like Beatrice, she is an intermediary of "the Virgin."

When asked what the first line meant, Eliot simply repeated it, insisting on the inseparability of form and meaning, despite his poem's envisaging separation of body from spirit ("bones" and "I"). Leopards proverbially cannot change their spots, but "white" ones have evidently done so. Beneath a juniper tree in the wilderness, Elijah asks for death in I Kings19; instead, an angel brings food sufficient to sustain a 40-day journey. The desert and its dry bones, so threatening in *The Waste Land*, here become transformative, just as that poem's intrusively audible women simplify, here, to the "Lady of Silences." There is, throughout, a certain sardonic humor: in discriminating the body's edible from its "indigestible" parts; in the twittering bones, seemingly anxious to please (not unrelated to the minstrel song's "dem dry bones," also alluding to Ezekiel); even God attempts a joke. There is a sense of language defining itself as gesture rather than communication: "The Lady is withdrawn / In a white gown, to contemplation, in a white gown" (white is this poem's only color). The central dimetrical passage, imitative of the Litany to the Blessed Virgin Mary, intensifies such effects, at times risking reductiveness: like a Wildean epigram, "The greater torment / Of love satisfied" offers a neatly formulaic reversal, without necessarily persuading that experience of "love satisfied" has been fairly assessed. Discussing the *Vita Nuova*, Eliot asserted as "fact" "that the love of man and woman . . . is only explained and made reasonable by the higher love, or else is simply the coupling of animals" (*SE* 234–35); but D. H. Lawrence, who admired animals, might applaud such unselfconscious sexuality. An almost jaunty self-dissociation is audible in the poem's final part, where "I who am here dissembled" hears the singing of his own bones and learns that "neither division nor unity / Matters" – and where the poem's impatience with categorical procedures of language is incipient, akin to Sweeney's "Death is life and life is death / I gotta use words when I talk to you" (*CPP* 84). The poem evokes "Speech without word and / Word of no speech": transcendent communication which only after his second marriage would Eliot allow to be achievable between man and woman (see "A Dedication to My Wife," *CP* 221).

This vision of the "Garden / Where all love ends" – here "ends" implies fulfillment of purpose, and "love" is a justifying singularity subsuming previously plural "loves" – is of a final destination that, in terms of *Ash-Wednesday*'s progress, remains unachieved. Therefore poem III (*CPP* 63) reengages with the fallen world of flesh – commencing on "the second stair," presumably, because preceding poems have equated to its first stage. This shortest poem of the sequence takes place indoors, contrasting with its predecessor but seeming to continue its self-dissociation: for the "shape twisted" below is interpretable as the speaker's self at an earlier or alternative stage (possibly alluding to Henry James's "The Jolly Corner," which Eliot knew well, where stairs figure significantly). The dominant rhyme of the poem continuously re-chimes with "stair"; the repetition of "turning" echoes the first poem but, denoting spiral movement, indicates ascent rather than circularity. Here sensual pleasures are persuasively evoked, through increased reference to colors and the natural world; beyond purely deterrent obstacles (devil and shark), now a pre-Raphaelite tableau glimpsed through the "slotted window" adds the impediment of sensory seduction. The "broadbacked" flute-player (therefore male, seen from behind through this "bellied" aperture) immediately suggests an erotics of association that interrupt the rhythm – as Pan's pipes cause panic – while the distracted climber pauses, then continues.

The next poem (*CPP* 64) makes more overt its religious and Dantean references, naming "Mary" and alluding to *Purgatorio* XXVI (where Arnaut Daniel, Provençal poet, expiates his sins of lust); violet is the liturgical color for penitence, newly decking the altar on Ash Wednesday. The first two lines rhythmically recall the beginning of the sequence, but the referent for their reiterated "who" is never exactly revealed; the grammatical parallelism imparts stationariness to this opening. The setting seems to be a garden emergent from a desert, but strong elements of dream prevail: "fiddles and . . . flutes" are borne away and sensory life in time amounts to a sumptuous funeral ("While jewelled unicorns draw by the gilded hearse"), allowing, nonetheless, opportunity to "Redeem / The unread vision in the higher dream." The "garden god" with breathless flute evokes the figure in the previous poem. The effect is of a still center (animation magically suspended, as in the line "White light folded, sheathed about her, folded") round which or by which the earthly pageant proceeds: the poem's dynamic is generated in its contrast between movement and stillness, the worlds of time and timelessness. Its repeated words and phrases and absence of articulated logic, together with the silently gesturing "sister" evoking "the word unheard, unspoken," indicate the outer limits of that range within which denotative language functions: in the resultant spiritual irrigation, bird, wind, or tree find equal eloquence. The final line, lacking terminal punctuation, abbreviates the "Salve Regina," a Roman Catholic prayer, to imply that "exile" will follow, rather than that revelation will follow exile.

In the fifth poem (*CPP* 65–66) "doctrine" apparently crowds out "poetry." The "Word" becomes capitalized, alluding to St John's gospel, and the resulting convolutions display negative residues from Andrewes's rhetoric, exploring possible accommodations between world, word, and Word. Eliot's ear seems to fail him, permitting fustily inert paradoxes of a pedantry that unstiffens only for worse disasters to occur, in calamitous double-rhymes ("silence"/"islands," etc.). This produces an extremely noisy poem supposedly in favor of uncontaminated silence. It offers various examples of what could be termed "bad faith"; what may be enacted here is a language of panicky over-control, reacting against a last, difficult "surrender" required: of reason and its categories, as embedded in words. The self-consciousness of its oratory seems the opposite of prayer, which, Eliot affirmed, involves the struggle to "forget self" (Spender 59); it may, then, embody fear of the final leap of faith, the vulnerability exposed in daring to believe one might, all undeservedly and wholly irrationally, be included in God's love. Entrenched within language, the poem must relinquish it; in 1933 Eliot would talk of his aspiration to write "poetry, with nothing poetic about it, poetry standing naked in its bare bones" (qtd. in *SP* 20); but even bones, *Ash-Wednesday* shows, must be discarded.

The final poem (*CPP* 66–67) reprises opening phraseology of the first, significantly altering "Because" to "Although"; other echoes inhabit the close. It is, perhaps surprisingly, situated in the world ("this brief transit") and like "Marina," his next poem, evokes Eliot's boyhood sea-coast. The abbreviation of the confessional formula, "Bless me, father," substitutes for the second part ("for I have sinned") an impassioned turning toward remembered places, connived at by the awakening rhythms of its sensory catalogue:

> And the lost heart stiffens and rejoices
> In the lost lilac and the lost sea voices
> And the weak spirit quickens to rebel
> For the bent golden-rod and the lost sea smell
> Quickens to recover
> The cry of quail and the whirling plover
> And the blind eye creates
> The empty forms between the ivory gates
> And smell renews the salt savour of the sandy earth (66)

That single "recover" counterbalances the reiterations of "lost"; it seems that "even among these rocks" grace can inhabit place. Although "empty forms" potentially imports a negativity, it does not inhibit these lines' affirmation of the natural world. The quail and the plover are precisely themselves, not symbolic like the earlier eagle or leopards; nor, seemingly, are they at odds with the holy mother at the end, who, as "spirit of the river, spirit of the sea," is agent of reconciliation between this world and the next. This is the first verifiably external location evoked by *Ash-Wednesday*, which otherwise unfolds in "The place of solitude where three dreams cross": that is, in the hollow round of the skull, where the drama of past, present, and future is played out.

The last line of the entire sequence quotes from Psalm 102, prescribed for Evensong of Ash Wednesday; notwithstanding, references to Roman Catholic liturgy increase in this poem, whose American evocations equally indicate what an unusual Anglican Englishman Eliot became. But, unlike Gerontion, he found his passion: *Ash-Wednesday* is concerned with worldly renunciation and the evocation of a discarnate love, surpassing that for "created beings" (*CPP* 74). As a poem of sublimation, it transcended the circumstances of Eliot's marriage and channeled his feelings for Emily

Hale toward her iconic role. Yet if this period commenced, iconically, with Eliot's veneration of a woman's statue, it also led, in time, to a real woman's reclaiming him for the world of flesh and blood: for, listening to John Gielgud recite "Journey of the Magi," a young Valerie Fletcher found *her* passion for its poet.

NOTES

1 Quotations from the Bible cite the Revised Version; quotations from the *Book of Common Prayer* cite the version issued for the reign of George V.

2 Eliot's supposition about Simeon's age, like his presumption that the Magi came out of the East, was based on longstanding extra-biblical tradition.

REFERENCES AND FURTHER READING

Bush, Ronald. *T. S. Eliot: A Study in Character and Style*. New York: Oxford UP, 1984.

Church of England. *The Book of Common Prayer*. London: SPCK, n.d.

Donoghue, Denis. *Words Alone: The Poet T. S. Eliot*. New Haven: Yale UP, 2000.

Holy Bible. King James Version. New York: American Bible Society, 1999.

Moody, A. D. *Thomas Stearns Eliot, Poet*. 2nd ed. Cambridge: Cambridge UP, 1994.

Raine, Craig. *T. S. Eliot*. New York: Oxford UP, 2006.

Schuchard, Ronald. *Eliot's Dark Angel*. New York: Oxford UP, 1999.

Seymour-Jones, Carole. *Painted Shadow: A Life of Vivienne Eliot*. London: Constable, 2001.

Shakespeare, William. *The Oxford Shakespeare: The Complete Works*. Ed. Stanley Wells et al. 2nd ed. Oxford: Oxford UP, 2005.

Spender, Stephen. "Remembering Eliot." *T. S. Eliot: The Man and His Work*. Ed. Allen Tate. London: Chatto, 1967. 38–64.

Woolf, Leonard. *Letters of Leonard Woolf*. Ed. Frederic Spotts. London: Bloomsbury, 1989.

17

"The inexplicable mystery of sound": *Coriolan*, Minor Poems, Occasional Verses

Gareth Reeves

"Unfinished," "minor," "occasional": the headings in the *Collected Poems* for the texts to be discussed in this chapter do not augur well. But, first, Eliot was an exceptionally self-critical writer: most poets would be proud to have written the "unfinished" *Coriolan* and many of the "minor" poems. The other "unfinished" work, *Sweeney Agonistes*, has begun to receive the critical attention it deserves, and therefore has its own chapter in this Companion. The present chapter maintains that *Coriolan*'s time has also come. Secondly, Eliot had a remarkable sense of mission, and everything he wrote can be seen, at any rate with hindsight, to take its place in the larger pattern of his life's work: all parts illuminate the whole, and the whole illuminates the parts. Many of the texts under discussion highlight the intensely auditory nature of Eliot's inspiration. Although the acoustic occasion changes from poem to poem, sound is at the heart of his poetry: in the vocal scenario of *Coriolan*, in the Symbolist "music" of the "minor" *Landscapes* sequence, and in the strategically conversational idiom of several of the "Occasional Verses."

Coriolan

The two parts of *Coriolan*, "Triumphal March" and "Difficulties of a Statesman," were first published, separately, in 1932, at a crucial juncture in Eliot's career. Both poetically and politically he was bewildered. Much is "hidden" in *Coriolan*, evidently from writer as much as from reader: "O hidden under the . . . Hidden under the . . ." (*CPP* 88). But the poetry's air of stunned mystification is essential to its meaning. That air should not be dispelled, however much readers may wish it away with the help of critics and commentators.

At the time he wrote *Coriolan* Eliot's politics were based on the conviction that liberal democracy inevitably degenerates into chaos and disorder. Consequently people yearn for order and authority, running after (then) popular ideas such as fascism and

A Companion to T. S. Eliot, First Edition. Edited by David E. Chinitz.
© 2014 John Wiley & Sons, Ltd. Published 2014 by John Wiley & Sons, Ltd.

communism, which are not really "ideas," sustainable ideologies, at all (Reeves 77).[1] This way of thinking was by no means confined to the conservative Right. For instance, W. H. Auden, from the opposite end of the political spectrum, was to conclude in 1940 that liberalism was totally ineffectual for the times, and arrived, like Eliot, at a Christian solution. Deeply distrustful of any form of populism, Eliot wrote in the *Criterion*:

> Order and authority are good. . . . But behind the increasing popular demand for these things, the parroting of the words, I seem to detect a certain spiritual anaemia, a tendency to collapse, the recurring human desire to escape the burden of life and thought. The deterioration of democracy has placed upon men burdens greater than they could bear . . . . And in this state of mind and spirit human beings are inclined to welcome any regime which relieves us from the burden of pretended democracy. Possibly also, hidden in many breasts, is a craving for a regime which will relieve us of thought and at the same time give us excitement and military salutes. ("Literature of Fascism" 287–88)

These sentences could be describing what happens in *Coriolan*; and they are as important for what they betray as for what they say, for the perspective shifts, no doubt unconsciously, from observer to observed, from analysis to compromised participant, from "I seem to detect" to "any regime which relieves us." That shift reflects the authorial bewilderment of *Coriolan*.

Presenting the "popular demand" for "order and authority," *Coriolan* is an echo-chamber which muffles even as it raises the issue of whether its words express a world of true order and authority, or whether they are not mere empty "parrotings" of conventional phrases about order and authority (Reeves 78). But *Coriolan* does not offer any resolution to the issue, and Eliot soon came to see the work as a cul-de-sac, for he consigned it, along with *Sweeney Agonistes*, to the "Unfinished Poems" section of *Collected Poems 1909–1935* (where the two parts were published together for the first time). At one time he envisaged two more parts following the fortunes of "young Cyril" under the leadership of Coriolan. The fourth part was to derive in some way from St. John of the Cross (Ackroyd 190). This suggests that Eliot originally wanted the work to achieve that visionary otherworldly peace which is "hidden" from the speaker in "Difficulties of a Statesman."

The general consensus has been to follow Eliot in calling the work unfinished. In terms of dramatic plot it may well be. But this does not justify the fairly common reaction typified by Peter Ackroyd's "promise unfulfilled" (191), for *Coriolan* represents an arresting poetic breakthrough, so that even today it is difficult to know how to describe it generically. Neither lyric, nor drama, nor poetic drama, nor dramatic monologue, it forces one to fall back with Eloise Knapp Hay on "dramatic poem" (Hay 108). But even this designation is not quite right. *Coriolan* is *sui generis*, and its lack of definition is its defining feature. To pin it down is to miss the point. It comes across primarily as a congeries of voices – voices of the people, voices of the leader, voices of opinion-makers, "parroted" and projected voices – that can be made to support or contradict one another depending on the listener's angle of hearing (Reeves 81–82). Coming after the intensely inward poetry of *Ash-Wednesday* and "Marina," *Coriolan* sounds like an attempt to move out of what, in his lecture "The Three Voices of Poetry" (1953), Eliot was to call the "first voice," that of "the poet talking to himself – or to nobody," into the "second," that of "the poet addressing an audience," and the "third," that of "the poet when he attempts to create a dramatic character" (*OPP* 89). Eliot also said in the lecture that "in every poem . . . there is more than one voice to be heard" (100), and in *Coriolan* those three voices coalesce, separate, and recombine bewilderingly. *Coriolan* may anticipate one thing, Eliot's drama, but it achieves another still to be properly appreciated. Grover Smith writes that *Coriolan* "suffers[s] from obfuscation" and that its obscurity "could have been moderated by the judicious insertion of quotation marks" (159–60). But this supposes that the poet would have known precisely where to put the quotation marks. Baffled obfuscation is essential to the work's meaning.

Shakespeare's presentation in *Coriolanus* of democracy's vagaries obviously provided the scenario for *Coriolan*. Less obvious is the fact that Eliot could well have taken the vocal cue for *Coriolan* from the play. When Coriolanus is reluctantly obliged to gain assent from the citizenry for the consulship, much is made of the fact that he must win their "voices." Although in this context the word simply means "votes," as in Plutarch (the play's main source; see *Cor.* 331), the central scenes persistently play on its vocally figurative potential. Coriolanus and the citizens reiterate and bandy the word "voices" about until the humiliation endured by Coriolanus fatally arouses his patrician contempt. The indignity of having to show the people his wounds, inflicted at Corioli, in order to win their "voices," becomes the occasion for much linguistic wit to do with speaking and tongues (*Cor.* 2.3.5–8; 2.3.46; 2.3.52–53). Coriolanus's appeal to "the tune of your voices" (2.3.84–85) is scornfully ironic, as if the people can be played upon like instruments (as indeed they are, by the tribunes). With scathing repetition he reduces them to their democratic function as voters:

> Here come more voices.
> Your voices! For your voices I have fought,
> Watch'd for your voices; for your voices, bear
> Of wounds two dozen odd. (2.3.124–27)

"Worthy voices!" is his mocking farewell (2.3.136). As the Second Citizen says, "He mock'd us when he begg'd our voices" (2.3.157). The tribune Sicinius says, "Sir, the people / Must have their voices" (2.2.139–40), and Eliot's text *Coriolan* must have its voices too, is indeed composed of voices, some of them "The tongues o' th' common mouth," as Coriolanus puts it (3.1.22).

The Waste Land had its "different voices" as well. (At one time Eliot thought of titling the poem "He do the police in different voices," from Dickens's *Our Mutual Friend*; see *WLF* 4–5). But the voices of *Coriolan* are less distinct, so that, particularly in "Triumphal March," it is uncertain where one voice stops and another starts, be it that of a narrator, or of the "press of people," or of Coriolan himself (Reeves 78); and that uncertainty is a vocal index of the probing uncertainty of Eliot's political thinking at the time. "Stone, bronze, stone, steel, stone, oakleaves, horses' heels / Over the paving" (*CPP* 85): who speaks these opening words? In keeping with what turns out to be the temporal conflation of the poem's setting – the triumphal march is simultaneously in Rome, in the City of London, and in France after World War I, the listed munitions being those surrendered by Germany after Versailles (Smith 162) – the opening voice comes disembodied out of nowhere. Is it a voice of impressive ritual, or a merely reportorial narrating voice, neutrally descriptive? The uncertainty becomes more pronounced with the repetitive phrasing at the start of line 3, although the tone seems to be turning into naïve awe: "And the flags. And the trumpets. And so many eagles. / . . . And such a press of people" (*CPP* 85). The voice gets mired in time and people, in personalities and exchanges, in questions and answers, exclamations and reactions: "How many? Count them," "So many waiting, how many waiting? what did it matter, on such a day?," "What comes first? Can you see? Tell us" (85). Tenses shift between present and past; pronouns shift between "we" and "you," and, in the midst of the list of munitions, to "I." The voice is above the crowd and then amongst it, narrator then participant. But it is impossible to tell at exactly what point the awestruck register takes over from the impartial one.

As described in the *Criterion* article, the voice starts to parrot the language of order and authority and take on the register of the thoughtless people, which, in a moment of dramatic irony, tells more about them than they suspect. The phrase "We hardly knew ourselves that day" betrays the truth about their ignorance (*CPP* 85; Reeves 79). Five lines later, the line "The natural wakeful life of our Ego is a perceiving" is another moment of dramatic irony, since on the one hand the reader wonders whether the people perceive anything beyond the triumphalism to which they are being subjected, and on the other the line echoes Edmund Husserl, a writer presumably beyond their ken (Smith 161–62). Later, at what sounds like a significant moment in "Triumphal March," where exactly does the change of voice happen, the change from naïve wonder back to something more impersonal, that voice out of nowhere? –

> And now come the Mayor and the Liverymen. Look
> There he is now, look:
> There is no interrogation in his eyes
> Or in the hands, quiet over the horse's neck,
> And the eyes watchful, waiting, perceiving, indifferent. (*CPP* 86)

The voice shifts this time from being among the crowd to being above it. But does this shift occur at the first "look," or at the second? Or perhaps the voice in the crowd is capable of saying, with awed incomprehension, "There is no interrogation in his eyes." Or has the poetry moved by this line entirely into the *de haut en bas* register; or do the two registers somehow coalesce at this point, leader and led in a conspiracy of deception and self-deception? A. D. Moody is more certain: "With that line we are no longer looking at but through the hero's eyes; and what is seen then, a purely poetic vision, has the intensity of something absolute." Moody goes on to quote the next lines, "O hidden under the dove's wing, hidden in the turtle's breast, / Under the palmtree at noon, under the running water / At the still point of the turning world. O hidden" (*CPP* 86), and comments: "That visionary awareness informs the remainder of ['Triumphal March'], but only as an ironical doubling of the merely literal perceiving" (165–66). But how can we be so sure we are looking *through* Coriolan's eyes at this point; and does their "indifference" denote vacancy, or lack of sympathy, or something more impartially commanding? Even, indeed especially, at this key moment, might not that intensity of vision be as subject to vocal and auditory ambiguity and uncertainty as the rest of this text? "There is no interrogation in his eyes" could be a powerful evocation of authority, or merely the people's parroting of such an evocation (*CPP* 85). We cannot be certain which; and that was Eliot's dilemma in the *Criterion* article: "Order and authority are good," but how can the true thing be distinguished from the false, the parrotings from the voice of authority itself? (Reeves 80). The fact that Hugh Kenner hears the three lines beginning "O hidden" as a parody, rather than an intimation, of Christ's entry into Jerusalem demonstrates how variously this poetry may be witnessed (Kenner 222).

The voice of "Difficulties of a Statesman" is Coriolan's, and so comes across as more unified than that of "Triumphal March," although again there are some arresting changes of register, especially into what the *Criterion* article calls "a certain spiritual anaemia." The different perceptions by the people in "Triumphal March" and by Coriolan here demonstrate Eliot's claim in the *Criterion* that "under democracy [authority] can always pretend that it is giving the people what the people demands" ("C [Apr. 1929]" 379). The initial exclamation, "Cry what shall I cry?" (*CPP* 87), from Isaiah 40, echoed at irregular intervals throughout "Difficulties," emphasizes that this is a vocal performance. The transitoriness ("All flesh is grass," also from Isaiah 40) of this "pretended democracy" is decried, as it were below the breath, even as it is being declared. The repeated cry shifts between, and mingles, inner lament and public protest. Another repeated vocal motif, "Mother," takes over halfway through "Difficulties," as a private phantasmagoria of imagery encroaches on, and possibly offers relief from, the public world of bureaucratic machinery and compromise. The meaning resides once again in the sound the poetry makes. The flat, world-weary officialese of the first half or so of "Difficulties" is interrupted in the second half by an increasingly internalized voice, as when Coriolan is briefly identified with the poet Sordello in *Purgatorio* VI: "Meanwhile the guards shake dice on the marches / And the frogs (O Mantuan) croak in the marshes" (88). In the *Purgatorio* Sordello addresses Dante's guide Virgil with the words "O Mantuan," and Dante goes on to lament Italy's chaos. This Dantean scenario gives a political dimension to those frogs in the marshes (they come from Virgil's *Georgics* I), which seem to be fleetingly identified with the plaintiff people; and the intriguingly awkward, seductive-sounding shift from "marches" to "marshes" withdraws Coriolan's voice from an exterior world to an interior world of lamentation, to issue in the plangently crepuscular line "Fireflies flare against the faint sheet lightning" (88). That interior world "hidden" in Coriolan's "breast" ("hidden in many breasts," in the words of the 1928 *Criterion* article) contains a wide tonal range, at times changing abruptly. One arresting leap is from "a sweaty torchbearer, yawning" to what sounds like a full-throated visionary moment, beginning "O hidden under the . . . Hidden under the . . . ," although whether that repetition conveys wonder, aspiration, bewilderment or frustration is open to question. Is there something too strenuous about the further repetitions, "a moment, / A still moment," "There the cyclamen, . . . there the clematis," or about the sonority of the line "Under the breast feather stirred by the small wind after noon" (88)? A few lines later the tone plummets again with "Noses strong to break the wind." This is poetic expression in search of a centre, of stability and order.

The parallel between those croaking frogs and the plaintiff people is not explicit, but that between "the small creatures" and the people in Coriolan's final inward communion sounds more so: "Hidden in the stillness of noon, in the silent croaking night. / . . . / 'Rising and falling, crowned with dust,' the small creatures, / The small creatures chirp thinly though the dust, through the night" (*CPP* 88). This moment of sympathy (which again echoes Isaiah 40, where the chirping creatures are grasshoppers) signals reconciliation, albeit in defeat, the phrases "crowned with dust" and "chirp thinly through the dust" coming to terms, in their different ways (acceptance and dismissal), with the transitoriness to which all are subject. This is a religious comprehension apparently absent from the invocation of "dust" in "Triumphal March." By the end of *Coriolan* the voices of the leader and his people combine in a vocal alliance of recrimination and self-recrimination, but with a sense of freedom at being released from this world where "all flesh is grass." It is too simple to say that with those final words "Resign Resign Resign" the voice of the people breaks in on Coriolan's solitary meditative voice (89). Rather, his voice merges with theirs, so that by the end he is as much shouting himself down as being shouted down by the people. If the people parrot the words presented to them by their leader, the leader parrots the words demanded of him by his people (Reeves 81). Their voices have become as one in this baffling and baffled echo-chamber.

Minor Poems

Eliot relegated thirteen short poems to a "Minor Poems" section of *Collected Poems 1909–1935*. In 1953 he recalled that "twenty years ago" – that is, at about the time when he would have been assembling this collection – "I seemed to myself to have exhausted my meagre poetic gifts, and to have nothing more to say" (*OPP* 91). This comment may reflect what the poet was feeling when he designated those poems "minor." But the heading "Minor Poems" takes on a different cast in the light of Eliot's pronouncement of 1944, in "What Is Minor Poetry?":

> The difference between major and minor poets has nothing to do with whether they
> wrote long poems, or only short poems – though the *very* greatest poets, who are few

in number, have all had something to say which could only be said in a long poem. The important difference is whether a knowledge of the whole, or at least of a very large part, of a poet's work, makes one enjoy more, because it makes one understand better, any one of his poems. That implies a significant unity in his whole work. (*OPP* 49–50)

In 1935 those thirteen short poems must have looked to the poet like the last sparks of a poetic fire that had produced "The Love Song of J. Alfred Prufrock," *The Waste Land*, and *Ash-Wednesday*, to name but the longest of his poetic triumphs. But years later those "minor" poems would have been regarded from a different perspective, as parts of a pattern that now included, among other works, the long poem (or sequence) *Four Quartets*. In the words of "Little Gidding" III, the "minor" poems would have "become renewed, transfigured, in another pattern" (*CPP* 142).

Likewise, a reader today, with "a knowledge of the whole . . . of [this] poet's work," can now "understand better . . . any one of his poems" – even, perhaps especially, the short "minor" ones. From this later perspective they can be seen to trace a trajectory from the conceptual phase of *The Waste Land* to *Four Quartets*. Under the title *Doris's Dream Songs*, the two poems "Eyes that last I saw in tears" (*CPP* 90) and "The wind sprang up at four o'clock" (90–91) first appeared, along with a third poem, "This is the dead land," in a periodical, *Chapbook*, in 1924. "This is the dead land" became Part III of the final version of "The Hollow Men" (1925), and some important motifs from the other two poems also found their way into "The Hollow Men." "The wind sprang up" looks back to *The Waste Land*, for seven of its twelve lines derive from an uncollected poem, "Song to the Opherian," which Eliot at one time considered incorporating into *The Waste Land* (*WLF* 98–99), inquiring of Pound, "Would you advise working sweats with tears etc. into nerves monologue . . . ?" Pound responded, "I dare say the sweats with tears will wait" (Pound 171). One can see Pound's point: those sweats with tears, and even more the line "The waking echo of confusing strife," sound like expressions of barely mediated emotional stress (*CPP* 90). That also is arguably the reason for the exclusion of "The wind sprang up" and "Eyes that last I saw" from "The Hollow Men," although they clearly belong in the same emotional terrain as that poem-sequence.

"Eyes that last I saw" and "The wind sprang up" may have been relegated to "minor" status, but they remain as evidence of Eliot's determined struggle to move his poetry on from *The Waste Land*. In 1935 they would have been part of what the poet had lived through, the backward prospect, whereas the other "minor" poems would have been part of what he was more nearly living through, the forward prospect. In later years, with his "knowledge of the whole, or at least of a very large part" of his work, he would have seen, if he looked, how those other poems, especially the small sequence headed *Landscapes*, fit into that whole. Only a poet as fastidious as Eliot would call this sequence, however brief, "minor," and its relegation to this status is no doubt largely responsible for its comparative neglect both as an important part of Eliot's oeuvre and as challengingly original in its own right.

Hindsight reveals that the *Landscapes* sequence anticipates in miniature, but in important respects, *Four Quartets*. Already in *Landscapes* is present the movement – back and forth, temporal, geographical, visionary, in memory and in actuality – between origins and destinations, beginnings and endings, at the heart of *Four Quartets*: "In my beginning is my end"; "In my end is my beginning" (*CPP* 123, 129). "New Hampshire," "Virginia" and "Cape Ann," the first two and the last of the *Landscapes*, were composed in America during Eliot's visit there in 1933, the other two, "Usk" and "Rannoch, by Glencoe," on his return. Thus, like *Four Quartets*, the *Landscapes* move between America and Britain; and their ordering must be deliberate, since they were not composed in the order in which they were published, with the American *Landscapes* encompassing the two British ones.

"New Hampshire" begins with "Children's voices in the orchard / Between the blossom- and the fruit-time" and ends with an "apple-tree" (*CPP* 93), thus anticipating the precise intimation of the ineffable at the close of the last of the *Quartets*, "Little Gidding," with its "children in the apple-tree / . . . heard, half-heard, in the stillness / Between two waves of the sea" (145). Though the music of "New Hampshire" is light, it has a somber note: "Twenty years and the spring is over; / To-day grieves, to-morrow grieves, / Cover me over, light-in-leaves" (93). The poem recognizes grief's ineluctability, that the spring of youth gets longingly replayed (in memory), whereas that intimation has "become renewed, transfigured, in another pattern" (142) by the close of "Little Gidding." "Twenty years and the spring is over" (93) is less grimly time-ridden than the "Twenty years largely wasted" of "East Coker" V (128); "New Hampshire's" suspension between the time-bound and the timeless sounds like an anticipatory but more bittersweet glimpse of the way "time stops and time is never ending" in "The Dry Salvages" I (131). At the close of "Little Gidding" a sense of time passing transforms into a sense of time transcended, so that "now" and "always" become as one: "Quick now, here, now, always – / A condition of complete simplicity" (145). But that condition has been briefly foreshadowed by the transparently simple music of "New Hampshire": "Cling, swing, / Spring, sing, / Swing up into the apple-tree" (93) – as if to sing spring might bring it back, thus both quickening and allaying grief. That line "Quick now, here, now, always," which repeats the conclusion of "Burnt Norton" (122), recollects the rose-garden episode (composed soon after *Landscapes*) at the start of that *Quartet*: "Quick, said the bird . . . / Through the first gate, / Into our first world" (117–18). In "New Hampshire" birds also entice ("Black wing, brown wing" [93]) into a first world, which is at one level the actual world of the poet's American homeland and youth. The rose garden's motifs of children and leaves ("the leaves were full of children" [118]), repeated at the end of "Burnt Norton" ("children in the foliage" [122]), are likewise prefigured in "New Hampshire." "Cape Ann," the fifth *Landscape*, is a small, virtuoso bird performance beginning "O quick quick quick, quick hear the song-sparrow," a line which likewise anticipates the rose-garden episode and its emotional quickening (95). But possibly augured too, in the recognition of "Cape Ann" that this childhood location must be put behind the poet, is the resignation of "The Dry Salvages": the seagull in the lines

"But resign this land at the end, resign it / To its true owner, the tough one, the sea-gull" (95), may pre-echo the seagull of Part I of "The Dry Salvages," with its magnificently "tough" poetic music conjuring up the sea (131).

These anticipations in *Landscapes* of *Four Quartets*, especially of "Burnt Norton," have a specific biographical context. When Eliot visited America in 1933 he renewed contact in Cambridge with his early love Emily Hale, whom he had not seen since 1914, nearly "twenty years" earlier, when he left for England; and the two met again in the summers of 1934 and 1935 on visits she made to England, when they visited Burnt Norton together (Gordon 56). The "quick" music of the birds in "Cape Ann," which finds its way into the rose garden, connects New England, place of this old flame whose memory had recently been rekindled, with old England, the land for which the poet had left her, in whose presence he had the visionary experience in the rose garden.

The fact that "New Hampshire" and the second *Landscape* poem, "Virginia," originally appeared in a pamphlet called *Words for Music* points to Eliot's preoccupation with the relationship between poetry and music; and in this respect also the *Landscapes* sequence presages some of the concerns and procedures of *Four Quartets*. "The palaver is finished," the concluding words to "Cape Ann" and to the sequence, hint with wry self-consciousness that at least as much attention should be paid to the sound of this poetry as to its sense (*CPP* 95).[2] The music of "Virginia" – the short-lined angularities, the vocal tensions and relaxations – is the most absolute of the sequence, and the poem is as uncompromisingly in the Symbolist mode as any Eliot had written or was to write. ("De la musique avant toute chose," begins the poem "Art Poétique" by the Symbolist Paul Verlaine – "music before all else" [172].) "Virginia" sounds like a demonstration of the Symbolist aesthetic that underlies the analogy between words and music in "Burnt Norton" –

> Words, after speech, reach
> Into the silence. Only by the form, the pattern,
> Can words or music reach
> The stillness (*CPP* 121)

– even if the "stillness" of "Virginia" sounds oppressive compared with that of "Burnt Norton." The music of "Virginia" is self-searching, and paraphrase is treacherous. Words proceed by stressful internal rhyme and assonance to convey emotional intransigence. For instance, the repeated rhyming words "will" and "still" sound locked together in tense stasis. The isolation of "still" at the start of line 4, without any certain syntactical connection with the previous line, lets it float free, but only to reify "stillness." Or later:

> Living, living,
> Never moving. Ever moving
> Iron thoughts came with me
> And go with me. (*CPP* 94)

"Never" triggers its opposite, "ever," but only to produce "iron thoughts," which, being "ever moving," never leave the speaker and are therefore immoveable – unless "go with me" intimates the final going, in which case, as with the trees earlier in the poem, "delay" can only mean, rhymingly, "decay." This is taut music, painstakingly – even, it seems, painfully – produced. It demands to be listened to, precisely because it sounds undemanding.

The two Old-World *Landscapes*, "Usk" and "Rannoch, by Glencoe," have their music too, although they do not depend on it for their meaning as much as does "Virginia." But again they contain motifs to be developed in *Four Quartets*. In "Usk," "The hermit's chapel, the pilgrim's prayer" (*CPP* 94) predicts "Little Gidding's" "You are here to kneel / Where prayer has been valid" (139). In "Rannoch, by Glencoe," the contemplation of ancient enmities *sub specie aeternitatis* ("Listlessness of ancient war / . . . / Clamour of confused wrong, apt / In silence" [94–95]) anticipates a preoccupation of "Little Gidding." "Memory is strong / Beyond the bone" in "Rannoch" (95), but already this poem sounds as though it is moving toward the double perspective of "Little Gidding" III, where "History may be servitude, / History may be freedom" (142).

Five-Finger Exercises, the other small sequence in the "Minor Poems" section, unremittingly develops a different weapon in Eliot's poetic arsenal: the art of allusion. Smith lists a phalanx of literary echoes, and dismissively concludes that the sequence holds little interest beyond what he calls this "counterpoint method" (254). Ackroyd more justly comments that the sequence's first three poems "evince the power of his music which is here linked to odd and discomfiting themes" (209) concerning mortality and the passage of time. But, addressed to a cat, a terrier, and a duck, they take on a quirkily macabre air, especially when combined with the jauntily witty allusiveness. The "music" can get exaggeratedly involved, the wordplay teeter on the absurd: "Here a little dog I pause / Heaving up my prior paws, / Pause, and sleep endlessly" (*CPP* 91–92). The comic "squirming worm" in "Lines to a Duck in the Park" gives way at the end of the poem to a graver Marvellian air: "soon the enquiring worm shall try / Our well-preserved complacency" (92). It is open to question whether some of the wordplay is as deft as it wants to be. But then the striking of attitudes and archly stylistic mirror-gazing are hallmarks of this sequence. "How unpleasant to meet Mr. Eliot" begins "Lines for Cuscuscaraway and Mirza Murad Ali Beg," the last, oft-quoted, poem of the sequence (93). But a poet who can write this knows he is not really unpleasant, especially as he is only playing with Edward Lear's "How pleasant to know Mr. Lear."

Occasional Verses

Unlike "Minor Poems," the modest heading "Occasional Verses" in the *Collected Poems* can be taken at face value, even though Eliot's introductory note to the first of the texts so headed immediately raises questions: "*Defense of the Islands* cannot pretend to be verse, but its date – just after the evacuation from Dunkirk – and occasion have for me a significance which makes me wish to preserve it" (*CP* 213). And it is true that, though invoking something called "English verse," "Defense of the Islands" is written in a loose-limbed rhythmical prose, with rangy and deliberately unfocused syntax – deliberately, one surmises, because Eliot was to remark a year later that "a great deal of bad prose has been written under the name of free verse" (*OPP* 37). The four other "Occasional Verses" rise at least to the level of "verse." Apart from the *terza rima* of "To Walter de la Mare" (whose last line, "The inexplicable mystery of sound" [*CP* 220], is applicable to the best of Eliot's own poetry), they are in the prosy, loping, conversational, at times buttonholing, at times preachy style which Eliot developed for use in parts of the last three *Quartets*. Those *Quartets* were written in wartime London, the first three "Occasional Verses" are to do with the war, and Eliot evidently considered the style of "a man speaking to men" particularly appropriate at a time of unprecedented communal stress.

Eliot's concern about the place and role of poetry in national life was particularly acute during the war, which presented a new and pressing context in which to consider the relation between tradition and the individual talent. The war may not have reduced the importance of that talent, but for Eliot it demanded humbling responsibilities. This is evident from the last three *Quartets*, which are invariably aware of their wartime context. "East Coker" V talks in military terms about the effort to learn to use words during "the years of *l'entre deux guerres*": "a raid on the inarticulate / With shabby equipment" among "Undisciplined squads of emotion"; "what there is to conquer / By strength and submission"; "There is only the fight to recover what has been lost / And found and lost again and again" (*CPP* 128). Eliot is not writing merely metaphorically here; he is thinking of poetry as taking its place in the effort to defend the British and European civilization he values and has made his own, and which preeminently includes a literary and poetic tradition. So when he writes in "Defense of the Islands" about "these memorials . . . of English verse" being "joined with the memory of this defense of the islands / and the memory" of sailors, pilots and soldiers, this is no mere rhetorical flourish (*CP* 213). However, as the second "Occasional Verse," "A Note on War Poetry," states, if the individual poetic talent is humbled by war, something "which we call 'poetry'" is not, for poetry is "Not the expression of collective emotion," but "the abstract conception / Of private experience at its greatest intensity / Becoming universal" (*CP* 215–16). The appeal here is to an absolute of some kind, beyond the immediate "situation" of war. "A Note" does not pretend to be "poetry," nor deal in anything other than abstractions, in terms that have already been arrived at through the poetic trials and tribulations of, for instance and especially, *Four Quartets*. It ends somewhat archly, therefore, with the statement that the conclusion about "poetry" which it has arrived at "May be affirmed in verse" – that is to say, merely in "verse," not in "poetry" itself. And that, it has to be said, is what the author of the last "Occasional Verse," "A Dedication to my Wife" (the dedicatory poem for *The Elder Statesman*), settles for. But again he is one move ahead of his audience. In "The Three Voices of Poetry" he had said that "a good love poem, though it may be addressed to one person, is always meant to be overheard by other people. Surely, the proper language of love – that is, of communication to the beloved and to no one else – is prose" (*OPP* 90). "A Dedication" ends, "But this dedication is for others to read: / These are private words addressed to you in public" (*CP* 221) – and therefore, according to Eliot's argument, not "the proper language of love." No doubt the hope is that those "private words" nevertheless constitute "a good love poem" to be "overheard" by us. But the self-consciousness of this appeal in the poem to decorum denotes uneasiness – albeit an uneasiness engagingly thought-provoking in its vulnerability.

NOTES

1   See also ELIOT'S POLITICS.
2   The British composer Thomas Adès (b. 1971) has set the sequence to music in a striking song cycle, "Five Eliot Landscapes," Op. 1, for soprano and piano.

REFERENCES AND FURTHER READING

Ackroyd, Peter. *T. S. Eliot*. London: Sphere, 1985.

Gordon, Lyndall. *Eliot's Early Years*. Oxford: Oxford UP, 1977.

Hay, Eloise Knapp. *T. S. Eliot's Negative Way*. Cambridge: Harvard UP, 1982.

Kenner, Hugh. *The Invisible Poet: T. S. Eliot*. London: Methuen, 1965.

Moody, A. D. *Thomas Stearns Eliot: Poet*. Cambridge: Cambridge UP, 1980.

Pound, Ezra. *Selected Letters of Ezra Pound 1907–1941*. Ed. D. D. Paige. New York: New Directions, 1950.

Reeves, Gareth. *T. S. Eliot: A Virgilian Poet*. Basingstoke: Macmillan, 1989.

Shakespeare, William. *Coriolanus*. Ed. Philip Brockbank. The New Arden Shakespeare. London: Methuen, 1976.

Smith, Grover. *T. S. Eliot's Poetry and Plays: A Study in Sources and Meaning*. 2nd ed. Chicago: U of Chicago P, 1974.

Verlaine, Paul. *Selected Poems*. Ed. and trans. Joanna Richardson. Harmondsworth: Penguin, 1974.

18
Coming to Terms with
Four Quartets

Lee Oser

Four Quartets was written in England between 1935 and 1942, with a hiatus of a little over four years between the first poem and the second (Gardner 16). It was not originally intended as a sequence of four poems. In fact, it was not originally intended. "Burnt Norton" grew out of some lines that didn't fit into *Murder in the Cathedral* (Gardner 82). Not until 1940 did Eliot glimpse the possibility of a long poem. This work of "magnificent orchestration" (Matthiessen 471) was largely improvised: its composition was shaped by unforeseen historical forces whose providential qualities became part of the poet's subject matter. What began with a chance visit to the old country estate at Burnt Norton grew into Eliot's spiritual autobiography, including his ancestral life at East Coker, his family's emigration to Massachusetts, and his return to England and its Church. Layered with all this history are echoes of Eliot's earlier poems, as well as intermingled strata of philosophy and theology.

Eliot was more comfortable talking about *Four Quartets* than about *The Waste Land*, and he made valuable comments on the poem's origins and history. In his 1959 *Paris Review* interview, he reflected on the intersections of life and art:

> In 1939 if there hadn't been a war I would probably have tried to write another play . . . . The form of the *Quartets* fitted in very nicely to the conditions under which I was writing, or could write at all. I could write them in sections and I didn't have to have quite the same continuity; it didn't matter if a day or two elapsed when I did not write, as they frequently did, while I did war jobs. (qtd. in Gardner 15)

Eliot's "war jobs" included volunteer work as an air-raid warden. Twice a week he stayed up through the night, walking the roof of the Faber & Faber building in Russell Square, while Stuka bombers menaced the city. The "familiar compound ghost" of "Little Gidding" II haunts London at the crossroads of history and poetry, and bears witness to this fateful convergence (*CPP* 140). Supernatural reality, the ghost seems to say, invades the order of nature when we confront and compose the words we live by.

A Companion to T. S. Eliot, First Edition. Edited by David E. Chinitz.
© 2014 John Wiley & Sons, Ltd. Published 2014 by John Wiley & Sons, Ltd.

At first glance, *Four Quartets* appears to be chiefly a poem of places. Burnt Norton is a country estate located near the town of Chipping Campden, in Gloucestershire, which Eliot visited in the summer of 1934 with a close American friend, Emily Hale.[1] Eliot came to East Coker, a village in Somerset, in August 1937. It was from East Coker that his ancestor Andrew Eliot sailed for New England around 1669. The Dry Salvages are two or three nubs of rock just off Pigeon Cove, a few miles north of the fishing town of Gloucester, on Cape Ann in Massachusetts. Eliot's family owned a summer house near the harbor in Gloucester, and the young poet used to sail by the Dry Salvages on his one-man outings along the coast. To this day, briar roses grow along the narrow streets of Gloucester, and the "distant rote in the granite teeth" (*CPP* 131) sounds along its beaches and harbors, which are flanked by impressive shelves of granite. Little Gidding, in Cambridgeshire, is home to a chapel where a small Anglican religious community, founded in 1625 by Nicholas Ferrar, gave refuge to King Charles I during the English Civil War.

But Eliot's connection to these places, though real, is fugitive. *Four Quartets* lies outside the tradition of country-house poems like Jonson's *To Penshurst* and Marvell's *Upon Appleton House*. It seems to touch but not to overlap the romanticism of Wordsworth's *Tintern Abbey*. Wordsworth's self, though psychologically traumatized, is solider than Eliot's self, largely because Wordsworth's sacramental approach to memory gives him a basis in the world that Eliot eschews. In all these poems, from Jonson to Wordsworth, the richness of time and place anchors the poet in the world. From the opening strophe of "Burnt Norton," with its reminiscence of an absent "rose-garden," Eliot is not writing from a place where he is securely grounded. He seems to have visited East Coker and Little Gidding only once (Gardner 58). His places in the world are real, but they hold their main significance as points of departure. In this essential respect, they are spiritual states and states of consciousness.

Even before we listen for Eliot's tone, we find a hint of his ghostly sense of place in his titles. "Burnt Norton," for instance, takes its name from a terrible fire that occurred in the 1740s, destroying a country house of which no trace remains (Gardner 36). Only in the name of the estate, not in the actual place itself, is the historical memory of the fire preserved. It is a small step from proper nouns to common nouns, and so we might find in Eliot's titles an affirmation of the poetic principle that "Every poem [is] an epitaph" (*CPP* 144). This principle speaks to the way in which time, ordering the poem both as an abstract concept and as a theme behind the imagery of seasons, paradoxically threatens to dissolve the meaning of *Four Quartets*. I will have more to say about the loss and recovery of meaning later on, but since the lost rose-garden represents the opening "chord" (more on musical analogies later as well) of the *Quartets*, a haunting chord that sets an elegiac tone, we should immediately be mindful of the problems with meaning that we face throughout the work. Because of time, every poem is an epitaph, every place is ghostly, and every poet is a ghost. History and poetry save the meaning from oblivion only through the unifying pattern that faith supplies.

After he was received into the Church of England, Eliot debated the question of belief with the eminent literary critic I. A. Richards. Rejecting Richards's theory that poetry consists of "pseudo-statements" (statements that give emotional satisfaction without reference to the facts), Eliot concluded, "I cannot, in practice, wholly separate my poetic appreciation from my personal beliefs" (*SE* 231). This debate with Richards animates the *Quartets*. It inspires Eliot's insight into the religious element in all poetry, including his own. Religious belief in *Four Quartets* is foundational. Neither art nor philosophy can cohere without it.

Eliot indicates the religious matrix of *Four Quartets* by taking his epigraphs from Heraclitus (*CPP* 117), who rose to fame in his native Ephesus (in modern Turkey) about 2,500 years ago. Helen Gardner notes that, in the Faber pamphlet *Four Quartets*, "the Greek epigraphs were printed on the reverse of the table of Contents, as if applying to the whole sequence. In the *Collected Poems 1909–1962*, they reverted to being the epigraphs to 'Burnt Norton' alone" (28). A. D. Moody, an important authority on Eliot, says in an unsubstantiated endnote, "Eliot's first thought and his last was to attach these epigraphs to 'Burnt Norton,' not to *Four Quartets* as a whole" (359). However, another distinguished critic, William Blissett, finds the "poetic suggestiveness" (Eliot's phrase) of Heraclitus to permeate all the *Quartets* (29). And as Benjamin Lockerd demonstrates, Eliot makes great structural use of the elemental scheme of earth, air, fire, and water on which Heraclitus focused. Following Blissett and Lockerd, I would argue that the epigraphs have significance relative to the whole, because no part of the total poem exists in isolation:

τοῦ λόγου δ'ἐόντος ξυνοῦ ζώουσιν οἱ πολλοὶ ὡς ἰδίαν ἔχοντες φρόνησιν.

But while the logos is common to all, the multitude [hoi polloi] live as though each had a private understanding.

ὁδὸς ἄνω κάτω μία καὶ ὡυτή.

The way up and the way down are one and the same.

What did Heraclitus believe? Mainly, that all things flow, and that opposites are related through a principle of unity expressing itself as fire. The "logos" that human minds can tap into is identical with this fire. By nature, things are bound to change, to be consumed by the cosmic flux, transformed elementally downward, toward water and earth, or elementally upward, toward air and fire. And yet, all things are held in counterpoise, reconciled and unified along the one fiery way. Heraclitus is not a relativist, because in his view the identity of the logos-fire persists through change (Lockerd 223). His central paradox is that "differences and unity are equally real" (Clubb 21).

Eliot's epigraphs do more than open a dialogue with Heraclitus. They resonate in our historical consciousness, awaking echoes and triggering associations, particularly through the word *logos*.[2] Translated variously as "word," "speech," "thought," or "reason," it appears throughout the philosophy and literature of classical Greece. It launches the Gospel of John: "In the beginning was the Word" (1:1). If Western culture can be imagined as an ancient building, the logos is its cornerstone: the foundation of science and rational theology. Its presence here suggests that Eliot intends to explore the reality that is "common to all."

But Eliot is not, in his epigraphs, invoking a realist metaphysic – a reality he can confidently grasp with his logical mind. He is not an outright philosophical realist in the tradition of Aristotle and Aquinas, guided by reason and the senses. (In the twentieth century, this tradition developed a grotesque mutation in the form of logical positivism, philosophical science-worship that Eliot despised.) Instead, Eliot pursues a middle course between alternatives. On the one hand, the first epigraph from Heraclitus suggests a denial of nominalism, the school of thought, moderate in William of Ockham and extreme in Jacques Derrida, that holds there are no universal truths, only names of things or individuals. For Eliot, as I have suggested, the act of naming is not empty nominalism but an opening for ghostly presences. On the other hand, the second epigraph suggests that there are severe limits to what reason and the senses can tell us about reality. If the way up and the way down are one and the same, then paradox trumps positivism.

Like the logos, paradox is a way of knowing, but its paths are by nature crooked, not straight. The truths of paradox are latent truths. There is a well-established critical tradition that links Eliot's meditations on time and eternity to St. Augustine's maddening paradoxes of time in the *Confessions* (see Rotsaert). And certainly paradox shapes a great deal of Christian thought, from Augustine to the sixteenth-century Spanish mystic St. John of the Cross, and from Dr. John Donne, the Dean of St. Paul's, to G. K. Chesterton – all of them influences on Eliot. The impact of religious paradox on modern philosophy is lasting and profound. Luther's Heidelberg Disputation is fraught with overwhelming paradox: "The law of God, the most salutary doctrine of life, cannot advance man on his way to righteousness, but rather hinders him" (31: 39). A sincere Lutheran, Kant showed that reason itself, if left to its own devices, ends in contradiction. Kant's breathtaking antinomies of pure reason demonstrate that reason terminates in paradox, because each of its highest assertions – about cosmogony and freedom and God – has a diametrically opposed counter-proof.

So Eliot presents the unusual spectacle of an anti-nominalist (not a realist) poet who promises to deal less in the proofs and forms of unaided reason, and more in paradoxes that have the mystery of God behind them. We are met with a sensibility that explores a middle way between Aristotle and Luther. The result is not so much a field of gray as it is darkness alternating with radiances of light along the path of experience: "a grace of sense, a white light still and moving" (*CPP* 119). In this paradoxical line from "Burnt Norton" II, Eliot is not denying reason and the senses. Both kinds of sense are suggested by "a grace of sense," which I understand grammatically as a genitive of material (cf. "a goblet of gold"), where sense is graced and given form. But sense and form are limited to what grace gives them. Without grace there is only darkness.

Eliot's Christianity is generally compared to that of Michel de Montaigne, the sixteenth-century essayist who charmingly mocked the pretensions of human reason. Montaigne, in his "Apology for Raymond Sebond," a work Eliot certainly knew, notes the irrational fervor for "sleight-of-hand, enchantments . . . communication with the spirits of the dead, prognostications, horoscopy . . . [and the] seat of Mars [being] located in the middle of the triangle of the hand" (510–11). Eliot may have had this passage in mind when he began the fifth section of "The Dry Salvages": "To communicate with Mars, converse with spirits, / To report the behaviour of the sea monster, / Describe the horoscope, haruspicate or scry" (*CPP* 135). Eliot and Montaigne, both aristocratic, conservative, and skeptical Christian humanists, are certainly close in temperament. But Eliot is more sympathetic than Montaigne toward philosophy and theology. Unlike Montaigne, he stands with Aquinas on the basic scholastic principle that good reasoning is never contrary to faith.

Eliot is, however, a writer who sometimes contradicts himself, and in his reaction against modernism, the Christian Eliot can baffle the student and the expert alike. There is, for example, the anti-modernist sermonizing of his "Choruses from *The Rock*," where we are instructed, "There is no life that is not in community" (*CPP* 101), and "You must not deny the body" (111). These tenets fly in the face of Eliotic modernism. True, Eliot expresses a more sympathetic view of community in *Four Quartets* than he expresses in, say, "The Love Song of J. Alfred Prufrock." But he continues to see community from the outside and does not live in it. As for Eliot's denying the body, we can turn to "Tradition and the Individual Talent," where Eliot describes the artist as the self-consciousness of "the mind of Europe" (*SE* 6). This typically modernist emphasis on isolated mental activity, as opposed to embodied communal activity, is inconsistent with the Christian sermonizing in his "Choruses from *The Rock*," yet quite consistent with the *Four Quartets*.

How, then, does Eliot manage to reconcile Christianity and modernism? The short answer is: it is not clear that he does. A great deal is left to the reader's interpretation, but it would be foolish to ignore the issue. Allow, if you will, that what mattered most intensely to Eliot before his conversion was his experience of art. Allow that what mattered most intensely to Eliot after his conversion was his experience of religion. What stays constant is this: throughout both halves of his career, *experience for Eliot has no physical, egotistical center*. Its fragmentary quality bespeaks a mind that knows reality not through action, but through the flux of language. Even in the *Quartets*, which forego the highly allusive, fragmentary technique of *The Waste Land*, Eliot does not entirely materialize. He remains invisible, a fugitive voice speaking behind a shifting tableau of situations. And if "Tradition and the Individual Talent" is Eliot's seminal essay, which he later criticized but never recanted, we find its avant-garde author on a strange foray: "The point of view which I am struggling to attack is perhaps related to the metaphysical theory of the substantial unity of the soul" (*SE* 9). This curious reference to "substantial unity" signals a conflict with the Thomistic–Dantean view of the embodied soul that is individually fashioned by God. Possibly it signals an openness to the ideas of Leibniz and Spinoza, who depersonalize the soul by making it part of a system. Most important (and here is where Eliot's difficulty lies), Christian literature is not "impersonal" in Eliot's sense, because the Christian writer's relationship to God is always personal.

Because it lacks a physical, egotistical center, Eliot's poetry is emotionally removed. With rare exceptions, it makes little or no claim on the body, which is the theater of emotion. Eliot tends to suppress what Aristotle's theory of catharsis assumes: a metaphysics of human nature. The wedding scene and dancing in "East Coker" II are described clearly and abstractly, by an almost bodiless observer, not by a flesh-and-blood narrator, like the friendly and humanely compassionate speaker of Spenser's *Epithalamion*. We may feel a mild sympathy for the fleeting couple in Eliot's description, we may even feel a mild sympathy for the "familiar compound ghost," but our experience of these figures is intellectual.

What Eliot offers in place of mimetic action is a meditation on the soul that is exquisitely lyrical and musical, and full of subtle and original effects. The form of the *Quartets* is self-consciously musical, with leitmotifs and moods set within distinct rhythmical movements. String quartets by Beethoven and Bartók appear to have influenced its composition (Barndollar 179–81). This musical element enriches the poet's meditation on time. By suggesting the timelessness of time, music seems to open a channel between time and eternity. It hints at the freedom of the divine vision. To quote Roger Scruton: "Music . . . offers an image of the subject, released from the world of objects, and moving in response to its own caprice" (149). Eliot's fluid four-beat line allows for shifting emphases according to one's rhythmic velleity or desire:

> There they were, dignified, invisible,
> Moving without pressure, over the dead leaves,
> In the autumn heat, through the vibrant air,
> And the bird called, in response to
> The unheard music hidden in the shrubbery,
> And the unseen eyebeam crossed, for the roses
> Had the look of flowers that are looked at. (*CPP* 118)

The "unheard music" emerges from behind or beyond the world of sense, much as an "unseen" being irradiates the roses with a presence that welcomes the soul into the garden, freed from the "pressure" of gravity, habit, and the fall of man. Here, and throughout the most intense lyrical passages of the *Quartets*, Eliot's symbolist procedures touch every layer of the verse, from its dreamlike indirection, to its musical atmosphere, to its self-referential language (see Everett). Words like "leaves" (pages are leaves in a book) and "air" (an air is a melody) feed an entrancing state of expanded self-consciousness as we ascend the stairs of being toward God. And so, "you are the music / While the music lasts" (136).

Eliot described the problem of the modernist long poem through an analogy to music. He told an audience in Glasgow on February 24, 1942, when "Little Gidding" still lay unfinished:

Dissonance, even cacophony, has its place: just as, in a poem of any length, there must be transitions between passages of greater and less intensity, to give a rhythm of fluc-tuating emotion essential to the musical structure of the whole; and the passages of less intensity will be, in relation to the level on which the total poem operates, prosaic – so that, in the sense implied by that context, it may be said that no poet can write a poem of amplitude unless he is a master of the prosaic. (*OPP* 32)

Behind this discussion stands the characteristic modernist tension between symbolist "intensity" and rational discourse. Much of modernism is an effort to overcome the restrictions of reason; unlike the poet of *The Waste Land*, however, the later Eliot begins with the logos. True to his past, he keeps faith with Walter Pater's finest epigram: "*All art constantly aspires towards the condition of music*" (1: 135; original emphasis). At the same time, he does not feast on irrationality or throw reason on the trash heap of historicism. Attuned to paradox, he finds a place for logic in "dissonance, even cacophony." A kind of painstaking logic, a grammatical parsing of experience, characterizes his poem's meditations and transitions (unlike *The Waste Land*, *Four Quartets* abounds in transitions). Through his "passages of less intensity," Eliot grows estranged, temporally and spatially, from the places – Burnt Norton, East Coker, The Dry Salvages, Little Gidding – where he starts. He grows estranged from his primary symbols, like the rose and the fire, sources of epiphanous power. But through these same passages, he reconsiders the "conceptual terms such as 'end,' 'beginning,' 'motion,' 'stillness,' and 'meaning'" (Perkins 28) that place the places and counter-point the symbols. Conceptual terms are less sensuous than symbols, but even con-ceptual terms become thematic through repetition, so that the musical idea holds for the total poem.

To understand better the rules of Eliot's game, it is helpful to consult the general structure of each *Quartet*, which echoes that of *The Waste Land*:

  I.   philosophical poetry: description of place, meditation on time, interplay of themes
  II.   a) high lyric; b) movement to discursive self-consciousness
  III. movement through darkness and paradox
  IV.   brief lyric
  V.   philosophical denouement, language about language (Kenner 307)

Taking "Little Gidding" as an example, we approach the chapel ("a husk of meaning") by way of a description of the environs (Little Gidding) and the season ("Midwinter spring") that is also a philosophical meditation on place and time (*CPP* 138–39). The high lyric section, beginning "Ash on an old man's sleeve," is actually somewhat less symbolist, less intensely musical and dreamlike, than its counterpart in "Burnt Norton," because Eliot in the last *Quartet* is building schematically toward his conclu-sion of the whole. By the same token, the movement to discursive self-consciousness that follows – that is, to the Dantean tercets of the ghost scene – is not as abrupt as in the other *Quartets*, though it is represented, as always, by a formal shifting of gears. In section three, we have darkness and paradox centering on King Charles I ("a king at nightfall") and the winners and losers of the English Civil War, who (paradoxically) are "United in the strife which divided them" (*CPP* 143). The brief lyric of section four, "The dove descending breaks the air," is elemental and religious and historical. The dove is the Holy Spirit in history, even in the shape of a German bomber plane. Here, Eliot's daring spirituality draws aid from the firmly liturgical fourth sections of "East Coker" and "The Dry Salvages," while catching a spiritually suggestive echo of "the kingfisher's wing" from "Burnt Norton" IV (121). And the fifth section of "Little Gidding" is a synthesis of all that has come before, where the linguistic (or poetic) aspects of "beginning" and "end" come to the fore, where the linguistic problem of synthesis is itself addressed ("The common word exact without vulgarity / The formal word precise but not pedantic" [144]), and where the major symbols of the poem – the fire and the rose – are revealed standing behind the whole.

Eliot's "prosaic style" is most pronounced in section II of the first three *Quartets*, with their recurring fall from high lyric to discursive self-consciousness. It is pronounced to the point of clever and appealing parody in Henry Reed's "Chard Whitlow":

> As we get older we do not get any younger.
> Seasons return, and today I am fifty-five,
> And this time last year I was fifty-four,
> And this time next year I shall be sixty-two. (279)

Playing directly off line 190 of "East Coker," Reed suggests that Eliot is mind-numbingly monotonous. Eliot might be said to invite such criticism: "You say I am repeating / Something I have said before. I shall say it again. / Shall I say it again?" (*CPP* 127). But to read Eliot well (as Reed does) is to pay attention to transitions that do not progress in a linear fashion. It is to enter into an experience of displacement and revision, not only of symbols and concepts, but of pronouns that include the self. The paradox in this passage from "East Coker" lies in the precise dissonance of the repetition; for the adverb "again" speaks to a different "I" with each turn of the verse. For Eliot, the accruing shifts in time and space alter one's identity until "the patient is no longer here" (134).[3] To quote "East Coker" again: "I am here / Or there, or elsewhere" (124). The enjambment makes all the difference, and the distance between "here" and "there" is definitive for the self in question. In fact the spatial adverbs "here" and "there" can have the paradoxical effect of disconnecting us from space, unless we are able to place ourselves in a larger pattern that has ultimate stability. Reed's perceptive joke, then, is to describe the "I" as mathematically and ploddingly constant. He measures out his life with coffee spoons, and then muddles the count. For Eliot, too, despite his poetic authority, the count is also on occasion muddled, and that is one reason why "humility is endless" (126).

Fusing the total poem is the connection Eliot makes between the spiritual and the aesthetic. This connection is the key to Eliot's poetic, including *The Waste Land*. We can approach it through the groundwork laid for Eliot by two nineteenth-century geniuses. Dealing in bold strokes, we can say that Pater was aesthetic, that Emerson was spiritual, and that Eliot unites the spiritual with the aesthetic: "the fire and the rose are one" (145). For Pater, the cliché is the index of a stereotyped world. Its verbal opposite is *le mot juste*, the exact right word that justifies the world as (in Nietzsche's phrase) an aesthetic phenomenon. For Emerson, conventionality means spiritual failure. "This one fact the world hates," Emerson writes in "Self-Reliance," "that the soul *becomes*" (158). Emerson, in other words, sees the soul as needing to escape the falsifying bounds of a routine identity. For Eliot, once the self and the world are stereotypically known, then it is spiritually imperative to move on, lest some form of idolatry ensnare us. Unlike Emerson, Eliot is Christian, elegiac, and fearful of self-idolatry. But their spiritual restlessness, open form – I am thinking of Emerson the essayist – and iconoclasm connect them. And so, by way of Pater and Emerson, when Eliot accuses himself of a lapse, it is not a sin or a vice in the ordinary sense. It is a "periphrastic study in a worn-out poetical fashion" (*CPP* 125). The failure is artistic: the spirit is caged in a dead style.

Eliot's union of the spiritual and the aesthetic tests and pushes the boundary between orthodoxy and heresy. Orthodox religion is liturgically present in the fourth sections of the middle poems. But dogma is also realized indirectly, in ways that do not precede experience or define it ahead of time. The aesthetic movement had challenged Christianity's ability to grasp new experience; this challenge is heard throughout modernism, in such important books as *A Portrait of the Artist as a Young Man* and *To the Lighthouse*. Eliot in the *Quartets* wants to show that a Christian can "bear . . . reality" (118). We have already noticed the incarnational grammar in "a grace of sense," from "Burnt Norton" II. It has the force, not of constriction, but of discovery. Here is a different case. When Eliot speaks of the "hardly, barely prayable / Prayer of the one Annunciation" (132), he does so at the end of a sestina that describes entropy and exhaustion: contextually, we are prepared for this climactic prayer by the building pressure of despair and loss. The effect can be compared with Tolstoy's breaking down of barriers to prayer in *Anna Karenina*. Both Tolstoy and Eliot prefer anticlimax to elevated sentiment. For both authors, to say the least, happy endings are hard to come by. "Little Gidding" offers further examples of Eliot's existential approach to dogma. The most stirringly affirmative of Eliot's writings, it shows Eliot weaving the fabric of his experience with a strong Christian thread (see Schuchard). But even in "Little Gidding" the tonic chord or "end" occurs provisionally, with a Pisgah vision that is a summons to further effort, prayer, and discipline.[4] There is no THE END.

When Eliot pushes orthodoxy to the breaking point, his language exhibits a metamorphic fecundity akin to pantheism. The river in "The Dry Salvages" I is described as "a strong brown god" (*CPP* 130), recalling, for instance, the River Xanthos in the *Iliad*. This deliberate use of myth can be justified, from the orthodox perspective, as a recapitulation of the Western mind's historical development. But there is more to it than that. Eliot displays his aesthetic spirituality, and his poetic method, through a bold juxtaposition:

> The sea has many voices,
> Many gods and many voices.
> The salt is on the briar rose,
> The fog is in the fir trees. (130–31)

At first it is a puzzling maneuver. What does the salt's being on the briar rose have to do with the sea's having many gods and many voices? But Eliot has prepared this back-and-forth movement with the opening lines of the verse paragraph: "The river is within us, the sea is all about us; / The sea is the land's edge also, the granite / Into which it reaches, the beaches where it tosses . . ." (130). Here the argument for the Heraclitean influence is most persuasive. The opposing elements of water and earth, the sea and the land, share an underlying identity. The sea is the land, because the sea is the "land's edge": "it reaches" into the "granite," a reach strengthened by the rhyme with "beaches," which extends the reach to the point that the sea actually becomes the land. A passing ambiguity in pronoun usage (the antecedent of the first "it") reinforces the effect of one divinity (the logos-fire) shifting through many forms: the way up and the way down are one and the same.

The sources for Eliot's pantheism include Heraclitus, Spinoza, Coleridge, Shelley, Woolf, and Pound. The collocation of gods and the sea's "many voices" echoes Tennyson's "Ulysses." Studying Eliot's pantheistic undertones, we may observe that the fire and the rose have "many voices" as well. This musical (as in the "voicings" of chords) and metamorphic principle is evident in the poet's reworking his two major symbols throughout the *Quartets*, from the fires of Hell and Purgatory, to the roses of Eden and Paradise. And the same metamorphic principle is active in Eliot's improvised uses of form. In "East Coker" IV, the paradoxical yoking of images and ideas recalls Donne and Crashaw: "If to be warmed, then I must freeze / And quake in frigid purgatorial fires / Of which the flame is roses, and the smoke is briars" (*CPP* 128). This metaphysical conceit may strike *Waste Land* enthusiasts as a little quaint, despite the exquisite versification. On a further reading, though, our eyes may detect an uncanny and powerful pattern, noticing, for instance, that the "briar rose" of "The Dry Salvages" I is foreshadowed by "roses . . . briars" in the last line above. Also, it happens that the "smoke" (fire and air) of these briars resembles the "fog" (water and air) in the fir trees, and the "fires" themselves anticipate the fir trees in several ways: in the material resemblance of "fir" to "fire"; in the fact that "fire" (as the *OED* attests) was an Early Modern or Tudor spelling of our modern "fir"; and, lastly, in the cyclical movement of "old timber to new fires / Old fires to ashes, and ashes to the earth" (123). Further still, these metamorphic firs foreshadow the human tree, whose "soul's sap quivers" (138), much as the "river is within us." The poem's unifying effects, observed through its myriad turnings of language and form, suggest that, if we could know the height of meditation ("the still point" [119]) and see the whole pattern of time in eternity, we would discover that the many, like the fire and the rose, are one.

But the many and the one is not necessarily a Christian metaphysic.[5] You will find it in metaphysical poetry – for example, in "The Phoenix and the Turtle." It is in

Leibniz and Spinoza. It is in William James, who considered himself a Christian, though of an unusual kind. Returning to Heraclitus, we see in him "the inevitable justification of a pantheistic philosophy – that everything is justified *sub specie aeternitatis*" (Copleston 1: 43). Historically, ideological critics have shown little sympathy for the theology of Eliot's last major poem. Christians may judge it to be of doubtful orthodoxy. In any case, the poet of *Four Quartets* is true to his art, insisting on the mystical and religious grounds of great literature.

NOTES

1 For Hale and her relationship with Eliot, see THE POET AND THE PRESSURE CHAMBER: ELIOT'S LIFE, or Gordon, passim.

2 The word ὁδός (hodos), or "way," also carries much historical weight.

3 This idea of self-disruption has numerous sources, from Buddha to Lucretius to Montaigne to David Hume. See, for example, Montaigne (554).

4 *Pisgah*: "The name of the peak of Mount Nebo, from which Moses saw the Promised Land" (*OED*). Eliot inherits the Mosaic mantle from his paternal grandfather, William Greenleaf Eliot (Oser 28).

5 Consider, however, the Christological (hence anthropocentric) language of 1 Corinthians 12.

REFERENCES AND FURTHER READING

Barndollar, David. "Movements in Time: *Four Quartets* and the Late String Quartets of Beethoven." *T. S. Eliot's Orchestra: Critical Essays on Poetry and Music.* Ed. John Xiros Cooper. New York: Garland, 2000. 179–94.

Bergonzi, Bernard, ed. *T. S. Eliot: Four Quartets: A Casebook.* London: Macmillan, 1969.

Blissett, William. "T. S. Eliot and Heraclitus." *T. S. Eliot and Our Turning World.* Ed. Jewel Spears Brooker. New York: St. Martin's, 2001. 29–46.

Bush, Ronald. *T. S. Eliot: A Study in Character and Style.* New York: Oxford UP, 1983.

Clubb, Merrel D., Jr. "The Heraclitean Element in Eliot's *Four Quartets.*" *Philological Quarterly* 40 (1961): 19–33.

Copleston, Frederick, S. J. *A History of Philosophy.* 9 vols. New York: Doubleday, 1985.

Davie, Donald. "T. S. Eliot: The End of an Era." 1956. Bergonzi 153–67.

Donoghue, Denis. *Words Alone: The Poet T. S. Eliot.* New Haven: Yale UP, 2000.

Emerson, Ralph Waldo. *Selected Writings.* New York: Modern Library, 1940.

Everett, Barbara. "Eliot's 'Four Quartets' and French Symbolism." *English* 29 (1980): 1–37.

"Fire." *The Oxford English Dictionary.* 2nd ed. 1989.

Gardner, Helen. *The Composition of Four Quartets.* London: Faber, 1978.

Gordon, Lyndall. *T. S. Eliot: An Imperfect Life.* New York: Norton, 1999.

Holy Bible. King James Version. New York: American Bible Society, 1999.

Kenner, Hugh. *The Invisible Poet: T. S. Eliot.* New York: Harcourt, 1959.

Lockerd, Benjamin G., Jr. *Aethereal Rumours: T. S. Eliot's Physics and Poetics.* Lewisburg, PA: Bucknell UP, 1998.

Luther, Martin. *Luther's Works.* Gen. Ed. Helmut T. Lehman. 55 vols. Philadelphia: Muhlenberg, 1955–86.

Matthiessen, F. O. "Eliot's *Quartets.*" 1943. *T. S. Eliot: The Contemporary Reviews.* Ed. Jewel Spears Brooker. Cambridge: Cambridge UP, 2004. 467–71.

Montaigne, Michel de. *The Complete Works.* Trans. Donald M. Frame. New York: Knopf, 2003.

Moody, A. D. *Thomas Stearns Eliot: Poet*. Cambridge: Cambridge UP, 1980.

Murray, Paul. *T. S. Eliot and Mysticism: The Secret History of Four Quartets*. New York: St. Martin's, 1991.

Oser, Lee. T. S. *Eliot and American Poetry*. Columbia: U of Missouri P, 1998.

Pater, Walter. *Works*. 10 vols. London: Macmillan, 1912–15.

Perkins, David. *A History of Modern Poetry: Modernism and After*. Cambridge: Harvard UP, 1987.

"Pisgah." *The Oxford English Dictionary*. 2nd ed. 1989.

Reed, Henry. "Chard Whitlow." *The New Oxford Book of Light Verse*. Ed. Kingsley Amis. Oxford: Oxford UP. 279–80.

Ricks, Christopher. *Decisions and Revisions in T. S. Eliot*. London: The British Library and Faber and Faber, 2003.

Rotsaert, Frank. "The Force of an Influence: Augustine and Eliot." *University of Dayton Review* 21 (1991): 145–59.

Schuchard, Ronald. "'If I think, again, of this place': Eliot, Herbert, and the Way to Little Gidding." *Words in Time: New Essays on Four Quartets*. Ed. Edward Lobb. Ann Arbor: U of Michigan P, 1993. 52–83.

Scruton, Roger. *An Intelligent Person's Guide to Philosophy*. New York: Penguin, 1999.

Smith, Grover. *T. S. Eliot's Poetry and Plays: A Study in Sources and Meaning*. Chicago: U of Chicago P, 1956.

19

"Away we go": Poetry and Play in *Old Possum's Book of Practical Cats* and Andrew Lloyd Webber's *Cats*

Sarah Bay-Cheng

In his 1936 essay on the poetry of Friedrich Hölderlin, philosopher Martin Heidegger remarked that "Poetry looks like a game and yet it is not. A game does indeed bring men together, but in such a way that each forgets himself in the process. In poetry, on the other hand, man is re-united on the foundation of his existence" (Heidegger 310). For Heidegger, poetry and games distinguish themselves not by presentation or form ("Poetry looks like a game"), but rather by what lies behind the playful exterior and, most significantly, by their effects on an audience. Whereas the game separates the viewer from his or her fellow observers through absorption in the game itself, poetry unifies a community of spectators. Whether or not T. S. Eliot read Heidegger's essay, he would have appreciated the comparison between poetry and games. The collective audience and the motif of games were important concerns of Eliot's throughout the thirties, and they provide perhaps the best lens through which to consider his critically neglected poetry collection, *Old Possum's Book of Practical Cats* (1939).

Begun in 1934–35 and dedicated to the children of friends, Eliot's collection details the personalities of several individual cats. "The Naming of Cats," which opens the sequence, and "The Ad-dressing of Cats," which concludes it, both speak directly to a human reader. From the outset, Eliot presents cats themselves as a kind of game or riddle. He introduces the collection in a tone of concealed playfulness, his words insisting on the seriousness of his subject even as his rhymes and figures of speech suggest the opposite:

> The Naming of Cats is a difficult matter,
> It isn't just one of your holiday games;
> You may think at first I'm as mad as a hatter
> When I tell you a cat must have THREE DIFFERENT NAMES. (*CPP* 149)

The reader is then confronted with the absurd challenge of learning the names of the cats and of discovering their secret world through their individual personalities and

A Companion to T. S. Eliot, First Edition. Edited by David E. Chinitz.
© 2014 John Wiley & Sons, Ltd. Published 2014 by John Wiley & Sons, Ltd.

clandestine rituals, such as the Jellicle Ball. These discoveries unfold through a series of 14 poems, leading to the ultimate aim, to call a cat "by his NAME" (171).[1]

Not surprisingly, their status as light verse written for children has marginalized the poems among Eliot's other work. Since their publication, most critics have tended either to ignore the poems or to dismiss them outright. Reviewer John Holmes asserted in 1939 that the collection "should have been prevented" (15), and most subsequent critics who have not disregarded the poems altogether have characterized them as instances of "the poet practicing his technique behind the mask of the comic versifier" (Moody 182). More recently, however, critics have noted a wider vein of humor in Eliot's writing, revealed in, for instance, "Effie the Waif" (1914), a mock film scenario (Trotter 248; McCabe 39–40), and in cruder verses written privately for friends throughout Eliot's career, such as his Bolo poems (see McIntire; Johnson). Contrary to the notion of the comic mask, Ronald Schuchard suggests, "In his bawdy, lighthearted moods, his more natural moods perhaps, [Eliot] would beg us, as 'Possum,' as Tom, not always to take him so seriously" (101).

For all its frivolity, *Practical Cats* returns to themes from Eliot's earlier poetry. Nursery rhymes and their eerie echoes of modern life can be found in *The Waste Land* ("London Bridge is falling down" [*CPP* 50]) and "The Hollow Men" ("*Here we go round the prickly pear*" [58]), and the cat as poetic metaphor emerges as early as "The Love Song of J. Alfred Prufrock" ("The yellow fog that rubs its back upon the window-panes" [4]). But the feline poems may owe more to Eliot's emerging drama of the thirties than to his poetry. Although what little critical attention Eliot's *Practical Cats* has received often rehearses what the poems are – jokes, regrettable folly, nonsense poetry, or serious revelation of talent – a more nuanced assessment might begin by noticing *when* they were written. Eliot began working in earnest on the collection in 1934, the same year he wrote his first full-length stage play, *The Rock: A Pageant Play*. While developing his cats poems between that year and their publication in 1939, Eliot completed two more plays, *Murder in the Cathedral* and *The Family Reunion*, both of which explore themes that appear in *Practical Cats*, particularly the importance of role-playing and the interplay between modern reality and illusion. Nearly all of Eliot's plays include metatheatrical references, which also appear throughout his feline verses. Eliot's collection of *Practical Cats* thus occupies a crucial place in the chronology of his oeuvre, connecting his early experiments with popular culture in poetry with his later attempts to integrate poetry into a popular theater. Considered as a link between his poetry and drama, the cats poems articulate a great deal about Eliot's changing sense of the audience in the thirties, his developing interest in the performing stage, and, ironically, the usefulness to be found in the apparent impracticalities of children's verse.

Old Possum's Book of Practical Cats began as a work exclusively for children. The idea for a collection of poems devoted to animals was set in motion with a birthday present to Thomas Earle Faber, the son of the publisher Geoffrey Faber and godson to Eliot. In a letter for Thomas's fourth birthday, in 1931, Eliot first wrote about his own "Lilliecat," named Jellylorum. In these initial playful lines, later reworked as

"The Old Gumbie Cat," Eliot describes his Jellylorum as a cat whose "one Idea is to be USEFUL!!" (*Cats* 7–8). His ironic wit is evident in the Lilliecat's performance as depicted in Eliot's accompanying drawings. While his text describes the practical work of the cat, his pictures visually contradict her supposed "usefulness." For example, the Lilliecat "straightens the pictures" by swinging from them; "does the grates" by scurrying over them; and "looks after" the larder and dustbin by eating out of them. (The drawings also reveal Eliot's self-mocking side, as when he caricatures his capacious ears by expanding one to accommodate a seat for the cat.)

Not long thereafter, Eliot further detailed the ironically practical cat in his *Five-Finger Exercises* of 1933, a series of charming poems devoted to friends and animals – among them, his "Lines to a Persian Cat." First mentioned in the touching "Lines to a Yorkshire Terrier," Jellicle cats would return in the Jellicle Ball of *Practical Cats,* following a similar pattern of robust rhythms, playful rhymes, and puns. Since the earlier Lilliecat portrait, Eliot's interest in animals has deepened, and they appear in these poems as reflections of human life and mortality, perhaps even representative of humans themselves. The narrator's voice, for instance, becomes intimately connected with the animals:

> Pollicle dogs and cats all must
> Jellicle cats and dogs all must
> Like undertakers, come to dust.
> Here a little dog I pause
> Heaving up my prior paws,
> Pause, and sleep endlessly. (*CPP* 91–2)

The early lines of the poem observe the ferocity of the environment ("Natural forces shriek'd aloud" [91]), but this descriptive voice yields by the end to that of the animal itself, in epitaph. Where exactly the human voice ceases and the animal's takes over, however, is difficult to pinpoint. Eliot's allusion to Robert Herrick's "Grace for a Child" ("Here a little child I stand / Heaving up my either hand" [336]) reinforces the implicit link between human and animal. In his self-deprecating poem "Lines for Cuscuscaraway and Mirza Murad Ali Beg," Eliot similarly weaves together his own attributes with those of his pets:

> How unpleasant to meet Mr. Eliot!
> With a bobtail cur
> In a coat of fur
> And a porpentine cat
> And a wopsical hat (*CPP* 93)

Where the unpleasant Mr. Eliot ends and his dog, his cat, and his fur coat begin, is again left deliberately unclear.

Following his initial mention of Jellicle cats and Pollicle dogs in 1933, Eliot began writing for a collection of children's verses in 1934. The animal verses were to have been published in time for Easter 1936 and titled "Mr. Eliot's Book of Pollicle Dogs and Jellicle Cats as Recited to Him by the Man in White Spats" (Gallup 363). This version never materialized, but its title suggests Eliot's growing interest in the popular audience. The poems were intended as entertainment, and they drew their influence from a number of sources in popular culture. According to biographer Burton Raffel, the "Man in White Spats" was Eliot's friend John Hayward, with whom the poet shared an almost fanatical devotion to Sir Arthur Conan Doyle's Sherlock Holmes stories (146). Although Eliot eventually revised both dogs and Hayward out of the title, rewriting the man in white spats as a cat, Bustopher Jones, the influence of Sherlock Holmes remained. "Macavity: The Mystery Cat" is based on Moriarty, Holmes's nemesis. Both Macavity and Moriarty are described as the "Napoleon of Crime" (*CPP* 164), and they share many physical attributes (Preston 398). In a letter to Frank Morley, Eliot confirmed, "I have done a new cat, modeled on the late Professor Moriarty but he doesn't seem very popular: too sophisticated perhaps" (*Cats* 8). Too much sophistication was not a problem for his other cats.

Eliot's animal verses in *Five-Finger Exercises* – a collection modeled on cat-lover Edward Lear – and his fondness for "inventing suitable cat names" suggest that his interest in nonsense poetry, noted by Elizabeth Sewell among other critics, was a particularly feline preoccupation (*Cats* 8). Like a cat with a mouse, Eliot enjoys a playful manipulation of language throughout *Practical Cats*, as in his description of cats' "ineffable effable / Effanineffable" names (*CPP* 149) and other invented words that contort the reader's tongue (e.g., "Firefrorefiddle, the Fiend of the Fell" [165]). His use of nonsense in *Practical Cats* differs radically from the disruptive, non-sequitur fragments of earlier verses such as *Sweeney Agonistes*, and instead constructs narrative upon the more soothing rhythms of "the child's fountain of voice" and the "verbal playground" of childhood rituals (Douglass 117). Eliot deploys heavy rhythmic stresses amid roughly variable metrical feet (often using triple or trochaic meters) to invoke both the feeling of a game with predictable rules and repetitive patterns, and the spontaneous creativity of children engaged in play. The rhymes are often surprising and sometimes rely on invented words ("She thinks that the cockroaches just need employment / To prevent them from idle and wanton destroyment" [*CPP* 151]). With their combination of thumping rhythms and madcap rhymes, the *Practical Cats* poems are intended not as moralizing directives to children, as some have claimed – see Hodge for an example of this argument – but rather as poems that revel in the pleasures of play, much like the Jellicle cats themselves, who "like to practice their airs and graces / And wait for the Jellicle Moon to rise" (155). One might even compare children and cats as two elements of civilized society granted the freedom to play, a liberty insufficiently afforded their adult human counterparts. The poems attempt, through verse technique, to envelop the reader, whether child or adult, in the experience of the cats. One simultaneously observes the cats and immerses oneself in their games.

Take, for example, the sensation of voices Eliot conveys by locating the reader in the midst of the excitement and play of Mr. Mistoffelees's magic show:

> Presto!
>   Away we go!
>   And we all say: OH!
>   Well I never!
>   Was there ever
>   A Cat so clever
>   As Magical Mr. Mistoffelees! (*CPP* 161)

Here Eliot lengthens the third line to create the impression of movement, only to lock the subsequent lines into a steady two-stress rhythm. The progressive shifting of the opening lines to the right echoes the thrilling takeoff of the magic act ("Away we go!"), while the clipped lines stacked on top of each other imply multiple simultaneous voices in a moment of shared experience and wonder. At the conclusion of these lines, the poem resumes its longer-lined pattern and accelerates into a dactylic meter, gathering momentum until the final exclamation mark. Eliot repeats this particular technique of metrical variation to convey shifts in the speaking voices within the diegesis of other poems – in "Mungojerrie and Rumpelteazer," in "Old Deuteronomy," in "Of the Awefull Battle of the Pekes and the Pollicles," and, in the final transition from the narrator's voice to that of the cat himself, in "Gus: The Theatre Cat":

> "But there's nothing to equal, from what I hear tell,
>   That moment of mystery
>   When I made history
> As Firefrorefiddle, the Fiend of the Fell." (165–66)

Recalling Charles Dickens's line "He do the police in different voices" – Eliot's working title for *The Waste Land* – these rhythmic devices effectively pull the reader into the experience of the poem, situating us as listeners among its sounds. Eliot do the cats in different voices.

Considering such playfulness in light of Eliot's earlier work, it is clear that his orientation to games changed with *Old Possum's Book of Practical Cats*. Games had previously appeared either as obstructions to human relationship or as foreboding riddles – think of *The Waste Land*'s "Game of Chess," the menacing role-playing on the cannibal isle in *Sweeney Agonistes*, or the ominous conspiratorial gamesmanship of "Sweeney Among the Nightingales." Inclusion in such games is threatening to the audience, as when Sweeney's role-playing spills over into the direct address of the concluding chorus: "you know the hangman's waiting for you" (*CPP* 85). Although the poems in *Practical Cats* occasionally echo the percussive rhythm of *Sweeney Agonistes*, their tone is invariably more cheerful: the verse treads lightly even in the seediest depictions. Growltiger's execution, for example, is surprisingly jocular: "He who a hundred victims had driven to that drop, / At the end of all his crimes was forced to go ker-flip, ker-flop" (153). Such an end seems not a death, but a game – playing possum perhaps. Play of this kind is inclusive, even reflective of its human audience, as when Eliot concludes "That Cats are much like you and me / And other people whom we find / Possessed of various types of mind." Humans learn about the cats through their "work and games" (169), and thus about themselves.

It is easy to attribute the difference in tone and pattern to Eliot's intended child audience and to the private origin of the poems, both of which allowed Eliot to work free from his weighty "Mr. Eliot" persona. Eliot was very much aware of his audience, and the deeper meanings in the poems are not meant to distract readers from their fun. He excluded one poem, "Grizabella: The Glamour Cat," because he thought it too sad for children, and he defended his cats to a disgruntled reader on the basis of their "charm": "And even my toughest characters, who gloat in doing harm, / Are not entirely destitute (admit it, please) of Charm" (qtd. in Campbell and Reesman 30) – a quality that defines the cats in a performative, even seductive relationship to the audience. Eliot plays to this audience himself. The change from the original title of poems "recited" to "Mr. Eliot" into a book created by "Old Possum" suggests a transition in poetic persona, not only from the staid, public veneer of Mr. Eliot to his goofier alter ego, but also from his role as the recipient of the poems to their creator. As either Mr. Eliot or Old Possum, Eliot contextualizes his poems as role-playing games, but with his final title he recasts himself in the roles of observer and participant in the animal world.

Eliot could thus take liberties in these poems that he rarely allowed himself in other works. At the same time, though, he may have had yet another reason for playing possum with his audience. By the mid-thirties, Eliot was deeply interested in role-playing and personae, not only in the context of poetry, but as essential elements of poetic drama. "Possibly the majority of attempts to confect a poetic drama," Eliot wrote, "have begun at the wrong end; they have aimed at the small public which wants 'poetry.'" A better approach, he argued, would be "to take a form of entertainment, and subject it to the process which would leave it a form of art" (SW 70). The populist variety theater of the English music hall, to Eliot's mind, provided the most promising model for a contemporary drama in verse.

Looking at the *Practical Cats*, one plainly sees the influence of the popular stage, and one finds in Eliot's poems the series of "turns" that structured music-hall comedy. "The Song of the Jellicles," for instance, is as much about dance as it is about song, incorporating a range of styles – "They know how to dance a gavotte and a jig" – and even rehearsal: "They like to practice their airs and graces" (CPP 155). Mungojerrie and Rumpleteazer are described as performers right off of the vaudeville stage, as "knockabout clowns, quick-change comedians, tight-rope walkers and acrobats" (156); Mr. Mistoffelees performs magic for adoring crowds; and Gus the Theatre Cat, an aging Victorian-era actor, boasts of his accomplishments: "I'd extemporize back-chat, I knew how to gag, / And I knew how to let the cat out of the bag" (165). With such cues inclining one's eye toward the popular stage, one can readily imagine the remaining poems in action, even when the cats are not explicitly playing the roles of performers. Thus Jennyanydots plays the matron, Growltiger the pirate anti-hero, and

Bustopher Jones the "Cat about Town" – all performances of human "types," even if not performances of performer-types.

Written as he began sustained work in drama, *Old Possum's Book of Practical Cats* follows Eliot's own dictates for dramatic writing, and it is his writing about the theater that reveals most about his poetic cats. In his essay "John Marston" (1934), for example, Eliot argues:

> It is possible that what distinguishes poetic drama from prosaic drama is a kind of doubleness in the action, as if it took place on two planes at once. . . . In poetic drama a certain apparent irrelevance may be the symptom of this doubleness; or the drama has an under-pattern, less manifest than the theatrical one. (*EED* 173)

The "apparent irrelevance" that Eliot anticipates in poetic drama might also characterize childish verses on cats. In light of these parallels to Eliot's thoughts on drama, the cats appear as personifications of theatrical doubleness – or tripleness. In 1933, Eliot described the reception of drama in ways that appear to reflect his characterization of cats:

> In a play of Shakespeare you get several levels of significance. For the simplest auditors there is the plot, for the more thoughtful the character and conflict of character, for the more literary the words and phrasing, for the more musically sensitive the rhythm, and for auditors of greater sensitiveness and understanding a meaning which reveals itself gradually. (*UPUC* 146)

Compare this scheme with Eliot's insistence in *Practical* Cats that a cat must have "three different names." The names that the family uses daily, like the plot, are designed for their usefulness; they are, as Eliot says, "[a]ll of them sensible everyday names" (*CPP* 149). These are followed by a list of more "particular" and stylish names, including that of his own cat, Jellylorum, and new names "[s]uch as Munkustrap, Quaxo, or Coricopat." These "more dignified" names echo the superficial cleverness of language, music, and character in the theater, but like the more common, useful names, they do not reveal the deepest meaning of the cat. At that most intimate level is the name that "THE CAT HIMSELF KNOWS, and will never confess" (149).

In *Practical Cats,* as in Eliot's plays, it is possible to see the deeper meaning as spiritual revelation. A Christian trinity appears in the cats' three simultaneous names, and the term "Jellicle" suggests "angelical." The name of the eldest cat, "Old Deuteronomy," derives from the book of the Bible that highlights the teachings of Moses. An unpublished fragment outlined a conclusion in which the cats achieve spiritual salvation, ascending "Up up up past the Russell Hotel, up up up to the Heaviside Layer" (*Cats* 9). The common root of *anima* (soul) and *animal* may not have been far from Eliot's mind. In his earlier Ariel Poem, "Animula," the "small soul" is described in a distinctly catlike manner: "The pain of living and the drug of dreams / Curl up the small soul in the window seat / Behind the *Encyclopedia Britannica*" (*CPP* 71).

For Eliot, who consistently rejected the Arnoldian idea that poetry would or could take the place of religion, books are more likely a refuge from the "pain of living" than a direct route to redemption. For the feline soul of "Animula," certainly, the *Encyclopedia Britannica* provides nothing more than a cozy retreat. It seems ironic, then, that Trevor Nunn should have defined the "Heaviside Layer," Eliot's representation of cat heaven, as a literally bookish joke: "The Russell Hotel sits right behind one of our big bookstores. Supposedly, the heaviest books were shelved on the very top floor. There's the Heaviside Layer the cats are talking about!" (Lawson 1). This conception of salvation found in books and bookshelves is only one of the critical misinterpretations Eliot's poems suffered in the 1981 adaptation by composer Andrew Lloyd Webber and director Nunn. Whereas Eliot's work conveys the essential elusiveness of cats — we never really see or understand them properly — the musical version of *Cats* came to define material theatrical excess in the 1980s.

Despite its simplification of Eliot's vision and its overindulgence in spectacle, however, Webber's *Cats* was not without its appeal. Webber was not the first to attempt a musical adaptation of *Practical Cats*, but he was by far the most successful. Reworking Eliot's verses into a kind of cats revue, Webber wrote a musical almost devoid of plot, but full of action and memorable tunes. Much like Eliot's verses, Webber's songs create an atmosphere of playful exuberance in which the audience is invited to participate. Dancing, tumbling, and playing with the audience, the cats ultimately celebrate the redemption of a waif who is chosen to ascend with Old Deuteronomy to the Heaviside Layer. In place of plot, Webber and his production team created a theatrical environment in which the audience was surrounded by singing, dancing cats in startlingly realistic costumes and a set that dominated every inch of playing space available, building out into the audience itself. Much like the earlier musical *A Chorus Line* (1975), *Cats* was essentially a dance show, in which the thin plot functioned primarily to introduce the next dance number. If the treatment of the text occasionally seemed odd, such difficulties were covered with performances that broke down any illusion of the theatrical fourth wall. Dances infiltrated the audience. A few rows of seating were integrated into the set. The show began with cats creeping through the theater, crossing catwalks, and chanting "The Naming of Cats." Audience members, particularly on the aisles, were regularly touched, sung to, and otherwise involved in the action. (One even sued for physical harassment.) The entire set was designed on a giant scale, so that the performers and audience members alike were reduced in proportion and assumed the perspective of cats in a junkyard. In the Broadway version's spectacular conclusion, requiring a budget four times that of the original London production, a giant tire lifted off the stage in a hydraulic cloud of fog and dazzling yellow lights, raising the chosen cat, Grizabella, and Old Deuteronomy "up up up" past the proscenium arch to the unseen Heaviside Layer. Theater critics disparaged this finale as the takeoff of a feline spaceship; audiences loved it.

The critical disdain for his efforts notwithstanding, few were better suited than Webber to adapt Eliot's verses. Drawn to *Old Possum's* book as a child, Webber saw them not as the works of a great poet, but perhaps more as Eliot intended them: as immersive, sensual experiences of play in a theatrical universe. By 1980, Webber had achieved success as a composer by integrating high-cultural material into popular musical theater. Indeed, he would spend nearly his entire career weathering accusations of plagiarizing Puccini to the unknowing masses. But for all his high-cultural aspirations, Webber was very much attuned to a child's world of play. His own production group, The Really Useful Theatre Company, was named after the children's books about Thomas the Tank Engine ("a really useful engine"), and Webber would follow *Cats* with his own toy-train musical, *Starlight Express* (1984). Perhaps because of his orientation to the theater as a kind of child's play, Webber recognized in Eliot what many of the middlebrow critics did not: that *Old Possum's Book of Practical Cats* is essentially a playground for the imagination in which the audience can participate and thereby be drawn into community with one another. The musical *Cats*, for all its excesses, attempted to capture the key elements of Eliot's original text, including his coded spiritual references and the engagement of the audience as collaborators in the making of theatrical meaning.

Well-read and well-meaning, Webber attempted to combine the poetic playfulness of the *Practical Cats*, popular music, and Eliot's dramatic interest in spirituality into a sensual theatrical experience. Following Eliot's range of allusions, Webber's music is a deliberate generic pastiche, including an homage to Puccini in the climactic ballad "Memory" (adapted from Eliot's "Rhapsody on a Windy Night"), music-hall-inspired tunes in "Mungojerrie and Rumpleteazer," and popular 1980s disco in "The Rum Tum Tugger." Every cat, it seems, gets not only its own musical number, but also its own musical genre. Webber extends Eliot's references to spiritual redemption in *Practical Cats* by adopting salvation itself as the dramatic structure for *Cats*. Webber was most excited by the unpublished fragment of "up up up to the Heaviside Layer" that would suggest "a coherent, albeit incomplete, structure for the evening" (*Cats* 9). To reinforce the spiritual themes for the angelical Jellicle cats and the redemption of Grizabella, Webber writes both the opening number and the final ascension to the Heaviside Layer as liturgical hymns. In four-part harmony with organ accompaniment, to a fitting crescendo, the cats intone: "The mystical divinity of unashamed felinity / Round the cathedral rang "Vivat" / Life to the everlasting cat!" (Webber). The life span – birth (naming), life, and redemption – of the cats gives the entire show its structure, both thematically and musically.

In an interview in 1986, Webber notes the cyclical structure of *Cats*: "Nobody, I hope, notices that the beginning of *Cats* is a fugue and that the middle of the Jellicle Ball is a fugue and that the resolution comes in a later theme. But for me it's the crucial thing on which the score depends, just as the whole of *Evita* is based on a tri-tone and goes round in a complete circle" (qtd. in Snelson 31–32). The circularity echoes the Christian concept of everlasting life, and it is no coincidence that Webber draws on the fugue, a Baroque compositional form often used to express the profound. That Webber uses this musical texture but wishes it to remain unnoticed reminds one of Eliot's desire for a drama that creates an invisible poetic "under-pattern, less manifest than the theatrical one" (*EED* 173). Like Eliot's ideal drama, Webber's adaptation engages a musical under-pattern to reinforce the meanings of the primary material, although his musical and theatrical references to spiritual salvation seem hardly "less manifest" than anything. Indeed, Webber intensifies both the spiritual and the theatrical themes, so that the audience is completely immersed in an overwhelmingly sensual – but not contemplative – experience. "There's a reason why 'Cats'" will play for a long time, wrote New York reviewer Frank Rich for the Broadway opening in 1982: "it's a musical that transports the audience into a complete fantasy world that could only exist in the theater and yet, these days, only rarely does" (3). Rich was correct. *Cats* went on to break the record for the longest-running musical on Broadway, closing after 18 years and 7,485 performances.

Despite the creative virtues of Webber's adaptation, *Practical Cats* ultimately achieves more than his musical. While Eliot might have appreciated *Cats'* playfulness and audience engagement, and probably would have enjoyed its commercial success (as well as the posthumous Tony award for his lyrics), the over-the-top designs and sensory overload in the theater were not what he had in mind for either his children's poems or his verse plays. As Eliot argued in "Poetry and Drama" (1950), verse drama should avoid "losing that contact with the ordinary everyday world with which drama must come to terms" (*OPP* 87). It was this everyday world that would unite the audience in its common existence. "It was the work of Shakespeare, more than any other writer," Eliot wrote, "to appeal to every audience, and so to keep them cohering" (qtd. in Moody 342). Significantly, Eliot chose to conclude his poems not with the mystical revelation of the Heaviside Layer, but with the more humble recognition that a human must earn the respect of a cat. Eliot leaves his audience not in thrall, but informed: "And there's how you AD-DRESS A CAT" (*CPP* 171). Webber, however, overpowers his audience by transforming them *into* cats who are ultimately left behind in a mass of fog machines, lights, and fugue. As Webber intended it, *Cats* "is an *experience*" – one that seeks to exceed all other forms of entertainment: "It's no good putting on something nowadays which people can see just as well on their video" (qtd. in Sternfeld 174). Whereas Eliot's cats humble the human to commonality, Webber reduces his audience to insignificance.

To return to Heidegger, it appears that Eliot writes his poetry with an eye toward the communal, ritual theater, but that Webber has created merely a game that looks like poetry but is not. Whereas Eliot aspired to a poetic theater that, by "imposing a credible order upon ordinary reality," would bring its audience "to a condition of serenity, stillness, and reconciliation" (*SP* 146), Webber's megamusical aspires to grandiose visual display. His adaptation of so-called "high art," including opera and poetry, into a popular theater instead creates the kind of overwhelming spectacle that Eliot once feared from the cinema. Far from a collaborative participant in the music hall, the spectator of Webber's *Cats* becomes immersed and overwhelmed in the fantasy of an all-out theatrical assault. The spectator gets lost among the spectacle. For Eliot, this loss of a common humanity, ironically to be found in the feline world, would be a significant loss indeed.

NOTE

1 An additional poem, "Cat Morgan Introduces
   Himself," was appended to the 1982
   reprinting.

REFERENCES AND FURTHER READING

Campbell, Jeanne, and John Reesman. "Creatures
of 'Charm': A New T. S. Eliot poem." *Kenyon
Review* 6 (1984): 25–33.

Cats: The Book of the Musical. New York: Harcourt,
1983.

Chinitz, David. *T. S. Eliot and the Cultural Divide.*
Chicago: U of Chicago P, 2003.

Douglass, Paul. "Eliot's Cats: Serious Play Behind
the Playful Seriousness." *Children's Literature* 11
(1983): 109–24.

Gallup, Donald. *T. S. Eliot: A Bibliography.*
London: Faber, 1969.

Heidegger, Martin. "Hölderlin and the Essence of
Poetry." *Existence and Being.* 1936. Ed. W.
Brock. Trans. D. Scott. Chicago: Regnery,
1949. 291–315.

Herrick, Robert. "Grace for a Child." *The Viking
Book of Poetry of the English-Speaking World.* Ed.
Richard Aldington. Rev. ed. Vol. 1. New York:
Viking, 1958.

Hodge, Marion C. "The Sane, the Mad, the Good,
the Bad: T. S. Eliot's *Old Possum's Book of Practical Cats.*" *Children's Literature* 7 (1978):
129–46.

Holmes, John. "Eliot on Roistering Cats." *Boston
Evening Transcript* 15 Nov. 1939: 15.

Johnson, Loretta. "T. S. Eliot's Bawdy Verse: Lulu,
Bolo and More Ties." *Journal of Modern Literature*
27 (2003): 14–25.

Lawson, Steve. "Trevor Nunn Reshapes 'Cats'
for Broadway." *New York Times* 3 Oct. 1982, sec.
2: 1.

McCabe, Susan. *Cinematic Modernism: Modernist
Poetry and Film.* Cambridge: Cambridge UP,
2005.

McIntire, Gabrielle. "An Unexpected Beginning:
Sex, Race, and History in Eliot's Columbo and
Bolo Poems." *Modernism/Modernity* 9 (2002):
283–301.

Moody, A. D. *Thomas Stearns Eliot: Poet.* London:
Cambridge UP, 1979.

Preston, Priscilla. "A Note on T. S. Eliot and
Sherlock Holmes." *Modern Language Review* 54
(1959): 397–99.

Raffel, Burton. *T. S. Eliot.* New York: Ungar,
1972.

Rich, Frank. "Theatre: Lloyd Webber's 'Cats.'"
New York Times 8 Oct. 1982: 3.

Schuchard, Ronald. *Eliot's Dark Angel: Intersections
of Life and Art.* New York: Oxford UP, 1999.

Sewell, Elizabeth. "Lewis Carroll and T. S. Eliot as
Nonsense Poets." *T. S. Eliot: A Collection of Criti-
cal Essays.* Ed. Hugh Kenner. Englewood Cliffs,
NJ: Prentice Hall, 1962. 65–72.

Snelson, John. *Andrew Lloyd Webber.* New Haven:
Yale UP, 2004.

Sternfeld, Jessica. *The Megamusical.* Bloomington:
Indiana UP, 2006.

Trotter, David. "T. S. Eliot and Cinema." *Modern-
ism/Modernity* 13 (2006): 237–65.

Webber, Andrew Lloyd. "The Journey to the
Heaviside Layer." *Cats.* Cond. René Wiegert.
Geffen, 1981.

20
Eliot's 1930s Plays: *The Rock,*
Murder in the Cathedral, and *The*
Family Reunion

Randy Malamud

Eliot's three plays from the 1930s are strikingly distinct. *The Rock* (1934), a large pageant play, is a loose, rambling work. Despite what sometimes seems a casual indifference – very unlike Eliot's earlier, intensely worked poetry – it offers some lively choral passages with a compelling new voice. *Murder in the Cathedral* (1935), the most durable of these works, is still performed regularly, often by amateur church-affiliated actors, and often in cathedrals. *The Family Reunion* (1939) introduces the last stage of Eliot's dramatic career, embracing the conventional realism of drawing-room drama, with a subtle strain of spiritual exploration and a newfound interest in family and social life.

Eliot's final productions (*The Cocktail Party, The Confidential Clerk,* and *The Elder Statesman,* discussed in the following chapter), smoothly constructed plays evoking the suave patter of Noel Coward, were written after Eliot had completed – or perhaps forsaken? – his career as a poet. The plays discussed in this chapter were conceived and composed while Eliot was still very much engaged in his poetic enterprise. The later plays have a more stable sense of dramatic tone and texture; these earlier works invite our attention precisely because their dramatic focus is less sure and confident. Eliot's plays of the 1930s hover uneasily, interestingly, between pure poetry and drama.

Is Eliot's drama a significant facet of his career, or just a sidebar? During the 1930s his literary identity is transitional. He is clearly attuned to crafting the final phase of his poetry, and many aspects of his plays resonate with the poems he was working on at the time. Throughout his career, Eliot demonstrated a strong and constant interest in the theater: he wrote copiously on dramatic topics, and one sees in many of these essays the temperament of a playwright, not just a literary critic.[1] Eliot extolled the centrality of drama in the English literary tradition and wrote of his quest to find "the most useful poetry, socially," concluding that "The ideal medium for poetry, to my mind, and the most direct means of social 'usefulness' for poetry, is the theatre" (*UPUC* 152–53).

A Companion to T. S. Eliot, First Edition. Edited by David E. Chinitz.
© 2014 John Wiley & Sons, Ltd. Published 2014 by John Wiley & Sons, Ltd.

What do these three plays have in common, if not their general form or style? Mainly, two things: an attempt at "poetic drama," and a Christian consciousness. As a sub-topic of the first, each features a Chorus, representing an important link to classical dramatic traditions. As a sub-topic of the second, these plays explore the dynamics and the value of community, in contrast to the solipsistic demeanor of Eliot's pre-conversion poetry, but very much in the spirit of his World War II-era valediction to poetry. In *Four Quartets*, the wartime devastation is an impetus toward community: amid such chaos, Eliot embraces poesis as a tool that can reinforce one's sense of community. In the darkening 1930s, Eliot's dramatic experiments represented another way of affirming community. Theater, of course, is inherently predicated upon community in terms of the nature of production and performance and the centrality of the audience. These plays elucidate the transformation from Eliot's early sensibility of isolation, muted despair, and cultural incoherence to a poetic of fortitude, pragmatic acceptance of chaotic external reality, and a determination to confront this chaos. They are an explicit declaration of Eliot's faith and of his commitment to Christian discourse, but more subtly they illuminate his quest to present a message worthy of (and inspirational to) a real, immediate audience.

Eliot's impulse towards sociability surfaces in his plays of the thirties as an awareness of the importance of ties among people, whether in a community, a church, or a family, anticipating the embrace of community spirit that will resonate in *Four Quartets*. There emerges here for the first time an awareness of the value and durability of social existence; hence, the pragmatic urging in *The Rock* to build churches. In 1922, Eliot described the specter of fallen towers, empty chapels, a decrepit urban infrastructure, and vanished (impotent, "unreal") imperial capitals. His initiative in the thirties follows from the lament in *The Waste Land*: instead of complaining about the fragments, Eliot now tries to inspire his audience to rebuild.

The Rock

With over 300 actors (mostly amateurs from local parishes), 22 scene changes, a choir, and an orchestra, *The Rock* was an ambitious undertaking. The enormity of the production and the challenge of developing the pageant from a scenario created by others contributed to Eliot's misgivings, and to his sense that he had gotten in over his head with a project that would have been difficult for anyone to control. Staged as a benefit for a London church-building fund, *The Rock* is, appropriately enough, about building churches. It opens as a Chorus laments the prominence of secular over spiritual concerns, with the consequence that the modern church has become generally unimportant. The Rock appears, extolling the eternal Christian condition and inspiring some workmen to exult in the glory of building new churches, though others, the unemployed, remain in despair. Three Cockney workmen who reappear throughout the pageant argue for the social and spiritual significance of the church they are constructing.

A series of tableaux and interpolations feature characters such as Saxons (describing the introduction of Christianity to England), ancient Israelites (rebuilding their temple against the threats of enemies), a Marxist agitator (ranting about an impending revolution when churches will become clubs and museums), and a Plutocrat (paying lip service to the church's glory but pandering to a mob that finds religion inconvenient). There are also medieval crusaders, Reformation-era preachers, nineteenth-century church builders, stone-carvers and other religious craftsmen, all of whom declaim the importance of sustaining England's religious tradition by erecting churches. At the end, after a tribute to Christopher Wren's magnificent St. Paul's Cathedral, the play presents an image of the completed church as a light on the hill amid a world of confusion and darkness, while The Rock reminds the audience that the church is only a reflection of God's greater glory.

At London's Sadler's Wells Theatre, audiences for the 1934 run of *The Rock* numbered as many as 1,500 per evening. Contemporary reviews were tepid: Michael Sayers wrote that the play "'stays on the ground'; it walks, with irregular steps, in a circle. It does not stir us by a bold advance" (231). Another reviewer objected, "The scanty action and copious talk are expressed partly in not very successful *vers libre* and partly in a cockney dialect with the omitted aspirates so laboriously indicated as to make the long speeches of the bricklayers exceedingly tiresome to read. Unhappily, there is little freshness and beauty of thought to mollify the exacerbating diction" (*Tablet*). Many perceived it as Christian propaganda – which is, indeed, exactly what it was.

The play certainly did not portend a successful future in the theater for Eliot. It was, David Ward writes, formally confusing, "an uneasy association of modes in which a crude expressionism alternates with rather flaccid experiments in the choric mode" (180). In Part II of *The Waste Land* (ll. 139–72), Eliot seemed to show a good ear for the rhythms and intonations of British working-class speech, but the more developed presentation of that voice fails in *The Rock*. A brief quotation (replete with "omitted aspirates") will suffice to illustrate the problem:

ETHELBERT. 'Ere, wot's this?
ALFRED. Blimey, Bert, you seem to 'ave 'it the nail on the 'ead this time! (16)

Discussing *The Rock* in "The Three Voices of Poetry," Eliot himself seems to apologize for the play, which fails to attain what he calls "the third voice," the apotheosis of dramatic address to the audience. He notes that the invitation to write this play "came at a moment when I seemed to myself to have exhausted my meager poetic gifts, and to have nothing more to say" (*OPP* 98). Although the opportunity to return to creative writing was revitalizing for Eliot, his creative exhaustion nevertheless shows through in the play.

If the play as a whole is often rough, its Choruses are much more fluent. Eliot recognized this by preserving the Choruses in his *Collected Poems*, while allowing the rest of the text to drift out of print. It makes sense that, given Eliot's poetic métier, the Choruses should be strong, and they are important as both poetry and drama. In a work that is fairly uneven, the Choruses provide the strongest sense of unity. Where the Cockneys' chatter is incontinently scattered, the Chorus speaks in precise, controlled measure. E. Martin Browne, who directed the 1934 production, writes that the Choruses combine "prophetic thunder with colloquial speech; and they use the orchestra of varied voices, male and female, to create continual dramatic contrast" (20). Eliot wrote many essays about the tradition of poetic drama, and all his subsequent plays were written almost completely in verse, though in a subtler mode than in the Choruses from *The Rock*. *Murder in the Cathedral*, *The Family Reunion*, and *The Cocktail Party* all feature their own versions of Choruses, formally prominent in the first of these, more subtly integrated with the verse drama in the second, and nearly vestigial in the last.

The origins of drama are, of course, poetic, and Eliot believed, as he wrote in "A Dialogue on Dramatic Poetry," that all drama tended toward poetry, and vice versa. The dramatists Eliot acclaimed as the greatest in the tradition, the Greeks and Elizabethans, wrote in a discourse that was heavily inflected by the form and style of poetry. In the plays of Eliot's more recent predecessors – Ibsen, Chekhov, and Shaw, for instance – a prosaic conversational tenor heightens the sense of realism; but Eliot was in sync with other contemporary poets who also wrote drama – Yeats and Auden are the most prominent – in carrying the tropes and forms of poetry with him as he moved to the stage. In "The Need for Poetic Drama," Eliot wrote that good poetic drama was not merely a play translated into verse but rather a play wholly conceived and composed in terms of poetry.

Eliot believed powerfully in the aesthetic and social importance of the Chorus. In an earlier and more antisocial phase of his life, he wrote that "Our dried voices, when / We whisper together / Are quiet and meaningless" (*CPP* 56). But the symphonic force of voices intoning in unison struck Eliot, in his more socially tolerant dramatic career, as an assertion of coherence. The lament of *The Waste Land* was that people could not speak together, or to each other: its terrain was a modern-day Babel, where characters chattered neurotically and at cross-purposes in different tongues and frail fragmentary shards of meaning. A choral poet *forces* the actors to speak together, and this discipline, Eliot felt, generated a communal appreciation of a common language.

In *The Rock*, the language of the Choruses is at the same time immediately contemporary and vatic. Some passages have the kind of hypnotically constructed cadences that anticipate the verbal choreography of *Four Quartets*, such as this one that begins the excerpted Choruses:

> The Eagle soars in the summit of Heaven,
> The Hunter with his dogs pursues his circuit.
> O perpetual revolution of configured stars,
> O perpetual recurrence of determined seasons,
> O world of spring and autumn, birth and dying!
> The endless cycle of idea and action,

> Endless invention, endless experiment,
> Brings knowledge of motion, but not of stillness;
> Knowledge of speech, but not of silence;
> Knowledge of words, and ignorance of the Word.
> All our knowledge brings us nearer to our ignorance,
> All our ignorance brings us nearer to death,
> But nearness to death no nearer to GOD.
> Where is the Life we have lost in living?
> Where is the wisdom we have lost in knowledge?
> Where is the knowledge we have lost in information? (*CPP* 96)

The theme of seasonality, intertwined with the philosophically situated consideration of language, knowledge, and being, echoes conspicuously in the *Quartets*. The style, too – foregrounding symbolic natural tropes, weighty yet elusive abstractions, paradoxical oppositions of motion and stillness, speech and silence – looks toward the poetic finale Eliot would complete over the coming decade.

Besides verse drama and choral drama, another important influence on *The Rock* was music-hall comedy. The various tableaux are filled with satire, slapstick, ditties, and burlesque; the Cockney ringleaders, resplendent caricatures who frame the historical scenes, are especially prone to exuberant (if cartoonish) verbal jousting. The whole undertaking is meant to be entertaining as well as didactic – in fact, all the more effectively didactic for its light comic surface. In a letter to Ezra Pound published in 1938 as "Five Points on Dramatic Writing," Eliot writes: "If you can keep the bloody audience's attention engaged, then you can perform any monkey tricks you like when they ain't looking" (10). The point of the pageant, fundraising for churches, was perhaps a "monkey trick" that Eliot felt was effectively cloaked in the razzle-dazzle of a carnivalesque spectacle. And as Browne explains, the work is directly indebted to the genre of the open-air pageant, a common contemporary undertaking, which celebrates the history of a place or institution by showing a chronological series of scenes, each introduced by a processional entry, and performed by a multitude of amateurs. The total effect is a display of panoply, a more relaxed and less disciplined version of a great parade (4).

Murder in the Cathedral

Many of the theatrical professionals who worked on *The Rock* joined Eliot again the next year for the production of *Murder in the Cathedral*, the story of Thomas Becket's spiritual apotheosis and martyrdom. The play's debut was presented in Canterbury Cathedral's chapter house, only 50 yards from where St. Thomas was actually killed in 1170 by four knights who perhaps misinterpreted (or, perhaps, did not) King Henry II's exasperation at the man who had been a dependable Chancellor, but began to assert the Church's independent authority after he became Archbishop of Canterbury. King Henry had hoped that Thomas would be his puppet and allow him to maintain control over religious affairs, but when Thomas rejected royal control of the Church, King Henry is reputed to have said something like, "Who will rid me of this meddlesome priest?" (words that do not appear in the play), which the knights took as justification for assassination.

Commissioned for the 1935 Canterbury Festival of Music and Drama, the play was originally performed with a sparse set (the only stage property was a simple throne) and designed to maximize the intimacy of the ecclesiastical setting: after the murder, Becket's body was carried out in a procession through the audience. The play had a long run in London's West End from 1935 to 1937, and enjoyed New York runs in 1936, produced by the Federal Theatre Project of the Works Progress Administration, and in 1938, on Broadway. One of the 1936 London performances was televised live in an early BBC production, and BBC radio also broadcast the play. *Murder in the Cathedral* was especially popular in England during World War II, where it was performed in such makeshift venues as cathedrals, schools, and even an air-raid shelter. One reviewer noted how the contemporary political climate colored the play: "the four knightly murderers of Becket would be recognized as figures of the day, four perfect Nazis defending their act on the most orthodox totalitarian grounds" (Dukes 114–15). Eliot himself said he wrote the play as anti-Nazi propaganda (Hayter 94).

Without forcing too heavy an autobiographical interpretation, it seems significant that the hero of this play, like its author, is a man named Thomas who has matured over the years from worldliness to a higher spiritual plane. At the opening, the Chorus worries about the Archbishop's return to the Cathedral after seven years in exile, and if we go back seven years from 1935, we are around the time of Eliot's conversion to Anglo-Catholicism (performed in 1927, and announced in 1928 in *For Lancelot Andrewes* [vii]). In the moment when the play is set, Thomas returns for what he suspects will be his martyrdom, and perhaps there is something – a forsaking of the worldly realm, an embrace of a more ethereal sense of faith – that Eliot, too, wants to stage, and to celebrate, as he comes to Canterbury Cathedral with this play. Peter Ackroyd writes that the play's hero "is not unconnected with the author himself, who has some special awareness of which others are deprived and yet whose great strengths are allied with serious weaknesses" (227), and Lyndall Gordon, too, sees autobiographical overtones in the character of Becket, whom Eliot found "not so different from himself. Here was a man to all appearances not born for sainthood, a man of the world . . . who moved from worldly success into spiritual danger" (28).

By any measure, *Murder in the Cathedral* is a much better structured and developed play than *The Rock*. Its two parts are balanced. In Part I, Thomas speaks in the language of Christian paradox about how the suffering and stasis of the masses, personified by the anxious Chorus, can be a pattern of action. Facing down the temptations that confront him, Thomas stands fast and places himself in God's hands. Between the two parts is the Archbishop's Christmas Day sermon about the connection between birth and death, which sets the stage for the impending martyrdom. In Part II, the Knights demand that Thomas leave England because he has undermined the King. When he refuses and retreats to the Cathedral, they follow him and kill him, then compound their ignominy with a series of almost comically tedious justifications. The Second Knight, for example, says:

> We are four plain Englishmen who put our country first. I dare say that we didn't make a very good impression when we came in. The fact is that we knew we had taken on a pretty stiff job; I'll only speak for myself, but I had drunk a good deal – I am not a drinking man ordinarily – to brace myself up for it. When you come to the point, it does go against the grain to kill an Archbishop, especially when you have been brought up in good Church traditions. (*CPP* 215)

(The Knights, pointedly, do not speak in the verse that constitutes the rest of the play.) After the Knights leave, while the Priests lament the desecration that has just occurred, they appreciate that the Church is strengthened by surviving this persecution, and the Chorus, too, comes to accept and understand the pattern of action that the play unfolds.

The characters are succinctly and effectively drawn, and, again, balanced: three priests, four tempters, four knights, and rising up above them, the hero. In *The Rock*, the Choruses provided coherence in an otherwise ramshackle dramatic enterprise; here, though the play is much better poised, still, a Chorus of Canterbury Women provides a forceful dramatic presence, balancing the thoughts and fears of the crowd against the force of personality, and the tragedy, of the saint; and they also balance the play's men – priests, tempters, knights, and saint – against the community of women. The play opens and closes with choral passages, indicating that the fundamental frame for this story of the saint is the society, the community, that witnesses and remembers what happens to the heroic figure. The Chorus "suggests the collectivity, the generality of mankind," writes Pieter Williams. "The stasis of the Chorus, compared with the movement, sometimes violent, of other characters and groups of characters, helps to isolate them visually in the kaleidoscope of power politics, and reinforces . . . the permanence of common humanity" (499–500).

As in the Choruses from *The Rock*, and even more prominently, the text of *Murder in the Cathedral* anticipates the tenor of the poetry that would comprise *Four Quartets*. There is much attention here to the poetics of time, and copious references to temporal markers: "Since golden October declined into somber November"; "The New Year waits"; "Seven years and the summer is over"; "Winter shall come bringing death from the sea"; "Why should the summer bring consolation / For autumn fires and winter fogs?" (*CPP* 175–76). The keen focus on months, years, and seasons pre-echoes the paradox of time that Eliot revisits in *Four Quartets*, the sense of human experience that time is very brief and immediate, and also eternal. Eliot's earlier philosophical study of F. H. Bradley reinforced the significance of temporal immediacy, while the Christianity he embraced emphasized the sense of eternity; both these notions of time are present, competing throughout his poetry and plays. In *Murder in the Cathedral*, the immediate moment resonates with uncertainty and potential danger, human folly and heroics; the longer-term scope of time embodies the sort of faith and strength

that a community derives when it has a historically coherent sense of how its traditions have endured and its moral values have remained vital as the months and seasons
have come and gone.

The rhythms of Ecclesiastes infuse this play, as they do *Four Quartets*. "The plough-
man shall go out in March and turn the same earth / He has turned before, the bird
shall sing the same song" (*CPP* 202). There are here again, as there were in the
Choruses from *The Rock* and as there would be throughout *Four Quartets*, the resonant
repetitions and Mobius-strip hypnotic twirls of language; the tropes that evoke
the ritual intonations of prayer (again, via repetition); the frequent scent of the
Audenesque, in its understated anticlimax.

The opening lines to "Burnt Norton," about time present, time past, and time
future, were originally written for *Murder in the Cathedral*; cut from the play, they
ended up in the poem. (Another line from the play, "Human kind cannot bear very
much reality," appears verbatim in the poem [*CPP* 118, 209].) The moments that
proliferate throughout *Four Quartets* – the moment of the rose, the moment in the
arbor, the hidden laughter of children in the foliage: instances where a paradoxically
intense consciousness, "the still point of the turning world," often manifests itself –
are prefigured in the same kinds of moments from *Murder in the Cathedral*: "When
the leaf is out on the tree, when the elder and may / Burst over the stream, and the
air is clear and high, / And voices trill at windows, and children tumble in front of
the door" (202). These little pieces of soothing, untroubled time are not obviously
profound, but in their pedestrian pace are all the more powerful for their quiet potential to facilitate a transcendence of the external world's busy chaos.

The opening of *Murder in the Cathedral* demonstrates a practical formulation of
Eliot's more philosophical exploration of the interrelation of past, present, and future:
time past, for the Chorus, is the seven years of the Archbishop's absence; time present
is the moment in which he returns and fulfills the anticipated martyrdom. Though
their lives had been orderly during Thomas's absence, they had been spiritually unremarkable; their task is to understand and transcend this little and empty piece of time
past, in their time present, to prepare for a meaningful time future. The play, like
Four Quartets, represents a meeting-ground between time and timelessness, which are
allegorically juxtaposed. Eliot presents a community that foundered in time past but
positions itself to fare better in time future: as he suggests in "Burnt Norton," the
promise of a favorable time future usurps and redeems time past in its renewal, acceptance, and understanding. And of course, time future for the Canterbury women is
time past for Eliot himself, and his twentieth-century audience, who bring their own
temporal consciousness alongside that of the twelfth-century Cantuarians. Eliot wrote
that he meant to present a vocabulary and structure for the play that were not quite
current but would not suggest to the audience any particular period style, so that his
language could be untethered, floating between the play's historical setting and the
audience's present. He imbued this play with the temporal transcendence he admired
in medieval drama, which "cared little about anachronisms and a great deal about the
permanent elements of humanity" ("Religious Drama" 9).

Finally, in Thomas's martyrdom, Eliot does not excessively idealize his hero: the play ends with a somewhat tepid strain of hagiography. Thomas has made some good and hard decisions, and certainly the audience knows that in the reaches of history he will garner profound regard, but for the moment it is pointedly the Chorus, the women of Canterbury, who have the last word, and these words are hesitant, deflationary. "Even with the hand to the broom, the back bent in laying the fire, the knee bent in cleaning the hearth," intone the women of Canterbury as they praise God in an exhortation that is overwhelmed with the qualifications and concerns of their daily struggle, "we, the scrubbers and sweepers of Canterbury, / The back bent under toil, the knee bent under sin, the hands to the face under fear, the head bent in grief / . . . praise Thee" (*CPP* 220–21). They acknowledge that they fear loneliness, surrender, deprivation, and the injustice of men less than the justice of God, and fear "the hand at the window, the fire in the thatch, the fist in the tavern, the push into the canal, / Less than we fear the love of God" (221). The etymological root of "martyr" is "witness," and these witnesses to the martyrdom seem underwhelmingly motivated to forget the many insults of time present in exchange for the benison of time future that, one would think, Thomas's devotion might have inspired in them. Instead, the play resonates with a pragmatic and tempered realism that reflects Eliot's modernist sensibility. The Chorus, and by implication the audience, have had a momentary experience of awareness and community in their witnessing of Thomas's martyrdom, but it is by no means profoundly cathartic, and it does not negate the oppressively mundane realities that still afflict their lives. In the schema of Eliot's overall poetic, we might regard the play's ending as *relatively* transcendent, or even salvational, to the extent that it is "better" than many of the other endings Eliot has formulated previously: "Till human voices wake us, and we drown"; "The last twist of the knife"; "Thoughts of a dry brain in a dry season"; "*Not with a bang but a whimper*" (*CPP* 7, 16, 23, 59). The experience of this community is a small victory, not as promising as one might have wished for, but certainly an improvement over all the barren and empty failures that resounded through Eliot's writing of the 1910s and 1920s. In an understated way (but perhaps more graspable because less resplendent), Eliot is moving toward the kind of affirmation he will make in "The Dry Salvages": of the rote of "prayer, observance, discipline, thought and action" (136), specifically "*right action*" (emphasis added), and the determination simply to go on trying: "Not fare well, / But fare forward, voyagers" (135).

The Family Reunion

If Thomas Becket was somehow a best-case inscription of T. S. Eliot's self-consciousness in the 1930s, the central figure of Harry from *The Family Reunion* is at the other extreme. Set in the country house of an aristocratic family, this play depicts its hero's struggles against the claustrophobic mannerliness of his family. Virginia Woolf wrote in her diary that she saw Harry as an incarnation of Eliot, and Harry's wife, who was drowned a year before the play's action begins, seems clearly indebted to Vivien Eliot. "Eliot's family, like Harry's, had looked on his marriage as an aberration" (85), Gordon writes, and both women exerted a disturbing control over their husbands even when they were no longer present. Gordon cites a letter Eliot wrote to Browne, the play's director, which "resonates with personal implications: Harry, he said, was partially de-sexed by the horror of his marriage" (49). In 1938, when the play was written, Eliot had been separated from his wife for five years and had barely seen her since then; she was institutionalized the month after he completed the play, and he never spoke with her again. The ambiguity of Harry's wife's disappearance, and of his culpability in her fate, seems to suggest Eliot's own complex feelings of guilt mixed with relief as he looked back on his unhappy alliance but also looked forward to the possibility of a life in which the burden of this marital failure might be relieved.

At the titular reunion, the first family gathering in many years, Harry's mother, Amy, attempts to convince her son to take his place in the family estate and resume the conventional life he had led before his marriage. The other family members, who form a Chorus that presents a darker view of the drawing-room machinations, see the event as a farce. Harry claims to have pushed his wife overboard, though his family responds that he is psychologically delusional, expressing this confession out of guilt at having wanted to escape from his wife. As the reunion unfolds, Harry bitterly rebukes his mother's vision for him and the pain she has caused him; his two brothers both have automobile accidents, suggesting the chaotic misdirection of their lives; and Harry, trying to piece together the mystery of his father's disappearance when he was a child, finds that his own isolation and numbness were experienced also by his father, who had been, like Harry, wholly unsuited to conventional family life. Finally, Harry experiences a vision of reconciliation, involving his acceptance of sin and expiation, and feels himself free from the demons who had been pursuing him. These ghosts are a reiteration of the Eumenides from the *Oresteia* of Aeschylus, which Eliot used as a model for the play; as in the Greek analogue, the hero's fate and guilt in Eliot's modern rendition were determined by his parents' crimes, and the curse from which his suffering emanated was brought to an end by the intervention of the gods, enabling a transformation from alienation to reconciliation. Harry's version of anagnorisis involves a vague sense of some spiritually meaningful commitment that will allow him to transcend the banality of the life he has led up to the present moment.

Like *Murder in the Cathedral*, *The Family Reunion* focuses on a central character who has experienced a range of tribulations and ends up changing course to follow a path of superior spirituality. Importantly, Eliot again uses a Chorus to put the individual experiences into a social context as people watch and respond. The major difference between the two works is the change from public historical drama to private drawing-room family melodrama. The resonantly stylized atmosphere of Eliot's modern medieval play gives way in *The Family Reunion* to a simpler naturalism and a subtler brand of poetic drama, with the possible exception of the Chorus (which, Browne felt, appeared too heavily evocative of classical Greek tradition and should instead have melded more smoothly with the rest of the play's conversational speech). The

Christian context foregrounded in *Murder in the Cathedral* similarly becomes a more understated element of *The Family Reunion*. This type of drama is where Eliot would remain, for better or worse, as he continued his playwriting for the next two decades.

While the play ends in a kind of soothing apotheosis for Harry, the atmosphere before that point recalls the depressing, banal tedium that Eliot's earliest poetry portrays. There is a strong whiff of the misogyny that permeates *Prufrock and Other Observations* and *Poems* (1920): just as the gentleman caller in "Portrait of a Lady" craves escape from the social confinement that is epitomized by the female sensibility, so too Harry's problem with family life seems to be mostly a function of what he sees as cloying, manipulative women. If the characters from Eliot's early poetry seem to inhabit the first circle of Dante's *Inferno*, the characters in *The Family Reunion* might be seen as residing just a step outside of Hell, but certainly quite far from anything approaching the more comfortably sustaining vision of community that his later plays and poetry will finally approach. The Chorus, in its first speech, laments its sense of a confusing and dismal atmosphere: "Why do we feel embarrassed, impatient, fretful, ill at ease, / Assembled like amateur actors who have not been assigned their parts? / . . . / We are here . . . to play an unread part in some monstrous farce, ridiculous in some nightmare pantomime" (*CPP* 231). The dramatic self-consciousness that frames the pervasive angst, evocative of the existentialist absurdity of Pirandello's *Six Characters in Search of an Author*, suggests that even in his third play Eliot's dramatic mission is still a work in progress. The entire play indeed resonates with a hapless and aimless spirit, making the choral plaint an apt assessment of the problem that Eliot represents in *The Family Reunion*.

In "Poetry and Drama," Eliot wrote an extensive self-critique of this play. He felt that using the same actors both as individual characters and as collective members of the Chorus was unsuccessful, and he judged two cryptic and incantatory passages to have failed because they disrupted the play's naturalistic flow. He felt that the first part of the play was good but too long, and then the second part unnecessarily explores the background in excessive detail, allowing the audience's attention to wander, while the conclusion was too abrupt. And he believed that there was an awkward disjunction between the play's Greek origin and the contemporary situation; he wished he had either stayed closer to the *Oresteia* as a model or else diverged more widely from it. The Eumenides, he acknowledged, did not fit well into the drama; he suggested that in future productions they might be understood as being visible only to certain characters and not to the audience. The play as a whole is finally unfocused, Eliot wrote, and the audience cannot be sure whether the play is about the mother's tragedy or the son's salvation (*OPP* 83–84). But he balanced this criticism with an affirmation of what he appreciated about the play: *The Family Reunion* successfully expressed the world of contemporary people living contemporary lives, and rather than using verse drama to bring the audience into an unreal poetic world for the play's duration, this play brought poetry into the real world of the audience.

Like all Eliot's plays of the 1930s, *The Family Reunion* has problems with its construction. One might consider all three of these plays experimental, or unstable, or at least partially failures, and certainly in Eliot's final three plays he has hit his stride and gotten rid of the structural unevenness and uncertainties that pervade all of his thirties drama in one way or another. But if these plays are less than completely successful on their own merits, they are still fascinating documents of T. S. Eliot's development as a writer. When we appraise Eliot's work of the 1930s, and how this decade acts as a fulcrum between his writing from the 1920s and that from the 1940s, it may initially seem that we are looking at contradictions, repudiations: Christianity instead of a weary agnosticism, drama upstaging poetry, community awareness and social interaction displacing solipsistic alienation. But the more enterprising (and, I think, the more accurate) way to see this is as an attempt to meld a challengingly diverse set of forms and cultural attitudes. Eliot is, after all, writing *verse* drama — which is both poetry and drama at the same time. This doubleness stands as a metaphor for the kind of bridging we see in Eliot's imperfect but impressively ambitious plays of the 1930s.

NOTE

1 In *T. S. Eliot's Drama: A Research and Production Sourcebook*, I annotate more than 60 of these essays (167–86). Some of the more important ones include, on specific writers, "Four Elizabethan Dramatists" (*SE* 91–99), "Christopher Marlowe" (100–06), "Shakespeare and the Stoicism of Seneca" (107–20), "Hamlet and His Problems" (121–26), "Ben Jonson" (127–39), "Thomas Middleton" (140–48), "Philip Massinger" (181–95), and, on dramatic theory, "A Dialogue on Dramatic Poetry" (*SE* 31–45), "The Future of Poetic Drama," "The Need for Poetic Drama," "Poetry and Drama" (*OPP* 72–88), "The Possibility of a Poetic Drama" (*SW* 60–70), and "The Three Voices of Poetry" (*OPP* 89–102).

REFERENCES AND FURTHER READING

Ackroyd, Peter. *T. S. Eliot: A Life*. New York: Simon, 1984.

Browne, E. Martin. *The Making of T. S. Eliot's Plays*. Cambridge: Cambridge UP, 1969.

Dukes, Ashley. "T. S. Eliot in the Theatre." *T. S. Eliot: A Symposium*. Ed. Richard March and Tambimuttu. Freeport, NY: Books for Libraries, 1968. 111–18.

Gordon, Lyndall. *Eliot's New Life*. Oxford: Oxford UP, 1988.

Hayter, Alethea. "Thomas à Becket and the Dramatists." *Essays by Divers Hands* n.s. 34 (1966): 90–105.

Malamud, Randy. *T. S. Eliot's Drama: A Research and Production Sourcebook*. Westport, CT: Greenwood, 1992.

——. *Where the Words are Valid: T. S. Eliot's Communities of Drama*. Westport, CT: Greenwood, 1994.

Rev. of *The Rock. Tablet* 4 August 1934: 138.

Sayers, Michael. "Mr. T. S. Eliot's *The Rock*." *New English Weekly* 21 June 1934: 230–31.

Smith, Carol H. *T. S. Eliot's Dramatic Theory and Practice*. Princeton: Princeton UP, 1963.

Ward, David. *T. S. Eliot Between Two Worlds*. London: Routledge, 1973.

Williams, Pieter. "The Function of the Chorus in T. S. Eliot's *Murder in the Cathedral*." *American Benedictine Review* 23 (1972): 499–511.

21

Eliot's "Divine" Comedies: *The Cocktail Party*, *The Confidential Clerk*, and *The Elder Statesman*

Carol H. Smith

It is clear from T. S. Eliot's earliest critical pronouncements that drama, especially poetic drama, held a special significance for him, both as a genre capable of formal order and coherence and as a literary form with deep roots in the ritual traditions of religious ceremony. And it is equally clear from his lifelong effort to master a variety of dramatic forms in verse – melodrama and burlesque in *Sweeney Agonistes*, pageant in *The Rock*, ritualized religious drama in *Murder in the Cathedral*, and stylized romantic comedy and farce in *The Cocktail Party*, *The Confidential Clerk*, and *The Elder Statesman* – that he regarded success in his dramatic writing to be one of his most important, if elusive, literary goals. Part of Eliot's commitment to dramatic writing can be explained by his wish to use the forms of popular drama to bring his religious ideas to a larger and more secular audience than his poems were likely to attract. But we can also see in Eliot's plays a revealing record of personal struggle with the competing demands of human obligations and the austerity of a spiritual life. Looked at in this light, the plays became for Eliot a public form in which to present, below the surface for those who could read it, a spiritual journey that he believed to be the defining meaning of his life.

In order to understand Eliot's sense of the importance of the dramatic form and its usefulness to his own literary project, we need to look back to his early ideas on the origins of drama. Along with others of his generation, he initially approached ancient drama from the perspective of the new views of culture introduced by the work of a generation of cultural anthropologists influenced by Sir James G. Frazer's *The Golden Bough*. In this view, the primitive sources of Greek comedy and tragedy formed one of the earliest cultural records of a ritual drama based on ancient fertility ceremonies that Frazer and his followers believed to be "universal." The later forms of comedy and tragedy thus not only revealed traces of mankind's primal religious rituals, but showed an innate need for spiritual expression by the "primitive" mind. The implications of these ideas for Eliot's drama were profound. A modern drama for a secular age might hide beneath its dramatic surface allusions to these origins, an idea which

A Companion to T. S. Eliot, First Edition. Edited by David E. Chinitz.
© 2014 John Wiley & Sons, Ltd. Published 2014 by John Wiley & Sons, Ltd.

Eliot developed into a theory of dramatic levels. The structure of his modern plays could be modeled on a Greek source (reflected in plot, characters, and theme), and the plays could be written to appeal to different levels of dramatic understanding in the audience. Eliot's view of the need to hide his religious meanings reflects his recognition of the unpopularity of religious ideas in a secular age. Nevertheless the general theme of all his plays remained consistent throughout his career: a protagonist's struggle to recognize and pursue a spiritual path in a world that fails to acknowledge his mission. The terms of this pursuit as well as the style of dramatic presentation changed significantly as Eliot's ideas of religious experience evolved, but in all the plays the goal of Christian illumination, captured in the Dantean sense of the term *comedy*, persisted.

Eliot's earliest dramatic experiment, *Sweeney Agonistes*, put forward his most negative view of the spiritual path, yet his most innovative and theoretically radical presentation. Sweeney, Eliot's favorite everyman figure in the early poetry, is impelled by his revulsion against the demands of the flesh to rehearse a Jazz-Age version of the spiritual advice of St. John of the Cross, to divest oneself of the temptations of the body by "do[ing] a girl in" and dissolving her body in a "lysol . . . bath" (*CPP* 83). We can see in this experiment an early model of Eliot's dramatic ideas. The characters are flat and speak in stylized jazz rhythms, and the hero remains isolated from his uncomprehending brothel companions. But "behind" the modern surface are hidden allusions to the ritual drama described by Frazer – the "cooking" of the sin-laden representative of the old order to make him new. In this early model of a Christian "comedy," the stylized rhythms and the Jazz-Age setting conceal the religious meaning underneath.

Eliot's first full-length drama, *Murder in the Cathedral*, because written for a religious setting and audience, openly explored the theme of the saint's progress amid secular tormentors. To reinforce the idea of the saint's spiritual isolation, Eliot included a chorus of unknowing women of Canterbury who must struggle to come to terms with the saint's journey and its meaning in their lives. His next play, *The Family Reunion*, marked Eliot's move to the popular stage of the West End, a venue where he faced the challenge of presenting his religious theme to the secular audiences of the commercial theater. Yet even here there are echoes of *Sweeney Agonistes* in Harry's fear that he has murdered his wife, or has wished to. Harry's pursuit by the Furies, presented on stage, suggested a visual allusion to Eliot's Greek source in Aeschylus. The appearance of the Furies was important to the dramatic situation of the play, for it makes clear to Harry that he cannot accept the promise of human love that his cousin Mary offers, a theme that Eliot explores in his later plays. However, the baffled reaction of West End audiences to the appearance on stage of the Furies forced Eliot to revise his ideas about how to dramatize the pursuit of the spiritually tormented hero. In his next play, *The Cocktail Party*, arguably Eliot's most original and successful comedy, we can see the result of that rethinking.

The move to comedy in *The Cocktail Party* (1949) shows Eliot's willingness to revise the dramatic tone of his plays radically in order to accommodate his audiences.

At the same time, it reflects a reconsideration of many aspects of his dramatic model. The stylized surface of comedy allowed the religious implications to be hidden in the symbolism and wit of double meanings and for characters to be flattened into representative comic types, yet at the same time to enact the ritualized roles of a drama of spiritual awakening. By modeling the situation of his modern play on a classical source that itself reflected ancient ritual sources, Eliot reproduced his earliest ideas on the multiple levels of history and ceremony in the dramatic form. Yet in his modern plays those layers of meaning were presented beneath a comic surface that would entertain his secular audiences yet exploit for his own purposes traditional features of comedy and farce, such as hidden identities, mysterious disclosures, and even buffoonery.[1]

Part of the challenge of Eliot's revised dramatic project was developing a verse form that could capture the tone of comedy and yet be flexible enough to allow for lyric moments or interludes that could explore the experience and the struggle of spiritual awakening. Eliot later described this revision in "Poetry and Drama" as an effort to tame his verse in order to fulfill his long-held goal of developing a viable poetic drama for the modern stage. Eliot's choice of comedy to express his Christian message also reflects a fundamental change of his view of spiritual experience from his earliest presentation of the violence of purgation in *Sweeney Agonistes*. He now saw the spiritual journey in more liberal terms, those closer to the Dantean model of the two paths to God, the negative way and the affirmative way, endorsed by Charles Williams and other contemporary Christian thinkers of his generation.

The Cocktail Party

The Cocktail Party's plot is structured by the comic reversals and disruptions of a romantic triangle consisting of Edward Chamberlayne; Lavinia, his wife; and Celia, his mistress. Edward's conviction that his marriage is a failure and that Celia could offer him permanent happiness is unsettled by the sudden disappearance of Lavinia and the mysterious presence of an unexpected guest, Sir Henry Harcourt-Reilly, at their cocktail party. With Sir Henry's (unwanted) help, Edward realizes that he wants his wife back, if only to find out who he himself is. Sir Henry makes Edward see that he has no real knowledge of his wife because our knowledge of others is always based on false memories of past moments. Peter, another guest at the party, confesses to Edward his own newly discovered love for Celia, not suspecting that she is Edward's mistress. After Peter leaves, Celia herself returns to discover Edward's change of heart. The comic reversals of the disrupted love affairs are matched throughout the first act with the interruptions of Julia, the busybody, and her friend Alex, both of whom have a mysterious relationship with Sir Henry. As doorbells and phones ring and intrusions to find misplaced umbrellas and eyeglasses interrupt every serious conversation about the nature of secular love and marriage, the audience is invited to witness the misjudgments and self-concealments that constitute modern relationships. There are also many hints that Sir Henry, Julia, and Alex are spiritual guardians whose mission is to provide insight through which the modern lovers may penetrate their unfortunate self-disguises.

In the second act, Sir Henry, now revealed as an eminent psychiatrist, leads Edward, Lavinia, and Celia to accept their different paths to spiritual health. Edward and Lavinia's spiritual illness results from their self-deception and inability to love others. Their cure is the affirmative way of Christian marriage, where they might follow Dante's model of seeing in the eyes of the beloved the reflection, not of self, but of God. For Celia, Sir Henry's diagnosis is different. As Eliot's figure for the potential saint, Celia sees the world as a delusion, feels a universal sense of isolation, and experiences a sense of sin. With Sir Henry's help, she recognizes a need to atone, a desire modeled on God's love; once she has experienced this higher form of love, she realizes that she can never be content with the compromises of secular love and marriage. Instead she chooses the negative way, the hard path of spiritual knowledge and the terrors of awareness that the saint's journey holds.

The third act, set two years later at another cocktail party held by the Chamberlaynes, reveals the results of these two decisions. Edward and Lavinia have transformed their marriage, and there are hints of a coming child to bless their union. Only Celia is missing from the celebrants at the earlier party. Alex, one of the guardians, announces Celia's terrible death in Kinkanja, as a sister in an austere nursing order who has been crucified near an anthill in a native insurrection. Sir Henry reveals that he foresaw her death and that it is not to be seen as a waste, as the others in their shock feel it to be, but a triumph that is part of God's design that they cannot know. The play ends with the departure of the guardians for another party and another act of divine intervention.

While the severity of Eliot's view of the saint's path alienated some critics and members of the audience, the play's conclusion seems intended to suggest the complementary relationship of the two ways to God. Edward and Lavinia's new understanding of Celia's suffering gives them a glimpse of the saint's vision and a recognition that although moments of spiritual insight are rare in ordinary life, they illuminate and give meaning to both the compromises and fulfillments of domestic experience. The libations and communion of the final party at the domestic hearth dramatically demonstrate that each approach to God involves the other.

Eliot used as his classical source for *The Cocktail Party* the *Alcestis* of Euripides, a play that reinforces the theme of death and rebirth carried out by divine agency. Like Sir Henry in *The Cocktail Party*, the god Heracles arrives as an unknown guest, disrupting with his drunken buffoonery and boisterousness the grieving household of Admetus and his newly dead wife Alcestis. Alcestis has chosen to die in her husband's place, and Admetus, recognizing her worth and his loss, wants her back. Heracles repays his host's hospitality by bringing her back from the dead, a feat that is echoed in Eliot's play by Sir Henry's return of Lavinia to Edward when he discovers his need of her. In another sense, Celia is also brought back from her spiritual death by Sir Henry's agency. Like Alcestis, Celia ransoms her life for others by enacting in her crucifixion the sacrifice of Christ, and her marriage to divinity is the counterpart of the secular marriage of the affirmative way.

The Cocktail Party was generally regarded as a theatrical success, and it seems to have fulfilled its author's dramatic model more fully than any of his other plays. The unity of the comic surface was matched with the rhythmic unity of a flexible conversational and often witty verse, one of Eliot's under-appreciated poetic achievements. The deeper religious meanings of the two Christian paths are revealed in both the patterned structure of the play and the translation into psychological language of Sir Henry's religious insights. The best example of Eliot's artful merger of dramatic levels is his adaptation of the ritual drama's spiritual doctor – a role reflected in the god Heracles in the *Alcestis* – in the figure of the modern psychiatrist who "plays God" and brings his unknowing clients to a religious cure in a modern world of secular isolation and lack of belief.

The Confidential Clerk

In Eliot's next play, *The Confidential Clerk* (1953), he chose an even more stylized form, the comedy of manners, and again modeled the dramatic situation on a play by Euripides, this time the *Ion*. Instead of the love triangle of romantic comedy, in *The Confidential Clerk* Eliot used a theme familiar in Greek comedy, the foundling's search for his true parentage, one that allowed him to explore again the potential conflict of the loyalty due to human relationships and that owed to the divine Father on whom all human relationships are founded. Rather than the lyrical passages or the overt dramatic signals of divine intervention of the earlier plays, the spiritual meanings are here conveyed by two of Eliot's most familiar metaphors for ecstatic or visionary experience, stepping through a private door into a secret garden and listening to the order and harmony of music.

The characters of *The Confidential Clerk* are the stylized characters of comedy of manners. Sir Claude Mulhammer, a London financier, and his eccentric wife, Lady Elizabeth, who dabbles in the occult, have both "mislaid" children in their earlier lives and now want them back. Much of the comedy of the play concerns their misdirected attempts to establish ties of parenthood. Sir Claude has a true but unacknowledged illegitimate daughter, Lucasta Angel, who is engaged to a brash young man, B. Kaghan, with an important future in the City. He is later revealed to be Lady Elizabeth's true son, despite her dislike of him. Both Sir Claude and Lady Elizabeth desire to adopt Colby Simpkins, Sir Claude's new confidential clerk, each mistakenly believing him to be his or her undiscovered child. In the climactic reversal scene, both discover and accept their true children, and Colby finds himself to be the child of his heavenly Father.

The characters who represent the spiritual guardians in this play, Mrs. Guzzard, the dishonest nurse who holds the key to everyone's identity, and Eggerson, Sir Claude's trusted former confidential clerk, preside over the resolution of the parental dilemmas. Only Eggerson fully understands that Colby's true vocation is to be church organist in Eggerson's own parish and that Colby will one day seek religious orders in the church.

While there are still two paths represented in the play, human family and more direct service to God, both paths have been softened, even domesticated, and the saint's path of martyrdom has been replaced by Christian service, a significant shift in Eliot's presentation of Christian mission. All the major characters experience spiritual longings, Lady Elizabeth in her pursuit of exotic religions and Sir Claude in his private passion for the beauty of ceramic forms, but these are revealed to be mere substitutes for genuine belief because they are separated from ordinary daily experience. Only Eggerson finds God in his garden and integrates its products into his daily life.

Eliot's choice of Euripides's *Ion* points up the importance of the theme of finding one's true identity by discovering one's relationship to the gods. In Euripides's play, Ion is the son of Apollo and Creusa, princess of Athens, who abandons him to die, but Apollo rescues him and installs him in his temple at Delphi. Years later, when the childless Creusa and her husband Xuthus travel to the oracle for aid, Apollo sends his reluctant son to claim his human birthright as prince of Athens. Interestingly, Eliot reverses the process in his play by having Colby give up the false secular identity that Sir Claude would impose on him in exchange for his divine role as a servant of God. While the two paths remain separate, the blessings of the guardians fall equally on the restoration of family ties and human obligations and on the humility of parish service rooted in the divine.

The Elder Statesman

The Elder Statesman (1958) was Eliot's last play, and while its tone and theme were generally seen to reflect a more openly personal expression of the happiness he had found in his second marriage, it followed the earlier plays in examining as well the painful journey that was necessary to arrive at forgiveness and purgation. Different as the mood of these two themes may seem, the play insists on the connection between the private joy of the discovery of love and its potential to expose and transform the painful deceptions and loss of self of an earlier life. The personal meanings for the playwright appear to be very close to the play's surface in this final comedy; the feelings of youthful rejuvenation expressed in the play are seen to mirror the release from the painful mask of the elder statesman that Eliot's reputation seems to have imposed on him. His personal poem of dedication to his wife Valerie in the printed version of the play hints at these personal meanings: "The words mean what they say, but some have a further meaning / For you and me only" (*Elder* 5).

The action of the play again centers on two kinds of love, but these are treated here in a new way. In *The Elder Statesman* a father's possessive demands for his daughter's love and service pose an obstacle to the young lovers' happiness. It is only when he is forced to acknowledge that his fame and success are built on the selfish use of others that a true bond of affection can be established between father and daughter. His honest confession of the secrets of his past wins her compassion and both generations are able to establish mutual bonds of family support. In this play, romantic love is celebrated rather than rejected and is seen as a foundation on which true selfhood can be established.

When the play opens, the lovers, Charles and Monica, express their love for each other in a lyrical duet that describes their awakening into a new shared identity. The only impediment to their engagement is the illness and enforced retirement from public life of Monica's father, Lord Claverton, a celebrated statesman of power and influence. He has come to depend on his faithful daughter and expects her to accompany him to an expensive convalescent home, Badgley Court, where he awaits death.

He is visited there by the ghosts of his past in the persons of Fred Culverwell and Maisie Montjoy. Culverwell blames Lord Claverton for his imprisonment for forgery and his loss of country and identity. Maisie Montjoy's grievance is that as her first lover, he abandoned her when their love affair became inconvenient. Both visitors blame Lord Claverton for corrupting their natures and violating their trust. Together they force him to acknowledge that his public self, his wealth and his honors, have been built on lies, lies which he himself chose to believe.

As their final revenge, they contrive to corrupt his wayward son Michael, using the same duplicity that was used to corrupt them. Michael's rebellious nature has led him to envy his father's success and to duplicate his failures. In one of his most painful lessons, Lord Claverton is brought to see his own responsibility for his son's nature and to vow, in a speech that echoes King Lear, that he will learn humility before it is too late. Finally he is willing to share his true self with his daughter and to find his way out of the isolation and hollowness of his false role as elder statesman.

Because of the transformation of Lord Claverton's relationship with his children, the young lovers recognize that their private love can become a circle of care and compassion. Monica looks ahead to her future role as a sister who can offer love and acceptance to her brother as he struggles with his own flawed choices in life. This ending, with its emphasis on a circle of family love, presents Eliot's dramatic rethinking of the separation of the negative and affirmative paths to God. Human love is now seen as an instrument to perfect the self at the end of a long life.

Eliot's choice of Sophocles's *Oedipus at Colonus* as the Greek source behind his last play suggests that the theme of purgation and forgiveness was important to its conception. It also suggests that Eliot conceived of the play as the completion of a purgative cycle, as Sophocles's play was. Long before, at the time of *The Family Reunion*, Eliot wrote to E. Martin Browne, the director of all his plays, that Harry's quest needed to be completed by an *Orestes* or an *Oedipus at Colonus* (Browne 107). The play can thus be read as a kind of personal farewell to the theater and as a final statement of resolution of the issue that Eliot had struggled with in all his plays – how to integrate the obligations to one's human family with the more austere demands of service to God.

In Sophocles's tragedy, the blind and exiled Oedipus has grown old expiating his youthful crimes of patricide and incest and has arrived at a state of reconciliation and acceptance. He is led by his faithful daughter Antigone to the sacred grove of the Eumenides, where it is ordained that he is to die. There, joined by his other daughter, Ismene, he makes his prayers to the gods. He begs Theseus, king of Athens, for asylum and protection, a request granted because Apollo has ordained his burial at Colonus. But Oedipus's peaceful death is threatened by the appearance of Creon, who desires to bring him back to Thebes so that he, Creon, may regain the crown that has been wrested from him by Oedipus's two sons. With the help of Theseus, Oedipus is able to resist all attempts to take him from the sacred grove. Oedipus is visited by his son Polynices, himself exiled by his brother, who asks his father's blessing in attacking Thebes. Instead Oedipus curses both his sons for thinking only of the throne. Thunder is heard, and, after a loving farewell to his daughters, Oedipus moves toward his fated place of death.

Eliot has included in his play numerous parallels to his Greek source. Lord Claverton, like Oedipus, has been blind to his own guilt. He has run over an old man, lived with his wife without recognizing her identity, and reared a son who, like Polynices, wants only power and wealth. As Oedipus is supported by his daughters, so Lord Claverton is supported and finally cured by his confession to Monica. And as Antigone vows to carry out the burial rites for Polynices, Monica promises to be her brother's link with his lost identity. Lord Claverton, like Oedipus, is drawn to the great beech at Badgley Court where he will find salvation, but first he bestows his wedding blessing on the love of Charles and Monica.

Eliot also includes elements of the ritual drama that was his initial model for all his experiments in verse drama. In *The Elder Statesman* the ritual scheme is quite literally translated into the surface action: the sin-laden protagonist near death retires to a "convalescent home" where his purgation and cure are conducted, just as the same process is displayed in *Oedipus at Colonus*. The dramatic effect is a closer unity between surface and depth than in Eliot's other comedies. In the same way the verse form and the theme of the play are brought closer together. In Eliot's earlier plays the love lyric was associated with the moments of human love that must be rejected in favor of a more ascetic path. The most extreme example of this rejection of human love appeared in *Sweeney Agonistes*, where the temptations of physical sexuality are caricatured in a debased jazz chant. In *The Family Reunion* the love duet between Harry and his cousin Mary is interrupted by the Furies as a sign to Harry that human love must be rejected. Similarly, in *The Confidential Clerk*, the love scene between Colby and Lucasta ends in a misunderstanding intended to show that another path awaits Colby. In *The Elder Statesman*, however, love and forgiveness are found through the human agency of marriage and family, and the lyric passages carry the major thematic meaning of the play: that the compassion and forgiveness that Monica offers her father is made possible by the transformation and completion that she experiences in her newfound love for Charles.

Evaluation

Looked at as a group, Eliot's three late comedies represent his most self-conscious efforts to present to the secular public his Dantean interpretation of the place of human love within the divine plan. As we have seen, Eliot's ideas about the role of love and marriage in a Christian life changed significantly from *The Cocktail Party* to *The Elder Statesman*. In the earlier play human love and marriage, the life of the domestic hearth, represented the affirmative way, and, while it was an acknowledged path to salvation, it was a poor second to the saint's sacrifice and torture of the negative way. The same spiritual hierarchy is presented in *The Confidential Clerk*; Colby's brief flirtation with Lucasta represents nothing more than a romantic interlude in his path of religious discovery. At the play's end, while the bonds of family affection embrace Lucasta and B. Kaghan in their coming marriage and return them to the restored circle of domestic attachment, Colby's path is clearly a separate one. It is only in Eliot's last play, *The Elder Statesman*, that the love of Charles and Monica is shown to hold the key to the redemption of Lord Claverton, the sin-laden representative of human pride and self-deception. The comic treatment in these three plays reflects the same transition. The witty buffoonery and antic stage business and dialogue of the ritualized figures of Sir Henry and the guardians of *The Cocktail Party* are replaced with the more consistent comic surface of society farce in *The Confidential Clerk*. In *The Elder Statesman*, the dramatic action and the meaning beneath it are more unified and the dramatic surface more transparent. The lyric passages of romantic awakening form the context for Lord Claverton's purification, reflecting a comic resolution in both ritual and Dantean terms. It is as if the playwright, in resolving the conflict of loyalties between human and divine obligations, found it less necessary to hide his spiritual meanings in the stylized banter and frivolity of stage comedy.

But satisfactory as this resolution may have been from the playwright's point of view, what were the reactions of contemporary critics and especially the audiences that Eliot sought to enlist in his efforts to bring religious drama to the popular stage? Although the critical reaction to Eliot's late comedies was mixed, the judgment often depending on the reviewer's sympathy with Eliot's religious message or with his choice of comedy to portray his religious themes, the plays would have to be judged a success in theatrical terms. *The Cocktail Party*, first presented at the Edinburgh Festival and later on Broadway in New York and in London's West End, had several hundred performances in each city. It also had impressive casts, including Alec Guinness, Irene Worth, Rex Harrison, Margaret Leighton, and Cathleen Nesbitt. According to E. Martin Browne, *The Cocktail Party* played to close to a million and a half spectators in all. *The Confidential Clerk*, like its predecessor, opened in Edinburgh, with a long and successful run both on Shaftesbury Avenue and on Broadway with a cast including Ina Claire, who came out of retirement to play Lady Elizabeth, Claude Rains as Sir Claude, and Joan Greenwood as Lucasta. *The Elder Statesman*, also first performed at Edinburgh, was less of a theatrical success, although it toured for three weeks after the Festival and had a two months' run in London, attracting Anna Massey in the role of Monica and later Vanessa Redgrave in a TV performance.

Certainly, this success with audiences and the press coverage it generated on both sides of the Atlantic supported Eliot's goal of introducing to mainstream audiences his concept of a drama linked to religious ritual and his determination to contrive a poetic drama that would attract and sustain the interest of a popular audience in spoken verse. Eliot's continuing efforts to develop a "transparent" dramatic verse reflected his conviction that to be stageworthy in modern times, poetry needed to be put on a "thin diet" in order to remain conversational for ordinary dramatic situations and yet to retain the potential to express important dramatic moments with the lyric intensity of poetry (*OPP* 75, 85).

Eliot's defense of his experiment with a new verse form for drama appears in "The Music of Poetry" and "Poetry and Drama." He explains that while only verse could convey the many levels of experience his plays required of his actors, he was nevertheless dissatisfied with the conventions of verse drama based on Shakespearean blank verse because it no longer captured the rhythms of contemporary speech. He wanted a verse that would be invisible to a modern audience, yet could intensify the dramatic meanings when necessary. He described the poetic line he developed in "Poetry and Drama":

> a line of varying length and varying number of syllables, with a caesura and three stresses. The caesura and the stresses may come at different places, almost anywhere in the line; the stresses may be close together or well separated by light syllables, the only rule being that there must be one stress on one side of the caesura and two on the other. (*OPP* 82)

Two examples cited by E. Martin Browne illustrate the flexibility of Eliot's poetic line. The first is from the opening speech by Amy, the matriarch in *The Family Reunion*, and captures her fear of death:

O Líght that was taken for gránted

When I was yoúng and stróng, // and sun and light unsoúght for
And the níght unféared // and the day expécted
And clócks could be trústed, // tomorrow assúred
And tíme would not stóp in the dárk! (Browne 297)

The second illustrates the firm rhythm and comic repartee of the guardians in *The Cocktail Party*:

ALEX You've míssed the point // complétely, Júlia:
          There *wére* no tígers. // *Thát* was the point.
JULIA Then what were you dóing, // úp in a trée:
          You and the Maharája? //

ALEX   My déar Júlia!
       It's perfectly hópeless. // You háven't been lístening. (300)

In his last comedies, Eliot worked to eliminate the poetic effects he felt had drawn attention to the verse in *The Family Reunion* – runic passages, lyric duets like those between Harry and Mary, and the choruses. In *The Cocktail Party*, to avoid the musical effects of spoken verse, he turned instead to other "poetic" effects such as extended images, repetition of phrases, and structural repetitions of all kinds available in the patterning of comedy. In *The Confidential Clerk* the verse is further "thinned," the dialogue less stylized and the comic effects limited to the traditional comic situations of misplaced children and divine intervention to solve issues of identity. In *The Elder Statesman*, while the verse form has been technically preserved, the tone is more somber, and the lyric passages are saved for the young lovers, to emphasize the theme of human love as an instrument of purgation and salvation.

If Eliot's dramatic program is to be weighed by his most ambitious goals of bringing poetic drama back to the English stage or establishing a permanent place for religious drama in the commercial theater, those goals were never fulfilled. His plays did not become the impetus for major changes in the theatrical world in the years that followed *The Elder Statesman*. Instead the postwar English stage tradition followed the more flamboyantly intellectual theatrics of Tom Stoppard and the cryptic minimalism of Harold Pinter. The popularity of Eliot's plays at the time of their production was probably explained by Eliot's reputation as the major modernist poet of his generation and the novelty of a stage career for the notoriously private and elite "Mr. Eliot," who had famously embraced labels of "impersonality" and invisibility in his early career. Nevertheless, the importance of the plays in any evaluation of his career cannot be denied. As we have seen, his early views of the religious origins of drama and its long and distinguished cultural history made him see this literary form as the final test for a poet who wished to speak to the deepest needs and values of his age. Eliot's determination to cast the conflicts of a spiritual life in the public form of drama seems to reveal a gradual stepping away from his earlier views of impersonality and an acceptance of the risks of exposure in exchange for the transformative message of his final plays. This, finally, may be the greatest importance of T. S. Eliot's plays – as a record of the evolution of his personal religious struggle and the dramatic methods he developed to make that quest available to a larger and more secular audience.

NOTE

1 For Eliot's theory of simultaneous levels of meaning in drama, see "AWAY WE GO": POETRY AND PLAY IN *OLD POSSUM'S BOOK OF* PRACTICAL CATS AND ANDREW LLOYD WEBBER'S *CATS*.

REFERENCES AND FURTHER READING

Browne, E. Martin. *The Making of T. S. Eliot's Plays*. New York: Cambridge UP, 1969.

Bush, Ronald. *T. S. Eliot: A Study in Character and Style*. Cambridge: Cambridge UP, 1991.

Chinitz, David E. *T. S. Eliot and the Cultural Divide*. Chicago: U of Chicago P, 2003.

Cornford, Francis M. *The Origin of Attic Comedy*. London: Arnold, 1914.

Gordon, Lyndall. *T. S. Eliot: An Imperfect Life*. New York: Norton, 1998.

Howarth, Herbert. *Notes on Some Figures Behind T. S. Eliot*. Boston: Houghton, 1964.

Jones, David Edwards. *The Plays of T. S. Eliot*. Toronto: U of Toronto P, 1960.

Malamud, Randy. *Where the Words are Valid: T. S. Eliot's Communities of Drama*. Westport, CT: Greenwood, 1994.

Miller, James E., Jr. *T. S. Eliot: The Making of An American Poet, 1888–1922*. University Park, PA: Pennsylvania State UP, 2005.

Smith, Carol H. *T. S. Eliot's Dramatic Theory and Practice*. Princeton: Princeton UP, 1963.

Williams, Charles. *Descent into Hell*. New York: Pellegrini, 1949.

22
Taking Literature *Seriously*: Essays to 1927

Leonard Diepeveen

In 1918, T. S. Eliot, chafing at the "slackness" of British literary culture typified by a recent *Times* article, attacked its "dodging of standards" through its "thoroughly British . . . avoidance of comparison with foreign literatures," and launched a strenuous defense of the "specialist." Damning "the man of mixed motives," which included such Victorian luminaries as Ruskin, Carlyle, Thackeray, and George Eliot, Eliot set off the last sentence of his article with a line of four asterisks: "But we must learn to take literature *seriously*" ("Professional" 61). While Eliot wrote this for the *Egoist*, a publication amenable to acerbity and typographic drama, the sentence typifies both how Eliot interacted with literary culture, and how his famous pronouncements surface in the context of local issues. "Seriously" tells much about Eliot's essays up to 1927. Indeed, to "take literature seriously" is not only an attitude that shapes Eliot's central aesthetic principles, it is an attitude that would help change how people wrote literary criticism. Eliot's notion of seriousness concerns itself with the parameters of criticism, with being explicit about what is and isn't the proper domain of criticism. Seriousness implied a move away from affect and an unproblematic belief that literature is a transparent communion between two souls, and a move toward a concern with evidence that would, eventually, lead to New Criticism.

Eliot's seriousness succeeded, and a sign of his success is that we don't argue with Arthur Clutton-Brock, author of the article that earned Eliot's ire. It's not just that Eliot is more canonical; it's that Eliot's prose is recognizable as literary criticism, eschewing affect, demanding the right level of particularity, displaying the anxieties of argumentative prose. By today's standards his writing does not make a category mistake, while Clutton-Brock's does. In response to critics like Clutton-Brock, Eliot recurrently insists on the "proper" definition of criticism. His essays ask relentless questions of careless critics, particularizing without mercy, pursuing nuance where the original genre would have contented itself with generalizations. These tendencies endow Eliot's essays with the peculiar qualities noted by David Perkins: "Eliot's prose gives the process of thinking, involves us, as readers, in the effort of definition,

A Companion to T. S. Eliot, First Edition. Edited by David E. Chinitz.
© 2014 John Wiley & Sons, Ltd. Published 2014 by John Wiley & Sons, Ltd.

qualification, analysis of examples, and redefinition by which thought develops" (123). (A practical consequence of this style is that quoting Eliot is a deceptive business. One may quote what looks like a definitive statement – but one sentence beyond the quotation Eliot recasts, qualifies, redirects it.)

Not all his ideas make the professionalist crossover, though. Eliot has some awkward allegiances: with art as the bearer of emotion, however redefined; with a sincerity that is not just based on technique, but also on morality; and with taste, although it is a taste that "cannot be had without effort, and without it, our likings remain insignificant accidents" ("Education of Taste" 521). And, though he regularly asserts the need for evidence, Eliot doesn't often provide it. Similarly, while Eliot castigates other critics for having no foundational principles, he is not a systematizer. Instead, he focuses on establishing boundaries for his inquiry, which, together with his turning to "phraseology suggestive of rigorous empirical method" (Jeffreys 99), makes his activities *within* his inquiry sound more systematic than they really are. Finally, we should keep in mind that Eliot was not after all a proto-New Critic; he did not write interpretations of literary works. He distrusted "the acrostic element in literature," and argued that "'interpretation' . . . is only legitimate when it is not interpretation at all, but merely putting the reader in possession of facts which he would otherwise have missed" (*SE* 20).

Canon

Where Eliot wrote his essays is central to understanding their argumentative style. Eliot's venues and topics show the startling diversity of a journalist. His writing ranges from early reviews of philosophy in the *Monist* to an awkwardly conservative tie to J. C. Squire at *The New Statesman* (for whom Eliot wrote "Reflections on *vers libre*"). Before his association with Squire was cold, he began to write for Harriet Weaver at the *Egoist*, and for *The Little Review* and *Athenaeum*, which he followed by vaulting upward and mainstream with his anonymous essays for the *Times Literary Supplement*, to the *Dial* (a very different sort of little magazine from the *Egoist*, with a significantly higher circulation and a less avant-garde agenda), to his writings while editor of the *Criterion*. Eliot selected some of the pre-*Criterion* essays for *The Sacred Wood*, where, with minor revising and to tepid reviews, he massaged them into a narrative form of telling juxtapositions and movement, loosely organized around the topics of the proper critic and the relation of artistic creation to belief and to the artist's surrounding society. Eliot's array of topics is remarkable (he later noted that his concerns were dictated by the books he was paid to review), ranging from philosophy, poetry, and drama to dance, the preservation of churches, and the state of contemporary letters. These pieces must be understood as journalism – not to diminish them, but to grasp how they functioned socially and rhetorically.

How critics have conceptualized the location of these essays over the years has affected what they think is the Eliot canon, the role and identity of its key concepts, and their own interpretive practices. There have been two different senses of Eliot's oeuvre. On one hand, there is that validated by New Criticism and based on *The Sacred Wood*, *Selected Prose*, and *Selected Essays*, with the result that "Tradition and the Individual Talent," "The Metaphysical Poets," "*Ulysses,* Order, and Myth," and "Hamlet and His Problems" dominate, and the objective correlative, the mythical method, and the dissociation of sensibility are treated as if they were systematic and unproblematically applicable to literary texts. Busy with canonizing high modernism and moving literary criticism away from belles-lettres toward something more professionalist, New Critics took hold of those ideas that seemed most generalizable and that worked best with modernist poetry. By the mid-1970s, though, beginning with Bernard Bergonzi's *T. S. Eliot* (1972), critics began to turn toward a more complex canon of amorphous boundaries and purposes, a canon which includes the uncollected essays, essays which are addressed to local conditions and popular culture. With essays located in hundreds of scattered places, this canon reveals Eliot's cultural criticism in its incipient form, makes visible his comments on popular culture, and sharpens his relationship with his immediate predecessors. This canon, congenial to current interest in the "new modernisms," opens up the diversity of Eliot's subject matter, gives his criticism a broader focus, and makes him less Olympian, more provisional. This canon also shows more clearly how key ideas are related. For example, the dissociation of sensibility, as it is seen in many different locations, is not a stand-alone concept, but is entangled with Eliot's ideas on perception and emotional expression, as well as his position on a homogeneous society, tradition, and the ritual of art, particularly performance-based art like dance.[1]

The different senses of Eliot's canon affect discussion about Eliot's consistency as a critic. Most who argue for Eliot's consistency base their claims on his thesis (published as *Knowledge and Experience in the Philosophy of F. H. Bradley*), and explore Eliot's positions on the nature of knowledge and perception. In the best case for the unifying force of the thesis, one which also has the advantage of keeping a close eye on the resultant poetry, Sanford Schwartz argues that "the dissertation displays the same dialectical relationship between emotions and objects, feelings and thought, that informs the 'objective correlative,' 'dissociation of sensibility,' and other crucial terms of his literary essays" (322). Consistency can, indeed, be found: Eliot had a consistent approach not only to subject/object relations, but also to emotion and to dramatic art as ritual. But one also needs to acknowledge that not only is the thesis very difficult and subject to widely differing interpretations, it also is idiosyncratic to his oeuvre, and early (though Eliot's dismissive comments about it late in life, like all his dismissive comments about his early work, should be taken with a grain of salt). Only the thesis is an extended meditation, and it is one of a very few pieces unconstrained by the pressures of a book to review or an editorial to write. Eliot was a journalist: we call his prose essays, but they started as targeted pieces, with topical, centrifugal pressures. That begins to explain why the big principles he enunciates are rarely the main point of the essay, and why often he doesn't explicitly return to them. So while there are congruencies, they do not bring terminological consistency with them. Eliot changed his mind about things as well, radically revising his judgments of Milton, Kipling, and Donne. He also left behind the idea of "pure" criticism, and increasingly became a social critic.

Professionalism

Eliot's early essays identify with professionalist concerns, most recurrently in assertions about how to write criticism properly. (I count at least 24 essays which turn to this topic, or 23 more essays than use the term "objective correlative.") This concern organizes much of *The Sacred Wood*. It must be admitted, however, that this is not the Eliot who engages current interest, and it's hard to gauge what the contemporary interest would have been in beginning an essay in the following manner:

> There are different purposes, motives, and methods possible in criticism. For the reading
> public some classification of these varieties would be useful: a classification which would
> enable the reader to determine immediately whether a critic fulfils any of the legitimate
> critical functions or fulfils more than one without confusion. ("Studies in Contemporary
> Criticism II" 131)

Indefatigably interested in the nature and boundaries of criticism, Eliot eagerly articulated what, and who, lay outside the pale. His list of outsiders includes Henry James ("Henry was not a literary critic"), Coleridge (at times a "corruptor" who provided "opinion or fancy"), Swinburne ("an appreciator"), Arnold ("he failed to ascend to first principles"), and Charles Lamb (a "baleful influence").[2] He did not attack other critics so much for their particular positions as for their category mistakes; his irritations are more with types of writing than with positions held. This obsession with the boundaries of criticism inflects his conflicted attitude to his own writing as well. Frequently grumbling about needing to write journalism, Eliot eagerly distinguished criticism from reviewing, which he saw as being too enmeshed in mass culture: "It [the public] will see, in the end, that the disease of contemporary reviewing is only a form of the radical malady of journalism. Criticism is a very different thing" ("Brief Treatise" 2).

What Eliot positively included in his definition of criticism he stated rarely, but he began the lead article of the October 1918 *Egoist* with: "The work of the critic is almost wholly comprehended in the 'complementary activities' of comparison and analysis. The one activity implies the other; and together they provide the only way of asserting standards and of isolating a writer's peculiar merits" ("Studies in Contemporary Criticism I" 113). This explains both a lot and not very much. On one hand, Eliot's emphasis on comparison explains why his essays so often set one writer next to another. Comparison is essential; when Eliot defined a critic as someone who is able "to treat a book austerely by criteria of art and of art alone" ("Criticism in England" 456), his standard was not the individual work as a self-enclosed system:

"Qua work of art, the work of art cannot be interpreted; there is nothing to interpret; we can only criticize it according to standards, in comparison to other works of art; and for 'interpretation' the chief task is the presentation of relevant historical facts which the reader is not assumed to know" (*SE* 122). On the other hand, Eliot never articulated what exactly he meant by "analysis." Clearly, he did not mean "analysis" in the New Critical sense of "interpretation of meaning," but instead postulated setting out "facts" – although his notion of what constitutes a "fact" is a little fuzzy. Both comparison and analysis, however, had the goal of properly estimating a writer's value.

Eliot charged the critic with keeping his "eye on the object" ("C [July 1924]" 373), an activity which he designated with the professionalist term "purity." For Eliot, "the opposite of the professional, the enemy, [was] the man of mixed motives" ("Professional" 61). Robert Lynd is as good an example as any:

> Mr. Lynd never does become *quite* serious. He obeys some inner check; perhaps he has been unconsciously bullied by the periodical public. He is never uninterested or uninteresting, he is never unintelligent; he never goes far wide of the mark, but his arrow does not flesh very deep. He never, that is, quite dares to treat a book austerely by criteria of art and of art alone. . . . ("Criticism in England" 456)

Writers like Lynd were in greasy contrast to Aristotle, whom Eliot exempted from "these impure desires to satisfy; in whatever sphere of interest, he looked solely and steadfastly at the object" (*SW* 11).

A second professionalist aspect of Eliot's writing is his position on aesthetic development, as when he famously asserted that Joyce's use of Homer "has the importance of a scientific discovery." The rigor lay not only in Joyce's method; it lay in realizing that Joyce's work had never been done before because "it has never before been necessary" (*SP* 177). By contrast, artists who were unaware of what was necessary were simply unserious, wasting culture's time:

> A poet, like a scientist, is contributing toward the organic development of culture: it is just as absurd for him not to know the work of his predecessors or of men writing in other languages as it would be for a biologist to be ignorant of Mendel or De Vries. It is exactly as wasteful for a poet to do what has been done already, as for a biologist to rediscover Mendel's discoveries. ("Contemporanea" 84)

But Eliot validated *organic* development. It's not that literature moved on a trajectory upward but that it found, in specific historical moments, better and inferior ways of responding to local conditions.

Modernity's local conditions had few requirements to which Eliot would commit, although *some* relationship was necessary. Eliot praised Stravinsky's *Rite of Spring* (which he saw in London in 1921, although without Nijinsky's original choreography) for its "quality of modernity." The music "did seem to transform the rhythm of the steppes into the scream of the motor horn, the rattle of machinery, the grind of wheels, the beating of iron and steel, the roar of the underground railway, and the other barbaric cries of modern life; and to transform these despairing noises into music" ("London Letter [Sept. 1921]" 452, 453). The conditions of modernity insisted even more clearly on the need for difficulty. In one of his famous asides, in his 1921 "The Metaphysical Poets," Eliot asserted:

> We can only say that it appears likely that poets in our civilization, as it exists at present, must be *difficult*. Our civilization comprehends great variety and complexity, and this variety and complexity, playing upon a refined sensibility, must produce various and complex results. The poet must become more and more comprehensive, more allusive, more indirect, in order to force, to dislocate if necessary, language into his meaning. (*SE* 248)

But Eliot resisted extending the necessities of modern development to what writers like Pound saw as an essential mechanism: group associations and movements. On one hand, Eliot cautiously supported modest alliances. In his "Brief Treatise on the Criticism of Poetry," he argued that "the practitioners of any art or of several arts who have a sufficient community of interests and standards" should be allowed to form their own journals and "should not be afraid of forming 'cliques,' if their cliques are professional and not personal" (9). But given his penchant for separating himself from others (a tendency all his biographers note), it is no surprise that Eliot ultimately held groups and movements at arm's length: "If we are passionately devoted to good literature, we look for individuals; but people who are keen on literature look for groups. They are easier to find, easier to talk about, and their multiplied activity is more inspiriting to watch than the silent struggles of a single man" ("Post-Georgians" 171). The danger of group association was its entanglement with publicity and fashion, leaving it the purlieu of the second rate, as Eliot pointed out in *Vanity Fair*: "writers who have positive faults in common, and who have only trifling varieties of silliness to distinguish them one from the other, must expect to be classified as a group" ("Preface to Modern Literature" 44).

Eliot's assaults on provincialism similarly spring from his professionalist tendencies. Routinely denigrating English literature unconnected to that of Europe, Eliot based his affinities on his belief in the capaciousness of language and in historical precedent, in tradition. In "The Classics in France – and in England," Eliot lambastes the claim that France's legacy is Latin while England's is Saxon. Without Latin, Eliot asserts, England has no culture, no literature. Not that England didn't come close. In *Tyro* in 1922, Eliot assaulted the "Three Provincialities" of Ireland, England, and America, which failed to realize that "literature is not primarily a matter of nationality, but of language; the traditions of the language, not the traditions of the nation or the race, are what first concern the writer" ("Three" 12). Given this emphasis, not only his position on the place of tradition, but also his assertion that the proper domain of criticism is comparison make sense. Eliot repeatedly argued that English letters were hopelessly amateur because they refused to do this kind of systematic work.

Knowledge

Eliot's professionalist concerns take in a large swath of his views on poetic production and the rise of modernism. But other central concepts, related to the nature of knowledge and the kinds of knowledge most useful for a society, live somewhat independently of these concerns. Not surprisingly, given the relativist thrust of his dissertation, these concepts all argue that there is no natural, unproblematic form of knowledge or expression. These propositions (except for his distinction between the classical and the romantic) also follow Eliot's distinctive rhetorical practice, in which he states then dissolves binary oppositions. Eliot repeatedly addresses his writing to the nature and articulation of knowledge, concerning himself not as much with the relationship between subject and object as with how a writer might *express* this relationship when attempting to communicate knowledge and feeling. One needs to begin here with Eliot's 1916 dissertation on Bradley, but with the caveat that the thesis didn't have much presence for scholars until its 1964 publication. New Critics bypassed it altogether, and this contributed to their seizing on some locally articulated ideas (such as the objective correlative, the dissociation of sensibility, and the impersonality of art) without taking into account the theory of knowledge that led to them.

The thesis attempts to provide a theory of perception/knowledge that balances personal subjectivity and crude realism, subjectivism and objectivism (as Schwartz points out, Eliot's poetic characters fail to negotiate this tricky balance). Objects have a real existence – but they are known only through a perceiver. There is no pure knowledge, and no purely existing object. As Eliot notes, knowledge is always knowledge *of* something, and, as soon as you are aware of something, it is mediated: "if we say feeling, we think of it as the feeling of a subject about an object. And this is only to make of feeling another kind of object" (*KE* 22). Thus, while there is a more primary state which Bradley and Eliot designate "immediate experience," in which one cannot distinguish subject from object, immediate experience cannot be represented. Knowledge, and the expression of knowledge, is always about separation, distance.

The poetic consequence is that emotion can be represented only as an object of knowledge. Art always has an "as if" character: unable to be direct, it always is about representation. By his terms Eliot is not anti-emotional; he opposes the illusion that emotions can be presented directly, and presents emotion as an epistemological issue. His criticism and poetry value awareness of emotion: "we know that those highly organized beings who are able to objectify their passions, and as passive spectators to contemplate their joys and torments, are also those who suffer and enjoy the most keenly" (*KE* 23). This, of course, resonates with his position in "Tradition and the Individual Talent," where he argues that "Poetry is not a turning loose of emotion, but an escape from emotion" (*SE* 10). The good poet, aware of how this interrelation happens, makes the slippage expressive. To pretend the disjunction does not exist is to act in bad faith, which is the problem of romanticism and its heirs. In one stage of an ongoing quarrel with Harold Monro, Eliot compares Monro to Jean de Bosschère, to Monro's discredit. The admirable quality of de Bosschère, Eliot maintains, was his "obstinate refusal to adulterate his poetic emotions with human emotions. Instead of refining ordinary human emotion . . . he aims direct at emotions of art" ("Reflections on Contemporary Poetry II" 133). Great writers create a "new art emotion" (*SE* 10), separate from the non-art emotion that may have instigated it.[3]

This theory of knowledge reaches far. The objective correlative, for example, which Eliot describes as "the only way of expressing emotion in the form of art," theorizes how to make one's emotion an object of knowledge for another person. Emotions need to anchor themselves in an object; the poet must find an objective correlative, "a set of objects, a situation, a chain of events which shall be the formula of that *particular* emotion; such that when the external facts, which must terminate in sensory experience, are given, the emotion is immediately evoked" (*SE* 124–25). As scholars have pointed out, Eliot was only one of several theorists who posited a causal connection between objects and emotions. But Eliot's version is stamped with his idiosyncrasies. The precision and necessity with which Eliot argues for this relationship come out of his professionalist mindset, and justify his belief that the relationship needs to be given in exact proportion, something which Donne was able to do. Citing Donne's lines about the "bracelet of bright hair about the bone," Eliot claims that

> the feeling and the material symbol preserve exactly their proper proportions. A poet of morbidly keen sensibilities but weak will might become absorbed in the hair to the exclusion of the original association which made it significant; a poet of imaginative or reflective power more than emotional power would endow the hair with ghostly or moralistic meaning. Donne sees the thing as it is. ("Reflections on Contemporary Poetry I" 118)

Romanticism, by contrast, lacks balance. Stressing feelings, it leaves them untethered to objects (the problem of naive realism is exactly the opposite). In an essay that lingers a little too long on the romanticism-based weaknesses of the minor critic George Wyndham, Eliot writes that "the only cure for Romanticism is to analyze it . . . . Romanticism is a short cut to the strangeness without the reality, and it leads its disciples only back upon themselves" (*SW* 31).

Eliot's often-cited but unverifiable assertions about the "dissociation of sensibility" come out of this complex theory of knowledge and emotional expression (they also have a political basis in social conditions, which I will address later). Only certain kinds of societies achieve a perfect unity of subject and object and an ability to link disparate experiences (what Eliot called "a mechanism of sensibility which could devour any kind of experience"). This state, Eliot initially believed, was last achieved by the metaphysical poets, after which a "dissociation of sensibility" set in (*SE* 247).

Before this time, sense and intellect could be aligned completely, resulting in a "quality of sensuous thought, or of thinking through the senses, or of the senses thinking" (*SW* 23).[4]

As one might expect, given Eliot's beliefs on the nature of perception, art could never be seamlessly inseparable from regular life. Art was never "natural," and thus it needed to exploit rather than hide its conventions. In the *Criterion* in 1924, Eliot noted that "the weakness of the Elizabethan drama is . . . not its conventions, but its lack of conventions":

> Anyone who has observed one of the great dancers of the Russian school will have observed that the man or the woman whom we admire is a being who exists only during the performances, that it is a personality, a vital flame which appears from nowhere, disappears into nothing and is complete and sufficient in its appearance. It is a conventional being, a being which exists only in and for the work of art which is the ballet. (*SE* 95)

The conventions of great art were always ones of simplification – the simplification characteristic of ritual. Eliot consistently gave this simplification both a social and an aesthetic component. He argued in 1923 that "the stage – not only in its remote origins, but always – is a ritual, and the failure of the contemporary stage to satisfy the craving for ritual is one of the reasons why it is not a living art" ("Dramatis Personae" 305–06). An enthusiast of the new ballet (he recalled restraining the "mirth" of audience members "with the point of an umbrella" during a performance of the *Rite of Spring*), Eliot argued that it presented a necessary "simplification of current life into something rich and strange" ("C [Oct. 1924]" 5; "London Letter [Aug. 1921]" 214).

Eliot's is a social theory of art. The audience participates in ritual, something which he saw happening, for example, in the music hall: "The working man who went to the music-hall and saw Marie Lloyd and joined in the chorus was himself performing part of the act; he was engaged in that collaboration of the audience with the artist which is necessary in all art and most obviously in dramatic art" (*SE* 407). Not only did Eliot believe that current middle-class art could never achieve this unity, he also believed in the necessity of a homogeneous society to make this kind of art possible. Eliot believed that contemporary conditions were not congenial to poetic drama; there was no contemporary audience that could create "a kind of unconscious cooperation" ("Poetic Drama" 635).

This sense of a collective leads to Eliot's most vexed opposition – the classical versus the romantic. His terms aren't primarily historical or even aesthetic designations; they are political/epistemological terms, with the romantic always denigrated in favor of the classical. This is one binary that Eliot did not problematize away into nothing. Romanticism for Eliot was not just an aesthetic category; more fundamentally, it was a political category aligned with the excesses of democracy: "We say democracy advisedly: that meanness of spirit, that egotism of motive, that incapacity for surrender or allegiance to something outside of oneself, which is a frequent symptom of the soul of man under democracy" ("C [Apr. 1924]" 235). Opposed to this was classicism, whose revival Eliot saw as necessary for the rejuvenation of art, and which took on an increasingly large place in his writing. Discussing T. E. Hulme's *Speculations*, Eliot saw Hulme's work as the symptom of "a new attitude of mind, which should be the twentieth-century mind, if the twentieth century is to have a mind of its own." Hulme's attraction was that he was "classical, reactionary, and revolutionary; he is the antipodes of the eclectic, tolerant, and democratic mind of the end of the last century" (231). But politics doesn't cover it completely: the split between romantic and classical forms of art was also an attack on unproblematized ideas of expressivism, and on lack of rigor and balance. Romanticism, in Eliot's system, had a lot to answer for.

The social and political ideas underlying the classical/romantic binary would, eventually, reorient Eliot's belief in the purity of criticism. Indeed, if the nature of a pure criticism dominates Eliot's early criticism, as time goes on it is eclipsed by the idea of a homogeneous society, in which people unconsciously work within a system of belief, act out roles, and participate in art. The idea of a homogeneous society had been on his mind all along, however.[5] As early as his 1917 "Reflections on *vers libre*," Eliot diagnosed *vers libre* as the symptom of a society in decay, to which he contrasted the advantages of a different kind of society: "Only in a closely-knit and homogeneous society, where many men are at work on the same problems, such a society as those which produced the Greek chorus, the Elizabethan lyric and the Troubadour canzone, will the development of such forms ever be carried to perfection" (*TCC* 189). This development of form in a homogeneous society demystifies Eliot's otherwise puzzling attachment to second-order artists and intellectuals. "Second-order minds" (*SW* xvi), indeed, are signs of and essential contributions to a healthy society.

Tradition

Virtually all of Eliot's major concepts are brought together in what remains the center of Eliot's criticism, his ideas on "tradition" as formulated in "Tradition and the Individual Talent." Eliot does not present tradition as a detachable, stand-alone concept, and he begins his complications immediately. The essay begins, as many of his do, with the current context, and an attack on amateurism: "In English writing we seldom speak of tradition, though we occasionally apply its name in deploring its absence . . . . You can hardly make the word agreeable to English ears without this comfortable reference to the reassuring science of archeology" (*SE* 3). Eliot then skewers his audience for disparaging the French for being "'more critical' than we," and because "we" (a disingenuous but rhetorically effective pronoun) "sometimes even plume ourselves a little with the fact, as if the French were the less spontaneous" (3). Unexamined criticism is not worth the writing, and from this Eliot turns to inspect the apparent virtues of originality and naturalness of tradition. To Eliot,

Tradition is a matter of much wider significance. It cannot be inherited, and if you want it you must obtain it by great labor. It involves, in the first place, the historical sense, which we may call nearly indispensable to anyone who would continue to be a poet beyond his twenty-fifth year; and the historical sense involves a perception, not only of the pastness of the past, but of its presence; the historical sense compels a man to write not merely with his own generation in his bones, but with a feeling that the whole of the literature of Europe from Homer and within it the whole of the literature of his own country has a simultaneous existence and composes a simultaneous order. (4)

Only trivial artists, bent on some mistaken notion of originality, try to escape this kind of comparative system. The poet "must be very conscious," and conscious that the "main current" of tradition "does not at all flow invariably through the most distinguished reputations" (5–6).

Eliot's essay also argues for what criticism should be. An awareness of tradition means that "No poet, no artist of any art, has his complete meaning alone. His significance, his appreciation is the appreciation of his relation to the dead poets and artists. You cannot value him alone; you must set him, for contrast and comparison, among the dead" (*SE* 4). This comparative awareness, as we have seen, springs from Eliot's ideas about the nature of perception and the problem of emotional expression. Positing what he asserts in many of his essays, Eliot argues that good art results in a "new art emotion" – "'emotion recollected in tranquility'" being "an inexact formula" (10). The distance also implies impersonality. The poet has "not a 'personality' to express, but a particular medium" (9): "What happens is a continual surrender of himself as he is at the moment to something which is more valuable. The progress of an artist is a continual self-sacrifice, a continual extinction of personality" (6–7). As Eliot would later write in "Shakespeare and the Stoicism of Seneca," "the great poet, in writing himself, writes his time" (*SE* 117). The chemical analogy Eliot uses to elucidate this "extinction" gives his essay the empiricist tone that many readers found so bracing after the great gulps of belles-lettres affect that had dominated criticism early in the century.

Eliot's idea of tradition as a system is given its most systematic expression in "Tradition and the Individual Talent," but the complicated foundation on which tradition rests supports virtually every one of his essays. As always, Eliot qualifies and entangles every idea. One doesn't get Eliot's "tradition" without his take on emotional expression, the nature of knowledge, and the perniciousness of amateurism. But, as is typical, Eliot directs more energy to clearing away false notions, and setting in place the correct terms for such clearing, than systematically building something new. This typical movement contributes to the self-consciousness and distancing that Eliot sees as central to artistic production. Nothing about art was ever "natural" for him. And for good reason. Without this realization, as Eliot insisted in the more occasional piece with which I began this essay, one is unable to "take literature *seriously*."

NOTES

1 Eliot is much richer than what is included in the essay collections, which encompass only a quarter of the roughly 200 listed in Donald Gallup's bibliography. Textual problems abound, and only Eliot's 1926 Clark lectures have been adequately edited, before which they existed only in manuscript form with little presence in scholarly understandings of Eliot. Until Ronald Schuchard's edited volumes come out, a sense of Eliot's oeuvre as a whole will remain elusive. For an exceptional reading of the issues that will be raised by a scholarly edition, see Schuchard (198–216) and Ricks.

2 "In Memory" 45; *SE* 21; *SW* 19; "C [Jan. 1925]" 162; "C [July 1924]" 373.

3 With this theory of the expression of knowledge, affect inevitably could not have a high place for Eliot in his criticism. Affect, as it was understood at the time, depended on an unproblematic understanding of the "personal" and of art as emotional expression.

4 In his 1926 Clark lectures Eliot placed the disintegration of intellect after Dante, and consequently radically revaluated Donne.

5 For a discussion of the continuity of the classic/romantic binary in Eliot and its social consequences, see Schuchard, especially 52–69.

REFERENCES AND FURTHER READING

Bergonzi, Bernard. *T. S. Eliot*. New York: Macmillan, 1972.

Brooker, Jewel Spears. *Mastery and Escape: T. S. Eliot and the Dialectic of Modernism*. Amherst: U of Massachusetts P, 1994.

Jeffreys, Mark. "The Rhetoric of Authority in T. S. Eliot's *Athenaeum* Reviews." *South Atlantic Review* 57 (1992): 93–108.

Materer, Timothy. "T. S. Eliot's Critical Program." *The Cambridge Companion to T. S. Eliot*. Ed. A. David Moody. New York: Cambridge UP, 1994. 48–59.

Menand, Louis. *Discovering Modernism: T. S. Eliot and His Context*. New York: Oxford UP, 1987.

Perkins, David. "Eliot's Criticism." *Central Institute of English and Foreign Languages Bulletin* 1 (1989): 120–32.

Ricks, Christopher B. *Decisions and Revisions in T. S. Eliot*. London: British Library, 2003.

Schuchard, Ronald. *Eliot's Dark Angel: Intersections of Life and Art*. New York: Oxford UP, 1999.

Schwartz, Sanford. "Beyond the 'Objective Correlative': Eliot and the Objectification of Emotion." *T. S. Eliot: Man and Poet*. Ed. Laura Cowan. Vol. 1. Orono, ME: National Poetry Foundation, 1990. 321–41.

23
He Do the Critic in Different Voices: The Literary Essays after 1927

Richard Badenhausen

Writing less than two years before his death, in a preface to a revised 1964 edition of *The Use of Poetry and the Use of Criticism*, T. S. Eliot complained about the staying power of his early literary criticism, a development expressed both in the preference of anthologists for essays like "Tradition and the Individual Talent" (1919) and the tendency of professors to overemphasize some of the more influential literary theories unfolded in those essays. This single-minded focus on work that was, in his words, both "juvenile" and the "product of immaturity" (*UPUC* vii–viii) exasperated Eliot, and so he was using this moment to express hope that some of the later prose might one day achieve similar renown. Readers, he feared, had a somewhat narrow understanding of his critical positions; and he sensed, too, to his own frustration, that he was not fully in control of the reception of his work and image. These concerns were among Eliot's preoccupations throughout his life.

Yet Eliot had no one to blame but himself for this development, which evolved over the years for a number of reasons. First, the early criticism is very different in tone and purpose from Eliot's later prose output. Attempting as a young writer to make a name for himself as an unknown foreigner in literary London, Eliot consciously adopted an aggressive manner, took iconoclastic positions with out-of-favor writers such as Donne and Jonson, and attacked revered texts like *Hamlet* in ways that were sure to make waves. For example, he called that most famous of plays the "'Mona Lisa' of literature," while also suggesting that it was ultimately an "artistic failure" and that Shakespeare was not up to the challenge of the material (*SE* 123–24). Eliot also had a particular talent for crafting clever-sounding expressions that seemed to offer special insights into texts – "objective correlative," "dissociation of sensibility," and "impersonal theory of poetry," to name a few – what he would late in his career refer to as those "few notorious phrases which have had a truly embarrassing success in the world" (*OPP* 106). Although this early writing served often as simply a way to pay the bills, Eliot was clearly after a reputation that would come from taking intentionally provocative stances in an assertive voice that caught readers' attention.

A Companion to T. S. Eliot, First Edition. Edited by David E. Chinitz.
© 2014 John Wiley & Sons, Ltd. Published 2014 by John Wiley & Sons, Ltd.

Yet after that reputation had been secured, Eliot adopted by middle age a more sedate, reflective tone suitable for the situations of his later pieces – many of which began as lectures – even though there were occasional eruptions of the familiar antagonistic posture in the later social criticism. Of the 16 essays that make up *On Poetry and Poets* (1957), for example, 11 of them started as addresses, while all 10 of the post-1927 essays collected in *To Criticize the Critic* (1965) originated as public talks.

The second cause of the ubiquitousness of Eliot's early essays was his habit of constantly republishing such pieces. In the case of "Tradition," it reappeared in volumes of Eliot's work on no fewer than four separate occasions after its initial appearance in the *Egoist*, most often in collections of his prose produced under his direction or that of his friend, roommate, and editor John Hayward, not to mention the more than three dozen separate translated versions of the essay or its position as a staple in anthologies of critical theory like Edwin Burgum's *The New Criticism* (1930) or the third edition of the very successful reader *The Great Critics* (1951), edited by James Harry Smith and Edd Winfield Parks. The essay stood out in other ways, as well: in the three editions of *Selected Essays* it was positioned first, while in Hayward's two edited volumes, *Points of View* (1941) and *Selected Prose* (1953), it was one of the few to be included in its entirety. This strategy suggested its importance and encouraged readers to interpret later criticism through the lens of "Tradition." When Eliot wasn't republishing early essays, he was spending plenty of time mulling over their implications, as at the start of *After Strange Gods* (1934), where he hoped to reformulate some of what he considered to be the more unsatisfactory ideas from "Tradition" (15). Similarly, his 1956 lecture at the University of Minnesota, which would eventually become "The Frontiers of Criticism," begins with a consideration of the early piece "The Function of Criticism" (1923).

Such a habit once led Tony Sharpe to remark that he could think of no other poet who had "during his own lifetime published so little so much" (160), though he had in mind Eliot's poetry more than his prose. While the entire body of serious, non-dramatic poetry in *The Complete Poems and Plays* runs to approximately 3,500 *lines*, his prose output exceeded 1,000 pieces, and ran the gamut from book reviews and straightforward examinations of single authors to more comprehensive considerations of larger artistic, cultural, and religious issues, to introductions of books by others. In addition, Donald Gallup's bibliography lists in excess of 130 letters to the editor, all but a handful of which were published after 1927, in that period when Eliot's role as "smiling public man" – to borrow a phrase from Yeats – really began to emerge in full force. Readers of the later prose should keep in mind that they cannot separate that work from the earlier literary criticism, not just because Eliot himself was at times intentionally writing against the ideas and tone of that criticism but because he also found himself either extending some of his early theories or adapting them to fit his later interests and positions.

While 1927 might seem an arbitrary date for carving up Eliot's literary criticism into two periods, it is a convenient one, marking as it does Eliot's conversion to Anglo-Catholicism and his taking of British citizenship, two steps signifying new personal paths that would also have a discernible effect on his writing. Indeed, the period immediately following Eliot's confirmation in the Church of England would see the publication of such explicitly religious poems as "Journey of the Magi" (1927) and *Ash-Wednesday* (1930), a long essay on the Christian poet Dante (1929), an extended meditation on the position and future of the Anglican Church in "Thoughts after Lambeth" (1931), and a reflection on the challenges of faith in the modern world through the figure of Pascal (1931).

The effects of Eliot's religious beliefs upon his work go way beyond the scope of this chapter, but there are a few points worth making. First, Eliot cultivated through much of his life a fascination with asceticism, suffering, and martyrdom. The later literature treats this subject explicitly in plays like *Murder in the Cathedral* (1935) and *The Cocktail Party* (1949), both of which ask what it means to stand alone and suffer with one's God. Eliot believed firmly that the Christian life should not be an easy one; rather, "[t]hought, study, mortification, [and] sacrifice" should be featured elements of the faith, which in turn might bring more people to the Church (*SE* 329). Such a context helps gloss Eliot's 1930 romanticized reading of Baudelaire's ability to attract "pain to himself" and then "study his suffering" (374). This example, like many others, demonstrates how hard it is to take the faith component out of Eliot's criticism. He even argued in "To Criticize the Critic" (1961) that it was "impossible to fence off *literary* criticism from criticism on other grounds, and that moral, religious and social judgments cannot be wholly excluded" (*TCC* 25). Second, Eliot's conversion might at least partially account for the change in tone in the later essays as well as an accompanying expansion in focus beyond some of the narrow concerns of the early work. It would be hard for Eliot not to think in broader terms, given the hope he articulates at the end of "Thoughts After Lambeth": that "Faith may be preserved alive through the dark ages before us; to renew and rebuild civilization, and save the World from suicide" (*SE* 342).

Ultimately, the later essays reflect an attitude about the function of literature and literary criticism that is captured perfectly in a 1932 reading of romantic poetry in which Eliot argues that "Any radical change in poetic form is likely to be the symptom of some very much deeper change in society and in the individual" (*UPUC* 66–67). In such work, Eliot often seems unable to avoid the realization that literature, individuals, and culture are inseparable, and that to discuss them otherwise would be to lose sight of the great challenges and possibilities of art in the twentieth century. Ultimately, we find Eliot in these essays arguing that literature has a fundamental place in the world because it is *useful*. He's perfectly willing to explore texts on aesthetic grounds, but just as often we find him coming back to a utilitarian argument. Such a position found its most extensive expression in the 1945 essay "The Social Function of Poetry," where he proposes that since emotion and feeling are common to all people, poetry can unify populations by evoking these commonalities (*OPP* 19); that great poetry also upholds a people's language, which in turn supports the culture and keeps it from being absorbed by another, stronger culture (21); and that vibrant poetry may allow work of European cultures to stimulate each other (23). In an essay on Byron, he sums up this dynamic as an "undeliberate collaboration between a great many people talking a living language and a very few people writing it" (201). The very survival of a language depends on this interaction.

This model has important implications for Eliot's reading of individual authors, for one of the ways he came to test their greatness was through their ability to participate in this exchange among people, culture, and literature. Those who helped advance the relationship were judged positively, while those who disrupted it – D. H. Lawrence, for example – were condemned. Thus, in "What Dante Means to Me" (1950), Eliot reads that medieval poet's work as demonstrating his ability "to find words for the inarticulate, to capture those feelings which people can hardly even feel, because they have no words for them," which has the ultimate effect of expanding the range of people's emotional response to the world (*TCC* 134) – a key benefit in a modern culture deadened by technology, industrialism, and spiritual emptiness. Dante's greatness turns on the rewards his treatment of language bestows upon the world. This preoccupation emerges also from Eliot's concern that he lived in "an age of uncertainty" where there was hardly any common ground (*OPP* 114), and in a modern period of literature in which there was no "common style," which helped exacerbate the "difficulty of communication" (188). Poetry that helped make some connections across these gulfs was work to be lauded and impelled Eliot toward a very different position than he had taken up in the early criticism, where he was just as often creating divides. Finally, this thread in his later essays grew out of Eliot's belief that in the fourth decade of the twentieth century "[n]ever were there fewer settled assumptions as to what poetry is, or why it comes about, or what it is for" (*UPUC* 17–18). It is also almost impossible, of course, to read these literary evaluations outside the context of a Europe ravaged by international conflict, with the poet searching for some kind of common ground through language as he observes and laments the many "falling towers" around him.

Attributing such a role to the poet lines Eliot up unexpectedly with the romantics who preceded him, in spite of the anti-romantic strain in his work. Reading Eliot arguing in "The Music of Poetry" (1942) that "poetry must not stray too far from the ordinary everyday language which we use and hear" and that the "music of poetry, then, must be a music latent in the common speech of its time . . . latent in the common speech of the poet's *place*" (*OPP* 29, 31) is somewhat shocking, given the previous attacks on Wordsworth and his circle. Those poets had not fit into Eliot's conception of literature in the early criticism for a variety of reasons, including their resistance to external, stabilizing systems, their interest in liberty, their supposed excessive eruptions of personality and egotism, and their rejection of tradition and attendant glorification of originality, imagination, and genius. Yet in light of the context established earlier in this essay, the alignment with romantic conceptions of language, culture, and place makes sense.

Eliot's evolving attitude toward Wordsworth highlights the fact that much of his prose criticism involves a struggle to understand influential precursors and his position relative to those earlier examples. This reminds us that Eliot most often wrote his literary criticism very self-consciously from the stance of the practicing poet, and that such a position influenced how his discussions of individual authors unfolded. At the start of his second essay on Milton (1947), for example, Eliot points out that writing criticism as a "practitioner" causes one to pay less attention to the author and more to the poem, to ask what is the "*use*" of the previous work "to poets writing to-day," and to try to make the "old masterpiece actual, give it contemporary importance" (*OPP* 147). Judging greatness in a writer on the basis of the lessons poets might learn from them, he elevates Dante and Chaucer, but finds Milton wanting due to his various idiosyncrasies (155).

Influence, of course, can work positively and negatively. While Spenser helped make Milton possible (*OPP* 58), Shakespeare and Milton made poetic drama and epic unattainable for succeeding generations, until the "danger" of imitation had passed (150). Positive influences make the ground more fertile for subsequent achievement by advancing the language, while negative influences function retrospectively as blocking figures for future writers struggling to get beyond the disruption of the anomalous example. One of the most revealing discussions of influence in his late criticism occurs in the opening four pages of "What Dante Means to Me," where Eliot reviews the various poets who have helped shape his work at different stages and the variety of ways in which those pressures have operated. Elsewhere, Eliot draws up a more contentious model of influence that turns on the idea of maturation, so that young, immature, "adolescent" writers engage in a thoughtless and emotional identification with a strong precursor. Later, they begin to develop the "power of self-criticism" that helps facilitate the broadening of one's taste (*OPP* 208) and finally reach a mature stage in which the "critical faculties" (*UPUC* 26) are fully awake. By applying these critical faculties to a work under consideration, the mature writer is able to separate that work from himself, a distance he could not achieve in the earlier stage of identification.

This model, which largely anticipates Harold Bloom's paradigm of psychological struggle in *The Anxiety of Influence*, was laid out most explicitly by Eliot in "Goethe as the Sage" (1955) and in his introduction to *The Use of Poetry and the Use of Criticism* (1933), but it informs many of his later discussions of his own authorial history and is also applied more broadly to different periods of literature. Thus, in "What is a Classic?" (1945), he argues that a "classic can only occur when a civilization is mature," by which he means that an evolution and sophistication in language, literature, and culture has reached its zenith (*OPP* 55). The accomplishments of Shakespeare, then, were facilitated by the work performed by predecessors who lived and wrote during a less fully developed period. This preoccupation with influence was also one of the few topics that would bring Eliot out of his reserved persona in the later prose, generating interesting reflections on his own influences, like a comment about the "invasion of the adolescent self by Shelley" (28) or his confession in his essay on Yeats (1940) that "only those who have toiled with language know the labour and constancy required to free oneself from such influences" (261).

In other places, Eliot considers his creative practices in a much more overt fashion, which suggests that the writer was more willing to explore personal issues in the post-1927 prose and that these occasions played an important role in helping Eliot understand his own writing process. The later criticism is quite direct in its contemplation of what Eliot called his "private poetry-workshop" (*OPP* 106). Early essays like "*Ulysses*, Order, and Myth" (1923) and "Marie Lloyd" (1923) can be read as providing oblique observations, respectively, about Eliot's poetic practices in *The Waste Land* and what he hoped to achieve in poetic drama, but they approach the topic of Eliot's own methods rather indirectly. "The Three Voices of Poetry" (1953), on the other hand, presents a detailed and extended first-person discussion of his previous work that is filled with fascinating asides, like his confession that the commission to write *The Rock* (1934) "came at a moment when I seemed to myself to have exhausted my meagre poetic gifts, and to have nothing more to say," and that the pressure of a performance deadline thus had "the effect that vigorous cranking sometimes has upon a motor car when the battery is run down" (*OPP* 91). In the essay, Eliot identifies three different poetic voices that are distinguished by their distance from the writer's voice and by the audience for whom the poetry is written. Thus the first voice represents the poet speaking to himself, the second the voice of the poet when he addresses a reader, and the third the voice of an imagined dramatic character who is addressing other characters. The discussion grows out of Eliot's experience writing for the stage and his difficulty in thinking about his relationship with the dramatic character. Whereas the poet's relationship to his non-dramatic poetic characters could be somewhat neatly tied up in the "impersonal theory of poetry," in "Three Voices" Eliot seems to understand that the dramatist's relationship with his characters is more complicated.

This discussion culminates in one of the most confessional moments in Eliot's late criticism, when he uses a passage from a lecture by the German poet Gottfried Benn as a jumping-off point to speculate about initiating imaginative invention. He leaves behind the consideration of audience that preoccupies him for much of the essay and focuses upon the writer, alone with his words at the start of the creative process. At that moment, the author couldn't care less whether anyone hears or understands his work; rather, he

> is oppressed by a burden which he must bring to birth in order to obtain relief. . . .
> [H]e is haunted by a demon, a demon against which he feels powerless, because in its
> first manifestation it has no face, no name, nothing; and the words, the poem he makes,
> are a kind of form of exorcism of this demon . . . he is going to all that trouble, not in
> order to communicate with anyone, but to gain relief from acute discomfort. (*OPP* 98)

This is remarkable on a number of fronts. First, the charged language describing demons, burdens, discomfort, and exorcism strikes a very different chord than most of the reserved prose of Eliot's essays from this period. Second, the direct revelation of the struggles Eliot faced as a writer signals a willingness to consider more overtly the challenges of his poetic practice, which he had only hinted at in earlier essays.

"Tradition and the Individual Talent," for example, tries to separate "the man who suffers and the mind which creates" (*SE* 8). Finally, the self-definition of the artist prostrate before an almost overwhelming challenge sets a strikingly different tone than one finds in the authoritative, commanding pronouncements of the early criticism. And yet it all seems more real and somehow more human, a sense that Eliot reinforces when he concludes his account by noting that once the writer has finally arranged the words in the proper order, "he may experience a moment of exhaustion, of appeasement, of absolution, and of something very near annihilation, which is in itself indescribable" (*OPP* 98). In this rendering, the creative process is one that is dangerous and even potentially destructive, yet it is also one that can potentially bring the writer to a state of peace and even grace, a condition suggested by the religious terminology. The model corresponds neatly with the type of post-conversion existence that Eliot had been leading, one of self-imposed asceticism that had as its goal the religious insight that can come, at least in his mind, from self-discipline, study, and suffering.

Eliot's reflections about his own poetry also encouraged him to associate his literary criticism with his verse. He claimed that critics who are also poets construct critical theories "with a view to justifying their poetic practice" (*UPUC* 20) and that his best literary criticism "consists of essays on poets and poetic dramatists who had influenced" him (*OPP* 106), a statement he would repeat regularly. It made sense that Eliot, a poet who wrote so much literary criticism, would spend time thinking about its place in the world, its effects on his own work, and its ultimate usefulness. Although he was sometimes prone to making rather exalted pronouncements, such as "literary criticism . . . is an instinctive activity of the civilized mind" (*TCC* 19) – a dictum reminiscent of comments made in early essays like "Tradition and the Individual Talent," where we learn that "criticism is as inevitable as breathing" (*SE* 3) – Eliot did spend quite a bit of time in the later essays thinking about the utility of literary criticism. Throughout *The Use of Poetry and the Use of Criticism*, Eliot argues that criticism and poetry work in concert in important ways, all of which center on advancing the language and collective thoughts of a people. More particularly, criticism can help readers "recognize [their] affinity with one poet" (*TCC* 21) and, if it is particularly good (by which he means "universal" or capable of transcending its own historical period), it can assist future generations in advancing their literature and critical acuity (17). Such beneficial outcomes suggest that readings of Eliot's prose and poetry can be enlarged by considering their relation to each other.

Eliot continued to theorize frequently about poetic drama – its form, its special advantages, and its effect upon the audience. In the late major essay "Poetry and Drama" (1951), Eliot opens by expressing surprise at finding that so much of his criticism of the previous three decades had been devoted to drama; but his astonishment is difficult to fathom, especially because he had spent much of his life writing plays. Whereas the early criticism on drama was devoted almost exclusively to Renaissance playwrights – especially their particular qualities and their relationship to

Shakespeare – the later essays tended to focus more on the benefits of verse drama and how these allowed the writer to achieve certain effects that were not attainable in prose drama. In "Poetry and Drama," Eliot argues that the rhythm of the verse in poetic drama acts unconsciously on the audience and has a powerful effect upon their emotions, a result he demonstrates through a reading of the opening scene of *Hamlet*, which now receives more favorable attention. In that scene, a "musical design" created by the poetry has "checked and accelerated the pulse of our emotion without our knowing it" (*OPP* 76). For Eliot, it is this *intensification* of the dramatic experience that is the main benefit of the form, and one that can't be achieved in prose drama, no matter how great the writer (Ibsen and Chekhov are mentioned as examples). As in some of the other late essays, "Poetry and Drama" contains an extended meditation upon Eliot's own work – in this case his first three full-length plays – which offers an extremely direct critique of his own successes and failures, as well as account of his creative method. Like the "Three Voices" essay, this consideration of his writing culminates in a passage that posits a very difficult world in which art is one of the few tools that enable us to overcome the daily challenges embedded in life. In Eliot's words, it is "the function of art, in imposing a credible order upon ordinary reality, and thereby eliciting some perception of order *in* reality, to bring us to a condition of serenity, stillness, and reconciliation" (*OPP* 87).

The portion of "Poetry and Drama" devoted to *Murder in the Cathedral* discusses, among other topics, Eliot's dependence on the chorus in that play.[1] This section of the essay is important not only because it reveals what had attracted Eliot to that special device but because it signals his continued interest in Greek drama, a pursuit that had originally emerged out of Eliot's study of Greek literature, his aspirations eventually to write for the stage, and the general revival of interest in the form due to Gilbert Murray's many verse translations of the originals. The chorus was particularly attractive to Eliot for two reasons. First, as he remarked elsewhere, it enabled "poets with no skill in the theatre, to make the most of their accomplishments, and thereby conceal some of their defects" (*OPP* 176). While Eliot is here adopting that overly modest voice that sometimes surfaces in the later prose, he is also offering an honest appraisal of the limitations of a play like *Murder in the Cathedral*, in which fairly stilted male characters surround a rich, vibrant chorus of Women of Canterbury. Second, the chorus of women, according to Eliot, "reflect[ed] in their emotion the significance of the action" (81), an effect that echoes an idea established in "John Marston" (discussed below) that poetic drama operates on two different levels, each reinforcing the other. This flexibility and accessibility of poetic drama is an important component of the form, for Eliot increasingly hoped later in his career that his writing would have an effect on as broad an audience as possible – another key change from his *Waste Land* days. Eliot believed that unlike "most poetry," dramatic verse "has as its function the making [of] an immediate, collective impression upon a large number of people gathered together to look at an imaginary episode acted upon a stage" (17).

In "To Criticize the Critic," Eliot tells his audience that in rereading his criticism on drama, he was much more pleased with the essays on Shakespeare's contemporaries than with those on Shakespeare himself. Characteristically, he does not identify specific features of those essays that make them superior; rather, he launches into an explanation of how those Elizabethan and Jacobean dramatists were much more influential to his work than Shakespeare. It was by those authors, he wrote, that "my imagination had been stimulated, my sense of rhythm trained, and my emotions fed" (*TCC* 18). One representative essay is the 1934 discussion of John Marston, where Eliot continues to explore one of his favorite topics, the differences between prose and verse drama. Here, he identifies the distinguishing feature of poetic drama as "a kind of doubleness in the action, as if it took place on two planes at once" (*SE* 229). This key idea, which would inform Eliot's own experiments on stage, is amplified later in the paragraph as an "under-pattern" that exists beneath the more obvious "theatrical" layer of the play. In the case of Marston, this gets expressed through an "underlying serenity" below the surface of the play that serves as a striking counterpoint to the "ferocity and horror" of the action in *The Wonder of Women* (232). In other cases, the two levels consist of the conscious existence of the characters and a deeper reality that is harder to express. This idea of doubleness in drama is developed in a number of essays, including most notably introductions to G. Wilson Knight's *The Wheel of Fire* (1930) and S. L. Bethell's *Shakespeare and the Popular Dramatic Tradition* (1944).

Because Eliot's conception of literature was animated by very particular ideas about tradition and history, he often characterized different literary periods through generalizations that tell us more about Eliot than about the eras themselves. He found the Middle Ages extremely attractive for their hierarchical society that ensured relative order; he located a unity in the culture that turned on religious purpose supposedly infusing everyday life, which allowed artists to employ a common language in their attempts to reinforce that effect. The longing Eliot expresses in his description of this period grows largely out of those medieval qualities he sees lacking in contemporary Europe and his frustration as a writer trying to operate in a less unified and more diverse culture. Eliot views the English Renaissance as a culmination of certain trends that end up facilitating a flowering of artistic accomplishment notable for artists collaborating together, for the maturity of its verse, and for Shakespeare's superior achievement. While the culture is far more chaotic than that of the Middle Ages, and the Elizabethans themselves are unaware of the climate of "social decay and change" (*SE* 178), Eliot sees this tension expressed productively in the drama of the period, even though he would always be bothered by the resultant "lack of conventions" this circumstance generated (94). In his later criticism, Eliot mostly held to the idea offered in "The Metaphysical Poets" (1921) that a "dissociation of sensibility" settled in during the seventeenth century, a condition in which thought and feeling were dislocated from each other and which was aggravated by Milton and Dryden. The 1936 essay on Milton still insists that we have yet to recover from the disruption (*OPP* 145) – a position Eliot modifies, however, when he revisits Milton in 1947 (152–53).

Not surprisingly, Eliot finds much that is attractive in the eighteenth century, for he projected onto its neoclassical writers both aspirations he had for his own poetic age and personal traits that he saw in himself. In "Johnson as Critic and Poet" (1944), for example, Eliot envisions a period in which "Eccentricity or uncouthness was reprehensible: a poet was prized, not for his invention of an original form of speech, but by his contribution to a common language" (*OPP* 165). Eliot tended to criticize the romantics for all sorts of faults, some of which have already been mentioned, though perhaps the greatest was their inability to contain excessive emotion in the form of their poetry, due in part to a rejection of tradition and an over-enthusiasm for originality. While admitting to finding this verse attractive as a young man, Eliot discovered many reasons as a maturing writer to cast aside such poets, as well as their Victorian successors, whose "philosophy of life," he writes in "Goethe as the Sage," "came to seem to me flimsy, their religious foundations insecure" (209–10).

One of Eliot's most interesting moves in his later prose was his attempt to reinsert himself into the American literary tradition after having spent so much time divorcing himself from it as a younger writer. While I have taken up this topic in detail elsewhere, the gist of the argument is that Eliot went to great lengths in his early life and criticism to distance himself from his homeland (Badenhausen). This pattern continued in mid-career in a cluster of essays around 1926–28 that use the figure of Whitman to reaffirm Eliot's antipathy toward American literature – a note struck particularly strongly in "Whitman and Tennyson" (1926) and his introduction to *The Selected Poems of Ezra Pound* (1928). Late in life, however, in remarks eventually published as "The Influence of Landscape upon the Poet" (1960), he attempts to reposition himself as a New England poet, in the line of Frost and Lowell. Here and elsewhere, Eliot speaks much more respectfully of the American literary tradition, writing key late essays on Poe and on American literature and language (both collected in *To Criticize the Critic*), and even an introduction to an edition of *The Adventures of Huckleberry Finn* (1950).

In his evaluation of individual writers, Eliot tended to use a variety of criteria that echoed his method of assessing literary eras and native traditions. At the top of the list was the issue of wholeness or unity, which means a consistent pattern in all the work even while that work is developing toward maturity. The supreme example of this quality is always Shakespeare, which is why Eliot consistently encourages readers to make their way through all of that poet's work, for the "whole of Shakespeare's work is *one* poem" (*SE* 179). In "Goethe as the Sage," he locates as the two distinguishing criteria of greatness in European writers permanence and universality; in other words, the great authors are those who are meaningful and influential to readers abroad as well as at home, and who make a lasting impression on successive generations of audiences. The only three who fulfill these criteria completely are Dante, Shakespeare, and Goethe (*OPP* 212). In two major essays on Dante in 1929 and 1950, Eliot explores the Italian poet's key features, focusing in the later essay upon three elements: his practice of the *craft* of poetry (*TCC* 132), the breadth of his *"emotional range"* (134), and his approachability, so that readers may make him their own (134–35). Importantly, Eliot believed Dante's poetry to be "the most persistent and deepest influence" on his own poetry (125). Virgil also comes in for high praise in "What is a Classic?," originally delivered as a lecture for the Virgil Society. Here Eliot identities three qualities in a classic – maturity, comprehensiveness, and universality – all of which happen to be present in Virgil. In order, these terms roughly suggest that a civilization, language, and writer mature simultaneously; that the work expresses the range of a people's feelings while also generating responses from the widest range of readers; and that the work, transcending the local and the national, has meaning across languages and cultures.

In his readings of individual authors, Eliot continues urging readers to separate the biography of a writer from the evaluation of his work. While the "impersonal theory of poetry" first established in the "Tradition" essay and other early pieces still partly underlies this argument, also relevant now is Eliot's belief that practicing poets will most benefit from a focused consideration of the work, and that distracting concerns about the authors' lives are best left to literary historians. Nevertheless, Eliot himself falls prey at times to the tendency he criticizes, as when he complains about how the life of a writer like Shelley gets in the way of dispassionate criticism, only then to attack him as "humourless, pedantic, self-centered, and sometimes almost a blackguard" (*UPUC* 80). For an even more unrestrained rant that begins with what can only be termed phrenological – and therefore pointedly personal – criticism, readers should consult his 1937 essay on Byron, even though Eliot laughably concludes the essay by assuring readers that he's not talking about the "private life" (*OPP* 206). Eliot somewhat implausibly defended moments like these by reminding readers that he is not elevating the importance of personality, but is rather "speaking of the men as they exist in their writings" (213), a defense he repeats in both "Goethe as the Sage" and "Byron" (206). Elsewhere he judges the "intensity" of the work on its relationship to the personality (*SE* 172–73, 179–80).

I have represented Eliot in this chapter largely through prose that is widely available in collected form, even though there exists another, perhaps more interesting or at least less predictable Eliot in his uncollected writings, one who will emerge more forcefully with the publication of Eliot's complete prose under the editorial directorship of Ronald Schuchard. That project, which should take the better part of a decade, will bring together over 700 previously uncollected prose pieces and will offer a much fuller portrait of Eliot as an essayist, a picture that is only sometimes hinted at in the more well-known criticism. There are moments that place Eliot in some unexpected locations, such as his dismissal of authorial intention in 1942 (*OPP* 30–31) and his comfort with letting the reader determine the meaning of a work (113). But perhaps the most representative moment, one I will leave you with, occurs in his marvelous late essay on Yeats. There Eliot finds himself writing as a very public man on the wrong side of 50, expressing astonishment (and perhaps even a bit of envy) at Yeats's capacity in his later poetry for brutal honesty and his ability to avoid the temptation so dangerous to aging poets of "becoming dignified, of becoming public figures with only a public existence – coat-racks hung with decorations and distinctions" (*OPP* 257). It is a struggle Eliot himself lived in his own writing and life.

NOTE

1 On Eliot's use of the chorus, see ELIOT'S 1930s
   PLAYS: *THE ROCK, MURDER IN THE CATHE-
   DRAL, AND THE FAMILY REUNION*.

REFERENCES AND FURTHER READING

Badenhausen, Richard. "In Search of 'Native Moments': T. S. Eliot (Re)Reads Walt Whitman." *South Atlantic Review* 57 (1992): 77–91.

Bush, Ronald. *T. S. Eliot: A Study in Character and Style*. New York: Oxford UP, 1984.

Gallup, Donald. *T. S. Eliot: A Bibliography*. London: Faber, 1969.

Kermode, Frank. Introduction. *Selected Prose of T. S. Eliot*. New York: Harcourt, 1975. 11–27.

Raine, Craig. *T. S. Eliot*. New York: Oxford UP, 2006.

Sharpe, Tony. "T. S. Eliot and Ideas of *Oeuvre*." *Modernist Writers and the Marketplace*. Ed. Ian Willison, Warwick Gould, and Warren Chernaik. New York: St. Martin's, 1996. 151–70.

24

In Times of Emergency: Eliot's Social Criticism

John Xiros Cooper

T. S. Eliot is now primarily remembered as one of the twentieth century's greatest poets. In his day, however, he was also an influential critic, a distinguished literary theorist, and a social and cultural critic of considerable renown. This chapter will examine what he had to say about culture and society. But first let's be clear about what we mean by these words. *Culture* should be understood primarily in its anthropological sense, denoting not simply the self-conscious productions of formal art, say operas, sonnets, and postmodern novels, but, as Eliot wrote, "all the characteristic activities and interests of a people" (*CC* 104) – activities as diverse as football, stand-up comedy, and going to college. We should also be careful with the word *society*. Eliot himself always took care to distinguish very clearly the day-to-day organization of social life from politics and government.[1] Inevitably the political must, to some extent, always intrude on the social, but this is not what primarily interested Eliot. Like Michel Foucault, but lacking the desolate determinism, he saw society as a complex web of activities, interactions, and meanings that should not be reduced to the formal structures of political power and authority. As Jeffrey Perl has put it, Eliot's politics were, in a word, "antipolitical": for him "political controversies were at best diversions 'from things of more importance'" (93; *CC* 158). It is with these so-called "things of more importance" in culture and society that this chapter is concerned.

Eliot was born in the late nineteenth century and lived through the barbarisms of war, genocide, and political upheaval in the twentieth. His sense of the world was pervaded by an awareness that he and his fellow citizens were living in a time of emergency (*CC* 5). This perception colored all his work, from the fractured consciousness of *The Waste Land* to his plea for the unity of European civilization after World War II. Disturbance and turmoil were not limited, in Eliot's view, to the larger historical events such as world wars, economic depressions, and mass executions. Personal and domestic life was also subject to general disarray. Social mobility, voluntary or forced migration, the reconfiguring of identities, the loosening of both traditional bonds and the bonding rituals of kith and kin all contributed to contradictory

A Companion to T. S. Eliot, First Edition. Edited by David E. Chinitz.
© 2014 John Wiley & Sons, Ltd. Published 2014 by John Wiley & Sons, Ltd.

impulses in individual lives. Liberation from inherited attachments often led to social isolation and new levels of anxiety. These, in turn, gave rise to new kinds of behavior and opened possibilities for fashioning new values or for finding oneself in a valueless world. In most respects, the muddles and promises of personal life were far more significant than the often distant and inscrutable operations of history over which people have very little power or control.

Eliot's thoughts about culture and society cannot be neatly separated from his literary work. All his thinking begins with the elementary anthropological observation that culture and society form an indivisible unity. This does not mean all societies are unified and harmonious, but that all social and cultural manifestations, including economic and artistic ones, are meaningfully related to each other. And the inner world of individuals, that is to say, their psychological and emotional well-being, is also meaningfully entangled in, say, the mechanization of work, or something a government might call a war on terror. One corollary of this general outlook is that a society cannot have great art without complementary achievements in many other areas – philosophy, for example, or a vital civic culture, or the cultivation of a good ear for music. Dante was a great poet because, as Eliot wrote in an early essay, he was sustained by a great public philosophy that was itself knitted to a common religion. Without that common culture to sustain him Dante would have shared the fate of a William Blake, a genius no doubt, but one left to his own devices to cobble together a makeshift mythology. Blake's exertions were symptomatic of both his genius and the more general failure of his culture and society (*SW* 155–58).

This generalization developed from Eliot's early introduction to the field of anthropology at Harvard University, where he was educated.[2] When one studies the culture and society of an ancient people, such phenomena as the rhythms of its music, the preparation of certain foods, and the character of its religion cannot be separated out and studied independently of one another. They are of a piece, and they remain that way no matter how developed or complex a society becomes. This was Eliot's greatest insight in his cultural and social criticism. The twentieth century accelerated the categorizing of knowledge brought about by growing specialization. A literary critic, for example, may not be able to see that changing attitudes toward and treatment of language in lyric poetry in a particular period may be related to what a sociologist might study in the area of changing sexual behavior, or a metaphysician see as a formal rift between word and thing. Eliot was never blind in that way. Blind he may have been about many other things, but the complex unity of social and cultural life was not one of them.

Eliot's interdisciplinary temper is visible in all his critical work, from his literary criticism right through to his more formal works on social themes. He articulates his general approach clearly in the first paragraph of *The Idea of a Christian Society*. Justifying his venture into social criticism, he writes that the subject

> could, no doubt, [be] handle[d] much better were I a profound scholar in any of several fields. But I am not writing for scholars, but for people like myself; some defects may

be compensated by some advantages; and what one must be judged by, scholar or no, is not particularized knowledge but one's total harvest of thinking, feeling, living and observing human beings. (*CC* 5)

His thoughts on society are concentrated in three works that make explicit his social vision. First, there is the intemperate *After Strange Gods* (1934), then *The Idea of a Christian Society* (1939) and, finally, *Notes towards the Definition of Culture* (1948). The last two put into more systematic form ideas about culture and society that are scattered here and there in essays, in letters, in his editorials in the *Criterion*, and in his many public lectures later in life. An extended study of his social criticism would, of course, examine all of these various forums. *After Strange Gods* need not detain us. It is a work that was delivered first as a series of lectures in Virginia and never reprinted after its initial publication in 1934. Now quite difficult to find except in the larger research libraries, its usefulness is limited by its self-righteous tone and the relative crudeness of its thought and language. These qualities may bare to public view a low side of Eliot's personality, but the book does not contribute a great deal to an exposition of his ideas. For our purposes, a look at his two other important publications will suffice.

The French Connection – and the English

First, though, we need to look a little at the intellectual sources that supply the background for these works. In his excellent book on Eliot as social theorist, Kenneth Asher emphasizes Eliot's roots in a French tradition of social thinking that dates back to the triumph of the French Revolution in 1789 and the fiery reaction of its conservative enemies. By overturning an established order of long standing, the Revolution transformed society from a slowly evolving organic whole into a mechanical object that could be manipulated by politically powerful elites as if it were a machine. The sweeping away of a historically rooted hierarchy both redefined what it meant to be a person in society and unmoored the individual from those psychological and emotional contexts that stabilized social identities. The collapse of inherited values, which included an unapologetic feudalism, social and political privilege for an entrenched nobility, and a religion dominated by priestly authorities, led inevitably, it was argued, to the excesses of the Revolution in the period after 1791 known as the Terror. The Revolution's liberal apologists saw the Terror as an aberration in an otherwise optimistic (and inevitable) historical process. The conservatives, on the other hand, saw it as intrinsic to revolutionary ruptures in general and to democratic secularism in particular. The Terror, they would say, is the black heart of liberalism.

Liberalism may be flawed at its core, but the conservative ideologue Joseph de Maistre asserted that this only reflected a prior malignancy, namely the state of disgrace into which individual human beings are born. Humanity's fallen nature, which the Church taught as original sin, colors every aspect of existence, in terms not only of the ethical but of the political and social as well. No individual human life nor any social organization of life can avoid this taint, and any society that operates as if this were not true yanks existence from its proper course. The problem as de Maistre saw it lay in a patently egotistical and self-blinding maneuver, the substitution of a purely human conception of reason for the idea of divine reason as basis of faith. He saw human reason as merely the servant of creaturely desires, most of which were, as Asher has put it, "uniformly perverse" (13).

De Maistre's attack on the Revolution helped shape the conservatism of two other nineteenth-century French thinkers, both latter-day apostates from liberalism: Ernest Renan and Hippolyte Taine. Both looked back to the Revolution from a later perspective shaped by the German military defeat of France in 1870 and the events of the Paris Commune in 1871. These debacles resulted, as far as they were concerned, from the revolutionary break of 1789. Renan was particularly exercised by the rampant individualism which the Revolution had made possible, breaking with traditional communal relationships of loyalty and duty. Self-interest, blatant materialism, and the pursuit of pleasure undermined the strength of the nation. Among many other criticisms, Taine was particularly disturbed, like de Maistre, by the effects of the Revolution on the French language. The enthroning of human reason, Taine argued, had had the effect on communicative practices of sucking local, regional, and class-based usages out of the language. Tradition's inertial drag on language resisted its transformation into a pure instrument of abstract reason, but resistance had failed. For the revolutionaries, the French language had been cleansed of ancient excrescences and monarcho-religious contaminations; for conservatives, the language was turned into a kind of colorless geometry suitable only for administration and theoretical acrobatics.

This conservative current led to a highly controversial, twentieth-century French intellectual who exerted a powerful influence on Eliot. No account of Eliot's social criticism is complete without taking notice of Charles Maurras. He too condemned the effects the Revolution exercised on French society. The sweeping away of the old hierarchies – "of throne, altar, and Pre-Romantic literary decorum" (Asher 161) – gave free rein to new regimes of desire, materialism, and individualism, the principal conduits through which original sin enters the world. What was needed, Maurras argued, was a "rappel à l'ordre," a call to Order, and the restoration of traditional social forms that realized the dictates of natural law. The social composition of the nation and inherited social structures were seen as the natural expression of the life and character of a people. The integrity and purity of a nation, now defined as distinct from the apparatuses of the state, became rallying points in the political expression of these general ideas. There is very little room for outsiders in this social vision. Racial or religious minorities, such as the Jews, are seen as dilutions or even threats to the national idea. Maurras labeled his restorative project "classicism" and ranged it against an implacable enemy he called "romanticism." Eliot took on board this "Manichean" (Asher 23) model of society in the 1910s and 1920s as he read through Maurras's works and the works of Maurras's predecessors. Democratic chaos, the prison-house of desire, the atomized equality of mass society, egotism, and revolution were ranged against Maurras's classical virtues – namely, political and religious hierarchy grounded in tradition; an organically evolving community marked by the continuity of its social, political, and cultural forms; and a commitment to Order throughout the whole of social life. Eliot's thinking evolved beyond this rather simple dichotomy, but he never completely abandoned the lessons taught by Maurras. The fact that Maurras, in the end, took up common cause with the collaborationist, neofascist government of Vichy France during World War II caused Eliot some embarrassment. But by the 1940s, his social thinking had matured and had been leavened by his residence in Great Britain, a country with a history very different from the politically divisive historical experience of France.

Of course, Great Britain was no stranger to political division, class conflict, and even civil war and revolution. But the commotions of history had not created the same kind of rift in Britain as was evident in France after the Revolution. Britain was a kind of hybrid nation, neither completely forged in revolutionary violence, nor completely suffocated by tradition. There was a parliament, but it was composed of a baffling mixture of oligarchic elements, genuine popular representation, and freewheeling independents. Not baffling to the British, mind you, but certainly to outsiders. There was a magnificent monarchy that many would defend to the death but also find risibly absurd. To be sure, there was an established Church to which everyone belonged but which seemed at times even more absurd than the monarchy. Britain was undoubtedly the first modern nation, but it was also crisscrossed by myriad institutions that had their roots in the Middle Ages (Scruton 10–11). It took Eliot some time to grasp the strange paradoxes of British society and to see the inapplicability of Maurras's schematic violence on the body politic. One can trace this process of understanding by examining Eliot's occasional editorials in the *Criterion* over the course of its 17-year run from 1922 to 1939.

Not all the influences on Eliot in the making of his views on culture and society were French. He had two important English predecessors: Samuel Taylor Coleridge and Matthew Arnold. Roger Kojecký, in his fine book, *T. S. Eliot's Social Criticism*, expounds their impact in an early chapter. Eliot felt drawn to Coleridge for a number of reasons. They were both social and political conservatives; they were both raised in the Unitarian faith, but migrated spiritually to the Church of England. Both felt that national life was in need of renewal and that only reaffirmation of Christian traditions could have the required effect. Most important for Eliot's thinking, though, was Coleridge's view that the conduit for revitalizing Britain by reaffirming Christian principles lay in the hands of a class of intellectual workers he called the *clerisy*. "Broadly speaking," as Kojecký explains, "the clerisy were the educated, who, having imbibed wisdom at the ancient 'halls of learning,' were able to communicate it to others throughout the country" (23). For Coleridge the clerisy represented a social force of considerable influence in shaping the culture of English society. Eliot was drawn to this idea and adapted it for the modern world as the "Community of Christians" in *The Idea of a Christian Society*.

Matthew Arnold's influence on Eliot was more limited in scope, but important nonetheless. Active in education (as a schools inspector) and in the spread of high culture (as critic and social theorist) in Victorian Britain, Arnold argued for a cultural activism that he had inherited from essentially liberal sources. In that respect, Arnold and Eliot were in opposed camps; yet Eliot appreciated many of the ideas and strategies suggested by his predecessor in situating society on a bedrock of universal values. Arnold put great stock in the social efficacy of elites, in the secular institutions of education, class, and the family, and in the formal pursuit of the arts. He was also a serious Christian, though perhaps not sufficiently so in Eliot's estimation. Differences aside, there are many points of congruence between the two men, but none more significant than their endorsement of the need for social order. Arnold's fear of social and political breakdown was expressed most vividly in *Culture and Anarchy* (1869). In the Conclusion, he affirms without qualification the need to repress "anarchy and disorder; because without order there can be no society, and without society there can be no human perfection" (168). By "anarchy and disorder," Arnold and Eliot had the example and the excesses of the French Revolution and its possible translation to Britain principally in mind. Both viewed revolutionary violence and the overturning of the state with horror.

The Idea of a Christian Society

Eliot's first systematic presentation of his ideas came in March 1939 when he delivered a series of lectures at Corpus Christi College, Cambridge, later published as *The Idea of a Christian Society*. In his short Preface to the book, Eliot declares in a sentence what has spurred the discourse. "My point of departure," he writes, "has been the suspicion that the current terms in which we discuss international affairs and political theory may only tend to conceal from us the real issues of contemporary civilization" (*CC* 3). But, he explains, the reader must not suppose that the book, its title notwithstanding, is a plea for a "religious revival" (4). He does not want to separate the institutions of spiritual life from political and economic activities. These form a complex whole, and concentrating on one does not imply ignoring the others. This is the practical result of his insight, gained from his early studies in anthropology, of the involved unity of cultures. As a result, in the current undertaking, he is not concerned with "spiritual institutions in their separated aspect, but the organization of values, and a direction of religious thought which must inevitably proceed to a criticism of political and economic systems" (4). The book may not satisfy specialists in any one discipline of thought, but it makes it possible to offer a more profound diagnosis of the state of contemporary civilization than is gained by an inventory of leading symptoms.

With his usual fastidiousness of language, Eliot begins his exposition by examining the key words of his title. He tells us that by the phrase "idea of a Christian society" he means what an affirmation of Christian values would require in order to produce, in the end, a society worthy of the name Christian. In a characteristic rhetorical move, he puts forward definition rather than persuasion as the primary goal of the exposition: "I am not at this moment concerned with the means for bringing a Christian society into existence; I am not even primarily concerned with making it appear desirable; but I am very much concerned with making clear its difference from the kind of society in which we are now living" (*CC* 6). By this stratagem, he hopes to nudge the wary reader, who may be suspicious of a Christian apologist's actual motives, into a state of benevolent receptivity. It doesn't take long for more urgent stipulations to emerge. Not definition only, then, but also the call for change – changes of "social attitude" leading to "changes in . . . organization of industry and commerce and financial credit" (8) – sharpens the text's designs. The argument cuts two ways: it continues Eliot's attack on liberal humanism (and especially on liberalism as an intellectual and political force), formulated more aggressively in *After Strange Gods*, and it elevates Christian tradition as the sole positive energy in a negative liberal society (13–16).

The attack on liberalism emphasizes two things. By loosening traditional bonds and loyalties, ones that stabilize and settle society, liberal sociopolitical organization inevitably moves toward a condition of chaos. At first the liberal mind sees only the positive advantages of such a process of "liberation." Equality, greater democratic participation, emancipation of the less privileged, and the opening of social, political, and economic space to develop one's potential to its fullest extent – these define the starting point of the liberal imagination. The weakness here lies in the fact that the liberal cannot foresee the end toward which liberalism is directed; he or she can only grasp the starting point because "[o]ur point of departure is more real to us than our destination." Where we end up in this process presents "a very different picture" (*CC* 12). The dawn of a liberal era, which begins in expansive optimism, descends over time into something less idealistic, something approaching the chaos of unchecked egotism, social fragmentation, and political despair. In 1939, it was rather easy to turn to the immediate political and economic realities of approaching war, totalitarianism, depression, and social stagnation and ask, what more proof of this descent do you need?

Eliot's second thrust at liberalism materializes from the first and is more devastating. Liberalism does not only tend to atomize society, it also produces its very opposite by a dreadful reversal of its logic:

> By destroying traditional social habits of the people, by dissolving their natural collective consciousness into individual constituents, by licensing the opinions of the most foolish, by substituting instruction for education, by encouraging cleverness rather than wisdom, the upstart rather than the qualified, by fostering a notion of *getting on* to which the alternative is a hopeless apathy, Liberalism can prepare the way for that which is its own negation: the artificial, mechanized or brutalized control which is a desperate remedy for its chaos. (*CC* 12)

Nazi Germany and Stalinist Russia, it turns out, are not wrong turnings or aberrations on the path to a benign liberal future, but the toxic outflows of its own gastrointestinal nature. As a consequence of its own logic, liberalism gives birth to political philosophies that deny it. These pernicious reversals, if nothing else, offer relief from the debauchery of liberalism. They revive in harmful ways and only partially satisfy what a Christian society offers in a more nourishing and valuable form, namely, a whole "way of life" (14).

A society founded on Christian values and traditions does not need to articulate itself as a party program or even as a political philosophy. A Christian society activates at a deeper level what Eliot calls "the substratum of collective temperament, ways of behavior and unconscious values" (*CC* 14). Religion sustains life, but not without exertion. Just because a society is nominally Christian does not mean that Christian values inform the life of individuals and of the community. Values have to be put into action, and this requires adjustments in social and political activity and organization. Eliot's principal sociopolitical forms in the new order are the Christian State, the Christian Community, and the Community of Christians.

A state would be Christian because the authorities in positions of power would act on Christian *principles*. They would not necessarily have to be Christian believers. Their executive, legislative, and administrative activities would be kept in check "by the temper and traditions of the people which they rule. . . . What the rulers believed, would be less important than the beliefs to which they would be obliged to conform" (*CC* 21–22). Education would be the primary author of the proper frame of mind. A Christian education would not simply inculcate faith, forcing even skeptics into insincere conformity; it would train people to think in Christian categories (22) and as a result to act within a Christian framework whether they believed or not.

The intellectual ability of a leadership elite to grasp the complex role assigned to it in a Christian society cannot be found in the larger Christian Community. The capacity of "the great mass of humanity" for thinking about faith and values is limited, and so "their Christianity may be almost wholly realized in behavior" (*CC* 23), both as customary practice and neighborly civility. To build a unified religious and social order and to counteract the atomization of society into isolated individuals, the traditional parish, weakened by urbanization and *sub*urbanization, must remain the social unit best suited to supporting both individuals and the larger aims of a Christian society (23). These ideas retrieve from the dustbin of history social forms that had provided the social cohesion and coherence of premodern society, last seen in more vivid form in preindustrial Britain. Eliot acknowledges that such a conception is seriously unhistorical, as it gropes back to that turning in the road which led to modernity (25). It wipes from the record the historical experience and dynamism of a people. Eliot's acknowledgment does not blunt this critical point.

The final element in the making of a Christian Society is a social formation Eliot calls, in contrast to the Christian Community, the Community of Christians. Coleridge's notion of the "clerisy" stands behind Eliot's formulation of this concept. What Eliot (and Coleridge before him) means is something like the modern term "intelligentsia." For Coleridge, this group included members of the ancient universities, the clergy, and grammar and public school teachers. Eliot's Community casts a wider net in terms of classes of people, but is also more restrictive. Teachers are included, but not all teachers – only those with "superior intellectual and/or spiritual gifts" (*CC* 30). The broad category of intellectuals, university teachers, writers, and artists, as well as the clergy, would also be included, but only if qualified by the highest intellectual and spiritual standards. This group would be the leading edge of society. It would advise the rulers and it would educate the people. It would disseminate a Christian view of the world and maintain its philosophical validity. Sharing a common background through a system of education, the Community would also propagate a common culture, such that they would collectively bring to life the consciousness and conscience of the nation (34). Every society has had a social formation of intellectuals as one of its leading elements, and Eliot's care in delineating their composition, beliefs, and responsibilities implies their historical importance.

From these elements Eliot develops a comprehensive idea of Christian society. He argues that there is no one strictly political form that ought to be considered Christian. The question of political and economic organization depends on "the character and the stage of intelligence and education of a particular people in a particular place at a particular time" (*CC* 45). Here Eliot's anthropological turn of mind again comes clearly into view. Differences in politics and economics from one society to another depend on the general cultural development of a people, not on deliberate application of political theories. Revolutionary states, from the French Revolution on, have attempted to impose political abstractions on the lived reality of a people with ghastly results. If a people are not ready intellectually and culturally for certain ideas to take root – the idea of democracy, for example – they must be guided by Church and State (45). If this means requiring conformity and even repression to some degree, then this is what Church and State, working together, must do. What the people are capable of accomplishing, not what people might think they want, is the central question at issue. For understanding *and* accepting that idea, culture is the key.

Notes towards the Definition of Culture

Eliot's social thought culminated almost ten years after the publication of *The Idea of a Christian Society* with a book that tackled the very question of culture head on. *Notes towards the Definition of Culture* was published in 1948, the work of a celebrated author who had achieved the status of a public sage and had been awarded the Nobel Prize for Literature that same year. As a reference point in certain political and ideological conflicts in the second half of the twentieth century, Eliot's ideas have been cited as significant statements of a generally conservative political cast, though they have had little influence on the subsequent development of modern society.

Notes towards the Definition of Culture formulates a defense of the concept of a Christian culture. As always in his critical writings, Eliot announces what seems a modest goal: the desire to define, distinguish, and relate "the three principal uses" of that troublesome word "culture" (*CC* 87). His starting point is the assertion that "no culture has appeared or developed except together with a religion" (87). Looking back at ancient societies and even at more recent ones, this anthropological observation is probably true. Eliot seems particularly annoyed by a turn in nineteenth-century social thought whereby religion was seen to be a product of culture rather than what Eliot believes is the true state of affairs: that a people's culture develops from its religion. Culture, he writes, is, "essentially, the incarnation . . . of the religion of a people" (101).

Perhaps the most important application of this startling proposition comes when Eliot turns his attention to the composition of society. Against the egalitarian and democratic tendencies of his time, he offers a stout defense of the concept of class. He is careful to distinguish two ideas that are sometimes confused: upper or socially dominant classes and social elites (*CC* 107–08). To sharpen his argument he takes on the social theories of Karl Mannheim, an important sociologist in the mid-twentieth century. Mannheim is criticized for confusing an elite of merit with higher social classes that maintain their position through the inheritance of wealth, status, and power (111). Elites come into being as groups of talented individuals who are brought together by possession of particular abilities and skills. Merit binds them in intellectual, spiritual, and moral activities and as a recognizable social group. Often the members of an elite come from a dominant social class, but the two formations are not identical. However, the two groups have a clear relationship. Elites produce ideas, science, art, and other intellectual, spiritual, and moral products; the dominant or upper classes consume what they produce. More importantly, the higher classes transmit what they have consumed as culture to the rest of society. This then comes to constitute the way of life of a people (113–15).

Elites form and re-form continuously. One cannot inherit a place in an elite; it is earned by palpable achievement. An upper class, by contrast, has a completely different historical presence. As the principal means for the transmission of high culture, this class must be deeply immersed in tradition, so that the practice of inheriting wealth, status, and power ensures both the continuity of the whole society and the continuous transmission of culture (*CC* 121–22). But Eliot is careful to avoid saying that an upper class is more beneficial for culture as a whole than the activities of other classes. An upper class may have "a more conscious and a greater specialization of culture" (121), but it does not have "*more* culture than the lower." The key is differentiation of cultural activity among the different classes. These thoughts are expressed very carefully because Eliot knows that a defense of what he calls "a graded society" may appear to devalue equality in a democratic society.

If the outstanding individual is the building block of an elite, the family serves the same role in the making of social classes. Eliot sees the family unit as the main channel in society through which culture is transmitted. We are all, he argues, products, to a not inconsiderable extent, of our early upbringing and environment (*CC* 115–16). But when he speaks of the family he does not mean the nuclear family of modern times, limited in extent and time-consciousness, but of an older conception:

I have in mind a bond which embraces a longer period of time than this: a piety towards the dead, however obscure, and a solicitude for the unborn, however remote. Unless this reverence for past and future is cultivated in the home, it can never be more than a verbal convention in the community. Such an interest in the past is different from the vanities and pretensions of genealogy; such a responsibility for the future is different from that of the builder of social programs. (116–17)

Reforms that are the product of social engineering cannot produce and sustain a culture worthy of the name.

Eliot's defense of the class structure and of the family resonates politically with the most traditionally conservative social theories of our time. And like a good conservative he also appreciates the value and vitality of the local region. A society is not one thing: it is an amalgam of various locales and regions that allows for greater or lesser degrees of cultural diversity. But, Eliot argues, it must be balanced by a clear unity as well (*CC* 125). Loyalty to a particular place, like loyalty to the family, is an important aspect of culture. Even a degree of religious diversity can be a very good thing, again as long as it is balanced by an appreciation of the fundamentals of faith as the progenitors of culture and society as a whole (157). In the making of these delicate social and cultural equilibria, education plays a vital *social* role, as opposed to the dominant view of education as a program primarily concerned with personal self-improvement. Education, in Eliot's view, ought to preserve the integrity and legitimacy of social class, and it should help to identify the deserving members of an elite (177). Eliot spends a good deal of time debunking modern educational theories as leading to the very condition of cultural breakdown which they are invoked to impede (185). He sees education as having a more limited role, not of making people happier, or stuffing their heads with expert knowledge, or equipping them for life in the modern economy. Education should make them more receptive to culture as the expression of the traditional life of their people. And this brings us back to religion as the source of culture. A people living with the faith and experience of their ancestors are better equipped to deal with everyday life and with whatever calamities and crises history puts in their path than societies of isolated egos who are encouraged to continuously concoct shrewd curricula of self-enlargement and self-promotion. Eliot saw no use for a religion that was simply one more tool for amplifying the self in the name of personal growth.

This social vision is deeply conservative, but not conservative in the modern neo-liberal sense. Eliot was as suspicious of the deleterious effects of capitalism as he was of what is now known as liberalism and the varieties of twentieth-century collectivist ideologies. He was conservative in an older sense given its first modern expression in England by Edmund Burke at the beginning of the nineteenth century and in France by the conservative thinkers who exerted a lasting influence on Eliot's thinking about society. Respect for tradition was the key principle, but by respect Eliot meant something other than an uncritical reverence of the past. He had spent his early years as a literary critic reflecting on the relation between tradition and the individual in the field of literature. Later, after his acceptance of the Church of England, his thoughts about tradition extended over a wider field of human experience. The individual he had in mind was no longer limited to the talented artist or writer, but now included ordinary citizens. On that larger canvas the egotistical impulse expressed itself in the most garish colors. The only alternative, he felt, to the dominance of the cult of self-absorption was religious orthodoxy. As early as 1933, when he gave the lectures that eventually become *After Strange Gods*, he saw the problem clearly: "Tradition by itself is not enough; it must be perpetually criticized and brought up to date under the supervision of what I call orthodoxy" (67). Baldly put, this may sound contradictory, and the relation between critical thought and the "supervision" of thinking may make us uneasy and may even hide from view an authoritarian tendency. But although Eliot never veered from this basic position, his subsequent extended meditations on society grew more sophisticated, and he developed a serious body of social criticism that in its day was much discussed but, as the world was headed in a different direction, was largely ignored by those who shaped Western societies after the cataclysm of World War II.

NOTES

1   See also ELIOT'S POLITICS.
2   See also MIND, MYTH, AND CULTURE: ELIOT AND ANTHROPOLOGY.

REFERENCES AND FURTHER READING

Arnold, Matthew. *Culture and Anarchy*. 1869. *Culture and Anarchy and other Writings*. Ed. Stefan Collini. Cambridge: Cambridge UP, 1991.

Asher, Kenneth. *T. S. Eliot and Ideology*. Cambridge: Cambridge UP, 1995.

Austin, Allen. *T. S. Eliot: The Literary and Social Criticism*. Bloomington: Indiana UP, 1971.

Chace, William M. *The Political Identities of Ezra Pound and T. S. Eliot*. Stanford: Stanford UP, 1973.

Craig, Cairns. *Yeats, Eliot, Pound and the Politics of Poetry: Richest to the Richest*. London: Croom Helm, 1982.

Kirk, Russell. *The Conservative Mind, from Burke to Eliot*. New York: Avon, 1968.

Kojecký, Roger. *T. S. Eliot's Social Criticism*. London: Faber, 1971.

Morrison, Paul. *The Poetics of Fascism: Ezra Pound, T. S. Eliot, Paul de Man*. New York: Oxford UP, 1996.

North, Michael. *The Political Aesthetic of Yeats, Eliot, and Pound*. Cambridge: Cambridge UP, 1991.

Perl, Jeffrey. *Skepticism and Modern Enmity: Before and After Eliot*. Baltimore: Johns Hopkins UP, 1989.

Scruton, Roger. *England: An Elegy*. London: Continuum, 2006.

Tratner, Michael. *Modernism and Mass Politics: Joyce, Woolf, Eliot, Yeats*. Stanford: Stanford UP, 1995.

Part III
Contexts

25
Eliot's Poetics:
Classicism and Histrionics

Lawrence Rainey

The vertiginous arc of T. S. Eliot's career can leave a later observer bewildered, even stupefied. In 1920, when Harold Monro (proprietor of the Poetry Bookshop in London and the editor of the literary journals *Poetry and Drama* [1913–1914] and the *Chapbook* [1919–1925]) published his survey of *Some Contemporary Poets*, he included discussions of W. B. Yeats, Ezra Pound, and Thomas Hardy – but not a word about Eliot. By 1924, instead, even a reviewer in a relatively provincial newspaper, the *Freeman's Journal* (Dublin), could call him "the most interesting of the younger school of English 'revolutionary' poets – understand by revolutionary a seeker after new forms and a radical experimentalist in technique" (J.M.H. 9), while only seven months earlier a reviewer writing in the *New York Evening Post* had called *The Waste Land* "the apotheosis of modernity" (Ransom 106). As if that abrupt change in Eliot's reputation and status in the course of only three to four years were not enough, more was to come: in his preface to a collection of recent essays published in 1928, Eliot announced that he was now "classicist in literature, royalist in politics, and anglo-catholic in religion" (*FLA* vii). Here was a startling change indeed. How could one reconcile "the revolutionary ... seeker after new forms and ... radical experimentalist," author of "the apotheosis of modernity," with classicism, royalism, and Anglo-Catholicism? Were these not deeply contradictory terms? Or were there two distinct and inimical Eliots lodged within the same mind? And did these develop different, equally contradictory poetics? Was Eliot's poetics really a singular entity, a stable core of doctrine gradually developed and extended over the course of his career, or was it really plural, a series of abrupt and radical excursions, each terminating in a dead end, followed by a new tabula rasa?

Nearly all accounts of Eliot's poetics turn on a conjuncture of three terms (tradition, impersonality, and classicism) and two phrases ("objective correlative" and "dissociation of sensibility"). The first two terms are used with considerable frequency in an early essay by Eliot, "Tradition and the Individual Talent" (1919), one often reprinted and widely assessed as the kernel of Eliot's poetics, a doctrinal core

A Companion to T. S. Eliot, First Edition. Edited by David E. Chinitz.
© 2014 John Wiley & Sons, Ltd. Published 2014 by John Wiley & Sons, Ltd.

subsequently elaborated over his long career. The essay begins by redefining the term "tradition." Whereas social theorists routinely distinguish between traditional and modern societies, between relatively static and dynamic organizations, between belief systems that are handed down and passively reproduced and those that are self-consciously acquired and self-reflexively transmuted, Eliot inverts and recombines these binary oppositions:

> Tradition is a matter of much wider significance. It cannot be inherited, and if you want it you must obtain it by great labour. It involves, in the first place, the historical sense, which we may call nearly indispensable to anyone who would continue to be a poet beyond his twenty-fifth year; and the historical sense involves a perception, not only of the pastness of the past, but of its presence; the historical sense compels a man to write not merely with his own generation in his bones, but with a feeling that the whole of the literature of Europe from Homer and within it the whole of the literature of his own country has a simultaneous existence and composes a simultaneous order. (*SE* 4)

Eliot's notion of tradition, in short, is not very traditional. In most accounts of it, tradition is inescapably bound up with place, with locale; the notion of an "international" or even a "global tradition" is a contradiction in terms. But by conflating tradition with "the historical sense," Eliot actually destroys tradition's embeddedness in the locale (or in this case, a temporal version of the locale, i.e., "the pastness of the past") and resituates it within the abstract grid of modernization ("a simultaneous existence" or "a simultaneous order"). What is being passed off as tradition is actually something quite different: that radical historicity associated with modernity, the systematic appropriation of the past marshaled to reshape the present and future.

"Impersonality" is another term that dominates "Tradition and the Individual Talent," even though the word itself appears only once in it, together with the adjective "impersonal" (twice) and the noun "depersonalization" (again, twice). Eliot can be positively ascetic in defining its implications:

> The progress of an artist is a continual self-sacrifice, a continual extinction of personality. (*SE* 7)

> Poetry is not a turning loose of emotion, but an escape from emotion; it is not the expression of personality, but an escape from personality. (10)

These are very striking formulations. Yet their metaphorical power may be purchased at the cost of analytical clarity: "self-sacrifice" invokes saintly renunciation, while "extinction" suggests a species of suicide, and "escape" simultaneously implies that personality is a prison and carries undertones of evasion. Between these remarks, however, Eliot offers an extended comparison that has aroused some controversy. The mind of the poet, he urges, is like "a bit of finely filiated platinum . . . introduced into a chamber containing oxygen and sulphur dioxide." The result is to "form sulphurous acid" (a material often used as a bleach or reducing agent), a new substance that nevertheless leaves the catalyst, the platinum unaltered: "the platinum itself is apparently unaffected; has remained inert, neutral, and unchanged" (*SE* 7). In this analogy, sulfurous acid is the new poem that results when "impressions and experiences," "the experience," "the passions," "emotions and feelings," or "numberless feelings, phrases, images" (8–9) – Eliot uses all these formulations – of the everyday man are conjoined via the shred of the platinum that is "the mind of the poet" (7). Eliot draws this analogy solely to emphasize the unchanging neutrality of the catalyst and its remoteness, its radical difference, from the poem. But Martin Scofield has expressed the bewilderment which this comparison has prompted even among Eliot's admirers: "Can we imagine that the mind of the poet is so inert in the process of composition? Can we imagine that it could be so totally unchanged by the process? Can the process of composition be so completely automatic as this would seem to make it?" (74). One might, however, lay stress on Scofield's phrase, a "process of composition . . . so *completely automatic*," juxtaposing it with Eliot's comment that "the poet has, not a 'personality' to express, but *a particular medium*, which is . . . not a personality" (*SE* 9; emphasis added), or his remark that "the mind of the mature poet differs from that of the immature one . . . by being a more finely perfected medium" (7). Together these recapitulate the rhetoric of automatic writing that takes place through mediums who surrender their identity to the demonic repetitions of the words of the dead, in spiritualist versions of it, or of the unconscious, in the Surrealist version that would be promulgated only five years after Eliot's essay. Eliot, summarizing his discussion of impersonality, describes it as "a passive attending upon the event." "Of course," he hastens to add in the next sentence, "this is not quite the whole story. There is a great deal, in the writing of poetry, which must be conscious and deliberate" (10). Yet that oscillation, between "a passive attending upon the event" and "a great deal . . . which must be conscious and deliberate," between "the awful daring of a moment's surrender" (*CPP* 49) and the hope that "history is a pattern / Of timeless moments" (144), constitutes a polarity that stands at the base of the two quite contradictory poetics that Eliot came to articulate over his career.

Though midway through the essay Eliot explicitly promises that he will "define this process of depersonalization *and* its relation to the sense of tradition" (*SE* 7; emphasis added), he executes only the first of these tasks: the term "tradition" never recurs in the rest of the essay, its relation to depersonalization left wholly implicit. Frank Kermode, trying to fill the lacuna with an innocuous formulation, says: "In this way a doctrine of 'impersonality' *is associated with* the doctrine of tradition" (*SP* 16; emphasis added), a formulation so vague that it could equally be applied to dogs and cats, or anything else brought together by mere contiguity. Others agree in urging that impersonality or depersonalization be conceived as a counterpart to "tradition." Somehow, in submitting to the claims of tradition – or so it is typically reformulated by commentators, who fail to note that Eliot actually proposes just the opposite: that tradition submit to the disembedding grid of modernization – the poet becomes impersonal. In a broader sense, such impersonality can seem to anticipate the way that some of Eliot's poems (especially *The Waste Land*) abound in quotation and allusion, rather than more direct expositions of feeling.

The radical passivity that exists in Eliot's early formulation of "impersonality" extends to the rhetoric in which he describes canon formation, or the interaction between novelty and tradition:

> [W]hat happens when a new work of art is created is something that happens simultaneously to all the works of art which preceded it. The existing monuments form an ideal order among themselves which is modified by the introduction of the new (the really new) work of art among them. The existing order is complete before the new work arrives; for order to persist after the supervention of novelty, the *whole* existing order must be, if ever so slightly, altered; and so the relations, proportions, values of each work of art toward the whole are readjusted; and this is conformity between the old and the new. (*SE* 5)

The difficulties in Eliot's account are concealed by his use of the passive voice in every clause that registers a critical moment:

> an ideal order . . . which *is modified*
> the *whole* existing order must *be* . . . *altered*
> the relations, etc. . . . *are readjusted*

At best, this presents a beguiling reciprocity between modernity and tradition, which now are no longer antithetical, but complementary terms. At worst, it presents oversimplifications that mystify the complex social and institutional constellations that shape and reshape traditions or canon formations. Women and spokespeople for various minorities object that a tradition that once excluded their writers is hardly as value-free or neutral as Eliot implies.

It was in 1923 that Eliot first began to adopt the term "classicism" to characterize his own beliefs, in an essay called "The Function of Criticism." It begins by quoting that same passage from "Tradition and the Individual Talent" cited above, urging that "the existing monuments form an ideal order among themselves"; then it offers an important qualification. The ideal order has a different aspect now: "There is accordingly something outside of the artist to which he owes allegiance, a devotion to which he must surrender and sacrifice himself in order to obtain his unique position" (*SE* 13). Further on, Eliot quotes from a recent essay by J. Middleton Murry: "Catholicism stands for the principle of unquestioned spiritual authority outside the individual; that is also the principle of Classicism in literature." This definition, Eliot adds, is "unimpeachable" (15), and his sympathies lie with "the writer [who] has admitted the existence of an unquestioned spiritual authority outside himself, to which he has attempted to *conform*" (17–18). Tellingly, such conformity now entails conscious activity: "[W]e are forced to conclude that what happens unconsciously we could bring about, and *form into a purpose*, if we made a conscious attempt" (13; emphasis added). It is difficult not to compare this with the earlier passage about the gases which, when mixed, "form sulphurous acid." For in the earlier passage, the verb "form" could be paraphrased as "become," as in the sentence, "Water forms ice when frozen." But in the later passage, the verb "form" can only be paraphrased as "organize or establish." What had once been "a passive attending upon the event" has been transformed into active, disciplined shaping.

Eliot's impulse to appeal to a standard "outside the individual" is best understood as an attempt to avoid the perils of psychologism, the philosophical attempt to establish truth – in this case, aesthetic or poetic truth, though the issue could extend to other realms as well – in the subjective elements of self-observation. Indeed, it was John Stuart Mill who famously tied both mathematics and logic to what he called "intuition."[1] The most damning (and persuasive) critique of this view was articulated by the philosopher Edmund Husserl, who wrote in 1913: "To refer to it [a number] as a mental construct is an absurdity, an offence against the perfectly clear meaning of arithmetic discourse, which can at any time be perceived as valid, and *precedes* all theories concerning it" (90). Or to put it more simply, Husserl is arguing that two plus two makes four, regardless of whether any individual mind chooses to believe it or not. The truth of mathematics is independent of experience, whether private or cultural. But the degree of our willingness to ascribe independent status to truth, while absolute in mathematics, and perhaps logic and physics, grows more attenuated when we turn to fields such as ethics, or aesthetics. Human rights campaigners come as close as possible to urging that certain rights really are universal, an a priori moral norm (in this they follow Kant), though others will rejoin that the very notion of human rights is very recent in origin. Eliot, in his notion that classicism stands "outside the individual," was trying to claim for aesthetics and/or poetics an a priori status of the same sort. Like Husserl, he was an antipsychologist.

It is amazing how often Eliot's capacity for coining a pithy phrase could generate discussion that lasted for years. The "objective correlative" is an instance. Eliot first used it in his essay on "Hamlet and His Problems," published in 1919, in which he urged that

> the only way of expressing emotion in the form of art is by finding an "objective correlative"; in other words, a set of objects, a situation, a chain of events which shall be the formula of that *particular* emotion, such that when the external facts, which must terminate in sensory experience, are given, the emotion is immediately invoked. (*SE* 124–25)

As subsequently adopted by other critics, the phrase became a tool of aesthetic judgment: the failure of a work to embody the "particular emotion" would be a by-product of the artist's failure to find an "objective correlative." And while the phrase was used by F. O. Matthiessen to produce sympathetic readings of Eliot's poetry, its status was already contested in Eliot's lifetime, and he himself lost interest in it. The idea that naming an object, or "a set of objects, a situation, a chain of events," will automatically present the reader with a sense-experience somehow analogous to that of the object, is not one that many critics would accept today. In effect, it becomes little more than a formula for urging the common-sense proposition that good writing should strive to be vivid, concrete, and richly detailed.

Yet another phrase by Eliot that enjoyed remarkable currency was "the dissociation of sensibility." Eliot used it in his essay on "The Metaphysical Poets," first published in 1921. In it, Eliot urges that

> something . . . happened to the mind of England between the time of Donne or Lord Herbert of Cherbury and the time of Tennyson and Browning. . . . Tennyson and Browning are poets, and they think; but they do not feel their thought as immediately as the odor of a rose. A thought to Donne was an experience; it modified his sensibility. (*SE* 247)

To diagnose this change Eliot proposed a theory: "In the seventeenth century a dissociation of sensibility set in, from which we have never recovered." As a result, "while the language became more refined, the feeling became more crude" (247). At the same time, from 1720 or so onwards, "The poets . . . thought and felt by fits, unbalanced; they reflected" (248). In short, a prelapsarian unity of thought and feeling had given way to a permanent divide, one in which both thought and feeling were exaggerated, extreme, unhealthy. Eliot tried to develop this insight further during the years that followed, culminating in his Clark Lectures given at Trinity College, Cambridge, in 1926, and subsequently recycled as the Turnbull Lectures, given at Johns Hopkins University in 1933. But he was sufficiently dissatisfied with both versions that he decided not to publish them. When he returned yet again to the idea in "Milton II," a lecture given in 1947, he no longer saw it as a purely literary matter:

> If such a dissociation did take place, I suspect that the causes are too complex and too profound to justify our accounting for the change in terms of literary criticism. All we can say is, that something like this did happen; that it had something to do with the Civil War; that it would even be unwise to say it was caused by the Civil War, but that it is a consequence of the same causes which brought about the Civil War; that we must seek the causes in Europe, not in England alone; and for what these causes were, we may dig and dig until we get to a depth at which words and concepts fail us. (*OPP* 153)

(Such were the sidelong mannerisms of Eliot's later prose!) Needless to say, later critics have largely dismissed the idea of a dissociation of sensibility. It is not an historical event that can be documented or verified in any useful way, and its presupposition of an idyllic, utopian world prior to the modern world amounts to little more than a sophisticated retelling of a familiar fall story. (In the olde days, things were better. . . .)

Eliot's poetics was developed not only through broad theoretical essays such as "Tradition and the Individual Talent" and "The Function of Criticism," but also through his occasional writings on individual authors. Consider his output in a single year. In 1921, at the suggestion of Bruce Richmond, editor of the *Times Literary Supple-*

ment, Eliot wrote the three essays "Andrew Marvell," "John Dryden," and "The Metaphysical Poets." Three years later he collected them into a small booklet issued by the Hogarth Press, *Homage to John Dryden*, appending a typically arch preface that summarized his approach: "I have long felt that the poetry of the seventeenth and eighteenth centuries, even much of that of inferior inspiration, possesses an elegance and a dignity absent from the popular and pretentious verse of the Romantic Poets and their successors" (9). It was through his often pointed comparisons that he advanced his most telling observations. After juxtaposing two poems by Marvell (1621–78) and William Morris (1834–96), both concerning a nymph, Eliot concludes:

> As for the difference, it could not be more pronounced. The effect of Morris's charming poem depends upon the mistiness of the feeling and the vagueness of its object; the effect of Marvell's upon its bright, hard precision. And this precision is not due to the fact that Marvell is concerned with cruder or simpler or more carnal emotions. The emotion of Morris is not more refined or more spiritual; it is merely more vague: if anyone doubts whether the more refined or spiritual emotion can be precise, he should study the treatment of the varieties of discarnate emotion in the *Paradiso*. (*SE* 258)

"Bright, hard precision," as opposed to "the mistiness of the feeling and the vagueness of its object." Such schematic dichotomies were often overdone, but proved extraordinarily powerful. In effect, they enabled educated readers to move from romantic and late Victorian assumptions about poetry to more elastic, more modern conceptions of poetry's possibilities. Still more astoundingly, they did so via a circuitous route that elevated writers of the sixteenth and seventeenth centuries, especially the metaphysical poets and the Elizabethan and Jacobean dramatists, and French poets of the nineteenth century (chiefly Baudelaire and Laforgue) to writers whose complexity and poetic precision made them compelling resources for the present – more compelling than any English poet of the preceding 100 years.

Only ten years after Eliot's trio of essays was first published, the distinguished American critic Edmund Wilson traced their effect:

> The extent of Eliot's influence is amazing: these short essays, sent out without publicity as mere scattered notes on literature, yet sped with so intense a seriousness and weighted with so wide a learning, have not only had the effect of discrediting the academic clichés of the text-books, but are even by way of establishing a new set of literary clichés. With the ascendancy of T. S. Eliot, the Elizabethan dramatists have come back into fashion, and the nineteenth-century has gone out. Milton's poetic reputation has sunk, and Dryden's and Pope's have risen. It is as much as one's life is worth nowadays, among young people, to say an approving word for Shelley or a dubious one about Donne. (116–17)

Wilson's words can remind us how swiftly Eliot's views became fashionable, and their influence was undiminished by the time of his death. In 1932, the same three essays on Marvell, Dryden, and the metaphysical poets were integrated into Eliot's *Selected Essays*, which opened with "Tradition and the Individual Talent" and "The Function of Criticism" – a volume intended to bolster the ever more monolithic image of the classicist, royalist, Anglo-Catholic Eliot. But did that image concretize a coherent poetics that Eliot advocated, or did it actually conceal a rather different one that he practiced? Consider those same three essays from 1921. They do indeed seem to anticipate the neoclassicism that Eliot would programmatically announce in 1928, when juxtaposed largely with works of the succeeding decade (1922–31). But would they look the same if, say, juxtaposed with his other essays from 1921?

That juxtaposition is unsettling, for it exposes the contours of a poetics deeply at variance with the decorum, repose, sobriety, and equilibrium associated with neoclassicism, and repeatedly emphasizing the importance of "surprise." In February 1921, Eliot observes "the high speed, the succession of concentrated images" in Marvell's "To His Coy Mistress," noting that these are the basis for another effect: "When this process has been carried to the end and summed up, the poem turns suddenly with that surprise which has been one of the most important means of poetic effect since Homer" (*SE* 254). Eliot remarks of another passage by Marvell: "There is here the element of *surprise* . . . the surprise which Poe considered of the highest importance, and also the restraint and quietness of tone which makes the surprise possible" (259). In early April, when he is well into work on part II of *The Waste Land*, Eliot praises Dryden's "Mac Flecknoe" because it offers "the most fun . . . the most sustained display of surprise after surprise of wit from line to line. . . . Dryden's method here is something very near to parody" (266). In the same essay a passage by Abraham Cowley is dismissed because it lacks "the element of *surprise* so essential to poetry" (267). Working on the first half of part III in mid-June, Eliot reiterates his stress on "surprise": "The strange, the surprising, is of course essential to art. . . . The craving for the fantastic, for the strange, is legitimate and perpetual; everyone with a sense of beauty has it" ("London Letter [July 1921]" 186). The strange, the surprising, the fantastic, something very near to parody – these terms hardly correspond with the cool sobriety conjured by "Tradition and the Individual Talent." No doubt that essay does encapsulate certain aspirations that will grow more prominent over time; but in 1921, while he was writing *The Waste Land*, those represented only one of several options facing Eliot. The strange, the surprising, the fantastic, something very near to parody . . . the aesthetic limned by these terms might almost be summarized as a poetics of the histrionic.

Similar terms, with a family resemblance, preoccupy Eliot over the course of 1921, with "ferocity" among the most conspicuous. Marie Lloyd, the music-hall star whose death a year later would elicit one of Eliot's finest essays, is praised for having "wit" that is "mordant, ferocious" ("London Letter [May 1921]" 168). Of Nellie Wallace, another admired music-hall star, Eliot writes: "The fierce talent of Nellie Wallace . . . holds the most boisterous music hall in complete subjection" (168). Related if more muted terms include "intensity," "intense," and "intensify," which appear 21 times in Eliot's essays from the first half of 1921 ("The Romantic Englishman," "The Lesson of Baudelaire," "Andrew Marvell," and "Prose and Verse"). Eliot, however, also deploys another term far more extreme than "intensity" and its cognates. He praises Baudelaire over Dryden because he "could see profounder possibilities in wit, and in violently joined images" (*SE* 273). Around the same time, he enthusiastically takes up Baudelaire's view on the distinctive trait of English comedy: "*le signe distinctif de ce genre de comique était la violence*" ("the distinctive sign of this kind of comedy was violence") ("London Letter [May 1921]" 169). A few months later, reversing Samuel Johnson's condemnation of the metaphysical poets, he applauds them because in their works "'the most heterogeneous ideas are yoked by violence together'" (*SE* 243). In ferocity, intensity, violence, compounded with the strange, the surprising, the fantastic, something very near to parody, we find the core of Eliot's poetics while he was writing *The Waste Land*. This of course explains why his essays of the time also highlight his responsiveness to caricature and music hall, modes of cultural production that thrive on wild exaggeration, hyperbolic repetitions that pivot on the play of likeness and illusion, a grotesque machinery of extremism.

Which poetics, then, is really Eliot's poetics: the poetics of classicism or the poetics of the histrionic? Or does formulating the question that way already falsify it? Might it not be better to urge that the two coexist nervously alongside one another, like an uneasy superego and an impish id? Or does the hypothesis of nervous coexistence obscure what in fact was a gradual chronological evolution, one in which his poetics of the histrionic, in the years after 1923, swiftly gave way to his poetics of classicism, to be glimpsed only in a few rare, unguarded comments issued in his later years? Perhaps these questions, however urgent, disguise another that is significantly more compelling. After all, it was Eliot himself, in "Tradition and the Individual Talent," who claimed that "the past should be altered by the present as much as the present is directed by the past" (*SE* 5). For a current generation of readers and critics, Eliot's poetics of classicism may have little to offer, lying as it does in close proximity to his later conservatism and his sometimes dogmatic theology. But his poetics of the histrionic – thriving on contradiction and multiplicity, and lying much closer to the demonic energies that drive his best verse – may well offer a great deal more. Eliot's stature and status in the past century cannot be altered or undone; but which of his two poetics we will want to attend to in the present century remains an open question.

NOTE

1 On mathematics, see Mill 7: 256–57. For Mill's claim that "[logic] is a part, or branch, of psychology," see 9: 359. For a reconsideration of Mill and psychologism, see David Godden, "Psychologism in the Logic of John Stuart Mill: Mill on the Subject Matter and Foundations of Ratiocinative Logic," *History and Philosophy of Logic* 26 (2005): 115–43. Godden concludes that "Mill's position on the subject matter of logic and psychology is, even at the best of times, neither transparent nor unequivocal" (117). He does not consider mathematics.

REFERENCES AND FURTHER READING

Husserl, Edmund. *Ideas: General Introduction to Pure Phenomenology*. Trans. W. R. Rocele. London: Allen, 1931.

J. M. H. "Poetry: New and Old." *Freeman's Journal* [Dublin] 9 Feb. 1924: 9.

Matthiessen, F. O. *The Achievement of T. S. Eliot*. Boston: Houghton, 1935.

Mill, John Stuart. *The Collected Works of John Stuart Mill*. Ed. J. M. Robinson. 33 vols. Toronto: U of Toronto P, 1963–91.

Monro, Harold. *Some Contemporary Poets*. London: Parsons, 1920.

Rainey, Lawrence, ed. *The Annotated Waste Land with Eliot's Contemporary Prose*. New Haven: Yale UP, 2005.

Ransom, John Crowe. "Waste Lands." *New York Evening Post Literary Review* 14 July 1923: 825–26. Rpt. in *T. S. Eliot: The Contemporary Reviews*. Ed. Jewel Spears Brooker. Cambridge: Cambridge UP, 2004. 106–08.

Scofield, Martin. *T. S. Eliot: the Poems*. Cambridge: Cambridge UP, 1988.

Wilson, Edmund. *Axel's Castle*. 1931. New York: Norton, 1984.

26

T. S. Eliot and Something Called Modernism

Ann Ardis

When he met T. S. Eliot for the first time in 1951, Donald Hall was an ambitious young poet who – like Eliot – had edited Harvard University's literary magazine, the *Advocate*, and had just won – like Eliot, in 1914 – a fellowship to Oxford University. Anxious about the prospect of meeting one-on-one with the recent Nobel Prize winner, Hall was "so convinced of the monumentality of this moment" that their conversation went badly. "I weighed every word as if my great-grandchildren were listening in, and I feared to let them down by speaking idiomatically, or by seeing the humor in anything," he writes (84). At the end of the interview, as Hall took his leave, Eliot appeared "to search for the right phrase with which to send [him] off" as he reflected on the parallels in their lives:

> "Let me see . . . forty years ago I went from Harvard to Oxford. Now you are going from Harvard to Oxford. What advice may I give you?" He paused delicately, shrewdly, while I waited with greed for the words which I would repeat for the rest of my life, the advice from elder to younger setting me on the road of emulation. When he had ticked off the comedian's exact milliseconds of pause, he said, "Have you any long underwear?" (87)

Ludicrously, Hall took Eliot seriously, purchased long underwear on the way back to his hotel – and awakened from his stargazing stupor to laugh at Eliot's joke six months later (88).[1]

This anecdote about an aspiring young poet-scholar's first encounter with the most famous modernist poet of his day epitomizes the contrasts I want to explore in this chapter in thinking about Eliot and modernism. Forty-odd years after Eliot's death, and more than fifty since he gave a lecture attended by nearly 14,000 people in a basketball arena (Matthews 166), it is actually hard to imagine a first-time reader of Eliot who is not aware of his celebrity status: a reader who can see Eliot outside the context of "seriousness" and "greatness" and "importance" that has built up around him, leaving young poets like Hall all but tongue-tied in his presence, incapable of

A Companion to T. S. Eliot, First Edition. Edited by David E. Chinitz.
© 2014 John Wiley & Sons, Ltd. Published 2014 by John Wiley & Sons, Ltd.

either recognizing Eliot's deadpan comedic wit or connecting it with his love of Groucho Marx. Today, as in 1951, it is difficult to experience Eliot's work without feeling pressured by a sense of his writing's cultural capital. This chapter, though, is about the roles that Eliot played in creating the aura of cultural authority that long surrounded a certain version of modernism. As the most influential aesthetic movement of the twentieth century, literary modernism has shaped the discipline of English studies in fundamental ways since the 1920s. As scholars wrestle now with historicizing modernism more thickly, Eliot remains a key figure of interest – though one whose work is being read through very different sets of critical lenses than those employed in the 1950s, when Donald Hall first met "Great Tom."

Defining and Historicizing Modernism

Somewhere between 1956 . . . and 1971 . . . the term {modernism} acquired a discernible currency among literary critics, shorthand to designate what {Graham} Hough had called "a revolution in the literature of the English language," a change which took place during "the years between 1910 and the Second World War." From literary studies the term migrated into other disciplines of the humanities, the history of art, music, and architecture. "Modernism is a term now frequently *used," Peter Faulkner could write in 1983, "in discussions of twentieth-century literature – indeed, of* all *forms of twentieth-century art." Such was the vertiginous history of a word. But what did it mean? Or perhaps we should ask, what has it meant in various times and places?*

— Rainey, *Modernism* xxi; emphasis added

So what is modernism, and what "has it meant in various times and places"? Some scholars argue that modernism is a "misleadingly singular rubric" for a "diverse synchrony" of artistic movements in the early twentieth century (Mahaffey 100), and point out the risks associated with attempting to formulate a unified formalist definition of modernism (North, *Reading* 209). Others trace key changes in the usage of this term over time and in different cultural contexts (Rainey, *Modernism* xx–xxv). Still others, while acknowledging such concerns, would nonetheless insist upon the continued usefulness of the term as a designation for literature written between 1910 and World War II that is formally self-conscious, experimental, and anti-representational (Felski 25). The latter also note that dating modernism isn't simply a matter of identifying beginning and end dates for a particular kind of artistic experimentation. Instead, it entails understanding how the work of an international set of late nineteenth- and early twentieth-century artists in self-imposed exile from bourgeois culture came to be comfortably ensconced in the academy, museum culture, and an international art market (Williams 35).[2]

I follow the lead of these last scholars here, since their work helps us recognize how Eliot figured in the construction of a highly selective twentieth-century literary canon that factored significantly in the institutionalization of English as an academic discipline in the 1920s and after. The "moment of modernism," Lyn Pykett writes, when "particular kinds of formal and linguistic experimentation" were privileged as defining "*the* canonical form of early twentieth-century literature," was also the moment

> in which a restricted group of texts and authors was removed from the complex social and cultural specificities of history and located in that transcendent ideal order of the literary tradition described (or invented) by Eliot in "Tradition and the Individual Talent"; a moment in which a particular "discipline of reading" was established by the "intellectual hegemony of Eliot, [F. R.] Leavis, [I. A.] Richards, and the New Critics."[3] (11)

Note the roles that Eliot plays in Pykett's argument about how modernist aesthetics and interpretive practices were stitched into the very fabric of English studies as the latter established its disciplinary credibility in the 1920s, 30s, and 40s. The year 1922 is often identified as the annus mirabilis of literary modernism because of two events: the first-time publication of James Joyce's *Ulysses* in book form, and the nearly simultaneous publication of Eliot's *The Waste Land* in two journals, the *Dial* in the United States and the *Criterion* in England, as well as in book form. As Ezra Pound proclaimed on many occasions, *Ulysses* and *The Waste Land* are literary modernism's masterworks: they epitomize "the 'movement' . . . our modern experiment, since 1900" (*Selected Letters* 180). Pykett's emphasis lies elsewhere, however. Eliot's literary criticism figures more prominently in her discussion than his poetry, because his critical essays model reading practices and interpretations of literary history that were championed by an extremely influential first generation of academics bringing contemporary literature into the formal curriculum of rapidly expanding systems of higher education in Britain and the United States.

"In the early 1920s," Terry Eagleton has noted, "it was desperately unclear why English was worth studying at all" at a prestigious institution such as Cambridge University. By the early 1930s, however, "it had become a question of why it was worth wasting your time on anything else" (31). As Gail McDonald argues in this collection and elsewhere, T. S. Eliot played a central role in this professionalization and elevation of literary studies in university curricula.[4] Through his own literary essays in the *New Statesman*, the *Egoist*, the *Times Literary Supplement*, and the *Criterion*, as well as through the influence of his work on British scholars such as Leavis and Richards and on the American New Critics, Eliot "changed the reading habits of . . . crucial audience[s]" (Diepeveen, "'I Can'" 55). Reshaping readers' "horizons of expectations" for modern poetry, he thereby guaranteed the critical success of his own work as well as of literary modernism more generally (40). Ezra Pound has been called the "impresario" of the London-based avant-garde because of his promotional efforts on behalf of writers such as Joyce, Eliot, and Wyndham Lewis (Rainey, *Modernism* 39). But if Pound played such a role in the 1910s, it was Eliot who oversaw the avant-garde's transformation into something called modernism through its "accession to cultural legitimacy" in the early 1920s (Levenson, *Genealogy* 213). It is thus worth considering in some detail how his poetry, specifically *The Waste Land*, and his literary-critical prose and editing work contributed to modernism's constitution as an idiom, a style of artistic expression deemed to be characteristic of the early twentieth century and presented as such in academic curricula as well as in public forums (e.g., periodicals and museum-based educational programming) reaching more general audiences.

Eliot and the Material Historical Production of Modernist Difficulty

{P}oets in our civilization, as it exists at present, must be difficult.

– Eliot, *SE* 248

I have undertaken the task of finding and selecting the contributors for a modest quarterly review which is subsidized to a moderate extent for three years. I propose that the quarterly should be simple and severe in appearance, *without illustrations, and my only ambition is that it should unite the best critical opinion in England, together with the work of the best critics whom I can find from other countries. Whilst I should admit other writing in very small quantity, I wish to make it primarily a critical review. To its ultimate financial success I am comparatively indifferent; but while it lasts, under my direction, I shall make its aim the* maintenance of critical standards and the concentration of intelligent critical opinion.

– Eliot, *Letters* 518; emphasis added

Why might it matter that *The Waste Land* was published first not in *Vanity Fair* or the *Little Review* but in both the inaugural issue of the *Criterion*, which Eliot himself edited, and the *Dial*, a highbrow arts magazine? Then as now, *Vanity Fair* was a "smart magazine" – that is, a high-quality, lavishly illustrated magazine appealing to a sophisticated urban elite, with a circulation of almost 100,000 (Douglas 117). The *Little Review* was a "little magazine," a noncommercial arts review founded for the express purpose of publishing "experimental works or radical opinions of untried, unpopular, or under-represented writers," whose print run never exceeded 1,000 (Churchill 8). Although the *Little Review's* in-your-face contempt for the status quo did not keep the magazine from running into the buzz saws of American censorship law in the late 1910s and 1920s, when it published work by Joyce and Wyndham Lewis, its masthead motto, "Making No Compromise with the Public Taste," exemplifies its stance toward both a social and a literary establishment. By contrast, the *Dial* (co-owned and coedited by Scofield Thayer, a wealthy New York lawyer and collector of modernist art, and James Sibley Watson, Jr.) was a "sober and authoritative" intellectual review with a circulation of between nine and ten thousand that "wanted to be in America what the *Mercure* had been in France" (Pound, "Small" 696).

As Jason Harding notes, the Viscountess Lilian Rothermere's purpose in funding the *Criterion* was to create a "London literary magazine that would have a social éclat among a select audience of writers, critics, and patrons of the arts"; Eliot's purpose in editing it, however, was to "consolidate the early groundwork of modernism and to combat the hostility or indifference of a highly commercialized industry of print journalism" to the work of London's literary avant-garde (9).[5]

So again: why might it matter that Eliot considered, and very deliberately rejected, both a little magazine and an upscale mass-market venue of publication for *The Waste Land*? What effect did the "bibliographic and contextual codes" of the *Dial* and the *Criterion* have on this poem's reception, and thus on the trajectory of Eliot's career?[6] In "The Price of Modernism," Lawrence Rainey argues that *The Waste Land*'s publication in the *Dial*, together with Eliot's receipt of the second annual Dial Award for poetry and a cash award of $2,000, marks "the crucial moment in the transition of modernism from a minority culture to one supported by an important institutional and financial apparatus" (91). But Michael Levenson's point that the founding of the *Criterion*, not the publication of either *Ulysses* or *The Waste Land*, marks modernism's true coming of age is equally germane to this discussion. The launching of this critical review, Levenson suggests,

> exemplifies the institutionalization of the movement, the accession to cultural legiti-
> macy. The journal provided Eliot, its editor, with a capacious forum; it had financial
> stability and intellectual weight; it constituted a respectable vessel for sometimes suspi-
> cious contents. *The Waste Land* appeared in the first issue of the journal, and its entry
> into the literary arena was no doubt eased by this context. If the poem threatened to
> outrage, the intellectual pedigree of the adjacent essays provided reassurance. These were
> reputable, restrained, even staid. (*Genealogy* 213)

I would connect both Rainey's and Levenson's arguments with recent scholarship on "material modernism" by George Bornstein to emphasize how the material historical practices of the periodical press and literary publishing contributed to the "shaping of taste" in the early twentieth century (Golding 43). Taken together, these three arguments underscore Eliot's considerable investments in the institutional "machinery of selective tradition" (Williams 32).

Writing in 1913 for the British little magazine the *Egoist*, Pound co-opted the rhetoric and the cultural authority of science for "the serious artist" when he argued that the arts "are a science, just as chemistry is a science," and give us "lasting and unassailable data regarding the nature of man" ("Serious" 42). In a letter to Sturge Moore on April 3, 1922 about his plans for the *Criterion*, Eliot emphasized that the focus of the new journal would be on the "maintenance of critical standards" rather than on the publication of original works of literature and the reproduction of con-temporary art (*Letters* 518). Yet when *The Waste Land* was published for the first time, in both the *Dial* and the *Criterion*, the "seriousness" of both Eliot's poetry and his critical standards was reinforced by the classical austerity of their presentation in these two settings, at a safe remove from, on the one hand, the aggressive anti-conformity of *The Little Review* and, on the other, the noisy visuality and overt commercialism of *Vanity Fair*. Publication in book form by Boni and Liveright, an upstart American publishing firm making its name by presenting contemporary American writers to American audiences, and then by Leonard and Virginia Woolf in a Hogarth Press limited edition, lent further support to *The Waste Land*'s reputation as a major cultural achievement. The point was underscored by *Vanity Fair*'s republication in June 1923 of poems by Eliot that had been published originally in the little magazines *Coterie*, the *Little Review*, and *Arts and Letters*, and its "intense campaign" of criticism on Eliot's work in its July and November 1923 and February 1924 issues (Rainey, *Institutions* 92, 200). As *Vanity Fair*'s managing editor noted in introducing the poetry reprints, "'[s]ince the publication of *The Waste Land*, Mr. T. S. Eliot has become the most hotly contested issue in American poetry.'" Eliot "had indeed become this," as Rainey observes, "in part because the *Dial* and *Vanity Fair* had said so themselves" – had made very conscious and deliberate investments in the dissemination of these views (*Institutions* 92).

Critical reputation is a function of interpretation, which can never entirely be separated from the history of institutional and material practices. Aesthetic value accrues to works of art as they circulate in culture and is directly related to *how* they circulate in culture. In Eliot's case, we might note that his status as "the most celebrated poet of his age" (Rainey, *Annotated* 2) is a function not only of how his poetry has been interpreted and reinterpreted but also of his success in shaping the critical standards by which his own creative work was evaluated, and the dissemination and reproduction of those standards in academic curricula for literary studies. Over the entire course of his career Eliot wrote only 2,700 lines of "major non-dramatic" poetry – roughly comparable to the first three books of *Paradise Lost* (Badenhausen 37). He wrote thousands of *pages* of prose criticism in the form of book reviews, introductions, public lectures, and essays. Between 1924 and 1965 he published "introductions, prefaces, forewords, critical notes, and similar documents" for the works of almost fifty contemporary or near-contemporary writers, including such figures as Pound, Joyce, Djuna Barnes, Marianne Moore, Wyndham Lewis, Christopher Isherwood, G. Wilson Knight, and David Jones (Jaffe 106, 107). His introductions, as Aaron Jaffe asserts, were "prized assets, partly prized for the highbrow cachet of Eliot's name, partly prized for his specific . . . ability to make obvious propaganda seem suitably critical and disinterested" (107). Through his editorial work for both the *Criterion* and Faber & Faber as well as by editing anthologies of periodical press writings – his own as well as those of peers such as Ezra Pound – Eliot contributed substantially to the redaction of a modernist canon.[7] And the support he expresses in essays such as "The Metaphysical Poets" for the social rhetoric of "difficulty," which is so central to the perception that modernism "was a sea change – not just in the properties of art works, but in the default and most useful ways of talking about and interacting with art" – figured crucially in the promulgation of literary modernism as *the* aesthetic of the twentieth century (Diepeveen, *Difficulties* xi).

The shaping power of modernist difficulty has been profound, as Leonard Diepeveen demonstrates. It was a "powerful aesthetic, then," and it "continues to be one, for aesthetic difficulty retains its legitimizing force today." Even now, "one's ability to move in high culture continues to depend, in large part, on how one reacts to difficulty" (*Difficulties* xi). It would certainly not be fair to say that Eliot created the prestige of modernist difficulty singlehandedly. Yet his work is part of the bedrock of that particular cultural formation. And that formation, as McDonald has shown, is complexly related to both the professionalization of literary studies and the curricular reorganizations of "modern" universities at the turn of the twentieth century.

Restoring Eliot to the "Fuller Context" of Modernism, Restoring Complexity to Eliot

But if Eliot's ambition to professionalize "both the creation and the study of literature" was "realized on a scale of which he probably never dreamed" by the 1960s and 70s (Chinitz 160), it is also the case that his familiar characterization as the human embodiment of elite culture fails to do full justice to the complexities of his life and life's work. As David Chinitz argues in *T. S. Eliot and the Cultural Divide*, the Eliot we inherited from the first several generations of scholarship on literary modernism "is *terribly* serious – a very paragon of solemn purpose, tormented vision, and lofty contemplation. And his milieu, while quite varied within its bookish limits, is altogether too polite" (12). One objective of Chinitz's study is thus "to restore Eliot to a fuller context": to ensure that twenty-first-century readers of Eliot recognize how popular artists and art forms such as comic strips, music-hall comedy, melodrama, and Jazz-Age song "belong to the mise-en-scène [of modernism] and have their parts to play in Eliot's cultural life – and in his writing" (12). The Eliot portrayed in his study is a "multidimensional thinker and artist" whose response to the popular genres of his day, "both as theorized in his critical essays and as practiced in his art, is supple, frequently insightful, and always deeply ambivalent" (5).

Chinitz's 2003 study exemplifies the move toward "richer, thicker" historicizations of modernism that distinguish what is sometimes known as "the new modernist studies" from the first several generations of scholarship on literary modernism (Levenson, *Companion* 1). In their different ways, Levenson's close study of the "micropolitics" of *The Waste Land* ("Does" 5); Jaffe's exploration of the interdependence of modernist literature – and Eliot's career – with modern celebrity culture (72–80); Patrick Collier's and Jason Harding's independent efforts to situate Eliot in relation to early twentieth-century journalism; and Michael North's restoration of *The Waste Land* (in *Reading 1922*) to a cultural moment that also saw essential developments in such diverse phenomena as travel writing, public relations, linguistics, and cinema also illustrate this form of criticism. As is clearly the case with the research cited in the previous sections of this chapter, recent scholarship in this vein reflects very self-consciously on both the interpretive paradigms and the mappings of literary history that we have inherited from modernists themselves, as well as from influential early readers and promoters of this work.

Emphasizing not only the plurality of modernisms but also the countercurrents, disagreements, and contestations *within* modernisms, much of this scholarship seeks to recover an early twentieth-century landscape in which modernism did not yet throw gigantic shadows. Demonstrating how literary modernism's rise to aesthetic hegemony paved the way for the institutionalization of English studies through the devaluation of *other* aesthetic practices, *other* modes of discursive production, this research is challenging us to remember the extent to which literature was an open field at the turn of the century: a highly unstable and fiercely contested discursive territory whose claims to authority over its objects of study were developed through the institutional networks its proponents sought to establish and the epistemologies they worked to naturalize. Reading modernist texts in tandem with literary and non-literary texts and cultural phenomena that the modernist avant-garde deemed extraneous or incidental to their own version of literary and cultural history, this work offers a "reappraisal of modernism as a whole" (Chinitz, "T. S. Eliot" 246) as it foregrounds issues of disciplinary organization of particular relevance today in the context of the current paradigm shift from literary into cultural studies.

In an important 1994 essay reviewing revisionary feminist scholarship on modernism, Deborah Jacobs contended that feminist scholars were reinforcing rather than challenging traditional modernist notions of aesthetic value (including but not limited to the privileging of "difficulty") as they recovered the work of female modernists such as Djuna Barnes, Mina Loy, Dorothy Richardson, Rebecca West, and Virginia Woolf. We have not yet managed "to *rethink* or *rechart* . . . modernism in terms other than those [it] narrated/laid out for itself," she argued. We continue "to read modernism from within its own politics and prejudices" rather than offering a more radical rethinking of them (277, 288). It is certainly true, as Aaron Jaffe has argued recently, that "rules of scarcity" continue to organize literary reputation, restricting the number of names and texts that "remain in heavy rotation" in modernist studies in spite of three decades' worth of revisionary scholarship. It is also true that what Jaffe terms the "imprimatur" of modernist literary self-fashioning has yet to be superseded by another modeling of aesthetic excellence. I would argue nonetheless that much of the recent scholarship I have cited in this chapter attempts to rethink modernism "in terms other than those [it] narrated/laid out for itself." That is to say, such scholarship is rising to some if not all of the challenges that Jacobs articulated so powerfully when she charted a new trajectory for further scholarship in the field.[8] A key feature of the new modernist studies in this regard has been its interest in rethinking modernism's relationship to popular culture and the popular ideologies of gender, race, and ethnicity of its day. In scholarship on Eliot this has involved developing readings of *The Waste Land* that focus, for example, on the influence of African-American dialect (North, *Dialect* 77–99), or of ragtime, jazz, and minstrel songs on Eliot's "poetic cadences" (Chinitz, *T. S. Eliot* 38, 41–49); or that situate the poem's typist and young man carbuncular in relationship to the constellation of popular genres – novels and plays, mainly – figuring the female office worker as a distinctively "modern" woman (Rainey, *Revisiting* 52–70). As Jonathan Freedman and Cassandra Laity both note, debating or redefining Eliot's relation to "low" culture, gender/sexuality, and race (specifically anti-Semitism) has been an occasion not simply for rethinking Eliot's life and life's work, but for debate about "the nature and shape of literary experience and expression itself for at least the past two generations" (Freedman 420; Laity 3).

Interest in reconceptualizing modernism's relationship to contemporary popular culture has also brought into the critical limelight works in Eliot's canon once acknowledged at best awkwardly – and even more frequently ignored entirely in major studies of his work (even though the industry of Eliot scholarship has never lagged at any point in time in the last 80 years). For example, Eliot's 1923 tribute to Marie Lloyd, the English music-hall performer whose funeral cortège was attended by nearly 100,000 people in October 1922, emerges as "a key document in a long series that embodies [Eliot's] genuine receptiveness to popular culture," not as a peripheral, eccentric, or anomalous piece of writing in Eliot's oeuvre, in *T. S. Eliot and the Cultural Divide* (Chinitz 15). Similarly, Eliot's first attempt to write a play, the two fragments we now know by the title *Sweeney Agonistes*, is garnering renewed attention for its Jazz-Age discourses of race, gender, and culture (DuPlessis 82), and for its campy, sardonically hyper-stylized evocations of the "American vulgar tongue" (Gates 289). Highbrow modernist friends like the Woolfs and Pound never quite comprehended why Eliot wrote verse dramas in the thirties, railing either publicly or privately against his "abandonment" of aesthetic quality in seeking large public audiences for his plays. After many years of critical reinforcement of such views, Eliot's forays into middle-class, middlebrow, mainstream theater are being perceived now not as a false move in an otherwise long and distinguished artistic career but as part and parcel of Eliot's lifelong interest in the dynamic give-and-take of highbrow and popular culture (Chinitz, *T. S. Eliot* 129–52). There is even a place in Eliot scholarship now for *Five-Finger Exercises*, *Old Possum's Book of Practical Cats*, and the crudities of the "Columbo and Bolo" poems.

For the first time, attention is also being given to Eliot's interest in reaching popular audiences through radio broadcasts for the BBC. When Eliot recorded his first series of talks for the BBC in July 1929, the latter was still a fledgling corporation, not an established institution whose prestige might have attracted a writer interested in enlarging his own celebrity status (Coyle 141). As Michael Coyle has established through careful review of the BBC archives, Eliot recognized early on the potential of radio as a means of mass communication, and respected it as an essentially oral medium, "capable of commanding a solidarity-building and oratic authority" (144). Although his attitude toward this emerging media form and his involvement with the BBC "puzzled" fellow modernists who "knew how pressed he was for time to write" at this point in his career, Eliot valued radio for its capacity to project pure voice – speech unmediated by writing – and he never expressed the kind of uniform hostility to mass media articulated so influentially by modernist critics such as Theodor Adorno (Coyle 141, 144). Choosing instead to distinguish radio from film and, later, TV because of what he saw as radio's potential as a medium of educational "uplift," Eliot made radio broadcasting a "regular and seriously regarded part of [his] working life" by the outbreak of World War II (152, 141).

Although the version of literary modernism that was instrumental in the institutionalization of English studies had no interest in, and no means of accounting for, Eliot's lifelong (albeit ambivalent) engagement with popular culture, current scholarship in the field is exposing the politics and prejudices driving such redactions of Eliot's career even as it identifies new archival resources for further research. As "more inclusive conceptions of modernism gain currency" in the field (Laity 2), and as modernism's relationship to modernity is being reimagined through this research, our portraits of T. S. Eliot are becoming more complexly multidimensional – Vorticist even – in their disruption of conventional perspective. An intriguing throwback to the monumentalizing notion of "Great Tom" that Donald Hall jettisoned in 1951 when he finally registered Eliot's joke about long underwear, Eliot the high-culture mandarin beams down at us in his four-piece suit from the murals of Barnes & Noble café bookstores all over the world (Jaffe 199–204). But Eliot the literary entrepreneur and the fan of Groucho Marx, the fox-trot, and detective fiction is an artist far better served in the twenty-first century by critical methodologies that attend to the material history of literary production, and that recognize contradiction, ambivalence, and multi-vocality, than by the reading practices and the social rhetoric of difficulty that he himself helped to normalize when something called modernism first entered the academy.

NOTES

1   Lawrence Rainey introduces his edition of *The Waste Land* with this anecdote, and I begin with it here to showcase the contrasts this chapter explores between the daunting monumentality of "Great Tom," the doyen of high culture, seriousness, and modernist difficulty that we inherited from the first several generations of scholarship on modernism, and the more complex – and human – figure emerging as "richer, thicker" historicizations of modernism reimagine Eliot (Levenson, *Companion* 1).

2   See also McDonald; Menand 97–132; and Scholes 3–32.

3   "Discipline of reading" is Richard Poirier's phrase, used in *The Renewal of Literature* (London: Faber, 1988) 95; "the intellectual hegemony of Eliot, Leavis, Richards and the New Critics" is Edward Said's phrase, used in "Criticism," *Boundary 2* 8 (1979): 17.

4   See also ELIOT AND THE NEW CRITICS.

5   See also KEEPING CRITICAL THOUGHT ALIVE: ELIOT'S EDITORSHIP OF THE CRITERION.

6   I borrow the terms "bibliographic and contextual codes" from George Bornstein, who uses them in *Material Modernism* to talk about how interpretation of a poem is affected by the material and sociohistorical contexts in which it is published and republished. "Bibliographic code" is Bornstein's term for the physical materiality of a text, as related to its distribution – the size and kind of paper it is printed on, the choice of typeface, use of graphics, choice of publisher, size of print run, price, etc. "Contextual code" is his term for all the historical epiphenomena that can shape a reader's interpretation of a given text – as, for example, when a reader reads "September, 1913" in *The Irish Times*, rather than in a modern teaching

edition of Yeats's poetry, and sees how it engages with that newspaper's coverage of "the most violent and prolonged labor struggles" in Irish history (55). Although Bornstein does not discuss Eliot in *Material Modernism*, I invoke his work here because it offers such a suggestive way of thinking about how the "aura" of *The Waste Land* in particular was created through its material production in its original sites of publication.

7 Jonathan Freedman's description of Eliot's impact on "the booming literary academy of the 1940s and 1950s, especially in America"

is particularly apt: "To be a college professor of English in this period was, perforce, to come to terms with a model of literary history and cultural value that placed Eliot, the work Eliot esteemed (e.g., metaphysical poetry), and the religious vision that Eliot affirmed at the center of critical and pedagogic practice" (420).

8 See Delap and DiCenzo, however, for an important discussion of how current work in modernist studies is still reinforcing rather than challenging modernist mappings of early twentieth-century literary and cultural history.

REFERENCES AND FURTHER READING

Ardis, Ann. *Modernism and Cultural Conflict, 1880–1922.* Cambridge: Cambridge UP, 2002.

Badenhausen, Richard. *T. S. Eliot and the Art of Collaboration.* Cambridge: Cambridge UP, 2004.

Bornstein, George. *Material Modernism: The Politics of the Page.* Cambridge: Cambridge UP, 2001.

Chinitz, David E. *T. S. Eliot and the Cultural Divide.* Chicago: U of Chicago P, 2003.

——. "T. S. Eliot and the Cultural Divide." *PMLA* 110 (1995): 236–47.

Churchill, Suzanne. *The Little Magazine Others and the Renovation of Modern American Poetry.* Aldershot: Ashgate, 2006.

Collier, Patrick. *Modernism on Fleet Street.* Aldershot: Ashgate, 2006.

Coyle, Michael. "T. S. Eliot on the Air: 'Culture' and the Challenges of Mass Communication." *T. S. Eliot and Our Turning World.* Ed. Jewel Spears Brooker. Basingstoke: Macmillan, 2001. 141–54.

Delap, Lucy, and Maria DiCenzo. "Transatlantic Print Culture: The Anglo-American Press and Emerging 'Modernities.'" *Transatlantic Print Culture 1880–1940: Emerging Media, Emerging Modernisms.* Ed. Ann Ardis and Patrick Collier. New York: Palgrave, 2008. 48–65.

Diepeveen, Leonard. *The Difficulties of Modernism.* New York: Routledge, 2003.

——. "'I can have more than enough power to satisfy me': T. S. Eliot's Construction of His Audience." *Marketing Modernisms: Self-Promotion, Canonization, and Rereading.* Ed. Kevin J. H.

Dettmar and Stephen Watt. Ann Arbor: U of Michigan P, 1996. 37–60.

Douglas, George H. *The Smart Magazines: 50 Years of Literary Revelry and High Jinks at Vanity Fair, The New Yorker, Life, Esquire, and The Smart Set.* Hamden, CT: Archon, 1991.

DuPlessis, Rachel Blau. *Genders, Races, and Religious Cultures in Modern American Poetry, 1908–1934.* Cambridge: Cambridge UP, 2001.

Eagleton, Terry. *Literary Theory: An Introduction.* Minneapolis: U of Minnesota P, 1983.

Easthope, Antony. *Literary into Cultural Studies.* London: Routledge, 1991.

Felski, Rita. *The Gender of Modernity.* Cambridge: Harvard UP, 1995.

Freedman, Jonathan. "Lessons Out of School: T. S. Eliot's Jewish Problem and the Making of Modernism." *Modernism/Modernity* 10 (2003): 419–30.

Gates, Henry Louis, Jr. *Figures in Black: Words, Signs, and the 'Racial' Self.* New York: Oxford UP, 1987.

Golding, Alan C. "*The Dial, The Little Review,* and the Dialogics of Modernism." *American Periodicals* 15 (2005): 42–55.

Hall, Donald. *Their Ancient Glittering Eyes: Remembering Poets and More Poets.* New York: Tichner, 1992.

Harding, Jason. *The Criterion: Cultural Politics and Periodical Networks in Inter-War Britain.* Oxford: Oxford UP, 2002.

Jacobs, Deborah. "Feminist Criticism/Cultural Studies/Modernist Texts: A Manifesto for the

'90s. *Rereading Modernism: New Directions in Feminist Criticism*. Ed. Lisa Rado. New York: Garland, 1994. 273–98.

Jaffe, Aaron. *Modernism and the Culture of Celebrity*. Cambridge: Cambridge UP, 2005.

Laity, Cassandra. "Introduction: Eliot, Gender, and Modernity." *Gender, Desire, and Sexuality in T. S. Eliot*. Ed. Laity and Nancy K. Gish. Cambridge: Cambridge UP, 2004. 1–22.

Levenson, Michael H., ed. *The Cambridge Companion to Modernism*. Cambridge: Cambridge UP, 1999.

——. "Does *The Waste Land* Have a Politics?" *Modernism/Modernity* 6 (1999): 1–13.

——. *A Genealogy of Modernism: A Study of English Literary Doctrine 1908–1922*. Cambridge: Cambridge UP, 1984.

Mahaffey, Vicki. "Heirs of Yeats: Eire as Female Poets Revise Her." *The Future of Modernism*. Ed. Hugh Witemeyer. Ann Arbor: U of Michigan P, 1997. 101–17.

Matthews, T. S. *Great Tom: Notes towards the Definition of T. S. Eliot*. New York: Harper, 1974.

McDonald, Gail. *Learning To Be Modern: Pound, Eliot, and the American University*. Oxford: Clarendon, 1993.

Menand, Louis. *Discovering Modernism: T. S. Eliot and His Context*. 2nd ed. New York: Oxford UP, 1996.

North, Michael. *The Dialect of Modernism: Race, Language, and Twentieth-Century Literature*. New York: Oxford UP, 1994.

——. *Reading 1922: A Return to the Scene of the Modern*. New York: Oxford UP, 1999.

Pound, Ezra. *Selected Letters, 1907–1941*. Ed. D. D. Paige. New York: New Directions, 1971.

——. "The Serious Artist." *The Literary Essays of Ezra Pound*. Ed. T. S. Eliot. New York: New Directions, 1935. 41–57.

——. "Small Magazines." *English Journal* 19 (1930): 689–704.

Pykett, Lyn. *Engendering Fictions: The English Novel in the Early Twentieth Century*. London: Arnold, 1995.

Rainey, Lawrence, ed. *The Annotated Waste Land with Eliot's Contemporary Prose*. New Haven: Yale UP, 2005.

——. *Institutions of Modernism: Literary Elites and Public Culture*. New Haven: Yale UP, 1998.

——. "Introduction." *Modernism: An Anthology*. Ed. Rainey. Malden, MA: Blackwell, 2005. xix–xxix.

——. *Revisiting The Waste Land*. New Haven: Yale UP, 2005.

Schenke, Celeste. "Exiled by Genre: Modernism, Canonicity, and the Politics of Exclusion." *Women's Writing in Exile*. Ed. Mary Lynn Broe and Angela Ingram. Chapel Hill: U of North Carolina P, 1989. 225–50.

Scholes, Robert. *The Paradoxy of Modernism*. New Haven: Yale UP, 2006.

Williams, Raymond. *The Politics of Modernism: Against the New Conformists*. London: Verso, 1989.

27

Conflict and Concealment: Eliot's Approach to Women and Gender

Cyrena Pondrom

Critics have differed sharply over the years about T. S. Eliot's views on women and gender. Few have regarded the matter as altogether unproblematic, but initial assessments generally saw him as reflecting traditional heterosexual attitudes toward gender roles in early poems concerned with the male speaker's inability to achieve satisfactory relationships with women. That view has survived to the present day, and it underlies the two vastly differing book-length studies of Eliot's view of women: Marja Palmer's *Men and Women in T. S. Eliot's Early Poetry* (1996) and Tony Pinckney's *Women in the Poetry of T. S. Eliot: A Psychoanalytic Approach* (1984). Palmer argues that in Eliot's early poetry the problems depicted in "portrayals of men" are "insecurity, lack of self-confidence, and emotional as well as sexual impotence." These issues deny the women any "affection and understanding between the sexes," but "the women themselves are seldom blamed" (228). She concludes that "both men and women" in *The Waste Land* "share the pain equally. It seems impossible to perceive any misogyny in the description of the women in the poem" (231). Pinckney, in contrast, paraphrases Eliot's own infamous lines (*CPP* 83) to argue "that any Eliotic text has to, needs to, wants to in one way or another, do a girl in; and if it fails to achieve that goal, it is itself murderously threatened by the girl" (18). Pinckney uses "post-Freudian developments in psychoanalysis" (49) to "focus critical attention on the commanding importance of representations of the mother and the female body in Eliot's text" (ix), and argues that "the murdered woman is never simply one's mistress, but is first and foremost recipient of unconscious phantasies pertaining to the most primitive stages of the infant–mother relationship" (49). Scholars like these, who operate on an underlying assumption of heterosexuality, have formed two divergent currents in recent scholarly discourse: those who argue for the misogyny of Eliot's texts, particularly but not exclusively feminist critics (Pinckney; Gilbert and Gubar; Nicholls; DuPlessis); and those who stress the importance of Eliot's vision of a Beatrice-like figure or "dark angel," usually explicitly female, with whom the poet's personae struggle in his early poetry and who ultimately

A Companion to T. S. Eliot, First Edition. Edited by David E. Chinitz.

becomes an intercessory presence or divine vision in his later writing (Gordon *Imperfect*; Schuchard).

Arrayed beside this in contemporary discourse are two other important currents: critics who see Eliot as an unacknowledged homosexual and found their analyses of his views of both women and gender upon this biographical assertion (Peter; Cole; Miller; Dean; Lamos), and critics who see Eliot as anticipating important elements of poststructuralism and argue, for instance, that he offers an example of *écriture féminine* (Badenhausen), or that he displays an understanding of gender as performative and that the anxiety of his modernism rests partially on the instability of identity such performativity produces (Pondrom). An extremely useful collection of a diverse range of views – most of them more recent – appeared in the 2004 anthology edited by Cassandra Laity and Nancy Gish. The efflorescence of nontraditional studies of Eliot and gender followed the publication of Eliot's notebooks, *Inventions of the March Hare*, in 1996, for this previously unpublished work contained the Bolo poems, arguably both misogynist and homosocial, and some poems or drafts with openly sadomasochist themes.

The apparatus with which Eliot introduced his early poems illustrates tendencies in his work that help to explain this vertiginous disparity in critical assessments. The dedication of *Prufrock and Other Observations* (1917) to Jean Verdenal, "mort aux [died at the] Dardanelles" is followed by a quotation from Dante that reads, in translation: "Now canst thou comprehend the measure of the love that warms me toward thee, when I forget our nothingness and treat a shade [ghost] as a solid thing" (*CPP* 3). There follows the individual poem title "The Love Song of J. Alfred Prufrock," and another Dantean epigraph which suggests that the speaker, burning in hell, is about to divulge secrets which must not be shared. This sequence places a decisive question mark beside Eliot's legal suppression in 1952 of John Peter's reading of *The Waste Land* as an elegy for a male friend, whom he identified in 1969 as Jean Verdenal, Eliot's friend during his critical year in Paris (1910–11), who was killed in World War I. We see here, I think, a paradigm case of Eliot as chameleon hiding in plain view, and we gain considerable insight into his poetic strategies. The same example illuminates the tirelessly discussed contradiction between Eliot's critical espousal of an impersonal theory of poetry and his later wry acknowledgment of surprise that *The Waste Land* had been taken as a statement of the modern mind when he in fact had regarded it as "only the relief of a personal and wholly insignificant grouse against life" (*WLF* 1). In short, Eliot believed – and demonstrated – that he could express the most completely personal emotions without a wide public linking them to his private feelings, when he did so by means of allusion, use of multiple languages, ellipsis, juxtaposition, irony, careful omission of gendered reference in some places, and rigorous deployment of a persona whose view the whole structure, rhetoric, and tone of his poems often critiqued. What he was particularly concerned to avoid in his poetry was the appeal to details of biography that lead the reader away from the poem and from experiencing the emotions it elicits. As he argued, "what a poem means is as much what it means to others as what it means to the author" (*UPUC* 122).

The productiveness of this view is clear in the popularity of Eliot's early poetry. Insecurity in approaching the Other, fears about being discounted by the opposite sex, and despair at the loss or uncertainty of love are common experiences, and the ambiguous source of the speaker's feelings in Eliot's poems enables them to resonate with the personal emotions of readers completely different from the poet. Nonetheless, Eliot's views of gender and struggles with his own are incxtricably bound up with his views of women, and what some readers have seen as misogyny may be more accurately read as anguish over conflicted sexual feelings that the poet seeks to order and control.

The Struggle for Masculinity: Gender Roles in the Early Poems

In fact, Eliot's conflicted views of women and gender and his chameleon-like self-concealment are outstandingly on display in "Prufrock." One of the standard interpretations of this poem is that at least at one level, it concerns the anguish and insecurity of a man who is uncertain how to perform the masculine role in social interactions between men and women and even whether he wishes or dares to do so (Drew 35; Palmer 23, 34–35). Gender offers itself here not as automatic, inborn and unreflective, but as a complex set of coercive cultural expectations that are performed in social behavior. The women of the poem appear alternatively as threatening and dismissive or as objects of compulsive desire mixed with a subtle revulsion. Even if we do not know that the poem was subtitled "Prufrock among the Women" in an early draft (*IMH* 39), the theme of a man seeking to define who he is in relationship to the other sex emerges in the poem almost immediately. First the speaker notes that the journey will take "us" past "one-night cheap hotels" – presumably the scenes of prostitution and one-night stands (*CPP* 3). Like the coercive expectations of gender roles, these streets seem to force him (with "insidious intent") toward his destination, which we immediately discover to be a drawing room populated, at least in part, by women. The jarring nature of the expected encounter is mimed by the disjunctive interpolation of the lines "In the room the women come and go, / Talking of Michelangelo" (4). Prufrock is not ready for this encounter, particularly, we come to suspect, with women whose expectation of masculine physical grace and power is shaped by the paintings of Michelangelo.

The speaker delays his intended entry, imagining the roles or façades that he will take up before he engages in the most conventional of encounters: "there will be time / To prepare a face . . . / Before the taking of a toast and tea" (*CPP* 4). This reverie is interrupted again by the Michelangelo lines, which now suggest an inexorable quality in the expected encounter, for their very repetition hints at forces beyond his control. Prufrock again recoils from his anticipated destination, and his reveries turn explicitly to his bodily insufficiencies. He imagines a future in which he will wear all the trappings of the well-suited, affluent male – morning coat, collar and necktie – but these "stage props" will not conceal his balding head and his skinny arms and legs. He is the antithesis of Michelangelo's muscular, young nude David, and he imagines that the women will turn from art to commenting on the unsatisfactory nature of his own body.

At this point Prufrock asks the pivotal question of the poem: "Do I dare / Disturb the universe?" (*CPP* 4–5). This question operates simultaneously within multiple frameworks. One of the most important is the philosophical, and these lines can be read as a potential challenge to the fundamental epistemological nature of human experience. In a dialectical world in which the self is shut off from absolute knowledge of the Other, subject from object, to seek real knowledge of the Other is an effort to alter the structures of human experience and possibility. (This view is shared at least in part by the major figures of philosophical idealism, including Descartes, Bergson, and Bradley, the latter the subject of Eliot's dissertation.) But the Other here is specifically female, and the fact compels the lines also to take on social meanings. One rendering portrays Prufrock's "universe" as a social and cultural one in which women dominate – a reading compatible both with Pinckney's psychoanalytic assertion of the power of the body of the mother in Eliot's poetry, and with Gilbert and Gubar's insistence that modernism was marked by a "battle of the sexes" brought on by the increasing entry of women into the public sphere in the first years of the twentieth century (31–34). In a reading projecting the speaker as banal, the question can be seen as the speech of a narcissistic, much too self-important and astonishingly fearful man who elevates the challenge of entering a room to engage in social discourse to the equivalent of a challenge to the universe – a man whose youth is implicit in the inexperience and naiveté of his reflections. But without losing the deflationary irony of such a treatment of the poem's persona, the lines also imply a more profound possibility, for the speaker may also be asking, "Do I dare disturb the universe of cultural expectations by refusing to perform my expected gender role – either by refusing to 'play the game' of courtship with the women, or more starkly by turning to a male companion for the support and personal enhancement of intimate friendship?"[1] Such a reading recognizes the coerciveness of gender roles, which are seen by the interpolated speaker to be both objectively part of the structure of the world and personally inherent, even as he summons gender into existence by his performance of it.[2] At this level the lines make vivid "the difficulties" Eliot saw "in constituting a gendered self" (Christ 31).

Prufrock believes that the women's "voices" and "eyes that fix you in a formulated phrase" have the power to construct and imprison him and to demand that he give an account of the way he has conducted his life (*CPP* 5). Nonetheless, their seductive allure interrupts his mental effort: he can't tear his mind away from an inner vision of perfumed women with "Arms that are braceleted and white and bare." The memory is accompanied by recollections as unappealing as the first thought was alluring, however, for he remembers seeing that the arms were "downed with light brown hair," and he wrenches his mind back to the task of giving an account of himself. The account he begins is of a male world – of walking urban streets and observing "the smoke that rises from the pipes / Of lonely men in shirt-sleeves." But this memory, too, fails him, and his next recourse is to the more elemental vision of himself as the "ragged claws" of a scuttling crab on the ocean floor (5).

The speaker finally is able to imagine himself actually seated in the room with a woman and he asks himself if he would "Have the strength to force the moment to its crisis?" (*CPP* 6). The question reflects the cultural rhetoric of masculine power, and though he imagines himself in the apocalyptic language of a John the Baptist sacrificed to Salomé, he confesses his failure in the language of a boxer snickered at by his second when he is afraid to enter the ring and fight (6). The following stanza confirms his despair. He cannot say in language what he means, but if some "magic lantern" could reveal his inner reality, could throw "the nerves in patterns on a screen," the woman would contemptuously dismiss him. He is not what she seeks: "That is not what I meant, at all." (6) Even the conclusion to this poem continues the metaphor of the *femme* literally "*fatale*," for his escapist imaginings are of mermaids, who drown the men who dare to love them.

One must emphasize the one-sidedness of this "love song." We know what Prufrock feels, but we do *not* know, except for brief quotations he attributes to them, what the women think. This painfully self-conscious speaker believes he will be seen as "a bit obtuse," "almost ridiculous" (*CPP* 7), but we cannot know reliably if this is the women's view. And we cannot say that Prufrock's attitudes constitute Eliot's own views of women. What we can say is that Eliot depicts Prufrock as a figure whose masculinity is constructed – and deconstructed – in the culturally defined behaviors of his dress, speech, body image, and social interactions. He *performs* his gender, and does so in a way that calls his potency into question, and at the same time he treats these conventions as coercive and beyond his control. Eliot also offers us here a portrait of a man so unable to focus his attention on his companion's feelings that the women of the poem practically merit compassion. That certainly is the case in the other long poem that constructs detailed images of women and gender in Eliot's first volume – "Portrait of a Lady."

Like "Prufrock," "Portrait of a Lady" was written during the critical period of 1910–11. A surprising number of critics have treated this poem as a more or less reliable account of the lady, whom they see as manipulatively trying to induce guilt in her young visitor so as to achieve companionship for herself (Miller 150; Palmer 54; Smith 298). But this poem is not made up of "double – male and female – monologues" "with equal legitimacy," as Palmer claims (54). As with "Prufrock," this is a poem entirely narrated by a male speaker, and the speech of the woman is placed in quotation marks while the silent monologue of the narrator goes unmarked. Although one must always bear in mind that these are the spoken words and the details of behavior and setting that the young man chooses or is able to see, hear, and remember, this poem is almost alone in Eliot's poetry in presenting a complex and nuanced female figure. Only in his later dramas are comparably ambiguous woman characters to be found.

The "Lady" appears to be a person of some education, culture, economic means, and sophistication, but the gender expectations for an unmarried woman of her years and class allow little more action than attending concerts and inviting friends to tea. The young man, whom she invites to tea, is subject to no such restraints. Nevertheless, he feels she threatens to control and humiliate him. From the second line – "You have the scene arrange itself – as it will seem to do," he sees her as a kind of master puppeteer, and himself as her writhing puppet, struggling to resist her control (*CPP* 8). The disjunction between the lady's lack of social freedom and young man's fear of her dominance is one of the elements of the poem that focus our attention on the power and meaning of gender roles.

In fact, this poem offers us a model of the differing kinds of power exercised in Eliot's world by women and men. The woman in this poem is manipulative, oblique. She seeks to compel intimacy by the appearance of volunteering great intimacy herself, and by imputing to the man keen insight into her own feelings. The young man reacts with the power he has – the power to go where he pleases, and, ultimately, the power of abandonment. As the first part ends, he seems to give no answer to the woman, but retreats to a masculine public world of tobacco, beer, and "monuments" (*CPP* 9).

In the second part the two are again in the lady's drawing room. She has become subtly accusatory, and when she implies he holds her life in his hands, the young man, like Prufrock, is quick to condemn himself. He hears the lady say "'And youth is cruel, and has no remorse / And smiles at situations which it cannot see'" and silently confesses, "I smile, of course" (*CPP* 9). Her comments again slip quickly from complaint to assertion of an understanding on the part of her visitor for which we see no evidence, and then to a hanging question: "'but what have I, my friend, / To give you, what can you receive from me?'" (10). Even her swift and proper suggestion that she can give "friendship" and "sympathy" cannot completely erase the erotic nuances the question conceals, and the young man immediately flees. He goes back to his routine of public spaces, and sturdily claims, "I remain self-possessed" except when a sound or smell reminds him of "things that other people have desired" (10).

The third section, in which the young man reveals to the lady his imminent departure "abroad," completes the themes that have been previously set in motion. He retains his self-possession as he resists the lady's pretenses of a close relationship, a pretense shattered when her mask is dropped and she confronts reality openly: "'I have been wondering frequently of late / . . . / Why we have not developed into friends'" (*CPP* 11). His own façade destroyed by her brief honesty, he struggles to construct a masculine persona that will restore his power, reverting to the "tobacco trance" that had earlier marked his withdrawal into the public space, while also caricaturing himself as an "ape." He then addresses the question which she implied in the second part, explicitly framing their relationship as a power struggle: "Well! and what if she should die some afternoon / . . . / Would she not have the advantage, after all?" (11).

Some critics have associated Eliot's sympathy with the woman, and others, often dogmatically, with the man (Smith 14; Miller 150; Palmer 70–71; Gordon, *Imperfect* 37). In fact, Eliot, chameleon-like, refuses to ally the poet's views with either figure in "Portrait" but instead offers a critique of the gender roles that each acts to the fullest, and suggests a bleak assessment of the possibility of genuine and compassionate human love.

Seductive, Manipulative, Pathetic: Images of Women before 1927

These themes are borne out in most of the other poems of this period that prominently involve women. Whenever a complex subjectivity is fully realized, it is masculine; female characters are generally presented in single dimension. These female figures fall in three general categories: images of desire or seduction to whom the male is unable to offer love; manipulative and sometimes threatening figures seeking male attention and often offering sexual commerce; and pathetic images of women merely exploited and used. In the first category are the innocent yet seductive girl imagined by the narrator in the important early poem "La Figlia che Piange" and "the hyacinth girl" of the first section of *The Waste Land*. In the first of these poems the narrator stages the girl with arms full of flowers at the head of a stair, and proceeds to "try on" the costumes of various images of male power as he imagines dismissing her. Some are cruel – "As the mind deserts the body it has used" – and others socially deft. He cannot tear his mind away from her image, but he confesses in the end that the only element about these fantasies that is true is the fact that "She turned away." The narrator has constructed around her memory nothing more than "a gesture and a pose" (*CPP* 20).

In *The Waste Land*, the narrator is struck dumb and blind before the image of proffered love represented by the figure called "the hyacinth girl," and in the face of his inability to respond to such a corporeal image of love he finds himself "neither / Living nor dead" (*CPP* 38). The perception of the erotic possibilities of the female has quite a different outcome in "Hysteria." Here a narrator, mesmerized by the laughter of his female companion, symbolically translates the experience into violently sexual terms. He feels himself engulfed, "lost finally in the dark caverns of her throat," and, as the poem ends, he seeks to salvage the encounter by directing his entire attention to the task of stopping "the shaking of her breasts" (19). The poem is a splendid example of Eliot's chameleon-like ambiguity: who manifests hysteria – the laughing lady or her terrified male companion?

The second category, a savage variant on the themes of "Portrait of a Lady," is exemplified in the exchange between husband and wife in section two of *The Waste Land*. Here a neurotic upper-middle-class woman demands repeatedly that her partner "[s]tay with" her and "[s]peak to" her (*CPP* 40). As in the earlier poem, the narrator quotes her words while representing his own silently, and his very refusal to speak becomes as much a passive-aggressive hostility as her threat to "rush out as I am, and walk the street / With my hair down, so" (41). A host of other female figures seek male attention or offer sexual favors, most of them simple characters who offer few glimpses of female subjectivity. Among these are Grishkin of "Whispers of Immortality" and the barmaids of "Sweeney Among the Nightingales." Grishkin's "promise of pneumatic bliss" offends the narrator almost as much, we suspect, as her "rank . . . feline smell" (33). In the latter poem the "nightingales'" slovenly commercializing of sex is matched by the almost pre-linguistic silence of "Apeneck Sweeney" (35). Such figures are too animalistic to rival the tragic adulteries of Agamemnon and Clytemnestra or the rape and revenge of aristocrats like Tereus and Philomela, but these classical allusions at the end underscore that mutual injury in sexual engagement continues from then to now.

Doris and Dusty of *Sweeney Agonistes* are further examples of women in Eliot's pre-conversion poetry who regard sex as economic exchange. Despite slightly higher class (they have a "flat," call themselves "Miss," and refer to the men who visit them as "Mr."), their expectations are much the same: they supply the men with sexual companionship and expect them to pay the rent or otherwise provide for them economically (*CPP* 74). It is here, in this unfinished drama, that the central character, a Mr. Sweeney quite different from those of the earlier poems, teases Doris in jazz-inflected rhythms, "I'll carry you off / To a cannibal isle. / . . . . / I'll gobble you up. I'll be the cannibal" (79–80), and later declares, in the midst of a story about a man who murdered a woman, that "Any man might do a girl in" (83). Surprisingly, many have read this work as misogynist, but there is little about the text *in its entirety* to suggest that it is meant to be taken literally. Instead this comic performance is, I believe, a savage unmasking of the implied erotic violence in traditional gender roles, especially in the automatic expectation of voracious male power. Eliot no more believed in the desirability of a man wishing to "do a girl in" than Swift recommended eating Irish babies, although at his most despairing Eliot did painfully observe that the struggle to establish selfhood in an erotic relationship could well look as if each sex desired to annihilate or maim the other.

Although the lady of "Portrait of a Lady," the neurotic wife of *The Waste Land*, and Doris and Dusty all have sufficient agency to do some exploiting of their own, others of the women of the early poetry seem too feeble to accomplish that, or even perhaps to wish for it. These figures are the pathetic images of women merely exploited and used. The "Thames maidens" who speak at the end of the third section of *The Waste Land* fall in this category (*CPP* 46), as do "the epileptic on the bed" of "Sweeney Erect" (26) and the "housemaids" whose "damp souls" sprout "despondently" in "Morning at the Window" (16).

Even in the pre-conversion poetry, a few female figures escape from erotic expectations that render them pathetic or threatening, to a neutral or mythic status. Eliot shows how culture and class confined women: Cousin Harriet is defined by the cultural world of "The *Boston Evening Transcript*," Aunt Helen by the rules of class and gender that order the lives of a well-to-do maiden New England woman, and Cousin Nancy, who "smoked / And danced all the modern dances," by her very rebellion against these same rules (*CPP* 17). The "ancient women / Gathering fuel in vacant lots" of "Preludes" (13), and the Cumaean Sibyl and Madame Sosostris of *The Waste Land* all suggest the mythic or prophetic, but each is gravely limited by circumstances. The scavenging women offer only the cyclic hope of those who convert refuse to fuel that can sustain life, while the Sibyl cannot escape the cage of life, even to die, and Madame Sosostris prophesies with the parodic equipment of the Tarot deck and the crystal ball.

Nonetheless, the pessimistic poetry of the years from 1908 to 1927 contains a few characters suggesting that a female figure may offer possibilities of bliss and even vision. In addition to the girl of "La Figlia che Piange" and the hyacinth girl, the most important of these are the "Eyes I dare not meet in dreams" of "The Hollow Men" (*CPP* 57). The only explicitly gendered characteristic of these disembodied eyes are their designation as "Multifoliate rose / . . . The hope only / Of empty men" (58). This direct comparison to Dante's Beatrice establishes the direction that Eliot's treatment of women would subsequently take.

A Revision of the Pattern: Women in Eliot's Later Work

In 1927 Eliot formally converted to the Church of England and pursued a high-church version of Anglo-Catholicism that emphasized the importance of the Virgin Mother. For a time, in fact, beginning in March 1928, Eliot took a vow of celibacy (Gordon, *Imperfect* 292). During these years he wrote *Ash-Wednesday* (1930), which recounts the speaker's almost intolerable struggle to renounce the demands of the flesh and to achieve union with God through meditation upon the visionary image of a woman like the Virgin Mary and through her intercession. This poem reaches new heights of doubleness of meaning at multiple levels, functioning at once as a confession of the speaker's inability to achieve carnal union with a beloved woman and spiritual union with God. The poem begins with a lament at the inadequacy of his efforts to "know / The one veritable transitory power" (*CPP* 60), a power that can be erotic or divine. The poem clearly shows that the speaker – here much closer to the poet himself – still finds himself anguished at his inability to achieve satisfying erotic union with a woman. The nuances of gender are still defined in performance, or in failure to satisfy society's prescriptions for performance. The woman still commands his attention, whether he wills it or not, but the woman as sensual attraction now clearly has a double – the woman transformed into a symbol of the Divine.

This figure is explicit when Eliot begins the second section with direct address to a "Lady." The image is that of an earthly woman much desired, from whom the speaker is unutterably separated. The analogy with Dante's Beatrice in the *Vita Nuova* is explicit (Bush, *Study* 138). The speaker in *Ash-Wednesday*, unlike many in the early poems, is determined to accept things as they are, but he can't, and his efforts to climb the purgatorial stairs are interrupted by the temptations of the sensual world: "brown hair over the mouth blown, / Lilac and brown hair" (63). In reaction, the speaker briefly envisions the earthly beloved transformed into something resembling the Virgin Mary, "White light folded, sheathed about her, folded," who walks the garden in white and "blue of Mary's colour" (64). As elsewhere throughout Eliot's work, such visions in which "the fountain sprang up and the bird sang down" are momentary only, and the section concludes with a line from the "Salve Regina," a prayer to the Virgin: "And after this our exile" (64). The speaker can sustain neither heavenly commitment nor earthly love, and he sees himself oscillating between affection and disaffection, belief and disbelief. He asks the "veiled sister" to "Pray for those who chose and oppose" at once (65). This prayer captures Eliot's career-long ambivalence in relationship to women. There is spiritual progression in the poem, and in the end the speaker affirms that *even though* he does "not hope to turn again" to either an erotic or a visionary unity, he still prays for "Our peace in His will" (66–67). The women, who were the occasion of temptation and failure in earlier poetry, have become a symbol of temptation, failure, *and* salvation, but this figure remains defined completely in terms of its meaning to the speaker. There is no inquiry into what the feelings of the woman might be.

Some critics (Schuchard 153; Gordon, *Imperfect* 235–38) root the Lady of *Ash-Wednesday* in Eliot's memories of Emily Hale, a woman in his Harvard milieu with whom, he later wrote, he thought himself in love after he had left for England (*Letters* xvii), and with whom he renewed friendship before he wrote *Ash-Wednesday*. Others trace the source of the imagery back to Eliot's memories of his Catholic nurse in St. Louis (Bush, *Study* 146–47). Most agree, however, that it is Hale who provides the model for the companion whom the speaker invites to join him in the rose garden in "Burnt Norton." This invitation, another in which the speaker is animated by vital memories of possibilities that were passed by, leads to another powerful moment of vision filled with many of the same symbolic elements encountered in *Ash-Wednesday*: a garden, a pool, birds, and white light (*CPP* 118). This scene, where "the lotus rose" and "The surface glittered out of heart of light" becomes a touchstone of the entire *Four Quartets*. There is, however, no transformation of this companion in "Burnt Norton" into something else. The Virgin to whom prayer for intercession is addressed in the fourth section of "The Dry Salvages" is the patron saint of the Portuguese fishermen of East Gloucester, and the women who are alluded to throughout the *Quartets* are drawn from history, as the speaker positions them in the pattern which is his meditative reconstruction of his own history, both of his generation and of his ancestors, personal, political, and intellectual.

After Eliot's conversion, major figures of three of his dramas torment themselves with an effort to come to terms with their failures in relation to a woman. Harry of *The Family Reunion* is pursued by Furies who represent his guilty recognition that he had wished his drowned wife dead, whether he actually pushed her or she fell. Edward in *The Cocktail Party* struggles to accept himself and his wife Lavinia in a loveless marriage, and the eponymous elder statesman faces the reappearance of the dancer he treated shabbily in his youth. The women, however, are portrayed more fully than before, and they demonstrate no comparable desire, or at least capacity, to possess or maim the male figures. Women now sometimes become images of relative wisdom

– a characterization seen in the chorus of women in *Murder in the Cathedral*, Agatha in *The Family Reunion*, and both Julia and Celia in *The Cocktail Party*. It is Celia who has the courage and vision to seek "atonement," which leads to her martyrdom. Although the characterization has been subject to the charge that Eliot is once more positioning his female characters as angels or devils, it is clear that Celia reached her vocation by *choosing* to resign her attachment to life, and that her commitment and discipline would be the way of the saint for either a man or a woman. Prior to her decision to "[w]ork out [her] salvation with diligence" (*CPP* 366), she was as embroiled in adultery and mindless cocktail parties as the characters whom she leaves spiritually behind.

Only in his last play, however, after his late marriage to Valerie Fletcher, his second wife, does Eliot offer a portrait of human love that is supportive and restorative within the historical moment. At the end of *The Elder Statesman*, Monica and Charles become "conscious of a new person / Who is you and me together" (*ES* 131). This love draws its being from divine love, for Monica perceives that "Before you and I were born, the love was always there that brought us together" (131). The Eliot of "Prufrock" or *The Waste Land* has given way here to something vastly different. It is undoubtedly, however, the men and women of Eliot's work who wrestle with questions of gender identity as they perform or combat stereotypical roles of the masculine or feminine who remain permanently memorable.

NOTES

1 Although some read "Prufrock" as a soliloquy of a divided self or an address to the reader, Eliot once affirmed in a letter that the "you" in the poem was "some friend or companion, presumably of the male sex" (qtd. in Miller 153). James Miller connects this assertion with the poem's dedication to Jean Verdenal, Eliot's frequent companion in Paris during some of the months in which the poem was being written.

2 For a full philosophical exegesis of such an understanding of gender, see Butler, *Bodies* and *Gender*.

REFERENCES AND FURTHER READING

Badenhausen, Richard. "T. S. Eliot Speaks the Body: the Privileging of Female Discourse in *Murder in the Cathedral* and *The Cocktail Party*." Laity and Gish 195–214.

Brooker, Jewel Spears, and Joseph Bentley. *Reading the Waste Land: Modernism and the Limits of Interpretation*. Amherst: U of Massachusetts P, 1990.

Bush, Ronald. *T. S. Eliot: A Study in Character and Style*. New York: Oxford UP, 1983.

——, ed. *T. S. Eliot: The Modernist in History*. New York: Cambridge UP, 1991.

Butler, Judith. *Bodies That Matter: On the Discursive Limits of "Sex."* New York: Routledge, 1993.

——. *Gender Trouble: Feminism and the Subversion of Identity*. 1990. New York: Routledge, 1999.

Christ, Carol. "Gender, Voice, and Figuration in Eliot's Early Poetry." Bush, *Modernist* 23–37.

Cole, Merrill. "Empire of the Closet." *Discourse* 19 (1997): 67–91.

Däumer, Elisabeth. "Charlotte Stearns Eliot and *Ash Wednesday*'s Lady of Silences." *ELH* 65 (1998): 479–501.

Dean, Tim. "T. S. Eliot, Famous Clairvoyant."
Laity and Gish 43–65.

Drew, Elizabeth. *T. S. Eliot: The Design of His
Poetry*. New York: Scribner's, 1949.

DuPlessis, Rachel Blau. *Genders, Races and Religious
Cultures in Modern American Poetry, 1908–1934*.
Cambridge: Cambridge UP, 2001.

Gilbert, Sandra, and Susan Gubar. *No Man's Land:
The Place of the Woman Writer in the Twentieth
Century*. Vol. 1. New Haven: Yale UP, 1988.

Gibert[-Maceda], Teresa. "T. S. Eliot and the Feminist Revision of the Modernist Canon." *T. S.
Eliot and Our Turning World*. Ed. Jewel Spears
Brooker. New York: St. Martin's, 2001.
191–202.

——. "T. S. Eliot on Women: Women on T. S.
Eliot." *T. S. Eliot at the Turn of the Century*. Ed.
Marianne Thormählen. Lund: Lund UP, 1994.
105–19.

Gordon, Lyndall. "Eliot and Women." Bush, *Modernist* 9–22.

——. *T. S. Eliot: An Imperfect Life*. New York:
Norton, 1998.

Laity, Cassandra, and Nancy K. Gish, eds. *Gender,
Desire, and Sexuality in T. S. Eliot*. Cambridge:
Cambridge UP, 2004.

Lamos, Colleen. "The Love Song of T. S. Eliot:
Elegiac Homoeroticism in the Early Poetry."
Laity and Gish 23–42.

Miller, James E., Jr. *T. S. Eliot: The Making of an
American Poet, 1888–1922*. University Park, PA:
Pennsylvania State UP, 2005.

Nicholls, Peter. *Modernisms: A Literary Guide*.
Berkeley: U of California P, 1995.

Palmer, Marja. *Men and Women in T. S. Eliot's Early
Poetry*. Lund: Lund UP, 1996.

Peter, John. "A New Interpretation of *The Waste
Land*." *Essays in Criticism* 2 (1952): 242–66.

——. "Postscript." *Essays in Criticism* 19 (1969):
165–66.

Pinckney, Tony. *Women in the Poetry of T. S. Eliot:
A Psychoanalytic Approach*. London: Macmillan,
1984.

Pondrom, Cyrena N. "T. S. Eliot: The Performativity of Gender in *The Waste Land*." *Modernism/
Modernity* 12 (2005): 425–41.

Schuchard, Ronald. *Eliot's Dark Angel: Intersections
of Life and Art*. New York: Oxford UP, 1999.

Smith, Grover. *T. S. Eliot's Poetry and Plays: A
Study in Sources and Meanings*. 2nd ed. Chicago:
U of Chicago P, 1974.

28
Eliot and "Race": Jews, Irish, and Blacks

Bryan Cheyette

There are, as yet, no comparative accounts of T. S. Eliot and "race."[1] At one end of the spectrum, Christopher Ricks argues convincingly that the question of racism and anti-Semitism should not be "isolated from the larger issues of categorizing and prejudice in Eliot's poetry" (61). But while Ricks's important book can be said to err on the side of generality, the work which has followed Ricks, at the other end of the spectrum, has tended to focus on particular racial representations. These studies of Jewish, Irish, and black representations in Eliot's poetry and prose have not been related to each other or read comparatively.[2] Instead, each of these racial groupings has generated a separate critical literature with its own internal debates, as if Eliot himself confined his various racial images to separate spheres. I will begin by looking at each of the three racial categories in Eliot's poetry and prose – Jew, Irish, and black – and will show the ways in which all three racial designations overlap and intersect in what Jonathan Freedman has characterized, in another context, as a series of "swirling Venn diagrams" (16).

Eliot and "Free-thinking Jews": The Prose Works

The response to "Eliot and anti-Semitism," as the discourse is commonly known, is far more polarized, over many decades, than the more recent critical literature on the representations of blacks or Irish.[3] Eliot's *After Strange Gods* (1934) and *Notes towards the Definition of Culture* (1948), especially, contain references to Jews that reinforce a coherent sense of Eliot's "Semitic discourse," as I have named it. I use "Semitic discourse" because this term recognizes that "anti-Semitism" or "philo-Semitism" are two relatively distinct aspects of a much broader history of differentiating Jews from other human beings. Instead of employing a predetermined "anti-" or "philo-" perspective that explains any given reading, "Semitic discourse" enables the literary critic to conduct a genuinely open dialogue about the complex nature of racial discourse

A Companion to T. S. Eliot, First Edition. Edited by David E. Chinitz.
© 2014 John Wiley & Sons, Ltd. Published 2014 by John Wiley & Sons, Ltd.

within literary texts which neither excuses nor accuses the writers under discussion (Cheyette 1–12).

The most notorious example of Eliot's use of a Semitic discourse in his prose works can be found in *After Strange Gods*, where Eliot refers to the makeup of a society in which "tradition" can thrive:

> The population should be homogenous; where two or more cultures exist in the same place they are likely either to be fiercely self-conscious or both to become adulterate. What is still more important is unity of religious background; and reasons of race and religion combine to make any large number of free-thinking Jews undesirable. There must be a proper balance between urban and rural, industrial and agricultural development. And a spirit of excessive tolerance is to be deprecated. (20)

Here we have the fundamental opposition in Eliot's political thought between heretical "free-thinking Jews" and a "homogenous" Christian "unity." Maud Ellmann has made the important connection between Eliot's aesthetic ideal of using "the right word in the right place" with his political quest to encourage "the great majority of human beings [to] go on living in the place in which they were born" (90). The search for clarity and order on both the levels of language and society was crucial for Eliot and, in these terms, the figure of "the Jew" embodies boundary-crossing disorder and uncertainty.

Eliot related the lack of clarity between "tradition and the individual talent" to the confusion of religion with culture which he associated especially with Matthew Arnold's *Culture and Anarchy* (1869). This was the reason for Eliot's concerted attack on Arnold, over nearly three decades, which culminated in the opening chapter of his *Notes towards the Definition of Culture*. It was in this work, too, that Eliot made clear the dangers of blurring the boundaries between religion and culture with reference to "the Jews":

> Since the diaspora, and the scattering of Jews amongst peoples holding the Christian Faith, it may have been unfortunate both for these peoples and for the Jews themselves, that the culture-contact between them has had to be within those neutral zones of culture in which religion could be ignored: and the effect may have been to strengthen the illusion that there can be culture without religion.[4] (*CC* 144)

It was this confusion that Eliot (writing during World War II) suggests might well have been the "unfortunate" cause of anti-Semitism. In his response to *Notes towards the Definition of Culture*, George Steiner has related this "oddly condescending footnote" to the "long-standing ambiguities on the theme of the Jew in Eliot's poetry" (34). Steiner is right to speak of ambiguity (Semitism) rather than monodimensional hatred (anti-Semitism), because Eliot, in line with other Christian thinkers, such as G. K. Chesterton, objected primarily to boundary-crossing, "free-thinking Jews" rather than overtly religious Jews, who, by living within distinct communities, would not threaten the unity of Christian culture (Cheyette 264–67). As Eliot argued in a 1940 correspondence with J. V. Healy, "It should be obvious that I think a large number of free-thinkers of any race undesirable, and the free-thinking Jews are only a special case." Healy replied tellingly that it was "unfortunate," repeating Eliot's euphemism, that "you should pick on Jews (free-thinkers or not) at a time when they are being hounded and tortured" (qtd. in Ellmann 88).

In the correspondence with Healy, Eliot attempted to clarify his remark about "deracinated," "free-thinking Jews" by explaining that "The Jewish religion . . . shorn of its traditional practices, observances and Messianism . . . tends to become a mild and colorless form of Unitarianism" (qtd. in Ricks 44). Eliot was raised as a Unitarian, and it is clear that the figure of "the Jew" represents an intimate aspect of his upbringing which he was attempting to expunge. As late as 1953, Eliot described the household of his childhood as if he had, himself, been one of the biblical Children of Israel: "The standard of conduct was that which my grandfather had set; our moral judgments, our decisions between duty and self-indulgence, were taken as if, like Moses, he had brought down the tables of the Law, any deviation from which would be sinful" (*TCC* 44). That Eliot encountered a very real hostility in England as a foreigner attempting to promote the modernist avant-garde could only reinforce these forms of repressed Jewish self-identification. C. S. Lewis, for instance, regarded Eliot Semitically as a "disguised" enemy who wheedled his way into key financial institutions and, with a few alien co-conspirators ("denationalized" "riff-raff"), attempted to bring about the collapse of European civilization (qtd. in Ricks 197–98). That Eliot embodied precisely what he disdained explains why in *For Lancelot Andrewes* (1928) he went on famously to define his "general point of view" as "classicist in literature, royalist in politics, and anglo-catholic in religion" (*FLA* vii). Such were the purifying national, racial, and spiritual boundaries needed to redeem himself from his cosmopolitan presence in London and his Unitarian background. In striving for "classical" exactitude and canonical authority, Eliot evoked a crudely racialized Semitic double – which could not, quite, be repressed – as the "other" to his ideals of "style and order."

Eliot and "the Jews": The Poetry

Critical response to the figure of "the Jew" in Eliot's poetry goes back at least to the *Survey of Modernist Poetry* (1927) by Robert Graves and Laura Riding and concerns some of Eliot's most significant work. As Steiner argued in 1971, "Eliot's uglier touches tend to occur at the heart of very good poetry" (qtd. in Ricks 28). This can be seen, especially, with the publication of Eliot's *Poems* (1920), which contains "Gerontion" and "Burbank with a Baedeker: Bleistein with a Cigar."

"Gerontion" was placed at the head of Eliot's *Poems*, and it was soon perceived to characterize the volume as a whole in much the same way as "Prufrock" had done in Eliot's earlier collection. The figure of Gerontion, however, far from developing a Prufrockian persona, is more accurately read as a withdrawal from the very idea of "persona" (Gray 211–14). In the opening lines of the poem, the figure of Gerontion is distinguished by what he was not: "I was neither . . . Nor . . . Nor . . ." (*CPP* 21). After these lines, "the jew" acts as an ostensible "other" against which the fragmented Gerontion can be clearly defined:

> My house is a decayed house,
> And the jew squats on the window-sill, the owner,
> Spawned in some estaminet of Antwerp,
> Blistered in Brussels, patched and peeled in London. (21)

Many critics have read "the jew" as the poem's antagonist, a squatting beast or insect (foreshadowing the "spider" or "weevil") who was not born but "[s]pawned," and who, because "blistered" and "peeled," is the embodiment of an unredeemed dryness. The figure of "the jew" is outside the "house" of a decayed Christendom and anticipates (in his excremental "squatting") the poisonous fertility of the "flowering judas" (21). "Jewish" frenetic cosmopolitan proliferation and arbitrary financial power (as "the owner") decays national boundaries and threatens the unity of Christian Europe. There is, as several commentators have noted, an implicit contrast between the bestial "jew . . . / Spawned in some estaminet of Antwerp," and the Christ-child, born in a manger, who emerges soon after this passage. The "jew," in these terms, can be read as an "anti-Christ," the ultimate antagonist, with the Christ-child symbolizing Oneness and centrality, and "the jew" plurality and disintegration (Maccoby 109–10).

But it is also possible to read the figure of Gerontion as a "jew" in the poem. The fractured and atomized Gerontion is, after all, an "old man driven by the Trades" (*CPP* 23), and his name recalls "Geruntus," a precursor for the character of Shylock. Resembling Gerontion, Shylockian Jews have been stereotyped, historically, as debased old men who, in stark contrast to a youthful Christianity, lack any spiritual vigor to renew mankind. From this perspective, Gerontion – "Being read to by a boy, waiting for rain" (21) – can be said to redouble a supposed fossilized, moribund Judaism in the poem. The multiple consciousness of Gerontion, which refuses to be limited by the Christian Logos, is, to this extent, "Jewish." Thus Gerontion is both an "other" to the crudely racialized "jew" and, at the same time, his repressed double. Such is the instability at the heart of the poem.

Instead of reading "the jew" as a settled racial "other," the figure of Gerontion reproduces a proliferating "semitic" vocabulary which he ostensibly opposes. A disconnected, rootless world is menacingly realized in his "wilderness of mirrors," "many cunning passages, contrived corridors," "whispering ambitions," "supple confusions," and "thousand small deliberations" (*CPP* 22–23). The cosmopolitan residents of Gerontion's rented house are also implicitly Judaized. Instead of the opposition between "the jew" and its racial "others," all in the poem are dispossessed and "devoured" by the "flowering judas / To be eaten, to be divided, to be drunk" (21–22). This inverse Communion is, above all, a betrayal ("[a]mong whispers") of the promise of the Christ-child, as the Word incarnate is negatively transfigured into the splintered remains of Gerontion's paranoid consciousness. One should not underestimate the very real terror in the poem of being Judaized, as witnessed by Gerontion's inability to separate himself completely from "the jew."

The protean "jew" is both a primitive force of nature, as can be seen from his animalistic appearance, and, simultaneously, "the owner," the embodiment of a failed, corrupt modernity. In "Burbank with a Baedeker," Eliot's "jews" are, likewise, hybrid creatures who are characterized by an originary primitivism beneath a cosmopolitan, moneyed modernity. The doubleness of Bleistein's animalism is condensed in the all-too-literal phrase "money in furs":

> But this or such was Bleistein's way:
> A saggy bending of the knees
> And elbows, with the palms turned out,
> Chicago Semite Viennese. (*CPP* 24)

Bleistein is both fixed as a stereotypical cartoon figure and dissolved in a welter of national and racial boundary-crossings, "Chicago Semite Viennese." His cigar smoke is, in this regard, an ideal figurative expression of "semitic" confusion (blurring religion and culture) which obscures the cultural significance of the past:

> The smoky candle end of time
>
> Declines. On the Rialto once.
> The rats are underneath the piles.
> The jew is underneath the lot.
> Money in furs. (24)

Bleistein is crudely associated with the devolution of a corrupt and disease-ridden European culture: "A lustreless protrusive eye / Stares from the protozoic slime / At a perspective of Canaletto" (24). The location of "the jew . . . underneath the lot," ravaging the foundations of Venice, ostensibly acts as the poem's nucleus, an explanation for the decline of Europe. But the epigraph of "Burbank with a Baedeker," as has been commonly noted, itself verges upon smoky incoherence – *"Tra-la-la-la-la-la-laire – nil nisi divinum stabile est; caetra fumus"* ["only the divine endures; the rest is smoke"] (23) – with references to six disparate accounts of Venice through the ages in almost as many lines. This kaleidoscopic, impressionistic account of Europe's crumbling center captures, in miniature, the poem as a whole, which dramatizes fragmentary and partial versions of Venice throughout history.

Sir Ferdinand Klein's repetition of Burbank's initial fall from grace escalates the biological and cultural descent inherent in the initial sexual encounter. Placed at the beginning of the line, the ironically drooping "Klein" (meaning "little") echoes both "declines" and the "small hotel" in the first stanza. Princess Volupine, like Bleistein, embodies the corrupting disease – "A meagre, blue-nailed, phthisic hand" (*CPP* 24) – which, in her case, has made it possible for the European aristocracy to become "adulterate" (*ASG* 20). Along with the German-Jewish financier, Sir Alfred Mond, whom Eliot evokes as a moneylender in "A Cooking Egg," Sir Ferdinand Klein represents that class of Edwardian plutocrat who buttresses, racially, a Bleisteinian Jewish bourgeoisie. Together such types were commonly seen to have destroyed a traditional sense of (aristocratic) order and continuity with the past.

The all-explaining "jew" appears at the beginning, in the middle, and at the end of time, in a myriad of contradictory guises: as a diseased eye, an eternal parasite, a cosmopolitan, a plutocrat, a usurer – Bleistein, Sir Ferdinand Klein, Shylock. In contrast, Burbank's Baedeker-inspired meditations on the Noachian "Time's ruins, and the seven laws" (*CPP* 24) are superficial acts of recuperation which are unable to expunge an utterly corrupt culture in a deep-seated spiritual crisis. What is, nonetheless, particularly ironic about "Burbank with a Baedeker" is that not only does the American Burbank himself contribute to the "ruins" of history (in his sexual encounter with Princess Volupine), but that "the jew" – explaining everything and nothing – can be said to infect the poem with the same "semitic" confusion which is condemned.

In the manuscripts to *The Waste Land*, Eliot revisits the figure of Bleistein in a more sustained redemptive context:

> Full fathom five your Bleistein lies
> Under the flatfish and the squids.
> Graves' Disease in a dead jew's eyes!
> When the crabs have eat the lids.
> Lower than the wharf rats dive
> Though he suffer a sea-change
> Still expensive rich and strange (*WLF* 121)

Ricks finds the reintroduction of Bleistein in "Dirge" and the seemingly gratuitous repetition of certain motifs from the earlier poem – "Graves' Disease in a dead jew's eyes! / . . . / Lower than the wharf rats dive" – to be "the ugliest touch of anti-Semitism in Eliot's poetry" (38). Other critics, however, understand "Dirge" as a poem that attempts to depict the "purgation" of Bleistein. The foundational "jew" in "Burbank with a Baedeker," who has confused and corrupted European civilization, is, in this reading, experiencing a "painful purgatory by water" (Maccoby 117). The vanquished Bleistein in "Dirge" is given a redemptive "sea-change," as he is rolled "gently side to side" (*WLF* 121) in a perverse act of baptism (echoing Eliot's implicit pun, which "gently" transforms "the jews" into "gentiles"). Bleistein in the poem is no longer saggily indistinct and smoke-ridden but is, literally, reduced to his bare bones – "(Bones peep through the ragged toes)" – although his unredeemed materialism ("gold in gold") remains "rich and strange."

Sweeney: Eliot and "the Irish"

Sweeney is the most consistently identified figure in Eliot's poetry, appearing in "Sweeney Erect," "Sweeney Among the Nightingales," the unfinished *Sweeney Agonistes*, *The Waste Land*, and "Mr. Eliot's Sunday Morning Service." He is both Eliot's Everyman and a crudely "simianized" Irish racial stereotype who "comes with borrowed blackness and apish qualities" (Du Plessis 684; Morse 136–40). Not unlike Eliot's "jews," Sweeney is bestialized and embodies a world of sexual depravity (he is usually surrounded by prostitutes). But unlike Bleistein or Sir Ferdinand Klein, who are figures of confusion, Sweeney is related to classical Greek culture. "Sweeney Erect," for instance, is saturated with references to Greece and Greek culture from the Cyclades (Aegean islands) to the mythological figures of Aeolus, Ariadne, Nausicaa, and Polyphemus. Their contrast with the racialized Sweeney is starkly made –

> Morning stirs the feet and hands
> (Nausicaa and Polypheme).
> Gesture of orang-outang
> Rises from the sheets in steam (*CPP* 25)

– except that Polyphemus is one of the Cyclopes, brutal one-eyed giants, who are not unconnected to the apelike Sweeney. While Sweeney "erect" is clearly a primitive who personifies a devolved humanity (*Homo erectus*), he is still placed in a clear relationship to Greek culture. There remains the possibility, in other words, of classical culture controlling the anarchy of contemporary reality. Figures such as Bleistein, on the other hand, make it impossible to utilize these traditions by corrupting them with "alien" modes of thought. This contrast is clear in "Sweeney Among the Nightingales," which evokes a paranoid and cosmopolitan world not unlike that of "Gerontion." More explicitly than in "Sweeney Erect," Sweeney in this poem is both animalized and, simultaneously, circumscribed by an epigraph – in translation, "Alas, I am struck deep with a mortal blow" – from the *Agamemnon* (35).

The question is not merely whether Sweeney's predicament is heightened or further demeaned by the allusion to the grandeur of Agamemnon. Either of these interpretations might be imposed on Sweeney, but the point is that he has some kind of connection, however tenuous, to the savage world of Agamemnon, who was tragically killed by his wife, Clytemnestra. The poem is full of cryptic characters (most unlike Sweeney), such as "the person in the Spanish cape," "the silent man in mocha brown," or "someone indistinct," who evoke an atmosphere of deadly paranoia and murderous savagery:

> Rachel *née* Rabinovitch
> Tears at the grapes with murderous paws;
>
> She and the lady in the cape
> Are suspect, thought to be in league;

> Therefore the man with heavy eyes
> Declines the gambit, shows fatigue,
>
> Leaves the room and reappears
> Outside the window, leaning in,
> Branches of wistaria
> Circumscribe a golden grin (*CPP* 35–36)

The wary "man with heavy eyes" echoes "the jew" in "Gerontion" in being outside the "house" of Christendom and confounds the redemptive power of nature with an underlying Bleisteinian materialism (as the last two quoted lines suggest). As with "Gerontion" and "Burbank with a Baedeker," the poem dramatizes a "semitic" confusion that prevents the reader from understanding the affiliation of Sweeney, his class and culture, to classical tradition.

That the poem is infected with uncertainty, in stark contrast to the dominant figure of Sweeney, can be seen in the "semitic" figure of "Rachel *née* Rabinovitch" who "tears at the grapes with murderous paws." Her rampant bestiality refers back to Sweeney in the opening stanza, but only to show the differences between them. Whereas Sweeney is positioned, however inscrutably, in an historical analogy with Agamemnon, Rachel is introduced precisely because she is outside of that history. "Rachel *née* Rabinovitch" is a category which sounds pedantically precise but is, on closer investigation, surprisingly vague. One does not say "*née*" in English while withholding the married name (Ricks 31). Such category confusions are reflected in a loss of control in the last verse, where the nightingales "let their liquid siftings fall / To stain the stiff dishonoured shroud" of Agamemnon (*CPP* 36). "Liquid siftings" evokes both the tragic grandeur of Agamemnon's "bloody" death and, in a telling ambiguity, the excremental "slime" which confounds such supposedly secure references to classical thought and feeling.

In the more enigmatic "Mr. Eliot's Sunday Morning Service," Eliot places Sweeney in the context of Boston Unitarianism. Guided by the epigraph from Marlowe's *The Jew of Malta* – "*Look, look, master, here comes two religious caterpillars*" (*CPP* 33) – a number of critics have emphasized the "semitic" element in this poem, which they find carried over into the first stanza:

> Polyphiloprogenitive
> The sapient sutlers of the Lord
> Drift across the window-panes.
> In the beginning was the Word. (33)

With reference to Eliot's neologism, "polyphiloprogenitive," George Monteiro has noted that the association between immigrant (or "drifting") Jews and "philoprogenitiveness" was a fairly common perception (20–22).

But it is unnecessary to fix Eliot's materialist "sutlers," who trade in words, as "jews." The "sutlers" or traders are condemned by their supposedly Hebraic proliferation of empty, meaningless words, rather than their racial Jewishness. This is especially apparent in the next stanza, when the opening of the poem is contrasted with the overly spiritualized deity of the Greek philosophers, "τὸ ἕυ," epitomized by the self-castrated "enervate Origen" (*CPP* 33–34). These two contrary versions of God – either Hebraically materialist or Hellenistically ethereal – are synthesized in the painting of the "Baptized God" in the third stanza (Maccoby 166–68). The need to control the "polyphiloprogenitive" reproduction of fragmented words as well as boundary-crossing peoples was later to be signified by the imposition of national boundaries on "free-thinking Jews." The devolution of the "sapient sutlers" into industrious worker-bees (who carry the pollen from the stamen to the pistil-like entrepreneurial middlemen) implicitly alludes to Marlowe's parasitic "religious caterpillars" and, also, prefigures much of the animal imagery used to construct Eliot's racial others and cosmopolitan drifters in his poetry. The modern-day Church, which is more concerned with "piaculative pence" than with "penitence," leaves Sweeney disinterested:

> Sweeney shifts from ham to ham
> Stirring the water in his bath.
> The masters of the subtle schools
> Are controversial, polymath. (*CPP* 34)

The muscular Sweeney shifting from "ham to ham" in his bath contrasts sharply with the "unoffending feet" of the "Baptized God," which "shine" "through the water." Whereas Sweeney in the earlier poems was juxtaposed with the origins of classical culture, he is here associated with the foundations of the Christian church. The unbridgeable gap between "the Flesh" and "the Word" in this last stanza is caused by the polymathic "masters of the subtle school," who, like the "polyphiloprogenitive" sutlers, merely commodify words. The unity of "the Word" is fragmented by the individualism and parasitic materiality of those in the established Protestant Church, such as Judaized Unitarians, who have dissociated the soul from the body of Christ.

While Sweeney is the mirror image of the "Baptized God," the "sapient sutlers" are, in contrast, part of an overly Judaized culture which includes Eliot himself. As Piers Gray has argued, "Mr. Eliot's Sunday Morning Service" is a curious paradox because it implosively "breeds exactly the form of exegesis which it satirizes" (197). The savage figure of Sweeney is needed to overcome a Judaic culture which has dissociated words from their spiritual origins. Primitivism could be salutary – the primitivism of poetry, which "begins . . . with a savage beating a drum in a jungle" (*UPUC* 148); of the artist, who is "more *primitive*, as well as more civilized, than his contemporaries" ("Tarr" 106); and of Eliot himself, whose ingrained Americanness might make him "a savage" (*Letters* 318). By the time he came to write *Sweeney Agonistes* (1926–27), he was quite explicit about "returning drama to its primitive origins" (Chinitz 120). His poetry had connected Sweeney to the ritualistic in both Greek tragedy and the foundations of the Christian Church. Even Sweeney's brief appearance in *The Waste Land* associates him with the perverse rite of spring which opens the poem: "But at my back from time to time I hear / The sound of horns and motors, which shall bring / Sweeney to Mrs. Porter in the spring" (*CPP* 43). Mrs. Porter, in turn, is linked both with the paganism of the moon – "O the moon shone bright on Mrs. Porter" – and the ambiguous salvific qualities of "soda water." Only the savagery of a sinful and suffering Sweeney, a version of the artist as primitive, can revitalize contemporary culture, a dysgenic "neutral zone" which merely trades in soulless words (*CC* 144).

This transformation of Sweeney is made explicit in the unfinished poetic drama *Sweeney Agonistes*, which attempts to reintroduce the ideal of "ritual" (but without "faith") back into Western culture through a self-conscious juxtaposition of popular and classical forms (Chinitz 121–25). Sweeney encompasses the extremities of high and low, classical and melodramatic, as can be seen in the opening of "Fragments of an Agon":

> SWEENEY.   I'll carry you off
>   To a cannibal isle.
> DORIS. You'll be the cannibal!
> SWEENEY. You'll be the missionary!
>   You'll be my little seven stone missionary!
>   I'll gobble you up. I'll be the cannibal (*CPP* 79–80)

Such exchanges combine jazz, vaudeville, and music hall – popular Anglo-American forms which Eliot valued as a method of revitalizing the culture and reaching the masses – with a classical sense of the transhistorical facts of life ("Birth, and copulation, and death" [80]). Sweeney's characterization of modern society as a living death – "Death is life and life is death" (84) – resonates with the earlier Sweeney poems. The perfect objective correlative for this sense of death-in-life is the violent purgatorial image of a murdered girl in limbo "kept . . . in a bath / With a gallon of lysol" (83). Whereas the viscosity of "the jew" leads to confusion and uncertainty, the image of the girl in the bath of the disinfectant Lysol leads to a savage clarity of vision. With Sweeney at the centre, Klipstein and Krumpacker, two Judaized cosmopolitan figures, are rather timid and marginalized and do not feel "at *home*" in London: "London's a little too gay for us / . . . we couldn't stand the pace" (79). All of the life-giving energy and timeless insight in the drama is with Sweeney.

Eliot originally considered subtitling his work "Fragments of a Comic Minstrelsy" (Chinitz 112), and many critics have noted the extent to which Sweeney is "blacked up" in the drama as if part of an American minstrel tradition (North 87–91). If Sweeney moves from "white" to "black" it is precisely to stress his "cannibal" primitivism and his distance from an empty modernity: "no telephones . . . no gramophones . . . no motor cars" (*CPP* 80). Eliot here reinforces the racialized figure of the working-class Irishman as a "white negro" (DuPlessis 684) or, equally, a noble savage. Described in "Sweeney Erect" as being "pink from nape to base" (*CPP* 25), he is now part of a "blackface" minstrelsy in which Swarts and Snow ("black" and "white") play Tambo and Bones, the traditional minstrel "end men" (North 88). These figures sing a version of the famous American popular song, "Under the Bamboo Tree," which, in line with the drama as a whole, raises profound spiritual questions in parodic form: "Two live as one / One live as two / Two live as three" (*CPP* 81). While Eliot eventually moves from Unitarianism to Trinitarianism, from Hebraism to Anglo-Catholicism, he is, in *Sweeney Agonistes*, no longer interested in merely satirizing the exegetics of theological difference (oneness versus threeness) as he had done in "Mr. Eliot's Sunday Morning Service." Sweeney's distrust of words is absolute: "I gotta use words when I talk to you / But if you understand or if you dont [*sic*] / That's nothing to me and nothing to you" (84). Words are no longer merely homeless, like Klipstein and Krumpacker, but have devolved, like Sweeney, into their inarticulate primitive essence:

> Hoo ha ha
> Hoo ha ha
> Hoo
> Hoo
> Hoo. (85)

King Bolo: Eliot and "the Blacks"

In a much-quoted letter to Herbert Read in 1928, Eliot wrote:

> Some day, I want to write an essay about the point of view of an American who wasn't an American, because he was born in the South and went to school in New England as a small boy with a nigger drawl, but who wasn't a Southerner because his people were northerners . . . and who so was never anything anywhere. (qtd. in North 78)

An increasing number of critics have rightly emphasized the influence of African-American culture and blackface minstrelsy on Eliot as a counter to the European heritage which is usually highlighted. Jonathan Gill has reminded us that Eliot, up until the age of 16, lived in St. Louis, which was an important center of African-American culture (65–68). The letter to Read is important in this context because it shows the extent to which Eliot's sense of himself as deracinated could take a "black" racial form in an American context as well as a "semitic" racial form in a European context. Michael North has made a convincing case for "black dialect" as a "private double" or "dirty secret" in the formation of modernist poetry as conceived by Eliot and Pound (77–78). This "black" double reached its apotheosis in *Sweeney Agonistes*, with Eliot, like Sweeney, moving from "black" to "white" and back again in his published and unpublished poetry and plays. That *Sweeney Agonistes* remained unfinished speaks to the difficulties which Eliot had in articulating a "nigger drawl," to signify homelessness, in a cultural context where he himself could easily be regarded as part of a "denationalized" "riff-raff" (Ricks 198).

In one of his most self-referential poems, "Mélange Adultère de Tout," Eliot represents his sense of deracination explicitly in relation to Africa. At the end of the poem, the speaker mockingly displaces his in-between identities onto the African continent, celebrating his birthday at an African oasis, dressed in a giraffe's skin. As North has argued, Africa in "Mélange Adultère de Tout" is the "place of placelessness" which resolves an impression of utter dislocation (84). This resolution, as we have seen in *Sweeney Agonistes*, yokes together a fearful inarticulacy ("Hoo hoo hoo") with an affect of primitive authenticity. That blackness reconciles a sense of boundary-crossing – in stark contrast to "semitic" difference, which unleashes endless religious, racial, and cultural crossings – is illustrated at the beginning of *After Strange Gods*. Here Eliot argues that "the chances for the re-establishment of a native culture are perhaps better [in Virginia] than in New England. You are farther away from New York and less invaded by foreign races; and you have a more opulent soil" (16–17). To be sure, Eliot here is following Pound in representing a "mythical 'lost' stability in American culture" which is "rural, repressive, stratified, and static": "a carefully chosen black model to block Jewish entry and influence in American life" (North 97).

It is in the context of such segregationist racial politics that the recent publication of Eliot's "King Bolo" verses is so crucial. These are a long cycle of bawdy, racist, and astonishingly vulgar doggerel which Eliot began writing for a few friends while a student at Harvard and was still writing a year before his death in 1965 (McIntire 287–88). These verses, many of which remain unpublished, begin with the mock discovery of the United States and the encounter between "Europe and America, the old world and the New, the modern and the primitive" (Gill 80). Eliot fantasizes that, after sailing to America from Spain, Columbus also discovered King Bolo and his "big black bastard queen." The first stanza is typical:

> Columbo he lived over in Spain
> Where doctors are not many
> The only doctor in his town
> Was a bastard jew named Benny
> To Benny then Columbo went
> With countenance so placid
> And Benny filled Columbo's prick
> With Muriatic Acid. (*IMH* 315)

Once again "the jew" is foundational ("underneath the lot"), killing Columbo only for him to be revived by Queen Isabella:

> The queen she took an oyster fork
> And pricked Columbo's navel
> Columbo hoisted up his ass
> And shat upon the table. (315)

As these lines indicate, Eliot's verses are outrageously scatological, with "anal excrement" the "great expendable form of currency and expression" throughout the sequence (McIntire 284). In fact Columbo's main cargo is "forty tons of bullshit" (318). Along with sexual activity of all kinds, from masturbation and rape to "buggery," disease and dirt circulates throughout the mock-epic cycle. King Bolo's infantilized, "swarthy" bodyguards wear a "big black knotty penis"; are "undaunted by syphilis"; and are "most disgusting dirty" as they climb a "banyan tree" to "sh[i]t upon their sovereign" (316).

The contrast between Eliot's transgressive "King Bolo" verses and his "stratified and static" political construction of blackness (North 97) could not be starker. Characterized by fluidity and boundary-crossing of all kinds, as well as outrageous forms of sexual and racial caricature, these poems use exactly the same motifs of sexual depravity, disease, and excremental sliminess which epitomize his Bleisteinian "jew." But whereas "the jew" is discounted as the creator of cultural confusion and uncertainty, King Bolo's "bullshit" is embraced by Eliot. It is not a coincidence that the cartoon pen drawing of the "racially ambiguous" King Bolo in Eliot's letters – smoking a cigar behind a "rocky landscape of contemporary Germany," where Eliot was then studying (McIntire 288–89) – is closely akin to the equally indeterminate figure of "Bleistein with a Cigar" (see Figure 28.1). As Gabrielle McIntire has noted, Eliot in 1921 was comparing the problems which he was having publishing his Bolo poems in a "limited edition" (*Letters* 455) with the analogous difficulties Joyce was having in publishing *Ulysses* (1922). His verse to Joyce, in this context, is most revealing: "Bolo's big black bastard queen / Was *so* obscene / She shocked the folk of Golder's [*sic*] Green" (*Letters* 455). Not unlike the timid Klipstein and Krumpacker in *Sweeney Agonistes*, the "folk" of the mainly Jewish North London suburb of Golders Green

Figure 28.1 "Viva Bolo," by T. S. Eliot (*Letters* 43)

(close to where Eliot worked as a teacher in Highgate School) are "shocked" by the appearance of Bolo's "big black" Queen. Outside the context of a "black" presence, Golders Green is represented entirely differently in "A Cooking Egg": "The red-eyed scavengers are creeping / From Kentish Town and Golder's Green" (*CPP* 27). (In an early version they are "feeding" rather than "creeping" to stress further an animal-like rapacity [*IMH* 359].) Earlier, in a 1916 letter to Conrad Aiken, Golders Green was again the site of invasion by King Bolo's "big black bassturd kween," who "led the dance on Golder's Green / With Cardinal Bessarian" (*Letters* 125). The Queen, as the pun ("bass-turd") indicates, is on the side of excremental indistinctness but has a Catholic cardinal with her to impose Christological boundaries on the largely Jewish suburb. Both Joyce and Eliot constructed "the jew" as a site for confusion and uncertainty, but only Joyce was to embrace this "semitic" ambivalence in the racially indeterminate figure of Leopold Bloom (Cheyette 206–34). Eliot, instead, displaced a sense of racialized subversion onto the transgressive figures of King Bolo and his Big Black Queen.

It was the black/white Sweeney who came closest to the Bloomian transgressive ideal in *Ulysses*, but *Sweeney Agonistes* remained unfinished. The arbitrary racial designations of "Jew," "Irish," and "black" were eventually superseded by the search for a fixed sense of tradition and a transcendent "order" which took the form of a fastidious Englishness, a devout Anglo-Catholicism, and an unyielding political conservatism. These national, religious, and political boundaries were all designed to keep Eliot's racial doubles – Bleistein, Sweeney, and Bolo – entirely in check.

NOTES

1   I would like to thank David Chinitz for his exemplary editorial work on this chapter.
2   Bornstein is a general exception to this rule, although he does not focus on Eliot.
3   For a range of scholarly responses, see the two special issues of *Modernism/Modernity* on "Eliot and anti-Semitism" (10.1 and 10.3 [2003]), and the sharply divided reviews of Anthony

Julius's "adversarial" *T. S. Eliot, Anti-Semitism and Literary Form* (New York: Cambridge UP, 1995).
4   Eliot rephrased this footnote in the 1962 edition of *Notes towards the Definition of Culture*, but the original wording was restored in later editions of this work published after his death.

REFERENCES AND FURTHER READING

Bornstein, George. "The Colors of Zion: Black, Jewish, and Irish Nationalisms at the Turn of the Century." *Modernism/Modernity* 12 (2005): 369–84.

Cheyette, Bryan. *Constructions of 'the Jew' in English Literature and Society: Racial Representations, 1875–1945*. New York: Cambridge UP, 1993.

Chinitz, David E. *T. S. Eliot and the Cultural Divide*. Chicago: U of Chicago P, 2003.

DuPlessis, Rachel Blau. "'Hoo, Hoo, Hoo': Some Episodes in the Construction of Modern Whiteness." *American Literature* 67 (1995): 667–700.

Ellmann, Maud. "The Imaginary Jew: T. S. Eliot and Ezra Pound." *Between 'Race' and Culture: Rep-*

resentations of 'the Jew' in English and American Literature. Ed. Bryan Cheyette. Stanford: Stanford UP, 1996. 84–101.

Freedman, Jonathan. *Klezmer America: Jewishness, Ethnicity, Modernity*. New York: Columbia UP, 2008.

Gill, Jonathan. "Protective Coloring: Modernism and Blackface Minstrelsy in the Bolo Poems." *T. S. Eliot's Orchestra: Critical Essays on Poetry and Music*. Ed. John Xiros Cooper. New York: Garland, 2000. 65–84.

Gray, Piers. *T. S. Eliot's Intellectual and Poetic Development, 1909–1922*. Atlantic Highlands, NJ: Humanities, 1982.

Maccoby, Hyam. *Antisemitism and Modernity: Innovation and Continuity*. New York: Routledge, 2006.

McIntire, Gabrielle. "An Unexpected Beginning: Sex, Race, and History in T. S. Eliot's Columbo and Bolo Poems." *Modernism/Modernity* 9 (2002): 283–301.

Monteiro, George. "Christians and Jews in 'Mr. Eliot's Sunday Morning Service.'" *T. S. Eliot Review* 3 (1976): 20–22.

Morse, Jonathan. "Sweeney, the Sties of the Irish, and *The Waste Land*." *Critical Essays on T. S. Eliot: The Sweeney Motif*. Ed. Kinley E. Roby. Boston: Hall, (1985). 135–46.

North, Michael. *The Dialect of Modernism: Race, Language and Twentieth-Century Literature*. New York: Oxford UP, 1994.

Ricks, Christopher. *T. S. Eliot and Prejudice*. London: Faber, 1988.

Steiner, George. *In Bluebeard's Castle: Some Notes towards the Re-definition of Culture*. London: Faber, 1971.

29

"The pleasures of higher vices": Sexuality in Eliot's Work

Patrick Query

Memory and *desire* are perhaps the most important terms in Eliot's work and in Eliot studies. They figure in numerous aspects of Eliot's thought and in key passages of his poetry, and they take on, in various places, philosophical, spiritual, emotional, historical, even political associations. They also provide an effective window into the role of sexuality in Eliot's writing and in his life. The term *sexuality* requires us to come very close to things like bodies and desire, action and pleasure, in a concrete way that another term, like gender, may not. Our attention shifts away from ideas of *masculinity* and *femininity*, the costumes people wear to affiliate themselves with one or another gendered tribe, and toward questions like: What do people, including T. S. Eliot, desire? How do they imagine their own and others' bodies? And how did Eliot express these things poetically? As I will discuss in the final section of this chapter, the debate is stronger than ever over whether we should be asking such questions about the man or the poetry. The topic of sexuality, though, invites us to do both at once, as sexuality depends not on abstractions but on passions, not on ideas but on objects of desire.

From Lower to Higher Vices

As biographer Peter Ackroyd writes: "For some writers, the family is merely something from which to escape, but for Eliot it was the formative influence" (16). Taking the long view of Eliot's career, it would certainly seem that his prevailing attitude toward sexuality was closest to the one he was taught as a boy by his Unitarian parents, whose views on earthly pleasures were effectively Puritan. The basic message about heterosexual sex they imparted to Tom was that it was sinful, dirty, and dangerous. Other kinds of sexual activity were unmentionable. Eliot learned early on to equate sex with sin, punishment, and injury; his father believed that syphilis was a divine punishment for sin and that the castration of his children would be preferable to their falling prey to sexual temptation (Seymour-Jones 38). It is thus little surprise to find

A Companion to T. S. Eliot, First Edition. Edited by David E. Chinitz.
© 2014 John Wiley & Sons, Ltd. Published 2014 by John Wiley & Sons, Ltd.

Eliot approaching sexuality in his early poems in tones ranging from timid to terrified, and to find ascetic self-denial holding more than abstract appeal as a relief from sexual tension. As Carole Seymour-Jones writes, "Sex lies at the heart of much of Eliot's poetry, becoming his personal synonym for sin. Sex attracts and repels, its urgency creating in the poet the same engulfing horror that he feels he, like Kurtz, deserves for breaking moral rules" (315).

If any single statement can encapsulate the treatment of sexuality in Eliot's work, it would have to be that, for all the various trajectories from which he approached the subject, nowhere in his writing does he present sex as something untroubled, natural, life-affirming, and pleasurable. Visible in his writings up through *Sweeney Agonistes* is an intense fascination with human sexuality but also shame over and mistrust of it. After that point the emphasis shifts gradually from the frenetic agitations of confronting sexuality head-on to an attempt to move above and beyond those worries into what the first Tempter in *Murder in the Cathedral* calls "the pleasures of your higher vices" (*CPP* 184), a pursuit still subject to human frailty but in which the stakes of the carnal are lowered in the face of a new concern with spiritual communion. The mistrust of physical intimacy, however, remains. The violent throbbing between the various poles of sexual experience in the early poems gives way over time to a hard-earned tranquility and detachment accompanying Eliot's decision to engage questions of human desire on a plane above the "thousand sordid images" of which his earlier sexual poetry was constituted (12). There is, however, a significant factor complicating this suggestion of a linear development of the sexual theme in Eliot's work, and that is the sexually explicit Columbo and Bolo poems, which remained unpublished until decades after his death. These poems, it must be acknowledged, constitute the longest sustained poetic project, in terms of years, in Eliot's life (McIntire 217). The light they shed on the place of sex in Eliot's imagination is considerable, despite the fact that they remained in virtual oblivion until quite recently and form no part of his canonical body of work.

The available biographical evidence suggests that Eliot began his independent life as a young man with little practical experience of the sexual, and with little clear sense of his own sexuality. In his early poems, certainly, sex and desire are fraught with anxiety, wonder, and fear. Eliot's first major poem, "The Love Song of J. Alfred Prufrock," composed in 1910–11, depicts physical desire from the point of view of one who is so excessively self-conscious that his desires are thwarted even before they achieve expression. Prufrock is the archetype of a figure Eliot would turn to again and again as the speaker in his poems: the aged, exhausted man, in this case thin, balding, and washed-up. Prufrock apparently desires contact – social as well as physical – with women, but he is so paralyzed by world-weariness ("For I have known them all already, known them all: – / Have known the evenings, mornings, afternoons") and self-doubt ("And should I then presume? / And how should I begin?") that he gets no further than contemplating its impossibility (*CPP* 5). Before he can begin, he is all but resigned to failure: "I have heard the mermaids singing, each to each. // I do not think that they will sing to me" (7). The failure to achieve human contact is also figured, as it would be later, in *The Waste Land*, as an inability to express oneself or to achieve communion through language ("It is impossible to say just what I mean!" "That is not what I meant at all. / That is not it, at all.") (6). The linkage is important to note, because there is in Eliot's later poetry a turning away from the difficult, and apparently painful, business of representing sexuality to thinking about questions of contact and desire in terms of the effective use of language.

A further aspect of sexuality in "Prufrock" that recurs throughout Eliot's work is the synechdochal description of bodies. The famous women who "come and go" in the poem never register as integrated wholes to Prufrock (*CPP* 4). Rather, he experiences – or at least remembers – them as isolated body parts: eyes, arms, heads, hair (5–6). This inability to perceive others as unified selves matches the speaker's sense that other people see him the same way; he worries over what they will say about his arms, his legs, and his hair, and even frets that his nerves are on display. He feels himself a specimen "sprawling on a pin" for their scrutiny, his body as incapable as his words of communicating his self. Prufrock's sexuality, such as it is, never gets beyond such paralyzing meditations (5).

Two other important poetic explorations of sexual themes from this period are "The Death of St. Narcissus" and "The Love Song of St. Sebastian," which were written around 1914 but were not published during Eliot's lifetime. Together these two poems effectively turn the wheel of sexual desire from a purely inward, intellectual struggle to an active imaginative adventure. The speakers in these poems try on various sexual selves rather than accepting the stasis of introspection, an important development in the way sexuality would function in Eliot's work. In "The Death of St. Narcissus," the sexuality of the speaker appears first as autoerotic –

> Then he knew that he had been a fish
> With slippery white belly held tight in his own fingers,
> Writhing in his own clutch, his ancient beauty
> Caught fast in the pink tips of his new beauty

– then as violent as well as autoerotic –

> Then he had been a young girl
> Caught in the woods by a drunken old man
> Knowing at the end the taste of her own whiteness
> The horror of her own smoothness
> And he felt drunken and old

– and finally as masochistic: "his flesh was in love with the burning arrows / . . . / his white skin surrendered itself to the redness of blood, and satisfied him" (*WLF* 97). The arrows also invite a homoerotic element into the poem, completing what Colleen Lamos calls "the link between male same-sex desire, self-love, and masochism" that often appears where sex comes up in Eliot's work ("Love Song" 36). In "The Love Song of St. Sebastian," a similar combination is present, as the speaker, who this time confesses a female object of desire, flagellates himself during "hour on hour of prayer / And torture and delight," spends the night with his beloved, and then strangles her to death (*IMH* 78). Richard Kaye has written at length on the homosexual resonance of St. Sebastian for poets of Eliot's era, and he points out that the object of desire in Eliot's "Love Song" is female only because of the "single detail of her breasts" (109).[1] In these two poems, then, Eliot gives voice to the major lessons about sexuality he learned as a child and establishes the themes that characterize virtually all of his subsequent poetic approaches to sex: self-love accompanied by self-loathing, mutual desire accompanied by contempt, and pleasure accompanied by punishment. The homoerotic element, fairly muted here, would begin to play a more prominent part in subsequent poems.

In "Gerontion," the speaker is consumed with the fact of his age, and he is even more painfully aware of his impotence than Prufrock. This "old man in a dry month" no longer even strives to strive for intimacy, and sensuality of any kind has ceased to signify:

> I have lost my passion: why should I need to keep it
> Since what is kept must be adulterated?
> I have lost my sight, smell, hearing, taste and touch:
> How should I use them for your closer contact? (*CPP* 23)

He dwells at length on his lack of traditional masculine virtues, having fought "neither at the hot gates / Nor . . . in the warm rain / Nor knee deep in the salt marsh" (21), adding to this the possibility of sexual deviance, perhaps, ironically, a result of traditional masculine codes: "Unnatural vices / Are fathered by our heroism" (22). "[D]epraved May" has shown him adulterated passions the very knowledge of which is not easily forgiven, and even his virtues are the result of "impudent crimes" (21–22). The movement suggested by the earlier poems from paralyzed sexuality to experimentation with perversity finds its logical conclusion in the figure of Gerontion, an old man without fertility, community, or peace, "a dry brain in a dry season," the veritable embodiment of a waste land (23).

Eliot's most famous and, sexually speaking, most controversial poem announces sexual tension at its outset. "April is the cruellest month" because of its propensity for "breeding," for "mixing / Memory and desire" and quickening the Gerontionesque "[d]ull roots" to life (*CPP* 37). Added to this tension is the gender ambiguity that comes from the constantly changing voices and the "failure to achieve union" in every instance of sexual possibility (Pondrom 427). The gender of many of the poem's speakers is not specified, but when it is, it is most often feminine: the aristocratic Marie, the hyacinth girl, Madame Sosostris, the pub gossip in "A Game of Chess," the Thames-daughters in "The Fire Sermon." Then there is hermaphroditic Tiresias, whom Suzanne Churchill characterizes as "a chiasmus of heterosexuality" who "'trans-genders' . . . the poem" (23). Eliot's Notes to the poem indicate that Tiresias, who has been at different times in his life both male and female, is "the most important personage in the poem, uniting all the rest" (*CPP* 52). It is thus extremely difficult to find solid ground from which to point to the poem's dominant sexuality. Still, there are some generalizations to be made, several of which arise from sexual themes in Eliot's earlier poems.

The Waste Land as a whole presents "an unproductive set of possibilities for male–female intercourse" and, what cannot be read as a positive alternative, cloudy hints of failed homoeroticism. Tiresias is witness to one of several "abhorrent, brutal, dispassionate, and futile" sexual scenes in the poem (Query 18). Like Prufrock, Tiresias is an observer of other people's sexuality, not a participant; his sexual life is all memory and prophecy, without the desire:

> I Tiresias . . .
> Perceived the scene, and foretold the rest –
> . . . .
> And I Tiresias have foresuffered all
> Enacted on this same divan or bed (*CPP* 44)

He watches as "the young man carbuncular" takes physical advantage of a young typist:

> The time is now propitious, as he guesses,
> The meal is ended, she is bored and tired,
> Endeavours to engage her in caresses
> Which still are unreproved, if undesired.
> Flushed and decided, he assaults at once;
> Exploring hands encounter no defence;
> His vanity requires no response,
> And makes a welcome of indifference. (44)

The young man leaves after bestowing "one final patronising kiss," the young woman thinking only, "'Well now that's done: and I'm glad it's over'" (44).

If this scene borders on date rape, other allusions in the poem to sexual assault are unambiguous. An earlier one is the mention of a picture depicting "The change of Philomel, by the barbarous king / So rudely forced," referring to the story in Ovid's *Metamorphoses* of the rape and mutilation of Philomel by her brother-in-law, Tereus (40). The reference to Philomel, after her victimization and transformation into a nightingale, "Fill[ing] all the desert with inviolable voice," suggests a rare productive, if ironic, outcome of a sexual act in Eliot's poetry (40). Sexuality and language are joined here, as they are in the exchange, if it can be called that, which follows. As in "Prufrock," it is sexual frustration and the failure of language that are paired:

> "My nerves are bad to-night. Yes, bad. Stay with me.
> "Speak to me. Why do you never speak. Speak.

"What are you thinking of? What thinking? What?
"I never know what you are thinking. Think." (40)

That these are as much sexual as social demands, that in this scene bodies and language form a common currency, is suggested by the preceding description of the woman's hair as "Glow[ing] into words" (40). Cyrena Pondrom reads this speaker's words as "a covert sexual demand, made in the oblique way permitted a middle-class woman of insistent libido, raised in the Edwardian era . . . [T]he woman pleads for a connection that is at once emotional and erotic" (431–32). (The man, who is locked in his own consciousness, does not respond.) Most critics have also seen in this section a representation of Eliot's marriage to his first wife, Vivien. As will be discussed below, sexual dysfunction as well as intense creative highs and lows were this marriage's hallmarks and lasting signs.

Another representation of what David Chinitz calls "the inadequacies of sexual passion [and] the failure of human compassion" comes in the songs of the three Thames-daughters (454). Both the sexual postures and the hollowness of the encounters are clear:

"By Richmond I raised my knees
Supine on the floor of a narrow canoe."

"My feet are at Moorgate, and my heart
Under my feet. After the event
He wept. He promised 'a new start.'
I made no comment. What should I resent?" (*CPP* 46)

Corruption, indifference, disappointment, violence, and again bodies as mere collections of parts: this is the sexual palette of *The Waste Land*.

The vacuity of human desire is unrelieved even by the rather more hopeful homo-erotically charged episodes in the poem. In the hyacinth-girl scene from "The Burial of the Dead," the word "Hyacinth" calls up the myth of the youth whom Apollo loved:

"You gave me hyacinths first a year ago;
"They called me the hyacinth girl."
– Yet when we came back, late, from the Hyacinth garden,
Your arms full, and your hair wet, I could not
Speak. . . . (*CPP* 38)

Here the scene's promising tenderness (a lover giving a gift), and images of fecundity (wet hair and arms full of flowers) are undercut by the indicators of frustrated hope: the strong " – Yet" and, once again, the failure of language. Whether the hyacinth "girl" is actually female has been a matter of considerable debate (see, for example, Pondrom, Churchill, Miller, and Query). There is nothing in the text to settle the matter definitively, though the Hyacinthus myth certainly admits the possibility of the homoerotic. In the last section of the poem, the lines beginning "*Datta*: what have we given? / My friend, blood shaking my heart / The awful daring of a moment's surrender" recount an intimate relationship (49); in an early draft, the passage began "DATTA. we brother, what have we given?" (*WLF* 77). Here the speaker and the addressee "think of the key, each in his prison." The precise nature of the "surrender" has kept scholars furiously busy for decades, but it is clear that it is a matter of both supreme importance ("By this, and this only, we have existed") and a source of shame ("Which an age of prudence can never retract"), and that it is to be kept secret ("Which is not to be found in our obituaries") (*CPP* 49). It also seems more possibility than realization, a combination of memory and desire: "your heart *would have* responded / Gaily, when invited, beating obedient / To controlling hands" (49–50; emphasis added). Unlike any of the scenes of heterosexual desire, this and the hyacinth-girl passage suggest reciprocal affection, and they retain passion and value in the memory of the speaker, but their potential, if it ever existed, to undo the corruption and disunity of the wasteland is undone by their status as missed opportunities. Less fondly remembered is Mr. Eugenides's coarser invitation "To luncheon at the Cannon Street Hotel / Followed by a weekend at the Metropole," which is presented as evidence of the roiling corruption of the City (43).

Colleen Lamos and Harriet Davidson have both called attention to the role of deviance and perversion, what Davidson calls "improper desire," in Eliot's work, particularly *The Waste Land*. "[T]he overriding tone of the poem," writes Davidson, "seems to yearn to be rid of improper desires" (122), which is consistent with Eliot's inherited view of sexuality. Eliot was not, however, without a forum in which he could freely explore, even embrace, "improper desires" of all kinds without the need for coding, disguising, or suppressing them. This was his long series of stanzas, alluded to earlier, of Columbo and Bolo poems. These verses, in which Eliot depicts the adventures, mostly sexual and scatological, of King Bolo and the explorer Columbo, were composed over the span of Eliot's career and privately circulated among a small group of male friends, including Ezra Pound, Wyndham Lewis, and James Joyce. Their public appearance, first in Eliot's *Letters* (1988) and then in *Inventions of the March Hare* (1996), has caused readers of Eliot to rethink the nature of sexuality not only in his poetry but in his imagination. They are bawdy pieces overwhelmingly concerned with masturbation, rape, sodomy, and scatology. I quote a representative example here:

> Now when they were three weeks at sea
> Columbo he grew rooty
> He took his cock in both his hands
> And swore it was a beauty.
> The cabin boy appeared on deck
> And scampered up the mast-o
> Columbo grasped him by the balls
> And buggered him in the ass-o. (*IMH* 317)

"Eliot's poetry and prose writings," as Churchill writes, "display an obsessive interest in sexual corruption and a particular fascination with homosexuality" (10). Whereas in his canonical work these fascinations "recur in more moderate incarnations," there is nothing moderate about the Columbo and Bolo poems (McIntire 38). Gabrielle McIntire argues that, beyond an interest in deviance, the poems also "highlight [Eliot's] ongoing obsessions with sex, race, and history," and that they are therefore of considerable value to our understanding of Eliot as both man and poet. Whereas most of Eliot's poetry tries to control (frequently deviant) sexual impulses, these private verses provide a comic space for indulging and enjoying those impulses – a space without which, one might conjecture, the rest of the poetry might not have been possible.

In Eliot's finished plays and published poetry after the mid-1920s, there is nothing like the intensity of sexual energy of the early poems. This is in part due to his aforementioned gradual shift from engaging sexuality directly to thinking of it as a question of communion to be achieved through poetic language. It is also linked to his increasing preference for thinking of earthly desire as a lower species of the desire for the divine, an idea that had been present to his mind since his youth but that was reinvigorated and clarified by his conversion to Anglicanism in 1927. The year after his conversion, Eliot took a vow of celibacy (Gordon 292), a step that likely enabled him to conceptualize more confidently his suspicions of human sexuality. Compared to union with the divine, as he wrote in "East Coker," "the coupling of man and woman" is scarcely different from "that of beasts. Feet rising and falling. / Eating and drinking. Dung and death" (*CPP* 124). In life the best a human might hope for is perfect expression in language, "where every word is at home, / . . . / The complete consort dancing together" (144).

Although the characters in Eliot's plays are placed in fairly traditional social and sexual situations, their wrestlings with questions of desire generally begin with the kinds of assumptions found in the early poems and make their way toward meditations on higher concepts. In *The Cocktail Party*, the possibilities for heterosexual union are only somewhat better than in *The Waste Land*. The separated Edward and Lavinia decide to reconcile, but marriage, while "a good life," is clearly not the *best* life (*CPP* 364). "The best of a bad job is all any of us make it – / Except of course, the saints," Reilly consoles them (356). This exception represents a new element in Eliot's economy of desire. Now there is the real possibility of redemption from the unsatisfying realm of earthly unions through pursuit of the divine union. Celia, Edward's mistress, throbs exactly between those two lives. She recalls the emptiness of her sexual relationship with Edward:

> And then I found we were only strangers
> And that there had been neither giving nor taking
> But that we had merely made use of each other
> Each for his purpose. That's horrible. (362)

Eventually she settles on a different path,

> In which one is exalted by intensity of loving
> In the spirit, a vibration of delight
> Without desire, for desire is fulfilled
> In the delight of loving. (363)

This path is not without human baggage, but, like marriage, it represents escape as well. As Reilly counsels:

> Each way means loneliness – and communion.
> Both ways avoid the final desolation
> Of solitude in the phantasmal world
> Of imagination, shuffling memories and desires. (365)

That shuffling, it seems, is the first but not the last marker of the human condition for Eliot. The "higher vices" available to the living, whether connubial or spiritual, provide intimations of the perfect absence of memory and desire that saints alone can claim.

The Critical Climate

Thus far I have spoken only in fairly general terms about the biographical background to some sexual themes in Eliot's poetry. Since the most intense critical speculation about Eliot and sexuality, however, routinely draws on a few key intimate relationships in Eliot's life, I will briefly highlight the ones that have seemed most pertinent to these investigations. The first is with Jean Verdenal, the French student with whom Eliot shared a rooming house from 1910 to 1911 in Paris. In Eliot's first year abroad, he found in Verdenal the very definition of a kindred spirit, a young man with a similar temperament, the same tastes in modern art, music, and poetry, similar religious yearnings, and a *joie de vivre* that seems to have carried the young American right along with it (Perinot 267–69; *Letters* 23, 28). After Eliot's departure from Paris, the two maintained a lengthy and intimate correspondence. Verdenal was later to be killed in World War I, a loss that struck Eliot to the core. The significance of their friendship is adequately suggested by two quotations. The first is the dedication of *Prufrock and Other Observations* (1917), Eliot's first book, to "Jean Verdenal, 1889–1915 / mort aux Dardanelles," accompanied by a passage from Dante (added in 1925) indicating "the quantity of love that warms me toward you" (*CPP* 3). The second comes from a *Criterion* "Commentary" Eliot wrote in 1934 in which he says that his "retrospect" of his days in Paris "is touched by a sentimental sunset, the memory of a friend coming across the Luxembourg Gardens in the late afternoon, waving a branch of lilac" ("C [Apr. 1934]" 452). His selection of this detail to exemplify his time in Paris, from among the countless new artistic, intellectual, and cultural experiences we know he had there, is as good an indicator as any of the central place of Verdenal's friendship in Eliot's imagination.

That there was a homoerotic quality to their relationship is beyond doubt. Whether there was a homosexual component has been a matter of fierce debate. Leaving the question open for the moment, I will offer for comparison the two great female loves of Eliot's life (apart from his second wife, Valerie, whom he married in his last years). Upon returning to Harvard from Paris in 1911, Eliot met the vivacious, well-bred, and talented Emily Hale. As Lyndall Gordon writes, Hale was the inspiration for several "moments of romantic attraction to a woman" in Eliot's poetry, including in "La Figlia che Piange," "Burnt Norton," and perhaps even *The Waste Land* (81). After an interval of several years, these two would reestablish contact and again become quite close, but it is clear that Hale's significance to Eliot was more as an ideal figure than as a potential sexual partner. In the meantime, Eliot had moved to London and, no more than a few weeks after receiving news of Verdenal's death in 1915, married Vivien Haigh-Wood, a young Englishwoman he had met only two months earlier. Vivien was fiery, creative, and thoroughly modern, not to mention, to Eliot, "a revelation of sexual and emotional life, and one in which he might lose all his doubts and anxieties" (Ackroyd 63). Despite this and their imaginative sympathy, their marriage was a near-total disaster. Vivien suffered from a number of physical and psychological ailments, as did Eliot, and their relationship was marked from very early on by mutual depression, anxiety, and sexual incompatibility. Eliot admitted later in life that "To her the marriage brought no happiness . . . to me, it brought the state of mind out of which came *The Waste Land*" (*Letters* xvii). For better or worse, his marriage to Vivien was the most crucial relationship of his life in terms of his development as a man and a poet.

These are the relationships, then, that loomed largest for Eliot during his most productive writing years, and that form the best basis we have for understanding his experience of sexual feeling, realized or not. Critics have only comparatively recently begun to make substantial inroads into understanding the significance of sexuality in Eliot's writing and into the links that exist between his writing and himself. By way of conclusion, I will note some of the more important ones.

A number of scholars have speculated, not without controversy, that the homoerotic scenes in *The Waste Land* are Eliot's attempt to come to terms with his memories of Jean Verdenal. Critical discussion of Eliot's own possible homosexuality was unofficially opened in 1952, when the journal *Essays in Criticism* published an article by John Peter, "A New Interpretation of *The Waste Land*," in which Peter argued that *The Waste Land* was in essence an extended elegy for a dead soldier with whom the speaker of the poem "has fallen completely – perhaps the right word is irretrievably – in love" (245). Although the essay itself makes no mention of homosexuality as such, Eliot moved immediately and forcefully to block its "further dissemination." Through his solicitors, he was able to get all existing copies of the July *Essays in Criticism* destroyed. The article was, however, republished in 1969, four years after Eliot's death, with an additional postscript describing Eliot's initial reaction, including the "amazement and disgust" with which he had read the piece. Peter also claimed in this postscript that the soldier elegized in *The Waste Land* is in fact Jean Verdenal.

It was not until 1977 that the first sustained critical study of Eliot's sexuality appeared. James E. Miller's *T. S. Eliot's Personal Waste Land: Exorcism of the Demons*, picks up Peter's initial suggestion about *The Waste Land* as an elegy for Verdenal and expands upon it, performing a detailed reading of *The Waste Land* that finds traces of Verdenal throughout and goes on to find the theme of mourning for a lost male love as underpinning most of the poet's work. Reading *The Waste Land* as a personal poem, contrary to its author's enormously influential doctrine of poetic impersonality, brought censure enough, but raising the theme of homoeroticism drew an additional measure of intensity from the book's many detractors.

The early response to Miller's book was indeed often hostile or dismissive. Many scholars saw it as an attempt to sully the reputation of a monumental figure, to capitalize on the suggestion of scandal in the life of a revered public person. Others objected to its apparent attempt to use *The Waste Land* and other poems as a key to the poet's life, as a biography in code. In the first authoritative biography of Eliot, published in 1984, Peter Ackroyd makes hardly any mention of Miller's book. More than thirty years after its appearance, *T. S. Eliot's Personal Waste Land* retains its ability to incite controversy, but it has also gained a new importance and relevance with the advent of Queer critical theory. Several contemporary critics have helped to ameliorate what had hitherto been an unproductive battle between those committed to the impersonal approach to criticism advocated by Eliot and those interested in making explicit connections between the poet's work and his life. The most influential recent investigations into the subject of Eliot's sexuality have not been afraid to note the apparent biographical resonances in Eliot's work, but they have generally disavowed interest in using the poetry as a key for unlocking the ostensible secrets of Eliot's life. Contemporary critical discussion of Eliot's sexuality is characterized by a nuanced attention to the interplay of the man's life and his work, to the ways in which texts and selves mutually influence one another.

It has been Eliot's emphatic reaction to John Peter's essay, as much as the essay's relatively mild insinuations of a homosexual relationship between Eliot and Verdenal, that has gotten the attention of critics. The vehemence of his denunciation of an article by a young, unknown scholar – an article that might very well have slipped quietly into oblivion – has understandably caused readers to wonder whether Eliot was protesting too much, and to ask whether something might indeed be hidden behind his denial. This has led to many attempts to answer the question of what biographical secrets the sexual screens throughout Eliot's work really hide. Queer theory, though, has kept critical discussion from degenerating into mere literary voyeurism. Merrill Cole, for instance, has seen in Eliot's dismissal of Peters as well as in *The Waste Land* a "closet rhetoric," which he faults Miller for overlooking in an attempt to bring "latent homosexuality to the surface in glittering positivity, virtually overlooking what its burial entails" (68–69).

Other critics have looked to Eliot's sexual masks not for what they conceal but for what they reveal. Tim Dean attempts to "[shift] the critical debate away from closet logic. . . . Sexuality in Eliot," he argues, "involves hiddenness not as a mode of concealment, but as an occult mode of access with erotic implications" (45). Colleen Lamos argues that "the structure of [homoerotic] desire" in Eliot's early poetry "is indicative of the configuration of melancholic homoeroticism between men characteristic of the early twentieth century" ("Love Song" 28; see also Kaye, Query). Some recent critics have also become seriously interested in reinvigorating the discussion about the relationship of the poet's life to his work, focusing on the idea of selfhood and just what that entails. In "Outing T. S. Eliot," Suzanne Churchill insists on treating Eliot as more than a purely discursive construction: "Eliot breathed, ate, wrote, and had sex (or didn't) in a particular body" (8). Yet she refuses to collapse his writing into his life in a purely biographical reading, arguing instead to balance attention to the poetry with a sufficiently "complex model of authorial identity" (8). David Chinitz has also fought to retain a sense of Eliot as a self and not merely a collection of texts. In a fascinating move, he suggests that the sexual and emotional scenarios in Eliot's poems are not the products of Eliot's real-life experiences, but rather that Eliot fashioned his actual relationships after patterns he had already imagined and written into his work: "Eliot's life took shape from his words and not the other way" (463). Of course, Chinitz is only following the lead of Eliot, for whom "the words sufficed / To compel the recognition they preceded" (*CPP* 141). Rather than having retreated into a stale was-he-or-wasn't-he, did-he-or-didn't-he debate, studies of sexuality in Eliot's work seem to have found new possibilities where there appeared to be dead-ends.

Such developments have not ended the debate about Eliot's "actual" sexual inclinations, however. Seymour-Jones's (2005) biography of Vivien, *Painted Shadow*, makes the most adamant case to date that Eliot was a – not-always repressed – homosexual. Seymour-Jones's book has been only slightly less controversial than Miller's, but, due to its use of substantial unpublished and private materials, it has earned the attention, and at times the respect, of Eliot scholars. And Miller himself has recently rejoined the fray with his *T. S. Eliot: The Making of an American Poet*, in which he backs down not at all from his earlier suggestions about the relationship between Eliot and Verdenal. With a good deal more of Eliot's writing in both poetry and prose yet to be published, it seems likely that there will be plenty of new evidence to fuel the ongoing discussion.

NOTE

1 Aware of St. Sebastian's status as a subcultural icon, Eliot felt it necessary to forewarn Conrad Aiken that there was "nothing homosexual" about his poem – or, presumably, about his fascination with St. Sebastian, paintings of whom he had made a study (*Letters* 44; see also 41, 376).

References and Further Reading

Ackroyd, Peter. *T. S. Eliot: A Life*. New York: Simon, 1984.

Chinitz, David E. "In the Shadows: Popular Song and Eliot's Construction of Emotion." *Modernism/Modernity* 11 (2004): 449–67.

Churchill, Suzanne W. "Outing T. S. Eliot." *Criticism* 47 (2005): 7–30.

Cole, Merrill. "Empire of the Closet." *Discourse* 19 (1997): 67–91.

Dean, Tim. "T. S. Eliot, Famous Clairvoyante." Laity and Gish 43–65.

Gordon, Lyndall. *T. S. Eliot: An Imperfect Life*. New York: Norton, 1998.

Kaye, Richard A. "'A Splendid Readiness for Death': T. S. Eliot, the Homosexual Cult of St. Sebastian, and World War I." *Modernism/Modernity* 6 (1999): 107–34.

Laity, Cassandra, and Nancy K. Gish, eds. *Gender, Desire, and Sexuality in T. S. Eliot*. Cambridge: Cambridge UP, 2004.

Lamos, Colleen. *Deviant Modernism: Sexual and Textual Errancy in T. S. Eliot, James Joyce, and Marcel Proust*. Cambridge: Cambridge UP, 1998.

——. "The Love Song of T. S. Eliot: Elegiac Homoeroticism in the Early Poetry." Laity and Gish 23–42.

Mayer, John T. *T. S. Eliot's Silent Voices*. New York: Oxford UP, 1989.

McIntire, Gabrielle. *Modernism, Memory, and Desire: T. S. Eliot and Virginia Woolf*. Cambridge: Cambridge UP, 2008.

Miller, James E. *T. S. Eliot: The Making of an American Poet*. University Park, PA: Pennsylvania State UP, 2005.

——. *T. S. Eliot's Personal Waste Land: Exorcism of the Demons*: University Park, PA: Pennsylvania State UP, 1977.

Perinot, Claudio. "Jean Verdenal: T. S. Eliot's French Friend." *Annali di Ca'Foscari* 35 (1996): 265–75.

Peter, John. "A New Interpretation of *The Waste Land*." *Essays in Criticism* 2 (1952): 242–66.

Pondrom, Cyrena N. "T. S. Eliot: The Performativity of Gender in *The Waste Land*." *Modernism/Modernity* 12 (2005): 425–41.

Query, Patrick. "'They Called Me the Hyacinth Girl': T. S. Eliot and the Revision of Masculinity." *Yeats Eliot Review* 18.3 (2002): 10–21.

Seymour-Jones, Carole. *Painted Shadow: The Life of Vivienne Eliot, First Wife of T. S. Eliot*. New York: Anchor, 2001.

30

"An occupation for the saint": Eliot as a Religious Thinker

Kevin J. H. Dettmar

Though primarily an onlooker when Wyndham Lewis and Ezra Pound dropped their *Blast* on London in 1914, his sly manner of coming out as a Christian in 1928 demonstrates that Eliot did in time develop his own genteel version of their polemics. His intentionally provocative pronouncement that he was, among other things, "anglo-catholic in religion," slipped into the preface of his essay collection *For Lancelot Andrewes*, took many of his peers by surprise, and frankly angered some. Eliot's capitulation to orthodoxy seemed to many a rejection of the very spirit of modernist experimentation that his 1922 landmark poem, *The Waste Land,* had helped to usher in. "Poor dear Tom Eliot . . . may be called dead to us all from this day forward," Virginia Woolf wrote to her sister; "there's something obscene in a living person sitting by the fire and believing in God" (457–58). Though elicited by a somewhat later (1934) and far more offensive tract (*After Strange Gods: A Primer of Modern Heresy*), the response of Eliot's former mentor and sponsor Ezra Pound further suggests the tenor of critical reaction to Eliot's conversion: "His diagnosis is wrong. . . . His remedy is an irrelevance" (qtd. in Gordon 104). Eliot's pugnacious declaration of religious orthodoxy, coming at the high-water mark of the literary modernism he had helped to establish as artistic orthodoxy, was perhaps as unsettling as Shelley's atheism a century earlier; in the same year that, for instance, Woolf's *To the Lighthouse* was published, Eliot seemed to be turning his back on experimentation in favor of the comforts of Tradition. Thus Eliot's June 1927 baptism into the Church of England had far more than a personal import: it was seen, at the time and subsequently, as a declaration of the failure of the modernist project.

Moments in and out of Time

T. S. Eliot was born into a family with deep, and deeply American, religious roots. Since Andrew Eliot of East Coker, Somerset, had established the family in Beverley,

A Companion to T. S. Eliot, First Edition. Edited by David E. Chinitz.
© 2014 John Wiley & Sons, Ltd. Published 2014 by John Wiley & Sons, Ltd.

Massachusetts in 1670, Eliot's forebears had included a number of important New England and St. Louis churchmen. The most important of those, whose influence Eliot felt keenly (though he died the year before the poet's birth), was his grandfather, the Rev. William Greenleaf Eliot. It was William Eliot who uprooted the family and brought them to the edge of the frontier: leaving his position at the Harvard Divinity School in 1834, he carried Unitarianism to the western banks of the Mississippi – St. Louis, Missouri. There, he also established Washington University (1853), named at its founding (and to its founder's dismay) "Eliot's Seminary." And the poet inherited a churchman's genes not just from the Eliots, but on the spindle side as well: he found an early model of the religious, devotional poet in his mother Charlotte, whose long poem *Savonarola* Eliot later arranged to have published, and for which he provided a loving introduction; and like his paternal grandfather, Charlotte's uncle, the Rev. Oliver Stearns, had taught at the Harvard Divinity School. Boston, Unitarianism, and Harvard were something like the three Magi in attendance at the poet's birth.

Eliot was born to a family with deep religious traditions: but the religion itself, American Unitarianism, Eliot thought anything but deep. Boston, the family's ancestral home, was the spiritual capitol of Unitarianism; and the Harvard Divinity School, from its founding in 1816, was a Unitarian seminary. It became an ostensibly nonsectarian department of the university in 1870; but an address delivered to students at the Eleventh Session of the Harvard Summer School of Theology, on July 22, 1909, serves to suggest just how closely the school hewed to Unitarian teaching for many years after its nominal separation. The speaker was none other than Charles W. Eliot, speaking in his last year as Harvard's president, and a month after T. S. Eliot had graduated with his AB; the two were related, if distantly (the President was the poet's grandfather's third cousin once removed). The lecture, published as *The Religion of the Future*, shows an American Unitarianism at its low tide: not only had the knotty doctrine of the Trinity has been abandoned, but through cross-pollination with its Boston neighbor Transcendentalism, along with a motley assortment of other belief systems and philosophies, Unitarianism had in essence abandoned any real notion of the divine. "In the future religion," Charles Eliot writes, "there will be nothing 'supernatural.' This does not mean that life will be stripped of mystery or wonder, or that the range of natural law has been finally determined; but that religion, like all else, must conform to natural law so far as the range of law has been determined" (31). The Harvard brand of Unitarianism had been gradually transformed into a capacious humanism, with human "pluck" its highest good:

> The future religion will pay homage to all righteous and loving persons who in the past have exemplified, and made intelligible to their contemporaries, intrinsic goodness and effluent good-will. It will be an all-saints religion. It will treasure up all tales of human excellence and virtue. It will reverence the discoverers, teachers, martyrs, and apostles of liberty, purity, and righteousness. (28)

This "natural supernaturalism" proved too thin a broth to feed either the imagination or the moral hunger of the younger Eliot; as Peter Ackroyd writes, Eliot ultimately "rejected" Unitarianism "as a bland and insufficient heresy" (17). This attitude persisted into the years when he began to write his first published poetry; "in 1916 and 1917," Lyndall Gordon reminds us, Eliot

> reviewed a number of books about the relation of philosophy to religion, criticizing writers who tried to reformulate Christianity so as to make it more palatable to the enlightened bourgeoisie. He criticised specifically their removal of asceticism and radicalism from Christianity — it made it too tepid, too liberal, too much like the enlightened Unitarianism of his family. "All that is anarchic, or unsafe or disconcerting in what Jesus said and did is either denied or boiled away," he complained. (109–10)[1]

Indeed, Eliot ultimately came to think the Unitarian church "outside the Christian Fold," as he put it in a 1927 letter to Bertrand Russell (qtd. in Gordon 19).

From an early age, then, Eliot recognized in himself an inchoate spiritual thirst that the liberal religious structures of his family and peers could not satisfy. "[I]n the first half of the twentieth century," Gordon writes, Eliot "sought an older, stricter discipline, unsoftened by nineteenth-century liberalism" (19). Before he had embraced a specific religious tradition within which to interpret them, however, Eliot was moved by experiences in which the constraints of terrestrial human existence came to seem fleeting, unreal: moments when the restrictions of time and space momentarily vanished. Gordon and Ronald Schuchard agree that the first time this kind of awareness finds its way into Eliot's writing is in the short poem "Silence," from June 1910, which records what Schuchard calls "an ecstatic visionary experience" (121). The poem closes on a tableau of "the ultimate hour," in which "life is justified":

> The seas of experience
> That were so broad and deep,
> So immediate and steep,
> Are suddenly still.
> You may say what you will,
> At such peace I am terrified.
> There is nothing else beside.[2] (*IMH* 18)

Whether Old Testament (Moses parting the Red Sea) or New (Jesus commanding the rough seas), the scene is redolent of biblical imagery, appropriate for an experience felt to carry an unidentified religious significance.

Such brief moments out of time, such visionary moments, occur repeatedly in Eliot's poetry: occasionally in the poems leading to and including *The Waste Land*, insistently and programmatically in his most fully realized Christian poem, *Four Quartets*. English poetry of course has a long tradition of recording such moments, going back to the very romantics from whom Eliot sought to distance himself. One of Eliot's great early critics, Helen Gardner, describes such passages as moments of religious expression unmoored from orthodox religious faith:

Religious experience finds sublime expression in many passages of Wordsworth's *Prelude*, and religious faith and dedication burns in Shelley's poetry. There is no comparable expression of the sublime or the ardent in those whose religious life is nourished by the Christian tradition. Nor, I think, after Wordsworth and Shelley, are such qualities often found in religious poetry outside the Christian tradition, or in nineteenth-century poetry generally. (162)

While Gardner restricts her comments to nineteenth-century poets, Eliot, discussing the prose writings of the Christian philosopher Blaise Pascal, calls such moments "mystical" and suggests that "what can only be called mystical experience happens to many men who do not become mystics." In the same essay, he calls Pascal's experiences "his illumination from God" (*SE* 357–58). And in this essay from 1931, Eliot leaves no doubt as to the reality, even primacy, of such experience:

[E]ven the most exalted mystic must return to the world, and use his reason to employ the results of his experience in daily life. You may call it communion with the Divine, or you may call it a temporary crystallization of the mind. Until science can teach us to reproduce such phenomena at will, science cannot claim to have explained them; and they can be judged only by their fruits. (*SE* 358)

Before his religious conversion of 1927, Eliot himself might have inclined to call such moments a "temporary crystallization of the mind"; by the time of the Pascal essay, however, he was convinced that they represented something much more, a "communion with the Divine."

From the English romantics onward, poetry (and later, literary prose) had sought after new ways to express the inexpressible, the ineffable. For the romantics, one side of this coin was their attraction to the sublime: those features of the natural world which, as Shelley writes in "Mont Blanc" (1817), connect us with a transcendent realm:

> Dizzy Ravine! and when I gaze on thee
> I seem as in a trance sublime and strange
> To muse on my own separate phantasy,
> My own, my human mind, which passively
> Now renders and receives fast influencings,
> Holding an unremitting interchange
> With the clear universe of things around. . . . (584)

The sublime arises from human encounters with those features of the natural world that dwarf our senses and intellect; but it's equally possible, and far more common, for us to become aware of our mental limitations in the encounter with outwardly unremarkable experiences. Wordsworth, in *The Prelude*, writes of "spots of time," moments when the restrictive prisms of human space and time seem suddenly, momentarily, to fall away:

> There are in our existence spots of time,
> That with distinct pre-eminence retain
> A renovating virtue, whence . . .
>
> > our minds
> Are nourished and invisibly repaired;
> A virtue, by which pleasure is enhanced,
> That penetrates, enables us to mount,
> When high, more high, and lifts us up when fallen. (XII, ll. 208–18)

These moments, Wordsworth writes, are "scattered everywhere," and a number of them appear in *The Prelude* itself: stealing a boat, in Book I; the death of Wordsworth's father in Book XI; climbing Mount Snowdon, in Book XIII.

Many subsequent writers, both of poetry and of prose, have followed Wordsworth in his concentration on these "spots of time"; Virginia Woolf called them "moments of being," and W. B. Yeats, ever hungry for mystical experience, writes of such an experience in "Vacillation," where he sits, "a solitary man, / In a crowded London shop":

> While on the shop and street I gazed
> My body of a sudden blazed;
> And twenty minutes more or less
> It seemed, so great my happiness,
> That I was blessèd and could bless. (251)

Similarly, the speaker of "The Second Coming" conveys a visionary experience in the poem's second stanza ("a vast image out of *Spiritus Mundi* / Troubles my sight"). But the modern writer who most insistently put such visionary moments on the agenda of modernist literature was James Joyce, in his concept of the epiphany. In *Stephen Hero*, an early version of *A Portrait of the Artist as a Young Man*, Joyce puts the recording of these evanescent epiphanies at the very center of the modern writer's job description: "By an epiphany [Stephen] meant a sudden spiritual manifestation, whether in the vulgarity of speech or of gesture or in a memorable phase of the mind itself. He believed that it was for the man of letters to record these epiphanies with extreme care, seeing that they themselves are the most delicate and evanescent of moments" (211). By the time Joyce gets his hands on Wordsworth's spots of time, they have been thoroughly secularized. Joyce's epiphanies may reveal timeless truths about human nature, but their source is entirely human: there's no trace of the transcendent about them. Hence the irony of Joyce's label for them, derived from the revelation of the infant Christ to the Magi, the divine incongruously appearing in the most humble of human settings.

Eliot's earliest attempts to fix these moments in his poetry, like "Silence," hover ambivalently between a spiritual and an entirely secular understanding of their etiology and significance. By the time of *The Waste Land*, however, any sense of spiritual import seems to have been drained off, save to the extent that the figure of a woman achieves a kind of quasi-spiritual status. Think of the terrifying epiphany in Part I:

> . . . when we came back, late, from the Hyacinth garden,
> Your arms full, and your hair wet, I could not
> Speak, and my eyes failed, I was neither
> Living nor dead, and I knew nothing,
> Looking into the heart of light, the silence. (*CPP* 38)

Eliot's doctoral work on the philosophy of the neo-idealist F. H. Bradley would have provided one context for understanding these experiences: "All significant truths are private truths. As they become public they cease to become truths; they become facts, or at best, part of the public character; or at worst, catchwords" (*KE* 165).

Though he never used the term, Eliot came increasingly to depend on these epiphanies, these spots of time: in this sense *Four Quartets* is Eliot's *Prelude* – which, it is well to remember, Wordsworth described as "a long poem on the formation of my own mind" (*Letters* 181). From Wordsworth to Yeats to Woolf and Joyce, these visionary moments became more and more thoroughly detached from any divine source; the trajectory of Eliot's poetic career, on the other hand, is precisely to restore to them the sense of their transcendent power, as his understanding of the commingling of the sacred with the profane deepens over the course of his own spiritual journey. This understanding is most dazzlingly on display, of course, in *Four Quartets*; the density of such moments in the poems beggars summary. Perhaps the best general evocation of these moments of epiphanic vision, and their importance, comes in "The Dry Salvages":

> But to apprehend
> The point of intersection of the timeless
> With time, is an occupation for the saint—
> . . . .
> For most of us, there is only the unattended
> Moment, the moment in and out of time,
> The distraction fit, lost in a shaft of sunlight,
> The wild thyme unseen, or the winter lightning
> Or the waterfall, or music heard so deeply
> That it is not heard at all, but you are the music
> While the music lasts. (*CPP* 136)

Earlier in the poem, they are described as "moments of happiness": "not the sense of well-being, / Fruition, fulfillment, security or affection, / Or even a very good dinner, but the sudden illumination" (132–33).[3]

But of course, like all good poetry, *Four Quartets* doesn't just tell us about these visionary experiences, but evokes them. The most famous of these – among the most famous passages in the poems – describes (and this a first for Eliot) not a moment of solitary revelation, but one experienced in the company of another. The passage is seemingly based on a trip that Eliot made with Emily Hale, in the summer of 1934, to Burnt Norton, Gloucestershire:

> Footfalls echo in the memory
> Down the passage which we did not take
> Towards the door we never opened
> Into the rose-garden. (*CPP* 117)

The figure of the rose garden, like its precursor the hyacinth garden in *The Waste Land*, becomes in the poem a figure for those timeless moments, rather like Wordsworth's "spots of time," which provide to the attentive intimations of immortality:

> To be conscious is not to be in time
> But only in time can the moment in the rose-garden,
> The moment in the arbour where the rain beat,
> The moment in the draughty church at smokefall
> Be remembered; involved with past and future.
> Only through time time is conquered. (119–20)

"Spilt Religion"

As a young man, Eliot was caught in something of a religious paradox – torn between the competing claims and authority of personal revelation and impersonal Tradition. Eliot thought purely subjective experience unreliable; one might point, for instance, to his rejection of John Middleton Murry's suggestion that the English writer should be led not by tradition, but by "the inner voice." In "The Function of Criticism" (1923), Eliot opposes to Murry's "immature" understanding of the process of poetic creation his own "classicist" view: "Those of us who find ourselves supporting what Mr. Murry calls Classicism believe that men cannot get on without giving allegiance to something outside of themselves" (*SE* 15). In this line of thought, Eliot adheres closely to the teaching of the British philosopher T. E. Hulme, whose thought Eliot knew well, and with whom Eliot may even have been acquainted in London before Hulme's untimely death in World War I (Schuchard 52–69). And although Eliot once called Hulme, with characteristic rhetorical brio, "the most remarkable theologian of my generation" (*Letters* 94), Hulme's great gift to Eliot's religious thinking wasn't a fully adumbrated religious system, but rather a single, pivotal concept: the doctrine of original sin.

Hulme wrote one of the most celebrated essays of the modernist period, "Romanticism and Classicism," apparently in 1913 or 1914. Therein he predicts, famously, a "classical revival" that would blow through the overripe romanticism cluttering London's chartered streets and deliver a poetry characterized by "accurate, precise and definite description," composed of "small, dry things" (132, 131). The colorful descriptions in Hulme's polemic insinuated themselves in all kinds of ways into the polemics written by Eliot and Pound in the teens; the almost comical binary constructed in Pound's critical prose between "hard" and "soft," for instance, has been the subject of much commentary. One significant feature of Hulme's essay is the way it allies traditional Christianity with the new classicism, and the forces of progress; for "the Church," Hulme wrote, "has always taken the classical view since the defeat of the Pelagian heresy and the adoption of the sane classical dogma of original sin" (117). Romanticism, on the other hand, is hamstrung by its manifestations of the religious impulse in improper channels: "Romanticism then, and this is the best definition I can give of it, is spilt religion" (118).

If we skip ahead ten years, we witness the definitive exiling of Christianity from the modernist vanguard, though arguably it had been but little in evidence before that, Hulme's aside notwithstanding. Certainly Pound had little use for Christianity; in a 1916 letter to H. L. Mencken, he wrote: "Christianity has become a sort of Prussianism, and will have to go. It has its uses and is disarming, but it is too dangerous. Religion is the root of all evil, or damn near all" (qtd. in Gordon 103). Eliot, it appears in retrospect, found himself until nearly the end of the 1920's in what Lyndall Gordon calls a state of "partial belief" (111). In the same year Pound aired his views on religion to Mencken, Eliot glossed Hulme's argument in an extension lecture at Oxford called "The Reaction Against Romanticism": "The classicist point of view has been defined as essentially a belief in Original Sin – the necessity for austere discipline" (qtd. in Schuchard 61). It is a "necessity" that Eliot understood, even before his celebrated conversion in 1927, but to which he had not yet subjected himself.

Then in one of the most profound acts of sleight of hand in modernist history, "in or about" the *annus mirabilis* 1922, Eliot declared the self-conscious, self-aware deployment of myth by modernist writers to be one of the hallmarks of the new writing. Part of the collateral damage caused by that preemptive strike, something rarely if ever talked about, is the way that religion gets left to one side when Eliot finds myth and comes to Frazer. In *"Ulysses*, Order, and Myth" (1923), Eliot famously declares that where religion was, myth will be: having briefly summarized the classicist position to which he adheres, and for which by implication he claims Joyce, Eliot goes on to argue in the review's famous closing paragraph that Joyce has followed on the lead of Yeats in developing the "mythical method" (*SP* 178): "It is simply a way of controlling, of ordering, of giving a shape and a significance to the immense panorama of futility and anarchy which is contemporary history" (177).[4] Eliot spells out the intellectual genealogy of the technique in a sentence: "Psychology (such as it is, whether our reaction to it be comic or serious), ethnology, and *The Golden Bough* have concurred to make possible what was impossible even a few years ago" (178).

Thus by 1923, myth is officially in, religion (except as a subject of anthropological curiosity) is out. It's a substitution Eliot would come to regret, if he ever regretted anything. Indeed, during Eliot's period of "partial belief," we see in his critical writing evidence of his own "spilt religion." "The instincts that find their right and proper outlet in religion," Hulme had written, "must come out in some other way" (118). During the official modernist prohibition on religion, before Eliot publicly broke with that orthodoxy in 1928, his critical prose becomes precisely that inappropriate outlet for his Christian impulses. Two quick indications from *The Sacred Wood* will have to suffice here. On the one hand, whereas William Blake himself declared "I must create a system or be enslaved by another man's," Eliot thought him wrong precisely on this count, comparing Blake's philosophical system, his original religious mythology, to "an ingenious piece of homemade furniture" (*SE* 279). "What his genius required, and what it sadly lacked," Eliot thought, "was a framework of accepted and traditional ideas which would have prevented him from indulging in a philosophy [read: religion] of his own, and concentrated his attention on the problems of the poet. . . . The concentration resulting from a framework of mythology and theology and philosophy is one of the reasons why Dante is a classic, and Blake only a poet of genius" (279–80). On the other hand, his commentary on Dante attributes his strength as a Christian poet precisely to his integration of experience, tradition, and faith: "Dante, more than any other poet, has succeeded in dealing with philosophy, not as a theory . . . or as his own comment or reflection, but in terms of something *perceived*. When most of our modern poets confine themselves to what they had perceived, they produce for us, usually, only odds and ends of still life and stage properties" (*SW* 170–71). By 1928, in his preface to the second edition of *The Sacred Wood*, Eliot was prepared to move in the direction toward which such arguments had long ago gestured. His thinking, he writes, has "passed on to another problem not touched upon in this book: that of the relation of poetry to the spiritual and social life of its time and other times" (viii). "[C]ertainly poetry is not the inculcation of morals, or the direction of politics; and no more is it religion or an equivalent of religion, except by some monstrous abuse of the words," he writes; yet, "on the other hand, poetry as certainly has something to do with morals, and with religion, and even with politics, perhaps, though what we cannot say" (ix–x).

Orthodoxy and its Discontents

If the doctrine of the Holy Trinity is the Christian doctrine most offensive to common sense and the Unitarian faith, the doctrine of original sin is most offensive to Americans' sense of pride and self-respect (and is eschewed equally by the Unitarians and their Boston neighbors, the Christian Scientists). But for Eliot, it seems to have comprised a bedrock component of his own life: his own experiences of depravity, of abjection, probably preceded his discovering it articulated in the Christian tradition. And in his writing, both critical and poetic, following his 1927 conversion, we find more frequent references to the antimodernist concepts of "sin" and "evil." In a 1930 essay on Baudelaire, for instance, Eliot rather improbably focuses on the French poet's well-developed moral conscience: "Baudelaire is concerned, not with demons, black masses, and romantic blasphemy, but with the real problem of good and evil" (*SE* 378).[5]

Baudelaire was hardly an orthodox pick as Eliot sought to restore the problem of evil to public debate. In the choruses from his pageant-play *The Rock*, however, Eliot suggests that it is precisely the role of the Church to keep such eternal truths in front of a public that would sooner deny them:

> Why should men love the Church? Why should they love her laws?
> She tells them of Life and Death, and of all that they would forget.
> She is tender where they would be hard, and hard where they like to be soft.
> She tells them of Evil and Sin, and other unpleasant facts.
> They constantly try to escape
> From the darkness outside and within
> By dreaming of systems so perfect that no one will need to be good. (*CPP* 106)

For Eliot, evil became real – took on a human face, we might say – neither through the teaching of the church, nor, as for Yeats, through the horrors of World War I and the Irish Civil War (Dettmar). Rather, Eliot's keen sense of moral evil was awakened by the sexual betrayal of his wife with their close friend Bertrand Russell. In a 1933 letter to his friend and confidante Ottoline Morrell, Eliot writes:

> Bertie, because at first I admired him so much, is one of my lost illusions. He has done Evil, without being big enough or conscious enough to Be [*sic*] evil. I owe him this, that the spectacle of Bertie was one contributing influence to my conversion. Of course he had no good influence on Vivienne. He excited her mentally, made her read books and become a kind of pacifist, and no doubt was flattered because he thought he was influencing her. . . . (qtd. in Schuchard 179)

The reality of evil, of sin – and the thorny question of how to deal with "sinners" – is a moral obstacle upon which many a Christian has stumbled. Eliot's view of humankind, dating back far before his conversion to Christianity, betrayed a tendency to misanthropy, from which his resistance to the humanism of Murry, Babbitt, and others issued, at least in part. Eliot could almost be talking about himself when he writes, in the 1930 essay on Baudelaire, that "[I]n much romantic poetry the sadness is due to the exploitation of the fact that no human relations are adequate to human desires, but also to the disbelief in any further object for human desires than that which, being human, fail to satisfy them" (*SE* 379). Eliot harbored, all his life, a profound sense of his own moral failings; this awareness, however, seems only imperfectly to have made him more sympathetic to failings and suffering of others. At the conclusion of the "Fire Sermon" section of *The Waste Land*, Eliot quotes from St. Augustine's *Confessions*, when the Lord has yanked him from midst of human contact, that "cauldron of unholy loves": "O Lord Thou pluckest me out" (*CPP* 46). The conclusion of the entire poem is equally uncompromising in its rejection of a sinful human race, as the speaker sits "upon the shore / Fishing, with the arid plane behind" him (50). This tableau establishes a pattern that will remain consistent through much of Eliot's later, more explicitly religious work: the believer is a solitary figure separated from human community, sitting on the banks, waiting for the advent of the Kingdom of Heaven. Surely there are other paths to sainthood, but Eliot seems to have struggled to imagine them. This is, perhaps, an occupational hazard of the mystic, and Eliot quotes the mystic St. John of the Cross in his epigraph to *Sweeney Agonistes*: "Hence the soul cannot be possessed of the divine union, until it has divested itself of the love of created beings" (*CPP* 74).

While Eliot seems to have come only with difficulty to embrace the notion of a community of humankind, he did become increasingly concerned, after his conversion, with his responsibility as a Christian intellectual, and took it upon himself to spur debate about the character and desirability of what he called "a Christian society." If one might somewhat schematically posit a distinction between "faith," as an act of personal conscience, intellect, and emotion, and "Religion," a formalized set of social and historical conventions, then Eliot's writing and attention, after his conversion, move largely from an exploration of the complicated dynamics of faith to the somewhat less compelling, and less personal, defense of his Religion. It's hard not to feel the emotional distance that sets in with essays on religious topics of the thirties like "Religion and Literature," "Thoughts after Lambeth," the "Modern Mind" section of *The Use of Poetry and the Use of Criticism*, and especially *After Strange Gods*. Gone is the anxious, vulnerable seeker, replaced by an impersonal font of orthodoxy. A rigid "us" vs. "them" schism takes hold, forcing out the honest ambivalence of Eliot's earlier writing – in this, for example, from the conclusion of "Lambeth": "The Universal Church is today, it seems to me, more definitely set against the World than at any time since pagan Rome" (*SE* 342). Those hypostasizing capitals say a great deal. Eliot's persistent defense of Christianity against the condescension and disdain of an increasingly secular world was courageous – certainly it put his reputation with his modernist cohorts and readers at risk – but it made him often defensive and at times even smug:

> The World is trying the experiment of attempting to form a civilized but non-Christian mentality. The experiment will fail; but we must be very patient in awaiting its collapse; meanwhile redeeming the time: so that the Faith may be preserved alive through the dark ages before us; to renew and rebuild civilization, and save the World from suicide. (342)

The difference between "faith" and "the Faith," one might suggest – or better, between the search for faith and embrace of "the Faith" – epitomizes the difference between Eliot's early and late writings on religion.

Eliot's most notorious experiment in religious writing, *After Strange Gods*, starkly demonstrates the confused impulses that undergird the larger project. "I do not wish to preach only to the converted," he writes early in the book, "but primarily to those who, never having applied moral principles to literature quite explicitly – perhaps even having conscientiously believed that they ought not to apply them in this way to 'works of art' – are possibly convertible." If not exactly ecumenical, Eliot here suggests the possibility of dialogue between believers and unbelievers. The pretense drops away, however, in the next three sentences: "I am not arguing, or reasoning, or engaging in controversy with those whose views are radically opposed to such as mine. In our time, controversy seems to me, on really fundamental matters, to be futile. It can only usefully be practiced where there is common understanding" (*ASG* 11). This is what counts as "reaching out" in his post-conversion religious writing.

Eliot criticism was for its first five decades characterized by a widespread unwillingness to engage seriously with Eliot's religious convictions and commitment. Most of this early work on Eliot and religion reads his Christianity (and his interest in comparative religion) into and out of his poetry, especially *The Waste Land* and *Four Quartets*; given the religious-quest framework of the former, famously illuminated by Eliot's own notes, and the explicitly Christian project of the latter, this seemed a sensible approach. Two books published in the last years of the twentieth century helped to turn the tide, however. Lyndall Gordon published the first volume of her biography of the poet in 1977, the second in 1988. Gordon's sympathy with Eliot's religious quest is explicit, and this thread of her presentation was only strengthened when, in 1998, the two volumes were republished in a revised one-volume edition. Gordon describes Eliot as "a man who conceives of his life as a spiritual quest despite the anti-religious mood of his age" (1), and this gets at something fundamental, and important, that much early criticism had overlooked. Gordon's critical biography was followed the next year by Ronald Schuchard's unapologetically biographical *Eliot's Dark Angel: Intersections of Life and Art*, his study of "the internal drama of shadows and voices that inhabit his [Eliot's] acutely personal poems and plays" (3). With these two studies, the depth, influence, complexity, and contradictions of Eliot's religious faith have finally begun to be taken seriously.

Putting aside the anti-religious prejudices of much early Eliot criticism, it becomes obvious that his two best-known and most accomplished poems are poems of religious quest: the first, *The Waste Land*, is that of a seeker weighing the claims of various traditions; the second, *Four Quartets*, is that of a believer seeking better to understand the burden of duty and obedience.[6] *Four Quartets* is arguably the most important Christian poem of the twentieth century, and it represents, along with *The Waste Land*, some of the most significant religious poetry in English of the era.

NOTES

1 Ronald Schuchard reads in these reviews not just a rejection of Unitarianism, but an incipient hunger for the Christianity he would later embrace: "Though Eliot's formal conversion to Anglo-Catholicism was eleven years away, his *sensibility* was religious and Catholic, and his primary critical concerns were moral in 1916, as his reviews for that year show" (68).

2 For further discussion of this poem, see SEARCHING FOR THE EARLY ELIOT: *INVENTIONS OF THE MARCH HARE*.

3 Elsewhere in *Four Quartets* Eliot writes, in a similar vein, of the

Whisper of running streams, and winter lightning.

The wild thyme unseen and the wild
strawberry,
The laughter in the garden, echoed
ecstasy
Not lost, but requiring, pointing to the
agony
Of death and birth. (*CPP* 127)

4   The term "mythical method" was actually
Joyce's, and was "leaked" to Eliot while he was
at work on the review.

5   In this declaration, however, Eliot was in some
ways simply reiterating the insight of a 1921
essay, "The Lesson of Baudelaire," published in
Wyndham Lewis's magazine *Tyro*: "More than
any poet of his time, Baudelaire was aware of
what most mattered: the problem of good and
evil."

6   On the Christian element of the *Quartets*, see
COMING TO TERMS WITH FOUR QUARTETS.

REFERENCES AND FURTHER READING

Ackroyd, Peter. *T. S. Eliot*. London: Hamilton, 1984.

Dettmar, Kevin J. H. "'Evil Gathers Head': Yeats' Poetics of Evil." *College Literature* 13 (1986): 71–87.

Eliot, Charles W. *The Religion of the Future*. Boston: Ball, 1909.

Gardner, Helen. *Religion and Literature*. New York: Oxford UP, 1971.

Gordon, Lyndall. *T. S. Eliot: An Imperfect Life*. New York: Norton, 1998.

Hulme, T. E. *Speculations: Essays on Humanism and the Philosophy of Art*. Ed. Herbert Read. London: Routledge, 1936.

Joyce, James. *Stephen Hero*. Ed. Theodore Spencer. New York: New Directions, 1963.

Pound, Ezra. *The Cantos of Ezra Pound*. New York: New Directions, 1972.

Schuchard, Ronald. *Eliot's Dark Angel: Intersections of Life and Art*. New York: Oxford UP, 1999.

Shelley, Percy Bysshe. *The Complete Poetical Works*. 1904. Cambridge: Chadwyck, 1992.

Woolf, Virginia. *The Letters of Virginia Woolf*. Ed. Nigel Nicholson and Joanne Trautmann. Vol. 3. New York: Harcourt, 1977.

Wordsworth, William. *The Prelude: A Parallel Text*. Ed. J. C. Maxwell. Harmondsworth: Penguin, 1971.

Wordsworth, William, et al. *Letters of the Wordsworth Family from 1787 to 1855*. Ed. William Angus Knight. Vol. 3. Boston: Ginn, 1907.

Yeats, W. B. *The Poems: A New Edition*. Ed. Richard J. Finneran. New York: Macmillan, 1983.

31

Eliot's Politics

Michael Levenson

Politics – as the legitimation of civic authority, the distribution of power, the apparatus of government, and the processes of legislation – placed an oblique, persistent, and complex pressure on Eliot's career. He recognized that political agitation dominated both his epoch and the discourse of his epoch, but he kept a self-conscious distance from its immediate demands. Eliot regarded himself as a radical thinker, one who pursued the deep-rooted questions of social life, especially questions ignored by those caught up in the superficiality of political debate. He preferred to keep free from the familiar identities of party and sect. But of course to refuse politics is not to escape it.

Two central issues impinge on Eliot's work from the start, though neither is cast initially as a political issue. These are a question of authority and a question of class. The former received its first sustained treatment through his work in philosophy, where it appears as a problem of knowledge and certainty. Writing at a moment of decisive transition, when the dominance of late nineteenth-century idealism was giving way to a resurgent empiricism, Eliot asked how authoritative knowledge could be possible.[1] How can we move from the immediacy of experience to a certainty of judgment? How might we advance from the subjective foundations of knowledge to a confirming objectivity? And while his dissertation on the philosophy of F. H. Bradley focused on these ancient epistemological questions, it is clear that Eliot was also concerned with their ethical significance. His early poetry broaches the question of authority as a matter of conduct and value. How might we gain authority over ourselves? And how might we reach definitive judgments about life's meaning? On the one hand, the works record moments of revelatory vision at "the ultimate hour / When life is justified" (*IMH* 18) or when the mind can glimpse "life that seems / Visionary, and yet hard" (51). On the other hand, the poems also dramatize the undoing of revelation. As Prufrock puts it, there is "time yet for a hundred indecisions, / And for a hundred visions and revisions, / Before the taking of a toast and tea" (*CPP* 4).

A Companion to T. S. Eliot, First Edition. Edited by David E. Chinitz.
© 2014 John Wiley & Sons, Ltd. Published 2014 by John Wiley & Sons, Ltd.

Eliot's first response to this dilemma is what his philosophy calls the "theory of points of view," which held that we can construct reliable – though never indubitable – judgments through the accumulation of many immediate perspectives. Cast in analogous terms a few years later, the concept of literary tradition reinterpreted "points of view" as the monuments of past literature that offer a pattern of authority determining the value of new works. Tiresias in *The Waste Land* – in whom, the notes tell us, "the two sexes meet" (*CPP* 52) – is a poetic figure for this early and developing position: the strenuous movement toward more inclusive, and therefore valid, perspectives. But the examples all suggest the stresses on this concept of authority. Eliot recognizes the threat of merely private judgment, but the attempt to build a principle of control – points of view, tradition, Tiresias – remains essentially unstable. A perspectival or composite authority always risks changing (or losing) its force, as new perspectives emerge. The very existence of an experiment such as *The Waste Land* has been taken as a sign of the tractability of Eliot's traditionalism: if it is pliant enough to accommodate such a radical work, one might say, then tradition cannot be a very severe principle of order. It is also worth noting that while the young Eliot is preoccupied with questions of authority, he has not yet made secure links to its political significance.

The other persistent early concern, the question of class, intersects with the issue of authority. The prewar poems betray a consistent suspicion of the genteel classes, the privileged and complacent elite, who enact shallow lives of brittle pleasure. Eliot's irony matures at the expense of this "porcelain land" of "sandwiches and ginger beer" ("Goldfish: Embarquement pour Cythère" [*IMH* 27]), a constellation of surfaces and superficial personalities. The privilege of the upper classes appears as a veneer covering an emptiness, though it is particularly women who become the objects of this critique, women who "come and go / Talking of Michelangelo" (*CPP* 4). Certainly, any appraisal of Eliot's politics must consider the abiding suspicion of moneyed privilege. His own comfortable background and elite genealogy did not prevent his estrangement from the gilded commercial classes who neither understood themselves nor their emotions and who came to stand as unworthy figures of authority.

In a letter written during World War I Eliot described his affection for the working-class students whom he taught in his extension classes and who were "very anxious to improve themselves" (*Letters* 166). Notably he characterizes these workers as a "class of people" that "is the most agreeable in England to me – you see I am by way of being a Labourite in England, though a conservative at home" (171). Yet at the same time he portrayed the English working classes as "impressive because of their fundamental conservatism; they are not, as a whole, aggressive and insolent like the same people in America" (169). These early affiliations are unstable and confused, but they do indicate a partiality (or at least a sympathy) toward the working-class cause – a partiality that quickly came up against its limits. In 1919, Eliot expressed worries over an imminent strike, remarking that "My own views are Liberal and strongly opposed to the Government in almost everything; but I cannot regard this present expression of labour discontent without grave apprehension and distrust" (*Letters* 336).

The stirring of collective revolt from below would become a chronic anxiety, appearing for instance as the "red-eyed scavengers" who are "creeping / From Kentish Town and Golder's [*sic*] Green" (*CPP* 27) or as "those hooded hordes swarming / Over endless plains" (48). In "A Game of Chess," the second section of *The Waste Land*, nothing seems worse than the hollowness of bourgeois privilege, unless it is the sterility of working-class life.

In these immediate postwar years Eliot became both more disenchanted with social life and more scathing toward the failures of the established order. His employment at Lloyds Bank brought him into daily contact with the economic machinery of the contemporary world, and the drafts of *The Waste Land* let us see the extent to which the work is, among many other things, an anti-finance poem. Eliot had entered London banking at a time when the City, the financial square mile, was at its extraordinary apogee. Through decades of industrial decline, finance was the prop and stay of the British economy, and as Eliot constructed the London of his poem, the City was the resistless magnet, drawing the laboring crowds on buses and underground trains. The streets of the district – Cannon Street, Lower Thames Street – give the poem its determinate geography.[2] An early version of "The Fire Sermon" indicates that the abandoned "Thames maiden" from Highbury had a father with an "anxious business" "somewhere in the city" (*WLF* 51), while the completed work portrays "the loitering heirs of city directors" as casual seducers of the "nymphs" (*CPP* 42). In a plaintive letter, Eliot had groaned in the face of the financial power: "So very few of one's acquaintance realize what it means to have sold . . . all of one's days, – except at most a month a year – and old age – to a huge impersonal thing like a Bank" (*Letters* 374). The degradations of commercial capitalism will remain an object of critique throughout his later career, with Eliot reacting to the appeasement at Munich by asking whether British society was "assembled round anything more permanent than a congeries of banks, insurance companies and industries, and ha[s] it any beliefs more essential than a belief in compound interest and the maintenance of dividends?" (*CC* 51).

Politics appears in another guise in *The Waste Land*, in the aspect of power, or more precisely, the absence of power. *The Waste Land* tells of an Archduke who long ago took Marie out on a sled, and a Coriolanus, who is now broken. Those loitering heirs of city directors have now departed, having left no addresses. There was a Fisher King. All these powers have receded, creating a landscape in which fearful selves are left to wander, at the mercy of forces no longer governed by once-formidable authorities, Kings and Generals, Directors and Dukes. Still, *The Waste Land*, with all its toppled towers of authority, displays power persisting. It lives on within the zone of personal intimacy, in the micro-society of intersubjectivity. The "barbarous king" who rudely forced Philomela is the terrible figure for the politics of intimacy, power between bodies, whose effects are written throughout the poem. Eliot envisions the couple, two flailing, flirting subjects, as a little system of submission and hierarchy, obedience and control. As the glimpsed idyll in the poem's final movements puts it, "your heart would have responded / Gaily, when invited, beating obedient / To controlling hands"

(*CPP* 49–50). Give, sympathize, and control – these are the imperatives of regulated subjectivity.

"Only from about the year 1926," Eliot wrote in retrospect, "did the features of the post-war world begin clearly to emerge – and not only in the sphere of politics. From about that date one began slowly to realize that the intellectual and artistic output of the previous seven years had been rather the last efforts of an old world, than the first struggles of a new" ("Last Words" 271). Within his own career, the moment of the middle twenties indeed marks a striking change. In "The Function of Criticism" (1923), the emerging position consolidates around an "Outside Authority" that can restrain and control the "Inner Voice" (Eliot borrows J. Middleton Murry's terms). He now demands a properly external order, no longer the construction of points of view, no longer simply the inheritance of tradition, and comes to call this order "Classicism" (*SE* 15). It is under the banner of classicism that he began his influential editorship of the *Criterion*. One of the most important sources of the position was T. E. Hulme, poet and critic, who had died during the war, but whose legacy Eliot celebrated in 1924, describing Hulme as the "forerunner of a new attitude of mind, which should be the twentieth-century mind, if the twentieth century is to have a mind of its own. Hulme is classical, reactionary, and revolutionary; he is at the antipodes of the eclectic, tolerant, and democratic mind of the end of the last century" ("C [Apr. 1924]" 231).

In 1927 Eliot was confirmed into the Church of England, and then in his preface to a new collection of essays, *For Lancelot Andrewes*, he made his celebrated avowal: he was "classicist in literature, royalist in politics, and anglo-catholic in religion" (vii). The significant change is away from authority as an assemblage of perspectives and toward authority as an enduring institutional power. The keywords of the emergent attitude are *Order, Discipline, Authority*, and *Control* – virtues now conceived not as primarily self-generated or even self-regulating, but as the products of external forces: a State and a Church. The special emphasis upon monarchy, but also the explicit turn to classicism and the Church, owed much to the conservative French thinker and activist Charles Maurras, whose work Eliot had been meditating upon for over a decade and who led the *Action française* in its demand for a return to French kingship. In the thirties *Action française* was proscribed by the Church, and though Eliot himself came to acknowledge the eccentricity and extremity of Maurras's campaign, his own political turn is scarcely conceivable without its precedent.

Gone is any dalliance with liberalism, which now becomes the name of political failure. By the mid twenties Eliot was describing himself as "personally . . . an old-fashioned Tory" (Letter 95), and in 1928 he stepped gingerly toward a consideration of Italian fascism. Even as he stayed clear from commitment or avowal, he was willing to

confess to a preference for fascism [to communism] in practice, which I dare say most of my readers share; and I will not admit that this preference is itself wholly irrational. I believe that the fascist form of unreason is less remote from my own than is that of

the communists, but that my form is a more reasonable form of unreason. ("Mr. Barnes"
690–91)

His religious faith, he attests, is what preserves him from the allure of Mussolini,
even as he acknowledges a "less remote" relation to fascism than to communism.
"Order and authority," he writes, "are good: I believe in them as wholeheartedly as
I think one should believe in any single idea; and much of the demand for them in
our time has been soundly based. But behind the increasing popular demand for
these things, the parroting of the words, I seem to detect a certain spiritual anaemia"
("Literature of Fascism" 287–88). The movement of thought here will become characteristic over the subsequent decade. As political life became more agitated, Eliot
acknowledged the conditions of historical emergency. But he refused to accept the
struggles – between communism and fascism, and between both movements and
liberalism – within the terms they themselves offered.

Partly, this self-conscious disengagement was a product of editorial principle. Eliot
held that a quarterly review such as the *Criterion* must be concerned with "political
philosophy rather than with politics, and the examination of the fundamental ideas
of philosophies rather than with problems of application," and he noted that his
journal had studiously "avoided the discussion of topical political issues, however
extensive" ("C [Jan. 1936]" 265). But more substantially, the abstention from the
immediate terms and topics of politics was an effect of his deepening involvement in
religion, as a matter not only of personal faith but at least as importantly as a question
of institutions and social order. Although Eliot's famous avowal of 1927 had given
equal weight to literature, politics, and religion, the balance quickly shifted. Roger
Kojecký and Peter Dale Scott have both noted how the Toryism of "Church and State"
shifted toward the absolute priority of religion, especially after the abdication crisis
of 1936 (Kojecký 123; Scott 69). Kojecký notes that Eliot calls for books that consider
the extent to which political belief "is a substitute for religion, and therefore a
muddle" ("Literature of Fascism" 282). Whatever privilege a monarch might enjoy,
it reached its limits in the authority of the Church. Similarly, the partisan literary
principle of classicism – the alternative to the "excess" of romanticism – lost its sharp
definition and aesthetic centrality. Literature, like politics, is now seen within the
encompassing framework of religious life. In a lecture on "Catholicism and International Order" (1933), Eliot set himself against those "who believe the public affairs
of this world and those of the next have nothing to do with each other":

> We, on the other hand, feel convinced, however darkly, that our spiritual faith should
> give us some guidance in temporal matters; that if it does not, the fault is our own; that
> morality rests upon religious sanction, and that the social organization of the world rests
> upon moral sanction; that we can only judge of temporal values in the light of eternal
> values. We are committed to what in the eyes of the world must be a desperate belief,
> that a Christian world-order, *the* Christian world-order, is ultimately the only one
> which, from any point of view, will work. (*EAM* 113–14)

The concept of orthodoxy now becomes the central pillar in his thought. Within the chaos of political life in the thirties, Eliot held fast to a principle of orthodox faith, from which he looked out onto a cataclysm. In the series of lectures given at the University of Virginia in 1933 and later published as *After Strange Gods*, he offered his "Primer of Modern Heresy." Beginning with the premise that contemporary society was "worm-eaten with Liberalism," he reevaluated the writings of the modernist generation – including Pound, Yeats, and Lawrence – which he now sees as rife with the errors of heresy (*ASG* 12). Having lost an "idea of Original Sin" (45), modern literature has given way to singular visions – private, eccentric, self-generated – that provide no genuine sense of Good and Evil, only ersatz substitutes for unreal human beings. Notoriously, the lectures in *After Strange Gods* called not only for the reanimation of a spiritual–ethical vision in literature, but also for the return to a single coherent Christian culture:

> The population should be homogeneous; where two or more cultures exist in the same place they are likely either to be fiercely self-conscious or both to become adulterate. What is still more important is unity of religious background; and reasons of race and religion combine to make any large number of free-thinking Jews undesirable. (20)

These infamous sentences were no doubt the chief reason for Eliot's decision to suppress the book soon after its publication. But the denunciative rhetoric, the intemperate proposals, and the anti-Semitism were not anomalies. Throughout his career Eliot's perception of political order required the extrusion of a poison, most often associated with women, Jews, or other "foreign populations," and during the thirties, he consistently tested the limits of extremity.

There is a *Church* whose authority is uncontested – "In matters of dogma, matters of faith and morals, it will speak as the final authority within the nation" (*CC* 38). There is a *public*, the "great mass of humanity" whose Christianity will be realized more in behavior than in beliefs, in "largely unconscious behavior" (23). There is an *elite*, the Community of Christians, "those of intellectual and spiritual superiority," the activists of a Christian society who exist to renovate the faith and to "form the conscious mind and the conscience of the nation" (30, 34). There is finally a *State* whose form is a matter of principled indifference: "What I mean by the Christian State is not any particular political form, but whatever State is suitable to a Christian society" (9). Thus: an authoritative Church; an unconsciously Christian public; a spiritual elect; a State of any kind that suits. This is the vision of 1939: it is *The Idea of a Christian Society*, which also first appeared as a series of lectures. The book, Eliot allows, is only a sketch of a Christian society, but then its sketchiness, its descriptive thinness and poverty of content, is no incidental feature. It is an act of radical simplification, which is a central act of Eliot's late politics.

Denis Donoghue has justly written that

> the entire rhetorical force of *The Idea of a Christian Society*, as of the books and essays surrounding it, is directed toward the conversion of political into religious terms, as if

to say that the ostensibly real political terms are in fact obfuscations or self-delusions; the real issue, in every case of a consideration of values, is a question of religious belief and practice. (226)

The conversion of political into religious terms: this is indeed the first motion, as we have seen, but its force can only be gauged when one acknowledges the second stroke, Eliot's reversion to politics armed with the categories of spirit. Here is the rhetorical dexterity of the tense discursive writings of the thirties: to ascend austerely to the religious plane only to turn and survey political life as it now shows itself to those above. Eliot wrote in this same year of war that for himself "a right political philosophy came more and more to imply a right theology," and it is no doubt in the spirit of that thought that he moved toward his most extreme positions. His poetry from "Gerontion" through "The Hollow Men" had presented varieties of catastrophe in the temporal sphere, and as early as 1931, in his reflection on the Lambeth conference of the Church of England, he had offered a dark prophecy:

> The World is trying the experiment of attempting to form a civilized but non-Christian mentality. The experiment will fail; but we must be very patient in awaiting its collapse; meanwhile redeeming the time: so that the Faith may be preserved alive through the dark ages before us; to renew and rebuild civilization, and save the World from suicide. (*SE* 342)

And yet because he remains responsive to the prevailing political crisis, Eliot does not see his faith as an abstention from worldly concerns, but rather as the basis for intervention in worldly failure. The widely shared perception of liberal society in terminal crisis was not something that he denied or avoided. Although he kept a fastidious distance from party controversies and legislative programs, he remained deeply concerned with the emergency of the thirties. Much as Eliot did not simply abandon worldly concerns in his poetry in order to compose devotional verse, he continued to address the ordering of temporal society, including "political" questions of elite and mass, leader and follower, authority and subject. Near the end of the decade, in a radio broadcast on "The Church's Message to the World," he laid out the terms for a spiritual politics – that is, a political intervention from the standpoint of religion. The Church "must struggle for a condition of society which will give the maximum of opportunity for us to lead wholly Christian lives, and the maximum of opportunity for others to become Christians" (qtd. in Kojecký 129). In "Catholicism and International Order," the politico-spiritual ambition is cast still more pointedly: "What we have to aim at is not merely an order which will not contradict the Christian order, an order in which Christians and non-Christians can accommodate themselves in perfect harmony; any program that a Catholic can envisage must aim at the conversion of the whole world" (*EAM* 123).

The name Christopher Dawson has still not been securely linked to Eliot – and this despite Eliot's acknowledgment of Dawson's Christian political example – despite, too, their participation in the Moot, the discussion group of Christian intellectuals who met for urgent talk as war approached. Dawson was no simple influence upon Eliot: he stands rather as the more daring plain speaker stands to the guarded voice, the willing controversialist to the cautious fellow traveler. To read Dawson's writing of the thirties, especially his work *Beyond Politics*, is to hear what Eliot dare not openly say, but what he often discreetly means. A method of allusion informs Eliot's discursive writings, one quite as important as the allusion in the poetry: it involves taking up a tone of relative moderation while making significant mention of the works of immoderate others. The writing achieves a kind of strategic banality, even as it invokes risk-taking confederates.

All through the late thirties, Dawson undertook to devise a theory of totalitarianism from the standpoint of Christian faith, and central to the theory was the claim that the framework of the modern secular state was insufficient to the transformations of the twentieth century. This was the political truth embodied by Stalin, more fully embodied by Hitler. It was mere moral preening for the so-called liberal democracies to parade their opposition to communism and fascism. Modern mass democracy is merely a polite name for totalitarianism. The ideal of the liberal state is obsolete; it is incapable of the necessary "social discipline," or "national unity." "We are witnessing," writes Dawson in the year the war began,

> the rise of new forms of social life and a new kind of community which aspires to be something more than the old State. We call it totalitarian in the bad sense, because it claims to absorb the individual and admits no rival. But what gives it its strength is that it aspires to be totalitarian in a higher sense: to go beyond the practical utilitarian functions of the individualist State and to embrace the whole of life. It seeks to be . . . a spiritual community, a fellowship through which the individual attains a higher and more complete life than he can realize by any form of private association. (130–31)

"If therefore," he continues, "If therefore Christians take up a negative attitude to this movement and attack and repudiate it, they may find that they are fighting against God and standing in the path of the march of God through history" (132).

Dawson's *Beyond Politics* appeared in January 1939, while the lectures for *The Idea of a Christian Society*, which nod meaningfully at Dawson's book, were delivered in the spring of that year. Although Eliot himself avoids saying so, his work is shadowed by Dawson's claim from late in *Beyond Politics* that the modern totalitarian regimes offer "new opportunities – new openings for the action of grace" (134). In the case of Eliot, as of Dawson, it is plain that the imminent catastrophe released a more aggressive refusal of the reigning social consensus. *The Idea of a Christian Society* is a book which imagines, and *desires* the uprooting of secular democratic politics. "No scheme for a change of society," writes Eliot, "can be made to appear immediately palatable, except by falsehood, until society has become so desperate that it will accept any change" (*CC* 18). Much of Eliot's rhetoric through the thirties involved a willing of desperation: when "East Coker" tells us that "to be restored, our sickness must grow worse" (*CPP* 127), the force of the metaphor is not only spiritual – it is political.

When Eliot speaks of a desperate society willing to accept any change, the passivity of the attitude deserves emphasis. The transformation is not conceived as something that the great social mass will enact for itself, but as something it will endure and then affirm. The agency lies elsewhere, specifically within the group of committed and conscious Christians, clergy and laity, who understand the relationship between spiritual and temporal authority. Against the structureless mass there will stand out a few starkly defined figures who will restore the Church militant. It is a vision that recalls the uncanny moment in *After Strange Gods*, when the ideal of orthodoxy shrinks to the very few and then shrinks again: "orthodoxy may be upheld by one man against the world" (32).

The fullest vision of the saving remnant, the redemptive minority, appears in *The Idea of a Christian Society* in its portrait of the Community of Christians, the spiritual elite, the superior few, who stand in telling relation to the early modernist avant-garde – an association confirmed by the no doubt deliberate echo of Stephen Dedalus in Eliot's statement of the Community's mission: to "form . . . the conscience of the nation" (*CC* 34). To acknowledge this transformation – from the aesthetic activism of 1918 to the spiritual activism of 1939 – is to recognize one of the most striking features of Eliot's mature politics: the conjunction of *opposition* and *orthodoxy*. From early in his career, the energies of radical opposition had remained close beside the defense of authoritative institutions, but it was only in the political writings of the thirties that Eliot discovered the reach of their intimacy. In "Thoughts after Lambeth," he notes how, within his cultural milieu, a turn to the Church can become a surprising form of exile: "any one who has been moving among intellectual circles and comes to the Church, may experience an odd and rather exhilarating feeling of isolation" (*SE* 325). By the time he articulates the portrait of the Community of Christians in *The Idea of a Christian Society*, it became possible to imagine all the oppositional force of an avant-garde devoted to an incontestably orthodox mission. The allure of this conjunction to Eliot is profound: protest sanctioned by orthodoxy, revolt dictated by obedience, insurrection in the service of authority.

The year 1939 should be taken as a moment in Eliot's political thought when this potent ideological compound was briefly displayed in its full ambition. It had been one thing for him to bait the liberals: this was scarcely notable in the hubbub of the thirties. But it was another and quite notable thing to follow Dawson toward the full repudiation of democracy, and to see fascism, as Eliot would put it in the Kipling essay, as "merely the extreme degradation of democracy" (*OPP* 246). In 1933, he had discharged from his favorite shooting spot – the middle of a long paragraph – this personal bullet: "I think that the virtue of tolerance is greatly overestimated, and I have no objection to being called a bigot myself; but that is an individual concern" (*EAM* 129). By 1939, when the ominous word returns, the matter is no longer indi- vidual; it is public, political. "However bigoted the announcement may sound, the Christian can be satisfied with nothing less than a Christian organization of society" (*CC* 27). And so, climactically, democracy withers as a positive, defensible value: "If you will not have God (and He is a jealous God) you should pay your respects to Hitler or Stalin" (50). We may regard this shift – from the partisan critique of liberalism to an apocalyptic politics that envisioned and willed the end of the secular democratic state – as a culmination of Eliot's militant orthodoxy.

On the eve of the war, Eliot allowed himself to imagine and to describe a final struggle. The excitement, breathed out softly in passionless prose, is that here at last, now finally, the contest can be met. The false compromise of the entire Enlightenment secular political project has been revealed as a snare and a delusion; God and Satan can play out their agon on the European terrain. And yet when the war started, the earthly war, Eliot's views underwent another notable change. The year 1939 marked a sharp fissure in his thought. The war weakened his taste for Armageddon and weakened too his conviction that the democratic state had come to the point of collapse. During the war years Eliot reimagined his politics, and the new views are codified in *Notes towards the Definition of Culture* (1948). But much of their interest lies in one surprising aspect of their provenance, namely from within the literary context – for instance in "Little Gidding," where the poem, in reflecting upon itself, speaks of the "sentence that is right (where every word is at home, / Taking its place to support the others," the "common word," the "formal word," "The complete consort dancing together" (*CPP* 144). As poetic doctrine the lines are unexceptional, but they serve as one epitome of Eliot's wartime reconsideration of the problem of totality – here the totality of the sentence that has all its parts dancing together. It is not too much to call this an aesthetic fetish, notable not only for its pervasiveness but for the unusual places in which it shows itself. The lecture "What is Minor Poetry?" of 1944 contains a rambling meditation on the importance of anthologies:

> Just as in a well arranged dinner, what one enjoys is not a number of dishes by themselves but the combination of good things, so there are pleasures of poetry to be taken in the same way; and several very different poems, by authors of different temperaments and different ages, when read together, may each bring out the peculiar savour of each other, each having something that the others lack. To enjoy this pleasure we need a good anthology. . . . (*OPP* 44)

During the catastrophe of the war Eliot came to brood ever more heavily, ever more obsessively, on Patterned Unity, Structured Wholeness, Total Form, aesthetic values refined until they became the basis of a politics. The image of the good society is formed in the course of reflections on the sentence that is right, the anthology that is successful, the dinner that is savory – or, to take a recurrent example, on the unity in the life of the great poet whose most incidental writings become part of one compacted whole.

In "The Music of Poetry" (1942) Eliot writes that the music of a word – and one might think of the word here as a citizen – "arises from its relation first to the words immediately preceding and following it, and indefinitely to the rest of its context. . . . Not all words, obviously, are equally rich and well-connected: it is part of the business of the poet to dispose the richer among the poorer, at the right points"

(*OPP* 32–33). This passage makes obvious what is in any case everywhere telling: that a social metaphorics hovers near, and often guides, what seems to be a strictly literary reverie. The problem of power, of order and disruption, of law and license, privilege and dispossession, is pondered in terms of the relations of rich and poor words, great and small poets, the classic and the contemporary, a native language and its foreign neighbors. And in seeking to understand Eliot's final political phase, the politics of life after wartime, life after the ascendancy of the Labour Party, we need to look toward these diverse improbable entities – the anthology, the sentence, the major poet, the musical verse, the Virgilian classic, the English language – which enact their own figural politics, the politics of an aesthetic totality which absorbs conflict and distributes the justice of form.

At least since Raymond Williams's *Culture and Society* it has been a commonplace to say of Eliot's *Notes towards the Definition of Culture* that it offers a social organicism, a political biology. But to say this is to pay Eliot the excessive compliment of taking him only at his own valuation. The language of organicism is indeed unrelieved – "culture," he never tires of repeating in one variation or another, "is something that must grow; you cannot build a tree" (*CC* 196). Eliot's studied aim is to conjure the image of a "living," a "natural" culture, but we might say that this is the ruse of every ambitious machine: to pretend to be an organism. In a revealing aside, he bemoans the persistence of the machine metaphor in social thought, but then, having moaned, he tinkers with that very metaphor, which sees his argument to its conclusion. The flourishing community is one which adjusts its "functions" (the functions of class), arranges its "units" (units of family, region, and nation), calibrates its "powers" (the power of a central Church and local parish), and in this way balances the "centripetal" and "centrifugal" forces of society. Within the medium of his literary reflections, Eliot constructs an alternative to the millenarian politics of the thirties and devises his last political testament, the post-apocalpytic vision of corporate equilibrium, which no longer makes bold to ask what may be achieved, only what may be preserved. "I would not belittle the importance," Eliot had written, "of the rearguard action" (*CC* 60).

Rearguard action is the condition of this final political phase – and also the condition of an exhausted modernism no longer prepared to make war with the infidels. Gone is the panting desire for the "conversion of the whole world"; in its place is the new talk of the "ecology of cultures," the balance of forces, Catholic and Protestant, Aristocrat and Democrat, Nationalist and Regionalist. "One needs the enemy," as Eliot puts it: "the universality of irritation" is a positive value (*CC* 133). Like the good anthology with its major and minor poets properly represented, like the elegant sentence with its words dancing together, like the poetical phrase with its rich and poor words balanced, the machinery of culture manufactures Totality out of Difference. It is a politics of incorporation that Eliot finally devises, incorporation into the social apparatus where irritation is universal, friction productive, and the enemy is your friend. We should recognize this cultural corporatism as a last sentence of revolutionary modernism, when both opposition and orthodoxy have given up the ghost.

NOTES

1 For more information on Eliot's epistemology, see YES AND NO: ELIOT AND WESTERN PHILOSOPHY and DISAMBIVALENT QUATRAINS.

2 Hugh Kenner observes that "One novelty of the new poem was to be a new specificity: a public focus on his new environment, the City of London" (27).

REFERENCES AND FURTHER READING

Asher, Kenneth. *T. S. Eliot and Ideology*. Cambridge: Cambridge UP, 1995.

Cooper, John Xiros. *T. S. Eliot and the Ideology of Four Quartets*. Cambridge: Cambridge UP, 1995.

———. *T. S. Eliot and the Politics of Voice: The Argument of The Waste Land*. Ann Arbor: UMI Research, 1987.

Dawson, Christopher. *Beyond Politics*. London: Sheed, 1939.

Donoghue, Denis. "The Idea of a Christian Society." *Yale Review* 78 (1989): 218–34.

Kenner, Hugh. "The Urban Apocalypse." *Eliot in His Time: Essays on the Occasion of the Fiftieth Anniversary of The Waste Land*. Ed. A. Walton Litz. Princeton: Princeton UP, 1973. 23–49.

Kojecký, Roger. *T. S. Eliot's Social Criticism*. New York: Farrar, 1972.

Levenson, Michael H. "Does *The Waste Land* Have a Politics?" *Modernism/Modernity* 6 (1999): 1–13.

North, Michael. *The Political Aesthetic of Yeats, Eliot, and Pound*. Cambridge: Cambridge UP, 1991.

Scott, Peter Dale. "The Social Critic and His Discontents." *The Cambridge Companion to T. S. Eliot*. Ed. A. David Moody. Cambridge: Cambridge UP, 1994.

32
Keeping Critical Thought Alive: Eliot's Editorship of the *Criterion*

Jason Harding

Ezra Pound thought that Eliot's 16-year editorship of the *Criterion* was a distraction from his true vocation as a poet. Eliot, who was not a prolific poet, believed that this kind of judgment "confuses energy with industry" ("C [May 1927]" 189). After all, *The Waste Land* was published in the first number of the *Criterion* in October 1922, without the epigraph, the notes, and the dedication to Pound, but it was essentially the poem that came to be celebrated as the epitome of postwar "modernist" experiment. Interestingly, Eliot had toyed with the idea of splitting the poem into two issues, and he had struggled with the printers over matters of punctuation, spacing, and spelling, complaining of "undesired alterations" (*Letters* 574). Still, few literary journals can boast such a remarkable poetic debut as the *Criterion*. Although editing the periodical would demand a great deal of Eliot's time, it continued to function as an outlet for his most experimental writing. In January 1925, the *Criterion* published "Three Poems" by "Thomas Eliot." Two of these poems were later reworked, with minor changes, as Parts II and IV of "The Hollow Men." In October 1926 and January 1927, Eliot published "Fragment of a Prologue" and "Fragment of an Agon" in the *Criterion*. After remaining dormant for some years, these unfinished "fragments" of verse dialogue were later reprinted together as the first and second sections of *Sweeney Agonistes*. In January 1928, Eliot offered the first British publication of "Salutation" in the *Criterion*. Stripped of its title and epigraph, this poem became the second of the six sections that comprise *Ash-Wednesday*. In this manner, the *Criterion* provided Eliot with an invaluable public forum in which he could experiment with the structural organization of his poems, assembling wholes from fragments that had previously been published separately.

Far from being a distraction from his work as a poet, Eliot's editorship of the *Criterion* can be seen as an extension of his engagement with the poetry written not only by British and American poets, but by advanced poets across Europe. Translations of Stéphane Mallarmé's "Heriodiade" and Paul Valéry's "The Serpent" followed *The Waste Land* in the next two numbers of the *Criterion*.[1] Pound's four "Malatesta"

A Companion to T. S. Eliot, First Edition. Edited by David E. Chinitz.
© 2014 John Wiley & Sons, Ltd. Published 2014 by John Wiley & Sons, Ltd.

Cantos completed the poetry published in the first volume, although Eliot cut the first line, "These fragments you have shelved (shored)," in order not to draw too much attention to the way in which these new *Cantos* "of a Long Poem" were in dialogue with the fragments that the editor of the *Criterion* had "shored" against his ruin in *The Waste Land*. Moreover, the pseudonymous contributions of the editor's wife, Vivien, to the early years of the journal frequently allude, as commentators have noted, to Eliot's published poetry. The second installment of Vivien's "Letters of the Moment" even contained 20 lines of verse which were adapted from the unpublished manuscript drafts of *The Waste Land*. The prose pieces Vivien published in the *Criterion* in 1924 and 1925 display her talent for witty, if rather slight, sketches of society life.[2] The *Criterion* carried more significant creative fiction by such accomplished exponents of the short story as Virginia Woolf, D. H. Lawrence, A. E. Coppard, and Aldous Huxley, as well as extracts from Marcel Proust's *A la recherche du temps perdu* and James Joyce's *Finnegans Wake*. The publication of fiction was not the *Criterion*'s strongest suit, but some of the stories, such as May Sinclair's tale of Eastern mysticism, "Jones's Karma," dealt with themes that were of great interest to the editor and stimulated his further thought on these areas – attested to by Eliot's reference to Sinclair's story in an editorial published almost a decade after the appearance of the tale ("C [July 1932]" 681).

The poetry published in the *Criterion* is interesting, not least since it bore Eliot's imprimatur. Experiments in the genre of the dramatic monologue by Herbert Read ("The Lament of Saint Denis"), Eugenio Montale ("Arsenio"), Hugh Sykes Davies ("Petron"), and F. T. Prince ("Epistle to a Patron") demonstrate how Eliot was attentive to younger poets who were seeking to develop a form he had reinvigorated. Many of the poets Eliot published in the *Criterion* hinted at their reading of *The Waste Land*. The case of Hart Crane is instructive in this regard. Eliot published "The Tunnel" section from *The Bridge* in the November 1927 *Criterion*. The purgatorial symbolism of this journey to the underworld resurfaces transfigured in the purgatorial London tube journeys of *Four Quartets*. Here a young poet deeply influenced by Eliot's "Unreal City" has entered into a creative dialogue with poetic tradition. The "familiar compound ghost" who speaks in *Four Quartets* is assembled from these voices – predominantly the great sage, W. B. Yeats, railing against old age in "The Tower" (published in the *Criterion* in 1927), but also young, unknown poets, like Robert Waller, whose "Apology" for the autumnal leaves of the urban waste land (published in the *Criterion* in 1938) is present in this phantasmagoria. The publication of Cantos from Laurence Binyon's translation of Dante's *Purgatorio* was clearly an important model for these ghostly visitations. If Eliot's own poetic contribution to the *Criterion* throughout the 1930s was limited to the light and whimsical *Five-Finger Exercises* he published in 1933, by then the periodical had become the testing ground and the clearinghouse for the unrivalled stable of young poets that Eliot had recruited for Faber & Faber: W. H. Auden, Stephen Spender, Ronald Bottrall, George Barker, Louis MacNeice, Charles Madge, Michael Roberts, F. T. Prince, and William Empson all had their poetry published in the *Criterion* before the appearance of full-fledged Faber volumes.

In retrospect, Eliot's achievement in the *Criterion* is inextricably bound up with the fortunes of the publishing house he joined in the autumn of 1925. (Faber reprinted the periodical in 18 weighty volumes in 1967.) However, the origins of the *Criterion* begin with Lady Lilian Rothermere, the estranged wife of the newspaper magnate Harold Harmsworth, the proprietor of the *Daily Mail*. It was Lady Rothermere who supplied the capital to launch Eliot's quarterly review in 1922. After the magazine was relaunched in 1926 as the *New Criterion,* under the Faber imprint, she continued as the major backer, now paying Eliot an editorial salary. She withdrew her subsidy at the end of 1927 after becoming dissatisfied with the character of the journal, not to mention the considerable financial losses that the *Criterion* was accruing. (Sales of the *Monthly Criterion,* which had been launched with a print run of 2,500 copies in May 1927, peaked at 1,200 copies sold – just over 200 by subscription – an insufficient number to make financial ends meet.) Eliot's editorial conception of the *Criterion* always placed a greater emphasis on serious analytical journalism with a pan-European perspective than on the offerings of radical chic that were more to the taste of Lady Rothermere, who complained of the dullness of the journal. The *Criterion's* austerity is evident in Eliot's prose contributions, which contain numerous intertextual nudges and winks to interlocutors in a select field of literary-critical journalism. It is not easy to extract Eliot's critical prose for the *Criterion* from its original periodical context and read it like the carefully chosen contents of *Selected Essays*. Only three of these articles were reprinted in that collection, and all of them – "Marie Lloyd," "The Function of Criticism," and "Four Elizabethan Dramatists" – were published in the first two volumes of the *Criterion*, during the period when Eliot was most anxious to secure the high critical standing of his fledgling quarterly review.

The well-known essay on the music-hall artist Marie Lloyd was first published as a "London Letter" in the New York monthly the *Dial*, but was reprinted in the *Criterion* in January 1923 as "In Memoriam: Marie Lloyd." It was Eliot's first prose contribution to the journal. His revisions to the essay, albeit minor in substance, revealed Eliot's greater intimacy with the *Criterion's* British readership than with the American audience of the *Dial*, who lacked firsthand acquaintance with the London music hall and its relation to English working-class culture. Collected as "Marie Lloyd" in *Selected Essays*, the essay sacrificed the topicality and the heartfelt appeal of the obituary address. "The Function of Criticism" also loses something when it is divorced from its original periodical context. This essay was, in many ways, an irritated response to John Middleton Murry's editorials in his new literary monthly, the *Adelphi*, founded shortly after the *Criterion* in the summer of 1923. Eliot's first editorial notes, published as "The Function of a Literary Review" in July 1923, unmistakably mocked Murry's opening manifesto, by challenging the terms of his belief in what Eliot called the "insidious catchword: 'life'" (421). In the next issue of the *Criterion*, "The Function of Criticism" voiced Eliot's severest Arnoldian scolding of the wide-eyed, soapbox oratory of those intellectuals who he felt were giving free rein to "personal prejudices and cranks" and turning serious critical journalism into a "Sunday park of contending and contentious orators." Eliot sternly remarked that he was "tempted to expel the lot," adding "I owe to Mr. Middleton Murry my perception of the contentious character of the problem" (*SE* 14). He clearly had Murry's rival magazine in mind as a competitor in this "contentious" field of literary periodicals, even if three decades later, in the lecture "The Frontiers of Criticism" (1956), he confessed that he was "bewildered" as to "what all the fuss had been about" (*OPP* 103). These 1923 exchanges were in fact the first blows of the protracted "romanticism and classicism" controversy that was aired, at times acrimoniously, in the pages of the *Criterion* and the *Adelphi* over the following years. Eliot saw the debate as a crucial one about the proper "elucidation of works of art and the correction of taste" (*SE* 13). His own standards of criticism were on display in "Four Elizabethan Dramatists," published as "A Preface" in February 1924, in anticipation of an unwritten, book-length study of dramatic verse, which was to survey the poetic techniques and conventions employed by Webster, Tourneur, Middleton, and Chapman, with an eye on the future possibilities of the modern theater. It was the critical complement to the creative experiments that issued in the *Criterion* in the form of the *Sweeney Agonistes* fragments, also to remain an unfinished project.

None of Eliot's 66 editorials for the *Criterion* were collected in his volumes of critical prose, presumably because they addressed contemporary literary, cultural, and political issues, thus rendering them somewhat ephemeral in the eyes of posterity. "The Idea of a Literary Review," published in the first number of the *New Criterion* in January 1926, was the most substantial statement of Eliot's editorial principles. The article was, in effect, a manifesto announcing a tighter editorial grip on his critical review. "The Idea of a Literary Review" rejected a sectarian program, or the vagueness of a miscellany, in favor of what he called a "classical" common tendency: "I believe that the modern tendency is toward something which, for want of a better name, we may call classicism. . . . [T]here is a tendency – discernable even in art – toward a higher and clearer conception of Reason, and a more severe and serene control of the emotions by Reason" (5). Eliot's comments echoed his praise, in an earlier editorial, of T. E. Hulme's posthumous collection of essays, *Speculations*, as "forerunner of a new attitude of mind . . . classical, reactionary, and revolutionary . . . the antipodes of the eclectic, tolerant, and democratic mind" of the nineteenth century ("C [Apr. 1924]" 231).[3] "The Idea of a Literary Review" went further by supplying a list of exemplary "classical" texts, comprising *Speculations* and books by Irving Babbitt and the French writers Charles Maurras, Georges Sorel, Julien Benda, and the Thomist philosopher Jacques Maritain. (In a later editorial, Eliot added a book by Wyndham Lewis.) The "modern tendency" most clearly supported by this disparate set of works was a marked distaste for liberal democracy. In truth, the new "classical revival" enunciated by Eliot in the *Criterion* had more in common with the right-wing "neo-classicism" of Maurras's *Action française* movement than it did with the classics in Latin and Greek.

"The Idea of a Literary Review" contained a barbed footnote aimed at the "religion of Mr. Middleton Murry, which I am totally unable to understand" (6). Suitably annoyed, Murry responded in the *Adelphi* in a lengthy article, "The 'Classical' Revival," in which he argued that Eliot's brand of "classicism" indicated he should join the Catholic Church. The *Criterion* then published three new articles by Murry on the "romanticism and classicism" controversy, beginning with "The Romantic Fallacy" in June 1926, and continuing a year later with the conciliatory essay "Towards a Synthesis," which sought to establish some rapprochement between romantic "intuition" and classicist "intelligence." It is significant that Eliot agreed to read and comment upon this essay in draft. Public controversy provides adversaries with the opportunity to advance their standing within the cultural field, yet the danger of collusion that affects such debate reveals the concord amid strategic discord which characterizes the limited field of literary periodicals.

Despite their partial cooperation, Eliot evidently did not share Murry's hope for a "synthesis." In fact, Conrad Aiken remembered the unfolding of the debate as a "carefully picked quarrel," and he believed that Eliot prolonged the controversy not simply with the intention of fully answering Murry, but to orchestrate what amounted to a literary "assassination" (Goldie 187). Eliot's editorial policy actively encouraged the free exchange of different points of view, but Aiken was correct to notice that the "romanticism and classicism" debate revealed the limits of his impartiality. Repeating his defense of "classicism" in his editorials, Eliot also published an article by Father Martin D'Arcy hostile to Murry, and personally translated two essays from French authors also highly critical of Murry. In "Mr. Middleton Murry's Synthesis," Eliot reiterated his inability to understand Murry's position and deployed the "polemic irony" which Eliot claimed "is a permanent weapon for the sensitive civilized man" ("C [Apr. 1933]" 469).

Murry was permitted a last, albeit disillusioned, word in the *Criterion*. In a letter to Eliot, he ruefully admitted that an abyss separated their ideas and convictions. Although motivated by conflicting editorial and critical principles, and even by personal antipathy, Murry himself realized that on the rarefied plane of serious critical journalism "enemies are *necessary* to one another" ("Notes [1929–30]" 81). Unfortunately, the "romanticism and classicism" controversy did little to boost sales and contributed to Lady Rothermere's decision to withdraw her subsidy from the *Criterion*.

The *Criterion* was involved at this time in an ill-tempered exchange with another entrant to the literary-cultural field, the *Calendar of Modern Letters*. In April 1927, the *Calendar* covertly criticized certain "English reviews" for supporting a "reactionary Latin philosophy" as a "repressive instrument of literary criticism" (qtd. in Harding 59). This was a thinly veiled reference to the *Criterion*. Eliot took up the gauntlet in his editorial by defending his publication of those French intellectuals – these included Henri Massis and Jacques Maritain – who were associated, by many English readers, with the "reactionary Latin philosophy" of the *Action française*. The *Calendar* reaffirmed its accusations: not only was the *Criterion*'s 'neo-classicism' reactionary and repressive, but Eliot's "stately editorial 'We'" often appeared self-deceiving and irritatingly superior (qtd. in Harding 60). Eliot was upset by these charges. He acknowledged the difficulty of employing the term "classicism" in an English cultural context, but he strongly denied any intention to repress the opinions of writers who disagreed with him. This editorial catholicity was illustrated by his decision to give space to Leo Ward's defense of the Vatican's condemnation of the *Action française*, although Eliot's disagreement was voiced in articles and editorials and buttressed by his decision to translate Maurras's lengthy "Prologue to an Essay on Criticism" for the *Criterion*.

Eliot believed that he possessed "some skill in the barren game of controversy" (qtd. in Margolis xv), but the question of the success – or otherwise – of his editorial controversies is a complicated one. Eliot praised the *Adelphi* and the *Calendar* as opponents with whom the *Criterion* shared "a common ground for disagreement" ("C [Sept. 1927]" 194). Nevertheless, Murry's public spat with the *Criterion* left him to complain that the "romanticism and classicism" debate had been interesting but only "in a negative way" ("Notes [1927–28]" 102). Meanwhile, the *Calendar*, in terminal financial difficulties, used its valedictory words to fire a parting shot at "the periodical which flaunts a pretension to philosophical righteousness and yet makes as many blunders with regard to the actual works of poetry or literature . . . as the most unenlightened of its Georgian predecessors" ("Valediction" 176). Leo Ward professed himself a friend of the *Criterion* who hoped that the journal would not turn into a "refuge where French philosophies go when they die" (372). This concern was echoed by some other readers of the *Criterion*. Desmond MacCarthy, for instance, wondered at the "Frenchified" neo-Thomism he found on display in Eliot's magazine. Traces of these bruising encounters can be detected in Eliot's uneasy admission, in the preface to the 1928 edition of *The Sacred Wood*, that a note of "pontifical solemnity" was assumed to be characteristic of his critical pronouncements (*SW* vii).

On the other hand, these controversies reveal Eliot's growing confidence to speak out on political subjects. During the early years of Lady Rothermere's patronage, the *Criterion* exhibited a dandyish reluctance to enter the political arena, although a series of pugnacious articles by Charles Whibley and his associates articulated Eliot's own "Tory" sympathies, as well as his hostility to nineteenth-century liberalism and the revolutionary utopia of communism. In "The Idea of a Literary Review," Eliot observed that a literary review "must protect its disinterestedness, must avoid the temptation ever to appeal to any social, political or theological prejudices" (4). However, in his June 1927 editorial "Commentary," Eliot announced under the Maurrassian heading "Politique d'abord": "It is a trait of the present time that every 'literary' review worth its salt has a political interest" (283). The *Calendar* considered this statement by a "disinterested" literary review as "an abuse of function" ("Valediction" 176); yet the *Criterion* would increasingly see its role as a public platform for the discussion of political philosophy.

The perceived threats from Soviet communism and the rise of Italian fascism were frequently canvassed in Eliot's editorials. They formed the poles of a symposium that took place in the *Criterion*. Eliot prepared the ground in his December 1928 review article "The Literature of Fascism."[4] In this article he dissociated himself from supporting either dictatorship or universal suffrage (achieved in Britain by the 1928 Representation of the People Act). Rather, Eliot wished for a political framework in which a restricted "democracy can live" (287). His disquiet about simply giving "the people what it wants" ("C [July 1930]" 589) was widespread among European intellectuals. Eliot thought that fascism was "an Italian regime for Italians" ("C [Feb. 1928]" 97). He did, however, encourage J. S. Barnes, Secretary-General of the International Centre of Fascist Studies, to expound the case for fascism in the *Criterion*, counterbalanced by a sympathetic essay from A. L. Rowse on the literature of communism. Eliot assessed both these essays in a further *Criterion* article, where he declared "a preference for fascism {to communism] in practice, which I dare say most of my readers share," adding that neither fascism nor communism was "new or revolutionary as *idea*" ("Mr. Barnes" 690–91). Such pronouncements betrayed his confusion between the philosophical dissection of political theories and the disturbing realpolitik of international foreign affairs, a failing that would soon become a poignant inability to estimate contemporary political forces at their true strength. By the end of the 1920s, as Bonamy Dobrée complained to Herbert Read, the *Criterion* had turned into a "Religio-Political Organ" (qtd. in Harding 178). The idealized vision of an alliance between Church and State – Eliot's "Tory" equivalent of the nationalism of the *Action française* – was not a viable political program for Britain during the 1930s and appeared highly unusual, not to say completely beside the point, to many observers.

Eliot would claim that he wanted to avoid "too distinct a theological cast to the *Criterion*" (qtd. in Margolis 135); nonetheless, the unavoidable hand of editorial commission and omission would tip the scales in several weighty debates. The extended discussion in the *Criterion* of Irving Babbitt's ethical philosophy of "New Humanism" was a case in point. Although Eliot published his strictures on his former Harvard teacher elsewhere, his commission of an extremely combative essay by Allen Tate, provocatively entitled "The Fallacy of Humanism" – which argued that religion was the "sole technique for the validating of values" (678) – would have been taken by most readers as the *Criterion*'s position on the subject. Similarly, although Eliot permitted Pound and other supporters of Major Douglas's Social Credit to propound this theory of monetary reform as the solution to endemic worldwide unemployment and the evil of poverty amid plenty, his editorials repeatedly asserted that the consideration of economic or political doctrines, or for that matter censorship, could not be divorced from ethical principles founded upon religious belief. In his closing editorial "Last Words," Eliot recalled that "For myself, a right political philosophy came more and more to imply a right theology – and right economics to depend upon right ethics: leading to emphases which somewhat stretched the original framework of a literary review" ("C [Jan. 1939]" 272).

The worsening politico-economic crisis that enveloped Europe during the 1930s certainly did restrict the cosmopolitan links with European periodicals that Eliot had taken considerable pains to establish. In his *Criterion* editorial for April 1926, Eliot spoke of the "European idea – the idea of a common culture of Western Europe" ("C [Apr. 1926]" 222). He returned to this common Latin–Christian culture of Western Europe in his editorial for August 1927. Eliot made clear that the defense of this

"European idea" was essential as a bulwark against the imminent spread of Soviet communism. In 1929, the *Criterion* could proudly claim to be the first English periodical to print the work of Proust, Valéry, Maurras, Maritain, Massis, Jean Cocteau, Jacques Rivière, Ramon Fernandez, Wilhelm Worringer, Max Scheler, and Ernst Robert Curtius. This was also the year in which the journal collaborated on a short-story prize with four like-minded European periodicals. But after 1929, the *Criterion* would be obliged to address a rather more divisive set of issues debated by European intellectuals – most notably, the problems besetting German (including German Jewish) writers under Nazi dictatorship, the Italian invasion of Abyssinia, the Spanish Civil War, pacifism, and the gathering storm clouds of World War II.

During the crisis-ridden 1930s Eliot commented: "Our occupation with immediate social, political and economic issues today is a necessity, but a regrettable one" ("C [Apr. 1934]" 452). These issues included the worldwide economic depression, which Eliot remarked could no longer "be ignored by literary critics" ("C [July 1932]" 676) and the threat to the unity of European culture presented by totalitarian governments. Eliot published Thomas Mann's "An Appeal to Reason" in the *Criterion* in 1931, in the wake of alarming gains made by Hitler's National Socialist Party in the German elections. A year later, Eliot praised Curtius's *Deutscher Geist in Gefahr*, which warned of the Nazi threat to education. In his editorial for October 1932, Eliot noted the menacing atmosphere which confronted German intellectuals – such as Curtius and the German Jewish scholar Friedrich Gundolf, who were both contributors to the *Criterion*. After Hitler's accession to power in 1933, Alec Randall discussed in his *Criterion* reviews of German periodicals the Nazification of the press and the harassment of Jewish writers; although in a short notice published in 1936, Montgomery Belgion treated with insensitivity the persecution of German Jews.[5] If the *Criterion* initially viewed the experiment of Italian fascism with interest, it cannot be said that the journal was sympathetic to Nazi Germany, which, like Soviet communism, Eliot criticized for stimulating religious fervor without an ethical system founded upon doctrinal beliefs. In his January 1936 editorial, Eliot considered pamphlets on the Italian invasion of Abyssinia. He rejected the partisan positions espoused by both right-wing supporters and left-wing opponents of the invasion, affirming: "All men are equal before God; if they cannot all be equal in this world, yet our moral obligation towards inferiors is exactly the same as that towards our equals" ("C [Jan. 1936]" 268). Eliot could not support Canon Dick Sheppard's pacifist Peace Pledge Union, but he thought that the zealous warmongering that infected British intellectual discussion of foreign affairs during the 1930s was deeply irresponsible.

His most forthright statement of this point of view was articulated in his editorials dealing with the Spanish Civil War. In a *Left Review* circular later published as *Authors Take Sides on the Spanish Civil War*, C. Day Lewis described the conflict as "quite simply a battle between light and darkness," indicative of the simplifying passions at work (qtd. in Harding 199). Eliot denied that authors were compelled to "take sides" on the Spanish Civil War – which to readers of the *Left Review* or the *New Statesman* meant unqualified support for the Republican government and the anti-fascist Popular

Front. It is strange that Eliot has been characterized as a secret admirer of Franco, since he openly praised Maritain's refusal to side with supporters of Franco, by disputing their claims that they were fighting a "Holy War." "Whichever side wins will not be the better for having had to fight for its victory," Eliot commented pointedly. "[A]ny eventual partisanship," he observed, "should be held with reservations, humility and misgiving" ("C [Apr. 1937]" 290). Eliot greatly admired "the just impartiality of a Christian philosopher" exemplified by Maritain's dignified and principled stance toward the Spanish Civil War ("C [Oct. 1938]" 58).

Faced with the increasingly volatile and sectarian political situation during the late 1930s, Eliot lamented in his editorial for October 1938: "There seems no hope in contemporary politics at all" (60). He was bitterly shaken by the Munich agreement between Chamberlain and Hitler, which produced in him a depression of feelings so profound that he no longer had the enthusiasm to edit the *Criterion*. In his valedictory "Last Words," Eliot remarked that "The 'European mind,' which one had mistakenly thought might be renewed and fortified, disappeared from view" (271). It is hard to recapture the twilit air of monastic gloom in which Eliot braced himself for the coming war. He placed his trust for the future not in the wide-circulation weeklies like the *New Statesman*, but in "the small and obscure papers and reviews, those which hardly are read by anyone but their own contributors." It would be these magazines that would continue the editorial work he had undertaken in the *Criterion*, seeking to "keep critical thought alive, and encourage authors of original talent" (274).

Keeping critical thought alive had not initially included book reviewing among the *Criterion*'s duties. A perfunctory review section was introduced in 1924, with Eliot contributing a notice of two anthropology books (his 1925 review of two studies of dance was printed as a freestanding article). The launch of the *New Criterion* in January 1926, with the magazine functioning as Faber's in-house literary journal, strengthened the emphasis on book reviews. There is no doubt that the *Criterion*'s standards of reviewing had been given a sharp jolt by the abrasive position-taking of the *Calendar of Modern Letters*. Eliot now used his own reviews for a severe public scrutiny of influential contemporary figures: George Bernard Shaw, H. G. Wells, Hilaire Belloc, Bertrand Russell and, almost inevitably, John Middleton Murry, were roughly handled. Bloomsbury critics Clive Bell and F. L. Lucas were unambiguously contradicted. Eliot expressed his distaste for what he considered to be voguish intellectual fashions. Even books by two valued contributors to the *Criterion*, Herbert Read and Ramon Fernandez, were criticized for placing too much emphasis on "the wipings of psychology" ("Mr. Read" 756). Freud's *The Future of an Illusion*, which had characterized religious belief as an antiquated illusion, was damned as "shrewd and yet stupid" ("Freud's Illusions" 350). Eliot's positive energies were released in lengthy batch reviews which anatomized the art of detective fiction. Yet his reviews for the *Criterion* can appear disappointing when judged alongside the revolutionary creative criticism that he had published in the *Egoist*, the *Athenaeum*, and the *Times Literary Supplement*.

During the short life of the *Monthly Criterion*, Eliot strove for the engaged topicality of belligerent monthlies like the *Calendar of Modern Letters*, but by 1928 the *Criterion* relaxed back into the leisurely urbanity of a quarterly review. The ample proportions of the "Books of the Quarter" section, which had swollen to take up to 80 pages (roughly one-third of each issue), functioned as a recruiting ground for Faber authors, and its judgments were perceived as an index of Faber & Faber's consecration of young writers. Although Eliot did not want an exact correspondence between his roles as an editor and as a publisher, he had told Geoffrey Faber in 1925 that he was anxious to avoid "publishing a book by some writer who had been consistently and steadily damned in the review" (qtd. in Schuchard 70). The connection encouraged the *Criterion* to display the augustness of authority, but it also stimulated newer entrants to the cultural field, such as *Scrutiny* and *New Verse*, to fits of pique. F. R. Leavis complained of the "particular weakness of the *Criterion* for the dead, academic kind of abstract 'thinking' . . . worth less than nothing if not related scrupulously to the concrete" (214). He perpetuated the myth among his disciples that Eliot permitted a coterie of left-wing poets to conduct a campaign against *Scrutiny* in the review pages of the *Criterion*.[6] The softening of Eliot's standards of reviewing during the 1930s can arguably be gauged by his increasingly favorable reviews of books by his old adversary, Murry. In *New Verse*, Geoffrey Grigson noted the demise of the *Criterion* as the fading of "a biennial after its seeds have matured and been dispersed." Grigson, who had published a mock obituary of Eliot in *New Verse* in 1938, was being unusually temperate. For his remarks reinforced a widespread belief that the *Criterion* had outlived its usefulness, an opinion forcefully expressed by Pound's complaint that "Criterion-ism" represented a "diet of dead crow" (114).

Retrospective valuations of Eliot's achievement as editor of the *Criterion* differ sharply. Eliot himself pointed to the distinguished list of international authors whom the journal introduced to the English reading public. He has been praised for the editorial catholicity with which he attracted established writers and encouraged younger talents. By the late 1920s, however, the *Criterion* was undoubtedly in retreat from experimental modernism. Eliot increasingly appeared in the periodical as a public moralist seeking to address the important social and political issues of the day, but with a barely disguised distaste for the practical realities of parliamentary politics and international affairs. His editorial pronouncements, which sought to define and defend the conservative religio-political orientation of the journal, were frequently dismissed as sententious and out of touch with the crisis-ridden political atmosphere of the 1930s. As Desmond Hawkins remarked in his 1939 obituary notice of the *Criterion*: "The most powerful group of young writers [in London] have not much in common with Eliot, and there is little public support for any literary review which is not nominally anti-fascist." It is fair to say that there had never been much public support for the *Criterion*, whose tiny circulation, elegiac editorial tone, and political naivety ensured that its rearguard action on behalf of the "European idea" seemed to most contemporaries a hopeless and forlorn undertaking. Even if a recent book champions the continuing relevance of the humanist "classicism" espoused in the *Criterion*

– especially during the 1920s – as a "source of inspiration" for our postmodern world (Vanheste 78), it is hard not to believe that we breathe a different intellectual air from the contributors of the *Criterion*. Yet the journal is not only testimony to Eliot's honorable and conscientious editorial engagement with complex and troubling areas of literary, cultural, and political debate. but a storehouse for some of the most significant essays, reviews, and original creative writing published in English throughout the interwar years.

NOTES

1   A section from Eliot's translation of St. J. Perse's *Anabase* appeared in the *Criterion* in February 1928.

2   One of these pieces, "On the Eve: A Dialogue," was published under Eliot's name, although it had been drafted by Vivien.

3   Eliot planned a special issue of the *Criterion* devoted to T. E. Hulme, but it did not materialize.

4   For further analysis of this essay and related pieces on the topics of fascism and communism, see ELIOT'S POLITICS.

5   For an account of Belgion's review of *The Yellow Spot: The Outlawing of Half a Million Human Beings*, wrongly attributed to Eliot, see Julius 167–70, 313–14.

6   Although Stephen Spender's review of *Revaluation* was hostile, Leavis conveniently overlooked Frank Chapman's praise of *Determinations*, as well as many other positive references in the *Criterion* to Leavis and the co-editors of *Scrutiny*.

REFERENCES AND FURTHER READING

Goldie, David. *A Critical Difference: T. S. Eliot and John Middleton Murry in English Literary Criticism*. Oxford: Clarendon, 1998.

Grigson, Geoffrey. "*Criterion* and *London Mercury*." *New Verse* ns 1 (1939): 62.

Harding, Jason. *The Criterion: Cultural Politics and Periodical Networks in Interwar Britain*. Oxford: Oxford UP, 2002.

Hawkins, Desmond. "London Letter." *Partisan Review* 6 (1939): 89.

Julius, Antony. *T. S. Eliot, Anti-Semitism, and Literary Form*. 2nd ed. London: Thames, 2003.

Leavis, F. R. " 'Under Which King, Bezonian?' " *Scrutiny* 1 (1932): 205–14.

MacCarthy, Desmond. "Frenchified." Letter. *New Statesman* 21 Jan. 1928: 460.

Margolis, John D. *T. S. Eliot's Intellectual Development, 1922–1939*. Chicago: U of Chicago P, 1972.

Murry, J. Middleton. "Notes and Comments." *New Adelphi* 1 (1927–28): 97–108.

——. "Notes and Comments." *New Adelphi* 3 (1929–30): 81–86.

Pound, Ezra. "Criterionism." *Hound and Horn* 4 (1930): 113–16.

Schuchard, Ronald. "T. S. Eliot at Fabers: Book Reports, Blurbs, Young Poets." *Areté* 23 (2007): 63–87.

Tate, Allen. "The Fallacy of Humanism." *Criterion* 8 (1929): 661–81.

"A Valediction Forbidding Mourning." *Calendar of Modern Letters* 4 (1927): 175–76.

Vanheste, Jeroen. *Guardians of the Humanist Legacy: The Classicism of T. S. Eliot's Criterion Network and its Relevance to the Postmodern World*. Leiden: Brill, 2007.

Ward, Leo. "L'Action française." *Criterion* 7 (1928): 364–72.

33
Making Modernism:
Eliot as Publisher

John Timberman Newcomb

Right Place, Right Time

T. S. Eliot joined the newly organized publishing firm of Faber & Gwyer as a director and literary advisor in September 1925, as he turned 37. This event was central to his life, not only marking its chronological midpoint, but giving him a stable professional and financial base over the next four decades, much as British citizenship and the Anglican Church would provide national and spiritual bases after 1927. His association with Faber is powerfully intertwined both with his growing prominence as poet, dramatist, and critic after 1930, and with the major events of his personal life, namely gradual detachment and eventual separation from Vivien Haigh-Wood, and much later, happy union with Valerie Fletcher. Peter Ackroyd claims reasonably that Eliot's publishing work at Faber "determined the shape of English poetry from the Thirties into the Sixties" (182). During those decades he cultivated and published a great many of the younger poets who became central to the mid-century canon, including W. H. Auden, Stephen Spender, Louis MacNeice, Robert Lowell, Ted Hughes, Sylvia Plath, and Thom Gunn. His editing and publishing of modernists of his own generation was hardly less significant. During his tenure Faber became not only the leading British publisher of serious contemporary literature, but, as longtime sponsor of James Joyce, Ezra Pound, Auden, Marianne Moore and, of course, Eliot himself, "the principal institutional legitimizer" (Gupta 35) of the particular version of early twentieth-century literature we call "high modernism."

At the time he was asked to join the firm, Eliot was at a low ebb of depression, exhaustion, and marital anxiety, and may have even suffered some sort of temporary "breakdown" in May 1925 (Ackroyd 150). He was still toiling in the dull office at Lloyds Bank that he had occupied since 1917. Although recommended by several well-known writers, including Hugh Walpole and Charles Whibley, he still had to work hard to win over the firm's founder Geoffrey Faber and the directors, who had not planned to add another to their ranks (Morley, "A Few" 99). His active

A Companion to T. S. Eliot, First Edition. Edited by David E. Chinitz.
© 2014 John Wiley & Sons, Ltd. Published 2014 by John Wiley & Sons, Ltd.

campaigning for the post, very unlike his usual temperamental diffidence, reveals his sense of the life-changing potential of the opportunity. Eliot's fame from *The Waste Land* (1922), whose impact on the youngest generation of British literati was immediate and galvanizing, may have piqued Faber's interest, although Eliot's friend and close colleague Frank Morley discounted this, proposing instead – ironically, given his misery at Lloyds – that it was Eliot's background in the City that most appealed to the publisher ("T. S. Eliot" 61–62).

Eliot had no previous experience in the book-publishing industry, but he was accustomed to dealing with authors in an editorial capacity through his post with the *Egoist* (1917–19), and of course through his ongoing editorship of the *Criterion* since 1922. The opportunity at Faber came at a fortuitous moment in the life of the *Criterion*, whose main financial sponsor, Lady Rothermere, was threatening to withdraw when her initial three-year subsidy ended in late 1925. Although Eliot scrupulously refrained from appealing to his new firm for financial aid (Morley, "A Few" 99), Faber decided to co-sponsor the journal anyway, and after a hiatus of one issue, the *New Criterion* debuted in January 1926. In late 1927 the firm would take over the journal's finances completely (Ackroyd 166). Faber's willingness to sponsor his review must have made Eliot feel he was not merely a functionary or figurehead, but already a valued insider in the firm – an unfamiliar experience for a personality who, despite his family's social prominence in America, felt himself a consummate outsider, "never anything anywhere" (qtd. in Read 15).

Eliot would find working at Faber as empowering as Lloyds had been dispiriting. If much of the power of his earlier poetry, from "Prufrock" through *The Waste Land* at least, came from an excruciating hypersensitivity to the effects of urban-industrial space upon the modern consciousness, the Russell Square offices of Faber & Gwyer (which became Faber & Faber in 1929) provided precisely what his earlier jobs had lacked, and which he may have imagined impossible in the "Unreal City": a working environment that was remunerative yet flexible, friendly and yet comfortably hierarchical, in which his contributions were appreciated, his position respected, his privacy protected. The contrast between the confusion, discomfort, and even terror of the unforgettable city flats and streets of his verse, and the various accounts of Eliot's sane and collegial life at Faber could hardly be greater.

Faber also functioned as a haven from the nightmare of his first marriage, which, as various episodes in *The Waste Land* make abundantly clear, colored his vision of modernity as a condition of intractable alienation and spiritual death, a "rats' alley" which reduced conversation to monologue, emotional intimacy to grim co-dependency. Eliot's first eight years at Faber were the last of his marriage to Vivien, which he ended (either gently or cravenly) in September 1932 by departing on an extended trip to the United States, intent upon not moving back in with her when he returned. In the painful interval after she learned this news and began haunting his steps with desperate attempts to reunite or recriminate, the Faber office played an especially crucial role. Well after their 1933 divorce, secretaries and colleagues remained on the lookout for Mrs. Eliot, and on multiple occasions interposed themselves to keep the two apart, undoubtedly following Eliot's wishes, whether or not he made these explicit (Ackroyd 217–18; Ridler 52).

In the three decades following the end of this pathetic but perhaps necessary spectacle, as Eliot's prominence grew into genuine cultural celebrity, Faber provided a near-ideal balance of connection with the world of modern letters and protection from its most wearying aspects. After his separation, Eliot went for almost 25 years without a domicile of his own, lodging with various friends. His Faber office was the closest thing he had to a permanent home during this period. There are various endearing accounts of his cramped top-floor office with an ancestor's nameplate on the door, and his openness and courtesy toward unknown admirers (see, for example, Levy and Scherle 9–14 and Davies 355), although his position allowed him to play the role of kindly eminence on his own terms. No doubt on many occasions never written about, his innate reserve prevailed, and the firm's semi-private office space became a shield from what his former secretary Anne Ridler calls "a continuous stream of hangers-on and impecunious poets," even if the latter were "never completely barred away" (52). After the war, one of his young admirers, as resolute as she was discreet, found her way to his office door and well beyond. Acting on a nearly lifelong fascination with Eliot, Valerie Fletcher came down from Leeds in 1949 expressly to become his secretary (Gordon 497–98). She served in that capacity through a long interval of growing mutual devotion, until they were quietly married in early 1957. The emotional Indian summer of Eliot's last years was thus a direct consequence of the office culture at Faber, which he had helped to create, and which returned to him the chance for a richer experience of life.

Clearly the publishing industry suited Eliot's temperament. Unlike schoolteaching and banking, this work among like-minded adults interested in ideas offered both financial security and intellectual purpose, freed the more playful aspects of his personality, and tempered his gentlemanliness with warmth instead of the chilly rectitude expected of a City banker. As a colleague he was well-liked and even spirited, gaining a reputation for elaborate practical jokes involving snowing cigarettes and miniature incendiary devices (Ackroyd 224; Morley, "T. S. Eliot" 69). By all accounts he took to his heavy workload with assiduity and even enthusiasm, becoming a "willing workhorse" (Morley, "T. S. Eliot" 68). He could now apply the fine judgments of his critical writings to questions that were both aesthetic and intellectual, yet also had real effects on the world. He relished the opportunity to scout young writers of promise, and this role dovetailed powerfully with his already magnetic presence among younger British writers and artists (see the account of James Reeves [38] and many others).

Eliot's purview at Faber included poetry, drama, and detective fiction, as well as economics, religion, and philosophy (Schuchard 68). Unsurprisingly, his authority on aesthetic matters became crucial to the firm's decision-making processes – not least because of the strong track record he established in advocating successful books. Yet he carried himself not as a Parnassian aesthete slumming in the business world, as some poets of his stature might have done, but as a serious professional believing in what he did. He was active in the Publishers' Association, working hard on questions of policy within the industry (Schuchard 65) and devoting substantial time and energy to projects involving the civic uses of poetry, such as the weekly poetry supplement to the BBC publication the *Listener* (Adam Smith, "T. S. Eliot" 333–34). Eliot wrote blurbs carefully and prolifically, and remarked late in his career that "every publisher who is also an author considers this form of composition more arduous than any other" ("Publishing" 1570). Ronald Schuchard's partial list of the authors Eliot blurbed includes Pound, Moore, Auden, MacNeice, Spender, Hughes, Djuna Barnes, Robert Graves, Henry Miller, Lawrence Durrell, F. Scott Fitzgerald, Herbert Read, William Saroyan, Robert Duncan, Charles Williams, and Jacques Maritain (83).

As this list indicates, the full meaning of Eliot's work in publishing is not entirely biographical, but also lies in his professional decisions and practices, which shaped the careers of many other writers as well as his own. He was renowned for personal kindness to young writers even or especially as he critiqued their work unsparingly. Accounts by various colleagues and friends attest that Eliot spent an enormous amount of time meeting with these aspirants, even those the firm had no interest in publishing, and he often tried to help those he thought promising to secure another publisher (Mairet 43). Kathleen Raine hints that fledgling poets used him as a source of free state-of-the-art criticism, knowing that their manuscript was unlikely to be accepted by Faber, yet also knowing that Eliot would strive to provide them insightful and encouraging suggestions even in rejection (80). He took a strong personal interest in poets such as Vernon Watkins and George Barker who were not as culturally advantaged as an Auden or a Spender, and who might otherwise have struggled to find a publisher. For Barker (1913–91) in particular, Eliot exhibited a strong personal, perhaps paternal, affinity, arranging loans and grants, campaigning for awards, and carrying the young man's poems around London in his jacket to show friends, much as a doting father might exhibit clippings of his son's accomplishments (Fraser 64–65). But while he had his favorites, Eliot was so universally kind and considerate to younger writers that among the thirties generation one finds virtually unanimous agreement with Spender, who (paraphrasing Auden) calls him "the most consistently friendly, the least malicious, envious and vain" of all the older writers they encountered (*T. S. Eliot* 51).

On the other hand, what is perhaps most striking about the professional work of this ostensibly retiring and unworldly figure is its ambition and even aggressiveness. With the firm's blessing Eliot set out to make a serious intervention in the literary scene, establishing Faber's credibility as a high-toned firm, and elevating the level of contemporary poetry publishing. From the beginning, many of his publishing initiatives seem calculated attempts to consolidate the achievements in avant-garde poetry of the previous 15 years, and to frame a distinctive view of modernist literary value as embodied by a few masterful figures, including himself. Within months of his debut as publisher he had deeply offended Virginia and Leonard Woolf not only by luring one of his more renowned poetic contemporaries, Herbert Read, away from the Hogarth Press, but also by contracting with Faber to reprint his own collected verse, including *The Waste Land*, which the Woolfs had tendered a standing offer to publish years before (Ackroyd 154; Gordon 219). He also lost no time in initiating a professional relationship with Ezra Pound. Two of his earliest publication projects, his own collection *Poems 1909–1925* (1925) and Pound's *Selected Poems* (1928), must be seen as powerful twinned efforts to assert a core canon of high-modernist poetry. Within a few years he would add to these canon-shaping efforts by securing Joyce's "Work in Progress," and by initiating a concerted campaign to elevate Marianne Moore into modernist canonicity. The only modernist contemporary whom he sponsored to this degree who did *not* achieve canonical status was Djuna Barnes, whose *Nightwood* was published with an enthusiastic introduction by Eliot in 1936. Even so, Eliot's advocacy helped Barnes maintain a foothold in modernist history which may now be growing into a role of greater importance.[1]

Difficulty in placing his own work had ended for Eliot years before, but still it would be a mistake to underestimate the importance of his dual role as Faber author as well as director. After 1925 all of Eliot's significant work went to Faber as a matter of course, and gave the firm instant and sustained credibility as a publisher of serious literature. The standard print runs of his Faber books were always healthy for books of poetry and criticism, and after the success of *Murder in the Cathedral*, which required multiple reprintings of several thousand copies each in 1937–38, they grew much larger still.[2] No doubt over the years Faber made a great deal more on books in other genres, but it's safe to say that Eliot did not lose the firm money. Being his own publisher allowed Eliot the freedom to craft the public presentation of his work exactly as he wished.

Shaping the High Modernist Canon

When Eliot joined Faber, Ezra Pound acquired a London publisher faithful through a tumultuous half-century of increasing political and psychological isolation, world war, treason charges, sanity hearings and incarceration, awards, and public furor. Noel Stock proposes that when Eliot took up his duties, he consciously set out "to give Pound a new start in England" (275) after the latter had seemingly burned his bridges there a few years earlier. Eliot made the 1928 selection of Pound's verse and introduced the volume himself. Another aspect of Faber's commitment to Pound was to invite him to create his own canon-of-the-moment in a compilation he called *Active Anthology* (1933). In typically antagonistic form Pound used this title to differentiate the volume from anthologies consisting of writing that has been generally accepted, instead confining himself to poems "that the British literary bureaucracy does NOT want to have printed in England" (9). The volume sought to raise the profile of several American poets – Moore, William Carlos Williams, Louis Zukofsky, George Oppen – among a British readership that barely knew they existed, and to conjoin them with Eliot and himself within a modern tradition of avant-garde stylistics. Despite this visionary goal, however, most of its contents register as fragments-in-progress or bleeding chunks carved from larger works. Of the 1,500 copies in the anthology's only printing, 750 remained unsold for years before being destroyed, rather ironically, in the Blitz (Gallup, *Ezra Pound* 157). The failure of the *Active Anthology* was perhaps a consequence of the economic times, but it also reveals Pound's diminishing power as an impresario of new verse in the 1930s, particularly compared to the growing stature of his friend and publisher.

Eliot's commitment to Pound remained undimmed. In 1933, perhaps the worst year of the Depression, Faber gamely published not only the *Active Anthology* but sections from Pound's sprawling masterwork-in-progress (*A Draft of XXX Cantos*) and the wayward but occasionally visionary *ABC of Economics*. This volume of socioeconomic theory was followed by multiple collections of prose handled primarily by Frank Morley (*Make It New: Essays by Ezra Pound* [1934], *Polite Essays* [1937]), and, in 1938, by a purportedly synoptic primer on aesthetics, *Guide to Kulchur*, which caused a good bit of trouble when, after binding the initial copies, the publisher balked at some of Pound's more vitriolic references to various English and American public figures, and pasted milder revisions in place of the offending pages (Stock 342, 354). Faber also drew the line at *Jefferson and/or Mussolini* (1935), which circulated through some 40 English publishers before landing at Stanley Nott. Still, the firm's standing order for cantos, and its willingness to issue most of Pound's other writings, represented an extraordinary commitment to one whose artistic identity was predicated upon his bitter opposition to the spinelessness of commercial publishers. Eliot's molding of Pound's *Cantos*, previously published piecemeal by various periodicals and small presses, helped to make the work's eventual canonization possible. In 1933 *A Draft of XXX Cantos* established a clear beginning and some powerful momentum, and the ensuing serial installments – *Eleven New Cantos* in 1935, *The Fifth Decad of Cantos* in 1937, *Cantos LII–LXII* in 1940, *The Pisan Cantos* in 1949 – filled gaps in readers' access, and made it possible to see the work not as a mere congeries of disparate elements but as an epic whole. All told, between 1932 and 1940 Faber averaged more than one Pound title a year, issuing a new grouping of his work, *A Selection of Poems*, as late as December 1940, while London was under aerial attack from the forces with which Pound had allied himself. Eliot's belief in Pound's importance to modern letters, and his unwavering personal loyalty to his old friend, trumped any concern for his own reputation. Indeed, it is not too much to propose that the advocacy of his preeminent friend was crucial to Pound's ability to maintain any sort of foothold in the mainstream literary world after 1940.

Through his editing of *Literary Essays of Ezra Pound* for publication by Faber in 1954, Eliot also figured significantly in Pound's extraordinary rise during the 1950s into the second central figure of modernist poetry. Michael Coyle describes Eliot's framing of Pound's life's work as a critic as "not simply a collected edition, but a concerted effort to transform the historically heterogeneous into the perfect artistic whole" (13). Eliot sought to make Pound's oeuvre not only aesthetically coherent but, perhaps more importantly, safe for the mid-century consensus of "post-ideological" New Criticism by portraying his most important prose contributions as *literary* essays, concerned with craft, *melos*, and beauty, and by carefully sealing them off from his explosive writings on politics, economics, and twentieth-century history. Coyle proposes that this editorial work fit into Eliot's larger postwar project of limning a "purely literary criticism" that would not only recuperate Pound but also repudiate "the sociopolitical ugliness of his own *After Strange Gods* (1934)" (19). The strategies Eliot's introduction employs to validate Pound's authority as a critic of poetry are subtle and ingenious. Perhaps the most distinctive of these strategies involves formulations that feint toward deauthorizing Pound, but then take unexpected turns that recuperate him by reframing the field of criticism in the terms of post-ideological formalism. This trope appears at least twice early in the introduction, but comes to fullest fruition late, at a moment where Eliot seems about to acknowledge Pound's "limitations" (xiii); encountering this word, the reader inevitably anticipates some concession to the bankruptcy of Pound's politics. Instead, Eliot continues, "The limitation of Pound's kind [of criticism] is in its concentration upon the craft of letters, and of poetry especially" (xiii). Here Pound's putative limitation (of political vision or social empathy) transforms into his self-aware choice to maintain an intense focus on a specific genre, which, Eliot has been arguing throughout, is precisely his greatest strength as a critic. Thus the expected concession becomes yet another version of Eliot's claim to Pound's centrality as *literary* critic, and effects the strategic erasure of his political sins. Such a strategy of "deliberate withdrawal" from mixing "the analysis of texts with social proscription" (Coyle 19) defined the postwar critical moment, and as in so many areas, Eliot both outlined its leading edge in his own poetic, critical, and editorial work, and inspired others to embrace it through theirs.

By 1928, with the publication of Pound's *Selected Poems*, Faber had become the primary English publisher of two members of the arch-modernist triumvirate, and the third was soon to come on board. Since 1922 Joyce had been publishing sections from his monumental "Work in Progress" in such small-circulation periodicals as the *Transatlantic Review* and *transition*, and also in various limited editions by small presses. But if the work was already a legend a decade before its completion, Faber brought it closer to the mainstream by publishing the 32-page section "Anna Livia Plurabelle" in June 1930, in an edition that eventually sold over 10,000 copies (Slocum and Cahoon 45–46). The next year Eliot contracted with Joyce to publish the whole book at around 200,000 words, though one more substantial section, "Two Tales of Shem and Shaun," would follow in 1932 under the Faber imprint. In May 1939, publishing the complete *Finnegans Wake* in all its elephantine strangeness, Faber culminated Joyce's publishing career – and one could argue, the entire project of high modernism.

Other than his work with Pound and Joyce, Eliot's most assertive and long-lasting act of modernist canon-making was to revive the profile of Marianne Moore's verse, which after the publication of one major volume, *Observations*, in 1924, had waned during the years she was busy editing *The Dial* (1925–29). Moore began to publish poems in periodicals again around 1932, but, never prolific, had no concrete plans for another book. Andrew Kappel suggests that by approaching her early in 1934 about a comprehensive volume that would reprint most of *Observations* along with whatever new work she wished to add, Eliot was redressing his felt failure to muster the advocacy he had promised Moore over a decade earlier, as well as gratefully reciprocating her consistent and insightful endorsements of his verse in a series of reviews in *Poetry* and the *Dial* since 1918 (129–32). Eliot explicitly framed the project to Moore as a parallel to the Pound *Selected Poems* of 1928 (Kappel 133), again suggesting his canny understanding of publishing formats capable of carrying canonizing force. The result was her own *Selected Poems*, issued in 1935 by Faber in Britain and Macmillan in the United States, for which Eliot not only orchestrated the publication process but arranged the poems and supplied a laudatory introduction. He did not edit the book in the sense of selecting its contents, since correspondence makes it quite clear that he gave Moore free rein to remove, revise, or add exactly what she wished. Both Kappel and Sheila Kineke conclude that his advocacy strongly shaped Moore's emergence as a canonical modernist for decades thereafter, although Kineke objects to Eliot's faintly diminishing characterization of Moore as an exotic creature whose elegant work could appeal only to connoisseurs of esoteric modern verse, which she argues helped to render Moore disembodied and sexless, a safe choice for female "mascot" within a high-modernist discourse dominated by patriarchal masculinism (134). Kappel emphasizes instead Eliot's nonchronological ordering of the poems (the basis of all subsequent Moore collections) as a strategy for constructing her oeuvre as a quintessentially *high-modernist* force, equally "brilliant" and "difficult" (135), in which hyperspecific acts of poetic observation and description foreground the sweeping epistemological issue of "how the mind orders reality" (141). Eliot's characterization of Moore thus laid a foundation for her standing, along with Pound, Eliot, Stevens, and eventually Williams, as the canonical epistemologists of the modernist imagination, in the central movements within postwar poetry scholarship from New Criticism through phenomenology and deconstruction.

The Next Generation

These projects involving established middle-aged modernist writers, while powerfully influential, were not the main emphasis of Eliot's publishing work. As Schuchard notes (85), Eliot understood Faber's commitment to poetry as a "responsibility toward society" and a necessary consequence of believing that "English poetry" is "the chief glory" of past literature (Eliot, "Publishing" 1568). His consistent approach was not primarily to poach already well-known figures, or to reward the isolated successes of middling poets, but to cultivate the young writers of greatest promise and patiently allow them to develop, confident that they "will be publicly recognized in ten or fifteen years' time" (1568). As Suman Gupta points out, Eliot's model of poetic value is predicated upon the cultivation of individual "genius" (33) which finally trumps even the concerns of the marketplace. Eliot acknowledged this sense of mission at various points, insisting in 1951 that "If we think a poet deserves our backing, we shall go on publishing his work whether it sells or not" (qtd. in Gupta 33), and the following year arguing that a poetry editor "convinced of the exceptional merit of a poet . . . should stick to him through thick and thin however disappointing the response of reviewers and readers" ("Publishing" 1569). Eliot's ability to think about publishing in the long term, and Faber's willingness to subsidize those years of growth with no expectation of immediate return, may now seem artifacts of a bygone and more enlightened literary culture, but even at the time they represented an extraordinary degree of commitment to the only genre from which, Eliot ruefully noted, publishers sought not to make money, but merely "to lose as little as possible" (1568).

Perhaps the most thoroughgoing influence of Eliot's publishing career was the cultivation of a group of young poets who became central to the mid-century canons of British poetry. Variously termed the Oxford poets, the Auden group, the "New Signatures," or the "Pylon boys" (Sternlicht 7), these closely associated men – Auden, Spender, MacNeice (and Christopher Isherwood, though he wrote little verse) – came to Eliot's notice soon after he joined Faber, and he followed their progress closely, providing space in the *Criterion* until he judged the time was right for publication of a volume by Faber. Auden was the first to surface, submitting poems to the quarterly in 1927 while still an undergraduate. Eliot soon became a serious advocate, remarking in January 1930 that Auden was the best new poet he had seen in years (Ackroyd 183). That October Faber issued Auden's first volume, *Poems*, followed by a second edition in 1933, and 13 more Auden titles in the next 11 years, including *Selected Poems* in 1938 (Bloomfield and Mendelson xv–xvi). A bit later Spender benefited from a similar trajectory, beginning with publication in the *Criterion* and a growing friendship with Eliot, a Faber volume entitled *Poems* (1933; 2nd edition 1934), and three further volumes culminating in a *Selected Poems* in 1940. MacNeice's *Poems* came in 1935, followed by two more volumes and his *Selected Poems* in 1940 (Smith 215). Through the 1930s this powerful nexus of energetic authors and adventurous publisher gave younger British verse a dynamism and coherence it had not enjoyed in decades, save perhaps for the borrowed glory of the expatriates led by Pound and Eliot twenty years earlier.[3]

The conservative Anglican publisher-poet might seem an unlikely match with the Auden group – iconoclastic about their social class, gay or sexually ambivalent, and identified with socially radical causes, including (during the 1930s, at least) communism. Yet he worked closely with them on the publication process (Marsack 24–25), stood proudly behind their work in later years (Smith 29), and maintained warm friendships with them until his death. In turn, despite diverging radically from his politics, they were devoted to him both as personal mentor and as the intellectual titan of their time. Spender's 1951 autobiography brings this across vividly, noting even in Eliot's business letters "a considerateness, a friendliness, a concern which at the time I must have ignored because I could not believe it to be there," and making clear Eliot's ability to detach political opinions from personal relationships (*World Within World* 148). For the Auden group, as for many younger American poets of the radical Left during the 1930s, Eliot's challenge to the modernity that had led to world war and economic catastrophe was powerfully energizing and comprehensive, far outweighing their rejection of his own personal politics.

At Faber Eliot also had a guiding hand in the creation of at least one crucial anthology of modern poetry. Anthologies are always implicit bids for canon-making in their very form, and from several decades' distance one can easily see which attempts have succeeded. Pound's *Active Anthology* of 1933 clearly failed to achieve the impact he sought. Soon after it was published, Eliot undertook to create a more orthodox and yet more inclusive sort of anthology, which would become *The Faber Book of Modern Verse*. In early 1935 he invited the critic and poet Michael Roberts, whom he had previously recruited to review poetry in the *Criterion*, to edit it (Adam Smith, "Mr. Eliot's Proposal" 726). Roberts's early critical work had positioned him as an enthusiastic acolyte and promoter of the Auden group, particularly in two anthologies issued by the Hogarth Press, *New Signatures* (1932) and *New Country* (1933), which had helped to establish them as the "leading 'movement'" among the younger British poets (Sutherland 133). Eliot cannot justly be accused of poaching Roberts from Hogarth as he had Read, but in recruiting him for his firm's anthology, as he had previously recruited the Auden poets themselves for the *Criterion* and for Faber, he was exercising a canonical force, gathering into his sphere of influence the elements he believed to be most significant in the next phase of modern verse writing. Roberts and Eliot worked together closely and cordially on the volume: their main disagreement came over Eliot's reluctance to occupy too many pages, and Roberts's quite natural insistence on including the whole of *The Waste Land* (Adam Smith, "Mr. Eliot's Proposal" 727). During their preparations, Eliot wrote to reassure Pound that everyone of importance would be included (Harding 163), but he may well have been humoring his eccentric friend, since he showed great confidence in Roberts's aptitude.

The finished anthology, published in early 1936, offered a strong selection of British and American poets. The British section dramatized the multiple approaches to modern verse by younger writers – not only the Auden group, just turning 30, but an even more precocious wave influenced by surrealism, including David Gascoyne, Charles Madge, and Dylan Thomas, who were barely out of their teens. The American roster included, besides Pound and Eliot, several poets then almost unknown in Britain, but soon to emerge as key figures, including Wallace Stevens, Hart Crane, E. E. Cummings, Allen Tate, Laura Riding, and John Crowe Ransom. Despite these prescient inclusions, the decision of Roberts and Eliot to limit the volume to only 36 writers constituted a potent act of canon-making, as did their handling of pre-1910 poetry. With Eliot's blessing, Roberts included extensive selections from one nineteenth-century precursor, Gerard Manley Hopkins, and a single figure of the *fin-de-siècle*, William Butler Yeats, before leaping straight to three avant-gardists of the 1910s, Eliot, Pound, and T. E. Hulme, categorically excluding the Georgians (Harding 163). The effect of this structure was to frame *Modern Verse* as a series of titanic individuals erupting from often inhospitable or unlikely conditions to achieve spectacular stylistic breaks, rather than as an incremental working-out of new principles by a larger number of poets.

In 1932, in the preface to his first anthology, *New Signatures*, Roberts had argued the need for modern poets to explore "the communist attitude" (19), using Spender's "The Funeral" as an exemplary instance. Whether due to Eliot's direct influence or to the broader disenchantment with communism affecting the young poets themselves by the mid-1930s, Roberts's preface to the Faber volume (which, not coincidentally, omits "The Funeral") exhibits a dramatic shift away from his earlier position, instead portraying the modern poet as a figure of specifically *aesthetic* opposition. In his first paragraph, Roberts characterizes the anthology's verse as coming from the "considerable body of poetry which excites an active animosity" because it departs from poetic conventions so drastically that many readers "feel compelled to argue that it is not poetry at all" (1). This account of modern poetry as a depoliticized avant-garde correlates with Eliot's own turn away from his previous attempts to conjoin politics and poetry, which can be traced to almost this same moment in the mid-1930s, and which would have such a powerful impact on the institutionalization of the high-modernist canon after World War II. *The Faber Book of Modern Verse,* a significant part of that canonical consolidation, would remain in print for over 50 years, its updated editions becoming important to generations of British poetry-readers.[4] As a measure of its familiar and even beloved status, Faber reissued the original edition "With an Account of Its Making" in 1983.

The anthology aptly exemplifies the extraordinary synergy between Eliot's already potent reputation when he joined Faber and the ways his position there allowed him to shape the formation of international high modernism over the next four decades. Through this synergy he came much closer than any other modernist to an integrated praxis of culture involving poetry, criticism, drama, social commentary, and publishing, which for a time reached across the entire English-speaking world. Today such integration is hardly imaginable, nor is Eliot's version of it especially desirable. But Eliot's publishing work helps us to understand better both this one man's strange magnetism upon the literary culture of his time, and the larger accomplishments and failures of modernism itself.

Notes

1 See, among other recent discussions of this relationship, Miriam Fuchs, "Djuna Barnes and T. S. Eliot: Authority, Resistance, and Acquiescence," *Tulsa Studies in Women's Literature* 12 (1993): 288–314; and Georgette Fleischer, "Djuna Barnes and T. S. Eliot: The Politics and Poetics of *Nightwood*," *Studies in the Novel* 30 (1998): 405–37.

2 The sizes of the print runs of Eliot's books are recorded in Gallup, *T. S. Eliot: A Bibliography.*

3 The only poets closely associated with the Oxford group whom Faber did not publish were C. Day Lewis and William Plomer, men slightly older than Auden and Spender who had already established relationships with the Hogarth Press by 1929.

4 "Like so many of my generation, I owe a very great deal to Roberts's anthology, and I would not want it to have been other than it was" (Birrell 519).

References and Further Reading

Ackroyd, Peter. *T. S. Eliot: A Life*. New York: Simon, 1984.

Adam Smith, Janet. "Mr. Eliot's Proposal: The Making of *The Faber Book of Modern Verse*." *Times Literary Supplement* 18 June 1976: 726–28.

——. "T. S. Eliot and *The Listener*." Tate 333–36.

Birrell, T. A. "A Reception of T. S. Eliot: Texts and Contexts." *English Studies* 69 (1988): 518–33.

Bloomfield, B. C., and Edward Mendelson. *W. H. Auden: A Bibliography, 1924–1969*. Charlottesville: UP of Virginia, 1972.

Coyle, Michael. *Ezra Pound, Popular Genres, and the Discourse of Culture*. University Park, PA: Pennsylvania State UP, 1995.

Davies, H. S. "Mistah Kurtz: He Dead." Tate 355–363.

Fraser, Robert. *The Chameleon Poet: a Life of George Barker*. London: Cape, 2001.

Gallup, Donald. *Ezra Pound: A Bibliography*. Charlottesville: UP of Virginia, 1983.

——. *T. S. Eliot: A Bibliography*. New York: Harcourt, 1969.

Gordon, Lyndall. *T. S. Eliot: An Imperfect Life*. New York: Norton, 1998.

Gupta, Suman. "In Search of Genius: T. S. Eliot as Publisher." *Journal of Modern Literature* 27 (2003): 26–35.

Harding, Jason. *The Criterion: Cultural Politics and Periodical Networks in Inter-War Britain*. Oxford: Oxford UP, 2002.

Kappel, Andrew J. "Presenting Miss Moore, Modernist: T. S. Eliot's Edition of Marianne Moore's *Selected Poems*." *Journal of Modern Literature* 19 (1994): 129–50.

Kineke, Sheila. "T. S. Eliot, Marianne Moore, and the Gendered Operations of Literary Scholarship." *Journal of Modern Literature* 21 (1997): 121–36.

Levy, William Turner, and Victor Scherle. *Affectionately, T. S. Eliot: The Story of a Friendship, 1947–1963*. Philadelphia: Lippincott, 1968.

Mairet, Philip. "Memories of T. S. E." *T. S. Eliot: A Symposium for His Seventieth Birthday*. Ed. Neville Braybrooke. New York: Farrar, 1958. 36–44.

March, Richard, and Tambimuttu, eds. *T. S. Eliot: A Symposium*. Chicago: Regnery, 1949.

Marsack, Robyn. *The Cave of Making: The Poetry of Louis MacNeice*. Oxford: Clarendon, 1982.

Moore, Marianne. *Selected Poems*. Intro. T. S. Eliot. London: Faber, 1935.

Morley, F[rank] V. "A Few Reminiscences of T. S. Eliot." Tate 90–113.

——. "T. S. Eliot as a Publisher." March and Tambimuttu 60–70.

Pound, Ezra. *Active Anthology*. London: Faber, 1933.

——. *Literary Essays of Ezra Pound*. Ed. and intro. T. S. Eliot. London: Faber, 1954.

Raine, Kathleen. "The Poet of Our Time." March and Tambimuttu 78–81.

Read, Herbert. "T. S. E.: A Memoir." Tate 11–37.

Reeves, James. "Cambridge Twenty Years Ago." March and Tambimuttu 38–42.

Ridler, Anne. "Working for T. S. Eliot: A Personal Reminiscence." *PN Review* 27 (2000): 51–53.

Roberts, Michael, ed. *The Faber Book of Modern Verse*. London: Faber, 1936.

——, ed. *New Signatures*. London: Hogarth, 1932.

Schuchard, Ronald. "T. S. Eliot at Fabers: Book Reports, Blurbs, Young Poets." *Areté* 23 (2007): 63–87.

Slocum, John J., and Herbert Cahoon. *A Bibliography of James Joyce, 1882–1941*. Westport, CT: Greenwood, 1971.

Smith, Elton Edward. *Louis MacNeice*. New York: Twayne, 1970.

Spender, Stephen. *T. S. Eliot*. New York: Viking, 1976.

——. *World Within World*. London: Hamilton, 1951.

Sternlicht, Sanford. *Stephen Spender*. New York: Twayne, 1992.

Stock, Noel. *The Life of Ezra Pound*. Berkeley: North Point, 1982.

Sutherland, John. *Stephen Spender: A Literary Life*. New York: Oxford UP, 2005.

Tate, Allen, ed. *T. S. Eliot: The Man and His Work*. New York: Delacorte, 1966.

Van O'Connor, William, and Edward Stone. *A Casebook on Ezra Pound*. New York: Crowell, 1959.

34
Eliot and the New Critics

Gail McDonald

Imagine that this year a few professors in a couple of universities – one in England and one in the United States – decide that the most exciting literature and criticism being produced at the moment is the work of a single poet and that it would be a first-rate idea to reconstruct English department curricula and revise teaching methods according to principles extracted from a few of his essays. The remarkable thing about T. S. Eliot and the New Critics is that a skeletal history of their association could be constructed along these lines. To be sure, such a story would be inadequate, but it would not be false. As preposterous as it may now seem, it is the case that professors at Cambridge in England and Vanderbilt in Tennessee saw Eliot – not just his works but what he himself seemed to be – as the poet and critic who could make the world, or at least the academy, safe for poetry.

In December 1965, the year of Eliot's death, the New Critic Cleanth Brooks summarized his contributions:

> In a time of grave disorder, Eliot has moved toward a restoration of order. Not the least important part of this work of restoration has been to clarify the role of poetry, not claiming so much for it that it is transformed into prophecy, or Promethean politics, or an ersatz religion; but at the same time pointing out its unique and irreplaceable function and defending its proper autonomy. ("T. S. Eliot" 330)

Brooks's praise for Eliot also neatly summarizes key vocabulary, assumptions, and motives of New Criticism, a way of reading literature that dominated the academy for nearly 40 years and continues to influence pedagogy today. Any critical methodology with this kind of longevity will eventually become hard to define. How does one recognize a New Critical reading? To put it somewhat reductively, such a reading will concern itself primarily with the formal properties of a text, often a poem. It will scrupulously attend to the interplay of effects within the text: such matters as rhythm, rhyme, connotations, tone, and so forth are considered as a set of relationships. The

A Companion to T. S. Eliot, First Edition. Edited by David E. Chinitz.
© 2014 John Wiley & Sons, Ltd. Published 2014 by John Wiley & Sons, Ltd.

objective of this close reading is to discover the means by which the text achieves its distinctive unity. Defining New Criticism in the *New Princeton Encyclopedia of Poetry and Poetics*, Brooks declares, however, that close reading is *not* the most distinctive trait of New Critical practice; rather, he defines New Criticism as the "application of semantics to literary study." What concerns Brooks are the means by which, in a given work of literature, heterogeneous elements are held together in a unified field. He asserts, further, that a reader's experience of this unity provides a "distinct kind of knowledge" (833).

When Brooks delivered his encomium, the many practitioners of New Criticism were adept at seeing a poem as a little world, one in which the disorderly energies of modernity had been masterfully shaped into a unity that was itself a form of knowledge, autonomous, irreplaceable, and as central to civilization as science, politics, or religion. Indeed, by the mid-sixties, critical opinion had begun to turn against the routines and formulas of New Criticism and, to a considerable extent, against its presumed progenitor, T. S. Eliot. Before we come to this turn, we must first understand why and how New Criticism came about. Clearly, something important for literary studies happened between 1920, when Eliot published *The Sacred Wood,* and 1965. This chapter considers the particular confluence of personalities and circumstances that accounts for the dominance of one poet over a group of critics and, in turn, for those critics' dominance in the academy during that period. Did Eliot "invent" New Criticism or did the New Critics invent "Eliot"? And what conditions fostered this interdependence?

New Criticism's ascendancy is normally dated from some point in the 1930s, but the story of its inception begins in the 1920s. There are two separate strands of the narrative: in England, the work of I. A. Richards, William Empson, and F. R. Leavis; in the United States, the work of John Crowe Ransom, Allen Tate, Robert Penn Warren, and, later, Cleanth Brooks and William K. Wimsatt. The catalog of American contributors must be truncated in the interest of space, but there are scores of other influential critics who have an affiliation with the New Critics – among them, R. P. Blackmur, Kenneth Burke, and F. O. Matthiessen. Most histories of New Criticism focus on the American strand, not only because of the sheer number of practitioners in the States but also because it was John Crowe Ransom who in 1941 published *The New Criticism*, the book that gave the "movement" its name. In general, the New Criticism was more broadly and enthusiastically adopted in the American academy than elsewhere. And there are other differences: for example, Richards and Empson made greater use of psychology than did most American critics, and were in significant ways laying groundwork for what would now be termed "reader-response" theory. Nevertheless, the shared interests of the English and American critics inform New Criticism from the beginning. Ransom's founding book discusses Richards, Empson, Eliot, and Yvor Winters, two of whom were Englishmen at Cambridge University. Though none of them was quite the "ontological" critic Ransom deemed necessary to the times, his selection of significant figures indicates that, whatever the national and intellectual differences among these thinkers, they shared a view that what then passed for literary criticism was unsatisfactory. It is on this point – a conscious design for improving the status of literature and literary criticism – that we see the interests of T. S. Eliot and the projects of critics in England and the United States converge.

This convergence was not, it is important to add, always a conscious one, nor one that either the New Critics or Eliot himself accepted without qualification. In a 1957 interview, Ransom questioned the grouping: "Let's name some of them – Richards, Eliot, Tate, Blackmur, Brooks, Leavis (I guess). How in God's name can you get that gang into the same bed? There is no bed big enough and no blanket would stay tucked" (qtd. in Asher 184). Similarly, in the 1956 lecture that became "The Frontiers of Criticism," Eliot wittily distanced himself from "the lemon-squeezer school of criticism" (*OPP* 113). (The New Critical method, he wrote, was to analyze poems "stanza by stanza and line by line, and [to] extract, squeeze, tease, press every drop of meaning out of it that one can.") Two phenomena are in evidence here: first, in the later phases of any movement, it is typical for those associated with it to say that there never was such a movement or that, if there was, its degree of organization and self-consciousness has been greatly exaggerated; second, the tendency of literary histories is to emphasize likenesses (of genres, periods, styles) whereas the tendency of artists is to treat temporary affiliations as enabling to their work or its promotion, but not as static entities to which some loyalty is owed. Ransom's evident exasperation with the interviewer's lumping together of critics is surely a function of the currency of New Criticism in the fifties, as is Eliot's little in-joke to an academic audience at Minnesota, many of whom were themselves well trained in lemon-squeezing.

Despite these denials, there are significant shared views among the group tussling for space in Ransom's imaginary bed. In *The New Apologists for Poetry* (1956), one of the most astute philosophical analyses of New Criticism, Murray Krieger carefully discriminates among the critics, yet he finds notable unity among them in their desire "to answer the need, forced on them by historical pressures, to justify poetry by securing for it a unique function for which modern scientism cannot find a surrogate" (6). In order to assess what Eliot was to the New Critics and they to him, we must attend to these "historical pressures."

Why this urgency on behalf of poetry? In writing the preface to the 1928 reissue of *The Sacred Wood*, Eliot, after the ritual apology for the book's air of "pontifical solemnity," remarks that whatever coherence the essays as a group may have lies in their treatment of "the problem of the integrity of poetry" (viii). "Integrity" is as important a word here as "poetry." That Eliot should have felt it necessary to issue pontifical edicts, that Krieger should describe the New Criticism employing a rhetoric of force, and that Brooks should characterize Eliot as restoring order to a culture under siege – such statements suggest that poetry's defenders were invested in more than how best to read a poem. As New Criticism developed, "poetry" became the symbolic citadel stormed by scientism, materialism, secularism, progressivism, utilitarianism, positivism, and other manifestations of modernity. To defend poetry, then, was to defend values opposed to the measurable achievements of science, technology, and business. It was, furthermore, to advance the notion that not all human accomplishments take a quantifiable form.

Of all Eliot's prose, the early essays gathered in *The Sacred Wood* (1920) were the most influential for New Criticism, in part because of their assertion that poetry had a "problem" and in part because they established Eliot's learned and authoritative tone. Even a quick browse through *The Sacred Wood* turns up many of the key principles governing New Critical practice. In "The Perfect Critic" Eliot explains what not to do. The critic should not try to be an artist. He should not impose his emotions upon art objects (6–7). "He must simply elucidate," for "there is no method except to be very intelligent" (11). The aim should be "to see the object as it really is" (14). In "Imperfect Critics" Eliot continues to instruct. The "tools of the critic" are "comparison and analysis." "The important critic is the person who is absorbed in the present problems of art" (37). The next essay in the volume is Eliot's most famous, "Tradition and the Individual Talent." In it, he reiterates the need for comparison and analysis and insists on a perspective that sees literature of the past and literature of the present as having a "simultaneous existence" composing "a simultaneous order" (49). The poet is, even in the act of innovation, "surrender[ing]" himself "to something which is more valuable" (52–53). Here, he first names the "Impersonal theory of poetry," that much-discussed division between "the man who suffers and the mind which creates," and he offers his equally well-known (and overtly anti-romantic) definition of poetry as "not a turning loose of emotion, but an escape from emotion . . . not the expression of personality, but an escape from personality" (52–53, 54, 58). Moving another 40 pages into this slim volume, the reader comes to "Hamlet and His Problems," wherein Eliot formulates the "objective correlative": "The only way of expressing emotion in the form of art is by finding an 'objective correlative'; in other words, a set of objects, a situation, a chain of events which shall be the formula of that *particular* emotion" (100).

The aforementioned essays all appeared in the *Athenaeum*, a literary review, between May 1919 and July 1920. (The final two sections of "Imperfect Critics" were published for the first time in *The Sacred Wood*.) One other essay would prove seminal for the New Critics: "The Metaphysical Poets," in which Eliot lays out his notion of "the dissociation of sensibility." This essay did not appear in *The Sacred Wood*, but followed soon after, in October 1921. Thus, between early 1919 and late 1921, Eliot had laid the groundwork for critical practices that would shape criticism and teaching for the next several decades. He could not have foreseen how powerful his essays would be in shaping critical practice. What he realized, however, was that the methods of critical reading available in 1919 were inadequate to the task of reading his poetry. In "Ben Jonson," another essay in *The Sacred Wood*, Eliot might easily have been speaking for himself in claiming that Jonson's criticism could be seen to "promulgate, as a . . . program of reform, what he chose to do himself" (117). Keenly aware that a book of critical essays could assist in creating a taste for the kind of poetry he wished to write, Eliot was also savvy about his role as an American "outsider" in the literary marketplace of London. A book, he knew, would be perceived as having more *gravitas* than occasional essays. He wrote to his friend Sidney Schiff in January 1920 that he wanted the book to be "small – one hundred fifty pages or so – both in order to get it done sooner and in order to make it a single distinct blow." As ever, a bit secretive about his own cunning and ambition, he admonished Schiff not to disclose the book's contents: "I do not want other people . . . to have any notion of what I want to say" (*Letters* 356).

How was it that *The Sacred Wood* became, as F. W. Bateson expressed it, "our sacred book" for students and professors in the late 1920s and 30s? What can account for the reception of Eliot's "small" book? *The Sacred Wood* – like many modernist works – is a symptom of change. Whether or not the world changed in Virginia Woolf's rather precise December 1910, the perception of change was widespread in the years immediately following World War I. For people inclined to notice intellectual trends, the alteration predated the Great War, but its horrors had put paid to simple notions of human progress. The eager reception of Eliot's early critical pronouncements derives in part from the growing sense that the modern world seemed, on the one hand, not to need poetry at all and, on the other, to need it more than ever. In addition, Eliot's status as a critic was significantly linked to his status as a poet, and his poetry to his status as a critic. Describing the fashion for Eliot among Oxford undergraduates in the twenties, Bateson declares, "It was Eliot the critic who prepared us to meet Eliot the poet" (637). Equally, though, Eliot's growing reputation as *the* poet of postwar cultural trauma sent readers, eager for understanding, to his criticism.

The university setting in which the New Criticism burgeoned is a vital dimension of poetry in the twentieth century. More and more frequently in the course of that century, and now in this century, the universities provided salaries to poets, degree programs in creative writing, venues for readings (and book sales), and training in how to read poetry. None of these conditions was customary in 1900. The fortunes of New Criticism were linked from the start to academic developments that were themselves effects of modernity. These included revision of the curriculum to include contemporary writing, the promotion of literary criticism as a professional practice, and an increase in the size and socioeconomic diversity of the student population. One of the great ironies of New Criticism's institutional success is that the conditions of modernization (Krieger's "historical pressures") that seemed to threaten poetry were in large part the same as those that made educational institutions so receptive to New Critical methodologies. New Criticism took criticism away from the gentleman amateur, replacing the vagueness of genteel appreciation with the specificity of teachable methods, enhancing the professionalism of the literature instructor through the publication of journals and textbooks, presenting its case at such organizations as the Modern Language Association, filling professorial positions in prestigious universities. At the same time, however, it offered what might be seen as a more specifically "humanist" and "aesthetic" dimension to literary studies, which had by the early decades of the century long been dominated by historical scholarship and philology. Allen Tate observed that when a young man "goes to graduate school, he comes out incapacitated for criticism. . . . He cannot discuss the literary object in terms of its specific forms; all that he can do is to give you its history or tell you how he feels about it" (*Collected Essays* 56). There was nothing new in Tate's complaint; such expressions of dissatisfaction had been circulating among students and at least some of their professors since the 1890s. William Morton Payne's *English in American Universities* (1895) made the point that students should be taught to see literature as art. The first use of the phrase "new criticism" was made by Joel Spingarn during an address at Columbia University in 1910, and while Spingarn did not intend precisely what Ransom did in using the phrase, he, too, wished to draw attention to the aesthetic dimension of literature.

For twenty-first-century students accustomed to courses in "British Fiction in the 1980s" and "Writing Screenplays," the history of English at Cambridge University will be surprising. In *The Muse Unchained*, E. M. W. Tillyard recalls the slow stages of change in the curriculum and examination systems that led, finally, to the English Tripos in 1917. English was not treated as a discipline of study until the late nineteenth century. In 1883, the English literature curriculum stopped at the end of the seventeenth century, and the basic approach was grammatical and philological. This emphasis on early periods and linguistics has to do with ideas about reading, especially the reading of contemporary literature. Reading was understood to be something a cultivated person did alone, a leisurely pursuit for which professorial guidance was unnecessary. To turn the appreciation of literature into a scholarly discipline risked tainting a gentlemanly pastime by association with paid labor. An important sign of modern times, however, came in 1911, when Sir Harold Harmsworth (later Viscount Rothermere) donated £20,000 to establish a Chair of English Literature in memory of King Edward VII, with the unusual specification that "the Professor shall treat this subject on literary and critical rather than on philological and linguistic lines" (Tillyard 38). Universities in the "provinces," such as Manchester, Liverpool, and Leeds, adopted literary-critical approaches with greater alacrity, an indication perhaps that issues of class and prestige slowed Cambridge's adoption of new methods.

Eliot was, for Tillyard,

> the man really responsible for introducing into Cambridge a set of ideas that both shocked and satisfied. I cannot think of anyone else who counted in this way. . . . [T]here was enough in *The Sacred Wood* for the young men in search of novelty to seize on and develop and to work up into a creed. (98)

Nor was the enthusiasm limited to the young men. Muriel Bradbrook, an accomplished scholar and contemporary of William Empson, recalled, "The poetry of *The Waste Land* gave us a new world. . . . 'Bliss was it in that dawn to be alive!'" (115). For students at Cambridge, Eliot symbolized the modernization and revitalization of literary studies. Eliot delivered the Clark Lectures, a series of eight talks on the metaphysical poetry of the seventeenth century, to a Cambridge audience in 1926. Even at this early stage of his career (*The Waste Land*, recall, was published only four years before), we see evidence of the tendency of academia to make Eliot into an icon, for good and ill. For detractors such as F. L. Lucas, Virginia Woolf reports, the lectures were evidence that Eliot had "thrown intellect to the winds" (65). For supporters such as I. A. Richards, however, Eliot was *the one hope* for the new School of English ("On TSE" 3). The lectures were well attended, especially by younger dons and undergraduates – further evidence that Eliot's poetry and criticism in those years seemed to point toward the future of English studies. His persona at this point had not acquired the aura of conservatism that would cause later generations of students to turn against him.

Richards was Eliot's most important advocate at Cambridge. Especially in *Practical Criticism: A Study of Literary Judgment*, Richards brought the methods of social science to the observation of reading practices, cataloging the kinds of misreading and misunderstanding of poetry typical of his students. His work serves two basic aims: first, describing the "experience" of reading a poem, and second, discovering the obstacles that interfere with the experience. For Richards, the value of poetry inheres in its invitation to a particular kind of experience not available outside literary discourse. He proposes that poetry offers not statements of truth (measurable against a correspondence to "reality") but "pseudo-statements" coherently expressed through the poem, such that the poem creates, as it were, a separate reality. By providing access to this kind of knowledge, he claims, poetry "is capable of saving us; it is a perfectly possible means of overcoming chaos" (*Science* 82–83). This conception of poetry as salvific highlight's Eliot's particular relevance to Richards. Eliot, the author of densely allusive poetry, had argued that difficulty was not a choice but a necessity:

> We can only say that it appears likely that poets in our civilization, as it exists at present, must be *difficult*. Our civilization comprehends great variety and complexity, and this variety and complexity, playing upon a refined sensibility, must produce various and complex results. The poet must become more and more comprehensive, more allusive, more indirect, in order to force, to dislocate if necessary, language into his meaning. (*SE* 248)

The notion of having to force language into one's meaning carries with it a sense of intellectual muscularity that, so to speak, raises the game of poetry, making its stakes and its players seem vital to cultural health. Images of wresting order from chaos imbue the activities of reading and writing poetry with heroic energy, and Eliot's creative work – especially *The Waste Land* – seemed to enact that courageous battle for the recovery of civilization.

Seven Types of Ambiguity, the tour de force of close reading by Richards's student William Empson, is a dazzling example of the engagement of a nimble mind with difficult texts. Like his teacher, Empson is interested in the reader, and his views are informed by psychology, a subject for which Eliot had little patience. The reader-centered focus of Richards's and Empson's work distinguishes them from most of the

American New Critics, as I have indicated. What links the English critics with the American New Critics are the following assumptions: poetry is a serious undertaking that demands from its readers their best attentions and most thoughtful analyses; the poet makes order out of chaos and, in doing so, models a response to the difficulties of modernity; a principal strategy of poetry is the balancing of contrary energies or tensions or ironies in a poem; a good poem conveys a sense of *achieved* unity; criticism of poetry requires the same kind of rigor and intelligence as other occupations and forms of learning; poetry's purposes are unrecognizable to solely materialist, positivist cultures – that is, poetry does not make money or effect cures. It does not "do" things in a quantifiable way, but it has an essential place in culture precisely for that reason. In short, these thinkers were making a hard case the hard way: by arguing that poetry is useful because it is useless.

It is a case made by negatives, the emphasis falling on what poetry is not. The same strategy of indirection informs the language of *The Sacred Wood*, in which Eliot himself found "the repeated assertion that when we are considering poetry we must consider it primarily as poetry and not another thing" (viii). Negative definition is crucial to the first phases of the American New Criticism. Before the New Critics came the Fugitives and the Agrarians, both groups setting themselves apart from mainstream culture. What began as a group of 16 men reading their poems to one another on Thursday nights in Nashville, Tennessee, eventuated in a little magazine called the *Fugitive*, its first issue appearing in the same year as *The Waste Land*. The magazine ceased publication in 1925, but the intellectual comradeship (not always entirely amicable) between two of the most gifted poets and thinkers in the group, John Crowe Ransom and Allen Tate, continued. Tate, the younger man, was especially taken with the work of T. S. Eliot. He and Ransom disagreed in print about the artistic worth of *The Waste Land*, but they did not disagree about the need for a criticism equipped to *read* poems like *The Waste Land*. Robert Penn Warren, another key figure of New Criticism, was then a sophomore at Vanderbilt whose talent was so prodigious that he was quickly taken up by Tate (then a graduate student) and brought into the Fugitive circle.

Apart from the desire to read and write poetry, the three men were united by their setting, a university in the American South. That this university was located in Tennessee helps to explain a second phase of Tate and Ransom's association: the Agrarians. The Agrarians were united not by poetry so much as by a set of shared principles; not all of them were poets or friends, and much of their communication occurred through letters and essays. Nor was Agrarianism a notion confined to Vanderbilt or even to the South. Rather, it was a point of view about how to organize life such that a link to nature, usually through farming, fostered independence and self-sufficiency. Some version of Arcadia or "green world" is conventionally imagined as a counterweight to courtly corruption or urbanization. Most pertinent to this discussion is the defensive position of this group of Southerners about the South and about the status of the arts. Heavily publicized events such as the so-called Scopes "monkey trial," in which a teacher was tried for teaching Darwinism in the

Bible-Belt South, harmed the already precarious reputation of the South as a home for intellectuals and artists. The introductory Statement of Principles to *I'll Take My Stand*, the book that came out of this Agrarian moment, declares an enmity between the arts and industry:

> Nor do the arts have a proper life under industrialism, with the general decay of sensibility which attends it. Art depends, in general, like religion, on a right attitude to nature; and in particular on a free and disinterested observation of nature that occurs only in leisure. Neither the creation nor the understanding of works of art is possible in an industrial age except by some local and unlikely suspension of the industrial drive. (xxv)

The critical and poetic works of Ransom and Tate particularly are inflected by the romanticization of the antebellum South. The Lost Cause of the Old South becomes in their hands a symbol of the vulgarization of American life. In such thinking they made common cause with Eliot, and he, in turn, expressed "sympathy" with the Agrarians and praised the South for having "at least some recollection of a 'tradition'" (*ASG* 15–18).

Ransom and Tate's active engagement with Agrarianism was short-lived, but not the sense that values eclipsed by forces of modernization should be restored to culture. The notion of a worthy "cause" remained central to the activities of the American New Critics. To fight their battle, they and their followers employed many of the strategies of the successful businessmen they mistrusted: they founded journals (the *Sewanee Review* and the *Kenyon Review*), held prestigious posts, received foundation grants to establish summer institutes for graduate students and junior lecturers, published best-selling textbooks such as *Understanding Poetry*, and engineered a kind of takeover of American university classrooms. Their timing was propitious: methodology fatigue had set in and younger scholars sought alternatives to philology and literary history; students were drawn to contemporary literature; the close-reading practices of New Criticism were perfectly suited to teaching students with little background in history or languages.

Thus an antimaterialist, anti-industrialist movement evolved into a commercially and institutionally successful enterprise – at least within the subculture of academic and literary life in the United States. It had become, as in Ransom's essay title, "Criticism, Inc." The contradictions between aims and methods are obvious. But we might consider whether any movement or strategy, if it is to have an impact at all, can be introduced to a broad audience without advertising, publishing, speeches, and financial support. The contradictions, it could be argued, suggest the inescapability of modernity – even by those who would resist its defining qualities. Literary modernism itself expresses such contradictions, sometimes apparently avant-garde, sometimes apparently reactionary. Thus the points of view gathered under the aegis of New Criticism can be described as on the leading edge of change, on the one hand, and as retrogressive, on the other. I. A. Richards and T. S. Eliot are the heroes of the young and intellectually adventurous. Allen Tate and T. S. Eliot are old fogies who regret the passing of classical humanism.

When it comes to the task of unraveling which of these caricatures comes closer to the truth, Eliot himself is not much help. His critical statements provide evidence in both directions. The view of many Eliot scholars is that Eliot's career should be viewed as having two phases: one before his conversion to Anglicanism in 1927 and one after, the latter phase evincing a growing philosophical and political conservatism. Other scholars, myself included, see the contrary impulses toward iconoclasm and conservatism as present even in Eliot's earliest thought and continuing throughout his career. Either view permits us to see Eliot as susceptible of conflicting interpretations and therefore suitable for all occasions. He was aware of the problem, conscious that he had been made a figurehead for New Criticism based largely on his earliest essays. In his 1964 Preface to *The Use of Poetry and the Use of Criticism*, he begins with the statement that Yeats had "had more than enough of 'The Lake Isle of Innisfree' as his anthology piece." He notes that his own poetry has been more fairly represented.

> But with my essays I have not been so fortunate. Just as any student of contemporary literature, putting pen to paper about my criticism, is certain to pass an examination on it if he alludes to the "dissociation of sensibility" and the "objective correlative," so every anthologist wishing to include a sample of my essays will choose "Tradition and the Individual Talent" – perhaps the most juvenile and certainly the first to appear in print.

With no wish to "repudiate" that famous essay, he nevertheless makes it clear that he has written rather a lot of criticism since then, little of which has attained the status of this early work. The New Critics had preserved the Eliot of *The Sacred Wood* in amber.

By the mid-1960s, when Cleanth Brooks praised Eliot's saving influence on poetry and criticism, the forces of opposition to Eliot and New Criticism had been gathering momentum for about a decade. The poet Delmore Schwartz complained about "The Literary Dictatorship of T. S. Eliot" in a *Partisan Review* essay of 1949. This essay appeared shortly after the controversy over the awarding of the Bollingen Prize to Ezra Pound for his *Pisan Cantos*. It does indeed seem odd that the Library of Congress should award a prize to a man who had recently faced a trial for treason against the United States and whose *Cantos* contained clear evidence of anti-Semitism. The award was taken as symptomatic of New Criticism's separation of the poem from the world, its words from its meaning. Karl Shapiro, a dissenting member of the prize committee, laid the blame at Eliot's door: "Eliot's criticism had by 1948 so far penetrated the critical mentality of his followers that they dared ignore the plain English in the poems for what they called their magnificent artistry" (82–83). Shapiro's comment encapsulates the most frequent accusation made against New Criticism: that its insistent focus on tensions and concordances among the words on the page precludes attention to poetic expression as communication of ideas. This is an ongoing and worthy debate in literary studies. However, much of the criticism after New Criticism effectively sanded down New Criticism's distinctive textures, making what had been various and interesting into something smooth, uniform, and dull. It is factually incorrect to say that New Critics had no interest in literary history or biography and equally incorrect to say that every New Critic was a closet conservative. Nevertheless, these accusations gained credibility with repetition.

Furthermore, the New Critics themselves were partly responsible for the routine and formulaic critical readings that proliferated in academic journals and student essays. Proliferation bred degeneration as "readings" became drearily predictable. The textbook "fallacies" outlined in William Wimsatt and Monroe Beardsley's *The Verbal Icon* and the "heresy of paraphrase" against which Brooks cautions readers in *The Well-Wrought Urn* gave credence to the view that New Criticism cared nothing for context. Seeming to forbid attention to biography, historical circumstances, and reader-response, it seemed also to grant permission to attend to artistic effects without regard for ideological import. Indeed, increasingly, the apparent lack of attention to ideology was deemed ideology in formalist disguise. That some of the New Critics were in fact socially conservative and religious, as was Eliot by this point, added weight to the suspicion that attention to the words on the page was not an innocent enterprise. On this reading, "impersonality" was not an antidote to subjectivity but a means of stifling individuality. Praising harmony in a poem looked suspiciously like code for supporting homogeneous societies. By the late sixties and early seventies, with the advent of women's studies, ethnic studies, and other forms of unapologetically political intellectual activity on university campuses, New Criticism seemed to students as sterile as philology had once seemed to their grandparents. Eliot's reputation, too, suffered during this period; he lost the association with energetic innovation that had once made him so appealing to undergraduates.

Among the critics associated with New Criticism is R. P. Blackmur. He is an odd man out in a number of ways. Entirely self-educated, he does not fit neatly into the academic context that shaped New Criticism. His work reminds us that no genuinely insightful criticism can be entirely governed by a template. In "A Critic's Job of Work," an essay in his *Form and Value in Modern Poetry*, Blackmur expresses a skeptical view of intellectual systems: "every formula of knowledge must fall the moment too much weight is laid upon it – the moment it becomes omnivorous and pretends to be omnipotent – the moment, in short, it is taken literally" (340). This is a sensible corrective to the view that Eliot was *"the one hope"* for English at Cambridge; or that one modest collection of essays should be responsible for an entire mechanism of reading, publications, prizes, and worldviews; or that any method of literary criticism can restore order to the chaos of modernity. Eliot was the poet and critic that the New Critics took him to be. And he was not. Maintaining this double vision is the best defense against a myopic view of either poetry or literary criticism – and of Eliot himself.

REFERENCES AND FURTHER READING

Asher, Kenneth. *T. S. Eliot and Ideology*. Cambridge: Cambridge UP, 1995.

Baldick, Chris. *The Social Mission of English Literary Criticism, 1848–1932*. Oxford: Clarendon, 1983.

Bateson, F. W. "T. S. Eliot: Impersonality Fifty Years After." *Southern Review* 3 (1969): 630–39.

Blackmur, R. P. *Form and Value in Modern Poetry*. Garden City, NY: Doubleday, 1957.

Bradbrook, M. C. "My Cambridge." *Women and Literature, 1779–1982*. Brighton, Sussex: Harvester, 1982. 113–23.

Brooks, Cleanth. *Modern Poetry and the Tradition*. Chapel Hill: U of North Carolina P, 1939.

——. "New Criticism." *The New Princeton Encyclopedia of Poetry and Poetics*. Ed. Alex Preminger and T. V. F. Brogan. Princeton: Princeton UP, 1993.

——. "T. S. Eliot: Thinker and Artist." Tate, *T. S. Eliot* 316–32.

——. *The Well-Wrought Urn: Studies in the Structure of Poetry*. New York: Harcourt, 1947.

Brooks, Cleanth, and Robert Penn Warren. *Understanding Poetry*. 3rd ed. New York: Holt, 1950.

Cowan, Louise. *The Fugitive Group: A Literary History*. Baton Rouge: Louisiana State UP, 1959.

Empson, William. *Seven Types of Ambiguity*. London: Chatto, 1930.

I'll Take My Stand: The South and the Agrarian Tradition. New York: Harper, 1930.

Jancovich, Mark. *The Cultural Politics of the New Criticism*. Cambridge: Cambridge UP, 1993.

Krieger, Murray. *The New Apologists for Poetry*. Westport, CT: Greenwood, 1956.

Leavis, F. R. *New Bearings in English Poetry*. London: Chatto, 1932.

Lentricchia, Frank. *After the New Criticism*. London: Athlone, 1980.

McDonald, Gail. *Learning to be Modern: Pound, Eliot, and the American University*. Oxford: Clarendon, 1993.

Ransom, John Crowe. *The New Criticism*. Norfolk, CT: New Directions, 1941.

——. *The World's Body*. New York: Scribner, 1938.

Richards, I. A. "On TSE." Tate, *T. S. Eliot* 1–10.

——. *Practical Criticism: A Study of Literary Judgment*. London: Routledge, 1929.

——. *Principles of Literary Criticism*. London: Kegan Paul, 1924.

——. *Science and Poetry*. London: Kegan Paul, 1926.

Shapiro, Karl. *In Defense of Ignorance*. New York: Random, 1960.

Spurlin, William J., and Michael Fischer. *The New Criticism and Contemporary Literary Theory: Connections and Continuities*. New York: Garland, 1995.

Tate, Allen. *Collected Essays*. Denver: Swallow, 1959.

——, ed. *T. S. Eliot: The Man and His Work*. London: Chatto, 1967.

Tillyard, E. M. W. *The Muse Unchained: An Intimate Account of the Revolution in English Studies at Cambridge*. London: Bowes, 1958.

Webster, Grant. *The Republic of Letters: A History of Postwar American Literary Opinion*. Baltimore: Johns Hopkins UP, 1979.

Wimsatt, W. K., and Monroe Beardsley. *The Verbal Icon: Studies in the Meaning of Poetry*. Lexington: U of Kentucky P, 1954.

Woolf, Virginia. *The Diary of Virginia Woolf*. Ed. Anne Olivier Bell. Vol. 3. New York: Harcourt, 1980.

35
"T. S. Eliot rates socko!": Modernism, Obituary, and Celebrity

Aaron Jaffe

T. S. Eliot rates socko!

What more do you say about Eliot and celebrity?

In 1958, *Variety*, trade paper of the entertainment industry, used precisely this headline, composed in its own patented *Variety* "slanguage" ("Hix Nix Stix Pix," etc.), to assess the significance of Eliot's draw on the lecture circuit: "Recent appearances of T. S. Eliot on Texas Campus showed the B.O. [box office] potential of the proper presentation of a literary biggie reading his own works. Rapt houses . . . heard the United States-born British poet give quiet, non-histrionic, but socko readings" (qtd. in Thompson 5.) Discovering Eliot's mass-entertainment "potential" – becoming suddenly aware that highbrow cultural goods are whammo – is somewhat akin to Molière's bourgeois gentleman's self-revelation about speaking in prose. Old news can be continually surprising. *Variety* had long run coverage on highbrow topics, and, not three years earlier, Eliot was garnering boffo exposure for packing in stadiums at the University of Minnesota (Ackroyd 317).

Before chalking up this reception to a typically American response to the return of its prodigal Nobel laureate, consider the press-clipping's existence in the files of the London offices of the International PEN Club. That PEN, the world association of writers, an international nongovernmental organization, and an official consultant on literary matters to UNESCO, hired a transnational press-clipping service to keep abreast of Eliot's star power should also be no surprise. Entities like PEN occupy an important, frequently ignored, middle space in the field of cultural production, where forms of elite and popular culture are collected, revalued, and promoted in various social, political, and economic ways. As such, the International PEN is as keen as *Variety* in tracking and celebrating what are, in *Variety*'s terms, the big names and pre-sold properties.

In due course, shortly after Eliot's death in 1965, for instance, PEN proposed rechristening its headquarters Eliot House – having first sounded the scuttlebutt

A Companion to T. S. Eliot, First Edition. Edited by David E. Chinitz.
© 2014 John Wiley & Sons, Ltd. Published 2014 by John Wiley & Sons, Ltd.

among the membership concerning Eliot's anti-Semitism. What quashed the scheme in the end was less the menace of bad publicity than the resistance of the literary executors. Making Eliot's name a standard for rallying donors rated as a step too mercenary to be plausibly denied as a form of publicity, which, as I have argued elsewhere, must be conspicuously cordoned off from elite modernist literary work.[1] This minor episode in the career of Eliot's reputation manifests a characteristic tension: promotion signals the wearing away of literary value, while literary celebrity modulates between strategies of control and feelings of ambivalence.

Eliot is hot; Eliot is cold. In all cases, the more exposed and diffused Eliot is as a cultural signifier before diverse publics, the more the signifier means, to borrow Simon Critchley's phrase, little, almost nothing.[2] Taking a cue from the film *Art School Confidential* (2005), Eliot's name may sound today like little more than a peculiar, atavistic incantation of a cultural form now past. It comes up during a TV interview, when an art instructor played by John Malkovich ponders an art student of his who has achieved something of a *succès de scandale*: "Should we judge an artist by what he does in his personal life? If he's an anti-Semite, like T. S. Eliot, or a bully, like Picasso, or in this case, a murderer, does that mean his art has any less value? I think not!" (175). Just as "Picasso" serves as little more than a byword for the endurance of the artist's name over objectionable bad manners, "Eliot" becomes a cliché for its precedence over objectionable bigotry. What Zygmunt Bauman calls "liquid life" – celebrity at its most ubiquitous extreme – draws little consequence from the difference between notoriety and fame. So too, it marks little distinction between Eliot and Picasso. The chief risk could be described as something like a semiotic red shift, to borrow a metaphor from astronomy for the observable shift in the spectrum of starlight, signaling an ever-expanding universe. The celebrity universe is similarly ever expanding, and death in the celebrity firmament happens not with a bang but a whimper, cold and quiet like interstellar background noise. The very ubiquity of the system – the numerosity of cultural means and ends – undermines its capacity to bear elite cultural value.

It is a critical commonplace that Eliot's passing happened well removed from the many scenes and achievements with which his name is associated. He died, in so many words, in the throes of postmodernism, far from the heady days of modernist innovation. Yet the obituaries that pursued him after death provide a crucial archive for charting his literary reputation *in extremis*, and, by extension, for exploring what happens to modernist celebrity beyond its death drive. What then do Eliot's obituarists – the first collectors of his posthumous reputation – have tell us about literary reputation as such? So much about what will be heard subsequently – the associations that circulate thereafter – is gathered and organized for this moment of Eliot's passing. After obituary, the writer becomes, in effect, his or her own notion, which, all too often, signals a foundational distortion (Alterno). Reputation is overburdened from the start by conditions of decay, and, despite the exaggerated posing of artistic consciousness in the production of modernist texts – or because of it – a modernist reputation presents itself in places of consumption beset by its own devaluation.

Specifically, this chapter concerns what this untimely archive might tell us about Eliot's cultural coinage, the afterlife of his literary reputation, and the afterlife of literary reputation per se. On this last topic, Eliot was, in his critical writings and elsewhere, among the archest strategists and the most influential thinkers of the twentieth century, only to be finally eclipsed, perhaps, by Harold Bloom, the prominent and prolific American literary critic, with his influential book *The Anxiety of Influence* in 1973. Yet, like Bloom, Eliot was a proponent of a model of literary reputation that functions beyond what is conventionally ascribed to authorial control. Indeed, one of the aims of this chapter is to show hidden historical continuity between two very different kinds of critics about a matter on which they are often held at odds.

Eliot's tremendous reputation was earned in many ways over his career, but it never rested on literary merits alone. It was also made by him and others in a speculative market of sorts, in modernism's critical regimes, material practices, and cultural institutions and in the many scenes where modernist value was materially formed, regulated, and promoted. With the big bang of cultural materials and consumers in the nineteenth century, making and retaining elite literary reputation was more problematic than ever, and one way to think about all the beguiling difficulty and intimidating originality that comes with modernism is as a strategic response in a culture of ubiquity, aimed at preserving high regard for rarefied aesthetic value. Paradoxically, modernist cultural signatures served as a promotional idiom for publicizing and disseminating a message about inscrutability and inaccessibility far and wide. Eliot had an active role in founding and preserving this idiom, and, following his death, with his own reputation no longer subject to active authorial involvement, his hand in institutionalizing this regime not only informed his immediate posthumous reception but also defined a controlling presence that continues to haunt the cultural economies of literary reputation and influence more generally.

T. S. E., the poet of multiple monuments, numerous cenotaphs, and repeated burials, is the very paragon for the distinctly modernist sense that literary lives, readers, and resources exist under threat of extinction. "In my beginning is my end / In my end is my beginning": so reads the expatriate Eliot's epitaph in a corner of an alien land simultaneously overdetermined as his ancestral parish (*CPP* 123, 129). His ashes were buried there in a private family funeral. "Thomas Stearns Eliot," C. Day Lewis writes in the *Times* obituary, "came [to England] of a New England family which had emigrated from the Somerset village of East Coker – a village which gave its name to one of his most famous poems and will now give the shelter of its church to his ashes." Thus, the uncanny circumscription of home and homelessness becomes as pronounced in the newspapers – wherein the circuit returning Eliot's name to its English origins is often remarked – as it ever was in the second of Eliot's *Four Quartets*. The bodiless second monument authorized with and animated by literary signatures is Eliot's memorial in Westminster, the much more public ceremony attended by the good and the great, a plaque unveiled the following year in Poet's Corner proximate the English literary pantheon. "The communication of the dead is tongued with fire beyond the

Figure 35.1 Photo by James R. Potts. Used by permission of the photographer

language of the living": thus reads the second epitaph (*CPP* 139). Both markers include fitting mottoes from the late Eliotic corpus – lines from "East Coker" and "Little Gidding," respectively – that supply the obituarists with ready-made modes of ingress into the lifework (see Figure 35.1). Eliot's reduction to clichés – the minting of his worn coins – begins with scenes of reading "Eliot," and *Four Quartets*, above all, as an impossible cache of instructions for his own burial ceremonies.[3]

The stone in Poets' Corner, "the crowning memorial," was laid January 4, 1967. During the ceremony, Christopher Fry read the pertinent lines from "Little Gidding" (Westminster 6–7). A number of the obituarists make hay of Eliot's neighbors there, Henry Wadsworth Longfellow and Robert Browning, and, according to biographer Lyndall Gordon, Eliot long coveted placement there, having obtained a photograph of Poets' Corner "with Dryden in the foreground" "some time after [his] arrival in England" (528). Literally speaking, the good and great at the public ceremony included Ezra Pound, Stephen Spender, Henry Moore, Peggy Ashcroft, and representatives of President Johnson, the Prime Minister, and the Queen. Alec Guinness, who starred in the original production of *The Cocktail Party*, recited passages from Eliot's later works, and the music included Stravinsky and Beethoven, the latter of which, according to Gordon, Eliot himself selected for the event as early as the late 1940s. Tellingly, it is here also that the now worn coin of the "objectionable Eliot" passes into circulation. "I said recently to a well-known Oxbridge don," Spender recounts,

> that I thought it strange that no member of the cultural branch of the British Labour government – neither Miss Jennie Lee nor Lord Snow – had attended the Westminster Abbey Memorial Service to Eliot. [He] replied that it was entirely appropriate that a

man with the liberal views of C. P. Snow should have abstained from paying homage to the author of the unfortunate "Burbank with a Baedeker: Bleistein with a Cigar." (59)

If Eliot had at least two burials, it only stands to reason that there be at least two Eliots. Pound's short obituary for Eliot takes this much for granted. Pound documents not only his attending two ceremonies but also his tending *two* missing companions:

> For T. S. E.
>
> His was the true Dantescan voice – not honored enough, and deserving more honor than I ever gave him.
>
> I had hoped to see him in Venice this year for the Dante commemoration at the Giorgio Cini Foundation – instead: Westminster Abbey. But, later, on his own hearth, a flame tended, a presence felt.
>
> Recollections? let some thesis-writer have the satisfaction of "discovering" whether it was in 1920 or '21 that I went from Excideuil to meet a rucksacked Eliot. Days of walking – conversation? literary? . . . Who is there now for me to share a joke with?
>
> Am I to write "about" the poet Thomas Stearns Eliot? or my friend "the Possum"? Let him rest in peace. I can only repeat, but with the urgency of 50 years ago: READ HIM. (109)

Something more than a missing readership is askew in this multiplication of Eliots. First, an Eliot who never arrives. Then, an Eliot lying in state. Then, a ghostly Eliot, alluding to "Little Gidding," perhaps:

> some dead master
> Whom I had known, forgotten, half recalled
> Both one and many; in the brown baked features
> The eyes of a familiar compound ghost
> Both intimate and unidentifiable. (*CPP* 140)

And then last, the rucksacked, playful Eliot. This last Eliot, then, the obscure, intimate Eliot, with whom Pound shared jokes and walks in southern France: is he the hidden biographical signified, the one that invites the most human treatment, akin to the object of desire Ian Hamilton describes so well in his account of his futile attempt to write J. D. Salinger's biography?[4] Is it this same Eliot who serves the hapless thesis-writer as an object of knowledge? Pound remembers the intimate, household Eliot chasing the troubadours in Southern France, that is, in the proprietary literary terrain of Ezra Pound. Who is buried where? Whom does Pound enjoin us to read? Thomas Stearns Eliot, the austere figure commemorated in Westminster, or "The Possum," the ghostly presence felt at the hearth? The public man and the private self – the familiar eulogistic dualism – won't easily reconcile. For T. S. E., there is no rest from scare quotes, no personal, private, or otherwise unmediated name, no uncirculated coin.

Of the dozen or so worn coins that circulate in the Eliot obituaries ("the Anglophile," "the Symptom," "the Originator," "the Pedant," "the Christian," "the Agèd Eagle," etc.), the one that seems to recycle most urgently is "the Possum." "The Possum" not only stands with his feet in southern France but also appears in nearly every one of the Eliot obituaries, in relation to all the other versions, and in the many economies of names, republics of letters, and literary firmaments there invoked. Rucksacked, solitaire-playing Eliot, connoisseur of cheeses, composer of children's verses: here, it seems, is the choice specimen in the collection that seems most "real" because it calls for actual human handling.

Yet, like the others, it trades on its spectral qualities, too. Like I. A. Richards's after him, William Empson's reminiscences – composed well before Eliot's literal death – begin with a sense of influence that is both invasive and illimitable, gesture toward "a universal rule of criticism," and quickly become "a witness to the Eliot legend," moving though a series of charmingly elusive, intimate, and obscure "Eliot anecdotes." Robert Giroux's trove of "trivial" anecdotes may be written to demonstrate that Eliot's demeanor was "wholly unlike the solemn pontifical manner that was generally ascribed to him," but the image that lingers is of Eliot as the Stone Guest ("like being invited to eat with a public monument and almost as frightening as shaking hands with the statue in Don Giovanni") (332). How personal can something be that is first experienced as a monument? For H. S. Davies, the first encounter also bespeaks an invitation to the living dead:

> [T]he effect of Eliot's poetry on me was in some ways oddly like what I had been assured I should get from *Dracula*, and had failed to find in it. [F]rom the imagery of deserts and waste places I got the kind of direct thrill which had failed to emerge from werewolves, ruined abbeys, and the rituals of necrophily. The language, too, struck me with that tang which, in the last analysis, can perhaps only be tasted fully from writing which is deeply and even violently contemporary. It was a shock wholly delightful to find that poetry could use "a selection of the language really used by men." The words were common, everyday, but what of that? They had behind them, to my mind, the terrific suggestiveness of words heard in dreams, of phrases spoken in nightmares. And my delight in this poetry was enhanced when my English master picked the book up from my desk one day, glanced at it for a few minutes, and handed it back with the advice that I should not waste my time on such "Bolshevik" stuff. (350)

The tang he tastes ("done by flashlight under the bed clothes") inevitably leads Davies to febrile experiments in "unspeakable and unreadable verses . . . full of desert scenery, red rocks, and rats' feet slithering over broken glass," to the society of "other young men from other schools with similar portfolios" up at Cambridge, and eventually – through Herbert Read – to an audience with Eliot himself. Bonamy Dobrée encounters a similar Eliot under different circumstances. This time "first awareness of Tom Eliot's existence" came at "the Palestine front" in 1917, E. M. Forster having slipped him a copy of *Prufrock and Other Observations*: "Here, I felt, was a poet who meant something in terms of today. I was becoming aware of a personality" (85–86). Only in 1924, invited to dine with Leonard and Virginia Woolf, does Dobrée meet Eliot in person, this time calling him the formal, sanctioned "T. S." (86).

The word *possum*, which means, the eulogists note, "I am able" in Latin, is also, of course, the familiar, vernacular form of *opossum*, an animal renowned for posing, for its ability to play dead. And there is something of a consummate performance (a "deliberate disguise," Richards calls it, quoting a phrase from "The Hollow Men") in the selecting of such an equivocal emblem as a sign of unmediated Eliotic authenticity (its origin conspicuously outsourced to better maker Pound) (26). "Sometimes I pose and sometimes I pose that I pose," writes Richards in this regard, suggestively applying to Eliot a phrase of Stella Benson's (26–27). Decisively, the redoubled pose does not return unmediated authenticity. That "the Possum" was equivocal, exaggerated, even impossible as a pose of presence is mentioned often in the Eliot obituaries. Eliot never quite seemed fully there even when he was. Dobrée writes, for instance, that his "Personal Reminiscence" comes from "a very individual sense of presence, which it is impossible to communicate," a sense conveyed by "the significance of that particular glance at that particular moment, the pressure of the handshake just then" (85). It is as if even the attempt to affirm the authenticity of Eliot's persona escapes definitive articulation. Richards recalls that Eliot had a "repertory of more or less confessed poses which his friends were not debarred from seeing through." Above all, he continues, Eliot had "the delicately perceptible trace, the ghostly flavor of irony which hung about his manner as though he were preparing a parody" (26). With Eliot gone, Richards is left recollecting phantasma of self-concealment. If Eliot's absence implies "delicately perceptible traces" of his presence, his presence also entails just as obscure traces of his inevitable absence, a feeling which connects fairly explicitly to notions of his posthumous reputation and influence.

Stephen Spender adds to the catalog of Eliots: "the Eliot of whom it was rumored that he was being converted to Christianity," "the unredeemed Eliot . . . more real to us," and the possibility of "a street-haunting dandified nightbird Eliot" (68). The last – Eliot in Nightown, in green face powder, perhaps – approximates the promise of "the Possum." Spender detects this particular foretaste in Eliot's personal exertions for younger poets: "Religiously, poetically, and intellectually, this very private man kept an open house. And all the rooms, and the garden, made clear sense. Yet in spite of all this, he was sly, ironic, a bit cagey, a bit calculating perhaps, the Eliot . . . called 'Old Possum'" (68). And, why this "in spite of all this"? The interpretive bridge between Eliot's deliberately solicitous disguises and the claims of Eliotic influence on new poets gets lost in Spender's syntactical about-face. Working through Eliotic influence as a mannered seduction means seeing these two particular Eliots – the one who attracts and the one who repels – as inextricably linked rather than at odds. Both the modernist regime of scarcity – its privileging of tightly controlled literary output and a small canon of innovators – and the modernist unease about plagiarism are paradigmatically connected with Eliot's name, because he was a noted strategist and practitioner of the former and because his citationally rich poetry, which inspired so much subsequent "imitation," actually elicited charges of the latter from certain quarters (Jaffe, *Modernism* 80–93). Condensing an argument I make more substantively elsewhere, modernist value – its tremendous cultural influence – depended in some part on the sense that its cultural objects and their producers were rarified and irreproducible originals and that the zones of influence, imitation, and literary proximity were therefore hazardous. In this vein, Spender recalls a nightmarish occasion when he is called on to give a lecture about Yeats with Eliot sitting in the respondent's chair; every time Spender comes to Yeats's name, he finds himself, to his horror, slipping and substituting Eliot's. Being Eliot is not merely a matter of not being Yeats, it also means prepossessing Spender.

"He abhorred disciples and his imitators bored him," writes Allen Tate (386). Such projected rejection is a fundamental condition of modernist value. Tate – correctly, I think – attributes its origins to Eliot himself; the structure of feeling may later become an "anxiety of influence," but it begins with modernism's exclusionary strategies of reputation and promotion. In *The Listener*, Auden's obituary follows suit:

> It is often said that *The Waste Land* has been the most influential poem of the twentieth century. So far as Anglo-American poetry is concerned, I am not sure that this is the case. That is to say, when reading a poet who found his own voice after 1922, I often come across a cadence or trick of diction which makes me say "Oh, he's read Hardy, or Yeats, or Rilke," but seldom, if ever, can I detect an immediate, direct influence from Eliot. His indirect influence has, of course, been immense, but I should be hard put to it to say exactly what it is. (5)

In his obituary in *The New Statesman*, Frank Kermode transforms Auden's assessment into the notable formula that "Eliot cannot be imitated, only parodied" ("Dialect" 227).

The feeling of resistance to Eliotic imitation and influence, pervasive in his obituaries, finds a counterbalance in an equally pervasive sentiment expressed by William Empson:

> I do not propose here to try to judge or define the achievement of Eliot; indeed I feel, like most other verse writers of my generation, that I do not know for certain how much of my own mind he invented, let alone how much of it is a reaction against him or indeed a consequence of misreading him. He has a very penetrating influence, perhaps not unlike an east wind. (152)

Auden and Empson, each in his way identified as an Eliot successor, are both haunted by Eliotic influence, but it is a sense of influence tempered by its failure, by a presence that never quite takes hold. Austin Warren echoes the Empson sentiment:

It is not possible for me to think of T. S. Eliot as dead. If this is for many reasons, it is chiefly because his transferable self has so entered mine that I no longer – for long – have needed to reread him and because I can no longer quote, from his criticism, without dubiety whether I am paraphrasing him or expressing my own views. (272)

Richards picks up on it, too:

In talking of a writer we have known – and to those whom he has mattered – how can we speak without feeling that he himself is by far the most important part of the audience? And indeed he is, not in any supernatural or transcendent sense, but as represented here now, in minds which are in a measure what they are through him, so that in their judgment and reflection he is active. Of no one is this more true than of TSE. In one degree or another we are all products of his work. (21–22)

There could not be a better description of the economics of modernist reputation than these foretastes and aftertastes of Eliot. A coherent line connects this TSE (internalized, ever-present, undead) to the comments about the "delicately perceptible trace" of absence when confronted with "the Possum" (externalized, anecdotal, dead), arcing back over numerous scenes of reading and criticism to the implied Eliot circumscribed in the "silent motto" of "East Coker": "In my beginning is my end . . . In my end is my beginning." This connection closes a circle of strategies of authorial control extending from Eliot's output to the multiple, seemingly uncontrollable scenes of Eliot's posthumous reception and reputation.

In effect, the worn Eliot coin that recycles most urgently has two sides: heads, in Kermode's words, is the feeling that "Eliot cannot be imitated, only parodied"; tails, in Empson's, is the feeling that "I do not know for certain how much of my own mind [Eliot] invented, let alone how much of it is a reaction against him or indeed a consequence of misreading him." In their obituaries, Richards, Kermode, Empson, Auden, Spender, Leavis, C. Day Lewis, Muriel Bradbrook, Helen Gardner, Allen Tate, Austin Warren, Robert Lowell, and others all invoke versions of sides one, two, or both. And then, there's Marianne Moore's obituary for Wallace Stevens that invokes them both vicariously for Stevens: Moore recalls a lecture by Stevens at Mt. Holyoke:

A moment of silence made conspicuous, [then] this question: "Mr. Stevens, what do you think of the *Four Quartets?*" The answer was quick: "I've read them of course, but I have to keep away from Eliot or I wouldn't have any individuality of my own" – an answer which in its scientific unevasiveness seemed a virtual self-portrait. (582)

On one level, Stevens's "scientific unevasiveness" – for owning up to his evasion of Eliot's influence, no less – says as much or more about Eliot than it does about Stevens. It puts a point on the clinical evasiveness of Eliotic influence, for one thing. The repeated "failures" of influence, read another way, become a *form* of influence. In fact, as demonstrated in anecdote after anecdote, this is the Eliotic brand of influence *par excellence.* Following the obituaries, in the almost 50 years after Eliot's death, this structure of feeling has become part of modernism's promotional idiom, formalized and bound up in the dehistoricized version of literary influence that is now the presumed model, a model so predominant that it defines whatever critical discussion that topic still elicits. What I am getting at here is a historical path from the notions of reputation circulating in T. S. Eliot's obituaries to the influential model of influence Harold Bloom advances eight years later in *The Anxiety of Influence*.

Eliotic influence is influence modulated by its failure, presence which never quite takes hold. Richards asks, "Would it not be an excellent thing if this sense of the presence of TSE compelling one to speak as though the author were here at one's side listening to one's every inflection, could become a universal rule of criticism?" (21–22). Crucially, it is a specific response that Eliot elicits that becomes the flaming sword across the gates of influence, something akin to a universal rule of criticism. In Kermode's obituary, among other places, the feeling becomes a governing "imperative of modernism" more generally. The lesson of Eliot, writes Kermode,

> was that the craft of poetry can no longer be a matter of perpetuating dialects and imitating what was well made; it lies in an act of radical analysis, a return to brute form; but last year's words will not find it. In consequence, the writing of major poetry seems more than ever before a ruinous and exhausting undertaking, and no poet deserves blame for modestly refusing to take it on, or even coming to think of Eliot and his peers as Chinese walls across their literature. ("Dialect" 228)

Given this feeling and the looming presence of, for instance, Yeats, Milton, and Johnson in the Eliot obituaries of 1965, it may not be too extravagant, I think, to speculate that much of Harold Bloom's Milton, the protagonist of *The Anxiety of Influence*, published in 1973, is in fact a displacement of Milton's literary nemesis, Eliot. A cartoon in *The New Statesman*, for instance, depicts Milton hanging out with Shakespeare in the literary firmament awaiting Eliot's arrival. "When he does get here," says Milton angrily, "I've got a bone to pick with him" (see Figure 35.2). Even as Eliot's reputation seemed to be "rapidly eroding among poets," the idea of internecine posthumous rivalry and contest was becoming *au courant* from out of the scenes of this erosion (Perkins 7).

If Milton is "the hidden side of Eliot," as Kermode writes ("his schismatic traditionalism, his romantic classicism, his highly personal impersonality"), then Eliot is – or, he will become – the Milton of Bloom ("Dialect" 228). Above all, it is the notion that greatness may be measured in terms of "bad influence" – the central preoccupation of Eliot's two essays on Milton – that ties this unlikely pair together (*OPP* 138–39). In the second Milton essay, Eliot approvingly cites Dr. Johnson on Milton (in turn citing Ben Jonson on Spenser): "he *wrote no language*, but has formed . . . a *Babylonish dialect*, in itself harsh and barbarous, but made by exalted genius and extensive learning the vehicle of so much instruction and so much pleasure, that . . . we find grace in its deformity" (*OPP* 154). Grace in deformity. Turning Eliot back on himself, Kermode titles his obituary "A Babylonish Dialect," thus reminding

Figure 35.2 "T. S. Eliot Dies," by Wally Fawkes ("Trog"). Used by permission of the cartoonist

readers that Eliot helped popularize the charge of which he stands much accused. In his second Milton essay, Eliot writes: "[T]here are the great poets from whom we can learn negative rules: no poet can teach another to write well, but some great poets can teach others some of the things to avoid" (155). The citations of bad influence – the layer cake of Kermode, Eliot, Johnson, Milton, Jonson, Spenser – lead us directly to Bloom and his great chains of literary being, as in, for example, "Milton is the central problem in any theory and history of poetic influence in English; perhaps more so even than Wordsworth, who is closer to us than he was to Keats" (33).

Where Bloom is overblown, "Possum" is overmodest, prudently framing his cognate theory as a rhetorical question: "Even if we assert, what can only be a manner of faith, that Keats would have written a very great epic poem if Milton had not preceded him, is it sensible to pine for an unwritten masterpiece, in exchange for one which we possess and acknowledge?" (*OPP* 152). Of course, for Eliot, the anti-Freudian, the schematic comes without the Oedipal drama (or, with it still latent, if you prefer). Yet, Bloom, the deliberate Freudian, can't help slipping into his own Oedipal complex with Eliot as influence. First, symbolic violence comes through omission: "Milton is the ancestor, Wordsworth the great revisionist; Keats and *Wallace Stevens* among others, the dependent heirs" (*Anxiety* 33; emphasis added). Later, it comes through resistance: as a self-described anti-Eliot ("Jewish, liberal, Romantic"), Bloom declares himself largely unmoved by Eliot's "polemical stance as a literary critic," unaffected by "his rhetorical stance as a poet," and absolutely churned up about "his cultural position [as] Anglo-Catholic, Royalist and Classical" ("Reflections" 70). And finally, it comes through the following subversion: "It is the pattern of Eliot's figurations that is most High Romantic, a pattern I suspect he learned from Tennyson and Whitman, who derived it from Keats and Shelley, who in turn were instructed by Wordsworth's crisis lyrics and odes, which go back yet further to Spenserian and Miltonic models" ("Reflections" 71–72).

At the moment of another commemoration of Eliot, the centenary, Bloom has what promises to be a moment of clarity. He goes so far as to tie his academic emergence – throwing in the Yale critics, by implication – to the symbolic death of Eliot (70–71). All this notwithstanding, one of the ways modernist valuation is smuggled under the "Chinese walls" into the present – among other cunning passages – is through Bloom's own highly Eliotic model of poetic reputation, with its desperately schematic insistence on prioritizing and economizing the minds which create. It is now possible to see these diagrammatic distortions of literary history as – to adapt Kermode's assessment of Eliot's critical work – "highly personal versions of stock themes in the history of ideas of the period," a period which we have not as of yet superseded (230).

NOTES

1 This information paraphrases materials held by the McFarlin Library at the University of Tulsa and the Ransom Center at the University of Texas. On imprimaturs, see Jaffe, *Modernism* 9–14, 18–20.

2 For a discussion of circulation of the posthumous literary name in post-literate culture, see Jaffe, "Joyce's Afterlives."

3 See, for example, the framing of Helen Gardner's *Art of T. S. Eliot* and Perkins 24–31,

especially the final paragraph. For the first Westminster ceremony, see Spender 59, Sencourt 235–36, Gordon 525–26, and Matthews 181–83. Also see Matthews for a full list of memorials and epitaphs.

4 The desire for such referents is particularly manifest in the Eliot obituary literature. Cf. the role of Emily Hale in Lyndall Gordon's *T. S. Eliot: An Imperfect Life* or Jean Verdenal in Carole Seymour-Jones's *Painted Shadow*.

REFERENCES AND FURTHER READING

Ackroyd, Peter. *T. S. Eliot: A Life*. New York: Simon, 1984.

Alterno, Letizia. "Raja Rao's Reputation: 'A Penniless Writer Amongst VIPs.'" Seminar Presentation. The Writer's Reputation: Gender, Time, Geography. Durrell School of Corfu. Corfu, Greece. 3–8 June 2007.

Auden, W. H. "T. S. Eliot, O.M.: A Tribute." *Listener* 7 Jan. 1965: 5.

Bauman, Zygmunt. *Liquid Life*. Cambridge: Polity, 2005.

Benjamin, Walter. "Unpacking My Library." *Illuminations*. Trans. Harry Zohn. New York: Schocken, 1968. 59–68.

Bloom, Harold. *The Anxiety of Influence: A Theory of Poetry*. Oxford: Oxford UP, 1973.

——. "Reflections on T. S. Eliot." *Raritan* 8 (1988): 70–87.

Clowes, Daniel. *Art School Confidential: A Screenplay*. Seattle: Fantagraphics, 2006.

Davies, H. S. "Mistah Kurtz: He Dead." *Sewanee Review* 74 (1966): 349–357.

Day Lewis, C. "Mr. T. S. Eliot, O.M., The Most Influential English Poet of His Time." *Times* 5 Jan. 1965: 12.

Dobrée, Bonamy. "T. S. Eliot: A Personal Reminiscence." *Sewanee Review* 74 (1966): 85–108.

English, James. *The Economy of Prestige*. Cambridge, MA: Harvard UP, 2005.

Empson, William. "The Style of the Master." *T. S. Eliot: A Collection of Critical Essays*. Ed. Hugh

Kenner. Englewood Cliffs, NJ: Prentice, 1962. 152–54.

Gardner, Helen. *The Art of T. S. Eliot.* 1949. London: Cresset, 1961.

Giroux, Robert. "A Personal Memoir." *Sewanee Review* 74 (1966): 331–38.

Gordon, Lyndall. *T. S. Eliot: An Imperfect Life.* New York: Norton, 1999.

Goux, Jean-Joseph. *Symbolic Economies After Marx and Freud.* Trans. Jennifer Curtiss Gage. Ithaca, NY: Cornell UP, 1990.

Hamilton, Ian. *In Search of J. D. Salinger.* London: Heinemann, 1989.

Jaffe, Aaron. "Joyce's Afterlives: Why Didn't He Win the Nobel Prize?" *James Joyce: Visions and Revisions.* Dublin: Irish Academic P, forthcoming 2008.

——. *Modernism and the Culture of Celebrity.* Cambridge: Cambridge UP, 2005.

Kenner, Hugh. *The Pound Era.* Berkeley: U of California P, 1974.

Kermode, Frank. "A Babylonish Dialect." *Sewanee Review* 74 (1966): 225–37.

——. "Eliot's Dream." *The New Statesman* 19 Feb. 1965: 280–81.

Matthews, T. S. *Great Tom: Notes towards the Definition of T. S. Eliot.* New York: Harper, 1973.

Moore, Marianne. *The Complete Prose of Marianne Moore.* New York: Viking, 1986.

Perkins, David. *A History of Modern Poetry.* Cambridge, MA: Harvard UP, 1976.

Pound, Ezra. "For T. S.E." *Sewanee Review* 74 (1966): 109.

Richards, I. A. "On T. S.E." *Sewanee Review* 74 (1966): 21–30.

Sencourt, Robert. *T. S. Eliot: A Memoir.* London: Garnstone, 1971.

Spender, Stephen. "Remembering Eliot." *Sewanee Review* 74 (1966): 58–84.

Tate, Allen. "Postscript by the Guest Editor." *Sewanee Review* 74 (1966): 383–87.

Thompson, J. M. N. "American News Letter." *Evening Standard* 27 May 1958: 5.

Trog. "T. S. Eliot Dies." Cartoon. *The New Statesman* 8 Jan. 1965: 36.

Warren, Austin. "Eliot's Literary Criticism." *Sewanee Review* 74 (1966): 272–92.

Westminster Abbey. *Order of Service in Memory of Thomas Stearns Eliot, Born 26th September 1888, Died 4th January, 1965, Thursday, 4th February, 1965, 12 noon.* London: Hove Shirley, 1965.

36

Eliot's Critical Reception: "The quintessence of twenty-first-century poetry"

Nancy K. Gish

Looking back from the twenty-first century on early reviews of T. S. Eliot, we may find it difficult to imagine the intensity of both outrage and enthusiasm he aroused. His poetry has for so long been a part of our aesthetic and cultural landscape that whether praised as a great poet, denounced as the spokesman for an outdated and reactionary modernism, or reimagined as a more complex and fascinating voice of modernity, Eliot is now simply there, a defining part of our consciousness. Writing in 1950, Helen Gardner aptly summarized both the history of Eliot's reception and his standing at mid-century:

> Although among older readers there lingers still a certain irritation at what is called his "obscurity," and although in more sophisticated circles there are signs of the expected revolt against an established reputation, among the young of both sexes, with whom poetry is a passion, there is an unquestioned recognition of his poetic authority and of the profound importance of his poetry. (1)

Not only had Eliot acquired unquestioned authority, Gardner claimed, he had "by now created the taste by which he is enjoyed" (1).

Mildred Martin's bibliography of Eliot criticism from 1916 to 1965 contains 2,692 entries (303). To address even a small sample of this material is thus to limit and, in a sense, simplify. Some patterns of critical interest, however, are considered and reconsidered. During Eliot's lifetime, critics primarily read his poetry through the lens of his own prose: What makes a poet really new? How is a poet to be evaluated in relation to the tradition of English literature, and how is that tradition defined? How do Eliot's "notes" to *The Waste Land* reveal his own way of incorporating that tradition? How can the fragmented modern world and modern consciousness be represented, and can they be made coherent in terms of myth? What is the "music of poetry" or the "visual imagination"? Is the relation of poetry to the poet "impersonal"? Eliot's criticism, because it foregrounded these aesthetic and intellectual terms, discouraged

A Companion to T. S. Eliot, First Edition. Edited by David E. Chinitz.
© 2014 John Wiley & Sons, Ltd. Published 2014 by John Wiley & Sons, Ltd.

attention to personal and social context, and mainstream critical analysis consistently affirmed his own judgment. This unquestioning acknowledgement, as Jewel Brooker notes, changed in the decades after Eliot's death in 1965 to increasingly intense critique, and "it became as fashionable to vilify him as it had once been to praise him"; yet by the late nineties "Eliot and his fellow modernists had settled down among the classics" (xiii). Classic or not, however, Eliot is no longer the authority by which he is read, and our expanding new knowledge of his life, work, and ideas has reopened questions once thought resolved.

Eliot among the Reviewers

Initial reactions were not at all clear or firm.[1] In 1915, when "Prufrock" and "Portrait of a Lady" first appeared in *Catholic Anthology*, Conrad Aiken called the collection an anthology that "blows the horn of revolution in poetry" and that is "worth while if only for the inclusion" of those two poems. He described both as "psychological character studies, subtle to the verge of insoluble idiosyncrasy, introspective, self-gnawing," and he praised Eliot's musical free rhyme and atmosphere (Brooker 3). Arthur Waugh, in the *Quarterly Review*, saw, instead, "the unmetrical, incoherent banalities of these literary 'Cubists,'" threatening poetry with anarchy (4). With the publication in 1917 of *Prufrock and Other Observations*, these extreme reactions were reiterated in many reviews. Eliot's new and revolutionary poetry was championed by Ezra Pound, Conrad Aiken, May Sinclair, and Marianne Moore for its genius, keen intuitions and subtle technique, poignancy, and honesty. It was derided in the *Times Literary Supplement* and the *Literary World* for its lack of any "genuine rush of feeling" and its "experiments in the bizarre and violent" (Brooker 6, 7). William Carlos Williams called Eliot "a subtle conformist" and denounced the ending of "La Figlia che Piange" as "warped out of alignment, obscured in meaning even to the point of an absolute unintelligibility by the inevitable straining after a rhyme" (16–17). The *TLS*, reviewing the clever satiric *Poems* of 1919, saw Eliot as "in danger of becoming silly," and the *Athenaeum* reviewer asked, "Is This Poetry?" (21).

Whether positive or negative, these evaluations nonetheless see Eliot as creating something distinctly new and modern. They see the poems, on the one hand, as internal, subjective, personal; and, on the other, as external, objective, and impersonal. They claim forms of unity or disintegration, and they discuss techniques of free verse, a new music, distinctive uses of rhyme, direct and often sordid images, and a style that cuts transitions and explanations. These topics help to frame the many ways of reading Eliot's poetry, for the work of early criticism provided a foundation on which new perspectives could be developed. Perhaps most significantly, they suggest the diversity of opinion Eliot's work can still evoke and the reasons it remains new and challenging.

With the publication of his first collected works as *Ara Vos Prec* in England and *Poems* (1920) in America, the continuing question of what to make of Eliot assumed a note of urgency, as of a central defining problem for literature far broader than the critical balancing of a young poet's slim production. Thus, when *The Waste Land* provoked vehement renewed controversy, it was controversy over an already acknowledged major author. Critiques of his fragmentation, disillusion, and failure to communicate appeared from such formidable sources as John Crowe Ransom, Louis Untermeyer, and J. C. Squire; F. L. Lucas reacted to the mass of allusions by announcing that "Among the maggots that breed in the corruption of poetry one of the commonest is the bookworm" (Brooker 115–16). But *The Waste Land* won the *Dial* prize and the adulation not only of reviewers but of a generation of readers who claimed that it spoke for them. Edmund Wilson, in "The Poetry of Drouth," said it best:

> Mr. T. S. Eliot's first meager volume of twenty-four poems was dropped into the waters of contemporary verse without stirring more than a few ripples. But when two or three years had passed, it was found to stain the whole sea. . . . Mr. Eliot, with all his limitations, is one of our only authentic poets. (Brooker 83)

Wilson and other reviewers went beyond praise to offer extended analyses of the structures, themes, and sources in the poem, seeking ways to read this radical new work.

As Eliot's poetry changed, the problem of how to read it changed: recognizing new poetry of concrete images gave way to appreciating poetry of increasingly abstract visions of faith. With the appearance of *Ash-Wednesday* in 1930, a new pattern was discerned, not only a new kind of rhythm and image but a philosophical, spiritual, and emotional development in a major poet. Again, whether the new style seemed greater or lesser, it was approached as a serious poetic issue to be studied and understood in the context of a life's work and poetry's history. William Rose Benét's revealing commentary in the *Saturday Review* defines the shifting grounds of Eliot's audience. Admitting his distaste for "another distillation of Eliot's despair mixed with a rather hopeless appeal for aid from the Christian religion," and calling him "a modern anchorite," Benét nonetheless concludes that his own fundamentally different attitude to life makes "more remarkable the strong impression that the writing of T. S. Eliot leaves on our mind" (Brooker 185). Those who found the new theme of faith compelling shared his admiration but added their satisfaction in reading Eliot's work as a unified whole: they saw in *Ash-Wednesday* "a new stage of his life" that might portend the return of the "main English tradition" (177–78), a move beyond irony and "superficial qualities" to beauty (178), and, in hindsight, a search for religious faith as the theme of all his work. For Morton D. Zabel, Eliot's "experience remains one of the few authentic records of intellectual recovery in our time," and *Ash-Wednesday* along with the "Ariel Poems" represented "the opening cantos of his *Purgatorio*" (182, 183). This comparison with Dante's journey through hell, purgatory, and heaven now identified *The Waste Land* and earlier poems as Eliot's *Inferno*, pointing forward to spiritual renewal. Edmund Wilson, who had celebrated the early work, found the new style "less brilliant and intense" but a continuation of "most of the qualities which made his other poems remarkable": "exquisite phrasing," "metrical mastery," and "peculiar honesty" (Brooker 181–82). The curve of Eliot's career had become a major focus of analysis.

The *Four Quartets* were published individually from 1936 to 1942, and as a single sequence in 1943. As Jewel Brooker states, the reviews were "unusually substantial" because by this time they represented a "cumulative understanding" of Eliot's work (xxxii). They were also almost universally positive, Eliot having attained a status as the most important poet in English of his time. As with earlier work, not everyone agreed: George Orwell objected to a worldview that "turns its eyes to the past, accepts defeat, writes off earthly happiness as impossible, mumbles about prayer and repentance and thinks it a spiritual advance to see life as 'a pattern of living worms in the guts of the women of Canterbury'" (Brooker 455). But the majority of reviewers shared the view of Kathleen Raine, who responded to Orwell that Eliot "writes of what is most human . . . about love" (458). And Horace Gregory, echoing those who had found in *The Waste Land* the voice of their own time, stated, "It has been Mr. Eliot's destiny to anticipate, without seeming overtly prophetic, the mutations of feeling which have taken place within the past twenty years" (471). By the publication of *Four Quartets*, Eliot's importance was no longer in question, and critical focus moved to consideration of his formal and thematic innovations.

Early Approaches

For purposes of definition, early critical approaches to Eliot can be loosely identified by decade from the 1930s through the beginning of the 1960s. Despite the broad range of readings and reactions, a trajectory can be traced in a series of influential texts. Their focus moves from evaluation and historic placement of Eliot's experimental new style to elucidation of specific poems, a search for design in his work as a whole, and interpretation of meaning as it is revealed in source studies. Although analyses often overlap, they do not reach consistent patterns of judgment. They represent, instead, major ways of reading that were influential for several decades. In the 1930s three major texts helped to frame critical discussion of Eliot for much of his life. Edmund Wilson and F. R. Leavis identified what made his work new and placed him in a moment of poetic revolution. Cleanth Brooks defined *The Waste Land* as a "modern" poetic form that could be understood through study of Eliot's own theoretical prose.

In 1931 Edmund Wilson devoted a chapter to Eliot in *Axel's Castle*. Taking his cue from Eliot's acknowledgement of French Symbolist influence, Wilson placed him – with W. B. Yeats, James Joyce, Gertrude Stein, Marcel Proust, and Paul Valéry – in "the culmination of a self-conscious and very important literary movement" (1). This movement he called "a counterpart to Romanticism" yet "entirely distinct." "Literature," he claimed, "is rebounding again from the scientific-classical pole to the poetic-romantic one" (10); for the Symbolists this meant that French poetry became "capable of the fantasy and fluidity of English" as it had been developed in Elizabethan poets and dramatists and in seventeenth-century poets. Symbolism sought to make poetry approximate music and to make it "even more a matter of the sensations and emotions of the individual than had been the case with romanticism" (20).[2] Most importantly, it used symbols differently from their traditional and conventional functions: "the symbols of the Symbolist school are usually chosen arbitrarily by the poet to stand for special ideas of his own – they are a sort of disguise for these ideas" (20). Thus Eliot and Joyce brought back into English literature qualities it once had, but with a French "complexion": "critical, philosophical, much occupied with aesthetic theory and tending always to aim self-consciously at particular effects and to study scrupulously appropriate means" (24).

By placing Eliot in literary history as a Symbolist, Wilson illuminates his style and aesthetic aims. Thus in "Prufrock" he emphasizes Eliot's use of verse rhythms like Jules Laforgue's as well as his use of new vocabulary and new ways of feeling. He more fully examines Eliot's themes, however, finding a sense that "human life is now ignoble, sordid or tame." Eliot is "haunted and tormented by intimations that it has once been otherwise" (100). The consciousness of such characters as Prufrock and the lady of "Portrait of a Lady" combines idealism and sensibility with an experience of emotional starvation – a contrast whose "most complete expression" is *The Waste Land*. Wilson described the poem in terms that remained a defining view: "In our post-War world of shattered institutions, strained nerves and bankrupt ideals, life no more seems serious or coherent – we have no belief in the things we do and consequently we have no heart for them" (106). Wilson found *Ash-Wednesday* less brilliant, but he would say, soon after its publication, that Eliot was a "leader" because he has "evidently been on his way somewhere" (125). Although many later writers found the change an aesthetic as well as a spiritual progress, Wilson's initial readings now sound familiar because they focused so early on what critics subsequently came to accept as key elements in the work.

Published one year after *Axel's Castle*, F. R. Leavis's *New Bearings in English Poetry* sets out, as the title indicates, to define specifically what is new in English poetry, and, like Wilson, Leavis finds it primarily in Eliot's almost singular awareness of his own age. "The peculiar importance of Mr. T. S. Eliot" he attributes to the invention of "techniques that shall be adequate to the ways of feeling, or modes of experience, of adult, sensitive moderns" (25). His influence is all the greater, Leavis adds, because his criticism and poetry reinforce one another (25). Like Wilson, Leavis sees in Eliot a complete break with English poetry of the nineteenth century, which defies "the traditional canon of seriousness," and emphasizes the debt to Laforgue (75, 79). Like Wilson and early reviewers, he emphasizes also a new form of consciousness in a postwar world changed by the machine age and sordid urban existence. And, like Wilson, he sees in Eliot the reappearance of psychological complexities, vocabulary, and rich imagery absent from English since the Renaissance. He finds in "Gerontion," for example, a major advance because it is dramatic in an impersonal way, while

"Prufrock" and "Portrait" he sees as concerned with the "directly personal embarrassments, disillusions and distresses of a sophisticated young man" (83). "Gerontion," he claims, "has neither narrative nor logical continuity, and the only theater in which the characters mentioned come together, or could, is the mind of the old man" (84). This new technique allows for the recurring theme of "mixing memory and desire," for creating fresh and startling contrasts, and – by the persona of the old man – for "projecting himself, as it were, into a comprehensive and representative human consciousness" (83). For Leavis, this impersonality is developed to its extreme limit in *The Waste Land*, which he calls "an effort to focus an inclusive human consciousness" represented in Tiresias (95). Given the presence of this unified sensibility, the poem was, in fact, not fragmented but unified through an organization that might be called musical (103).

Both Wilson and Leavis define the literary history of their own time through the dramatic shift Eliot's poetry created. Moreover, by using Eliot's own notes and terminology, both set a style of criticism sustained through Eliot's lifetime and still central to critical debate. That critical debate had already, in reviews, moved increasingly toward elucidation and interpretation. A third major study of Eliot in the 1930s, Cleanth Brooks's "*The Waste Land*: A Critique of the Myth," took Eliot's Notes as a starting point. Brooks offered a systematic reading of the poem, explaining its overall meaning, explicating individual sections, and demonstrating a unified theme as well as a pattern of parallel and contrasting images and allusions. Moreover, in providing what he called a "scaffolding," Brooks framed an alternative reading of *The Waste Land* as not only unified and clearly structured but as beginning Eliot's poetic search for faith. According to Brooks, most critics, even and especially Edmund Wilson, had entirely missed the theme and structure of the poem. In reading it as a representation of disillusion and despair they had, he argued, provided a stock interpretation that not only failed to understand the poem but – in a profound and widespread failure – led to far more pervasive misconceptions: "the general interpretations of post-War poetry which begin with such a misinterpretation as a premise" (156). Thus *The Waste Land*, for Brooks, as for others, defined modern poetry; seeing Eliot as "a man of his own age," Brooks claimed Eliot could "indicate his attitude toward the Christian tradition" only as the "rehabilitation" of a system of beliefs (160–61).

The Waste Land, according to Brooks, depicted a spiritual waste land, but one whose images were not a simple contrast of glorious past and sordid present; rather, the images and allusions could all be understood in relation to the plan of Jessie Weston announced in Eliot's notes. All aspects of the poem – the "protagonist" who seeks spiritual renewal; the role of Madame Sosostris, who carries lost knowledge even though degraded herself; the allusions to dryness, rocks, bones, and especially sterility in sex and spiritual life – can be understood as modern spiritual versions of an ancient and universal myth. Similarly, the hyacinth girl, St. Magnus Martyr and the fishmen, the water, the reenactment of the drowned god, and the Fisher King can be seen in terms of potential renewal.

These associations are now familiar, but when Brooks wrote his analysis, he did so to critique most reviewers' conception of the poem as devoid of faith and belief. His essay became a classic treatment of the poem as a unified work of art based on ironic contrasts, a "prose meaning" identified in Eliot's notes, and a "protagonist" whose presence provides a continuing thread of experience. Most importantly, however, it defined Eliot's "modern" work as already grounded in a Christian meaning, one that became, for many critics, a lifetime's development revealed in the pattern of Eliot's poetry and a redefinition of postwar experience.

Entering the Books

Tracing this pattern of development formed the focus and method of the first complete books on Eliot. One, F. O. Mattheissen's *The Achievement of T. S. Eliot*, had appeared before Brooks's essay on *The Waste Land*. Like Brooks, Matthiessen developed a way of reading Eliot that remained classic for several decades. "His criticism," Matthiessen wrote, "steadily illuminates the aims of his verse, while his verse illustrates many aspects of his critical theory" (99). Devoting each chapter to a critical principle such as "Tradition," "The Objective Correlative," "The Auditory Imagination," or "The Sense of His Own Age," Matthiessen examines individual poems as illustrations of these principles, often placing extended commentary in his notes in order to leave the main text focused on theory. His primary purpose is to emphasize technique and poetic form as it is revealed in Eliot's work as a whole. Sharing Wilson's view of Eliot as "evidently on his way somewhere," Matthiessen also sees that movement as a sustained "Sense of His Own Age." Reading Eliot chronologically, he claimed, was to see him "become expert in one mode of presentation only to move on to something else" (134). In his first edition, Matthiessen's chronology ran from "Prufrock" through *Ash-Wednesday* and represented a move from "the dark consequences of loneliness and repression" to "the purified vision" (9, 150). By 1947, the date of the second edition, *Four Quartets* had been published; it served as a culmination in its "reconciliation of opposites" and its "resolution of man's whole being" (195). In *Four Quartets* Matthiessen saw the creation of a modern form for meditation: the poems reflect Eliot's own sense of the "music of poetry" as including transitional material with passages of greater or lesser intensity. Matthiessen defines Eliot's career through his development of formal techniques to articulate his changed experience and intentions.

Three other key texts of the 1940s define Eliot's overall poetic development. In Helen Gardner's *The Art of T. S. Eliot*, technique remains primary, while a final chapter formulates "An Approach to the Meaning." Elizabeth Drew, in *T. S. Eliot: The Design of His Poetry*, and Kristian Smidt, in *Poetry and Belief in the Works of T. S. Eliot*, emphasize meaning. What these three authors share with Matthiessen is a focus on the poetry as a single whole, revealing an aesthetic and thematic progress.

Elizabeth Drew begins with an explicit assumption that *"design"* is the impulse for all art, and that the function of criticism, using Eliot's term, is "elucidation": "Any exploration of the techniques of poetry is inextricably intermingled with the exploration of another element in design, 'the figure in the carpet,' and the attempt to elucidate that" (xi). Like Matthiessen, she takes her starting point from Eliot, adding to "design" an overarching study of myth and Eliot's theory that myth, by "manipulating a continuous parallel between contemporaneity and antiquity," could provide "a way of controlling, of ordering, of giving a shape and significance to the immense panorama of futility and anarchy which is contemporary history" (*SP* 177). She links this, however, with Carl Jung's psychology, which, she argues, reveals Eliot's own pattern of development as "the archetype of transformation" and "in non-symbolic language as the process of Individuation or the Integration of the Personality." This process involves detachment from "the world of objective reality as the centre of existence" and discovery of a new center other than ego: it describes a process of death to an old life and birth to a new life (12), and it parallels the myth described by Jessie Weston in *From Ritual to Romance*. Drew's analyses of the poems compare Eliot's images to Jung's dream symbols. She describes a move from early images of imprisonment in "futility and anarchy" to spiritual renewal in the "new redeeming symbols" of *Four Quartets* (99). Distinctive in its reliance on Jung, Drew's reading is nonetheless similar to others in an increasing elevation of Eliot as a figure of religious and spiritual as well as poetic authority.

Like Matthiessen and Drew, Kristian Smidt reads Eliot's work as a whole, drawing on both his own work and other sources. He focuses, however, less on Eliot's aesthetic theory than on his beliefs. Significantly, he emphasizes the personal sources of those beliefs in a way that Eliot's theory of impersonality had largely displaced. Though Eliot claimed to show in his poetry, not beliefs themselves, but what it feels like to believe in something, Smidt argues that to "feel positively" is itself to believe, and that Eliot's beliefs, drawing on "years of philosophical and theological studies" do affect readers "in other ways besides poetic enjoyment" (78). Thus, for Smidt, the poems, especially the longer ones, bear "the impress of permanently held ideas or a settled attitude to life" (77). Moreover, he claims, "the way in which a poet writes is an aspect of his beliefs" (78). This astute analysis of Eliot's aesthetics allows Smidt to recognize personal sources in the poetry, for beliefs as well as emotions are personal. Thus he writes that "we can hardly avoid recognizing some of the author's features under the mask of Prufrock" (86). And he argues that with *Four Quartets* "Eliot appears to have given up his impersonal theory and his technique of concealment almost entirely" (95).

Smidt's book is structured on concepts – Eliot's and those of philosophers and mystics he read. Notwithstanding an emphasis on the disparity and complexity of Eliot's thought structure, he concludes with a chapter on "Eliot's Synthesis": "If we view the attitudes and ideas of Eliot's poetry as a whole, we do find a striking correspondence and inter-relationship between those of the seemingly most disparate derivations" (223). In affirming the work as a synthesis, he shares with Matthiessen,

Drew, and Gardner a focus on wholeness. His wholeness, however, carries with it conflicting ideas and feelings, and is inseparable from the personal. For Smidt, Eliot's early poetry presents "something intermediate between objective description and personal confession" (87); Prufrock, for example, is "the poet and his fictitious character in one person," and "Eliot is present in this creature of his imagination" (86). Thus, in early works, Eliot's own voice is represented, in part, as a persona, while in later poetry it moves to the surface without disguise.

Helen Gardner's *The Art of T. S. Eliot* sustains the view of Eliot's life work as a "fundamental unity." With the benefit of hindsight and the influence of Matthiessen and Leavis, she offers new insights by focusing on *Four Quartets* and the development of Eliot's prosody. Her work added to the now-standard perception of Eliot as not only a great poet but one who "effected a modification and an enrichment of the whole English poetic tradition" (2). While Gardner's almost hyperbolic praise reflects the extraordinary standing Eliot had achieved, she justifies it, within Eliot's terms, by her rigorous and acute analysis of his style. It is the "style" – in all its complex elements – to which she attributes his status. She does not hesitate to link him even with Dante, as one who also, if with less range and scope, found a "*dolce stil nuovo*," a "sweet new style" (186).

The development of this style, because it finds its fullest expression in *Four Quartets*, frames Gardner's book. And because she focuses on style and form, she organizes her text, like Mattheissen's, on Eliot's own theoretical terms, primarily those that address language: "The Auditory Imagination," "The Music of Poetry," "Poetic Communication." Perhaps Eliot's greatest poetic achievement, she claims, is his creation of the characteristic meter of *Four Quartets*, which made possible "the variety of the diction, the union of the common word and the formal, the colloquial and the remote, the precise and the suggestive" (15). She traces this characteristic meter back to Spenser and the "new poetry" of the sixteenth century. In her exacting metrical analysis, Gardner demonstrates concretely the forms that had, from Wilson through Matthiessen, been seen as central to Eliot's revolution in style. For Gardner, this new style emerges in the later work, from *Ash-Wednesday* on: "One meaning of this, if not the principal one, is that from now on he will try to speak in his own voice, which will express himself with all his limitations, and not try to escape those limitations by imitating other poets" (20).

Thus, throughout the 1940s, a series of major critical studies emphasized Eliot's poetry as a unified achievement, to be read as an integrated design. It was Gardner who articulated the criteria for a "major poet," by which she placed Eliot in the position of "leader": he must, she claimed, "have bulk," a variety of "the greater poetic forms," subject matter of "universally recognized importance," "originality," something to say on human experience that is both "personal and of general relevance," and – most important – a "new and individual" idiom and rhythm "which become a classic" (3, 4). Critics in the following decades largely accepted these criteria and moved to developing what now seem standard readings of individual poems.

Establishing Standard Readings

Two books in particular – George Williamson's *A Reader's Guide to T. S. Eliot* and Grover Smith's *T. S. Eliot's Poetry and Plays* – provided massive research into the allusions, quotations, and sources comprising Eliot's own mining of Western literature. Of the two, Williamson's earlier study employs the more exacting – even restrictive – method of analysis. Working, like Drew, from an aesthetic principle that art *is* a form of order, Williamson offers a way of reading Eliot as formally ordered in individual poems and in the work as a whole. He argues for a fairly extreme form of coherence, order, and reason, rejecting outright the possibilities of multiple readings or poetry of the unconscious. While allusions can enrich the poet's meaning, he states, they cannot replace it, and for Williamson that meaning is rational and discovered through a formal pattern of syntax or the intentional sequence of ideas and feelings. Although "the more obvious signs of connection . . . may be missing," he insists the connections are "mental or psychological rather than verbal or grammatical" (17). In *The Waste Land*, for example, all the disparate images, scenes, and sources can be recognized as a logical structure which, "reduced to its simplest terms . . . is a statement of the experience that drives a character to the fortune-teller, the fortune that is told, and the unfolding of that fortune" (129–30). By translating what had been read as subconscious, nonrational, spatialized, and internal into a more familiar conscious, rational, linear, and openly intentional form, Williamson offered an Eliot understood as comprehensible if less dramatically experimental. At the same time, however, he provided often-astute readings of passages in the work.

One of the most thoroughly developed and extensively researched studies of all Eliot's work, and perhaps still the most detailed treatment of his sources, is Grover Smith's *T. S. Eliot's Poetry: A Study in Sources and Meaning*. Although Smith cites the influence of the other books discussed here, his "Preface" distinguishes his purpose from theirs. He is not, he makes clear, concerned with the relation of Eliot's poetry to his prose, or with biography. Rather, he "considers in particular the creative ideas behind each work and the literary echoes which enrich meaning" (vii). Moreover, to the extent that he addresses the work as a whole, he acknowledges a general shape rather than a continuous progression: "Yet, though his earlier poems now seem to point to this ultimate formulation [the "reconciliation" of *Four Quartets*], they were individual efforts to reach it themselves, every one a separate attempt to fulfill its own potentiality" (296).

Smith's readings, then, emphasize each poem's distinctive meaning and use of allusion and quotation. He does, however, see a standard poetic theme in "the idealist's quest for union with the vision forever elusive in this world" (6). And though he does not focus on biography, he challenges the long acceptance of "impersonality," which he calls a cliché; he sees, in the poetic personae, masks or forms of displacement in which early versions of desire as strictly sexual move toward a combination of sexual and spiritual motivation (28–29). Smith's use of terms like "spokesman," "Eliot's poetic voice," and "Dantean speaker" reflect his view that for Eliot impersonality was a series of masks and displacements. What the poems share, he claims, is not a continuing quest but themes of love, redemption, history, and poetry itself: these he considers Tiresias's "four categories of doubt," "permutations" of which appear from "The Hollow Men" through *Ash-Wednesday* and supply the four themes of *Four Quartets*.

Although Smith's book is primarily a study of sources, using Eliot's allusions and quotations as central, he takes a balanced stand on what works or fails, and his concluding evaluation is not uncritically admiring. He is refreshingly willing to challenge standard assumptions, expressing, for example, a certain sympathy with and even admiration for the vitality of a Sweeney and finding that "The Prufrockian temperament . . . does not come off well when put alongside the champions of fleshly joy" (29). Indeed, he concludes that Eliot's poetic vision "falters . . . because of its peculiar privacy, which admits no wide sympathies" (298). Even acknowledging that apart from W. B. Yeats's, Eliot's poetry "may include the greatest written in the contemporary age," Smith finds his vision remains that of the "isolated self" (298–99), one that uses "impersonality" as "dramatic camouflage" and only once, in "Portrait of a Lady," ever fully realizes an external character. Smith's overall estimate is thus a revealing attempt to reconsider the poetry outside the framework of Eliot's own terms.

By the end of the 1950s, Eliot's poetry had been intensively studied, yet its fascination remained. Other major critics continued to address it in new terms. Hugh Kenner, in 1959, called his book *The Invisible Poet*. Dismissing all prior criticism as having left Eliot uncomprehended, he rejected biography, personality, source study, and line-by-line explication to focus on, in his words, "the *nature* of what [Eliot] wrote and published in those early years, examining as minutely as we like what we are under no compulsion to translate or 'explain'" (xii). Eliot is concerned, he asserts, not with ideas but with effects, and he focuses on what he finds on the page. While Kenner concentrated on individual readings of the poems, in 1963 Northrop Frye published a critical biography with an early commentary on Eliot's cultural theories, which he found both "repellent" and present in the poetry. Frye, nonetheless, emphatically states that Eliot's poetic representations of "squalid mongrelism" and Jews, and his belief in "blood kinship" can be "clearly separated from Eliot's permanent achievement" (6, 10).

In the 1960s, critical anthologies on Eliot's work presented extensive overviews of major critical positions. What remain hardly visible are the cultural questions discussed elsewhere in this book. However Eliot is now read, these issues can no longer seem to be "clearly separated from" his achievement. In "Tradition and the Individual Talent," Eliot quoted an unnamed writer as saying "The dead writers are remote from us because we *know* so much more than they did." "Precisely," he added, "and they are that which we know"(*SE* 6). We now know so much more about Eliot than the reviewers and critics writing from 1916 to 1965 did that their specific analyses can seem misleading or even false. The facsimile edition of *The Waste Land*, with its mass of poems and sections not used in the published version, was unavailable at the time of Eliot's death. His early poems in *Inventions of the March Hare* were unpublished, and his Clark and Turnbull lectures, eventually published as *The Varieties of Metaphysical Poetry*, were uncollected and little noted. Almost nothing of his life was known beyond that of the public figure and some background on family and scholarly influences. Only in the 1970s were major biographical works to appear, including memoirs and initial scholarly studies along with challenging new readings based in Eliot's life. With the appearance of these revealing texts, broad but similar readings of the poems as impersonal, universal, unified in a quest for spiritual meaning, and based in a European high-art tradition no longer seem definitive or complete.

From the 1930s through the 1960s, Eliot's own authority largely defined how his poetry was to be read and what issues were significant. His own theory of impersonality, especially, effectively framed and even blocked discussion of his representations of gender, race, ethnicity, and culture. With increasing biographical information, the publication of early poems and prose, and changing ideas about the place of literature in culture, this authority gave way to new ways of reading. If we no longer doubt that "Prufrock" is poetry or wonder how to understand anything in *The Waste Land*, we doubt the certainties of much earlier analysis. In a sense, we have returned to the open questioning and sense of complexity in early reviews. Eliot remains a subject of continuing debate; as this book reveals, his work is still current, challenging, exciting, and controversial. A reviewer in 1917 (Brooker 9), admittedly puzzled by "The Love Song of J. Alfred Prufrock," remarked that "Mr. Eliot may possibly give us the quintessence of twenty-first-century poetry." Given the increasingly complicated figure we now see, that reviewer may have been prophetic.

NOTES

1 For the reviews cited here, I am relying on Jewel Brooker's edition, *T. S. Eliot: The Contemporary Reviews*. Her astute and thorough introduction covers reviews of all Eliot's work, including the criticism. For an overview of contemporary debates, see Cassandra Laity's rich and insightful introduction in Cassandra Laity and Nancy K. Gish, eds., *Gender, Desire, and Sexuality in T. S. Eliot* (Cambridge: Cambridge UP, 2004).

2 *See also* T. S. ELIOT AND THE SYMBOLIST CITY.

REFERENCES AND FURTHER READING

Brooker, Jewel Spears, ed. *T. S. Eliot: The Contemporary Reviews*. Cambridge: Cambridge UP, 2004.

Brooks, Cleanth. "*The Waste Land*: Critique of the Myth." 1937. *T. S. Eliot: The Waste Land*. Ed. C. B. Cox and Arnold P. Hinchliffe. London: Macmillan, 1969. 128–61.

Drew, Elizabeth. *T. S. Eliot: The Design of His Poetry*. New York: Scribner's, 1949.

Frye, Northrop. *T. S. Eliot*. 1963. New York: Capricorn, 1972.

Gardner, Helen. *The Art of T. S. Eliot*. 1950. New York: Dutton, 1959.

Kenner, Hugh. *The Invisible Poet: T. S. Eliot*. New York: Harcourt, 1959.

Leavis, F. R. *New Bearings in English Poetry*. 1932. Ann Arbor: U of Michigan P, 1960.

Martin, Mildred. *A Half-Century of Eliot Criticism: An Annotated Bibliography of Books and Articles in English, 1916–1965.* Lewisburg: Bucknell UP, 1972.

Matthiessen, F. O. *The Achievement of T. S. Eliot.* 1935. 3rd ed. Oxford: Oxford UP, 1958.

Smidt, Kristian. *Poetry and Belief in the Work of T. S. Eliot.* 1949. Rev. ed. London: Routledge, 1961.

Smith, Grover. *T. S. Eliot's Poetry and Plays: A Study in Sources and Meaning.* Chicago: U of Chicago P, 1956.

Williamson, George. *A Reader's Guide to T. S. Eliot.* 1953. 2nd ed. New York: Noonday, 1966.

Wilson, Edmund. *Axel's Castle.* New York: Scribner's, 1931.

37

Radical Innovation and Pervasive Influence: *The Waste Land*

James Longenbach

Proposition: when we consider what precedes it and what follows it, *The Waste Land* emerges as the most radically innovative and pervasively influential poem written in the twentieth century.

"I am often asked whether there can be a long imagiste or vorticist poem," wrote Ezra Pound in 1915 (*Gaudier* 94). The prescriptions that produced imagist poems made no mention of length; shorter poems were not inevitably to be preferred to longer poems. But the second and most important of Pound's famous "Don'ts" – "to use absolutely no word that does not contribute to the presentation" – inevitably encouraged a discipline that shied away from the discursive presentation of information, dismantled the illusion of a speaking voice, and shrank lyric utterance to its pithiest core (*Literary Essays* 3). When Pound made his earliest versions of Chinese poems, working exclusively from H. A. Giles's English translations, his imagist procedures transformed this poem –

> O fair white silk, fresh from the weaver's loom,
> Clear as the frost, bright as the winter snow –
> See! friendship fashions out of thee a fan,
> Round as the round moon shines in heaven above,
> At home, abroad, a close companion thou,
> Stirring at every move the grateful gale.
> And yet I fear, ah me! that autumn chills
> Cooling the dying summer's torrid rage,
> Will see thee laid neglected on the shelf,
> All thoughts of bygone days, like them bygone. (Giles 101)

– to an utterance that some ears could not recognize as poetry at all. Pound's poem is called "Fan-Piece, for her Imperial Lord," and the final line of this three-line utterance ("You also are laid aside") says everything, the word "also" bearing weight that Giles could not conceive (*Personae* 111).

A Companion to T. S. Eliot, First Edition. Edited by David E. Chinitz.
© 2014 John Wiley & Sons, Ltd. Published 2014 by John Wiley & Sons, Ltd.

"Fan-Piece, for her Imperial Lord," carved from Giles's clunky pentameters, would stand apart even if Giles's poem were well made. Gone is explanation, dramatic context, narrative tissue; what had been spelled out is here strongly implied. Poems like Pound's "Fan-Piece" appealed to an avant-garde sensibility that had tired of Victorian discursiveness while at the same time confirming a different and equally powerful nineteenth-century inheritance: imagist poems burn always with a gem-like flame, as Walter Pater said every moment of our experience must (Pater 189).

Pound published "Fan-Piece" in 1914, and less than a year later he needed publicly to admit that he was chafing against the limitations of imagist brevity. Pound's ambition was to write a long poem, since he recognized (as would Eliot) that his stature would ultimately rest not on a collection of pristine lyric utterances but on a poem driven by an epic impulse – a poem that would inevitably be seen as a successor to works as different as *The Prelude*, *In Memoriam*, and *Leaves of Grass*. But his ambition stood at odds with his aesthetic: how could he write a poem of immense length while at the same time preserving the condensed economy of means, the linguistic and emotional intensity, that distinguishes a poem like "Fan-Piece, for Her Imperial Lord"?

The Waste Land, first published in 1922, is the answer to this question. Pound called *The Waste Land* "the longest poem in the English langwidge" and "the justification of the 'movement,' of our modern experiment, since 1900" (*Selected Letters* 180). He might have said that the poem was the justification of the modern movement precisely because it is, in a sense, the longest poem in the English language. The ways in which Eliot (with Pound's assistance) achieved the structure of this poem – and the ways in which this achievement has shaped our apprehension of long poems ever since – is the subject of this chapter. For unlike any poem in the language preceding it (but like many to follow), *The Waste Land* is not a poetic sequence but an expression of what Roland Barthes would call the "syntagmatic" imagination, a poem "whose fabrication, by arrangement of discontinuous and mobile elements, constitutes the spectacle itself" (Barthes 211). The fact that we have by and large lost the ability to register the unprecedented strangeness of *The Waste Land* is part of the story I have to tell.[1]

"I am wracked by the seven jealousies," said Pound to Eliot when their work on *The Waste Land* was finished (*Selected Letters* 169). Pound did write several fascinating long poems between 1915 and 1922: why did *The Waste Land* emerge as the poem that answered Pound's question about the viability of a long poem? In the first three cantos, published in 1917 and later scuttled when Pound reorganized this very long poem's opening, Pound returned to the Browningesque discursivity that he had previously abandoned for the shock of imagist condensation:

> Another's a half-cracked fellow – John Heydon,
> Worker of miracles, dealer in levitation,
> In thoughts upon pure form, in alchemy,

Seer of pretty visions ("servant of God and secretary of nature");
Full of plaintive charm, like Botticelli's,
With half-transparent forms, lacking the vigor of gods. (*Personae* 241)

This mode ultimately offered no solution, and Pound's subsequent efforts at long poems either fall back on nineteenth-century precedent or lurch forward into unrepeatable feat. The gorgeous *Homage to Sextus Propertius* (1919) is a cannily reconfigured translation of certain of the Roman poet's elegies, and *Hugh Selwyn Mauberley* (1920), though immensely powerful both structurally and thematically, is precisely what *The Waste Land* is not: a long poem made, like *In Memoriam* or *Leaves of Grass*, out of a sequence of discrete shorter poems.

"What we term a long poem is, in fact, merely a succession of brief ones," said Edgar Allan Poe in "The Philosophy of Composition" (Poe 22). This wisdom came increasingly to be the case throughout the nineteenth century. Think not only of Tennyson and Whitman but of Rossetti's *House of Life* or Meredith's *Modern Love*: the disparate poems of these sequences are unified by a consistent lyric voice. More seductively fragmented in its movement was the first edition of *Leaves of Grass*, in which the many pieces of "Song of Myself" were not numbered but simply laid side by side, a procedure that blurs the boundaries of the lyric utterances and makes the movement of the entire poem feel more intricate, less a matter of arranged wholes than of interwoven pieces. Still, the indomitable presence of the lyric "I" mitigates this effect, allowing us to process the accumulating pieces of "Song of Myself" without registering the full effect of their disparity.

Listen in contrast to a passage from "The Burial of the Dead," the first of the five movements of *The Waste Land*:

> What are the roots that clutch, what branches grow
> Out of this stony rubbish? Son of man,
> You cannot say, or guess, for you know only
> A heap of broken images, where the sun beats,
> And the dead tree gives no shelter, the cricket no relief,
> And the dry stone no sound of water. Only
> There is shadow under this red rock,
> (Come in under the shadow of this red rock),
> And I will show you something different from either
> Your shadow at morning striding behind you
> Or your shadow at evening rising to meet you;
> I will show you fear in a handful of dust.
> > *Frisch weht der Wind*
> > *Der Heimat zu*
> > *Mein Irisch Kind,*
> > *Wo weilest du?*
>
> "You gave me hyacinths first a year ago;
> "They called me the hyacinth girl."

> – Yet when we came back, late, from the Hyacinth garden,
> Your arms full, and your hair wet, I could not
> Speak, and my eyes failed, I was neither
> Living nor dead, and I knew nothing,
> Looking into the heart of light, the silence.
> *Oed' und leer das Meer.*
>
> Madame Sosostris, famous clairvoyante,
> Had a bad cold, nevertheless
> Is known to be the wisest woman in Europe,
> With a wicked pack of cards. Here, said she,
> Is your card, the drowned Phoenician Sailor,
> (Those are pearls that were his eyes. Look!) (*CPP* 38)

Here, Eliot moves from 12 lines in a strongly prophetic tone, reminiscent of Ezekiel: "What are the roots that clutch, what branches grow / Out of this stony rubbish?" These lines are immediately superseded by four lines in German; their sound is radically at odds with what we have just heard, and if we know their source (a sailor's melancholy lament from the beginning of Wagner's opera *Tristan und Isolde*), then their meaning seems at odds with the prophetic warning as well. Next comes the recalled encounter in the hyacinth garden – a fragment that, although brief, suggests just enough dramatic context to make it feel like a complete scene. But however explicable this scene may be, the "I" who speaks the passage bears no obvious relationship to the "I" who would show us fear in a handful of dust. Then the "I" shifts again: with the swift introduction of Madame Sosostris, we move from the heartbroken to the broadly comic, only to find that the tone of this fragment not only contrasts with what we've heard so far but is itself interrupted by a different tone, suddenly lyrical and achingly sincere: "Those are pearls that were his eyes" – Ariel's song to Ferdinand in *The Tempest*. Moving through the passage, we're negotiating a tangle of precisely discernable but oddly dislocated tones, not a juxtaposition of complete or coherent utterances. The fragmentary pieces are not much like imagist poems, but they retain the particular value of imagist poems: all immediacy and impact, no background, no explanation.

My purpose here is not simply to describe the workings of these well-known lines but to remind us of their strangeness. While the five movements of *The Waste Land* are definitively numbered and titled, the movements themselves are made up of interwoven pieces, pieces that feel coherent in themselves not because of narrative continuity or dramatic situation but because of a swiftly established certainty of tone. These pieces are not only strategically different from one another, thwarting any effort to fold them into a continuing lyric utterance; each piece so strongly resists closure that the movement between them is a disjunctive leap not between one short poem and another but between one provocatively clipped fragment and another. As a result, the developing movement of the poem feels simultaneously assured and out of control, a stream whose turns and eddies we cannot predict, though we can follow it assuredly.

It is instructive to recall that some of the opening lines of this passage were originally the opening lines to a poem called "The Death of St. Narcissus," completed
around 1915 but not published until many years later. Folding this poem into the
texture of his long poem, Eliot used only a piece of it, not the whole; the whole would
have established a more clearly identifiable speaker and subject matter. At large, *The
Waste Land* feels as if it were made of pieces that carry, because of their sharpness of
tone, echoing remnants of contexts from which they've been rent. The poem accumulates coherence as we move through its texture not because there is an underlying
schema (there isn't one, despite many readers' efforts to put one there), but because
the various pieces of the poem become a chamber in which subsequent pieces
resonate.

For instance, when we reach these lines in the second movement of the poem, "A
Game of Chess" –

> "Do
> "You know nothing? Do you see nothing? Do you remember
> "Nothing?"
>
> I remember
> Those are pearls that were his eyes. (*CPP* 41)

– we suddenly give more weight to this line from *The Tempest* (and its suggestion of
the possibility of resurrection and transfiguration), recalling as we do its earlier appearance in the Madame Sosostris passage. The connection is associational, a matter of
considering the implications of connections made both within and without the poem.

Had Eliot retained an earlier version of these lines –

> I remember
> The hyacinth garden. Those are pearls that were his eyes, yes!
> (*WLF* 13)

– the connection would be made on the level of narrative, since we would be encouraged to think of the "I" speaking these lines as the same "I" that could not speak to
his beloved in the hyacinth garden. But with Pound's encouragement, Eliot cut the
suggestion of such continuities from *The Waste Land*. The poem would not be bound
together by narrative tissue or continuity of voice, and neither would the negotiation
of the poem's variously juxtaposed pieces be aided by a strong sense of the boundaries
of those pieces.

This particular cut from the manuscript of *The Waste Land* was Eliot's doing, but
as Pound and Eliot worked together on the poem, Pound pushed Eliot in this direction, slicing large passages of narrative verse and organizing what remained around
highly charged fragmentary instants. It is precisely in this sense that Pound could
think of *The Waste Land* as the longest poem in the language, for if all of the

implications of the poem's various instants were spelled out, then the poem would indeed be much longer. By cutting down the poem, Eliot made it feel immense.

Such radical condensation was unprecedented even in Pound's work. Unlike Pound, Eliot was deeply schooled in post-Hegelian philosophy, and in retrospect it makes sense that the formal design of *The Waste Land* would come to a mind that believed (as Eliot wrote in his dissertation for the Harvard philosophy department) that "[f]acts are not merely found in the world and laid together like bricks, but every fact has in a sense its place prepared for it before it arrives, and without the implication of a system in which it belongs the fact is not a fact at all" (*KE* 60). All knowledge was for Eliot relational and contingent, and in *The Waste Land* he forged a poetic structure that allowed his readers not simply to understand but to experience this conviction.

This is why the astonishingly cacophonous and beautiful final lines of *The Waste Land* —

> London Bridge is falling down falling down falling down
> *Poi s'ascose nel foco che gli affina*
> *Quando fiam uti chelidon* — O swallow swallow
> *Le Prince d'Aquitaine à la tour abolie*
> These fragments I have shored against my ruins
> Why then Ile fit you. Hieronymo's mad againe.
> Datta. Dayadhvam. Damyata.
>   Shantih   shantih   shantih (*CPP* 50)

— feel like a satisfying conclusion while also pushing the poem's strategies of radical condensation and juxtaposition to their highest pitch. *The Waste Land* does not conclude by folding its disparate pieces into a whole: instead, it concludes with its most extravagant act of discontinuity, an act into which its readers are initiated through their experience of the poem's unfolding structure. *The Waste Land* takes a shape inevitable to a poet who believed that "the self is a construction" (*KE* 146).

To say so makes Eliot sound like a proto-postmodernist, though it is more responsible to say that what we've come to think of as modern and postmodern aesthetics were always fully implicated in each other. More crucial is the need to understand why we've come to underestimate or overlook the astonishing nature of Eliot's achievement in *The Waste Land*, thinking of the poem as an easily mapped monolith of modernism rather than a poem of truly unprecedented boldness, a poem that opened a thousand doors for subsequent poets.

Eliot was of course an influential critic as well as poet, and probably more than any other poet-critic in the English language, he had the fortune — as well as the misfortune — to have created the taste by which he was judged. A few months after *The Waste Land* appeared, Eliot published a review of James Joyce's *Ulysses*, and Eliot's readers immediately applied the terms of this review to Eliot's inexplicable long poem:

In using the myth, in manipulating a continuous parallel between contemporaneity and antiquity, Mr. Joyce is pursuing a method which others must pursue after him. They will not be imitators, any more than the scientist who uses the discoveries of an Einstein in pursuing his own, independent, further investigations. It is simply a way of controlling, of ordering, of giving a shape and a significance to the immense panorama of futility and anarchy which is contemporary history. . . . It is a method for which the horoscope is auspicious. Psychology (such as it is, and whether our reaction to it be comic or serious), ethnology, and *The Golden Bough* have concurred to make possible what was impossible even a few years ago. Instead of narrative method, we may now use the mythical method. (*SP* 177–78)

It is clear that *The Waste Land* does not employ a narrative method, but does it employ a mythical method, manipulating a continuous parallel between contemporaneity and antiquity? Does *Ulysses*? Pound didn't think so, or at least he didn't think that Joyce's use of Homer was terribly significant. "These correspondences," said Pound in his own review of *Ulysses*, "are part of Joyce's mediaevalism and are chiefly his own affair, a scaffold, a means of construction, justified by the result" (*Literary Essays* 406). What interested Pound was the roiling texture of Joyce's novel, not the scaffold, and what interested him in *The Waste Land* was the same thing, since there is no scaffold underlying Eliot's poem. Other readers, eager to manage the poem's chaotic energies, tried to elevate the presence of myth, transforming one of the poem's many ingredients, the Grail legend, into a kind of key. The proposed presence of a key turned the poem into a lock.

Eliot was partly responsible for this misleading way of reading the poem. He must have suspected that readers would link his remarks about a mythical method with his notes for *The Waste Land*, especially the head note in which he pointed eager hermeneuts to *The Golden Bough* and *From Ritual to Romance*, Jessie Weston's book about the Grail legend. That this manner of reading *The Waste Land* was strategic, not inevitable, is suggested by the chronology of the poem's gestation, for during the many years of its making, the Grail legend played no part in the poem's structural or thematic design. Even the poem's title (its most potent reference to the myth) was a late addition. The poem Eliot handed over to Pound in manuscript was called "He Do the Police in Different Voices," a title that elucidates the poem's texture but also simplifies it as well: even to say that this long poem is made of multiple "voices" is to stabilize its chaotic energies, transforming a delicate interplay of disembodied tones into map of human consciousness.

Why were readers eager to find ways to make *The Waste Land* seem less strange, more manageable? Eliot's literary criticism was one of the crucial influences on what came to be called the New Criticism, the umbrella under which critics as unique as John Crowe Ransom, Allen Tate, R. P. Blackmur, Cleanth Brooks (and sometimes Kenneth Burke and William Empson) were collected.[2] These writers read Eliot in very different ways. Ransom had been highly impressed by *The Sacred Wood*, Eliot's first collection of essays, published in 1920, but when confronted by *The Waste Land* two years later he declared that Eliot's early work had been "merely precocious" (Ransom 179). Influenced by Eliot's more programmatic critical values, Ransom wanted poems to be impersonal, unified, classical, autotelic, and *The Waste Land* was none of these things. He couldn't understand how Eliot could be rigidly coherent in his prose but chaotic in his poem.

Responding to Ransom, Allen Tate maintained that *The Waste Land* was essentially ironic: that is, it dramatized a failure to achieve the values that Eliot upheld in his critical prose. In a very influential reading of the poem, Cleanth Brooks later maintained that *The Waste Land* was really not chaotic at all: it was clearly organized by the mythical method. This way of reading did make the poem (and much else in modernist literature) more palatable to an unsympathetic audience, but it did so at a price. The most prominent New Critical readings of *The Waste Land* laid a highly schematized version of Eliot's more notorious critical pronouncements over the poem. And in subsequent decades, as the linked fortunes of Eliot and the New Criticism rose and fell, it became difficult for readers to know if they were responding to *The Waste Land* as such or to the manner in which certain powerful critics had claimed the poem for a narrow vision of the modernist achievement.

This dynamic is most obviously apparent in the work of more recent critics. For the Marxist critic Terry Eagleton, for instance, *The Waste Land* is structured around "totalizing mythological forms" in order to produce a "closed, coherent, authoritative discourse" (150). This reading of the poem reproduces Cleanth Brooks's reading, except that it deplores what Brooks approves. Neither critic is responding to the actual texture of Eliot's writing – both assume that the poem is structured by an underlying scaffold – and Eagleton has more or less substituted a New Critical distortion of the poem for the poem itself.

If this kind of misreading is to a degree inevitable, it appears more interesting, more fruitful, less merely oppositional, when we see it played out in the work of other poets – writers who were interested not merely in placing Eliot in the past but in figuring out ways to harness his achievement for the future. As early as 1923 Hart Crane could speak of "the settled formula of Mr. Eliot," and in the wake of Eliot's review of *Ulysses*, Crane conceived of *The Bridge* as a response to *The Waste Land* as he had come to understand it through Eliot's criticism (Crane 311). Unlike *The Waste Land* itself, *The Bridge* can be read according to the program of "*Ulysses*, Order, and Myth": the poem is built from a narrative that lasts a single day (a man wakes up in Brooklyn, crosses the bridge to Manhattan, goes to work, stops in a bar on the way home, and takes the subway to Brooklyn at dawn), and each aspect of that day corresponds to various aspects of a macrocosm of history, geography, and myth.

The Waste Land has no such coherence. And inasmuch as *The Bridge* was designed by Crane as a response to Eliot's vision, the great irony of its reception is that various New Critics (especially Crane's friends Allen Tate and Yvor Winters) judged Crane's long poem to be chaotic and disorganized. In fact, *The Bridge* is far more logically structured than Eliot's poem, built from a sequence of well-made shorter poems whose position in time and space is clearly delineated. *The Bridge* is a masterpiece, but in order to write it, Crane did not need to harness the most radical means by which *The Waste Land* answered the question "can there be a long imagiste or vorticist poem?"

The writer of a less infamous but equally important long poem of the twenties did harness those means:

> The
> Voice of Jesus I. Rush singing
> > in the wilderness
> A boy's best friend is his mother,
> It's your mother all the time.
> Residue of Oedipus-faced wrecks
> Creating out of the dead, –
> From the candle flames of the souls of dead mothers
> Vide the legend of thin Christ sending her out of the temple, –
> Books from the stony heart, flames rapping the stone,
> Residue of self-exiled men
> By the Tyrrhenian.
> > Paris.
> But everywhere only the South Wind, the sirocco, the broken Earth-face.
> The broken Earth-face, the age demands an image of its life and contacts,
> Lord, lord, not that we pray, are sure of the question,
> But why are our finest always dead? (Zukofsky 3)

These are the opening lines of Louis Zukofsky's *Poem beginning "The"* (1928). Like *The Bridge*, *Poem beginning "The"* was conceived as a response to *The Waste Land*, but unlike *The Bridge* it is not so much a sequence of poems as kaleidoscope of different tones. Line by line, the poem leaps, folds back on itself, simultaneously establishing tentative lines of continuity while also disrupting them. The poem lurches from the lyrical to the broadly comic, from high to low, spooky to dorky, and, as is the case with *The Waste Land*, this intricate interplay of tones is in part established through quotation and allusion. Zukofsky's notes for just these opening lines of *Poem beginning "The"* send us to Sophocles, Aldous Huxley, James Joyce, Norman Douglas, Ezra Pound, the Bible, and popular songs. A few lines later, the notes send us to Eliot: "And why if the waste land has been explored, traveled over, circumscribed, / Are there only wrathless skeletons exhumed new planted in its sacred wood" (4).

Like Crane, Zukofsky wanted to his readers to think of his poem as a corrective response to *The Waste Land*. But however different Zukofsky's vision may be from Eliot's, especially in its inclusion of ethnic and social tones to which Eliot was deaf, Zukofsky's formal procedures are unthinkable without Eliot's precedent. *The Waste Land* offered this young poet the crucial example of a long poem built from the interplay of parts rather than a synoptic vision of the whole. Because of the ways in which the literary history of modernism usually gets told, however, we assume that Crane is the far more Eliotic writer, and that Zukofsky's project is merely opposed to Eliot's. In fact, Zukofsky's difference from Eliot is the mark of his debt. More than *The Bridge*,

Poem Beginning "The" reveals a young poet intensely aware of what was most astonishing about *The Waste Land*: not its supposed pretension to a mythical method but the texture of its language and the ways in which that texture becomes a structuring device in the absence of the more typical marks of a poetic sequence. The title of Zukofsky's poem, which encourages us to think about the parts rather than the whole, highlights procedures toward which Eliot had groped in the dark.

The revision of literary history I'm implying here may please nobody. Readers devoted to a timeworn vision of Eliot's legacy usually disdain Zukofsky, and readers devoted to the Objectivist line in American poetry are usually not interested in Eliot except inasmuch as he may be trotted out as a dependable whipping boy. But we are nearly a decade into the twenty-first century, and it's time we all got down off our stilts and looked around. If I think of poets now writing at the height of their powers – poets as different from each other as Louise Glück, Susan Howe, and Frank Bidart – it's clear that their poems have been shaped by their reading of Eliot, just as Eliot's poems were shaped by his reading of Whitman. Overcoming an antipathy, discovering that one is learning from an artist whom one had previously found useless, is one of the great human experiences. It's like the discovery of love in the wilderness – no, in the village where you've lived your entire life.

Proposition: when we recognize *The Waste Land* as the most radically innovative and pervasively influential poem written in the twentieth century, we experience what precedes and follows it as if for the first time.

NOTES

1 *See also* "Fishing, with the arid plain behind me": Difficulty, Deferral, and Form in *The Waste Land*.

2 *See also* Eliot and the New Critics.

REFERENCES AND FURTHER READING

Barthes, Roland. *Critical Essays*. Trans. Richard Howard. Evanston, IL: Northwestern UP, 1972.

Breslin, James E. B. *From Modern to Contemporary: American Poetry, 1945–1965*. Chicago: U of Chicago P, 1984.

Brooks, Cleanth. *Modern Poetry and the Tradition*. Chapel Hill: U of North Carolina P, 1939.

Bush, Ronald. "T. S. Eliot and Modernism at the Present Time: A Provocation." *T. S. Eliot: The Modernist in History*. Ed. Bush. Cambridge: Cambridge UP, 1991. 191–204.

Conte, Joseph. *The Forms of Postmodern Poetry*. Ithaca: Cornell UP, 1991.

Crane, Hart. *Complete Poems and Selected Letters*. Ed. Langdon Hammer. New York: Library of America, 2006.

Eagleton, Terry. *Criticism and Ideology*. London: Verso, 1985.

Giles, H. A. *A History of Chinese Literature*. New York: Appleton, 1901.

Grant, Michael, ed. *T. S. Eliot: The Critical Heritage*. Vol. 1. London: Routledge, 1982.

Hammer, Langdon. *Hart Crane and Allen Tate: Janus-Faced Modernism*. Princeton: Princeton UP, 1993.

Litz, A. Walton. "Literary Criticism." *Harvard Guide to Contemporary American Writing*. Ed. Daniel Hoffman. Cambridge: Harvard UP, 1979. 51–83.

Longenbach, James. *Modern Poetry After Modernism*. New York: Oxford UP, 1997.

Pater, Walter. *The Renaissance: Studies in Art and Poetry*. Ed. Donald Hill. Berkeley: U of California P, 1980.

Perloff, Marjorie. *21ˢᵗ-Century Modernism: The "New" Poetics*. Walden, MA: Blackwell, 2002.

Poe, Edgar Allan. *Literary Criticism of Edgar Allan Poe*. Ed. Robert Hough. Lincoln: U of Nebraska P, 1965.

Pound, Ezra. *Gaudier-Brzeska: A Memoir*. New York: New Directions, 1970.

——. *Literary Essays*. Ed. T. S. Eliot. New York: New Directions, 1968.

——. *Personae: The Shorter Poems*. Ed. Lea Baechler and A. Walton Litz. New York: New Directions, 1990.

——. *Selected Letters, 1907–1941*. Ed. D. D. Paige. New York: New Directions, 1971.

Ransom, John Crowe. "Waste Lands." *New York Evening Post Literary Review* 14 July 1923: 825–26. Rpt. in Grant 172–79.

Tate, Allen. "A Reply to Ransom." *New York Evening Post Literary Review* 4 Aug. 1923: 886. Rpt. in *Grant* 180–82.

Zukofsky, Louis. *Selected Poems*. Ed. Charles Bernstein. New York: Library of America, 2006.

Bibliography of Works by T. S. Eliot

After Strange Gods: A Primer of Modern Heresy. New York: Harcourt, 1934.

"The Aims of Poetic Drama." *Adam: International Review* Nov. 1949: 10–16.

"American Prose." *TLS* 2 Sept. 1926: 577.

"The Art of Poetry, I: T. S. Eliot." Interview with Donald Hall. *Paris Review* 21 (1959): 47–70.

"The Ballet." *Criterion* 3 (1924–25): 441–43.

"The Beating of a Drum." *Nation and Athenaeum* 6 Oct. 1923: 11–12.

"Beyle and Balzac." *Athenaeum* 30 May 1919: 392–93.

"A Brief Treatise on the Criticism of Poetry." *Chapbook* Mar. 1920: 1–10.

"Christianity and Communism." *Listener* 16 Mar. 1932: 382–83.

Christianity and Culture. New York: Harcourt, 1968.

"The Classics in France – and in England." *Criterion* 2 (1923–24): 104–05.

Collected Poems 1909–1962. New York: Harcourt, 1971.

"A Commentary [Apr. 1924]." *Criterion* 2 (1923–24): 231–35.

"A Commentary [July 1924]." *Criterion* 2 (1923–24): 371–75.

"A Commentary [Oct. 1924]." *Criterion* 3 (1924–25): 1–5.

"A Commentary [Jan. 1925]." *Criterion* 3 (1924–25): 161–63.

"A Commentary [Apr. 1926]." *Criterion* 4 (1926): 221–23.

"A Commentary [May 1927]." *Criterion* 5 (1927): 187–90.

"A Commentary [June 1927]." *Criterion* 5 (1927): 283–86.

"A Commentary [Sept. 1927]." *Criterion* 6 (1927): 193–96.

"A Commentary [Feb. 1928]." *Criterion* 7 (1928): 97–99.

"A Commentary [Apr. 1929]." *Criterion* 8 (1928–29): 377–81.

"A Commentary [July 1930]." *Criterion* 9 (1929–30): 587–90.

"A Commentary [July 1932]." *Criterion* 11 (1931–32): 676–83.

"A Commentary [Apr. 1933]." *Criterion* 12 (1932–33): 468–73.

"A Commentary [Apr. 1934]." *Criterion* 13 (1933–34): 451–54.

"A Commentary [July 1935]." *Criterion* 14 (1934–35): 610–13.

"A Commentary [Jan. 1936]." *Criterion* 15 (1935–36): 265–69.

"A Commentary [Apr. 1937]." *Criterion* 16 (1936–37): 560–64.

"A Commentary [Oct. 1938]." *Criterion* 18 (1938–39): 58–62.

A Companion to T. S. Eliot, First Edition. Edited by David E. Chinitz.
© 2014 John Wiley & Sons, Ltd. Published 2014 by John Wiley & Sons, Ltd.

The Complete Poems and Plays 1909–1950. New York: Harcourt, 1952.

"Contemporanea." *Egoist* June–July 1918: 84–85.

"Criticism in England." *Athenaeum* 13 June 1919: 456–57.

"Dramatis Personae." *Criterion* 1 (1922–23): 303–06.

"The Education of Taste." *Athenaeum* 27 June 1919: 520–21.

"Eeldrop and Appleplex, I." *Little Review* 4 (1917): 7–11.

The Elder Statesman. London: Faber, 1959.

Essays Ancient and Modern. London: Faber, 1936.

Essays on Elizabethan Drama. 1932. New York: Harcourt, 1956.

"Five Points on Dramatic Writing." *Townsman* 1.3 (1938): 10.

For Lancelot Andrewes: Essays on Style and Order. Garden City, NY: Doubleday, 1929.

"Freud's Illusions." Rev. of *The Future of an Illusion*, by Sigmund Freud. *Criterion* 8 (1928–29): 350–53.

"The Function of a Literary Review." *Criterion* 1 (1922–23): 421.

"The Future of Poetic Drama." *Drama* 17 (1938): 3–5.

Homage to John Dryden. London: Hogarth, 1924.

The Idea of a Christian Society. 1939. *Christianity and Culture* 1–77.

"The Idea of a Literary Review." *Criterion* 4 (1926): 1–6.

"The Idealism of Julien Benda." Rev. of *The Treason of the Intellectuals*, by Julien Benda. *New Republic* 12 Dec. 1928: 105–07.

"In Memory [of Henry James]." *Little Review* Aug. 1918: 44–47.

"The Influence of Landscape upon the Poet." *Daedalus: Journal of the American Academy of Arts and Sciences* 89 (1960): 420–22.

Introduction. *Literary Essays of Ezra Pound.* Ed. Eliot. London: Faber, 1954. ix–xv.

Introduction. *Savonarola: A Dramatic Poem.* By Charlotte Eliot. London: Cobden-Sanderson, 1926. vii–xii.

Introduction. *The Wheel of Fire.* By G. Wilson Knight. London: Oxford UP, 1930. xi–xix.

Inventions of the March Hare: Poems 1909–1917. Ed. Christopher Ricks. New York: Harcourt, 1996.

"John Dryden – II. Dryden the Dramatist." *Listener* 22 Apr. 1931: 681–82.

"John Dryden – III. Dryden the Critic, Defender of Sanity." *Listener* 29 Apr. 1931: 724–25.

"Kipling Redivivus." *Athenaeum* 25 Apr. 1919: 297–98.

Knowledge and Experience in the Philosophy of F. H. Bradley. London: Faber, 1964.

"Last Words." *Criterion* 18 (1938–39): 269–75.

"The Lesson of Baudelaire." *Tyro* 1 (1921): 4.

Letter to Henry Eliot. 1 Jan. 1936. Houghton Library, Harvard University, Cambridge, MA.

Letter. *Transatlantic Review* 1 (Jan. 1924): 95–96.

The Letters of T. S. Eliot, Vol. I: 1898–1922. Ed. Valerie Eliot. San Diego: Harcourt, 1988.

"The Literature of Fascism." *Criterion* 8 (1928–29): 280–90.

"London Letter [May 1921]." *Dial* June 1921: 686–91. Rpt. in *The Annotated Waste Land with Eliot's Contemporary Prose.* Ed. Lawrence Rainey. New Haven: Yale UP, 2005. 166–71.

"London Letter [July 1921]." *Dial* Aug. 1921: 213–17. Rpt. in *The Annotated Waste Land with Eliot's Contemporary Prose.* Ed. Lawrence Rainey. New Haven: Yale UP, 2005. 183–87.

"London Letter [Sept. 1921]." *Dial* Oct. 1921: 452–55. Rpt. in *The Annotated Waste Land with Eliot's Contemporary Prose.* Ed. Lawrence Rainey. New Haven: Yale UP, 2005. 188–91.

"London Letter [Apr. 1922]." *Dial* May 1922: 510–13.

"Marianne Moore." Rev. of *Poems* and *Marriage*, by Marianne Moore. *Dial* Dec. 1923: 594–97.

"Mr. Barnes and Mr. Rowse." *Criterion* 8 (1928–29) 682–91.

"Mr. Middleton Murry's Synthesis." *Criterion* 6 (1927): 340–47.

"Mr. Read and M. Fernandez." Rev. of *Reason and Romanticism*, by Herbert Read, and *Messages*, by Ramon Fernandez. *Criterion* 4 (1926): 751–57.

"The Need For Poetic Drama." *Listener* 25 Nov. 1936: 994–95.

"The New Elizabethans and the Old." *Athenaeum* 4 Apr. 1919: 134–36.

"The Noh and the Image." *Egoist* Aug. 1917: 102–03.

Notes towards the Definition of Culture. 1948. *Christianity and Culture* 79–202.

On Poetry and Poets. London: Faber, 1957.

Poems Written in Early Youth. New York: Farrar, 1967.

"The Poetic Drama." Rev. of *Cinnamon and Angelica: A Play*, by John Middleton Murry. *Athenaeum* 14 May 1920: 635–36.

"The Post–Georgians." *Athenaeum* 11 Apr. 1919: 171–72.

"A Preface to Modern Literature." *Vanity Fair* Nov. 1923: 44+.

"Professional, Or ..." *Egoist* Apr. 1918: 61.

"The Publishing of Poetry." *Bookseller* 6 Dec. 1952: 1568–70.

"Reflections on Contemporary Poetry I." *Egoist* Sept. 1917: 118–19.

"Reflections on Contemporary Poetry II." *Egoist* Oct. 1917: 133–34.

"Religious Drama: Mediæval and Modern." *University of Edinburgh Journal* 9 (1937): 8–17.

Rev. of *All God's Chillun Got Wings*, by Eugene O'Neill. *Criterion* 4 (1926): 395–96.

Rev. of *Group Theories of Religion and the Religion of the Individual*, by Clement C. J. Webb. *International Journal of Ethics* 27 (1916): 115–17.

Rev. of *The Growth of Civilization* and *The Origin of Magic and Religion*, by W. J. Perry. *Criterion* 2 (1923–24): 489–91.

The Rock: A Pageant Play. London: Faber, 1934.

"The Romantic Englishman, the Comic Spirit, and the Function of Criticism." *Tyro* 1 (1921): 4.

The Sacred Wood: Essays on Poetry and Criticism. London: Methuen, 1960.

"A Sceptical Patrician." *Athenaeum* 23 May 1919: 361–62.

Selected Essays. 1932. New ed. New York: Harcourt, 1964.

Selected Prose of T. S. Eliot. Ed. Frank Kermode. London: Faber, 1975.

"Studies in Contemporary Criticism I." *Egoist* Oct. 1918: 113–14.

"Studies in Contemporary Criticism II." *Egoist* Nov.–Dec. 1918: 131–33.

"Tarr." *Egoist* Sept. 1918: 105–06.

"The Three Provincialities." *Tyro* 2 (1922): 11–13.

To Criticize the Critic. 1965. New York: Octagon, 1980.

"T. S. Eliot Talks About Himself and the Drive to Create." Interview with John Lehmann. *New York Book Review* 29 Nov. 1953: 5+.

"T. S. Eliot Talks About His Poetry." *Columbia University Forum* 2.1 (1958): 11–14.

The Use of Poetry and the Use of Criticism. London: Faber, 1933.

The Varieties of Metaphysical Poetry. Ed. Ronald Schuchard. New York: Harcourt, 1993.

The Waste Land: A Facsimile and Transcript of the Original Drafts Including the Annotations of Ezra Pound. Ed. Valerie Eliot. New York: Harcourt, 1971.

Index